Table of Contents
Instructor's Manual with Test Bank
White/Terrorism and Homeland Security, 8th Edition

Instructor's Resource Manual with Test Bank

Terrorism and Homeland Security

EIGHTH EDITION

Jonathan R. White
Grand Valley State University

Prepared by

Vanessa Escalante
LA College International

WADSWORTH
CENGAGE Learning·

Australia • Brazil • Japan • Korea • Mexico • Singapore • Spain • United Kingdom • United States

WADSWORTH
CENGAGE Learning·

ISBN-13: 978-1-285-06842-8
ISBN-10: 1-285-06842-4

Wadsworth
20 Davis Drive
Belmont, CA 94002-3098
USA

Cengage Learning is a leading provider of customized learning solutions with office locations around the globe, including Singapore, the United Kingdom, Australia, Mexico, Brazil, and Japan. Locate your local office at:
www.cengage.com/global

Cengage Learning products are represented in Canada by Nelson Education, Ltd.

To learn more about Wadsworth, visit
www.cengage.com/wadsworth

Purchase any of our products at your local college store or at our preferred online store
www.cengagebrain.com

Printed in the United States of America
1 2 3 4 5 6 7 16 15 14 13 12

CHAPTER 1

Defining Terrorism in Modern History

Learning Objectives

After reading this chapter, students should be able to:

1. Explain the reason *terrorism* is difficult to define.
2. Summarize the impact of context on definitions of *terrorism*.
3. Explain the impact of the Enlightenment on democracy and potential revolutionary thought.
4. Summarize the origins of modern terrorism from the Enlightenment through the Napoleonic wars.
5. Explain why terrorism became defined as a revolutionary activity after the European experience in 1848.
6. Define socialism, anarchism, and communism.
7. Summarize the differing meanings of terrorism in Russia from the Peoples' Will through Lenin and Trotsky.
8. Summarize the early history of the Irish Republican Army.
9. Define *selective terrorism* as used by Michael Collins.

Key Terms

Social construct, p. 4
Academic consensus definition, p. 4
Social context, p. 4
Selective terrorism, p. 5
Nidal Malik Hasan, p. 5
Enlightenment, p. 6
Estates General, p. 8
National Convention, p. 8
Committee of Public Safety, p. 8
Reign of Terror, p. 8
Spain in 1807, p. 9
Radical democrats, p. 9
Socialists, p. 12
Anarchists, p. 12
Communists, p. 11
Bourgeois, p. 13
Hohenzollerns, p. 13

Academic consensus definition is a complex definition based on the work of Alex Schmid. It combines common elements of the definitions used by the leading scholars in the field of terrorism.

Anarchists: Those in the nineteenth century who advocated the creation of cooperative societies without centralized governments. There were many forms of anarchy. In the popular understanding of the late nineteenth and early twentieth centuries, anarchists were seen as violent socialist revolutionaries. Today anti-globalists, calling themselves anarchists, have little resemblance to their earlier counterparts.

Bourgeois: The middle class. *Bourgeoisie* (plural) in Marxist terminology refers to trades-people, merchants, artisans and other non-peasants excluded from the upper classes in medieval Europe. Marx called the European democracies, after the French Revolution, bourgeois governments, and he advocated a democracy dominated by workers.

Committee for Public Safety: Assembled by Maximilien Robespierre (1758–1794) to conduct the war against invading *monarchal* powers, it evolved into the executive body of France. The Committee for Public Safety initiated the Reign of Terror.

Communists: Socialists who believed in a strong centralized economy controlled by a strong central government. Their ideas were summarized in *The Communist Manifesto,* written by Karl Marx and Friedrich Engels in 1848.

Enlightenment: An eighteenth-century intellectual movement following the Scientific Revolution. Also called the Age of Reason, the Enlightenment was characterized by rational thought and the belief that all activities could be explained.

Estates General: An assembly in pre-revolutionary France consisting of all but the lowest class. The Estates General had not been called since 1614, but Louis XVI assembled them in 1789, in response to demands from the Assembly of Notables, who had been called to address the financial problems of France. Radical elements in the Estates General revolted, and the disruption led to the French Revolution.

Free State: The name given to the newly formed Republic of Ireland after Irish independence in the Tan War.

Hapsburg: The ruling family of Austria (1282– 1918), the Austro-Hungarian Empire (1437–1918), and the Holy Roman Empire (1282–1806). Another branch of the family ruled in Spain (1516–1700). Reference here is to the Austrian royal family.

Hohenzollern: The ruling family of Brandenburg and Prussia that ruled a united Germany from 1871 to 1914.

Joseph Stalin: The dictator who succeeded Lenin. Stalin solidified communist control of Russia through a secret-police organization. He purged the government of all suspected opponents in the 1930s, killing thousands of people.

Leon Trotsky: A Russian revolutionary who led foreign affairs in Stalin's government, and later became the commander of the Red Army. He espoused terrorism as a means for spreading revolution. He was thrown out of the Communist Party for opposing Stalin, and was assassinated by communist agents in Mexico City in 1940.

National Convention: Elected in 1792, it broke from the Estates General and called for a constitutional assembly. The Convention served as the major legislative body of France until it was replaced by the Directory in 1795.

Nidal Malik Hanson (1970-) an American soldier of Palestinian descent. Hasan was an Army psychiatrist who apparently became self-radicalized, embracing militant Islám. He went on a shooting spree at Fort Hood in Texas on November 5, 2009, killing thirteen people and wounding almost three dozen others. He was wounded, arrested, and charged with several counts of murder.

Radical democrats: Those who tried to bring democracy to all classes. They sought a more equitable distribution of wealth throughout all economic classes, believing that concentrated wealth and class inequities prevented societies from becoming truly democratic.

Reign of Terror: The name given to the repressive period in France 1794–1795. The revolutionary government accused thousands of French nobles and clergy of plotting to restore the monarchy. Executions began in Paris and spread throughout the countryside. Large mobs attacked and terrorized nobles in rural areas. Summary executions (executions on the spot without a trial) were quite common.

Royal Irish Constabulary (RIC): The police force established by the United Kingdom in Ireland. It was modelled after the London Metropolitan Police, but it represented British interests. After the Free State formed, the RIC became the RUC, Royal Ulster Constabulary. In turn, the RUC gave way to the Police Service of Northern Ireland (PSNI) as part of Irish and British attempts to bring peace to Northern Ireland after 1995.

Selective terrorism is a term used by Michael Collins during the Irish War of Independence (1919-1921). Collins did not launch indiscriminate terror attacks; he selectively targeted the British military, the police force it sponsored, and people who supported the United Kingdom.

Sinn Fein: The political party of Republicans. Critics claim it represents terrorists. Republicans say it represents their political interests. Despite the debate, Sinn Fein historically has close connections with extremism and violence.

Social construct refers to the way people view reality. Groups construct a framework around a concept, defining various aspects of their lives through the meanings they attribute to the construct.

Social context describes the historical, political, and criminological circumstances at a given point in time. The social context affects the way terrorism is defined. The text examines the impact of history, war, political power and repression, media coverage, crime, religion, and specific forms of violence on the definition of terrorism.

Socialists: Radical democrats who sought wealth equality in capitalist societies. Some socialists sought governmental guarantees of living standards. Others believed that the state should control industry and divide profits among all members of society. Others believed that people would form cooperative relationships on their own with no need of a government.

Spain in 1807: The Peninsula War (1808–1814), which began when Spanish and French forces divided Portugal in 1807. Napoleon, whose army entered Spain in 1807, attempted to use his forces to capture the Spanish throne in 1808. British forces under Sir Arthur Wellesley, later Duke of Wellington, joined Spanish forces, loyal to the king of Spain, and Spanish partisans to fight the French.

Supreme Council of the IRB: The command centre of several Republican terrorist organizations, including the Irish Republican Army. and the Provisional Irish Republican Army. The name was transposed from the Irish Republican Brotherhood.

Vladimir Lenin: The Russian revolutionary who helped lead a revolution in February 1917,and who led a second revolution in October, bringing the communists to power. Lenin led the communists in a civil war, and set up a dictatorship to enforce communist rule in Russia.

Vladimir Putin: (1952–) a former KGB officer and second President of the Russian Federation from 1999 to 2008. He began serving as Russia's prime minister after the end of his presidential term.

Workers Councils (or Soviets): The lowest-level legislative body in the Soviet Union following the October Revolution. *Soviet* is the Russian word for "council."

Chapter Outline

I.   **The Difficulty with Definitions.**

   LO 1: **Explain the reason *terrorism* is difficult to define.**

   LO 2: **Summarize the impact of context on definitions of *terrorism*.**

   A. Defining terrorism has generated numerous debates.
   B. Terrorism is difficult to define in that the meaning changes within social and historical contexts.
   C. The term terrorism is a *social construct* – groups construct a frame work around a concept, providing a definition through the meanings they attribute

4

to the construct. The *social context* surrounding the term terrorism influences how it is defined – the historical, political, and criminological circumstances at a given point in time affect the way in which terrorism is defined.

1. U.S. State Department considers Hezbollah to be a terrorist organization while the Jordanian police consider Hezbollah to be a militia fighting Israeli Defense Forces.
2. Given their past experiences with terrorism, Israel keeps a close eye on militant activities in Lebanon, including violating Lebanese air space. Lebanese consider this an act of terrorism.
3. The definition becomes more complicated in war zones. NATO forces are fighting two major enemies in Afghanistan; however, the military, politicians and the media combine the two groups as one organization.
   a. al Qaeda
   b. Taliban
4. *Nidal Malik Hanson*, a U.S. Army Major went on a shooting spree at Fort Hood in Texas. Some view Hanson as a terrorist; others view him as a mentally deranged soldier.

D. There is no standard meaning of *terrorism.* Schmid (2005) posits an academic consensus definition, stating that most definitions of the term have two characteristics:
   1. Someone is terrorized
   2. The meaning of the term is derived from the terrorists' targets and victims.

A. Terrorism is a *pejorative term,* meaning that the term is laden with derogatory meanings.

II. **The Origin of Terrorism in Western History.**

LO 3: Explain the impact of the Enlightenment on democracy and potential revolutionary thought.

LO 4: Summarize the origins of modern terrorism from the Enlightenment through the Napoleonic wars.

LO 5: Explain why terrorism became defined as a revolutionary activity after the European experience in 1848

A. Historical Circumstances – meaning of terrorism has changed with political tides in Western history.
   1. Modern terrorism originated from the French Revolution.
      a. Term used to describe the repressive actions of the French government.
   2. The meaning of terrorism soon transformed to refer to guerilla tactics in the Napoleonic wars.
      a. In guerrilla war, guerrillas use terrorist tactics against their enemies, and may terrorize enemies and their supporters into submission.

5

3. Mid-19th century, the term shifted to encompass the actions of revolutionaries which were copied by Nationalists.
4. The meaning is seen as having come full circle, when Communists in the Soviet Union used terrorism to subjugate the population.

B. Social Revolution and the Enlightenment
1. Historians often call the eighteenth century the Age of Reason, or the Enlightenment, in spite of the vast amount of contradictions, inconsistencies, and political turmoil that occurred during the period.
   a. Radical changes in thinking threatened the ruling class, which sparked tension with the governed peoples.
   b. Increased demand for democracy led to violent rebellions.
2. The Enlightenment was an international intellectual movement.
   a. Theology lost its grip on being the one *true* source of answers.
   b. A rise of science and a new age of discovery.
   c. Deductive logic was gradually replaced by empirical observation.
3. Philosophers of the period produced a common idea about government.
   a. Governments should exist to protect individual rights
   b. The best form of government was democracy.
   c. Governments' had a duty to grant and protect citizens' rights.
   d. Common people were to control government by social contract.

C. The American Revolution, 1775-1783
1. American colonists felt Britain was denying their basic rights.
   a. Demand for American democracy led to battle between the Continental Congress and the British in 1775.
   b. The desire for independence came late in the war, and it was not supported by the majority of Americans.
   c. The Second Continental Congress declared independence from Britain on July 4, 1776.
   d. Great Britain and the United States signed a peace treaty in 1783.
2. The American Revolution was important to Europe.
   a. A "conservative: revolution created a real life Enlightenment democracy.
   b. Americans created a republic based on a representative democracy.
3. Terrorist attacks occur more frequently in democratic nations.

D. The French Revolution, 1789-1799
1. Based on the same principles of enlightment as the American revolution. France represented a radical shift in power structures.
   a. Inequitable class structure – nobles and clergy paid no taxes.

6

  b. Class violence ripped through France as middle- and working-class revolutionaries tore power from the hands of the social elite and the state-sponsored Roman Catholic Church.

 2. King Louis XVI's Estates General gave way to a new National Assembly, which dissolved and formed an assembly to create a new government in 1791.

  a. National Convention elected in 1792

  b. Committee of Public Safety formed in 1793, executed thousands of nobles and clergy – period known as *Reign of Terror*.

 3. Napoleon came to power amid the socio-political turmoil, ending the revolution through military authoritarianism.

E. Guerrillas and the Spanish Peninsula

 1. Napoleon invaded Spain in 1807.

  a. The French army encountered a new style of battle, guerilla warfare, being waged by the Spaniards.

  b. The Napoleonic Wars continued until 1815.

  c. The Spanish called the partisans patriots, but the French referred to them as terrorists.

  d. The meaning of *terrorism* shifted away from governmental repression to the resistance of some people to governments.

III. **1848 and the Radical Democrats**

LO 5: Explain why terrorism became defined as a revolutionary activity after the European experience in 1848.

LO 6: Define socialism, anarchism, and communism.

A. Western minds began to view terrorism differently, due in large part to the nature of European violence, in the 1800s.

B. Europe continued to experience political struggles and demands for freedom in spite of the flourished democracies in Britain and America.

 1. The democrats of the early 1800s were not united.

 2. Royalists were reasserting their power in the rest of Europe.

 3. Facing continued failure, democratic forces began to think radically.

C. Formation of radical democrats, socialists, anarchists and capitalists.

 1. Radical democrats demanded immediate and drastic change. They were not only interested in developing constitutions, but also wanted to distribute evenly the wealth created by trade and manufacturing.

 2. Socialists argued for centralized control of the economy.

 3. Anarchists sought to reduce or eliminate centralized government

 4. When the level of terrorism is identified, the level of response can be determined.

D. Radical democrats called for class revolution.

 1. Constitutional movements had failed in many countries.

7

2. Parisians revolted in 1848, followed by almost every other European capital, as working-class distaste for the distribution of wealth and power increased.
3. The rebel efforts failed, creating an underground movement, signaling the beginning of modern terrorism.

E. Socialists
1. Three strains of radical democrats coalesced after the failed revolutions of 1848: communists, socialists, and anarchists.
   a. Socialists wanted to completely democratize society and assume control of industrial production.
   b. Karl Marx (father of communism) advocated a strong centralized government, the elimination of all classes except the working class, and a complete state monopoly over all forms of industrial and agricultural production.
   c. Anarchists viewed government as evil and sought to eliminate it.

F. Anarchists
1. The term *anarchy* originated with Greek philosophers speaking of government elimination.
2. Pierre Joseph Proudhon (1809–1865) was one of the advocates of modern anarchism. He called for:
   a. An extension of democracy to all classes.
   b. The elimination of property and government.
   c. Property was to be commonly held.
   d. Families living in extended communes were to replace centralized government.
3. Anarchists of the era came to see themselves as revolutionaries.
   a. anarchists favored strikes, demonstrations, and other mass actions.
   b. They would have growing influence on terrorism in the second half of the nineteenth century..

IV.   **Anarchism and Nationalism**

   LO 5: Explain why terrorism became defined as a revolutionary activity after the European experience in 1848.

A. The 1800s witnessed the growth of anarchism and the rise of Nationalism in the West. Terrorism in the modern sense came from violent anarchists in the late 1800s.
1. Anarchists called for an end to government.
2. Nationalists demanded the right to self-government.
3. Nationalists, who adopted "philosophy of the bomb", began using the terrorist tactics of violent anarchists. Nationalists believed that they were fighting patriotic wars. They adopted only the tactics of the anarchists, not their ideology.

8

B. Lindsay Clutterbuck (2004) states that most analysts believe that modern terrorism derived from the blend of anarchism and nationalism in Russia after the assassination of Czar Alexander II in 1881.

C. The nineteenth-century anarchists caused a panic.
    1. Terrorist activities, such as assassinations and bombings, were routine.
    2. Their activities were sensationalized by the press.
    3. People feared anarchism.
    4. People believed that anarchists were involved in an international conspiracy designed to topple Western governments.

V. **Terrorism and Revolution in Russia: 1881–1921**

   LO 7: Summarize the differing meanings of terrorism in Russia from the Peoples' Will through Lenin and Trotsky.

A. Late-nineteenth-century Russia differed significantly from the other great powers of Europe.
    1. As opposed to other European countries, class distinctions remained intact .
    2. Russia was inadequately prepared to manage the impact of the industrial revolution.
    3. Three groups in Russia after 1850 felt that they could reform and modernize the Russian state:
        a. One group aligned with Czar Alexander for modernizing Russia from the top down.
        b. A second, intellectuals, wanted Russia to become a liberal Western democracy.
        c. A third, Narodnaya Voyla (the People's Will), advocated violent socialist revolution.
    4. The People's will followed the philosophy of Mikhail Bakunin and Sergey Nechaev.
        a. They murdered the police chief of Moscow, and went on a campaign of bombing and murder.
        b. In May 1881, they succeeded in striking their ultimate target; they killed Czar Alexander II.

B. Czar Nicholas and the Revolutions of 1905 and 1917
    1. Russia experienced a revolution in St. Petersburg in 1905 - a time of economic and political turmoil following a lost war with Japan. The rebellion was suppressed by Czar Nicholas' forcesAfter entering WWI, a second revolution broke out, as Russian citizens grew tired of the economic state and Czarist rule. The army joined the people this time, creating a new government.
    2. Workers Councils (Soviets) were established.
    3. The February revolutionaries (Mensheviks) were unpopular as they kept Russia in the war.

9

4. Vladimir Lenin (1870–1924), backed by Germans, pulled Russia from the war, and began forging policy by force of will, in his desire to create a better socialist state. He saw terrorism as a useful instrument to overthrow governments and control enemies.

VI. **Selective Terrorism and the Birth of the Irish Republic**
      LO 8: Summarize the early history of the Irish Republican Army.
      LO 9: Define *selective terrorism* as used by Michael Collins.

A. The Irish have never ruled their island as a single political entity.
   1. The Irish have experienced some type of foreign domination since a series of Viking incursions in 800 A.D.
   2. English colonization of Ireland in the 1500s created friction on two fronts: colonizers vs. colonized, and Protestants vs. Catholics. The tension increased in 1801 as the UK formed and absorbed Ireland, forcing British rule upon the Irish.
      a. Unionists - people who wanted to remain in the United Kingdom of Great Britain and Ireland.
      b. Republicans - people who wanted independence from Britain.

B. The Early Irish Republican Army (IRA).

   1. Irish Republican Brotherhood (IRB) formed in the 1850s (made up primarily of Irish Catholic exiles and ex-patriots).

   2. Due to Irish nationalistic feeling in the homeland, and the hope of home rule, the IRB waged a campaign of bombing and assassination from 1870 until 1916.

C. The Easter Rising.
   1. At Easter in 1916, Patrick Pearse and James Connolly (1868–1916) led a revolt in Dublin.
   2. The revolt failed so the pair sought terms with the British.
   3. Sinn Fein, the political party of Irish republicanism, continued its activities in spite of the failure of the Easter Rising.
   4. The IRB had transformed itself into an army: the IRA, with Michael Collins soon to take the lead.
   5. Forcing the issue of self rule, the British fought with IRA forces in the Black and Tan War.

E. Selective Terror.
   1. Michael Collins, leader of the IRA, studied the tactics of the Russian Peoples' Will, and the writings of earlier anarchists and terrorists.
   3. He felt revolution could be successful, but not from a popular uprising. He felt that it needed to be systematic, organized, and ruthless.

4. Collins developed a strategy called "selective terrorism." To be effective, terrorism had to selectively, and ruthlessly, target security forces and their symbols of authority.

Chapter Summary

- The term *terrorism* refers to a social construct, and not a physical entity. Furthermore, the term is pejorative because it evokes a variety of politically charged responses. The way *terrorism* is defined often has life or death consequences.
- *Terrorism* is defined within social and political contexts, and it means different things in different time periods. The meaning even changes within a historical timeframe as contexts change. This is the primary reason that no single definition of *terrorism* will ever be successful.
- The eighteenth century Enlightenment provided the intellectual climate to support modern democracy. The ideology spawned revolutions in the American colonies and France, but the French Revolution brought a new government that ruled by the fear of terrorism. The French would change the meaning of the word again by calling guerrillas terrorists.
- European governments and capitalists came to fear class revolution as a series of uprisings swept across Europe in 1848. After governments restored order, by the use of force, they remained leery of groups calling for economic equality and full democracy. A small minority of the radical democrats called for violence and terrorism. People with political power began to label all types of activism as terrorism whether it was violent or not.
- Socialism refers to controlling an economy by direct democracy, and utilizing economic profits to ensure the well-being of citizens. Anarchism is a philosophical concept originating in ancient Greece. In the eighteenth century anarchists generally disavowed the power of national governments. Some anarchists were violent and they engaged in bombing and assassination. Communism in its ideal form is socialism, where economic production and profits are owned and distributed by workers.
- Modern revolutionary terrorism is closely associated with a series of revolutionary activities that began with the Peoples' Will and continued through the Communist Revolution. After the Communists seized power, they returned to the practice of the French revolutionaries using terrorism to maintain political power.
- Irish revolutionaries fought for independence for several centuries. The Irish Republican Brotherhood was created in the mid-nineteenth century. They soon adopted the tactics of the 1848 revolutionaries, waging a campaign of terrorism that culminated in the Black and Tan War.
- *Selective terrorism* was a term used by Michael Collins after the failure of the Easter Rising. His intention was to specifically target government officials and supporters. He sought to terrorize them until they accepted IRA terms.

11

Discussion Questions

1. If you were asked to develop a definition of terrorism, what political aspects would you apply in your definition? Do you believe that the definition of terrorism used by the United States is concise? Explain your position. (LO1)

2. Mr. Gibbs is angry with his insurance company. He hacks into the company's data base causing the system to crash. Would you consider this to be an act of terrorism? Explain. (LO 1, 2, and 7)

3. Imagine yourself having a conversation with some friends about the American Revolution, when someone states, "they were a bunch of terrorists". How might you respond? Be sure to expand on your answer. (LO 1, 2, 3, and 5)

4. Historical circumstances have had a powerful impact on the meaning of terrorism. Do you believe that the meaning of terrorism will change again in the future? What would need to occur in order to change the definition? Explain. (LO 1 and 2)

5. Do you believe U.S. Army Major Nidal Hasan was acting as a terrorist, or do you believe him to have been mentally ill at the time of shooting at Fort Hood? Explain. (LO 1, 5, and 9)

Class Activities

1. At the start of class, have your students write on a piece of paper a definition of terrorism in their own words. Have the students share their definitions with the class. Allow time to discuss student responses, as well as to discuss how the responses align with what White has written. Or post a Discussion Question addressing this topic on Blackboard or Moodle, and have the students discuss via this medium. (LO 1)

2. As a review, play jeopardy using the key terms and/or theorists. (LO 1 through 9)

3. In small groups have the students create a chart that displays the evolution of modern terrorism. (LO 3, 4, 5, 7, and 9)

4. Have students monitor nightly news, news magazines, or newspapers (local, national and/or international) in regard to broadcasts/stories on terrorism. Have them report their findings at the end of the course, or have them present a weekly current events article summary on a terrorism related article.
(LO 1 through 9)

12

5. Have each student comb through http://onlinelibrary.wiley.com/browse/publications (or another virtual library or website as approved by the instructor) for terrorism related news, and select an article that relates to one or more of the chapter's core concepts. Have students provide a journalistic summary and a personal opinion/reaction to the article. Have students orally present the article to the class, field Q & As from their fellow students, and provide a copy of the original source article following the presentation. Optional: Have students complete peer assessments at the end of each presentation. (OBJ 1 - 9)

Media Tools

1. 7 Things you should know about Wikis. Retrieved from the Web Jun 29, 2012 at http://net.educause.edu/ir/library/pdf/ELI7004.pdf

    This document offers easy to understand instruction on the history, development, and potential uses of Wikis.

    Have students develop a *Webliography* (resource list) using a Blog or Wiki that provides a short description, and link to a scholarly resource pertaining to course concepts. For example, have students add two to three resources each and ask them to add their assessment of at least one of their peers' contributions. If desired, allow time to discuss Blogs/Wikis. This activity can be reused throughout the course, by asking students to add/revise their contributions each week, bi-weekly, etc. (LO 1 through 9)

2. Global Issues:. Social, Political, Economic and Environmental Issues That Affect Us All. Full List in War on Terror Section. Retrieved from the Web Jun 29, 2012 at http://www.globalissues.org/article/358/war-on-terror-articles.

    This document offers an exhaustive list of links to articles reposted from other sites that detail numerous terrorism related events that have occurred during America's "War on Terror". This resource can additionally serve as an example for media tool sample #1. (LO 2, 4, 5, and 9)

    Divide class into two groups. Have each half select an article from the list and discuss it among their group. Direct their focus to the law enforcement response during each event, and reflect upon what they might (should) have done differently, if anything. After each group has completed their discussions, have each group present a summary of their discussions to the other group. Once completed, have the entire class compare and contrast both groups' consensus of the events. (LO 4, 5)

3.   The FBI's Terrorism Screening Center. Retrieved from the Web Jun 29, 2012 at http://www.fbi.gov/about-us/nsb/tsc.

This site offers a substantial array of information on terrorism related topics including postings of most Wanted Terrorists and Domestic Terror Fugitives. It additionally provides several links to related agencies in the War on Terror. In addition, the site also offers information on careers with the FBI, virtual tours, as well as a fun & games page.

Have students visit the photo gallery section and select three photos that they feel best represent America's War on Terror". Have students create a PowerPoint presentation that includes each photo as well as commentary on why they chose the way they did.   Be sure to give instruction on source citation for images. (LO 1, 2)

Chapter 1—**Defining Terrorism in Modern History**

TRUE/FALSE

1. Terrorism is considered a violation of law in all nations.

ANS: F   REF: p. 4   OBJ: 1

2. The Taliban and al Qaeda are one and the same organization.

ANS: F   REF: p. 5   OBJ: 2

3. Theology gained greater appreciation by the masses during the Enlightenment.

ANS: F   REF: p. 6   OBJ: 3

4. Terrorism came into existence during the American Revolution.

ANS: F   REF: p. 6 - 10   OBJ: 3, 4, and 5

5. The French Revolution was much more violent than the American Revolution.

ANS: T   REF: p. 6 - 10   OBJ: 4

6. Terrorist attacks occur more frequently in democracies than in countries with any other form of government.

ANS: T   REF: p. 7   OBJ: 3

7. Guerilla warfare originated in Spain.

ANS: F   REF: p. 5 and 9   OBJ: 4

8. European capitalists of the 1800s opposed all forms of socialism and anarchy.

ANS: T   REF: p. 10   OBJ: 3 and 6

9. Modern terrorism surfaced with violent anarchists in the late 1800s.

ANS: T   REF: p. 5 and 10   OBJ: 4 and 5

10. German born immigrant Most's *philosophy of the bomb* is a call for violence to produce change in government.

ANS: T   REF: p. 13   OBJ: 7 and 8

11. The definition of terrorism fluctuates according to the interests of the group defining the term.

ANS: T   REF: p. 5 and 17   OBJ: 1

12. Russia was the site of *The Easter Rising* of 1916.

ANS: F   REF: p. 22   OBJ: 8

13. Guerilla tactics were used throughout the Napoleonic Wars.

ANS: T   REF: p. 5   OBJ: 4

14. European governments and capitalists came to fear class revolution as a series of uprising swept across Europe in 1848.

ANS: T   REF: p. 25   OBJ: 3, 4, 5, and 7

15. David Bell believes that total war began with the 1789 French Revolution.

ANS: T   REF: p. 26   OBJ: 5

MULTIPLE CHOICE

1. "Selective terrorism" as strategy was developed by _____.
   a. Michael Collins of the IRA
   b. Karl Marx
   c. Karl Heinzen
   d. Peter Prokoptin

ANS: a   REF: p. 1 - 5   OBJ: 8, 9

2. The violence of the French Revolutionary period is colloquially known as _____.
   a. Bloody Sunday
   b. The Reign of Terror
   c. The Rule
   d. Black October

ANS: b   REF: p. 8 - 9   OBJ: 3, 4, 5

3.   _____ do not support centralized control of the economy.
       a. Communists
       b. Socialists
       c. Anarchists
       d. Capitalists

ANS: c   REF: p. 10 - 13   OBJ: 6

4.   The Irish Republican Army (IRA) developed out of a _____ desire.
       a. Nationalistic
       b. Socialistic
       c. Economic
       d. Capitalistic

ANS: a   REF: p. 15 - 16   OBJ: 8

5.   Modern terrorism, as defined in the text, surfaced with violent anarchists in the late
       _____.
       a. 1900s
       b. 1700s
       c. 1600s
       d. 1800s

ANS: d   REF: p. 12 - 18   OBJ: 4, 5

6.   Modern terrorists largely strike at governments by _____.
       a. Propaganda
       b. Killing citizens
       c. Embargos
       d. Cyber strikes

ANS: b   REF: p. 15   OBJ: 8

7.   Who is considered the father of is considered the father of communism?
       a. Karl Marx
       b. Friedrich Engels
       c. Joseph Stalin
       d. Leon Trostsky

ANS: a   REF: p. 10 - 12   OBJ: 6

8.   What was the hallmark of anarchist groups in the mid to late 1800s?
       a. Political assassinations
       b. Espionage
       c. Riots
       d. Poisoning

ANS: a   REF: p. 13   OBJ: 4, 6, and 7

9. The Peoples' Will advocated for a violent socialist revolution in what country?
   a. France
   b. England
   c. Russia
   d. Spain

ANS: c   REF: p. 18 - 19   OBJ: 7

10. While the U.S. State Department considers Hezbollah a terrorist organization, the Jordanian police view Hezbollah as _____?
    a. As a militia
    b. As a terrorist organization
    c. As a religious group
    d. As a law enforcement agency

ANS: a   REF: p. 4   OBJ: 1, 2

11. Who, of the following, claims terrorism constitutes the illegitimate use of force to achieve a political objective by targeting innocent people?
    a. Brian Jenkins
    b. Walter Laqueur
    c. David Rapoport
    d. Edward Herman

ANS: b   REF: p. 4   OBJ: 3

12. Which of the following was NEVER a formal ruler of Russia?
    a. Lenin
    b. Putin
    c. Stalin
    d. Trotsky

ANS: d   REF: p. 19   OBJ: 4

13. The definition of terrorism is not only produced from various social constructs, it also developed through the application of_____?
    a. War
    b. Political power
    c. Police power
    d. Censorship

ANS: b   REF: p. 6 and 25   OBJ: 1

14. According to Schmid terrorism is a _____; that is, terrorism is defined by different people within vacillating social and political realities.
    a. Military concept
    b. Social context
    c. Social construct
    d. Truth construct

ANS: c   REF: p. 4   OBJ: 1

18

15. The Black and Tan War was fought in what country?
   a. England
   b. Ireland
   c. Wales
   d. Scotland

ANS: b   REF: p. 23 - 24   OBJ: 8

16. To preserve following the Thirty Years' War (1618–1648), several European rulers agreed to tolerate different sects of _____ within the same realm.
   a. Islam
   b. Christianity
   c. Judaism
   d. Hinduism

ANS: b   REF: p. 6   OBJ: 3, 4, 5, and 7

17. Michael Scheuer (former director of the CIA's bin Laden unit) contends there are two types of terrorist experts—retired governmental and military officials and informed commentators, the latter group being made up of _____.
   a. Politicians
   b. Social workers
   c. Religious leaders
   d. Academics and journalists

ANS: d   REF: p. 20   OBJ: 2

18. What group was responsible for the assassination of Czar Alexander II?
   a. The IRA
   b. The Peoples' Will
   c. Mensheviks
   d. Hohenzollerns

ANS: c   REF: p. 16   OBJ: 7

19. According to the text, the definition of _____ changes with social and historical circumstances.
   a. War
   b. Anarchism
   c. Terrorism
   d. Violence

ANS: c   REF: p. 4   OBJ: 1, 2

20. Modern terrorism developed out of the _____.
   a. French Revolution
   b. Civil War
   c. American Revolution
   d. World War II

ANS: a   REF: p. 5 and 10   OBJ: 4 and 5

21.   After which event did nationalistic groups begin to be labeled as terrorists?
       a. French Revolution
       b. Civil War
       c. American Revolution
       d. World War II

ANS: d   REF: p. 15   OBJ: 2, 8

22.   The Taliban is also referred to as _____.
       a. The Students
       b. The Teachers
       c. The Professors
       d. The Pupils

ANS: a   REF: p. 5   OBJ: 2

23.   The theological tradition of the Taliban differs from al Qaeda's infatuation with a violent
       interpretation of a twentieth-century militant _____ theologian.
       a. Egyptian
       b. Saudi
       c. Iranian
       d. Turkish

ANS: a   REF: p. 5   OBJ: 2

24.   Historians often call the eighteenth century the Age of Reason or the _____.
       a. Engagement
       b. Existence
       c. Illumination
       d. Enlightenment

ANS: d   REF: p. 6   OBJ: 3

25.   From 1794 to 1795, the French government conducted more than _____ legal
       executions.
       a. 1,700
       b. 17,000
       c. 700
       d. 170,000

ANS: b   REF: p. 9   OBJ: 3, 4

26.   Napoleon's army's first encounter with guerrilla tactics came with its invasion of which
       country?
       a. Spain
       b. Russia
       c. England
       d. Austria

ANS: a   REF: p. 9 - 10   OBJ: 4

20

27. Who was the primary force behind Russia's removal from World War I?
    a. Vladimir Lenin
    b. Vladimir Putin
    c. Karl Marx
    d. Czar Alexander II

ANS: c   REF: p. 19 - 20   OBJ: 7

28. Two issues dominated media consciousness about terrorism in the 1970s: the cold war and violence around Israel and _____.
    a. Iraq
    b. Iran
    c. Afghanistan
    d. Palestine

ANS: d   REF: p. 20   OBJ: 2

29. Leon Trotsky (1879–1940), believed that _____ should be used as an instrument for overthrowing middle-class, or bourgeois, governments.
    a. terrorism
    b. diplomacy
    c. propaganda
    d. negotiation

ANS: a   REF: p. 20   OBJ: 3 and 7

30. According to Schmid, there is no true or correct definition because terrorism is a(n) _____ concept with no real presence.
    a. Abstract
    b. Real
    c. Concrete
    d. Power

ANS: a   REF: p. 4   OBJ: 1 and 2

31. A simple definition of terrorism involves all of the following EXCEPT:
    a. Use of force
    b. Innocent people
    c. Political purposes
    d. Counterterrorism

ANS: d   REF: p. 4   OBJ: 1, 2, and 5

32. Historically, the violence in Ireland has been largely intertwined with conflict between these two religions:
    a. Anglicanism and Hinduism
    b. Protestantism and Catholicism
    c. Judaism and Paganism
    d. Islam and Catholicism

ANS: b   REF: p. 21   OBJ: 8

33. Hezbollah members are primarily _____ .
    a. Shi'ite
    b. Sunni
    c. Christian
    d. Agnostic

ANS: a   REF: p. 4   OBJ: 2

34. Many Lebanese believe _____ to be the true source of terrorism.
    a. Jordan
    b. Palestine
    c. Iran
    d. Israel

ANS: a   REF: p. 4   OBJ: 2

35. On November 5, 2009, U.S. Army Major Nidal Malik Hasan went on a shooting spree at _____, killing thirteen people.
    a. Tacoma Mall, WA
    b. Fort Hood, TX
    c. Virginia Tech, VA
    d. Washington, DC

ANS: b   REF: p. 5   OBJ: 2

36. Terrorism began as government repression in what country?
    a. The United States
    b. France
    c. Canada
    d. England

ANS: b   REF: p. 5   OBJ: 4

37. _____ was thrown out of the Communist Party for opposing Stalin and was assassinated by communist agents in Mexico City in 1940.

    a. Karl Marx
    b. Friedrich Engels
    c. Vladimir Lenin
    d. Leon Trostsky

ANS: d   REF: p. 20   OBJ: 7

38. Due to the carnage of the _____, many European rulers opted to tolerate different sects of Christianity within the same realm to achieve peace.
    a. Thirty Years' War
    b. Eighty Years' War
    c. Nine Years' War
    d. One Hundred Years' War

ANS: a   REF: p. 6   OBJ: 4

22

39. The Irish Republican Army (IRA) was founded in the _____ century.
    a. 19th
    b. 17th
    c. 18th
    d. 20th

ANS: a.   REF: p. 22   OBJ: 8

40. Who wrote of principles of revolution in his "Catechism of the Revolutionary."?
    a. Nechaev
    b. Rubenstein
    c. Marighella
    d. Bakunin

ANS: a.   REF: p. 19   OBJ: 6, 7

Case 1.0

The Enlightenment was an 18th century international intellectual movement that gave rise to rise to science and a new age of discovery - deductive logic giving way to empirical observation. Although diverse in political opinions, the philosophers of the Age of Reason produced a common idea about government - they believed that governments should exist to protect individual rights. Philosophers argued that citizens had rights and that governments' duty was to protect those rights. Common people were to control the government by a social contract, or constitution, that spelled out the rights of citizens and limited governmental power.

41. The form of government that best exemplifies the ideals of the Enlightenment is a(n):
    a. Democracy
    b. Oligarchy
    c. Dictatorship
    d. Theocracy

ANS: a   REF: p. 6   OBJ: 3 and 6

42. The movement of the period was seeking to increase the political power of:
    a. Ruling/Upper classes
    b. Military
    c. Middle/lower classes
    d. Clergy

ANS: c   REF: p. 6   OBJ: 3 and 6

43. During the Enlightenment, which group lost its monopoly on providing answers to all human questions?
    a. Ruling/Upper classes
    b. Military
    c. Middle/lower classes
    d. Clergy

ANS: d   REF: p. 6   OBJ: 3 and 6

44. Which of the following statements might NOT be popular among the philosophers during this period?
   a. The Church is the only source of truth
   b. The Earth revolves around the sun
   c. The sun is the center of the universe
   d. All writings are to be subjected to censorship by Church and state

ANS: c   REF: p. 6   OBJ: 3 and 6

Case 1.1

The political activities of Pierre Joseph Proudhon (1809–1865) eventually landed him in a French prison, but Proudhon was not a man of violence. He called for the extension of democracy to all classes, to be accomplished through the elimination of property and government. Property was to be commonly held, and families living in extended communes were to replace centralized government.

45. Proudhon's philosophy would most appropriately classify him as a(n):
   a. Socialist
   b. Anarchist
   c. Communist
   d. Terrorist

ANS: b   REF: p. 11 - 12   OBJ: 3 and 6

46. Which of the following statements would Proudhoun likely disagree?
   a. All classes should have equal authority
   b. A Centralized government is a necessary evil
   c. Violence is necessary to promote change
   d. Capitalism should be supported by the masses

ANS: b   REF: p. 11 - 12   OBJ: 3 and 6

47. Which individual would you suspect NOT to support Proudhoun's endeavors?
   a. Karl Marx
   b. Prokoptin
   c. Nechaev
   d. Heinzen

ANS: a   REF: p. 11 - 12   OBJ: 3 and 6

Case 1.2

After being released from prison in a general amnesty, IRA's Michael Collins studied the tactics of the Russian Peoples' Will and the writings of earlier anarchists and terrorists. Collins developed a strategy called "selective terrorism." Collins reasoned that indiscriminate terror was of no value - random or large-scale attacks would alienate public opinion. Conversely, launching an attack and waiting for the population to spontaneously rise to rebellion was equally futile.

48. Which of the following acts is an example of Collin's "selective terrorism"?
    a. Mass bombing in a public park
    b. Sniper shooting at officers leaving a police department
    c. Taking a politician hostage
    d. Poisoning of a city's water supply

ANS: b   REF: p. 24   OBJ: 9

49. Which of the following would NOT be a likely target for Collins?
    a. Foreign diplomat
    b. Police officer
    c. Irish national
    d. Government worker

ANS: C   REF: p. 24   OBJ: 8 and 9

50. Collins viewed himself as a:
    a. Terrorist
    b. Anarchist
    c. Nationalist
    d. Socialist

ANS: c   REF: p. 24   OBJ: 8 and 9

Completion

1. According to Alex Schmid's academic consensus definition of terrorism, most definitions of the term have two characteristics: (1) someone is terrorized and (2) the meaning of the term is derived from _____.

ANS: the terrorists' targets and victims   REF: p. 4   OBJ: 1

2. The main objective of most European middle-class democrats from approximately 1815 to 1848 was to obtain constitutions to _____.

ANS: ensure liberty   REF: p. 10   OBJ: 3

3. The primary targets of the IRB's 1870 terrorist campaign were _____.

ANS: Unionists and British forces   REF: p. 22   OBJ: 8

4. Historically, American military preparedness had been based on the axiom that U.S. Armed Forces should be able to fight two independent major wars while maintaining a _____.

ANS: Strong continental defense   REF: p. 3   OBJ: 2

5. The synthesis of various positions on the definition of terrorism is known as the _____ Definition.

ANS: academic consensus   REF: p. 4   OBJ: 1 and 2

6. _____ reports that terrorism constitutes the illegitimate use of force to achieve a political objective by targeting innocent people.

ANS: Walter Laqueur   REF: p. 4   OBJ: 1 and 2

7. Modern terrorism originated from the _____ revolution.

ANS: French   REF: p. 5   OBJ: 4

8. Czar Nicholas of Russia faced his first revolution in _____.

ANS: 1905   REF: p. 19   OBJ: 3 and 7

9. *The Minimanual of the Urban Guerrilla* was written by _____.

ANS: Carlos Marighella   REF: p. 19   OBJ: 3, 4, and 5

10. During the Enlightenment, Europeans masses sought to increase the political power of the _____ classes.

ANS: lower   REF: p. 6   OBJ: 3, 4, and 5

11. _____ was the site of the start of the First Russian Revolution in 1905.

ANS: St. Petersburg   REF: p. 18   OBJ: 4

12. Anarchism is a philosophical concept that originated in _____.

ANS: ancient Greece   REF: p. 25   OBJ: 6

13. The political party of Irish republicanism is called _____.

ANS: Sinn Fein   REF: p. 23   OBJ: 8

14. The Estates General of prerevolutionary France included members from all classes except those from the _____ classes.

ANS: lower   REF: p. 8   OBJ: 4

15. The dividing of _____ by Spanish and French forces sparked the beginning of the Peninsula War (1808–1814).

ANS: Portugal   REF: p. 9   OBJ: 4

16. Karl Marx and Friedrich Engels immortalized their communist ideals in their 1848 writing, _____ .

ANS: *The Communist Manifesto*   REF: p. 10   OBJ: 6 and 7

26

17. _____ in Marxist terminology refers to the middle class - trades-people, merchants, artisans and other non-peasants excluded from the upper classes in medieval Europe.

ANS: *Bourgeoisie*   REF: p. 13   OBJ: 6

18. _____ led the October 1917 Russian revolution, bringing the communists to power.

ANS: Vladimir Lenin   REF: p. 55   OBJ: 4

19. _____ is the Russian word for "council."

ANS: *Soviet*   REF: p. 19   OBJ: 6

20. The Royal Irish Constabulary (RIC) was the police force established by _____ in Ireland.

ANS: the United Kingdom   REF: p. 22   OBJ: 8

Essay

1. Describe some major differences between the Taliban and al Qaeda.

ANS: Al Qaeda functions internationally, with a violence-focused theological base, whereas the Taliban form divergent regional militias and use selective terrorism to support guerrilla operations.

REF: p. 5   OBJ: 2 and 9

2. Explain why there is confusion when trying to define terrorism. Provide examples to illustrate your answer.

ANS:
- Terrorism is defined by different people within vacillating social and political
- realities
- Definition of social construct changes with the social reality of the group
- providing the definition
- Groups construct a framework around a concept, defining various aspects of their
- lives through the meanings they attribute to the construct
- Meaning of terrorism changes within social and historical contexts
- Meaning of terrorism has changed over time
- Examples will vary

REF: p. 4   OBJ: 1 and 2

3.   Compare and contrast the definitions of terrorism offered by Walter Laqueur and Alex Schmid. Do you agree with Laqueur or Schmid? Explain

ANS:
- Laquer
    - Terrorism constitutes the illegitimate use of force to achieve a political objective by targeting innocent people
    - Attempts to move beyond the simple definition are fruitless because the term is so controversial
    - Laquer promotes a simple definition because the meaning of terrorism changes constantly as social contexts change
    - Simple definition includes 3 parts: 1) use of force, 20 against innocent people, 3) for political purposes
- Schmid
    - There is no true or correct definition because terrorism is an abstract concept with no real presence
    - A single definition cannot possibly account for all the potential uses of the term
    - Leading definitions have some common elements and most definitions have two characteristics – someone is terrorized and the meaning of the term is derived from terrorists' targets and victims.
    - Definition closely related to the group searching for meaning
- Opinions will vary based on arguments presented.

REF: p. 4   OBJ: 1 and 2

4.   Explain the impact the Enlightenment on democracy and potential revolutionary thought.

ANS:
- Historians often call the eighteenth century the Enlightenment.
- Also called the Age of Reason, the Enlightenment was characterized by rational thought and the belief that all activities could be explained.
- Europe had been exhausted by the carnage of the Thirty Years' War (1618–1648).
- To preserve peace, several rulers agreed to tolerate different sects of Christianity within the same
- realm.
- During the Enlightenment, theology lost its monopoly on providing answers to all human questions.
- This gave rise to science and a new age of discovery. The deductive logic of the former age was gradually replaced by empirical observation.
- Europe and America experienced tremendous economic, political, and social
- change during this time.

- Changes in the approach to political power. Before the Enlightenment, a large segment of the European population was tied to a class of nobles, and smaller groups of people were part of emerging trade and professional classes or free farmers.

28

- During the Enlightenment, many Europeans began to question how they were governed, and they sought to increase the political power of the lower classes.
- Evolving legal authority in England began to limit the power of the monarch,
- and the French questioned the authority of their king even more directly.
- The forces of change during the Enlightenment brought a new way of thinking about
- citizenship. Ordinary people came to believe that the state existed to protect everybody,
- not just the nobles. The nobles and other people who held power were frightened
- by this line of thinking.
- The Enlightenment was an international intellectual movement.
- Although diverse in political opinions, the philosophers of the Age of Reason produced a common idea about government.
  - governments should exist to protect individual rights
  - the best form of government was democracy.
  - citizens had rights and that government's duty was to protect those rights.
  - common people were to control the government under a social contract, or constitution,
  - that spelled out the rights of citizens and limited governmental power.

- The Enlightenment brought an increased demand for democracy. Such thinking
- produced tension between the ruling class and the governed, and some of the

REF: p. 6   OBJ: 2, 5, and 7

5.   What is meant by the term official context? Provide examples.

ANS:
- The definition of terrorism is related to the government entity defining terrorism.
- U.S. Legal Code
- FBI
- U.S. Department of State
- Department of Defense
- DHS

REF: p. 4   OBJ: 1 and 2

6.   Karl Marx, founder of communism, is often labeled as a terrorist. Do you feel this is a correct assessment? Why or why not?

ANS
- The author takes a position that Marx has historically been erroneously labeled as a terrorist given that Marx never sought for violent action to create change.
- Marx referred to "revolutionary" change, but he never clarified what he meant by revolution.
- Further, he did not advocate political bombing or assassination. In fact, on most occasions he publicly condemned it.

29

- He believed socialism was to be a reflection of democracy, not violence.
- A massive seizure of power by the general population might be justified, but individual acts of murder were not.

REF: p. 12   OBJ: 6

7.   Compare and contrast socialist, communist, and anarchist movements of the mid 1800s.

ANS:
- o   Socialists
- o   Three strains of radical democrats coalesced after the failed revolutions of 1848: communists, socialists, and anarchists.
- o   Socialists wanted to completely democratize society and assume control of industrial production.
- o   Karl Marx (father of communism) advocated a strong centralized government, the elimination of all classes except the working class, and a complete state monopoly over all forms of industrial and agricultural production.
- o   Anarchists viewed government as evil and sought to eliminate it.
- o   Anarchists
  - The term *anarchy* originated with Greek philosophers speaking of government elimination.
  - Pierre Joseph Proudhon (1809–1865) was one of the advocates of modern anarchism. He called for:
- o   An extension of democracy to all classes.
- o   The elimination of property and government.
- o   Property was to be commonly held.
- o   Families living in extended communes were to replace centralized government.
- o   Anarchists of the era came to see themselves as revolutionaries.
- o   anarchists favored strikes, demonstrations, and other mass actions. They would have growing influence on terrorism in the second half of the nineteenth century.
- o   Violent Anarchists
- o   Fueled by a lack of change, anarchists turned to violence in the 1880s.
- o   They began to assassinate heads of state.
- o   The elimination of property and government.
- o   Property was to be commonly held.
- o   Families living in extended communes were to replace centralized government.
- o   Anarchists of the era came to see themselves as revolutionaries. They would have growing influence on terrorism in the second half of the nineteenth century.

REF: p. 11 - 13   OBJ: 2

8.   Trace the evolution of the People's Will.

ANS:
- Three groups in Russia after 1850 felt that they could reform and modernize the Russian
- state, but they disagreed about the ways to do it.
  - One group, whose views Czar Alexander shared, wanted to modernize Russia from the top down.
  - Another group, the intellectuals, wanted Russia to become a liberal Western democracy. Violent anarchists took another path. They believed that Russian problems could be settled through revolution.

- Narodnaya Voyla (the People's Will) advocated violent socialist revolution.

- When it launched a campaign of revolutionary terrorism in the 1870s, it faced confrontation with conservative elements such as the church, police, and military.

- Members of the People's Will came to believe that it was necessary to terrorize
- these conservative organizations into submission.

- The motivations behind the People's Will evolved from Russian revolutionary
- thought. According to Laqueur (1999, pp. 15–16), the philosophy of anarchist terrorism
- in Russia was embodied by Mikhail Bakunin and Sergey Nechaev.
  - Their revolutionary thought developed separately before they met each other in the 1860s, when they formed an intellectual union.
  - Both spoke of revolt against the czar, and both endorsed violence as the means.
  - Yet, even in the nation that would experience a violent anarchist campaign and eventually a communist revolution, Bakunin and Nechaev basically stuck to rhetoric.

- Although they were ideologically linked to anarchism in Western Europe, they
- were distinct from their Western supporters.

- Russian anarchists were writing for a general population in the hope of sparking a democratic revolution. Laqueur says that their significance lies in their influence on later revolutionaries and the violence and assassinations those later revolutionaries committed.

- They were not radical revolutionaries in Laqueur's view.

REF: p. 18   OBJ: 3

31

9.   Chart the organizational structure/hierarchy of the Supreme Council of the IRB.

ANS:
- Any illustration that displays a command center that includes several Republican terrorist organizations, specifically:
    o The Irish Republican Army
    o The Official Irish Republican Army
    o The Provisional Irish Republican Army.

REF: p. 22   OBJ: 3

10.   Compare and contrast the socialists, anarchists, and communists of the 18th and 19th centuries.

ANS:
- Socialism refers to controlling an economy by direct democracy and utilizing economic profits to ensure the well-being of citizens. Socialists:

    o Radical democrats who sought wealth equality in capitalist societies

    o Sought governmental guarantees of living standards

    o Believed that the state should control industry and divide profits among all members of society

    o Believed that people would form cooperative relationships on their own with no need of a government

- Communism in its ideal form is socialism where economic production and profits are owned and distributed by workers. Communists:
    o Socialists who believed in a strong centralized economy controlled by a strong central government

    o Followers of *The Communist Manifesto,* written by Karl Marx and Friedrich Engels

- Anarchism is a philosophical concept originating in ancient Greece. In the eighteenth century anarchists generally disavowed the power of national governments. Anarchists:

    o Advocated the creation of cooperative societies without centralized governments

    o Violent socialist revolutionaries

    o Some anarchists were violent and they engaged in bombing and assassination.

REF: p. 10 - 15   OBJ: 6

CHAPTER 2
The Social Underpinnings of Terrorism

Learning Objectives

After reading this chapter, students should be able to:

1. Outline differing approaches for understanding social reality
2. Define the elements of netwar
3. Describe terrorism as a religious process
4. Define practical criminology as used by security forces
5. Describe the differences between terrorist and criminal behavior
6. Explain the reason terrorists and counter terrorists need to justify violence
7. Summarize studies of the ways terrorist violence is justified
8. Describe three views in the profiling debate
9. Outline differing points of view about radicalization and alienation

Chapter Key Terms

Social process, p. 29
Meaning framework, p. 29
Theory of action, p. 30
Structural framework, p. 31
Social geometry, p. 31
Netwar, p. 31
Node, p. 31
Eschatology, p. 33
Cesare Beccaria, p. 36
Profiling, p. 40
Routes to terrorism, p 43
Radicalization, p. 43
Violent radicalization, p. 43
Alienation, p. 43
Umar Farouk Abdulmutallab, p. 48
James W. von Brunn, p. 48
Omar Hammami, p. 49
Al Shabaab, p. 49

Al Shabaab (also known as the Harakat Shabaab al-Mujahadeen, the Youth, Mujahadeen Youth Movement, and Mujahadeen al Shabaab Movement) was formed as a militant wing of a federation of Islamic courts in Somalia in 2006. Its senior leadership is affiliated with al Qaeda.

Cesare Beccaria (1738-1794) was one of the founders of the discipline of criminology. His work *Of Crimes and Punishments* (1764) is the classic Enlightenment study of the discipline.

Eschatology (pronounced es-**ka**-taw-low-gee) is a Greek word used to indicate the theological end of time. In Judaism and Christianity it refers to God bringing creation to an end. In some Shi'ite Islamic sects and among Christians who literalize biblical eschatological literature, believers contend that Jesus will return to lead a final battle against evil. Other major religions also have end-time theologies.

James W. von Brunn (1920-2010) was an American white supremacist and anti-Semite. He entered the Holocaust Museum on June 10, 2009 and began shooting. He killed a security officer before he was wounded and subdued. He died in federal custody while awaiting trial.

Meaning framework is the social construct providing definitional boundaries for a particular social meaning.

Netwar refers to one network fighting another network.

Nodes in counterterrorism or netwar discussions refer to crucial points in a system where critical components are stored or transferred. The importance of a node is determined by its relationship to the network.

Omar Mammami (b. 1984) is an American leader of al Shabaab. He also goes under the name of Abu Mansoor al-Ameriki.

Profiling is a practical criminological process designed to identify the behavioral attributes of certain types of criminals.

Radicalization as used in this context refers to the psychological process of adopting extremist positions.

Routes to terrorism (as used by John Horgan) refer to the psychological and social factors that motivate people to join, and remain, in terrorist groups.

Social geometry (as used by Black) is the social space occupied by a structure, and the direction in which it moves.

Social process refers to the way individuals and groups structure themselves, interpret reality, and take action based on those interpretations.

Structural framework refers to the idea that social constructs are based on systems that provide order. The systems are social structures that accomplish functions necessary to survive. Human activity is taken to accomplish the functions required to maintain the social structure of the system.

Theory of action is a social science theory based on the assumption that human beings take action based on the subjective meanings they attribute to social settings.

Umar Farouk Abdulmutallab (b. 1986), according to a federal indictment, smuggled a chemical bomb and igniter onto a Northwest flight from Amsterdam to Detroit on December 25, 2009. He was born into a family that practiced Islam, but became radicalized while attending school in the United Kingdom. He was allegedly trained by terrorists in Yemen who supplied the explosive compound.

Violent radicalization refers to the process of adopting extremist positions and engaging in violence based on a new set of beliefs.

Chapter Outline

I.   **Terrorism as a Social Process: Two Frameworks**
       OBJ 1: Outline differing approaches for understanding social reality

    A. Terrorism is a *social process* involving groups of people forming associations, defining social realities, and taking actions based on the meanings given to those realities.

    B. Terrorism is violent, and it is conducted in situations where violence is not expected.

    C. Two schools of thought dominate the scholarly literature on terrorism:
        1. One group tends to focus on the meaning of the activity.
        2. The other school looks at the structure of action.

    D. The meaning framework.
        1. Many social scientists study group behavior by looking at the *meaning* of actions.
        2. Social scientists, who study group and individual behavior this way, believe the way we interpret the world motivates the actions we take.
        3. When this method is used to study terrorist organizations, it can be called a *meaning framework.*
            a. Mark Juergensmeyer uses this approach to study the impact of religion on terrorism.
            b. Michael Arena and Bruce Arrigo study meaning by looking at the ways terrorists view symbols to develop their concepts of self.
            c. Gregory Lee uses a meaning framework to develop a

method of classifying terrorist organizations, so as to assist law enforcement officers in conspiracy investigations.

4. Historians often use this methodology – Bernard Lewis examines the rise and demise of the Ottoman Turks.
    a. Lewis argues that the trouble between Islam and Western modernity can be attributed to the meanings each group attributes to historical change.
        i. Middle Eastern Muslims tend to search for a lost ideal, whereas the West embraces modernity.
5. Samuel Huntington believes that a new political order emerged at the end of the cold war, and future conflicts will take place between the world's major civilizations.
6. Thomas P.M. Barnett believes the world is divided into three economic groupings, and conflict will be based on the distribution of wealth.
7. Malcolm Nance advances a *theory of action,* while dealing with the practical aspects of counterterrorism.

E. The structural framework
1. This methodology maintains that human societies need to accomplish certain functions, so they create organizations to do them.
2. Approaches to understanding terrorist behavior by looking at the way organizations function can be called a *structural framework.*
3. Donald Black:
    a. Argues that explaining terrorist behavior is no different than explaining any other aspect of human action.
    b. All groups, including terrorist organizations, take action because they belong to a structure that operates for a specific purpose – *social geometry*.
4. The structure and movement of groups explain terrorism – terrorism develops when an inferior group moves against a superior group, inducing mass civilian casualties.
5. Terrorism was rare in the past because geography would not allow it to develop.

II. **Structural Approaches and Netwar**
   OBJ 2: Define the elements of netwar

A. Vito Latora and Massimo Marchioni:
1. Terrorist organizations are complex systems that can be modeled mathematically and projected by computer simulations.
2. According to their thesis, terrorist organizations are structured in the same manner as communication and transportation systems.
3. Latora and Marchiori's position reflects a new theory in modern warfare called *netwar.*

4. Sub-national criminal, terrorist, or revolutionary groups organize themselves in a network of smaller logistical structures, groups, or command posts.
5. Any point where information, weapons, or personnel are gathered or exchanged is called a *node*, and the node is the critical target for counterterrorist operations.

III. **Terrorism as a Religious Process: Anthropological and Sociological Approaches**
   OBJ 1: Outline differing approaches for understanding social reality
   OBJ 3: Describe terrorism as a religious process
   OBJ 6: Explain the reason terrorists and counter terrorists need to justify violence
   OBJ 7: Summarize studies of the ways terrorist violence is justified

   A. Tanja Ellingsen says two primary reasons account for the continued influence of religion.
      1. First, religion has always been an important factor in the history of humanity.
      2. Second, modernization tends to break down communities, families, and social orientation.
   B. Susanna Pearce believes that strong religious beliefs increase not only the likelihood of religious conflict, but also the intensity of fighting.
   C. *Eschatology* plays a major role because messianic warriors in the end-time correct the heresies of the past, and fight for the ideal divine order of a deity.
   D. Marvin Harris believes human beings have experienced two types of religions: killing and non-killing.
      1. Killing religions developed during the food-gathering cycles of pre-agrarian and early agricultural societies; they embraced enemies and developed elaborate theologies to justify violence as a last resort.
      2. In the killing religions, gods slaughtered enemies; the non-killing religions appeared in order to try to transcend everyday experience.
   E. Jessica Stern:
      1. States that people around the world are returning to their religious roots as a means to escape the complexity of modern life.
      2. When mythological truths compete, violence often results.
      3. Individuals come to a group because they believe they have been called to the story of an entire people; they join a cosmic struggle, a holy cause.
      5. The power of the myth becomes less important, and the day-to-day job of terrorism grows.

7. Religion helps to produce the "lone wolf avenger," a person striking out with an ideology but no group; they are the most difficult type of terrorist to deter or detain.

F. Mark Juergensmeyer:
1. Terrorism is created by the meanings subjects attach to social situations producing a common pattern in religious terrorist organizations.
2. Believers must identify with a deity, and think they are participating in a struggle to change history.
3. The call to violence is a call to purify the world in a holy war that eliminates the nonbeliever and the incorrect interpreters of tradition.
4. The holy terrorist is victorious either by killing the enemy or dying in the struggle.

G. Eli Berman:
1. Argues that it is possible to understand religious terrorism by looking at the economic factors that cause groups to prosper and grow.
2. The internal economic dynamics of a religious terrorist group are the key to its success, it has very little to do with theology.
3. His findings have important information for security specialists:
   a. Religious terrorists are lethal; religious terrorists are deadlier than their secular counterparts.
      i. Counterterrorism programs should focus on radical ideology. Reduce the violent rhetoric and the level of terrorism goes down.
   b. There are twenty active religious terrorist organizations in the world. Eighteen of them are based in Islam, and less than a dozen are very effective.
      i. Counterterrorist policy should be aimed at studying the internal ability of a selected group to operate effectively.

IV. **Terrorism as Practical Criminology**
   OBJ 4: Define practical criminology as used by security forces
   OBJ 5: Describe the differences between terrorist and criminal behavior

A. There are two branches of criminology in the practical world of criminal justice.
   1. Classic criminology, tracing its origins to *Cesare Beccaria*, and using the most modern theories of individual and group behavior.
   2. Practical criminology focuses on the common actions of lawbreakers.
      a. The second use of *criminology*, the applied actions, is utilized in crime prevention and apprehension.

B. Terrorists differ from ordinary street criminals.

C. Law enforcement personnel must recognize the differences between typical criminal behavior and terrorist activity if they want to prevent crime and apprehend criminals.

D. Law enforcement officials are frequently the first governmental agents on the scene of a terrorist incident.

E. The FBI has created localized terrorism task forces—Joint Terrorism Task Forces (JTTFs)—around the country. This allows the FBI to coordinate law enforcement resources in the face of domestic terrorism, and to expand investigations.

F. D. Douglas Bodrero offers a comparative analysis between terrorist behavior and that of ordinary criminals.
   1. Criminals are unfocused. Terrorists focus their actions toward a goal.
   2. Criminals may live in a criminal underworld, but they are not devoted to crime as a philosophy. Terrorists are dedicated to a cause.
   3. Criminals will make deals to avoid punishment. Terrorists rarely cooperate with officials because they do not wish to betray their cause.
   4. Criminals usually run when confronted with force. Terrorists tend to attack.
   5. Criminals strike when the opportunity to do so is present. Terrorists strike against symbols after careful planning.
   6. Criminals rarely train for crime. Terrorists prepare for and rehearse their operations.

G. These differences influence the ways criminal intelligence is gathered in the process of criminal investigations.

H. Law enforcement, military, and security officials need to focus on ideology, group and individual behavior, and sharing information over broad geographical regions to successfully investigate terrorism.

V. **Justifying Terrorism**

   OBJ 6: Explain the reason terrorists and counter terrorists need to justify violence

   OBJ 7: Summarize studies of the ways terrorist violence is justified

   A. Every person who uses force must seek to justify it. As the amount of force increases, the need to justify it becomes greater.

   B. Terrorists have a need for social approval, but they rarely obtain it because their actions are not sanctioned by the governments they attack.

   C. Early studies of reinforcement in terrorist groups.
      1. The terrorist group must develop its own parameters of ethical normalcy, and go through a process of moral justification.
      2. Jerrold Post:
         a. Believes there is no single terrorist personality, but that terrorists do follow similar behavioral patterns:

   i. The most important pattern has to do with group and individual acceptance.

   ii. Terrorists reinforce one another, and the pattern holds true across cultures.

   iii. Terrorists are usually people who have been rejected by mainstream society, and who fall in with like-minded individuals, resulting in an us-against-them mentality.

   iv. The rejection of external authority results in the acceptance of internal authority because behavior must be reinforced somewhere.

  b. The key point for conversion in terrorist organizations is when the group shifts from violent rhetoric to action.

  c. Criminal activity marks the true beginning of a terrorist group.

D. Recent studies and expanded theories of justification.

 1. Randy Borum:

  a. Says that researchers have come to the conclusion that there is no standard rationale for justifying behavior.

  b. It is profitable to distinguish three different phases of self-justification: reasons for joining, reasons for remaining, and reasons for leaving the group.

E. Jeff Victoroff:

 1. Agrees that a multiplicity of factors is used to justify violence, but he does not believe current research to be comprehensive.

 2. There are multiple theories and suggestions, but few empirical studies of the motivational factors that support terrorist violence. He offers a few tentative conclusions:

  a. Terrorism is caused by a variety of social and psychological factors, including biological predispositions toward violence.

  b. Terrorists operate and justify violence because they emotionally attach themselves to an ideology, they cannot tolerate moral ambiguity, and they have the capacity to suppress instinctive and learned moral limitations on behavior.

  c. There is a need to study the impact of leadership on group behavior; terrorists must justify violent behavior but we do not yet know all the ways they do it.

F. Research by Brock Blomberg, Gregory Hess, and Akila Weerapana concludes that terrorist groups form because they are not happy with the economic status quo.

 1. Terrorists exhibit a collective frustration about poverty, and believe violence is justified to redress denial of economic opportunity.

 2. Increased access to economic activity decreases the level of violence, and decreased opportunities in high-income countries increase the probability of terrorism.

G. Jessica Stern:
1. Several factors must be in place for group cohesion to be effective:
    a. The group must identify an enemy, and create an us-against-them atmosphere in daily life.
    b. The group must have "a story," an almost mythological element, which inspires and guides its membership.
    c. The group needs its own language, or symbolic words, to demonize the enemy.
2. Leaders must be able to inspire members to action and constantly search for more demonized enemies – terrorists and their leaders reinforce each other in the process.
H. Motivation prior to engaging in violence means that the process of justifying illegitimate violence begins before individuals actually engage in acts of terrorism. This leads some researchers to believe that such behavior can be profiled.

VI. **Classification Systems: Can the Terrorist Personality Be Profiled?**
OBJ 8: Describe three views in the profiling debate

A. Attempts to find psychological profiles of terrorists continue in the 21st century.
B. Ervin Staub states that terrorists come from three types of social groups:
1. Those that identify with a suffering group.
2. Those who respond to suffering in their own group.
3. Alienated individuals who find purpose by joining a terrorist group.
C. Clark McCauley sees four types of personalities:
1. Revolutionaries drawn to a cause.
2. People who wander among terrorist groups.
3. People who have a sudden conversion experience.
4. People who are attracted by peers.
D. Many law enforcement agencies, including the Behavioral Science Unit in the FBI, have attempted to develop practical models for *profiling* terrorists, based on individual psychological characteristics.
E. Police officials in the United Kingdom make practical decisions based on profiles of terrorists and the classification of each incident.
F. There is no general consensus in regard to profiling terrorists.
G. Rejecting terrorist profiles.
1. Walter Laqueur says that no one can develop a composite picture of a terrorist, because no such terrorist exists – terrorism fluctuates over time and the profile of the terrorist changes with circumstances.
2. Nationalistic movements produce terrorists from the lower classes, but religious terrorists come from all classes.
3. Laqueur believes it is impossible to profile a terrorist personality because terrorism is not the subject of criminology.

41

4. Randy Borum states that there is no single terrorist personality, and that terrorists represent a variety of physical types.
5. With so many variables, critics believe that profiling is impossible.
H. Proposing a multivariate profile.
1. Jeffrey Ian Ross says it may be possible to conceptualize terrorism in a model that combines social structure with group psychology.
2. Ross believes five interconnected processes are involved in terrorism:
   a. Joining the group.
   b. Forming the activity.
   c. Remaining in the campaign.
   d. Leading the organization.
   e. Engaging in acts of terrorism.
3. Two factors are involved in the rise of terrorism at any point in history:
   a. The first centers on social structure; modernization, democracy, and social unrest create the structural conditions that facilitate terrorism.
   b. Structural factors interact with the psychological makeup of potentially violent people to produce terrorism.
   c. Ross identifies five psychological and other factors involved in the development of terrorism:
      i. Facilitating traits.
      ii. Frustration/narcissism-aggression.
      iii. Associational drives.
      iv. Learning opportunities.
      v. Cost-benefit calculations.
   d. Psychological factors change constantly and interact with each other – fear, anger, depression, guilt, antisocial behavior, a strong ego, the need for excitement, and a feeling of being lost.
4. Ross's ideas explain the transformation of terrorism across history, and provide social and psychological indicators of terrorism.
5. Laqueur says a profile cannot be obtained because terrorism is a political activity, but Ross counters by demonstrating both political and psychological factors.
I. Paths and routes.
1. John Horgan believes researchers should search for the *routes to terrorism*.
2. Horgan is concerned with the psychological processes that lead people to terrorist groups, the issues that keep them in the group, and providing support for people who want to leave.
3. The process of becoming a terrorist involves three distinct phases:
   a. In the first phase, a person must decide to become a terrorist.
   b. This is followed by a decision to remain in a terrorist group.
   c. The third process, disengagement, is the behavior of people who decide to abandon terrorism.

VII. **Radicalization: Mixed Opinions**
   OBJ 9: Outline differing processes of radicalization and alienation

A. One of the psychological and social issues surrounding terrorism is *radicalization* – the process that changes a person's socially acceptable behavior into terrorism.
   1. *Violent radicalization* is the problem of terrorism.
   2. Brian Jenkins believes that since it is a process, people moving toward violent radicalization exhibit observable signs.

B. Many analysts began looking at radicalization in the first part of the 21st century, and their focus tended to be on individuals attracted to Islamic extremism.

C. Paths to radicalization developed differently for different causes and different types of groups.
   1. Ethnic, nationalistic, political, and religious terrorists were radicalized in a multitude of ways.

D. Group processes.
   1. Marc Sageman presents radicalization as a six step framework:
      a. Alienated young man.
      b. Meets other alienated young men and form bond.
      c. Groups gravitate to religion.
      d. Religion interpreted in militant terms.
      e. Militant group meets terrorist contact.
      f. Militants join terrorists as a group decision.

E. Groups in prison.
   1. Prison recruitment is similar to the procedures used by street gangs.
   2. Terrorists also recruit from the outside – this is most frequently associated with religion, and the person who recruits and radicalizes potential terrorists is a visiting chaplain.
   3. Mark Hamm found five common patterns of converting people to violent radical causes:
      a. Potential radical converts in prison.
      b. Crisis convert.
      c. Protection seeking convert.
      d. Searching converts.
      e. Manipulating converts.
      f. Free world converts.
   4. Radicalization tends to take place among two factions and three major groups.
      a. The first faction involves various Muslim groups who use cut-and-paste versions of the Qur'an.
      b. The second faction centers on white supremacy.
         i. Islamic extremism.
         ii. Christian extremists.
         iii. White supremacists.

43

5. Patterns of prison radicalization in other countries seem to follow similar patterns, but the level of the threat they represent varies.
6. Prison radicalization is a growing threat in Central Asia.
F. Individual radicalization.
1. There is evidence to suggest that radicalization is not always a group process. It often involves individual reflection whether a group plays a role or not.
2. Individual psychological and sociological factors create the framework for interpreting reality.
3. The probability of individual radicalization increases when a relatively weak group feels that its existence is threatened, and that it has been victimized by a superior power.
4. Radicalization is the result of the social and psychological interpretation of reality.
5. All types of criminology help to explain the processes of individual radicalization, because the social sciences focus on the complexity of human behavior, and practical criminology gives security forces a tactical view of the challenges they face.
G. Commonalities in radicalization.
1. Empirical research suggests that even though radicalization resembles other forms of behavior, there are some distinct issues.
   a. In religious radicalization, people tend to exhibit distinctive forms of behavior, and these may appear in any sequence.
      i. They adopt rigid, literalist interpretations of religion, trusting only selected radical sources of theological information, and they tolerate no deviance from their interpretation.
      ii. These patterns can be seen across many religions.
2. When Islam is involved there are other behavioral indicators.
   a. People being radicalized accept the idea of the clash of civilizations, and they believe the West is at war with Islam.
3. It is virtually impossible to control all the factors that may radicalize a person, but there are points when terrorists want to leave the organization.

Chapter Summary

- Social scientists examine actions from a variety of perspectives, and this impacts the way researchers look at terrorism. Some analysts look at the manner in which groups attach meanings to actions. Another accepted method is to look at the social structures that support action.

- Netwar is a structural method for examining terrorism. The analogy assumes that terrorism takes place within a network of social connections. Actions take place at nodes, or connections in the network. The goal of counterterrorism is to disrupt the network.

- Scholars and analysts, who use religion as a way of examining terrorism, use meaning and structural frameworks. They believe that religion influences behavior. It does so by placing terrorism within the context of a sacred story giving new meanings to the actions a group takes, or the social structures supporting the organization.

- Law enforcement, intelligence, and military communities use both meaning and structural approaches to understand terrorism. Security forces do not look for theories about behavior. They look for practical results to neutralize terrorism. Therefore, they approach criminology from a practical perspective.

- The behavior of criminals and terrorists differs. Criminals tend to be un-focused and not dedicated to a cause. Terrorists are focused and dedicated. Some analysts believe that religious terrorists are more dedicated than political terrorists.

- All people, including terrorists, must feel that they are justified in their behavior. Socially, terrorists are justified by the use of group reinforcement, ideology, and symbols.

- Some scholars believe that terrorist behavior cannot be profiled because it fluctuates with historical, political, and social circumstances. Others believe that profiles are possible, if social factors are matched to a behavioral profile.
- Some scholars have developed models of alienation and radicalization. They believe that models help researchers understand terrorism. Models differ, but social alienation seems to be a common element among models. Other researchers believe that terms like radicalization and alienation are too broad.

DISCUSSION QUESTIONS

1. Do you feel that the United States is sufficiently prepared to defend against netwar? Why or why not? (OBJ 2)

2. Do you believe that the world is facing a surge of religious violence? Why or why not? Be prepared to defend your position. (OBJ 3)

3. Do you believe that some criminal groups could also be considered terrorists? Discuss some examples to support your answer. (OBJ 4, 5, and 8)

4. Compare and contrast the three views in the profiling debate offered by White. (OBJ 8)

5. In what ways does criminal behavior differ from terrorist behavior? What similarities do the two share? Should law enforcement approach the two in the same manner? Provide examples to demonstrate your reasoning. (OBJ 4 and 5)

ASSIGNMENTS

1. Before beginning the section on profiling the terrorist personality, have the students break into groups and develop a terrorist profile. Discuss the various profiles the students produce, and then discuss whether they believe it is possible to profile individual terrorists and/or terrorist organizations. (OBJ 8)

2. Give students time to discuss the elements of netwar. Provide students with flipchart paper and have them list potential U.S. targets that they feel are most susceptible to netwar. Poll the class offerings, and then reduce the list to their 'top 5'. Have them debate the reasoning for their selections. Time permitting; segue into possible solutions to mitigate netwar attacks. (OBJ 2)

3. Have each student comb through http://www.nationalterroralert.com (or another website as approved by the instructor) for terrorism related news, and select an article that relates to one or more of the chapter's core concepts. Have students provide a journalistic summary and a personal opinion/reaction to the article. Have students orally present the article to the class, field Q & As from their fellow students, and provide a copy of the original source article following the presentation. Optional: Have students complete peer assessments at the end of each presentation. (OBJ 1 - 9)

4. Have the students break into three groups, assigning each group one of the three views in the profiling debate. Give them time to research and prepare arguments for a mock debate of the profiling issue. Have the class select a "judge" for the challenge, then have each group select one *panelist* from their respective groups to be the debater. Recap post debate on the strengths and weaknesses of each of the three views. (OBJ 1, 3, 4, 5, 8, and 9)

5. As a review, play jeopardy using key terms and/or concepts from the chapter. (OBJ 1 – 9)

MEDIA TOOLS

1. *"Wikis"*
   7 Things you should know about Wikis. Retrieved from the Web Jun 29, 2012 at http://net.educause.edu/ir/library/pdf/ELI7004.pdf

This document offers easy to understand instruction on the history, construction, and potential uses of Wikis.

Have students develop (or make additions to a previously created one) a *Webliography* (resource list) using a Blog or Wiki that provides a short description, and link to a scholarly resource pertaining to course concepts. For example, have students add two to three resources each, and ask them to add their assessment of at least one of their peers' contributions. If desired, allow time to discuss Blogs/Wikis. This activity can be reused throughout the course, by asking students to add/revise their contributions each week, bi-weekly, etc. (OBJ 1- 9)

2. ***"Current Events Article Summary with Peer Assessment"***
Article The Council on Foreign Relations. Defense/homeland Security Issues. Retrieved from the Web Aug 8, 2012 at http://www.cfr.org/issue/135/

This website offers an exhaustive list of articles related to defense and homeland security issues, as well as information on other global issues. This resource can additionally serve as an example for media tool #1.

Use the Article Summary Template, which can be obtained on the instructor companion website, for this assignment. The template offers information on Internet research, outside resources, identification of credible sources, and detailed directions on completing an assessment of a news article. It also includes a peer evaluation tool.

(OBJ 1-9)

3. ***"Biographies"***
The FBI's Terrorism Screening Center. Retrieved from the Web Jun 29, 2012 at http://www.fbi.gov/about-us/nsb/tsc

This site offers a substantial array of information on terrorism related topics, including postings of most Wanted Terrorists and Domestic Terror Fugitives. It additionally provides several links to related agencies in the War on Terror. In addition, the site also offers information on careers with the FBI, virtual tours, as well as a fun & games page.

Split the class in two groups. Designate group A to complete a 1 – 2 page biography on an individual terrorist selected from the FBI's "Most Wanted" list. Have group B do the same, but select a non-terrorist criminal from the list. It is recommended to provide a completed biography for example purposes. Be sure to give instruction on source citation for images. (OBJ 1 - 9)

Chapter 2—The Social Underpinnings of Terrorism

TRUE/FALSE

1.   Criminals become involved in terrorist groups for economic gain, and they have a low level of commitment to a cause.

ANS: T   REF: p. 28   OBJ: 5

2.   Terrorism is a social process.

ANS: T   REF: p. 28   OBJ: 3

3.   Terrorism develops when a group with inferior power moves against a superior group, inducing mass civilian casualties.

ANS: T   REF: p. 31   OBJ: 5

4.   Terrorist organizations can be modeled mathematically and projected by computer simulations.

ANS: T   REF: p. 31   OBJ: 2

5.   Radicalization is the process that changes a person's socially acceptable behavior into terrorism.

ANS: T   REF: p. 43   OBJ: 9

6.   Counter-terrorism efforts need to share information over broad geographical regions to be successful.

ANS: T   REF: p. 38   OBJ: 2 and 4

7.   It is not necessary for terrorists groups to be isolated from mainstream society for social acceptance to work.

ANS: F   REF: p. 39   OBJ: 8

8.   Research suggests that economic factors do not play a role in justifying terrorist violence.

ANS: F   REF: p. 39   OBJ: 5

9. Violent political extremists are considered to present the most dangerous of all potential threats.

ANS: T   REF: p. 40   OBJ: 8

10. Statistics have shown that religious terrorist groups killed more people with fewer attacks than secular terrorists.

ANS: T   REF: p. 35   OBJ: 3

11. Nodes are critical targets for counterterrorist operations.

ANS: T   REF: p. 31   OBJ: 2

12. When governments fail to address the socio-economic pressures of its citizenry, the likelihood of terrorism increases.

ANS: T   REF: p. 41   OBJ: 7

13. Alienation is the process that changes a person's socially acceptable behavior into Terrorism.

ANS: F   REF: p. 43   OBJ: 9

14. Prison sentences, negotiations, concessions, and the threat of death are effective in reducing the attachments such people feel toward their group's purpose.

ANS: F   REF: p. 29   OBJ: 1, 3, and 5

15. A 2004 study by Marc Sageman shows that a majority of al Qaeda members were radicalized in the West and had no prior history of violence.

ANS: T   REF: p. 42   OBJ: 9

MULTIPLE CHOICE

1. Theories about terrorism in the _____ focus on the interpretation individuals and groups give to the actions of others as well as their own actions.
   a. Meaning framework
   b. Structural framework
   c. Secular framework
   d. Political framework

ANS: a   REF: p. 29   OBJ: LO1

2. Juergensmeyer sees the clash between _____ as one of the reasons for terrorism.
   a. Capitalism and poverty
   b. Education and income
   c. Modern values and traditional culture
   d. Christianity and Islam

ANS: c   REF: p. 29   OBJ: 1 and 7

3. Of the top twenty currently active religious terrorist organizations in the world, the majority are based upon a militarized version of which religion?
   a. Judaism
   b. Islam
   c. Buddhism
   d. Catholicism

ANS: b   REF: p. 35   OBJ: 1

4. _____ is a social science theory based on the assumption that human beings take action based on the subjective meanings they attribute to social settings.
   a. Theory of action
   b. Theory of meaning
   c. Theory of society
   d. Theory of subjectivity

ANS: a   REF: p. 30   OBJ: 1 and 3

5. _____ is defined as the idea that social constructs are based on systems that provide order.
   a. Meaning framework
   b. Structural framework
   c. Organizational framework
   d. Functional framework

ANS: b   REF: p. 31   OBJ: 1, 3 and 7

6. When religious groups feel they must purify the world for a new epoch, such thinking is termed _____.
   a. Violent eschatology
   b. Peaceful eschatology
   c. Religious eschatology
   d. Fanatic eschatology

ANS: a   REF: p. 33   OBJ: 3

7. The _____ is the critical target for counterterrorism.
   a. Node
   b. Unit
   c. Mode
   d. Cell

ANS: a   REF: p. 31   OBJ: 2

8. _____ refers to one network fighting another network.
   a. Interwar
   b. Netwar
   c. Group battle
   d. Net battle

ANS: b   REF: p. 52   OBJ: 2

9. _____ religions were based on the premise that a deity would help the community in times of crisis.
   a. Killing
   b. Non-killing
   c. Primitive
   d. Civilized

ANS: a   REF: p. 33   OBJ: 3

10. In the killing religions, _____ slaughtered enemies.
   a. No one
   b. Military
   c. Women
   d. Gods

ANS: d   REF: p. 33   OBJ: 3

11. Jerrold Post reports that radicalization is passed on through _____.
   a. Social processes
   b. Generations
   c. Missionary activity
   d. Political groups

ANS: b   REF: p. 39   OBJ: 9

12. It can be argued that religion often helps to produce the _____, a person striking out with an ideology but no group.
   a. Crazed avenger
   b. Solitary avenger
   c. Independent avenger
   d. Lone wolf avenger

ANS: d   REF: p. 34   OBJ: 8

13. With religious terrorism, the struggle must be a _____ struggle; that is, the outcome of the struggle will lead to a new relationship between good and evil.
   a. Secular
   b. Cosmic
   c. Sacred
   d. Profane

ANS: b   REF: p. 34   OBJ: 3

14. According to John Horgan, _____ refers to the psychological and social factors that motivate people to join and remain in terrorist groups.
   a. Routes to terrorism
   b. Social geometry
   c. Religious indoctrination
   d. Structural factors

ANS: a   REF: p. 43   OBJ: 9

51

15.   _____ criminology focuses on the common actions of lawbreakers.
a. Practical
b. Political
c. Legal
d. Historical

ANS: a   REF: p. 36   OBJ: 4

16.   Who are usually the first government agents on the scene of a terrorist incident?
a. Local police officials
b. The JTTF
c. Homeland Security
d. The FBI

ANS: a   REF: p. 36   OBJ: 2, 4 and 8

17.   Terrorists may select targets of opportunity, but the target has a primarily _____ value.
a. Financial
b. Religious
c. Symbolic
d. Military

ANS: c   REF: p. 37   OBJ: 4 and 7

18.   The _____ becomes the primary source of social reality for individual terrorists.
a. Terrorist leader
b. Terrorist group
c. Larger society
d. Religious leader

ANS: b   REF: p. 39   OBJ: 1 and 5

19.   Which of the following is NOT one of Ross's (1999) five identified factors involved in the development of terrorism:
a. Learning opportunities
b. Frustration/narcissism-aggression
c. Cost-Benefit Analysis
d. Race

ANS: d   REF: p. 41   OBJ: 8

20.   Two schools of thought dominate the scholarly literature on terrorism. One group tends to focus on the meaning of activity, and the other school looks at the _____.
e. Structure of action
b. Political implications
c. Social implications
d. Religious ideology

ANS: a   REF: p. 29   OBJ: 1

52

21.   Approaches to understanding terrorist behavior by looking at the way organizations function can be called a _____.
    a. Meaning framework
    b. Tactical framework
    c. Applied framework
    d. Structural framework

ANS: d   REF: p. 31   OBJ: 1 and 9

22.   Johnny Ryan (2007) posits that radicalization is the result of "Four Ps:" persecution, precedent, piety, and _____.
    a. Pacifism
    b. Perseverance
    c. Palatability
    d. Paltriness

ANS: b   REF: p. 45   OBJ: 9

23.   According to Huntington, _____ refers to the cultural conflicts among the world's eight dominant civilizations.
    a. Clash of civilizations
    b. Cultural paradigms
    c. Social processes
    d. Radicalization

ANS: a   REF: p. 50   OBJ: 1

24.   According to the text, terrorists achieve social justification for their actions by group reinforcement, ideology, and _____.
    a. Symbols
    b. Finances
    c. Media
    d. Promotion

ANS: a   REF: p. 52   OBJ: LO8

25.   _____ is considered a founding father of criminology.
    a. Max Weber
    b. Bruce Hoffman
    c. Cesare Beccaria
    d. Karl Marx

ANS: c   REF: p. 36   OBJ: 1 and 4

26.   Which of the following is NOT one of the three elements of social geometry of terrorism according to Black?
    a. An ability to travel
    b. An aggrieved party
    c. A process of structural procedures
    d. An access to weapons

ANS: c   REF: p. 31   OBJ: 1

27. The _____ is a federal agency created in 2004 to integrate all information gathered on international terrorism.
   a. Department of Homeland Security
   b. Federation of Law Enforcement
   c. National Counterterrorism Center
   d. Joint Terrorism Task Forces

ANS: c   REF: p. 50   OBJ: 4

28. Ross (1999) posits that the more facilitating traits a person exhibits, the more likely that the person will engage in terrorism. His list of facilitating traits include: fear, anger, depression, guilt, antisocial behavior, a strong ego, the need for excitement, and _____.
   a. Bravery
   b. A feeling of being lost
   c. Integrity
   d. Benevolence

ANS: b   REF: p. 42   OBJ: 4

29. _____ and _____ are the primary influences upon single event terrorists such as suicide bombers.
   a. Politics, cultural paradigms
   b. Religion, economics
   c. Social structure, ideology
   d. Ideology, religion

ANS: d   REF: p. 37   OBJ: 3, 7 and 8

30. International terrorism took long to develop as it was inhibited by _____.
   a. Government
   b. Geography
   c. Military
   d. Religious leaders

ANS: b   REF: p. 31   OBJ: 2

31. Which of the following al Qaeda membership profiles is INCORRECT as identified by Marc Sageman's 2004 study?
   a. Members were almost exclusively male and were radicalized in the West
   b. Most members came from the lower class families
   c. They had no history of violence
   d. Few members had arrest records

ANS: b   REF: p. 42   OBJ: 4, 5, and 8

54

32. Which of the following is NOT a basis for one of the three dominant models surrounding research in radicalization?
   a. Social and economic deprivation
   b. Long-term learning
   c. Psychological interpretations
   d. Political oppression

ANS: d   REF: p. 46   OBJ: 9

33. Who conducted the 2007 definitive study of prison radicalization in the United States?
   a. Mark Hamm
   b. Marc Sageman
   c. Michael King
   d. Donald Taylor

ANS: d   REF: p. 46   OBJ: 9

34. A prison inmate joining a radical terrorist group out of fear is referred to as a _____ convert.
   a. Crisis
   b. Protection-seeking
   c. Free-world
   d. Searching

ANS: b   REF: p. 46   OBJ: 9

35. Which of the following is NOT one of the three major identifications of prison radicalization "converts"?
   a. Islamic extremism
   b. Christian extremists who use selected biblical passages to justify their views
   c. White supremacists who have adopted the Norse pantheon
   d. Left-wing extremism

ANS: d   REF: p. 47   OBJ: 9

36. *The New York Times* reports that most international attacks against the United States in the twenty-first century have come from _____ (Mackey, 2010).
   a. Well-educated terrorists from the middle class
   b. Poorly-educated terrorists from the middle class
   c. Well-educated terrorists from the upper class
   d. Poorly-educated terrorists from the lower class

ANS: a   REF: p. 49   OBJ: 3, 4, 5, 8, and 9

37. Which of the following is NOT a descriptor of persons *at-risk* for radicalization according to Sageman's six-step model?
   a. Well socialized youth
   b. Seek orientation in religion
   c. Their religion is militarized
   d. They encounter an actor who knows terrorists

ANS: a   REF: p. 49   OBJ: 3, 4, 5, 8, and 9

38. _____ religions developed during the food-gathering cycles of pre-agrarian and early agricultural societies.
    a. Killing
    b. Non-killing
    c. Cosmic
    d. Terrestrial

ANS: a   REF: p. 33   OBJ: 3, 6, and 7

39. The most difficult type of terrorists to deter or detain are _____.
    a. Lone-wolf avengers
    b. Jihadists
    c. Separatist revolutionaries
    d. Narco-terrorists

ANS: a   REF: p. 34   OBJ: 3, 5, 6, 7, and 9

40. Nationalistic movements produce terrorists from the lower classes - religious terrorists come from _____ classes.
    a. Upper
    b. Middle
    c. Lower
    d. All

ANS: d   REF: p. 41   OBJ: 5, 8, and 9

Case 2.0

Bodrero (2002) says terrorist behavior differs from standard patterns of criminal behavior because terrorists are highly motivated and loyal to a particular cause. Whereas ordinary criminals are opportunistic, terrorists are focused. They may select targets of opportunity, but the target has a symbolic value. Terrorists use crime to make a symbolic statement about a political cause.

41. After conferring with several like-minded extremists, a suspect places a bomb under the seat of local politician. The suspect would most accurately be classed as a (n) _____.
    a. Criminal
    b. Terrorist
    c. Lone-wolf avenger
    d. Anarchist

ANS: b   REF: p. 37   OBJ: 5

42. A reclusive individual leaves home following a television documentary on the biblical sins of man over the ages. He decides to shoot randomly at persons in his neighborhood as he claims he was inspired by the show to "cleanse the area". The suspect would most accurately be classed as a (n) _____.
    a. Criminal
    b. Terrorist
    c. Lone-wolf avenger
    d. Anarchist

ANS: c   REF: p. 37   OBJ: 5 and 8

43. A group of armed and dangerous teenagers are returning home late at night and come across several seemingly unoccupied homes. They enter one home and before taking numerous valuable, spray paint racial slurs on the walls. The suspects would most accurately be classed as a(n) _____.
   a. Criminal
   b. Terrorist
   c. Lone-wolf avenger
   d. Anarchist

ANS: a   REF: p. 37   OBJ: 5 and 8

44. Buford Furrow (entered a Jewish day care center in August 1999 and began shooting people) would most accurately be classed as a(n) _____.
   a. Criminal
   b. Terrorist
   c. Lone-wolf avenger
   d. Anarchist

ANS: c   REF: p. 37   OBJ: 5 and 8

Case 2.1

Many law enforcement agencies, including the Behavioral Science Unit in the FBI, have attempted to develop practical models for profiling terrorists based on individual psychological characteristics. They work to assess and/or classify potential terrorists and terrorist threats.

A practical example of such classification systems comes from the United Kingdom. Police officials there make practical decisions based on profiles of terrorists and the classification of each incident. When faced with an act of terrorism, the local ranking police official makes an assessment of the event. If it is classified as a criminal activity or the result of a mentally deranged individual, the local police commander handles the incident. If the commander deems the action to be the result of political terrorism, the central government is informed, and the incident is handled on the prime minister's level. In addition, if the level of the threat is sufficiently high, the matter may be referred to the national government.NARREND

45. A local police station receives a call of a drive-by shooting in the neighborhood. The witness reports recognizing the suspect car as a local gang member and the victim - a 12 year old girl. According to the UK classification system outlined in the above scenario, who (or at what level) would handle the incident?
   a. National government
   b. The local police commander
   c. Central government
   d. Prime Minister level

ANS: b   REF: p. 40   OBJ: 2

46.	The Prime Minister's executive secretary receives a letter in the mail that calls her derogatory terms.
	a.	National government
	b.	The local police commander
	c.	Central government
	d.	Prime Minister level

ANS: d		REF: p. 40		OBJ: 5

47.	Several local government offices begin to receive a series of anthrax laden packages in the mail.
	a.	National government
	b.	The local police commander
	c.	Central government
	d.	Prime Minister level

ANS: a		REF: p. 40		OBJ: 5

48.	Blueprints of a main water supply plant and several gallons of toxic chemicals are discovered in a university dorm.
	a.	National government
	b.	The local police commander
	c.	Central government
	d .	Prime Minister level

ANS: a		REF: p. 40		OBJ: 5

Case 2.2

Assume that you are assigned to patrol within a mid-size American police agency of 120 personnel. You and your partners have recently been trained in the Sageman's six-step model for radicalization. Recall that this is: (1) alienated youth, (2) join other alienated youths, (3) they seek orientation in religion, (4) their religion is militarized, (5) they encounter an actor who knows terrorists, and (6) the actor introduces them to the terrorists and they join. *As there are many differing paths to radicalization, there are many models to consider. For the purposes of this scenario, we are using Sageman's model for illustrative purposes.*

You are on your first day post-training and are now looking for these behavioral patterns during investigations and routine patrol operations. In each of the following scenarios, how many of the six indicators exist?

49.	Ellen, student council president, leaves her gymnastics class that she has attended with her best friend since childhood, to spend some time by herself in the library researching Buddhism. She meets Karen, a loner and terrorist (unbeknownst to Ellen), who suggests that she extend her research to include Islam. Ellen does and over time the two become friends.
	a.	Four
	b.	One
	c.	Five
	d.	Six

ANS: a		REF: p. 49-50			OBJ: 5, 8 and 9

58

50. George is a young African-American inmate serving time in Folsom after living a difficult life moving from foster home to foster home, never really connecting with anyone or bonding with another individual. Having just returned from serving extended periods of time in administrative segregation, George is feeling angry and wants revenge. He is approached in the yard by another inmate who suggests that he seek the counsel of Raffi, an in-house Imam of sorts. Raffi spends hours with George, sensing George's vulnerability to suggestion – Raffi channels George's anger, convincing him that he (George) is a victim of "the evils of West" and that George can do something about it. Raffi says he will show George how if George is willing to prove himself worthy. George begins to spend more time reading militant Islamic writings and meeting with other converted inmates. George believes he has now "found his way" and "is worthy" and seeks out Raffi for guidance on "how". Raffi then introduces him to others in the group and assigns George a "very important job".

   a. Four
   b. Three
   c. Five
   d. Six

ANS: d   REF: p. 49-50   OBJ: 5, 8 and 9

Completion

1. Psychologist Clark McCauley sees four types of personalities: revolutionaries drawn to a cause, people who wander among terrorist groups, people who have a sudden conversion experience, and people who are attracted by _____.

ANS: peers   REF: p. 40   OBJ: 8 and 9

2. For social acceptance to work, terrorist groups must be _____ from mainstream society.

ANS: isolated   REF: p. 39   OBJ: 8

3. The text points to the lack of quantitative and qualitative _____ studies as one of the current weaknesses in terrorism research

ANS: behavioral   REF: p. 39   OBJ: 1 - 9

4. Juergensmeyer sees the clash between _____ and traditional culture as one of the reasons for terrorism.

ANS: modern values   REF: p. 29   OBJ: 1

5. Any point where information, weapons, or personnel are gathered or exchanged is called a _____.

ANS: node   REF: p. 31   OBJ: 2

59

6. _____ , as used in the text, refers to the psychological process of adopting extremist positions.

ANS: radicalization   REF: p. 43   OBJ: 9

7. _____ is the social construct providing definitional boundaries for a particular social meaning.

ANS: meaning framework   REF: p. 29   OBJ: 1

8. _____ is the social space occupied by a structure and the direction in which it moves.

ANS: Social geometry   REF: p. 31   OBJ: 1

9. The creation of _____ Forces allows the FBI to coordinate law enforcement resources in the face of domestic terrorism and to expand investigations.

ANS: Joint Terrorism Task   REF: p. 37   OBJ: 4 and 5

10. Jeffrey Ian Ross (1999) believes that five interconnected processes are involved in terrorism: joining the group, forming the activity, remaining in the campaign, leading the organization, and _____.

ANS: engaging in acts of terrorism   REF: p. 41   OBJ: 3, 5, 6, 7, 8, and 9

11. According to _____ theory, sub-national criminal, terrorist, or revolutionary groups organize themselves in a network of smaller logistical structures, groups, or command posts.

ANS: Netwar   REF: p. 31 - 32   OBJ: 2

12. Donald Black (2004) states that all groups, including terrorist organizations, take action because they belong to a structure that operates for a specific purpose, a concept he calls _____ .

ANS: Social geometry   REF: p. 31   OBJ: 1 and 7

13. Although there are many approaches to the study of social explanations of group behavior, two schools of thought dominate the scholarly literature on terrorism. One group tends to focus on the meaning of activity, and the other school looks at the _____ .

ANS: structure of action   REF: p. 29   OBJ: 1

14. The _____ were the last great Islamic empire.

ANS: Ottoman Turks   REF: p. 30   OBJ: 1

15. Terrorism develops when a group with inferior power moves against a superior group, Inducing _____.

ANS: mass civilian casualties   REF: p. 31   OBJ: 5

16. _____ occurs when an individual or group becomes separated from the dominant values of society at large.

ANS: alienation   REF: p. 43   OBJ: 9

17. In the killing religions, _____ slaughtered enemies.

ANS: gods   REF: p. 33   OBJ: 1

18. _____has changed the face of terrorism by shrinking distances and providing weapons.

ANS: Technology   REF: p. 31   OBJ: 3

19. _____ terrorists view themselves as victorious either by killing the enemy or by dying in the struggle.

ANS: *holy* or jihadist   REF: p. 35   OBJ: 3, 6, and 7

20. Chaplains outside of the prison system who spread literature and preach radicalization are referred to as _____.

ANS: Free-World Converters   REF: p. 46   OBJ: 3 and 9

Essay

1. What are the common patterns of converting people in prison to violent radical causes as posited by Mark Hamm? What does Hamm say lies behind most all prison conversions?

ANS:
- Hamm found five common patterns of converting people to violent radical causes
- Crisis convert: The first contains people in crisis, and they will respond to religious overtures for emotional support.
- Protection seeking convert: A second type involves people seeking protection in the prison environment; these people will convert because the radical group offers safety.
- Searching converts: The third group of potential converts, searchers, has had little exposure to religion, and they are fascinated by both the multiplicity of religious expressions inside prison and the feeling of belonging for members of the group.
- Manipulating converts: The fourth personality is common in prison; it involves manipulating people for personal gain.

61

- Free world converts: Hamm classifies chaplains from the outside as free world recruiters.
- Classification of chaplains from the outside as free world recruiters.
- Behind almost every conversion, according to Hamm, lies a friendship or kinship link, but sometimes a new inmate simply meets somebody in the yard and converts to a new faith.

REF: p. 46-47   OBJ: 3, 5, and 9

2.   What is David Rapoport's position on the influence of religion on terrorism? What is your view on the religion's influence on terrorism?

ANS:
- Rapoport believes that religion has influenced terrorism because of eschatological expectations.
- Belief in end-of-the-age theology and the coming of a deity serves to justify violent behavior.
- Although this seems to separate religious and political terrorists, Rapoport argues that both sets of behavior are similar.
- Political ideology plays the same role for political terrorists as eschatology does for religious ones.
- There is little difference in behavior between secular and religious terrorists, and both types of terrorists are intensely dedicated to a cause.
- Stated views will vary.

REF: p. 35   OBJ: 3, 8, and 9

3.   What is the difference between killing and non-killing religions? Which of these is associated with modern-day terrorism? Explain.

ANS:
- Killing religions developed during the food-gathering cycles of pre-agrarian and early agricultural societies.
- They were premised on a deity helping the community in times of crisis
- In the killing religions, gods slaughtered enemies.
- These beliefs gave way to the non-killing religions because the older, killing religions did not, in fact, protect early villages from the ravages of war and natural disasters.
- The non-killing religions embraced enemies and developed elaborate theologies to justify violence as a last resort.
- The non-killing religions appeared in order to try to transcend everyday experience.
- The non-killing transcendence is often transformed into a militant ideology designed to protect a state or some other social group by this rationalizing of the use of violence as a last resort.
- Explanations will vary.

REF: p. 33-34   OBJ: 3, 6, and 7

4.   Discuss Mark Juergensmeyer's views on religious terrorism.

ANS:
- Juergensmeyer approached several militants from differing religious traditions around the world.
- Discussions are categorized to find commonalities.
- The findings are based on the meanings his subjects attach to modernity.
- Terrorism is created by the meanings subjects attach to social situations producing a common pattern in religious terrorist organizations.
- Believers must identify with a deity and think they are participating in a cosmic struggle to change history – the outcome of the struggle will lead to a new relationship between good and evil.
- When they feel the struggle has reached the critical stage, violence may be endorsed and terrorism may result.
- The call to violence is a call to purify the world in a holy war that eliminates the nonbeliever and the incorrect interpreters of tradition.
- The lines of battle are clear and positions cannot be compromised.
- Such a war allows only one way of thinking: those people who do not stand with the holy warrior are evil.
- The holy terrorist is victorious either by killing the enemy or dying in the struggle.

REF: p. 34   OBJ: 3, 6, and 7

5.   According to Bodrero, what are the practical behavioral differences between terrorists and criminals? What is the significance of Bodrero's argument in regard to investigative responses to terrorism?

ANS:
- Criminals are unfocused. Terrorists focus their actions toward a goal.
- Criminals may live in a criminal underworld, but they are not devoted to crime as a philosophy. Terrorists are dedicated to a cause.
- Criminals will make deals to avoid punishment. Terrorists rarely cooperate with officials because they do not wish to betray their cause.
- Criminals usually run when confronted with force. Terrorists tend to attack.
- Criminals strike when the opportunity to do so is present. Terrorists strike against symbols after careful planning.
- Criminals rarely train for crime. Terrorists prepare for and rehearse their operations.
- Police officers can take advantage of the behavioral characteristics of typical criminals when investigating a crime; however, these tactics do not work in countering terrorism. Law enforcement, military, and security officials need to focus on ideology, group and individual behavior, and sharing information over broad geographical regions to successfully investigate terrorism.

REF: p. 37-38   OBJ: 4 and 5

6.   Discuss the new theory in modern warfare known as Netwar.

ANS:
- According to this theory, sub national criminal, terrorist, or revolutionary groups organize themselves in a network of smaller logistical structures, groups, or command posts
- Any point where information, weapons, or personnel are gathered or exchanged is called a node
- The node is the critical target for counterterrorist operations
- Latora and Marchiori argue that once an organization is modeled as a network, the nodes will appear as movement is monitored
- If the node is destroyed, the network is disrupted
- To understand this approach to terrorist organizations, consider the traffic pattern in a major city. If you monitor cars moving through the city at rush hour, you will soon find critical points where traffic must keep flowing or the city will become locked in a traffic jam. The traffic pattern on the highway is like a network, and the crucial intersections, merge ramps, and expanded traffic lanes are nodes. If vehicles begin clogging at a node, traffic slows or comes to a standstill at many points in the network.

REF: p. 32-33   OBJ: 2

7.   Discuss Sageman's six-step radicalization model. Would you agree with this model? Why or why not?

ANS:
- It starts with an alienated young man.
- Meets other alienated young men and form bond; outdoing each other in zeal to express love for the group.
- They "discover" religion as a way of giving meaning to their lives.
- Terrorism enters the equation, if the new found religious orientation turns to violence. Most groups stop at this point.
- They must meet a broker, an activist who knows actual terrorists, and be accepted by an actual terrorist group.
- Militants join terrorists as a group decision.
- Views will vary.

REF: p. 44   OBJ: 8 and 9

8.   According to Brock Blomberg, Gregory Hess, and Akila Weerapana, what is the importance of economic factors in the justification of violence?

ANS:
- Terrorist groups form because they are not happy with the economic status quo.
- The individual socioeconomic position of a single terrorist is less important than economic welfare and opportunity at large.
- Terrorists exhibit a collective frustration about poverty, whether or not they are impoverished.

64

- Consequently, they believe violence is justified to redress denial of economic opportunity.
- Increased access to economic activity decreases the level of violence, and in contrast, decreased opportunities in high-income countries increase the probability of terrorism.

REF: p. 40   OBJ: 7

9.   Why does Laqueur (1999) state that it is impossible to profile a terrorist personality? Do you agree? Why or why not?

ANS:
- No one can develop a composite picture of a terrorist because no such terrorist exists.
- Terrorism fluctuates over time and the profile of the terrorist changes with circumstances.
- There can be no terrorist mosaic because there are different types of terrorism.
- Most terrorists are young, but their actions and psychological makeup vary according to social and cultural conditions.
- Nationalistic movements produce terrorists from the lower classes, but religious terrorists come from all classes.
- Individual and group profiles are the result of political and social conditions.
- Terrorism is not the subject of criminology; terrorism is a political phenomenon different from ordinary crime or psychopathology.

REF: p. 40   OBJ: 8

10.   Describe the factors involved in the development of terrorism as presented by Jeffrey Ross (1999).

ANS:
- Facilitating traits include fear, anger, depression, guilt, antisocial behavior, a strong ego, the need for excitement, and a feeling of being lost; the more of these traits a person exhibits, the more likely that the person will engage in terrorism.
- Frustration/narcissism-aggression means that a person has suffered a blow to the ego and reacts hostilely. Frustration refers to aggression channeled toward another person or symbol.
- This, in turn, interacts with structural factors to cause more violence.
- Associational drives are developed in group settings; when potential terrorists perceive benefits from particular groups, they tend to join those groups. Once inside, violent behavior is likely to increase because the group's acts of terror reinforce it.
- The existence of groups that engage in acts of terrorism create an environment for teaching terrorism to others. As learning opportunities increase, the amount of terrorism increases.
- Violence takes place after a cost-benefit analysis; terrorists evaluate whether the cost of an attack is worth the result.

REF: p. 41   OBJ: 3, 5, 8 and 9

CHAPTER 3

The Organization and Financing of Terrorism

Learning Objectives

After reading this chapter, students should be able to:

1. Summarize rural, urban, and insurgent models of terrorism
2. Trace the evolution of terrorist organizational structures
3. Discuss the challenges involved in leading a terrorist group
4. Describe the issues involved in terrorist financing
5. Describe legal and illegal sources of income
6. Explain the ways funds are disbursed in an underground economy
7. Describe the hawala system
8. Summarize views on the political economy of terrorism
9. Outline the manners in which drugs and terrorism overlap

Chapter Key Terms

Ernesto "Che" Guevara p. 56
Cuban guerrilla war, p. 57
Carlos Marighella, p. 58
Cells, p. 62
Active cadre, p. 62
Pyramid, p. 62
Column, p. 62
Umbrella, p. 64
Virtual organizations, p. 64
Chain organizations, p. 64
Networks, p. 64
Tribal areas, p. 68
Capone discovery, p. 69
Forensic accounting, p. 70
Expropriation, p. 71
Triborder Region, p. 73
Globalization, p. 73
Black Market Peso Exchange, p. 74
Hawala system, p. 75
New economy of terrorism, p. 78
Failed state, p. 78
Shell state, p. 78
Narco-terrorism, p. 80

Active cadre: a military term that describes the people actually carrying out terrorist activity in an organizational hierarchy. The active cadre refers to the small terrorist group at the top of a pyramid.

Capone discovery: a term used by James Adams to explain the Irish Republican Army's entry into organized crime.

Carlos Marighella (1911–1969): a Brazilian communist legislator and a revolutionary theorist. Marighella popularized urban terrorism as a method for ending repression and eliminating U.S. domination of Latin America. He was killed in a police ambush in São Paulo in 1969.

Cells: the basic unit of a traditional terrorist organization. Groups of cells form columns. Members in cells seldom know one another. In more recent terrorist structures, the term cell is used to describe a tactical group dispatched by the network for selected operations.

Chain organizations: temporary associations of diverse groups. Groups in a chain come together for a particular operation and disband after it is over.

Cold War: a standoff between the United States and the Soviet Union from 1945 until 1991. Each nation fought for influence through surrogates around the world, and would not confront each other directly for fear a massive nuclear destruction. It ended with the economic and political collapse of the Soviet Union in 1991.

Column: groups of cells in a terrorist or guerrilla organization.

Cuban guerrilla war: a three-step process as described by Che Guevara: (1) revolutionaries join the indigenous population to form guerrilla *foco*, as Guevara called them, (2) small forces form columns and control rural areas, and (3) columns unite for a conventional offensive to overthrow government.

Cuban Revolution: the guerrilla revolution led by Fidel Castro. Castro initially failed in 1956 and left for Mexico after a brief prison sentence. He returned with a small group of guerrillas and built a large guerrilla army. He overthrew the Cuban government in 1959, embracing communism shortly after taking power.

Ernesto "Che" Guevara (1928–1967): Fidel Castro's assistant and guerrilla warfare theorist. Guevara advocated guerrilla revolutions throughout Latin America after success in the Cuban Revolution. He was killed in Bolivia in 1967 when trying to form a guerrilla army.

Expropriation: a term used by Carlos Marighella for armed robbery.

Failed state: a geographical area outside of a government's control. Failed states operate under differing warlords, criminal groups, or competing governments.

Forensic accounting: an investigative tool used to track money used in illegal activities. It can be used in any crime involving the exchange, storage, or conversion of fiscal resources.

Frantz Fanon (1925–1961): a writer, psychiatrist, and revolutionary theorist. He was also one of the most influential philosophers in the awareness of colonialism. Fanon grew up in the French colony Martinique in the Caribbean, and he became acutely aware of racism and colonialism in experiences there. He joined the French Army in World War II, and won one of France's highest military decorations. After the war he studied psychiatry. Believing that mental illness was a result of imperialism, Fanon campaigned against racism and colonialism. He supported Algerian rebels in their struggle with France and advocated for violent revolution. He died of leukemia, but his ideas influenced anti-colonial revolutionaries for decades.

Globalization: a common global economic network ideally uniting the world with production and international trade. Proponents believe it will create wealth. Critics believe it creates corporate wealth and increases distance between the rich and poor.

Hawala system: a system of exchanging money based on trust relationships between money dealers. A chit or promissory note is exchanged between two hawaladars, and it is as valuable as cash or other traded commodities because the trust between the two parties guarantees its value.

Insurgency: as used by the text, refers to various forms of conflict that pits sub-national forces or groups of forces against recognized a nation state or allied states. It incorporates multidimensional guerrilla, terrorist, and political tactics. Insurgencies range from small revolts in a region of a country to international terrorist operations against a group of countries.

Mao Zedong (1893–1976): also known as Mao Tse Tung, the leader of the Chinese Communist Party. He seized power in a revolution in 1949 and ruled China until his death in 1976.

Narco-terrorism: a controversial term that links drugs to terrorism in one of two ways. Either drug profits are used to finance terrorism or drug gangs use terrorism to control production and distribution networks.

Netwar: refers to one network fighting another network.

Network: refers to organizations of groups, supplies, weapons, and any structure that supports an operation. Much like a traffic system or the World Wide Web, networks do not have central leadership, and they operate under a variety of rules.

New economy of terrorism: a term used by Napoleoni. The term describes the evolution of terrorist financing from the beginning strategies of the cold war to the present. Economic support and anti-terrorist policies interact to form the new economy.

Pyramid: as used in the text - an illustration of the way terrorists organize themselves into hierarchies. It is an analogy showing a large base of support culminating in the small group of terrorists at the top.

Reference group: the values of the primary group with which individuals or other groups identify. It is an idealized group of peers that serve as a model for behavior.

Shell state: a political situation where a government nominally controls its own state but where large regions are either anarchic or under the control of others. A government is unable to enforce law or provide for other forms of social order in a shell state.

Tri-Border Region: as used in the text, is the area where Brazil, Paraguay, and Argentina join. The major city is Cuidad del Este.

Umbrella: as used in the text, is a group which shelters, supports, and inspires smaller terrorist groups. The RAND Corporation refers to this as a hub.

Urban terrorism: a four-stage process described by Carlos Marighella: (1) unorganized violence accompanied by passive disruption, (2) governmental repression to stop violence, (3) massive uprising in response to repression, and (4) toppling of government.

Virtual organizations: as use in the text, develop through communication, financial, and ideological links. Like a network, a virtual organization has no central leadership.

Chapter Outline

I.   **Models of Terrorism**
       OBJ 1: Summarize rural, urban, and insurgent models of terrorism

   A.   The first wave of modern terrorism appeared in Africa and Asia after 1945.
   B.   Around 1965 ideological terrorism brought a more urban model, employing terrorism as a strategy, because no other weapons were available; religious terrorists began employing the same urban model in the 1980s.
   C.   The three models – rural, urban, and insurrection – represent general trends from 1945 to the present.
   D.   Guerrilla warfare and rural terrorism

1. Several nationalistic rebellions after World War II were based on guerrilla war, including a long campaign that toppled the Chinese government in 1949.
2. Left-wing ideologues came to view guerrilla war as a statement of struggle against capitalist powers. Terrorism had a special role in the *Cuban Revolution*.
    a. The Cuban Revolution popularized guerrilla warfare throughout the world.
    b. *Ernesto "Che" Guevara* served the communist regime of Guatemala in 1954, but fled to Mexico City when communists were purged from the government.
    c. Ernesto Guevara and Fidel Castro worked together to oust the Cuban military dictator Fulgencio Batista.
E. Guevara: on guerrilla warfare
    1. Guerrilla revolutions based on the Cuban experience are typified by three phases; each one designed to progress from, and complement, the previous one.
        a. In the first phase the revolution begins with isolated groups.
        b. In phase two, the isolated groups merge into guerrilla columns.
        c. The final phase brings columns together in a conventional army.
    2. Terrorism plays a limited role in Guevara's guerrilla framework.
    3. The main purpose of terrorism is to strike at the government's logistical network; the secondary purpose is to demoralize the government.
F. Debray: expanding guerrilla warfare
    1. The theory of guerrilla war came after the appearance of Guevara's work, and it was popularized by a French socialist named Regis Debray.
        a. According to Debray, poverty threads through the entire fabric of Latin American life, and entwines divergent cultures and peoples in a common knot of misery
        b. Revolution is essentially an affair for poor peasants, and it can begin only in a rural setting with regional guerrilla forces.
G. Urban terrorism
    1. The model for modern *urban terrorism* was intellectually championed by *Frantz Fanon*.
        a. Fanon believed the pressures caused by exploitative imperialism were the primary causes for mental illness in Algeria.
        b. Native culture is forgotten by the middle class, as native intellectualism is replaced by Western traditions.
        c. Fanon argued that the natives had one course of action – violent revolt -- which included guerrilla warfare and acts of terrorism.

70

       d. Fanon's concept of guerrilla warfare was based in rural revolution, but urban terrorism would become the major weapon rendering colonial administration impotent.

      e. Proposed targets for terrorism: white settlers and the native middle class.

H. *Carlos Marighella* and the urban model

  1. Marighella was a Brazilian legislator, a leader of the nationalistic communist party, and eventually, a revolutionary terrorist.

      a. Marighella designed practical guides for terrorism that have had more influence on recent revolutionary terrorism than any other set of theories.

      b. Marighella believed the basis of revolution was unstructured and uncoordinated.

  2. *Urban terrorism* was to begin with two distinct phases: one designed to bring about actual violence; and the other designed to give that violence meaning.

      a. A campaign of revolutionary terrorism in an urban setting could be used to destabilize governmental power.

      b. A psychological assault would convince the government and the people that the status quo no longer held – the government would be forced to declare some form of martial law.

  3. Any form of urban violence is desirable because a violent atmosphere creates the political environment needed for success; therefore, terrorism is the primary strategy of the urban guerrilla.

  4. The main operational group of a terrorist organization should be the firing group, which is composed of four to five terrorists each.

      a. Several firing groups are needed to construct a terrorist organization.

        i. The firing group is the basic weapon of the urban guerrilla.

  5. *Globalization*, modern communications, and new weapons technology allow sub-national groups to wage another type of campaign, an insurrection. Some military theorists believe this is a third model of terrorism.

I.   An American understanding of *insurgency*.

  1. Given experiences in the 21st century, some American military officers have concluded that guerrilla war, and various forms of modern terrorism, have changed the nature of sub-national conflict.

  2. Insurgencies represent a new mix of operations and tactics made possible by sweeping technological changes and globalization.

  3. It is impossible to fight insurgencies with military tactics designed for guerrilla war or terrorism, even though insurgents use guerrilla and terrorist tactics.

      a. If modeled after guerrillas or terrorists of the past, an insurgency will be viewed as a law enforcement and military problem.

      b. Insurgents require few personnel, but a security force needs to be massive.

      c. Utilization of force may increase the power of insurgents.

    4. Insurgencies developed at the end of the Cold War.

    5. Technology and weapons helped many insurgencies grow, and instantaneous communications and travel provided a means for creating large networks of support.

      a. The new political atmosphere made the rise of organizations like al Qaeda possible.

    6. The comprehensive nature of network to network confrontations suggests that the insurgent model will be one of the dominant factors in the future of terrorism.

II.   Changing Dynamics and Structures
OBJ 2: Trace the evolution of terrorist organizational structures

A.   The invention of dynamite and the formation of tactical groups, were the two most important developments in the history of modern terrorism.

B.   Michael Collins, leader of the IRA, studied revolutionary tactics from the 18th and 19th centuries, and developed a method of isolating small units of terrorists. He called the small units cells.

    1. Each cell had its own mission, and it operated without knowledge of others cells in the area; this organizational method reemerged after World War II, and dominated the structure of terrorism until the 1990s.

C. The evolution of cells

    1. James Fraser discusses the organization of terrorist groups by analyzing two factors: the structure of the organization and its support.

    2. The typical organization is arranged in a *pyramid*.

    3. The majority of people who work in terrorist organizations serve to keep terrorists in the field; the most common job in terrorist groups is support.

    4. According to James Fraser and Ian Fulton, the hierarchical structure of terrorist groups is divided into four levels:

    a. The smallest group, at the top of the pyramid, is responsible for command.

    b. The second level is the *active cadre*, or the people responsible for carrying out the mission of the organization.

    c. Under the active cadre is the second largest, and perhaps the most important level of a terrorist organization: the active supporters.

    d. The last and largest category is difficult to identify and characterize; it is the organization's passive supporters.

    5. Most terrorist groups number fewer than fifty people as active supporters, cadre, and command, and are incapable of mounting a long-term campaign.

6. Larger groups are guided by the same organizational principles, but they have major subunits capable of carrying out extensive operations.
7. Anthony Burton describes the basic structure of subunits. Terrorist organizations have two primary types of subunits: the *cell* and the *column*.
8. The only terrorists who do not follow typical organizational models are individual terrorists who operate without a group.
D. New models: *Umbrella* organizations and modern piracy
   1. Around 1982, new types of organizational styles developed from the pyramid, and organizational transformations continue today.
      a. The first change came with the birth of the umbrella organization; in this style of organization, several small pyramids gather under a sheltering group that manages supplies, obtains resources, creates support structures, and gathers intelligence.
      b. *Virtual organizations* are created through computer and information networks.
      c. *Chain organizations* involve small groups linked by some type of communication and whose members periodically cooperate.
   2. A complex all-channel *network* is composed of groups, logistical systems, and overlapping relationships among groups, individuals, and technology.
   3. The second concept in the network is the node – any critical function in the network ranging from a group to support systems.
      a. The network is a series of nodes held together with communication.
   4. The RAND approach reveals the structure of networks: they involve terrorist, extremist, criminal, and disruptive-activist groups.
   5. Operations are characterized by the dual nature of the network – violence takes place on two levels:
      a. Organized small groups.
      b. Disruptive violence from demonstrations.
   6. A command group can recruit, train, plan, supply, and launch an attack within a network.
E. Umbrella groups and pirates
   1. Most people incorrectly assume that piracy is an activity of the past; today's pirates are armed with global positioning systems, satellite phones, machine guns, rockets, and grenades.
   2. Most currently work for organized crime syndicates and provide an ideal model for terrorists: a seemingly legitimate business provides cover for pirates, while denying all connection with illegal activities.
   3. By 2005 terrorist networks in the Horn of Africa established links with maritime pirates.
   4. The problem of piracy is endemic to the political struggle in Somalia; piracy off the coast of the Horn of Africa is caused by the multifaceted

conflict brought on by the breakup of legal authority and social systems.

III.   **Managing Terrorist Organizations**
      OBJ 3: Discuss the challenges involved in leading a terrorist group

   A. Terrorist leaders face operational problems, and they seek to solve them with the same strategies taught in a management class.
      1. The first problem is the need for secrecy.
         a. Because the need for secrecy is so great in any terrorist organization, subgroups are generally allowed a relatively high degree of autonomy.
      2. Terrorism is a decentralized affair, and the larger the group, the greater the degree of decentralization.
         a. Decentralization offers relative security: very few people know many other members of the organization.
   B. To prevent factionalism and excessive autonomy, terrorist commanders turn to internal discipline for control.
      1. Internal discipline can become a major factor in the demise of a terrorist organization.
      2. There are two opposing dynamics at work, one pulling for cohesion and cooperation through fear, and the other pulling for autonomy through decentralization and secrecy.
   C. Another problem of terrorist management is that of gaining immediate tactical support for operations.
      1. The most important element of a terrorist campaign is the number and structure of active supporters.
   D. Marc Sageman believes that operations are managed by the social organization of networks and finds four major clusters, or nodes, connected by a central staff cluster:
      1. Friendships and social relations form the communication and managerial nexus of the organization.
      2. These relations are enhanced by cliques within the group.
      3. Hierarchies are more difficult to manage because power is concentrated; they are more vulnerable to counterterrorist techniques.
      4. The formation of command structures within the networks creates a method for overcoming some of the difficulties inherent in managing terrorist organizations.
      5. Even when a hierarchy is created inside a network, it does not necessarily insure that cells or individuals can be managed effectively.

IV.   **Group Size and Length of Campaign**
      OBJ 3: Discuss the challenges involved in leading a terrorist group
      OBJ 4: Describe the issues involved in terrorist financing

A. The size of a group affects its ability to operate over time; large groups last longer than small ones.

B. Groups that had sponsors survived, and independent groups fell apart or were destroyed.

C. It is also important to consider the religious and ideological factors that hold international networks together.

D. The majority of successful groups embrace other doctrines, such as nationalism.

V. **Financing Modern Terrorism**
   OBJ 4: Describe the issues involved in terrorist financing
   OBJ 5: Describe legal and illegal sources of income

A. Terrorists need money to run an operation; political violence requires financial backing.

B. When modern terrorism began to emerge after World War II, security forces frequently concentrated on investigative measures, military force, and tactics to counter terrorism; financing was often overlooked.

C. Methods of terrorist financing had changed over time; many terrorist organizations began using petty crime, money laundering, and transfer of illegal contraband to finance operations.

D. The awareness of the importance of financing began to evolve slowly; a terrorist operation does not cost a lot of money, but the overall budget for a campaign is quite high.

E. The financial investigative debate.
   1. There is a debate about whether a financial strategy can be effective.
   2. Martin Navias argues that the major strategy of counterterrorism should be waging "financial warfare" with financial weapons.
   3. There are three primary reasons that traditional financial criminal investigative techniques are ineffective:
      a. First, terror attacks would be expensive for a normal individual, but not for a group.
      b. Second, freezing assets does not work because terrorists can find sources, and investigators lose the ability to follow a particular link once it is frozen.
      c. Finally, if financial weapons are to be effective, they must be based on international agreements.
   4. Law enforcement agencies have successfully used *forensic accounting* for many years.

VI. **Illegal Funding Methods**
   OBJ 4: Describe the issues involved in terrorist financing
   OBJ 5: Describe legal and illegal sources of income

OBJ 6: Explain the ways funds are disbursed in an underground economy

OBJ 7: Describe the hawala system

A. Financing terrorism is not a single proposition; it involves multiple layers of organizations and activities operating in a variety of ways.

B. Three major categories help explain the structure of financing:
1. The first element deals with the unlawful raising and distribution of funds.
2. Terrorists also use another source of income, the formal regulated economy.
3. The third category has little to do with financing, but has much to do with financial effectiveness – using financial weapons against terrorists.
   a. It is necessary to consider the ways terrorists can turn the tables and use the costs of terrorism as a weapon.
4. In the past two decades, the links between criminal networks and terrorist organizations have increased all over the globe.
   a. In central Asia terrorist organizations trade illegal arms, launder money, and distribute drugs.
   b. Latin American terrorism is tied to drug production and public corruption.
   c. In the United States domestic terrorists engage in fraud schemes and robberies to finance political violence.

C. Criminal methods of funding and distribution
1. Carlos Marighella argued that "urban warfare" begins with a campaign of *expropriation*; that is, robbery.
2. Terrorists around the world use a variety of criminal methods to raise funds.
   a. Violent activities involve kidnapping, extortion, and robbery.
   b. Less violent methods include fraud, larceny, smuggling, dealing in contraband, forgery, and counterfeiting.
3. Counterfeiting and fraud are common weapons of the American extremist right.
4. The Internet has become a tool for fraud. Terrorists use online activity in identity theft and gaining access to bank and credit card accounts.
5. Terrorists use extortion and protection rackets to raise money.
6. Large embezzlement schemes in the global economy represent a source of income for small groups as well as large organizations.

D. Underground networks and organized crime.
1. When terrorists move goods, people, weapons, money, or contraband, they must do so in underground networks.
2. The FBI estimates the underground economy produces $500 billion per year.

3. Frederich Schneider states that the underground economy, and its ties to crime, are so important to terrorists because all the transactions remain hidden.
4. Tamara Makarenko says that Russian organized-crime groups trade weapons for drugs in Colombia; she also finds that both terrorists and criminals take advantage of political instability in regions like central Asia and the *Triborder region* in South America.
5. The globalization of crime and terrorism has created opportunities for vast profits in the diamond trade.

E. Legal Sources of Funding: Charities
   1. Terrorists do not limit their financial activities to underworld networks and illegal revenue sources; many groups engage in legitimate business activities to raise and distribute money
   2. According to several researchers charities have been involved in funding terrorism.
   3. Many people who contribute to charities do not know they are supporting terrorist organizations; others believe the efforts they are supporting are not terrorist operations but legitimate military operations.
      a. Non-traceable funding: The hawala system.
   4. While primarily based in Pakistan and India, many international terrorist groups move money through an ancient trading network called the *hawala system*.
   5. The hawala system is a legitimate means of transferring money.
      a. Legitimate business operations.
   6. Sometimes terrorists fund activities through legitimate businesses or localized marketing of specialized products.
   7. According to FBI officials, European Islamic extremists finance terrorism through a variety of legitimate businesses – one group ran a car-repair shop, and a group in Germany ran a used-car dealership.
   8. Domestic violent political extremists use small markets to raise cash; some violent right-wing extremists sell videos, propaganda, and firearms at gun shows.
      a. The extremist right benefits from small-business marketing as well as the Internet.

F. The Political Economy of Terrorism
   OBJ 8: Summarize views on the political economy of terrorism

   1. The financial aspects of terrorism have influenced the changing nature of the international economy.
   2. Promoting an economic system that emphasized international production, trade, and consumption, American economic policies focused on reducing the trade barriers between nation-states.

77

3. Loretta Napoleoni:
   a. Argues that terrorism has evolved as an economic entity.
   b. The fall of the Soviet Union, and subsequent globalization, have produced what she calls the *new economy of terrorism*.
   c. The origins of the new economy of terrorism can be traced to anti-colonial revolts. The desire for autonomy led terrorist groups to join criminals in an underground economy.
   d. Globalization has created pockets in the world where failed or weak states are left to govern with little economic and political power.
   e. The ETA changed the structure of terrorist finance; instead of seeking links to an underground economy, the ETA tried to gain control of the economy.

G. The Narco-terrorism Debate

   OBJ 9: Outline the manners in which drugs and terrorism overlap

   1. One of the heated issues surrounding the discussion of terrorist financing is the relationship between terrorism and drugs, *narco-terrorism*.
   2. Terrorists are involved in the international production and distribution of drugs; the narcotics trade is one of their primary sources of money.
   3. The link between drugs and terrorism.
      a. According to David Adams, Hezbollah and Hamas use the Latin American drug trade to raise funds.
      b. The military's prime concerns are the Tri-border region, the Venezuelan island of Margarita, and the areas controlled by FARC in Colombia.
      c. The French Ministry of Defense issued a report stating that drugs are the primary currency used to finance international terrorism.
      d. Afghanistan is the primary source of heroin in Europe, and the profits from these drug sales fund all international Islamic terrorist groups.
      e. According to many in the Indian government, militant Islamic groups are funded by the drug trade.
   4. Narco-terrorism: Another view.
      a. The use of the term *narco-terrorism* is an attempt to take political advantage of the fear of terrorism.
      b. The Taliban used narcotics trafficking to support Afghanistan.
      c. David Kaplan says the financing of militant Islamic groups has very little to do with the drug trade.
      d. The term narco-terrorism is too vague to describe either drug traffickers or terrorists.
      e. Charities are responsible for the bulk of terrorist financing, and the money funds radical mosques, militant schools and Islamic centers that support the jihad movement.

f. Pierre-Arnaud Chouvy argues that the term *narco-terrorism* is too vague to describe either drug traffickers or terrorists; the problem with drugs involves supply and demand.

g. Civil libertarians see the attempt to link narcotics and terrorism as a ploy by states.

Chapter Summary

- Modern terrorism can be characterized by three overlapping models. A rural model is associated with anti-colonial guerrilla war, and an urban model emerged from ideological terrorism. The insurgent model combines both approaches and associates them with networks, technology, and globalization.

- Organizational structures evolve over time. Hierarchies gave way to umbrella or hub organizations. Terrorism continued to develop into leaderless networks. Failed states have given terrorists the ability to create a hub or umbrella organization within a network.

- Modern piracy is related to organized crime, however, in the Horn of Africa it has become linked with terror networks.

- Large groups or networks are more effective than smaller ones outside a network.

- Analysts slowly developed an appreciation of the importance of terrorist financing. Today it is commonly assumed that good counterterrorist policy involves strategic efforts to deny fiscal resources to terrorists.

- One group of analysts and scholars believes that a financial strategy against terrorism will reduce violence. Another group argues that this approach is too simple because terrorists operate in an underground economy, immune from formal governmental sanctions.

- The relationship between terrorism and economic systems is multifaceted. One way to approach this complexity is to look at illegal funding and networks and legal methods of participating in the economy.

- Terrorists raise money through traditional criminal methods, and exchange resources in underground networks.

- Terrorists also raise money through legal operations. They divert funds to support terrorist operations. Charities and business operations are the most frequent legal activities.

- The hawala system is based on an old method merchants used to exchange money without risking transport of actual cash. Today, some terrorists use this system to fund operations.

- The political economy of terrorism involves groups that have the ability to act autonomously in shell states and failed states. Becoming a *de facto* government power, they control the movement of money, goods, and services.

- The idea of narco-terrorism is controversial. Proponents believe that terrorists use drugs to finance operations; opponents argue that governments use the term to increase its power.

DISCUSSION QUESTIONS

1. Explain the views on the political economy of terrorism as offered by White. Do you agree with White's assessments? Expand on your answers. (OBJ 8)

2. Discuss the positions concerning narco-terrorism as offered in the text. What are your views? Explain. (OBJ 4, 5, and 9)

3. Compare and contrast the rural, urban, and insurgent models of terrorism. List examples. (OBJ 1, 2, 3, and 8)

4. Describe the relationships among the structure, management and financing of terrorist organizations. Describe the impact of each upon planning and controlling a terrorist campaign. (OBJ 1 - 9)

ASSIGNMENTS

1. Have each student comb through http://www.justice.gov/dea/pubs/pressrel/narcoterrorism_index.html (or another website as approved by the instructor) for terrorism related news and select an article that relates to one or more of the chapter's core concepts. Have students provide a journalistic summary and a personal opinion/reaction to the article. Have students orally present the article to the class, field Q & As from their fellow students, and provide a copy of the original source article following the presentation. Optional: Have students complete peer assessments at the end of each presentation. (OBJ 1 - 9)

2. Before the class, have the students explore the possible methods terrorists use to fund their organizations. Write the ideas on the board, and discuss with the class which of the methods they have chosen would be most applicable to current

terrorist groups. Have them compare and contrast terrorist and criminal enterprise finance methods. (OBJ 3, 4, 5, 6, 7, and 9)

3. Have students choose a topic from this chapter, and write a study guide/handout to present and share with the class. For example, students may focus their study guide on describing the emergence of modern piracy. Allow time to discuss topics to eliminate duplication. (OBJ 1 – 9)

4. Discuss the varying positions of the narco-terrorism debate, and have the students take a position. Once they have chosen which side of the debate to argue, have the students research drugs and terrorism, and find evidence that supports the position they have taken. Have students pair up with a classmate of an opposing view and debate their positions. Switch pairs two or more times, then recap the experience with the class. (OBJ 4, 5, and 9)

5. "Guess who". Using a flip chart, describe three different terrorist organizations using a series of bullet points, moving from generalities to specifics. Cover the bullet points with paper, exposing one bullet point at a time. Encourage students to uncover the identity of the organization in as few bullet points as possible. (OBJ 1, 2, and 3)

MEDIA TOOLS

1. *"Wikis"*
   7 Things you should know about Wikis. Retrieved from the Web Jun 29, 2012 at http://net.educause.edu/ir/library/pdf/ELI7004.pdf

   This document offers easy to understand instruction on the history, development, and potential uses of Wikis.

   Have students develop (or make additions to a previously created one) a *Webliography* (resource list) using a Blog or Wiki that provides a short description, and link to a scholarly resource pertaining to course concepts. For example, have students add two to three resources each and ask them to add their assessment of at least one of their peers' contributions. If desired, allow time to discuss Blogs/Wikis. This activity can be reused throughout the course, by asking students to add/revise their contributions each week, bi-weekly, etc. (OBJ 1 - 9)

2. *"What if? Scenarios"*

   Target America: opening eyes to the Damage Drugs Cause. Retrieved from the Web Aug 08, 2012 at http://www.targetamerica.org/resources/exhibitteaching.html

This website offers a host of educational resources relating to the effects of narcoterrorism. This link can additionally serve as a resource for media tool #1.

Divide the class into small groups, and provide each group with a sheet of five to ten *what if?* Scenarios, either downloaded or instructor created. After each group has completed their discussions, have each group present a summary of their discussions to the other group(s). Once completed, have the entire class compare and contrast their combined discoveries. (LO 4, 5, and 9)

3. *"PowerPoint presentation"*
   The Terror Finance Blog. Retrieved from the Web Jun 29, 2012 at http://terrorfinance.org/

   This site offers a substantial array of information on terrorist financing including government measures, programs, academic studies, and related articles. It additionally provides several links to biographical information on the authors.

   Have students probe the blog, taking note on information about the hawala system. Have students create a 5 – 7 slide PowerPoint presentation that describes the system and demonstrates how it works. (LO 3 - 7)

4. *"Current Events Article Summary with Peer Assessment"*

   Use the Article Summary Template, which can be obtained on the instructor companion website, for this assignment. The template offers information on Internet research, outside resources, identification of credible sources, and detailed directions on completing an assessment of a news article. It also includes a peer evaluation tool.

   Have each student comb the Internet for terrorism related news and select an article that relates to one or more of the chapter's core concepts. Be sure selections are an article of interest from a credible source (*more on credibility can be found in the article summary template above).* Fill out an article summary template. The *template asks for generic info about the article, a journalistic summary, as well as a personal opinion/reaction to the article.* Have each student summarize the article and present it orally to the class and field Q & As from their fellow students. Have students complete peer assessments at the end of each presentation. Have students submit templates, original source article, and peer-reviews prior to the end of class. (OBJ 1-9)

Chapter 3—The Organization and Financing of Terrorism

TEST BANK

TRUE/FALSE

1. The Cuban Revolution created guerrilla warfare.

ANS: F   REF: p. 55   OBJ: 1 and 2

2. The most basic type of terrorist subunit is called a column.

ANS: F   REF: p. 57   OBJ: 1 and 2

3. According to Ted Robert Gurr, group size is not an important issue for a terrorist organization.

ANS: F   REF: p. 68   OBJ: 2 and 3

4. Terrorist networks in the Horn of Africa established links with maritime pirates.

ANS: T   REF: p. 66   OBJ: 2

5. The National Strategy for Combating Terrorism endorses investigation into terrorist organization finances, targeting the source of funding, and the mechanisms to transfer money.

ANS: T   REF: p. 69   OBJ: 4

6. Many international terrorist groups move money through an ancient trading network called the hawala system.

ANS: T   REF: p. 75   OBJ: 4, 6 and 7

7. Carlos Marighella believed that all violence could be urban-based and controlled by a small group of guerrillas.

ANS: T   REF: p. 59   OBJ: 1, 2 and 3

8. When terrorist move goods, people, weapons, money, or contraband they must do so in underground networks.

ANS: T   REF: p. 72   OBJ: 4, 6 and 7

9. All countries have prospered through globalization.

ANS: F   REF: p. 77   OBJ: 8

10. Many scholars agree that the narcotics trade is a primary source of money for terrorist organizations.

ANS: T   REF: p. 80   OBJ: 4, 5 and 9

11. Terrorists often move in the same circles as organized criminals, smugglers, and drug dealers.

ANS: T   REF: p. 80   OBJ: 4, 5, 6 and 9

12. Hezbollah and Hamas use the Latin American drug trade to raise funds.

ANS: T   REF: p. 80   OBJ: 4, 5, 6 and 9

13. Mexican drug cartels have established operations in 48 American states.

ANS: T   REF: p. 84   OBJ: 9

14. Globalization has facilitated a global underground economy – providing for illegal trade routes for drugs, arms smugglers, contraband dealers, and human traffic.

ANS: T   REF: p. 78   OBJ: 6 and 8

15. Most terrorist groups number fewer than twenty people.

ANS: F   REF: p. 63   OBJ: 2 and 3

MULTIPLE CHOICE

1. Which of the following does NOT represent general trends in terrorism post 1945?
   a. Rural
   b. Urban
   c. Insurrection
   d. Patriotic

ANS: c   REF: p. 55   OBJ: 1

2. Who is the Brazilian communist legislator and revolutionary theorist who popularized urban terrorism as a method for ending repression and eliminating U.S. domination of Latin America?
   a. Ernesto Guevara
   b. Frantz Fanon
   c. Fidel Castro
   d. Carlos Marighella

ANS: d   REF: p. 58   OBJ: 1 and 2

84

3. _____ refers to various forms of conflict that pits sub-national forces or groups of forces against a recognized nation state or allied states.
   a. Politic tactics
   b. Insurgency
   c. Guerilla warfare
   d. Economic sanctions

ANS: b   REF: p. 60   OBJ: 1 and 2

4. Which of the following is NOT a management problem faced by terrorist organizations?
   a. Secrecy
   b. Training
   c. External discipline
   d. Financing

ANS: c   REF: p. 67   OBJ: 3

5. What is the smallest element of James Fraser's structure of terrorist organizations?
   a. Active cadre
   b. Command structure
   c. Passive support
   d. Active support

ANS: b   REF: p. 62   OBJ: 2 and 3

6. A _____ is an illustration of the way terrorists organize themselves into hierarchies.
   a. Pyramid
   b. Command structure
   c. Organizational chart
   d. Military circle

ANS: a   REF: p. 62   OBJ: 3

7. Which is NOT true of most terrorist organizations?
   a. They number more than one hundred people
   b. They are divided into groups with specific tasks
   c. They are incapable of a large terrorist campaign
   d. They are controlled by a few people

ANS: a   REF: p. 63   OBJ: 3

8. A _____ refers to groups of cells in a terrorist or guerilla organization.
   a. Unit
   b. Column
   c. Chain
   d. Combat cell

ANS: b   REF: p. 62   OBJ: 2 and 3

9. The Triborder region referred to in the text is where these three countries join.
a. Brazil, Paraguay, and Argentina
b. Argentina, Chile, and Mexico
c. Belize, Guatemala, and Argentina
d. Nicaragua, Brazil, and Argentina

ANS: a   REF: p. 73   OBJ: 3, 4 and 6

10. A system of exchanging money based on trust relationships between money dealers is called _____.
a. Money laundering
b. The hawala system
c. Charitable fronts
d. Expropriation

ANS: b   REF: p. 75   OBJ: 4 and 6

11. Counterfeiting and fraud are common weapons of the _____.
a. Asian extremists
b. South American extremists
c. American extremist right
d. Eastern Europe extremists

ANS: c   REF: p. 71   OBJ: 4 and 5

12. Which of the following is based in the belief that international trade barriers should be removed so that commerce and industry can develop in an international free market?
a. The new economy
b. Globalization
c. Financial terrorism
d. Global industry

ANS: b   REF: p. 73   OBJ: 4 and 5

13. According to Loretta Napoleoni, _____ is a term that describes the evolution of terrorist financing from the beginning strategies of the cold war to the present.
a. The new economy of terrorism
b. Globalization
c. Financial terrorism
d. The global industry

ANS: a   REF: p. 77   OBJ: 4, 5 and 6

14. Much like the World Wide Web or a traffic system, a _____ does not have central leadership and they operate under a variety of rules.
a. Pyramid
b. Unit
c. Network
d. Command

ANS: c   REF: p. 65   OBJ: 3

15. According to Mario Ferrero, what do modern radical Islamic groups use as a means of providing economic stability?
a. Violent activity
b. Unregulated diamond trading
c. Drug trading
d. Document fraud

ANS: a   REF: p. 79   OBJ: 4 and 5

16. Which of the following theories suggests that counterterrorism policies should be aimed at providing the world's people with economic stability, opportunity, and participation in the mainstream economy?
a. Microeconomic theory
b. Globalization theory
c. Macroeconomic theory
d. Global economic theory

ANS: c   REF: p. 79   OBJ: 4, 5, 6 and 8

17. Which of the following is NOT an economic policy to counter terrorism?
a. Supporting states in threat of failure
b. Increasing loans to Third World Nations
c. Providing opportunities for people to participate/benefit from economic systems
d. Eliminating underground economic networks

ANS: b   REF: p. 79   OBJ: 8

18. According to _____, charities are responsible for the bulk of terrorist financing.
a. David Kaplan
b. Loretta Napoleoni
c. Joshua Krasna
d. David Adams

ANS: a   REF: p. 81   OBJ: 4 and 5

19. Who does David Kaplan (2003) blame for funding the spread of an intolerant form of Islam?
a. Iraq
b. Afghanistan
c. Libya
d. Saudi Arabia

ANS: d   REF: p. 81   OBJ: 4, 5 and 8

20.   The _____ aspects of terrorism have had the greatest influence upon the changing nature of the international economy.
a. Religious
b. Financial
c. Political
d. Social

ANS: b   REF: p. 82   OBJ: 8

21.   _____ are the most frequent legal activities used by terrorists to fund their activities.
a. For-profit education facilities
b. Stock trading
c. Charities and business operations
d. Real estate investments

ANS: c   REF: p. 83   OBJ: 5

22.   _____ exist through computer and information networks.
a. Virtual organizations
b. Hub organizations
c. Chain organizations
d. Wheel organizations

ANS: a   REF: p. 64   OBJ: 2 and 3

23.   _____ involve small groups linked by some type of communication where members periodically cooperate.
a. Virtual organizations
b. Hub organizations
c. Chain organizations
d. Networks

ANS: c   REF: p. 64   OBJ: 2 and 3

24.   Capone discovery is a term used by James Adams to explain the entry of _____ into organized crime.
a. Irish Republican Army
b. Jihadist movement
c. Animal Liberation Front
d. al Qaeda

ANS: a   REF: p. 69   OBJ: 4 and 5

25.   Which of the following countries is NOT a member of the Triborder Region of Latin America?
a. Brazil
b. Paraguay
c. Chile
d. Argentina

ANS: c   REF: p. 73   OBJ: LO8

26.   Guerrilla revolutions based on the Cuban experience are typified by _____ phases; each designed to progress from and complement the previous one.
a. Four
b. Three
c. Six
d. Five

ANS: b   REF: p. 57   OBJ: 1

27.   Which of the following activities are terrorist organizations LEAST likely to pursue to finance its operations?
a. Smuggling
b. Fraud schemes
c. Charitable donations
d. Money laundering

ANS: d   REF: p. 30   OBJ: 4 and 5

28.   _____ is a term describing a political situation where a government nominally controls its own state but where large regions are either anarchic or under the control of others.
a. Globalization
b. Shell state
c. Weak state
d. Failed state

ANS: b   REF: p. 54   OBJ: 2

29.   Carlos Marighella argued that "urban warfare" begins with a campaign of _____.
a.   Expropriation
b.   Initiation
c.   Laundering
d.   Investment

ANS: a   REF: p. 71   OBJ: 1

30.   _____ off the coast of the Horn of Africa is caused by the multifaceted conflict in Somalia accompanied by the breakup of legal authority and social systems.
a. Prostitution
b. Piracy
c. Drug trade
d. Weapons trade

ANS: b   REF: p. 54   OBJ: 1 and 8

31.   What country is the primary source of heroin in Europe?
a. Afghanistan
b. Iraq
c. Saudi Arabia
d. China

ANS: a   REF: p. 80   OBJ: 5

89

32.   The Sinaloa Drug Cartel is based in what country?
      a. Mexico
      b. Columbia
      c. Nicaragua
      d. Brazil

ANS: a   REF: p. 84   OBJ: 9

33.   The Cuban Revolution occurred during what years?
      a. 1918-1921
      b. 1956-1959
      c. 1991-1994
      d. 1965-1969

ANS: b   REF: p. 55   OBJ: 1

34.   What is the preferred method of fighting among Latin American revolutionaries?
      a. Cyber warfare
      b. Guerilla warfare
      c. Biological warfare
      d. Trench warfare

ANS: b   REF: p. 56   OBJ: 1

35.   1965 saw the end of Algeria's war with what country?
      a. France
      b. Libya
      c. Tunisia
      d. Egypt

ANS: a   REF: p. 58   OBJ: 1 and 2

36.   Who were the leading forces of the Cuban revolution?
      a. Ernesto 'Che' Guevara and Fidel Castro
      b. Fulgencio Batista and Fidel Castro
      c. Ernesto 'Che' Guevara and Fulgencio Batista
      d. Regis Debray and Fidel Castro

ANS: a   REF: p. 5   OBJ: 1 and 2

37.   Who were the leading forces of the Cuban revolution?
      a. Ernesto 'Che' Guevara and Fidel Castro
      b. Fulgencio Batista and Fidel Castro
      c. Ernesto 'Che' Guevara and Fulgencio Batista
      d. Regis Debray and Fidel Castro

ANS: a   REF: p. 55   OBJ: 1 and 2

38.   The most common job in terrorist groups is _____, not combat.
       a. Networking
       b. Administration
       c. Support
       d. Propaganda

ANS: c   REF: p. 62   OBJ: 3

39.   The largest cross section of a terrorist organization is its _____?
       a. Commanders
       b. Active Cadre
       c. Passive supporters
       d. Active supporters

ANS: c   REF: p. 62   OBJ: 3

40.   RAND refers to a terrorist organization's ability to quickly assemble members, strike,
       and return to obscurity as _____.
       a. Ghosting
       b. Enlisting
       c. Swarming
       d. Hiving

ANS: c   REF: p. 65   OBJ: 3

Case 3.0

According to Fraser and Fulton, the hierarchical structure of terrorist groups is divided into four levels. The smallest group, at the top of the pyramid, is responsible for command. As in military circles, leadership makes policy and plans and provides general direction. The second level of the hierarchy is the active cadre, or the people responsible for carrying out the mission of the organization - the striking arm of the terrorist group. The third are the active supporters. They maintain communication channels, provide safe houses, gather intelligence, and ensure that all other logistical needs are met. The last and largest category is the organization's passive supporters. This group is extremely difficult to identify and characterize because passive supporters do not readily join terrorist groups; they simply represent a favorable element of the political climate.

Imagine you are a security analyst for the Department of Homeland Security and have just been given several intelligence briefs that describe the activities of several individuals, described below:

91

A young college student (Adain) has just left a meeting with the niece (Bella) of a well known HAMAS member (Mahmud) who has been in hiding after a series of videos had been leaked to the press showing him overseeing a terrorist training camp. Adain immediately goes to a hardware store and purchases several bomb making items which he delivers to a nearby farm. The hardware store owner (Mansour) intuitively aware of Adain's impending plan offers his goods at a deep discount and wishes him well on his *journey*. The farmer (Shari) accepts the items and wishes Aiden goodbye. Shari creates the bomb and calls for Adain to return. Adain returns and detonates the bob in a local café and dies in the process. Ross, Glen, and Keary (uninvolved in the incident) view Adain's activities as brave and offer words of respect to the family.

41. Your supervisor asks you to classify each individual's according to Fraser and Fulton's levels outlined above. Reflecting upon the scenario, at what level in the terrorist organization would you classify Adain?
    a. Command
    b. Active cadre
    c. Active supporter
    d. Passive supporter

ANS: b   REF: p. 62   OBJ: 2 and 3

42. Your supervisor asks you to classify each individual's according to Fraser and Fulton's levels outlined above. Reflecting upon the scenario, at what level in the terrorist organization would you classify Bella?
    a. Command
    b. Active cadre
    c. Active supporter
    d. Passive supporter

ANS: c   REF: p. 62   OBJ: 2 and 3

43. Your supervisor asks you to classify each individual's according to Fraser and Fulton's levels outlined above. Reflecting upon the scenario, at what level in the terrorist organization would you classify Mahmud?
    a. Command
    b. Active cadre
    c. Active supporter
    d. Passive supporter

ANS: a   REF: p. 62   OBJ: 2 and 3

44. Your supervisor asks you to classify each individual's according to Fraser and Fulton's levels outlined above. Reflecting upon the scenario, at what level in the terrorist organization would you classify Mansour?
    a. Command
    b. Active cadre
    c. Active supporter
    d. Passive supporter

ANS: c   REF: p. 62   OBJ: 2 and 3

45.   Your supervisor asks you to classify each individual's according to Fraser and Fulton's levels outlined above. Reflecting upon the scenario, at what level in the terrorist organization would you classify Shari?

   a.   Command
   b.   Active cadre
   c.   Active supporter
   d.   Passive supporter

ANS: b   REF: p. 62   OBJ: 2 and 3

46.   Your supervisor asks you to classify each individual's according to Fraser and Fulton's levels outlined above. Reflecting upon the scenario, at what level in the terrorist organization would you classify Ross, Glen, and Keary?

   a.   Command
   b.   Active cadre
   c.   Active supporter
   d.   Passive supporter

ANS: a   REF: p. 62   OBJ: 2 and 3

Case 3.1

   Asadullah is an operative for the Lashkare-Taiba, a Kashmiri terrorist group. Asif, Asadullah's contact in Peshawar, needs $500 to buy AK-47s. After raising funds in the United States, Asadullah visits a *special* shop owner, hands over $500, and asks him to get the money to Asif. The Peshawar shop owner gives Asif the money, not knowing its use. Asif buys the weapons and delivers them to contacts in the Lashkar-e-Taiba. There is no record of the transaction.

47.   The financial transaction above is an example of the _____ system.
   a.   Shwarma
   b.   Hawala
   c.   Falafel
   d.   Salama

ANS: b   REF: p. 75   OBJ: 6 and 7

48.   Why does this situation present special challenges for counterterrorism efforts?
   a.   There is no way to trace the flow of funds
   b.   The system gives terrorists unlimited funds
   c.   Governments are not able to impart taxes on the transactions
   d.   No challenge exists – such transactions are common in international banking

ANS: a   REF: p. 75   OBJ: 6 and 7

Case 3.2

Ernesto 'Che' Guevara, following the overthrow of Batista in Cuba, wrote *Reminiscences of the Cuban Revolutionary War* in which he described the success of the revolution as being a three-step process (1) revolutionaries join the indigenous population to form guerrilla *foco*, as Guevara called them, (2) small forces form columns and control rural areas, and (3) columns unite for a conventional offensive to overthrow government.

49.   What style of warfare was Guevara describing in his three step process?

        a. Cyber warfare
        b. Guerilla warfare
        c. Biological warfare
        d. Trench warfare

ANS: b   REF: p. 57   OBJ: 1

50.   Which of the following would NOT be a likely strategy for Guevara?
        a. Ambush
        b. Sabotage
        c. Diplomatic negotiations
        d. Raids

ANS: c   REF: p. 57   OBJ: 1

COMPLETION

1.   The second level of Fraser and Fulton's hierarchy is the _____.

ANS: active cadre   REF: p. 62   OBJ: 1, 2,and 3

2.   The _____ is one method used to transfer money from one person to another without leaving a record of the transaction.

ANS: hawala system   REF: p. 75   OBJ: 7

3.   Illegitimate groups form _____ states, organizations that acts like a government in a place where the government is not strong enough to act.

ANS: shell   REF: p. 78   OBJ: 2 and 8

4.   _____suggests that counterterrorism policies should be aimed at providing the world's people with economic stability, opportunity, and participation in the mainstream economy.

ANS: macroeconomic theory   REF: p. 79   OBJ: 8

5. The term _____ refers to terrorists using either terrorist tactics to support drug operations or drug trade profits to finance terrorism.

ANS: narcoterrorism   REF: p. 80   OBJ: 4, 5 and 9

6. _____ describes the evolution of terrorist financing from the beginning strategies of the cold war to the present.

ANS: New economy of terrorism   REF: p. 78   OBJ: 2, 4, 5, 8 and 9

7. According to Tamara Makarenko, terrorist and criminal organizations have grown into _____.

ANS: global enterprises   REF: p. 73   OBJ: 8

8. According to the text, the two most important developments in the history of modern terrorism are the invention of _____ and the formation of tactical groups.

ANS: dynamite   REF: p. 61   OBJ: 2

9. _____ is considered the founding father of the Irish Republican Army (IRA).

ANS: Michael Collins   REF: p. 62   OBJ: 1 and 2

10. _____ involve small groups linked by some type of communication and whose members cooperate.

ANS: chain organizations   REF: p. 64   OBJ: 3

11. An estimated ninety percent of the weapons used by the cartels are purchased in ____.

ANS: the United States   REF: p. 84   OBJ: 9

12. Most of Hezbollah's funds come from state funding, with _____ acting as the principal sponsor.

ANS: Iran   REF: p. 77   OBJ: 4 and 5

13. Inside Lebanon is an extensive protection racket that charges legitimate businesses to ensure that their property will not be damaged and that their personnel are not harmed. The charges are collectively known as a _____.

ANS: "Hezbollah tax"   REF: p. 77   OBJ: 5

14. The problem of modern day piracy is endemic to the political struggle in _____.

ANS: Somalia   REF: p. 66   OBJ: 5

95

15. *Legitimate* organizations that do not directly become involved in terrorism, but support and/or shelter terrorists are known as _____ organizations.

ANS: umbrella   REF: p. 82   OBJ: 4

16. The first suicide attacks in Western Europe in 2005 when three young men detonated bombs in separate trains on _____.

ANS: the London Underground REF: p. 68   OBJ: 1 and 2

17. Interpol estimates that counterfeiting and intellectual property theft is responsible for $_____ in illegal profits in the United States.

ANS: 200 billion   REF: p. 71   OBJ: 5

18. The practice of purchasing stocks, providing false information to inflate the stock, and selling off the stock before the stock drops back to its normal level is known as _____.

ANS: "pump and dump"   REF: p. 71   OBJ: 5

19. North American cars, especially SUVs, are attractive to _____ because they can be heavily packed with explosives and have a high cash value ($100,000+).

ANS: terrorists   REF: p. 71   OBJ: 5

20. The FBI estimates that the underground economy produces $_____ billion per year.

ANS: 500   REF: p. 72   OBJ: 5, 6 and 8

ESSAY

1. Explain how Carlos Marighella believed a campaign of revolutionary terrorism in an urban setting could be used to destabilize governmental power. Evaluate his beliefs.

ANS:
- A psychological assault would convince the government and the people that the status quo no longer held.
- They would come to feel that the terrorists were in control.
- When this situation developed, Marighella believed, the government would be forced to show its true colors.
- With its authority challenged and the economic stability of the elite eroded, the government would be forced to declare some form of martial law.
- This would not be a defeat for terrorism but rather exactly what the terrorists and their supporters wanted.
- Marighella believed the public supported governmental policies because they did not realize the repressive nature of the state.

- The terrorist campaign would force the government to reveal itself, thereby alienating the public.
- With no place to turn, the public would turn to the terrorists, and the terrorists would be waiting with open arms.
- As the ranks of the urban guerrillas grew with the rush of public support, the revolutionaries would gradually abandon their terrorist campaign.
- Their efforts would focus more and more on the construction of a general urban army, an army that could seize key governmental control points on cue.
- When the urban army had reached sufficient strength, all its forces would be launched in a general strike.
- Student evaluations will vary.

REF: p. 59   OBJ: 1

2.   Explain the hawala system, its origins, and what are the advantages that would make this system appealing to terrorists?

ANS:
- A system of exchanging money based on trust relationships between money dealers.
- A chit, or promissory note, is exchanged between two hawaladars, and it is as valuable as cash or other traded commodities because the trust between the two parties guarantees its value.
- The system originated several hundred years ago in China under the name of Feng Chin, or "flying money."
- Today it is primarily based in Pakistan and India, but there are hawala dealers around the world.
- It is a legitimate means of transferring money without using money or moving funds across international borders, although it may violate currency transfer regulations in some countries.
- Money moves with no record and crosses international borders with ease.
- It is based on trust, and long-term trusting relationships are in place.
- Money can easily be bartered for contraband.
- No tax records exist.

REF: p. 75   OBJ: 7

3.   Explain how the RAND approach reveals the structure of networks.

ANS:
- They involve terrorist, extremist, criminal, and disruptive-activist groups.
- The key to networks, according to this approach, is their ability to operate in a technological setting.
- Operations are characterized by the dual nature of the network.
- Violence takes place on two levels: organized small groups and disruptive violence from demonstrations.
- Another characteristic is the structure of the group.
- It is not a traditional hierarchy; it is a network.

97

- Members can be quickly assembled although they operate from diverse locations, and group structures are temporary.
- They are designed to fit a particular situation.
- They appear seemingly from nowhere, strike, and return to obscurity.
- RAND refers to this as the ability to swarm.

REF: p. 65   OBJ: 2 and 3

4.   Describe the three primary reasons that traditional financial criminal investigative techniques are ineffective. What is your view on why these investigative techniques are not effective? Explain your view.

ANS:
- First, terror attacks would be expensive for a normal individual, but not for a group.
- Some attacks cost a few thousand dollars while major operations can be conducted for less than $500,000.
- This amount of money can be moved within the financial system.
- Second, freezing assets does not work because terrorists can find sources and investigators lose the ability to follow a particular link once it is frozen.
- Links inside networks should be the focus of terrorism investigations, and known financial links may reveal an unknown node.
- Finally, if financial weapons are to be effective, they must be based on international agreements.
- Student views will vary.

REF: p. 70   OBJ: 4, 6 and 7

5.   Describe the three major categories that help explain the structure of financing. Illustrate how terrorist utilize these three categories.

ANS:
- The first element deals with the unlawful raising and distribution of funds.
- It is necessary to examine the illegal sources of income and the underground networks used to disburse the funds.
- Terrorists also use another source of income, the formal regulated economy. Therefore, it is necessary to examine activities that appear to be legitimate.
- The third category has little to do with financing but has much to do with financial effectiveness.
- Some analysts propose using financial weapons against terrorists, and some terrorists have learned that economic targeting is a technological force multiplier.
- In other words, it is also necessary to consider the ways terrorists can turn the tables and use the costs of terrorism as a weapon.
- Student illustrations will vary.

REF: p. 70   OBJ: 4, 6 and 7

6.   Explain how the Internet has become a tool for fraud. Provide a specific example.

ANS:
- Terrorists use online activity in identity theft and gaining access to bank and credit card accounts.
- They also sell items at Internet auctions.
- Security fraud is another method of raising funds.
- For example, a group might buy a large amount of stock in a company that is fairly inactive.
- They then fill the Web with stories of new products, new technology, or some other item that will cause the company's stock to increase.
- As the stock value increases, terrorists sell the stock at an inflated price even though the company had no real increase in value.
- Before the stock drops back to its normal level, the terrorists make a huge profit.
- This process is known as "pump and dump," and it is frequently used by dishonest stock speculators and other criminals
- Examples will vary.

REF: p. 71   OBJ: 5 and 6

7.   What does Loretta Napoleoni mean by the term new economy of terrorism? Describe her theory about the financing of terrorism.

ANS:
- A term used to describe the evolution of terrorist financing from the beginning strategies of the cold war to the present.
- Economic support and antiterrorist policies interact to form the new economy.
- Loretta Napoleoni found links between organized crime networks and terrorism; terrorism has evolved as an economic entity.
- The fall of the Soviet Union and subsequent globalization have produced what she calls the new economy of terrorism.
- The origins of the new economy of terrorism grew from the cold war (1945–1991).
- Napoleoni sees this as the beginning of a macroeconomic shift.
- Western nations began to use underground methods to fund their struggles in the colonies, and revolutionaries sought their own sources of money.
- The origins of the new economy of terrorism can be traced to anti-colonial revolts.

REF: p. 71   OBJ: 4 and 8

8.   Explain how macroeconomic theories of terrorism may have meaning for the nature of counterterrorism. Do you agree with this theory? Why or why not?

ANS:
- Macroeconomic theory suggests that counterterrorism policies should be aimed at providing the world's people with economic stability, opportunity, and participation in the mainstream economy.

- Economic policies to counter terrorism would involve supporting states in danger of failure, providing opportunities for people to participate and benefit from economic systems, and eliminating underground economic networks.
- When a state fails and a terrorist group creates its own shell state, the group has no incentive to participate in legitimate economic enterprises.
- When economic globalization threatens the ability of ordinary people to meet their needs, they will find other ways to survive.
- Poverty does not cause terrorism, but economic and political failures may result in a shell state where terrorism can be organized and funded.
- Views will vary.

REF: p. 79   OBJ: 8

9.   Who was Ernesto "Che" Guevara? Describe the three phases through which guerrilla revolutions based on the Cuban experience are typified. What was the goal of Guevara's strategy?

ANS:
- Guevara was born in Argentina in 1928.
- Earned a medical degree at the University of Buenos Aires.
- Turned his attention from medicine to the plight of the poor.
- He believed poverty and repression were problems that transcended nationalism and revolution was the only means of challenging authority.
- He served the communist regime of Guatemala in 1954 but fled to Mexico City when communists were purged from the government where he met Castro.
- Fidel Castro's assistant and guerrilla warfare theorist.
- Wrote *Reminiscences of the Cuban Revolutionary War* which appeared in the United States in 1961; the book enjoyed mass distribution at the end of the decade.
- Guevara-style revolution begins with isolated groups.
- In phase two, the isolated groups merge into guerrilla columns.
- The final phase brings columns together in a conventional army.
- The goal of the strategy is to develop a conventional fighting force, or at least a force that renders the conventional opponent impotent.

REF: p. 56   OBJ: 1

10.   Describe the four levels of the hierarchical structure of terrorist groups as posited by James Fraser and Ian Fulton. Evaluate Fraser and Fulton's levels.

ANS:
- The smallest group, at the top of the pyramid, is responsible for command.
- As in military circles, leadership makes policy and plans and provides general direction.
- The command structure in a terrorist organization is not free to communicate openly with its membership; therefore, it cannot exercise day-to-day operational control.

- The second level is the active cadre, or the people responsible for carrying out the mission of the organization.
- Depending on the organization's size, each terrorist in the cadre may have one or more specialties.
- Other terrorists support each specialty, but the active cadre is the striking arm of the terrorist group.
- After the command structure, the cadre of active terrorists is the smallest organization in most terrorist structures.
- Under the active cadre is the second largest and the most important level of a terrorist organization: the active supporters.
- They maintain communication channels, provide safe houses, gather intelligence, and ensure that all other logistical needs are met.
- This is the largest internal group in the organization.
- The last and largest category is the organization's passive supporters.
- This group is extremely difficult to identify and characterize because passive supporters do not readily join terrorist groups.
- Passive support complements active support.
- Student evaluations will vary.

REF: p. 62   OBJ: 2 and 3

CHAPTER 4
Terrorism and the Media

Learning Objectives

After reading this chapter, students should be able to:

1. Discuss the role of the media in constructing social reality.
2. Explain the tension between security forces and the media.
3. Describe how the media can be viewed as a weapon.
4. Explain how news frames are used to present a story.
5. Describe the special relationship between terrorism and television.
6. Explain how the Internet has impacted terrorism.
7. Summarize various positions about bias in the news media.
8. Define the contagion effect.
9. Debate the issues of freedom of the press and censorship.

Chapter Key Terms

news media, p. 87

news frames, p. 90

reporting frame, p. 91

postmodern, p. 92

infotainment telesector, p. 93

made-for-TV drama , p. 94

al Jazeera, p. 95

al Manar, p. 95

al Asqa Intifada, p. 95

steganography, p. 97

Salafi movement, p. 97

critical media consciousness, p. 101

copycats, p. 102

longitudinal studies, p. 104

Freedom of Information (FOI) Act, p. 105

Al Asqa Intifada: an uprising sparked by Ariel Sharon's visit to the Temple Mount with a group of armed escorts in September 2000. The area is considered sacred to Jews, Christians, and Muslims. Muslims were incensed by the militant aspect of Sharon's visit.

Al Jazeera: an international Arabic television network and news organization based in Qatar.

Al Manar: Hezbollah's television network.

Copycat: refers to people who imitate other criminals after viewing, hearing, or reading a story about a crime. A copy cat copies the targets and methods of another criminal.

Critical media consciousness: the public's understanding of the media and the way stories are presented. A critically conscious audience would not simply accept a story presented in a news frame. It would look for the motives for telling the story, how the story impacted social constructs and actions, and hidden details that would cause the story to be told another way.

Freedom of Information Act: a law ensuring access to government records.

Infotainment telesector: a sarcastic term to describe cable news networks. It refers to news organization producing stories to entertain their audiences under the guise of presenting objective information.

Longitudinal studies: social science examinations of the same subjects over long periods of time.

Made-for-TV-drama: refers to any news story that will keep viewers attention. H.H.A. Cooper was among the first analysts to recognize the drama terrorism presented for television.

News frames: visual, audible, or written packages used to present the news. Communication scholars do not agree on a single definition, but news frames generally refer to the presentation of the news story. They contain a method for beginning and ending the story, and they convey the importance of characters and actions as the story is told.

News media: as used in this text, refers to television, radio, and print journalism. It also refers to newer sources on the Internet, including news reporting services, the blogosphere, WebPages, and propaganda broadcasts.

Postmodern: refers to the belief that modernism has ended. Some events are inexplicable, and some organizations and actions are naturally and socially chaotic and defy explanation. A postmodern news frame leaves the consumer thinking there are many possible conclusions.

Reporting frame: the simplest form of a news frame. It is a quick, fact-driven report that summarizes the latest information about a story. It does not need to contain a beginning or an end, and it assumes that the consumer understands the context of the facts.

Salafism: a reform movement in Islam that started in North Africa in the 19th century. Its purpose is to purify Islam by returning to the practices of Mohammed and his followers.

Steganography: embedding a hidden encoded message on an Internet site.

Chapter Outline

I.   **The Media and the Social Construction of Images**
      OBJ 1: Discuss the role of the media in constructing social reality
      OBJ 2: Explain the tension between security forces and the media
      OBJ 3: Describe how the media can be viewed as a weapon

   A. Additional research addressing the relationship between the media and terrorism is needed.
   B. Terrorism involves symbolic communication usually aimed at an audience far beyond the immediate victims of violence.
   C. Communication develops in three primary manners:
      1. Reporting of terrorist events
      2. Creating the social definition of terrorism
      3. The World Wide Web becoming a basis for propaganda and communication
   D. Popular media misconceptions
      1. The myths circulated by television news shape the world view of consumers.
      2. If social constructs are created by collective definitions, the power of the media helps to define the boundaries of those constructs.
      3. Media view of terrorism is dominated by several simplified stories, presented and re-presented on twenty-four hour cable news networks. a.   Viewers are encouraged to accept simple facts about complicated
           Issues, and to accept misappropriated labels.
      4. Phrases like "broken borders" and "war on terrorism" create images that become reality after they are used again and again.
      5. Topics selected for coverage not only distort images; unselected topics go unnoticed.
   E. Tension between security forces and the media
      1. Police and security forces frequently find themselves at odds with this media power.
         a. They compete for favorable media coverage.
         b. Governments exhibit strong distain for the press because media social constructions often run counter to government objectives and policies.
      2. Law enforcement and military goals often conflict with the goals of the reporters.
      3. Police and military forces frequently try to take advantage of the media's ability to define social reality.
   F. The media as a weapon
      1. Richard Clutterbuck once concluded that the media were similar to a loaded weapon lying in the middle of a street – the first person to pick it up got to use it.
      2. Ayman al Zawahiri's use of the media as a weapon
         a. Any attack, especially if it is sensational, can dramatize the struggle.
         b. Zawahiri can turn to his own media relations group.
         c. Zawahiri uses his own writings to justify terrorism.
         d. Along with other jihadists, he uses the Internet.

104

3. An analysis of Jihadist media and communication goals, from their own writings, shows that Jihadists are keenly aware of the media's ability to influence the social construction of reality.
4. Jihadist texts reveal three media strategies:
   a. They seek legitimacy for their movement, especially wanting to justify acts of violence to other Muslims.
   b. They want to spread their message and increase sympathy for their militant interpretation of religion.
   c. Their opponents, both the West and Muslims with a different interpretation of Islam, are targeted for intimidation.

II. **News Frames and Presentations**
OBJ 4: Explain how news frames are used to present a story

A. Reporting patterns are packaged in segments called <u>news frames</u>.
   1. The purpose of a news frame is to assemble words and pictures to create a pattern surrounding an event.
B. News frames form the basis for communicating symbols.
C. The news frames provide the "correct" symbolism for the consumer.
D. News frames help "mediatize" the presentation of terrorism; that is, it shapes the way an event is communicated.
E. The classic approach for television is the <u>reporting frame</u>. It is usually short, and designed to provide the latest information.
F. Types of frames
   1. A dominant frame presents a story from a single point of view.
   2. The conflict frame presents a story frame with two views, each side having experts or witnesses to support a position.
   3. A contention frame summarizes a variety of views.
   4. Investigation frames champion the role of the press as the protectors of democracy.
   5. Television news presents a mythic frame, which reinforces deeply held values; frequently used to depict those people who have sacrificed their lives for a cause.
G. Ambiguous stories and news frames
   1. News frames give the story a structured meaning, but sometimes a story defies structure.
   2. The news frame works when a report is based on sources with definitive explanations of an event.
   3. Ambiguity destroys the ability to create a sustainable news frame.
      a. If terrorism is reported in well-defined news frames, both the media and the consumer will assume that there is a political beginning, a violent process, and a logical end.
      b. If there is ambiguity about the story, the method by which reporters gather the story and present it becomes the story, because there is no logical conclusion.

H. Beating the war drum
1. After September 11, television beat the war drum, and called in a variety of terrorism experts who reflected a single view.
2. Radio engaged in sensationalistic propaganda.
3. A military solution may well have been the proper answer to 9/11, but news frames presented no other option.

III. **Terrorism and television**
   OBJ 2: Explain the tension between security forces and the media
   OBJ 5: Describe the special relationship between terrorism and television

A. Benjamin Barber argues that the media flourishes on one overriding factor: entertainment.
1. Barber calls the twenty-four hour news networks the Infotainment Telesector, designed to create revenue.
2. The contexts of the infotainment telesector, and the desire to beat the other networks, have a negative effect on homeland security.
B. H. H. A. Cooper was one of the first analysts to point to the issues explaining that terrorist acts were made-for-TV dramas.
C. David Levin says the purpose of television news coverage is to keep the audience primed with emotion and excitement.
D. The drama pattern is designed to keep the viewer tuned to the station.
E. The overriding message of the drama is "stay tuned."
F. Control of the drama pattern has been held in a Western monopoly until recently.
1. New networks such as al Jazeera and al Arabia have challenged the Western hold on international news.
2. Localized networks present other perspectives and definitions of terrorism.
   a. Al Jazeera is an international Arabic television network and news organization based in Qatar.
   b. Al Manar is Hezbollah's television network.
G. Television makes the viewing audience participants in a terrorist attack.
1. Viewers have short and long term psychological damage after seeing terror attacks on television, and it shapes anxiety and attitudes.

IV. **The Internet and Terrorism**

   OBJ 6: Explain how the Internet has impacted terrorism

A. The Internet impacts news coverage of all events, and often exceeds the ability of the established media to report an event; it is also used to present terrorism.
B. The Internet is used most frequently as a communication device, and nonsecure e-mail is the most common form of usage for terrorists.
C. Terrorists run their own Web sites, and they sometimes hack into existing sites to broadcast propaganda videos.

D. <u>Steganography</u> is frequently said to be one of the Internet's greatest vulnerabilities to criminal and terrorist communication.
 1. The process refers to embedding hidden information in a picture, message, or other piece of information.
E. There are numerous potential methods to use steganography in terrorism.
 1. Hide communications.
 2. Steal information from security forces or an organization within the critical infrastructure.
 3. Provide opportunities for electronic attack.
I. There are two positions on the steganographic threat to the United States:
 1. Steganography is used by terrorist groups to communicate and launch cyber-attacks.
 2. It will be used in denial of service attacks, or to deface Websites.
J. Stephan Lau argues that the real threat lies with the government's enhanced ability to decipher private communications based on a threat that does not exist.
K. In the areas of propaganda, reporting, and public relations, the Internet has been a boon; allowing terrorist groups to present messages and portray images that will not appear in mainstream media.
L. The Internet can also be used for recruiting and training.
M. The Internet is also used in target selection, reconnaissance, and sometimes as a tool to support an attack.
N. Security forces also effectively use the Internet.
O. The Internet can be used against terrorism and other forms of criminal activity.

V. **Issues in the Media**

 OBJ 7: Summarize various positions about bias in the news media

A. Because the media is so powerful, many of the issues surrounding reporting and communication are hotly debated.
B. Liberal and conservative biases in terrorism reporting?
 1. Most mainstream media claim objectivity when presenting information about terrorism.
 2. All news comes with a slant, and reporters are expected to create news frames reflecting their outlet's orientation.
 3. At one end of the spectrum critics claim the media have a liberal bias.
 4. Others claim that the media have been taken over by conservatives.
 5. Daniel Sutter
  a. A news organization, a profit-making entity, has the incentive to attract the largest possible audience.
   i. If the news moved either to the right or left, it would be threatened with the loss of mainstream viewers.
  b. If the entire media were to exhibit a bias, some owner would need to have a monopoly on all media outlets.
  c. Journalism is a profession.

d. As news organizations expand, there will be pressures for bias to develop special audiences among liberals and conservatives.

e. News organizations are increasingly led by boards and groups of owners driven by the desire to make money.

6. David Baron suggests bias appears on two levels:

a. The individual discretion of the reporter collecting information for a story.

b. The public's desire to watch or read the most captivating story.

7. Tim Groseclose and Jeffrey Milyo

a. The American media have a liberal bias.

b. The news media cited the think tanks referenced by liberal members of Congress more than conservative members.

8. Fouzi Slisli

a. Adjectives introduce bias into the news.

9. David Levin

a. The news is aimed at particular audiences, and different organizations approach audiences in different ways.

10. Richard Miniter

a. The media used to have a conservative bias, and now it has tilted toward liberalism.

b. The issue for the media is that it is spreading incorrect information about terrorism.

   i. He identifies twenty-two misconceptions about terrorism which are accepted as truth by most newspapers, magazines, and broadcasters.

11. Todd Fraley and Elli Roushanzamir

a. The current conditions of sub-national and supranational violence is shifting and distorting all media presentations of violence, including terrorism.

b. The mass media are spreading more propaganda than news.

   i. The flow and amount of information, however, could serve to raise the awareness of news consumers, creating a new <u>critical media consciousness</u>.

VI. **The Contagion Effect**
OBJ 8: Define the contagion effect

A. Some analysts are not as concerned about the content of press coverage as they are about its role in spreading terrorist violence.

B. M. Cherif Bassiouni – terrorism is contagious: media-reported terrorism caused more terrorism.

C. A few years later, research suggested that media images produced emotional behavior, but not in ways that were completely predictable.

D. More recent research indicates that the effects of media exposure are even more complex.

1. Many researchers believe that the fear generated by media reporting is contagious.

E. Other findings demonstrate that media reports might inspire a person to engage in terrorism, but so do stories from friends and families.

F. There may be a contagious relationship between a terrorist event and the level of violence in later events.

G. Some researchers believe that if a contagion effect exists, it might be used to counter terrorism.

H. Other problems in media-induced violence appear with differing methodologies.
   1. Variables are unknown.
   2. Consumers may prefer media violence as entertainment, while never accepting violent behavior in everyday life.
   3. Casual relationships are often oversimplified.

VII. **Censorship Debate**
   OBJ 9: Debate the issues of freedom of the press and censorship

A. Debates over censorship arise because many people assume that acts of terrorism are induced by reckless media coverage, and that media outlets provide terrorists with information.

B. Paul Wilkinson believes that governments face three choices when it comes to freedom of the press and terrorism:
   1. A popular position is to assume a *laissez-faire* attitude.
   2. A second choice is censorship.
   3. A final choice is self-regulation.

C. The arguments about censorship are heated and deal with core issues in democracy.

D. The censorship debate also focuses on truth or factual information.

E. Doris Graber
   1. Freedom of the press is crucial during times of national crisis, but that   is when the media are most vulnerable.
   2. Arguments used to encourage censorship.
      a. National security.
      b. The public wants information withheld.
      c. Restraints not censorship.
      d. Anti-censorship argument.
         i. Mainly journalists presented the anticensorship view.

F. Gabriel Weimann argues that two issues come into play when debating government regulation.
   1. Terrorists use the media, but they have access to their own forms of communication.
   2. Censorship, regulation, and gathering data from communication threaten the basis of democracy.

Chapter Summary

- Media stories help impact the ways consumers construct social reality. Images of terrorism are frequently simplified, skewing social constructions.

- There are a number of scholarly works on terrorism and the media, and most agree that reporting magnifies the power of terrorism.

- This frequently creates tension between security forces and the media. Law enforcement and other security forces represent the power of social order, and they are responsible for maintaining governmental authority. Media outlets feel that they are responsible for informing the public, and providing a check on governmental power. Despite these differences, media reports tend to show security forces in a favorable light simply because they show them responding to an emergency.

- Both terrorists and security forces seek to manipulate the media by using it as a weapon. In addition, terrorists have found that they can directly control the media by creating their own information outlets. This can backfire because terrorist propaganda frequently contains important intelligence information that can be used by security forces.

- News frames shape stories about terrorism. They set the stage for the story, introduce the characters, give a narrative of the action, and either provide a conclusion or lead consumers to a variety of conclusions.

- There is a special relationship between terrorism and television. Terrorism has a close relationship with television because it provides an unfolding drama. Television news reports are often designed to entertain and excite audiences. Some critics maintain the television reporting focuses more on entertainment than information. New international outlets often provide sympathetic views of terrorism.

- The Internet has a complex relationship with terrorism. It can be used like other media to report an event, but it has many other functions, including serving as a means for communication, propaganda, recruiting, and training. It can also be used as a tactical weapon. Information on the World Wide Web can be used for sending embedded messages, and as a tool to support an attack.

- Some media commentators believe that there is a liberal bias in television news reporting. Others feel that conservative views dominate the airwaves. There are some networks on cable television that cater to particular political audiences, and they adjust their reports to match the opinions of their viewers. Gender roles are also shaped by the way terrorism is covered. The power of media has prompted some security experts to call for censorship when reporting about terrorism.

- Because many news consumers experience an event only through the media, all forms of media play an important role in the social construction of reality. They provide information for a construct.

DISCUSSION QUESTIONS

1. What do you believe is the role of the media in the "War on Terror"? Do you believe that the media should provide U.S. citizens with more or less information regarding terrorist organizations and operations? Explain. (OBJ 1 – 9)

2. Do you believe the media should be censored to protect Homeland Security? Explain. (OBJ 1 – 9)

3. Do you believe that steganography is a true threat to the United States, or just an "urban myth"? Explain. (OBJ 2, 3, 5, and 6)

4. Explain your view of objective reporting. For example, do you believe that print media is more, or less, objective in their reporting than televised reporting? Do you believe there is more, or less, objective reporting during times of crises? (OBJ 1, 4, 5, 7, and 9)

ASSIGNMENTS

1. Have each student comb through http://topics.nytimes.com/top/reference/timestopics/subjects/t/terrorism/index.html (or another website as approved by the instructor) for a current event and select an article that relates to one or more of the chapter's core concepts. Have students provide a journalistic summary and a personal opinion/reaction to the article. Direct them to give consideration as to whether the articles are favoring the U.S. Government, security forces, or the terrorist organization(s). Have students orally present the article to the class, field Q & As from their fellow students, and provide a copy of the original source article following the presentation. Optional: Have students complete peer assessments at the end of each presentation. (OBJ 1 - 9)

2. Bring in a news video reporting a story related to terrorism (via the Internet or television). Have the students discuss the different frames that are presented, including reporting frame, dominant frame, conflict frame, contention frame, and mythic frame. (OBJ 1, 2, 3, 5, and 7)

3. Have students choose a topic from this chapter and write a study guide/handout to present and share with the class. For example, students may focus their study guide on describing the contagion effect. Allow time to discuss topics to eliminate duplication. (OBJ 1 – 9)

4. Play "Bingo" as a review. Provide students with a checklist of the following TV drama patterns:

   - *Change:* The situation is changing and the outcome is unknown.

   - *Information:* The latest news and breaking news about the situation is on this station.

   - *Stay tuned:* You must keep watching; the best is yet to come.

- *Expertise:* Only this station is qualified to explain the situation. *On   scene reports:* Reporters are there telling you what is happening, even when they do not know.

- *Control:* The anchor controls the information from the studio, giving you a vicarious feeling of control.

- *Participation:* You are allowed to vicariously participate in the event.

- *Money:* The station breaks away to sponsors but promises even more drama after the commercial.

Play a segment of a news frame, and have students raise their hands when they recognize one of the patterns during the segment, earning a letter B..I...N... for each correct response. (OBJ 1 – 9)

MEDIA TOOLS

1.   *"Wikis"*
     7 Things you should know about Wikis. Retrieved from the Web Jun 29, 2012 at
     http://net.educause.edu/ir/library/pdf/ELI7004.pdf

     This document offers easy to understand instruction on the history, development, and potential uses of Wikis.

     Have students develop (or make additions to a previously created one) a *Webliography* (resource list) using a Blog or Wiki that provides a short description and link to a scholarly resource pertaining to course concepts. For example, have students add two to three resources each, and ask them to add their assessment of at least one of their peers' contributions. If desired, allow time to discuss Blogs/Wikis. This activity can be reused throughout the course, by asking students to add/revise their contributions each week, bi-weekly, etc. (OBJ 1 – 9)

3.   *"Video…discussion & debate"*

     Kooistra, Paul. (2012). The bias of TV News. Retrieved from the Web Aug 08, 2012 at
     http://www.youtube.com/watch?v=KO1z4DAauPs.

     This video presents Paul Kooistra, Professor of Sociology from Furman University discussing media bias with a diverse audience.

     View the video with the class. At the end of the video open the floor to discussion with the class on media bias. (OBJ 1 and 7)

4.   *"Video...PowerPoint"*

Information War: Internet Jihad and Hacking. Retrieved from the Web Jun 29, 2012 at http://www.youtube.com/watch?v=cTmUzz7UP3E&feature=related

The video interview with Andrew Colarik, a cyber security expert and author of Cyber Terrorism: Political and Economic Implications speaks to the dangers of cyber-terrorism.

Have students view video, and then conduct independent research on Colarik's "digital tsunami". Have students prepare a 2 – 3 slide Powerpoint presentation illustrating explaining Colarik's "digital tsunami". (OBJ 3 and 6)

5.   *"Video...Q & A"*

PBS Teacher Center. Retrieved Aug 16, 2012 at http://www.pbs.org/wgbh/pages/frontline/teach/terror/classroom/7.html

The website offers a variety of activities that can be used with any of PBS's FRONTLINE programs on terrorism, except where otherwise noted, as well as links to related web materials and curriculum standards.

Play one of PBS's FRONTLINE videos on terrorism, then prompt students with questions, either from the instructor, or derived from the activity linked above (example question from the activity. "In "Looking for Answers" we see footage of Egyptian Jihad leader Ayman al-Zawahiri. Why is he speaking in English? In other films, where else do you see English used (e.g., signs in crowds of protesters)? What does this tell you about the intended audience for the message?"). (OBJ 1 – 9)

5.   *"Current Events Article Summary with Peer Assessment"*

Use the Article Summary Template, which can be obtained on the instructor companion website, for this assignment. The template offers information on Internet research, outside resources, identification of credible sources, and detailed directions on completing an assessment of a news article. It also includes a peer evaluation tool.

Have each student comb the Internet for terrorism related news and select an article that relates to one or more of the chapter's core concepts. Be sure selections are an article of interest from a credible source (*more on credibility can be found in the article summary template above*). Fill out an article summary template. The *template asks for generic info about the article, a journalistic summary, as well as a personal opinion/reaction to the article.* Have each student summarize the article, present it orally to the class, and field Q & As from their fellow students. Have students complete peer assessments at the end of each presentation. Have students submit templates, original source article, and peer-reviews prior to the end of class. (OBJ 1-9)

113

Chapter 4—Terrorism and the Media

TEST BANK

TRUE/FALSE

1. Terrorism involves symbolic communication usually aimed at an audience far beyond the immediate victims of violence.

ANS: T   REF: p. 87   OBJ: 1 and 3

2. Some researchers are of the belief that the contagion effect might be used to counter terrorism.

ANS: T   REF: p. 103   OBJ: 8

3. Police and security forces and the media enjoy consistently cooperative relationships.

ANS: F   REF: p. 89   OBJ: 5

4. Ambiguity strengthens the ability to create a sustainable news frame.

ANS: F   REF: p. 92   OBJ: 1 and 7

5. Most of the studies on media-induced contagion are dated or focus on areas other than terrorism.

ANS: T   REF: p. 103   OBJ: 8

6. Censorship, regulation, and gathering data from communication threaten the basis of democracy.

ANS: T   REF: p. 106   OBJ: 6 and 9

7. An American Navy Seal captured Osama Bin Laden.

ANS: T   REF: p. 86   OBJ: 4

8. Police and military forces rarely attempt to take advantage of the media's ability to define social reality.

ANS: F   REF: p. 90   OBJ: 2, 7 and 9

9. Counterterrorist researchers from the Combating Terrorism Center at West Point find that literature from violent extremists rarely reveals important information about their organizations and strategies

ANS: F REF: p. 90 OBJ: 3 and 5

10. Television and the Internet give terrorists an immediate international audience.

ANS: T REF: p. 94 OBJ: 3 and 5

11. Al Jazeera is Lebanon's national television network.

ANS: F REF: p. 95 OBJ: 1, 5, and 7

12. Television generates the same stereotypes for female terrorists and politicians.

ANS: T REF: p. 96 OBJ: 1 and 7

13. Sending unsecure e-mail is the most common usage of the Internet by terrorists.

ANS: T REF: p. 96 OBJ: 6

14. Luckily for counterterrorist forces, terrorists do not comprehend the power of the Internet.

ANS: F REF: p. 96 OBJ: 6

15. "Stay tuned" is an example of a television network's drama pattern.

ANS: T REF: p. 94 OBJ: 4

16. Studies have shown American news media to have a strong conservative bias.

ANS: F REF: p. 100 OBJ: 4, 6 and 7

17. American television reports on terrorism are highly objective.

ANS: F REF: p. 101 OBJ: 1, 2 and 3

18. Steganography is frequently said to be one of the Internet's greatest vulnerabilities in light of criminal and terrorist communication.

ANS: T REF: p. 97 OBJ: 3 and 6

19. Terrorists rarely use the Internet for propaganda.

ANS: F REF: p. 97 OBJ: 8

20.   In ancient Roman times, generals would shaved the head of a slave, tattoo a secret message on the slave's head, and wait for the slave's hair to grow back as a means to send coded messages.

ANS: T   REF: p. 97   OBJ: 5 and 6

21.   Female holy warriors are known as mujahideen.

ANS: F   REF: p. 97   OBJ: 6

22.   Al Qaeda's underground video network, known as As Sahaab, wages an effective propaganda campaign using the Internet.

ANS: T   REF: p. 98   OBJ: 3 and 6

23.   In its own media offensive, the United States launched al Hurra, an Arabic-language twenty-four-hour satellite station, in early 2004.

ANS: T   REF: p. 98   OBJ: 1, 2, and 9

24.   Terrorists use the Internet for target selection.

ANS: T   REF: p. 98   OBJ: 6 and 8

25.   The United States effectively uses the Internet for spreading propaganda.

ANS: F   REF: p. 98   OBJ: 2 and 6

MULTIPLE CHOICE

1. Al Manar is the television network of which country?
    a. Lebanon
    b. Oman
    c. Afghanistan
    d. Iraq

ANS: a   REF: p. 107   OBJ: 5

2. According to Thussu, the _____ circulated by television news shape the worldview of consumers.
    a. Truths
    b. Myths
    c. Facts
    d. Opinions

ANS: b   REF: p. 88   OBJ: 1

3. Fouzi Slisli believes adjectives introduce _____ into the news.
    a. Bias
    b. Myths
    c. Understanding
    d. Truth

ANS: a   REF: p. 100   OBJ: 7

4. Which famous theorist once concluded that the media were similar to a loaded weapon lying in the middle of a street?
    a. Richard Clutterbuck
    b. Simon Cottle
    c. Walter Laqueur
    d. Douglas Keller

ANS: a   REF: p. 90   OBJ: 3 and 5

5. One of the first criminal justice scholars to study media contagion was _____.
    a. Ana Lisa Tota
    b. Jeffrey Ross
    c. Allan Mazur
    d. M. Cherif Bassiouni

ANS: d   REF: p. 103   OBJ: 8

6. _____ refers to the visual, audible, or written packages used to present the news.
    a. News frame
    b. Reporting frame
    c. Communicating frame
    d. Media frame

ANS: a   REF: p. 91   OBJ: 4

7. _____ refers to a quick, fact-driven report that summarizes the latest information about a story.
    a. News frame
    b. Communicating frames
    c. Reporting frame
    d. Dominant frame

ANS: c   REF: p. 91   OBJ: 4 and 7

8. The _____ reports a story from the broadcaster's opinion.
    a. Reportage frame
    b. Dominant frame
    c. Campaigning frame
    d. Investigation frame

ANS: c   REF: p. 91   OBJ: 4 and 7

117

9.   The _____ presents a story frame with two views, each side having experts to support a position.
      a.   Reportage frame
      b.   Dominant frame
      c.   Conflict frame
      d.   Contention frame

ANS: c   REF: p. 91   OBJ: 4 and 7

10.   News frames form the basis for _____ symbols.
      a.   Communicating
      b.   Understanding
      c.   Defining
      d.   Producing

ANS: a   REF: p. 91   OBJ: 4

11.   According to Cottle, television news presents a _____ frame, which reinforces common values.
      a.   Contention
      b.   Dominant
      c.   Mythic
      d.   Cultural recognition

ANS: c   REF: p. 91   OBJ: 1, 4, and 7

12.   Critics believe National Public Radio (NPR) _____.
      a.   Has a conservative bias
      b.   Has a liberal bias
      c.   Fails to address terrorism
      d.   Is objective in reporting terrorism

ANS: b   REF: p. 99   OBJ: 7 and 9

13.   According to Durham, _____ destroys the ability to create a sustainable news frame.
      a.   Reality
      b.   Ambiguity
      c.   Facts
      d.   Opinion

ANS: b   REF: p. 92   OBJ: 4 and 7

14.   According to Barber, what is the largest overriding factor through which the media flourishes?
      a.   Entertainment
      b.   Drama
      c.   Money
      d.   Information

ANS: a   REF: p. 93   OBJ: 1, 2, 4, 7, and 8

15.   According to the text, reporters are expected to create news frames reflecting _____.
        a. Fair reporting
        b. Balanced reporting
        c. Their outlet's orientation
        d. A sense of drama

ANS: c   REF: p. 99   OBJ: 1 and 4

16.   _____ refers to embedding hidden information in a picture, message, or other piece of information.
        a. Steganography
        b. Encryption
        c. Spyware
        d. Norton

ANS: a   REF: p. 97   OBJ: 3 and 6

17.   _____ is Hezbollah's television network.
        a. Al Hurra
        b. Al Fajir
        c. Al Jazeera
        d. Al Manar

ANS: d   REF: p. 95   OBJ: 5

18.   _____ refers to news organizations producing stories to entertain their audiences under the guise of presenting objective information.
        a. News frames
        b. Investigative
        c. Infotainment telesector
        d. Communication

ANS: c   REF: p. 93   OBJ: 1 and 7

19.   Most mainstream media claim _____ when presenting information about terrorism.
        a. Subjectivity
        b. Objectivity
        c. Prejudice
        d. Partisanship

ANS: b   REF: p. 99   OBJ: 7

20.   Tim Groseclose and Jeffrey Milyo conclude that the American news media _____.
        a. Has a strong liberal bias
        b. Has a strong conservative bias
        c. Is fair and balanced
        d. Presents coverage as a dramedy

ANS: a   REF: p. 100   OBJ: LO9

119

21.   According to _____, the news is aimed at particular audiences, and different organizations approach audiences in a variety of ways.
        a. Daniel Sutter
        b. David Baron
        c. Fouzi Slisli
        d. David Levin

ANS: d   REF: p. 100   OBJ: 7

22.   In television news coverage, the _____ is designed to keep the viewer tuned to the station.
        a. Drama pattern
        b. Control pattern
        c. Expertise pattern
        d. Information pattern

ANS: a   REF: p. 94   OBJ: 4

23.   In one of the best standard setting studies, _____ and Jany deGraaf report that the relationship between terrorism and the media is so powerful that Western democracies may need to take drastic actions and even implement censorship.
        a. Yassen Zassoursky
        b. Alex Schmid
        c. H.H.A. Cooper
        d. David Levin

ANS: b   REF: p. 94   OBJ: 9

24.   _____ occurs when media reports promote fear and magnify threats, thereby causing fear to spread.
        a. The contagion effect
        b. The terror effect
        c. The stereotype effect
        d. The security effect

ANS: a   REF: p. 102   OBJ: 8

25.   Which of the following is not a governmental choice when faced with censorship?
        a. Criminalization
        b. Hands-off
        c. Complete censorship
        d. Self-regulation

ANS: a   REF: p. 104   OBJ: 9

26.   The arguments about censorship are heated and deal with the core issue of _____.
        a. Privacy
        b. Freedom
        c. Security
        d. Democracy

ANS: d   REF: p. 105   OBJ: 9

27. Which of the following is NOT an argument used by the government to encourage censorship?
   a. National security
   b. The public wants information withheld
   c. The truth makes the government look bad
   d. They are asking for restraint, not censorship

ANS: c   REF: p. 105   OBJ: 9

28. Sonia Liff and Anne Sofie Laegren state that cybercafés _____ because they make communication untraceable.
   a. Enhance the Internet's striking power
   b. Recruit new members
   c. Are the source for all email correspondence
   d. Provide crucial information for building bombs

ANS: a   REF: p. 97   OBJ: 6

29. _____ is used to describe the public's understanding of the media and the way stories are presented.
   a. Crucial media consciousness
   b. Critical media consciousness
   c. False media consciousness
   d. Class media consciousness

ANS: b   REF: p. 101   OBJ: 1 and 4

30. Thussu refers to the power of the media to create and sustain the social image of terrorism as _____.
   a. Media monsters
   b. Mythmaking
   c. Storytelling
   d. Illusionism

ANS: b   REF: p. 88   OBJ: 1

31. Journalists who join combat units are known as _____ reporters.
   a. Embedded
   b. Insync
   c. Entrenched
   d. Implanted

ANS: a   REF: p. 89   OBJ: 2

32. Counterterrorist researchers from the Combating Terrorism Center at West Point find that _____ from violent extremists frequently reveals important information about their organizations and strategies
   a. Literature
   b. Testimony
   c. Videos
   d. Family history

ANS: a   REF: p. 90   OBJ: 3

33. The classic approach for television is the _____. It is usually short and designed to provide the latest information.
    a. Dominant frame
    b. Reporting frame
    c. Collective interest frame
    d. Conflict frame

ANS: b   REF: p. 91   OBJ: 4

34. A news frame that draws largely upon the broadcaster's opinion is called a(n) ___ frame?
    a. Investigative
    b. Campaigning
    c. Dominant
    d. Reporting

ANS: b   REF: p. 91   OBJ: 4 and 7

35. What terrorist group created the underground video network known as As Sahaab?
    a. Al Qaeda
    b. Hezzbollah
    c. LTTE
    d. Taliban

ANS: a   REF: p. 98   OBJ: 6

36. Stephen Ulph (2006a) sees terrorists increasingly using Internet searches to find _____ targets.
    a. Economic
    b. Political
    c. Religious
    d. Military

ANS: a   REF: p. 98   OBJ: 6

37. Concern about the impact of images of violence began with movies in the _____, and it continues today.
    a. 1920s
    b. 1940s
    c. 1960s
    d. 1980s

ANS: a   REF: p. 104   OBJ: 1, 5, and 8

38. Law enforcement networks in the _____have the ability to share criminal investigative information.
    a. Rational Ideological Support System
    b. Regional Information Support System
    c. Regional Information Sharing System
    d. Rational Ideological Sharing System

ANS: c   REF: p. 98   OBJ: 6

39.   Terrorists selected targets for maximum _____.
        a. Death toll
        b. Property damage
        c. Publicity
        d. Repair cost

ANS: c   REF: p. 103   OBJ: 3 and 5

40.   Following the 9-11 attacks, media began reporting several _____ attacks across the
      nation.
        a. Smallpox
        b. Cyanide
        c. Anthrax
        d. Saran Gas

ANS: c   REF: p. 103   OBJ: 5 and 8

Case 4.0

Reporting patterns are packaged in segments called news frames. The purpose of a news
frame is to assemble words and pictures to create a pattern surrounding an event. The
news becomes a symbolic representation of an event in which the audience is allowed to
participate from a distance. Television and other media spin the event so that it can be
translated into the understanding of popular culture.

There are several types of news frames - reporting frames: superficial, short, and laced
with facts; dominant frames: one authority's view; conflict frames: two sides, with
experts; contention frames: a variety of positions; investigative frames: exposing corrupt
or illegal behavior; campaigning frames: the broadcaster's opinion; reportage frames: in-
depth coverage with background; community service frames: information for viewers;
collective interest frames: reinforce common values; cultural recognition frames: a
group's values and norms; and mythic tales frames: hero stories.

41.   A television network provides coverage of the political primaries, followed by a thirty
        second clip of the network's anchor providing her personal thoughts on who the front
        runner is and why. The thirty second clip is an example of what type of news frame?

        a. Dominant
        b. Investigative
        c. Campaigning
        d. Collective interest

ANS: c   REF: p. 91   OBJ: 4, 7, and 9

123

42. A news report displays a TV anchor sandwiched between two criminologists debating the legitimacy of the U.S. government utilizing Guantanamo Bay for housing suspected terrorists. The broadcast is an example of what type of news frame?
    a. Conflict
    b. Reporting
    c. Contention
    d. Investigative

ANS: a   REF: p. 91   OBJ: 4, 7, and 9

43. A television network airs a 10 minute segment demonstrating a U.S. customs officials taking bribes from a Mexican cartel.
    a. Dominant
    b. Investigative
    c. Conflict
    d. Community service

ANS: b   REF: p. 91   OBJ: 4, 7, and 9

44. A news network provides a bulletin notice advising the public about local hospitals offering free vaccines. The bulletin would be an example of what type of news frames?
    a. Dominant
    b. Investigative
    c. Community service
    d. Collective interest

ANS: c   REF: p. 91   OBJ: 4, 7, and 9

45. A news network breaks into regular programming to report that the President has been shot. Such a report is an example of what type of news frame?
    a. Dominant
    b. Investigative
    c. Conflict
    d. Community service

ANS: b   REF: p. 91   OBJ: 4, 7, and 9

46. A local radio station airs a 10 minute segment where a think tank member gives her analysis of al Qaeda's future plans.
    a. Dominant
    b. Investigative
    c. Conflict
    d. Community service

ANS: a   REF: p. 91   OBJ: 4, 7, and 9

124

Case 4.1

A scholarly examination of literature from militant Islamic groups to determine their media strategies showed that jihadists are keenly aware of the media's ability to influence the social construction of reality. Jihadist texts reveal three media strategies. First, they seek legitimacy for their movement, especially wanting to justify acts of violence to other Muslims. Second, they want to spread their message and increase sympathy for their militant interpretation of religion. Third, their opponents, both the West and Muslims with a different interpretation of Islam, are targeted for intimidation.

47. Terrorist members hand out flyers to members at a recruitment rally, disguised as a service at a local mosque. They listen intently to the attendees who dismiss the flyer's information and watch carefully to see who throws away the literature. Which media strategy was most prominently being employed by the terrorists after they handed out their flyers?
    a. Legitimacy for their movement
    b. Spread their message
    c. Increase sympathy for their militant interpretation of religion
    d. Identify opponents for targeted intimidation

ANS: d   REF: p. 90   OBJ: 1, 3, and 5

48. A terrorist group bombs a local café. The group's leader circulates a videotape of the café's owner wearing a catholic cross, driving lavish cars, living in a lush residence, surrounded by opulence. Which media strategy was most prominently being employed by the videotape release?
    a. Legitimacy for their movement (justify acts of violence)
    b. Spread their message
    c. Increase sympathy for their militant interpretation of religion
    d. Identify opponents for targeted intimidation

ANS: a   REF: p. 90   OBJ: 1, 3, and 5

Case 4.2

Al Manar television provided twenty-four-hour coverage of the al Asqa uprising following Ariel Sharon's September, 2000 visit to the Temple Mount, sympathetic to Hezbollah. The news was interspersed with inspirational religious messages. Hezbollah was able to get al Manar to focus on Hezbollah's role in the Intifada and to run programs on its former glories. In an effort to demoralize the Israelis, al Manar broadcast pictures of Israeli casualties and ended with the question: "Who will be next?"

Power came in the form of visual images. Through reports via al Manar, Lebanon came to believe that faced with heavy fighting in a West Bank village, Israeli forces withdrew. The Israeli Defense Forces (IDF), using Israeli mass media, denied it had abandoned the village. Al Manar presented another view. When the Israelis withdrew, Hezbollah fighters entered the village along with Palestinian mujahideen. Hezbollah raised its flag over the village, and someone took a picture. As the IDF was denying it had retreated al Manar showed the village with the Hezbollah flag flying high overhead. Hezbollah achieved a media victory.

49. From the above information, what types of news frames was al Manar television using to in reference to Hezzbollah?
a. Mythic tales (hero stories)
b. Community service
c. Reporting
d. Investigative

ANS: b   REF: p. 91   OBJ: 4, 7, and 9

50. The harnessing of media power by Hezzbollah in the case above is an example a _____ multiplier.
a. Strength
b. Recruitment
c. Force
d. Mass

ANS: c   REF: p. 91   OBJ: 3, 4, and 7

COMPLETION

1. Terrorism is a method of _____ communication.

ANS: symbolic   REF: p. 87   OBJ: 1 and 5

2. News consumers need to develop _____ that look beyond the news frame and examine the issues behind terrorism and other political events.

ANS: analytic abilities   REF: p. 101   OBJ: 1 and 7

3. The infotainment telesector is not geared for depth; it is designed to create _____.

ANS: revenue   REF: p. 93   OBJ: 1, 4, and 7

4. _____ influences on the media have eliminated the West's monopoly on news programming and information dissemination.

ANS: International   REF: p. 95   OBJ: 1, 4, and 7

5. Specialized command units are often created in police agencies to portray a favorable image to reporters, and U.S. military forces include _____ when they go to war.

ANS: public relations units   REF: p. 95   OBJ: 2

6. The _____ frame presents a story frame with two views, each side having experts or witnesses to support a position.

ANS: conflict   REF: p. 91   OBJ: 4

7.   The purpose of a _____ is to assemble words and pictures to create a pattern surrounding an event.

ANS: news frame   REF: p. 91   OBJ: 4

8.   _____ says the purpose of television news coverage is to keep the audience primed with emotion and excitement.

ANS: David Levin   REF: p. 94   OBJ: 1 and 4

9.   Some researchers believe that if a contagion effect exists, it might be used to counter _____.

ANS: terrorism   REF: p. 103   OBJ: 8

10. _____refers to embedding hidden information in a picture, message, or other piece of information.

ANS: Steganography   REF: p. 97   OBJ: 3

11. The _____ Act ensures public access to governmental records.

ANS: the Freedom of Information (FOI)   REF: p. 105   OBJ: 9

12. Following the 2002 takeover of a Moscow theater by Chechen terrorists, the Chechens delivered a prepackaged video tape to the _____ television network.

ANS: al Jazeera   REF: p. 107   OBJ: 5

13. On May 2, 2011, the U.S. Navy's elite SEAL Team ____ landed in a compound north of Islamabad, capturing and killing Osama bin Laden.

ANS: six   REF: p. 86   OBJ: 1, 2, and 4

14. Television, radio, print journalism as well as newer sources on the Internet, including news reporting services, the blogosphere, Web site pages, and propaganda broadcasts are collectively referred to as _____.

ANS: news media   REF: p. 87   OBJ: 1

15. The public depends on the _____ for information about issues.

ANS: mass media   REF: p. 93   OBJ: 1 and 4

16. Analyst H.H.A. Cooper was the first to terrorist acts as, "_____" dramas.

ANS: made-for-TV   REF: p. 94   OBJ: 1, 4, and 5

17. Edward Herman (1999), in examining the media, claims existing bias is economic and it is dominated by _____.

ANS: multinational corporations   REF: p. 99   OBJ: 7

18. Terrorist groups have an underground communication system, but they need the _____to spread their messages.

ANS: mainstream media   REF: p. 104   OBJ: 5

19. According to Ross, terrorists will increasingly use _____ to communicate as the relationship between the media and terrorism grows stronger in the future.

ANS: the Internet   REF: p. 105   OBJ: 3 and 6

20. Jihadist texts reveal three media strategies: seeking legitimacy for their movement, spreading their message, and _____.

ANS: targeting opponents   REF: p. 90   OBJ: 3, 5, and 6

ESSAY

1. According to Simon Cottle, other frames complement the reporting frame. List and explain Cottle's communication frames and how these influence viewers.

ANS:
- Reporting frames: superficial, short, and laced with facts
- Dominant frames: one authority's view
- Contest frames: two sides, with experts
- Contention frames: a variety of positions
- Investigation frames: exposing corrupt or illegal behavior
- Campaigning frames: the broadcaster's opinion
- Reportage frames: in-depth coverage with background
- Community service frames: information for viewers
- Collective interest frames: reinforce common values
- Cultural recognition frames: a group's values and norms (can be used for the opposing group to avoid "us" versus "them")
- Mythic tales frames: hero stories
- Student views will vary.

REF: p. 91   OBJ: 4

2. Explain Edward Herman's view on the social construction of reality and political bias when examining the media. Provide an example illustrating his view.

ANS:
- The bias is economic and it is dominated by multinational corporations.
- The American media is part of a vast propaganda machine promoting the values and goals of business corporations.

- Herman conducts case studies examining advertising, ownership, and content to demonstrate the point.
- Stories affecting corporate profits are manipulated in a positive way.
- Dictators are portrayed as moderate or benign when they favor corporate investments and profits, even as the same leaders repress or massacre their own citizens.
- Newspapers use catchphrases such as "free trade," "third world elections," and other simplifications to hide the powerful economic forces behind political action.
- The political bias is neither liberal nor anti-American; it is based in market orientation.
- Student examples will vary.

REF: p. 99   OBJ: 1

3. Describe Anat Shoshoni and Michelle Sloan's research on anxiety and attitude in regard to terrorism reporting. Provide your personal analysis of his research.

ANS:
- Shoshoni and Sloan measured the reactions of 300 university students in Israel after they had been exposed to terrorist violence on television.
- Looking at levels of anxiety and anger, they also wanted to see if attitudes in perceptions of the enemy and the willingness to accept negative group stereotypes would be affected.
- Unlike the immediate experiences of anxiety and anger, attitudes are generally formed over a long period of time.
- The experiment began with a survey to measure anxiety and attitude.
- After this students were shown two seven minutes video clips, one of a terrorist attack and the other of non-terrorist violence from the same group, and they conducted a second set of measurements.
- Shoshoni and Sloan found that anger and anxiety increased, but they also that long-term attitudes changed within the same time frame.
- They concluded that the power of television makes the audience part of the event.
- Student views will vary.

REF: p. 95   OBJ: 1, 4, 5, 7, and 9

4. Discuss the infotainment telesector; how does it negatively affect homeland security? Provide examples to support your answer.

ANS:
- Infotainment telesector refers to news organization producing stories to entertain their audiences under the guise of presenting objective information.
- It is not geared for depth; it is designed to create revenue.
- "News" becomes banter between a news anchor and guest, and debates evolve into shouting matches between controversial representatives.
- Issues are rarely discussed.
- Hosts perpetually interrupt their guests or provide answers to their own questions.
- Morning news shows are full of interviewers who discover issues obvious to the rest of the world and who shake their heads in wonderment when common knowledge is revealed.

129

- These contexts of the infotainment telesector and the desire to beat the other networks have a negative effect on homeland security.
- Documents are leaked, confidential plans are unveiled, and vulnerabilities are exposed.
- Terrorism becomes more horrific to create better drama.
- News film is constantly replayed, giving the illusion that attacks are repeated time and time again.
- News hosts spend time interviewing reporters from the field who speculate on the facts surrounding an event leading to a dilemma for policy makers.
- Student examples will vary.

REF: p. 93　　　　　　　　　　OBJ: 5

5. According to the text, how is the Internet used for recruiting, training, and target selection? In answering the question, provide examples of each.

ANS:
- Salafi-jihadists using websites and e-mail to make training manuals available.
- The Internet has become more important as growing numbers of females join the Salafi movement.
- Claims are made that the Internet gives women the opportunity to become *mujahidat* (female holy warriors).
- Some sites are specifically aimed at recruiting or retaining females.
- Other sites encourage suicide bombings.
- Discussion groups examine tactics and provide basic weapons orientation, and some militant scholars provide in-depth theological apologies to justify religious violence.
- One site has an entire first-aid course to deal with battlefield wounds.
- Maps, satellite imagery, and diagrams provide ready-made intelligence sources.
- Economic targets can be found using Internet searches.
- Terrorist groups are attracted to data mining opportunities; one terrorist training manual points out that it is possible to gather enough information on enemy targets.
- Terrorists want to take hacker warfare to their enemies.
- Groups post methods to steal passwords and instructions for breaking into secure areas.
- There are instructions on systems and denial-of-service attacks.
- As a logistical tool, the Internet can also be used to assemble people for a violent action.
- Student examples will vary.

REF: p. 96　　　　　　　　　　OBJ: 6

6. What, according to the text, is the essence of the drama pattern? List and explain the different type of TV drama patterns.
ANS:
- The drama pattern is designed to keep the viewer tuned to the station. The attention-getting theme is the essence of the drama.
- Change: The situation is changing and the outcome is unknown.
- Information: The latest and breaking news about the situation is on this station.
- Stay tuned: You must keep watching; the best is coming.

130

- Expertise: Only this station is qualified to explain the situation.
- On-the-scene reports: Reporters are there telling you what is happening, even when they do not know.
- Control: The anchor controls the information from the studio, giving you a vicarious feeling of control.
- Participation: You are allowed to vicariously participate in the event.
- Money: The station breaks away to sponsors but promises even more drama after the commercial.

REF: p. 94   OBJ: 4

7.   Explain the tension between the media and the government, police and security forces. Provide an example.

ANS:
- On the one hand, they compete for favorable media coverage. On the other hand, governments exhibit strong disdain for the press because media social constructions often run counter to governmental objectives and policies.
- Governments seek to harness the power of the media for social control.
- The social meanings created by news segments favor governmental policy, security forces come to the opposite conclusion.
- Chiefs of police and military commanders generally do not respect or trust media figures and reporters, and their attitudes are reflected by line personnel.
- Specialized command units are often created in police agencies to portray a favorable image to reporters, and U.S. military forces include public relations units when they go to war.
- For example, in hostage situations security forces are responsible for the fate of the victims.
- Reporters often do not focus on the security mission of such incidents because they are under tremendous pressure to be first with the story, and they have their own agendas when reporting the story.
- As a result law enforcement and military goals often conflict with the goals of the reporters.

REF: p. 106   OBJ: 2

8.   Explain steganography and its use in terrorism. What are the two positions on the steganographic threat to the U.S?

ANS:
- The process refers to embedding hidden information in a picture, message, or another piece of information.
- It could be used to hide communications, steal information from security forces or an organization within the critical infrastructure, or provide opportunities for electronic attack
- One position claims that steganography is used by terrorist groups to communicate and launch cyberattacks.

131

- Some believe that it will be used in denial-of-service attacks or to deface websites.
- The other position claims that fear of steganography is the stuff of urban legends.
- Although steganography programs are readily available and difficult to detect or prevent with security hardware, statistical analysis programs of data contained in any Internet transmission readily reveal irregularities and the location of a hidden image.
- The belief is that the threat is not in the hidden image, the real threat is that the ability to decipher private communications based on threat that does not exist.

REF: p. 97   OBJ: 3 and 6

9.   Discuss Paul Wilkinson's analysis of the media. Do you agree with his analysis? Why or why not?

ANS:
- Paul Wilkinson argues that terrorists must communicate their efforts and they use the media to do so.
- Terrorists and the media have an interdependent relationship.
- Terrorist groups have an underground communication system, but they need the mainstream media to spread their messages.
- Mass media serve as a psychological weapon by creating fear and anxiety.
- Terrorists may trap the media into spreading their message.
- The media may inadvertently shift blame for an incident from terrorists to victims or governments.
- Governments benefit when media sources portray the savage cruelty of terrorist groups.
- Views will vary.

REF: p. 97   OBJ: 1, 4, 7, and 9

10.   Discuss the arguments used to encourage media censorship as well as the anticensorship view. Do you agree or disagree with censorship concerning terrorism? Explain.

ANS:
- The first was national security, a powerful excuse used in times of emergency.
- According to this position, information must be controlled to ensure the survival of the state.
- Another position was to claim that the public wanted the information withheld.
- Democratic senator Joseph Lieberman voiced his support for controlling information, claiming the American people overwhelmingly supported governmental efforts.
- According to this logic, America was fighting a new type of war and some form of censorship was required.
- The other arguments asked Americans to behave patriotically.
- Ultimately, governmental officials claimed they were asking for restraints, not censorship.
- Mainly journalists presented the anticensorship view.
- They cited a variety of governmental mistakes and misdeeds all hidden under the rubric of national security.

132

- They also argued that the terrorism was essentially a war of information.
- Instead of trying to silence sources, the government should focus efforts on getting out the facts.
- Every governmental clampdown cast officials in a bad light.
- The anticensorship camp reserved its harshest criticism for media outlets that decided to self-censor as a governmental service.
- Editors according to Doris Graber should hold back information to protect citizens and security forces, but those decisions belong to the media, not the government.

REF: p. 104   OBJ: 9

CHAPTER 5

Gender Roles, Tactics, and Force Multipliers in Terrorism

Learning Objectives

After reading this chapter, students should be able to:

1. Summarize the tactics of modern terrorism.
2. List and describe four force multipliers.
3. Discuss historical and current roles of women in terrorism.
4. Outline the tactical importance of female terrorists.
5. Define the types of threats posed by technological terrorism.
6. Explain the effects of biological, chemical and radiological weapons.
7. Characterize the possibility and possible outcomes of nuclear terrorism.
8. Discuss the role of the media as a force multiplier.
9. Summarize transnational economic targeting in the tourist, energy, and transportation industries.
10. Summarize theories of suicide bombing.

Chapter Key Terms

six tactics of terrorism, p. 110
force multipliers, p. 110
Triborder region, p. 111
philosophy of the bomb, p. 111
thermobaric bomb, p. 111
racial terrorism, p. 112
international focus, p. 113
domestic issues, p. 113
Ulricke Meinhof, p. 113
Leila Khalid, p. 113
cyber-terrorism, p. 116
bacterial weapons, p. 118
viral weapons, p. 118
highly enriched uranium, p. 120
radiation sickness, p. 120
nuclear black market, p. 123
endemic terrorism, p. 127
altruistic suicide, p. 128
theory of suicide terrorism , p. 129

Altruistic suicide refers to the willingness of individuals to sacrifice their lives to benefit their primary reference group, such as a family, military unit, ethnic group, or country. It may involve going on "suicide missions" in combat, self-sacrifice without killing others, or sacrifice while killing others.

Bacterial weapons are enhanced forms of bacteria which may be countered by antibiotics.

Domestic terrorism the term is used by Margaret Gonzalez-Perez to refer to groups within a country fighting to change the social or political structure of that nation.

Endemic terrorism refers to terrorism that exists inside a political entity. For example, European colonialists created the nation of Rwanda by combining two tribes that literally hate one another. The two tribes fight to eliminate one another. This is endemic to political violence in Rwanda.

Force multiplier is a method of increasing striking power without increasing the number of combat troops in a military unit. Terrorists have four force multipliers: (1) technology to enhance weapons or attacks on technological facilities, (2) transnational support, (3) media coverage, and (4) religious fanaticism.

Highly enriched uranium (HEU) is a process that increases the proportion of a radioactive isotope in uranium (U-235) making it suitable for industrial use. It can also be used to make nuclear weapons. Most nuclear weapons are made from HEU or plutonium.

International terrorism the tem is used by Margaret Gonzalez-Perez to refer to terrorist groups operating across national boundaries to resist foreign intrusions on traditional social systems.

Leila Khalid (b. 1944) was a member of the Popular Front for the Liberation of Palestine. In 1969 she was part of a team that hijacked four aircraft that were destroyed after the passengers and crews disembarked. Arrested in 1970 after another attempted hijacking, she was released as part of a prisoner exchange.

Nuclear black market refers to the period when the Soviet Union collapsed; it was difficult to account for all the nuclear weapons that were in the control of military officials and the newly independent states. People feared these weapons would be sold to terrorists. Similar fears exist for Pakistan's nuclear bombs and nuclear development programs in North Korea and Iran.

Philosophy of the bomb is a phrase used by anarchists around 1848. It means that social order can only be changed through violent upheaval. Bombs were the first technological force multiplier.

Racial terrorism a dominant group using violence to intimidate a racial minority. Tactics would include lynching, murder, beatings, and other forms of violence against a minority group. For example, the Ku Klux Klan historically has practiced racial terrorism.

Radiation sickness is caused by exposure to high doses of radiation over a short period of time. It is characterized by nausea, diarrhea, headaches, and fever. High doses produce dizziness, weakness, and internal bleeding. It is possible to treat patients who have been exposed to doses of radiation, but higher doses are usually fatal. Other than the two nuclear bombs used in World War II, most radiation sickness has been caused by industrial accidents.

Six tactics of terrorism are defined by Brian Jenkins. They include (1) bombing, (2) hijacking, (3) arson, (4) assault, (5) kidnapping, and (6) hostage taking.

Theory of suicide terrorism was developed by Robert Pape. The theory states that a group of people occupied by a democratic power are likely to engage in suicide attacks when there are differences in the religions of each group and the occupied religious community supports altruistic suicide.

Thermobaric bomb is a two-stage bomb. The first stage spreads either a fuel cloud or finely ground powder through the air. The explosive material mixes with the oxygen present in the atmosphere and becomes explosive at that point. The second stage denotes the cloud; pressure explodes in all directions in a series of shock waves. The cloud can penetrate a number of barriers. A person breathing the material explodes from the inside out when the material is ignited.

Triborder region refers to the area where Brazil, Paraguay, and Argentina join. The major city in the area is Cuidad del Este.

Ulricke Meinhof (1934-1976) co-created the Red Army Faction with Andreas Baader in 1970. She was co-leader of the group. Arrested in 1972, she committed suicide in prison.

Viral weapons are enhanced forms of viruses. The virus is "hardened" so that it can live for long periods of time and enhanced for deadlier effects.

<u>Chapter Outline</u>

I. **Gender and Mission**
    OBJ 3: Discuss historical and current roles of women in terrorism
    OBJ 4: Outline the tactical importance of female terrorists

A. Social aspects of the organized group are an important consideration.
B. Ideology and mission affect operations.
C. Gender impacts tactics, and in turn, is often related to ideology.
D. Women have been active in historical and contemporary terrorism – role is often overlooked.
1. Margaret Gonzalez-Perez
   a. Political and social ideology is closely related to the roles women play in terrorist groups.
   b. Women are more attracted to domestic terrorist organizations than international groups.
   c. Women in domestic groups gravitate toward combat and leadership.
   d. Every geographical area produced a common trend; domestic groups emphasized the role of women even when they have no stated feminist agenda.
2. Cindy Ness
   a. Most terrorism analysts ignored the role of women, thus missing critical information that could have been used to increase security.
      i. Ulricke Meinhof
      ii. Leila Khalid
   b. Conservative male dominated religious terrorists relegated females to secondary status.
   c. Women may begin organizing and taking leadership roles, or they may take charge out of necessity, when male leaders are captured or killed.
3. Kathleen Blee
   a. Women played an indirect role when *racial terrorism* emerged in the South after the Civil War.
   b. Role changed in the early 20th century as women became prominent in lynchings and other forms of racial violence.
   c. Depending on the direction of White Supremacists in the 21st century, women's roles in terrorism may change again.
E. Overlooking female terrorists
1. Researchers tend not to to think of women as terrorist or criminals.
2. Women have been overlooked because it is generally assumed that terrorism is a violent male occupation.
3. Katharina von Knop – women are following a male model instead of assuming roles they would define on their own.
4. Laura Sjoberg – females are discussed in gendered terms.
   a. Women are not "terrorists", they are "women involved in terrorism."
5. One of the ironies in Central Asia is that women working in traditional support roles have developed a new path to radicalization and have the organization to sustain it.

II. **The Tactics of Terrorism and Multiplying Force**
   OBJ 1: Summarize the tactics of modern terrorism
   OBJ 2: List and describe four force multipliers

   A. Ian Lesser – terrorism is defined by a situation, and it changes with each new situation.
   B. Brian Jenkins – *six tactics of terrorism:*
      1. Bombing
      2. Hijacking
      3. Arson
      4. Assault
      5. Kidnapping
      6. Hostage taking
   C. Force multiplies
      1. Increase striking power without increasing the number of combat troops in a military unit.
      2. Terrorists have four force multipliers:
         a. Transnational support
         b. Technology
         c. Media coverage
         d. Religion
      3. Cyber-terrorism and potential WMD attacks are examples of technological force multipliers.
   D. Most common weapon of terrorism is still the bomb.
      1. *Philosophy of the bomb* – the only way to communicate with the social order was to destroy it.
   E. Middle Eastern terrorist groups were working on two types of military style weapons called mini-nukes.
      1. One type spreads fuel in the air then ignites it.
      2. *Thermobaric bombs* explode the air in the blast area.
   F. Terrorists create terrorism because they are designed to attack civilians and symbolic targets exclusively.

III. **Technology**
   OBJ 1: Summarize the tactics of modern terrorism
   OBJ 5: Define the types of threats posed by technological terrorism
   OBJ 6: Explain the effects of biological, chemical and radiological weapons
   OBJ 7: Characterize the possibility and possible outcomes of nuclear terrorism

   A. Terrorism is influenced by technology.

B. Some view the technological impact as a strategy; others believe it confuses the issue.

C. Cyber-terrorism – term coined by Barry Collins
   1. The use of computers to attack technological targets or physical attacks on computer networks.
   2. Cyber-terrorism is an attractive low-risk strategy.
   3. Most common usage today is defacement of Websites.
   4. Potential targets for cyber-terrorists
      a. Computer virus
      b. Logic bombs
      c. Trojan horses

D. Violent political activists use the Internet as a command-and-control mechanism.

E. Biological Agents
   1. Biological weapons have been used for centuries.
   2. Modern arsenals contain *bacterial weapons* and *viral weapons*, with microbes cultured and refined, or *weaponized*, to increase their ability to kill.
   3. Biological agents are difficult to control, but relatively easy to produce.
   4. Four types of biological agents:
      a. Natural poisons or toxins
      b. Viruses
      c. Bacteria
      d. Plagues
   5. The Centers for Disease Control and Prevention (CDC) classifies the most threatening agents as:
      a. Smallpox
      b. Anthrax
      c. Plague
      d. Botulism
      e. Tularemia
      f. Hemorrhagic fever
   6. The United States has experienced two notable biological attacks since 1980.
   7. Congressional commission concluded that the United States had no structure in place to respond to a biological attack.

D. Chemical and Radiological Weapons
   1. Radiological poisoning and "dirty" radioactive devices are forms of chemical alterations.
   2. Chemicals are usually easier to deliver than biological weapons, and they are fast acting.
   3. There are four types of chemical agents:
      a. Nerve agents
      b. Blood agents

139

c. Choking agents
d. Blistering agents
4. Radiological weapons are closely related to chemical weapons.
5. Radiological poisoning takes place when a contaminated material comes in contact with any source that conducts radiation.
6. Most dirty-bomb scenarios are based on the premise that a radiological agent will be used with a conventional explosive.
7. Most nuclear weapons are made from highly enriched uranium (HEU) or plutonium.
8. Most dirty bombs would not cause radiation sickness or an upsurge of cancer rates; the primary danger of such a bomb is the psychological effects.
9. Since dirty bombs are less effective than popularly believed, an attack on a nuclear facility with conventional weapons presents a more tempting target.
E. Nuclear Terrorism
1. The most fearful scenario with WMD involves a nuclear explosion.
2. There are two methods for constructing a nuclear device – HEU and plutonium.
3. Some scholars suggest the probability of nuclear terrorism is low; others say the possibility of nuclear terrorism is real.
4. The United States should approach nuclear terrorism in two manners:
   a. Debunking popular myths about the subject.
   b. Revamp defense systems.

IV. **The media as a force multiplier**

OBJ 2: List and describe four force multipliers
OBJ 9: Discuss the role of the media as a force multiplier

A. Governments and terrorists benefit when media sources portray the savage cruelty of terrorist groups.
B. Every group involved in a terrorist conflict tries to manipulate images, seeking to use the media as a force multiplier.
C. Brigitte Nacos states most terrorist groups have objectives beyond publicity, and public attention is not the only goal of terrorism.
D. Gadt Wolfsfeld says that media victories are crucial for terrorism.
   1. The media is the primary tool for demonizing the enemy, and the most powerful tool is the way television reports casualties.
E. All forms of media can be used to multiply force. The Internet is one of the most important force multipliers, and is easily available to terrorists.
F. Natalya Kransoboka reports that the Internet does not have an overwhelming impact in democratic countries, but it is a powerful tool for opposition forces in authoritarian regimes.

G. Governments try to control the Internet for their own purposes, seeing its potential as a weapon for opposition and revolution.

H. Cinema presents another venue for both assisting terrorism and distorting issues.

   1. Unlike the news, movies can be completely grounded in fiction and are responsible for strong emotional projections.

I. Terrorists and security forces battle for media control by:

   1. Creating organizations to place stories in a good light.

   2. Demonizing their enemies.

   3. Creating the best images for the media.

   4. Appearing to support peace proposals.

V. Economic Targeting and Transnational Attacks

OBJ 9: Summarize transnational economic targeting in the tourist, energy, and transportation industries

A. Terrorists may use transnational support or transnational operations as a force multiplier.

B. Terrorists have found that striking transnational economic targets increases the effectiveness of operations.

C. Three types of transnational attacks can be used to illustrate the issue:

   1. Tourism

   2. Energy

   3. Shipping

D. Tourism – a relationship exists between terrorism and tourism; however, it is not simple.

   1. Terrorism against tourists has a negative economic impact.

E. Energy – terrorists have a vested interest in disrupting oil and gas production.

   1. Fossil fuels present tempting targets for two reasons:

      a. They are representative of the power and strength of the industrialized world

      b. Strikes against oil refineries or transfer facilities have an economic impact on the West.

   2. Oil plays crucial roles in violence:

      a. It is used to fund endemic terrorism and corrupt governments.

      b. It becomes a target of those who cannot control production.

      c. Oil companies investing in the area have a greater incentive to focus on security than the debilitating poverty engulfing the region

   3. The Niger Delta is one of the largest oil-producing areas outside the Middle East, and it is beset with *endemic terrorism*.

      a. Oil in the Niger Delta simultaneously funds terrorists and other violent groups, while serving as a target for terrorism.

141

F. Transportation
    1. Transportation systems present a tempting economic target because they produce mass casualties with minimal effort.
    2. Costs of protecting transportation are staggering.
       a. Attacks on aviation, shipping, and transportation facilities increase the cost of security.

VI. Suicide Attacks – Conflicting Opinions
OBJ 10: Summarize theories of suicide bombing

A. Sometimes warriors are sent on missions where they know their lives will be lost, while at other times, people intentionally sacrifice their lives for a greater cause.

B   Diego Gambetta developed three types of suicide attacks:
    1. Suicide in warfare
    2. Suicide for a principle without killing others
    3. Suicidal terrorism

C. Suicide attack is not a method chosen simply to end one's life; it is a freely given sacrifice in the form of altruistic suicide.

D. A theory of suicide terrorism
    1. Robert Pape suggests that suicide terrorism be considered as a strategic tool, and believes three factors must be in place before a suicide terror campaign can take place:
       a. A nationalistic or ethnic group must be resisting the occupation of a foreign power.
       b. The foreign power must have a democratic government whose voters will not routinely allow the indiscriminate slaughter and total repression of the people in the occupied area.
       c. There must be a difference in the religions of the occupying power and the people living under occupation.
    2. Pape states that it is difficult to test this theory because there are so many differing factors; however, he argues that it might be possible to test it by focusing on the evidence from case studies:
       a. Israeli occupation of the Shiite areas of Lebanon.
       b. The Sinhalese (Buddhist) control of the Tamil (Hindu) region of Sri Lanka.
       c. The fighting between Sunni Kurds and Sunni Turks in eastern Turkey.
       d. The Indian (Hindu) struggle with the occupied Sikhs.
    3. Domenico Tosini believes the link between suicide and religion has been disproved, given that secular terrorist groups have employed the tactic.
       a. Suicide bombing takes place through a social process that endorses self-sacrifice as a legitimate expression of normal behavior.

4. Sara Jackson Wade and Daniel Reiter believe that Islam is an important factor in suicide bombings
   a. Muslim states suffer more suicide attacks than Western states, and more Muslims are targeted in suicide attacks than any other group.
E. Models for suicide bombing.
   1. There is a debate about modeling attacks.
   2. Rohan Gunaratna sees three things that all attacks have in common:
      a. Secrecy
      b. Reconnaissance
      c. Rehearsal
   3. Others suggest that models may exist, but there are so many factors that a single set of precursors cannot exist. It is also suggested that different models have emerged over time.

Chapter Summary

- The six basic tactics of terrorism are: bombing; arson; hijacking; assault; kidnapping; and taking hostages. Terrorists employ these tactics in a variety of ways.

- Terrorists use force multipliers to increase their attacking power. Force multipliers include technology, transnational support, media coverage, and religious fanaticism.

- Women have been involved in terrorist groups throughout the history of modern terrorism, and their role has been ignored. Many researchers, and the general public, have found it difficult to believe that women could become terrorists. More inclusive studies of gender in terrorist activities will increase the understanding of terrorism.

- Female terrorists impact tactics, and security forces often overlook the threats they pose. Different types of groups tend to use females in differing manners. Nationalistic and ethnic groups tend to use them in supporting roles, but women emerge as warriors and leaders in revolutionary groups. The importance of women in terrorism is growing. Some male-dominated traditional groups are openly recruiting females for suicide bombings and other operations.

- Technology can enhance striking power when it is employed as a weapon or is the target of an attack. Any form of technology may be used. Cyber-terrorism is a growing threat. Computer systems can be infected, or data can be stolen. Terrorists, or other enemies, might attack cybernetic control systems to cause a catastrophic failure in the economic sector or infrastructure.

- Technology also increases the lethality of potential weapons, giving them the potential for mass destruction. Biological agents include bacterial and viral weapons. There are four types of biological agents: (1) natural poisons, or toxins that occur without human modification; (2) viruses; (3) bacteria; and (4) plagues. There are four types of chemical agents: nerve agents; blood agents; choking agents; and blistering agents. Radiological weapons are closely related to chemical weapons, and they could be used by dispersing high doses of radiation in a conventional manner.

- Nuclear terrorism involves the potential employment of a nuclear bomb. There are two methods for constructing a nuclear device. The simplest method is to use HEU in a homemade bomb. The other method would be to gain control of an existing device. Some scholars and analysts believe that this will not happen, and others think that it will. Regardless, America is not prepared for nuclear terrorism. The country needs to develop a cooperative climate among security bureaucracies, and create a multifaceted defense in depth.

- Terrorists use the media as a weapon for enhancing the power of attacks, by using it to broadcast a political message, thus gaining publicity for a violent political movement, and providing respectability for their cause.

- The force of terrorism can be multiplied by the selection of transnational economic targets. Tourism, energy, and transportation present excellent opportunities for increasing the economic impact of an attack.

- Pape's theory of suicide terrorism is based on examining religious differences when a democracy occupies a foreign country or the enclave of an ethnic group. Local religious leaders must create a climate where martyrdom is supported. Other research suggests that religion has no link to suicide bombings. It is difficult to model suicide terrorism because there is no single group or individual profile of suicide attackers. Different groups use different methods, and suicide bombers come from a variety of backgrounds.

DISCUSSION QUESTIONS

1. Of the differing views presented on the role of women's participation in terrorist activities, which do you find most appropriate and why? What is your view as to why women's role in terrorism has been overlooked? Explain. (OBJ 3 and 4)

2. The author discusses the use of cyber-terrorism and the potential effects on American society. What are some potential counterterrorist policy strategies that could assist in the prevention of cyber-terrorism? (OBJ 1, 2, and 5)

3. According to Pape, the differences in religion are important in suicide bombing. If this is true, what policies or counterterrorist tactics may be implemented to reduce the number of suicide attacks? Do you believe that any intervention could potentially increase or decrease the number of suicide attacks? Explain. (OBJ 1 and 10)

4.	Describe the effects of chemical and radiological WMD as opposed to the effects of biological weapons. Which do you believe poses the most serious threat? Explain. (OBJ 1, 2, 6, and 7)

ASSIGNMENTS

1.	"Mix and match". Prepare flash cards listing a variety of biological, chemical, radiological and nerve agents and their symptoms. Have students match each vector (i.e. virus, bacteria, nerve agent, etc.) to the correct corresponding category or symptom (i.e. biological, chemical, etc.). Wrap up the activity with discussion on preventative measures to reduce exposure to bioterror attacks. (OBJ 1, 6, and 7)

2.	Suicide bombing is one of the most popular terrorist tactics used today. Have the students bring print media articles to class regarding suicide bombers. Students may also bring the URL of online videos addressing suicide bombers. Discuss the reasons as to why this tactic is used, and possible ways to defend against suicide attacks. (OBJ 1, 3, 4, and 10)

3.	Give students a minute or two to silently reflect on what type of targets may be the most desirable to terrorists, and then break them into small groups to discuss their reflections. Equip each group with a flip chart and markers. Have them choose a scribe from their group to write down the group thoughts, and a presenter to share the group's work with the class when finished. Open the floor to discussion when all groups have finished their presentations. (OBJ 1, 2, 5, 6, 7, and 9)

4.	Divide the class into four groups. Have each group address one of the four force multipliers discussed in the chapter. Each group should list the ways in which the force multiplier is and can be utilized as well as strategies to combat that use. Have each group select a presenter to share their findings with the class. (OBJ 1, 2, and 8)

5.	Have each student comb through http://www.cnn.com/search/?query=terrorist+weapons&primaryType=mixed&sortBy=relevance&intl=false (or another website as approved by the instructor) for a current event, and select an article that relates to one or more of the chapter's core concepts. Have students provide a journalistic summary and a personal opinion/reaction to the article. Have students orally present the article to the class, field Q & As from their fellow students, and provide a copy of the original source article following the presentation. Optional: Have students complete peer assessments at the end of each presentation. (OBJ 1 - 10)

MEDIA TOOLS

1. ***"Wikis"***

   7 Things you should know about Wikis. Retrieved from the Web Jun 29, 2012 at
   http://net.educause.edu/ir/library/pdf/ELI7004.pdf

   This document offers easy to understand instruction on the history, development,
   and potential uses of Wikis.

   Have students develop (or make additions to a previously created one) a
   Webliography (resource list) using a Blog or Wiki that provides a short
   description and link to a scholarly resource pertaining to course concepts. For
   example, have students add two to three resources each, and ask them to add their
   assessment of at least one of their peers' contributions. If desired, allow time to
   discuss Blogs/Wikis. This activity can be reused throughout the course, by asking
   students to add/revise their contributions each week, bi-weekly, etc. (OBJ 1 – 10)

2. ***"Terrorist Fact Sheets"***

   National Consortium for the Study of Terrorism and Responses to Terrorism.
   Terrorist Organizational Profiles. Retrieved from the Web Aug 20, 2012 at
   http://www.start.umd.edu/start/data_collections/tops/

   This website offers a comprehensive database of terrorist organizations,
   containing detailed information on structure, organization, major players and
   tactics. This resource can additionally serve as an example for media tool sample
   #1.

   Have the class comb through the database and select a terrorist organization to
   research. Have each student create an organizational profile 'fact sheet' of the
   group to present to the class, with special focus on the role of women within the
   organization. Once completed, have the entire class compare and contrast their
   combined discoveries. (OBJ 1, 3, 4, and 10)

3. ***"Biological Weapons Portfolios"***

   Science How Stuff Works. 10 Scariest bioweapons. Retrieved from the Web
   Aug 08, 2012 at http://science.howstuffworks.com/bioweapon.htm

   The article explores the history of biological weapons as well as an examination
   of 10 of the most virulent viruses and bacteria that can be fashioned into weapons
   of terror.

Have students peruse the article and select one of the top 10 bioweapons. Have students complete some further independent research on their selection, and prepare an informative "fact sheet" to provide to their classmates. As a class project, have the students combine their fact sheets into a single portfolio. (OBJ 2, 6, and 7)

4.   *"Current Events Article Summary with Peer Assessment"*

Use the Article Summary Template, which can be obtained on the instructor companion website, for this assignment. The template offers information on Internet research, outside resources, identification of credible sources, and detailed directions on completing an assessment of a news article. It also includes a peer evaluation tool.

Have each student comb the Internet for terrorism related news, and select an article that relates to one or more of the chapter's core concepts. Be sure selections are an article of interest from a credible source (*more on credibility can be found in the article summary template above*). Fill out an article summary template. The *template asks for generic info about the article, a journalistic summary, as well as a personal opinion/reaction to the article.* Have each student summarize the article, present it orally to the class, and field Q & As from their fellow students. Have students complete peer assessments at the end of each presentation. Have students submit templates, original source article, and peer-reviews prior to the end of class. (OBJ 1 - 10)

TEST BANK

TRUE/FALSE

1. Women played leading roles during emerging racial terrorism in the South after the Civil War.

ANS: F   REF: p. 112   OBJ: 3

2. Examples of force multipliers include technology and reserve units 'at the ready'.

ANS: F   REF: p. 125   OBJ: 2 and 8

3. Although terrorist tactics change through time, the most common weapon of terrorism has been and remains the bomb.

ANS: T   REF: p. 111   OBJ: 1 and 5

4. All researchers have determined that the frequency of violence is more important than the severity of terrorist attacks.

ANS: F   REF: p. 126   OBJ: 1

5. Researchers have found no relationship between terrorism and tourism.

ANS: F   REF: p. 126   OBJ: 9

6. The most common tactic of cyber-terrorism to date has been the defacement of Web sites.

ANS: T   REF: p. 116   OBJ: 16

7. The media can be used as a force multiplier.

ANS: T   REF: p. 111   OBJ: 8

8. Most dirty-bomb scenarios are based on the premise that a radiological agent will be used with a conventional explosive.

ANS: T   REF: p. 120   OBJ: 6 and 7

9. The role of females in terrorist groups is decreasing around the globe.

ANS: F   REF: p. 109   OBJ: 3

10. All researchers have determined that the severity of terrorist attacks is more important than the frequency of violence.

ANS: T   REF: p. 126   OBJ: 1

11. Media coverage can make a minor group appear to be politically important.

ANS: T   REF: p. 110   OBJ: 8

12. Women often receive combat or leadership positions in international terrorist organizations.

ANS: F   REF: p. 113   OBJ: 3 and 4

13. All hackers are terrorists.

ANS: F   REF: p. 116   OBJ: 1 And 5

14. Only the government and military have access to highly enriched uranium (HEU).

ANS: F   REF: p. 120   OBJ: 6 and 7

15. Radioactive poisoning is highly contagious.

ANS: F   REF: p. 121   OBJ: 6 and 7

MULTIPLE CHOICE

1. The National Conference of State Legislature defines _____ as, "the use of information technology by terrorists to promote a political agenda."
    a. Narco-terrorism
    b. Cyber-terrorism
    c. Domestic terrorism
    d. Transnational terrorism

ANS: b   REF: p. 116   OBJ: 5

2. The first known female suicide bomber (employed against an Israeli convoy) occurred in which decade?
    a. 1970s
    b. 1980s
    c. 1990s
    d. 1960s

ANS: b   REF: p. 109   OBJ: 10

3. Margaret Gonzalez-Perez found that the role of women in terrorist groups is more closely determined by the _____ orientation of an organization than its tactics.
   a. Gender
   b. Economic
   c. Religious
   d. Political

ANS: d   REF: p. 113   OBJ: 10

4. What is the name given a technological program that typically copies itself and moves through a computer system in order to disrupt a computer or computer network?
   a. Cyber worm
   b. Computer virus
   c. Cyber bomb
   d. Logic bomb

ANS: b   REF: p. 117   OBJ: 5

5. Treatments of antibiotics are a suitable defense against _____ attacks.
   a. Bacterial
   b. Chemical
   c. Viral
   d. Nuclear

ANS: a   REF: p. 118   OBJ: 6

6. There are four types of biological agents: (1) natural poisons, or toxins that occur without human modification, (2) viruses, (3) bacteria, and (4) _____.
   a. Radiation
   b. Plagues
   c. Nerve gas
   d. Plutonium

ANS: b   REF: p. 118   OBJ: 6

7. Which of the following tactics is most often employed by terrorists?
   a. The bomb
   b. Kidnapping
   c. Hijacking
   d. Arson

ANS: a   REF: p. 111   OBJ: 1

8. According to the text, _____ is the only group that has made an effort to obtain a nuclear device.
   a. LTTE Black Tigers
   b. Hezbollah
   c. Al Qaeda
   d. Kurdistan Workers Party

ANS: c   REF: p. 122   OBJ: 7

9. Which of the following is NOT a type of bacterial agent?
   a. Salmonella
   b. Botulism
   c. E. coli
   d. E. bola

ANS: d   REF: p. 118   OBJ: 6

10. Ebola virus is considered a/an _____.
   a. Bacterial infection
   b. Food borne illness
   c. Radiological weapon
   d. Hemorrhagic fever

ANS: d   REF: p. 118   OBJ: 6

11. Gadt Wolfsfeld believes the media is a primary tool for demonizing the enemy, with the most powerful tool being the way _____ reports casualties.
   a. Television
   b. Email
   c. Internet blogs
   d. Radio

ANS: a   REF: p. 124   OBJ: 8

12. What biological agent infected citizens through the mail in the wake of the September 11, 2001, attacks?
   a. Anthrax
   b. Smallpox
   c. Plague
   d. Botulism

ANS: a   REF: p. 118   OBJ: 1 and 6

13. Anthrax is considered a _____.
   a. Vermin
   b. Virus
   c. Bacteria
   d. Chemical

ANS: c   REF: p. 118   OBJ: 2, 6, and 7

14. _____ enter the body through ingestion, respiration, or contact.
   a. Blood agents
   b. Blistering agents
   c. Nerve agents
   d. Choking agents

ANS: c   REF: p. 118   OBJ: 6

15.   Most dirty-bomb scenarios are based on the premise that a _____ agent will be used with a conventional explosive.
    a. Bacterial
    b. Viral
    c. Chemical
    d. Radiological

ANS: d   REF: p. 120   OBJ: 7

16.   The _____ in eastern Turkey conducted the least deadly attacks in the course of modern suicide bombing, killing an average of two people per incident.
    a. Black Tigers
    b. Kurdistan Workers Party
    c. Tamil Hindus
    d. Russian Orthodox Christians

ANS: b   REF: p. 130   OBJ: 1 and 10

17.   The major factor in deciding to employ suicide terrorists is the _____ of the group.
    a. The social structure and culture
    b. Religion
    c. Rational choice
    d. Economic strength

ANS: a   REF: p. 130   OBJ: 10

18.   As the world moves closer to a global economy, terrorists have found that striking _____ increases the effectiveness of operations.
    a. Economic targets
    b. National targets
    c. Symbolic targets
    d. Security targets

ANS: a   REF: p. 126   OBJ: 1 and 9

19.   Which of the following is NOT a target of transnational attack?
    a. Tourism
    b. Energy
    c. Transportation
    d. Consumerism

ANS: d   REF: p. 126   OBJ: 9

20.   J. Bowyer Bell refers to _____ terrorism, which is a form of violence that occurs in Africa where arbitrary national boundaries have been drawn through ethnic and tribal divisions.
    a. Endemic
    b. Ethnic
    c. Epidemic
    d. Evident

ANS: a   REF: p. 127   OBJ: 9

21.	_____ is considered a non-contagious bacterial infection.
a. Smallpox
b. MRSA
c. Hemorrhagic fever
d. Anthrax

ANS: d	REF: p. 118	OBJ: 6

22.	According to the text, the _____ have conducted more suicide bombings than any other group.
a. Buddhist Sinhalese
b. Sunni Kurds
c. LTTE Black Tigers
d. Hezbollah

ANS: c	REF: p. 129	OBJ: 3, 4, and 10

23.	Gender impacts terrorist tactics and is often related mostly to the _____.
a. Social standing of the terrorist organization
b. Ideology of the terrorist organization
c. Economics of the terrorist organization
d. Media influence upon the terrorist organization

ANS: b	REF: p. 114	OBJ: 3, 4, and 10

24.	Rohan Gunaratna sees three things that all suicide bombings have in common:
a. Secrecy, reconnaissance, and rehearsal
b. Secrecy, religion, and political agendas
c. Political agendas, chance of success, and secrecy
d. Secrecy, rehearsal, and chance of success

ANS: a	REF: p. 131	OBJ: 1 and 10

25.	Terrorists use _____ to increase their attacking power.
a. Force multipliers
b. Tactics
c. Large memberships
d. Secrecy

ANS: a	REF: p. 132	OBJ: 1, 2, and 8

26.	Muslim states suffer more _____ than Western states.
a. Bombing attacks
b. Kidnappings
c. Suicide attacks
d. Biological attacks

ANS: c	REF: p. 131	OBJ: 10

27. More _____ are targeted in suicide attacks than any other group.
    a. Catholics
    b. Muslims
    c. Jewish
    d. Atheists

ANS: b   REF: p. 131   OBJ: 10

28. The United States has experienced _____ notable biological attacks since 1980.
    a. Zero
    b. One
    c. Two
    d. Ten

ANS: c   REF: p. 118   OBJ: 2 and 6

29. In 2004, *New Scientist* reported that Middle Eastern terrorist groups were working on a two-stage military-style weapon called a _____.
    a. IED
    b. Mininuke
    c. Drone
    d. Dirty bomb

ANS: b   REF: p. 111   OBJ: 2 and 6

30. The National Conference of State Legislature defines _____ as, "the use of information technology by terrorists to promote a political agenda."
    a. Narco-terrorism
    b. Cyber-terrorism
    c. Domestic terrorism
    d. Transnational terrorism

ANS: b   REF: p. 116   OBJ: 5

31. In 2003, Al Qaeda began targeting oil facilities in what country?
    a. Iran
    b. Saudi Arabia
    c. Iraq
    d. Kuwait

ANS: b   REF: p. 127   OBJ: 1, 2, and 9

32. Daly says that the Taliban believes that the most effective way to destroy the Pakistan government is to attack _____.
    a. Political targets
    b. Women and children
    c. Economic targets
    d. Allies of the Pakistani government

ANS: c   REF: p. 127   OBJ: 9

33. After the September 11 attacks, the federal government immediately budgeted $ 4.8 billion to protect the ____ industry.
    a. Shipping
    b. Aviation
    c. Computer
    d. Banking

ANS: b   REF: p. 128   OBJ: 9

34. ____ terrorists are responsible for sixty-five percent of all political assassinations.
    a. Child
    b. Female
    c. Male
    d. Ecological

ANS: b   REF: p. 133   OBJ: 3 and 4

35. Which of the following is NOT a target for cyber-terrorism: computers, computer networks, and information storage and retrieval systems.
    a. Computers
    b. Freeways
    c. Computer networks
    d. Information storage and retrieval systems

ANS: b   REF: p. 116   OBJ: 5

36. HEU stands for _____.
    a. Heavily elongated uranium
    b. High evolution utilities
    c. Harsh environmental usage
    d. Highly enriched uranium

ANS: d   REF: p. 120   OBJ: 10

37. Nerve agents, blood agents, choking agents, and blistering agents are all examples of _____ agents.
    a. Bacterial
    b. Chemical
    c. Viral
    d. Radiological

ANS: b   REF: p. 118   OBJ: 6

38. Which of the following is NOT considered one of Jenkins' six tactics of terrorism?
    a. Kidnapping
    b. Bombing
    c. Espionage
    d. Assault

ANS: c   REF: p. 110   OBJ: 1

39.   Congress mandates that all radioactive waste from America's nuclear power plants be transported to a repository in what state?
        a. Nevada
        b. Arizona
        c. Alaska
        d. Colorado

ANS: a   REF: p. 121   OBJ: 6

40.   The type of bomb used at Hiroshima employed _____.
        a. Highly enriched uranium (HEU)
        b. Plutonium
        c. Neptunium
        d. Deuterium

ANS: a   REF: p. 122   OBJ: 7

Case 5.0

Terrorists tend to increase their effectiveness in bombing by applying improved explosive technology to their weapons just as conventional military forces constantly improve the killing power of their munitions. In 2004, *New Scientist* reported that Middle Eastern terrorist groups were working on a two-stage military-style weapon called a mininuke. This type of explosive is designed to spread fuel in the air and then ignite it. Known as a thermobaric bomb, it actually explodes the air in the blast area. One analyst speculated that an attack on a Tunisian synagogue in 2002 used this technology (Hambling, 2004).

41.   A thermobaric bomb is a force multiplier of what classification?
        a. Transnational support
        b. Technology
        c. Media coverage
        d. Religion

        ANS: b   REF: p. 132   OBJ: 1, 2, and 6

42.   In which targeted environment would you suspect a thermobaric bomb to be a terrorist's most desirable weapon of choice?
        a. A small classroom
        b. An underground tunnel
        c. An open air market
        d. Middle of the ocean

        ANS: c   REF: p. 132   OBJ: 1, 2, and 6

Case 5.1

Brian Jenkins says that the six tactics of terrorism can be enhanced by force multipliers. In military terms, a force multiplier increases striking power without increasing the strength of a unit. He labels four kinds of force multipliers: *Transnational support, Technology, Media coverage* and *Religion*. Terrorists routinely use force multipliers because they add to their aura. All political terrorists want to give the illusion that they can fight on a higher, more powerful level.

For each of the scenarios below, select which force multiplier is being utilized:

43.   A terrorist group receives a large sum of cash from a charity organization from another country that enables them to purchase weapons.
        a. Transnational support
        b. Technology
        c. Media coverage
        d. Religion

      ANS: a   REF: p. 132   OBJ: 2 and 8

44.   A terrorist leader sends coded messages to members of the organization during a televised interview with a local journalist.
        a. Transnational support
        b. Technology
        c. Media coverage
        d. Religion

      ANS: c   REF: p. 132   OBJ: 2 and 8

45.   Terrorists break through Homeland Security's firewalls, highjack and destroy several drones.
        a. Transnational support
        b. Technology
        c. Media coverage
        d. Religion

      ANS: b   REF: p. 132   OBJ: 2 and 8

46.   A suicide bomber explodes in a local supermarket.
        a. Transnational support
        b. Technology
        c. Media coverage
        d. Religion

      ANS: a   REF: p. 132   OBJ: 2 and 8

47.   Terrorist cell members receive instructions from within the shelter of a local church.
        a. Transnational support
        b. Technology
        c. Media coverage
        d. Religion

      ANS: a   REF: p. 132   OBJ: 2 and 8

48.   Terrorists activate a dirty bomb explodes within a military outpost.
        a. Transnational support
        b. Technology
        c. Media coverage
        d. Religion

      ANS: b   REF: p. 132   OBJ: 2 and 8

Case 5.2

Terrorism by WMD presents a potential strategic and include biological agents, or biological weapons, which have been used for centuries. Modern arsenals contain bacterial weapons **and** viral weapons, with microbes cultured and refined, or weaponized, to increase their ability to kill. Because bacterial agents are susceptible to antibiotics, nations with bacterial weapons programs have created strains of bacterial microbes resistant to such drugs. Viral agents are produced in the same manner, and they are usually more powerful than bacterial agents. Biological agents are difficult to control but relatively easy to produce. Terrorists may find them to be effective weapons.

There are four types of biological agents: (1) natural poisons, or toxins that occur without human modification, (2) viruses, (3) bacteria, and (4) plagues. The Centers for Disease Control and Prevention (CDC) classifies the most threatening from the groups as smallpox, anthrax, plague, botulism, tularemia, and hemorrhagic fever.

49.   Smallpox is classified under which category?
       a. Toxin
       b. Virus
       c. Bacteria
       d. Plague
   ANS: b   REF: p. 118   OBJ: 6

50.   Hemorrhagic fever is classified under which category?
       a. Toxin
       b. Virus
       c. Bacteria
       d. Plague
   ANS: b   REF: p. 118   OBJ: 6

COMPLETION

1.   _____ present an attractive weapon for terrorists because they are easy to control and the users can avoid the area they attack.

ANS: chemicals   REF: p. 119   OBJ: 6

2.   Nerve agents enter the body through ingestion, respiration, or ____.

ANS: contact   REF: p. 119   OBJ: 2 and 6

3.   When people are victims of a bacterial attack, _____ may be an effective treatment.

ANS: antibiotics   REF: p. 118   OBJ: 6

4.   Radiological poisoning and "dirty" radioactive devices are forms of _____ alterations.

ANS: chemical   REF: p. 119   OBJ: 2 and 6

5. _____ systems present a tempting economic target because they produce mass casualties with minimal effort.

ANS: transportation   REF: p. 128   OBJ: 9

6. _____ refer to snippets of computer program code that lie dormant for years until they are instructed to overwhelm a computer system.

ANS: logic bombs   REF: p. 117   OBJ: 5

7. _____ is a phrase used by anarchists around 1848. It means that social order can only be changed through violent upheaval.

ANS: philosophy of the bomb   REF: p. 111   OBJ: 1, 5, and 10

8. _____ suicide refers to the willingness of individuals to sacrifice their lives to benefit their primary reference group, such as a family, military unit, ethnic group, or country.

ANS: altruistic   REF: p. 128   OBJ: 10

9. Jenkins says that there are six tactics of terrorism: _____, arson, assault, kidnapping bombing and hostage taking.

ANS: hijacking   REF: p. 110   OBJ: 1

10. The formal name of the terrorist group referred to as PKK is the _____.

ANS: Kurdish workers' Party   REF: p. 130   OBJ: 4

11. The Pakistani Taliban and Al Qaeda formed female suicide cells after the first female suicide bomber struck in _____ in 2010.

ANS: Pakistan   REF: p. 109   OBJ: 4 and 10

12. The block formation of ancient Greek fighting methods is called a _____.

ANS: phalanx   REF: p. 110   OBJ: 1

13. _____ increases the ability of terrorist groups to move and hide across a nation.

ANS: transnational support   REF: p. 110   OBJ: 1, 2, and 9

14. In the campaign against the U.S. military in Iraq after 2003, suicide bombings and _____ became the weapons of choice.

ANS: roadside bombs   REF: p. 111   OBJ: 1

159

15. _____ terrorism involves organized groups from a dominant race violently intimidating racial minorities to keep them from achieving higher social standing and political power.

ANS: racial   REF: p. 112   OBJ: 3

16. Energy, shipping, and _____ industries are the most likely targets for a transnational attack.

ANS: tourism   REF: p. 126   OBJ: 9

17. _____ terrorism is a form of violence that occurs in Africa where arbitrary national boundaries have been drawn without regard to ethnic and tribal divisions.

ANS: endemic   REF: p. 127   OBJ: 1 and 9

18. The popular conception in Lebanon is that _____ causes suicide terrorism.

ANS: militant Islamic theology   REF: p. 129   OBJ: 10

19. Force multipliers include _____, transnational support, media coverage, and religious fanaticism.

ANS: technology   REF: p. 132   OBJ: 2

20. There are four types of chemical agents: nerve agents, blood agents, choking agents, and _____.

ANS: blistering agents   REF: p. 132   OBJ: 6

ESSAY

1. Name and summarize the effects of the most threatening biological agents indicated by the Center for Disease Control and Prevention. Describe the two biological attacks on U.S. soil.

ANS:
- The Centers for Disease Control and Prevention (CDC) classifies the most threatening agents as smallpox, anthrax, plague, botulism, tularemia, and hemorrhagic fever.
- Smallpox is a deadly, contagious virus. Many people were vaccinated against smallpox in their childhood, but these old vaccinations are no longer effective against the disease.
- Anthrax is a non-contagious bacterial infection, and plague is transmitted by insects.
- Botulism is a kind of food borne illness, and other bacteria can be modified to serve as weapons.
- Hemorrhagic fevers are caused by viruses. One of the most widely known hemorrhagic fevers is the Ebola virus.
- The first modern use of biological terrorism in the United States was engineered in 1984 by followers of a religious group in Oregon.

160

- The group spread bacteria in area salad bars in attempt to sicken voters during a local election.
- Their intent was to elect their religious followers to local office.
- Hundreds of people suffered food poisoning as a result.
- The second attack involved anthrax and came in the wake of 9/11.
- It began in Florida when two tabloid workers were infected by anthrax through the mail. One of the victims died.
- In the following days anthrax appeared again as NBC *Nightly News* received spores in the mail.
- Staffers at the office of former Senate majority leader Thomas Daschle noticed a white powdery substance in a letter.
- The powder contained anthrax spores, and although there were no fatalities, legislative offices were closed in Washington, D.C., for several weeks.
- Mysteriously, other people died on the East Coast with no explanation of how the anthrax was spreading.

REF: p. 118   OBJ: 6

2.   Describe cyber-terrorism and its targets; why is it attractive to terrorist? How can Cyber-terrorism be utilized by terrorists?

ANS:
- Cyber-terrorism refers to the use of computers to attack technological targets or physical attacks on computer networks; The National Conference of State Legislatures defines cyber-terrorism as the use of information technology by terrorists to promote a political agenda.
- Barry Collin coined the term in the early 1990s, believes it involves disrupting points where the virtual, electronic realm of computer networks and programs intersects with the physical world.
- There are targets for cyber-terrorism: computers, computer networks, and information storage and retrieval systems.
- Terrorists differ from hackers, the council argues, because their purpose is to launch a systematic attack for political purposes.
- Cyber-terrorism is an attractive low-risk strategy.
- Computers allow terrorist groups to remain connected, providing a means for covert discussions and anonymity.
- Computer networks are also much less expensive and work intensive than the secretive infrastructures necessary to maintain terrorist groups.
- Modern Western society needs information and the flow of information to function, so cyber-terrorists threaten to interrupt or confuse that flow of information.
- The most common tactic to date has been the defacement of websites.
- There are many potential targets for cyber-terrorists.
- Computer virus is implanted in an enemy's computer.
- "Logic bombs," or snippets of program code that lie dormant for years until they are instructed to overwhelm a computer system.

161

- Bogus computer chips sold to sabotage an enemy's computer network.
- Trojan horses can contain malevolent code that can destroy a system, and "back doors" in computer systems can allow terrorists to enter systems thought to be secured.
- Shahar believes that conventional attacks, such as overloading an electrical system, threaten computer security.

REF: p. 116   OBJ: 1, 2, and 5

3.   Discuss why Margaret Gonzalez-Perez states that women are more attracted to domestic terrorist organizations than international groups.

ANS:
- Domestic organizations are focused on revolution and social change – women are attracted to such groups because they have a chance to redefine their roles, and males and females welcome them since they want the same change.
- Some groups have a feminist agenda.
- Women have opportunities for leadership in revolutionary groups.
- International terrorists resist outside forces such as capitalism and imperialism – they try to defend a traditional culture that limits the role of women.
- Women in domestic groups gravitate toward combat and leadership.
- Women in international groups are given more limited roles -- international terrorists tend to employ women as supporters, sympathizers, and spies, seldom receiving combat or leadership positions.
- This pattern remains constant even in social systems that emphasize male dominance.
- For example, it is thought that the *machismo* influence in Central and South America would blunt female leadership and combat roles, but the opposite is true.
- Most Central and South American groups have a left-wing revolutionary focus.
- Women move into active roles because the groups are seeking to restructure their culture and political structure.
- Every geographical area produced a common trend; domestics groups emphasized the role of women even when they have no stated feminist agenda.

REF: p. 113   OBJ: 3 and 4

4.   Describe the four types of chemical agents as well as the problems they present. When are chemical weapons most effective?

ANS:
- There are four types of chemical agents: nerve agents, blood agents, choking agents, and blistering agents.
- Nerve agents enter the body through ingestion, respiration, or contact.
- Blood and choking agents are usually absorbed through the respiratory system.
- Blistering agents burn skin and internal tissue upon contact.
- Chemicals present an attractive weapon for terrorists because they are easy to control and, unlike biological weapons, the users can avoid the area they attack.

162

- Chemical weapons present four problems.
- First, terrorists must have a delivery mechanism; that is, they need some way to spread the chemical.
- The second problem is related to the first. Bombing is a popular tactic, but the heat of most explosives incinerates chemical agents.
- It takes a lot of chemicals to present a threat.
- Finally, weather patterns, air, and water can neutralize a chemical threat.
- Chemical weapons are most effective when used in a confined space, and they are difficult to use effectively in large outdoor areas.

REF: p. 119 OBJ: 6

5. How does oil in the Niger Delta represent a different opportunity for economic attack?

ANS:
- Oil in the Niger Delta represents a different opportunity for economic attack as it simultaneously funds terrorists and other violent groups while serving as a target for terrorism.
- Dilapidated storage facilities and pipelines have become an ecological disaster for the impoverished local residents.
- The result is an environment that encourages sub-national violence and that might serve as a base for international terrorism.
- The energy environment in Africa represents an interesting paradox.
- If poverty, endemic terrorism, and criminalized politics are not addressed by the industrial world, areas like the Niger Delta will evolve in two directions.
- They will become the base for the emergence of new international terrorist groups, providing excellent resources for training and eluding detection.
- At the same time, the energy resources in the delta provide a target-rich environment for terrorists.

REF: p. 127 OBJ: 9

6. What is a force multiplier? List and explain force multiplier and how they are used.

ANS:
- Force multipliers are a method of increasing striking power without increasing the number of combat troops in a military unit.
- Terrorists have four force multipliers: (1) technology to enhance weapons or attacks on technological facilities which allows a small group to launch a deadly attack, (2) transnational support which increases the ability of terrorist groups to move and hide, (3) media coverage, which can make a minor group appear to be politically important, and (4) religious fanaticism which transcends normative political and social boundaries, increasing violence and decreasing opportunities for negotiation.
- Cyber-terrorism and potential WMD attacks are examples of technological force multipliers.

- Media coverage and interpretation of terrorist events often serve as force multipliers – one incident can be converted into a "campaign" as electronic media scrambles to break the latest news.
- The triborder region in South America demonstrates that transnational support networks multiply the striking power of terrorists.
- A new force multiplier has been the introduction of religious fanaticism in terrorist activities.
- The introduction of religion has introduced suicide attacks into the arsenals of terrorism.
- Other examples are provided throughout the chapter.

REF: p. 132   OBJ: 2

7.   What are Michael Levi's five goals for policy makers? How does Levi suggest the U.S. approach nuclear terrorism?

ANS:
- Support international efforts to stop the proliferation of nuclear weapons.
- Address nuclear terrorism in conjunction with all other terrorist threats.
- Mandate nuclear threat analysis based on the most probable dangers.
- Create a cooperative multiagency defense system.
- Audit the defense system and reward cooperation.
- Levi suggests that the United States should approach nuclear terrorism in two manners.
- The first involves debunking popular myths about the subject.
- Policy makers and the public need to understand the basic aspects of nuclear security and must realize that it is never 100% effective.
- Fear should be rationalized.
- Levi believes it is more logical to look at several realistic scenarios and aim preventive measures at high probability targets.
- It is not enough to limit the focus on nuclear terrorism – Levi argues for a comprehensive approach to a terrorist group and all its activities as this provides a better threat analysis than limited attention to nuclear terrorism.
- The second response is to revamp defense systems.
- Protection against any form of terrorism does not involve a single agency working against a single group.
- Defense involves a multitude of agencies and organizations at all levels of government and liaison with private organizations.
- Levi argues that the current bureaucracy does not provide protection because agencies protect turf, they do not share information, and administration is confused and competitive.
- Oversight of defense systems needs to be clarified and streamlined, and agency managers should be routinely evaluated on the ability to work with other agencies and to share information.

REF: p. 122   OBJ: 7

8.   What is Laura Sjober's view of the scholarly literature that covers women and terrorism? Do you agree with Sjober's view that the field would be enriched through feminist perspectives? Why or why not?

ANS:
- Studies of women in terrorism are generally ignored, and when females are discussed it is in gendered terms.
- They are not "terrorists," they are "women involved in terrorism."
- There are exceptions, but most scholars and analysts conclude that women play some type of nebulous role in terrorism.
- They cannot define the role, and they do not seem to care to do so.
- Media presentations follow the same track – women are neither significant nor worthy of analysis.
- Sjoberg vehemently disagrees with such characterizations.
- Women do have a special place in terrorism; women are terrorists just like men who do the same thing.
- There are terrorists who happen to be women, and they have been around for quite some time.
- There is also no feminist perspective of terrorism; there are feminists who study terrorism in a variety of ways.
- Sjoberg says that scholars and other researchers are reluctant to study political and criminal violence among women because it violates idealized notions of womanhood.
- Their behavior should be studied from a variety of feminist perspectives, Sjoberg concludes. Such literature would enrich the field.
- View will vary.

REF: p. 115   OBJ: 3 and 4

9.   Discuss Gadt Wolfsfeld's position on the media and terrorism.

ANS:
- Gadt Wolfsfeld states that media victories are crucial for terrorism.
- In the al Asqa Intifada both sides tried to use the media.
- Struggles for the way a battle is reported are as important as combat on the battlefield.
- Neither side wants to be portrayed as the aggressor.
- The Palestinians know that sensational television coverage presents one of their best chances to receive outside intervention, leaving Israel to practice damage control.
- Both sides have structures to capture media attention and present their respective views.
- Wolfsfeld also believes the media is the primary tool for demonizing the enemy, and the most powerful tool is the way television reports casualties.
- Both sides use the same pattern – each side compassionately presents its own casualties and describes how they got their injuries in horrific terms, whereas the other side's killed and wounded are described as statistics.
- Although radio and print media are important, television takes center stage because it can show bloody images.

165

- The worst images are shown many times over on the twenty-four-hour networks.
- The media makes conflict worse in a subtle way because drama dwindles when news organizations report peace efforts.
- Most reports about peace efforts are stories of the breakdowns.
- When an explosion threatens peace talks or terrorists behead a hostage after fighting has ended, television, radio, and newspaper reporters flood the world with gruesome stories.
- Negotiations during civil unrest are not dramatic, but explosions and machine gun fire are riveting.

REF: p. 124 OBJ: 8

10. Explain Domenico Tosini's beliefs regarding suicide, religion, and terrorism.

ANS:
- Tosini believes the link between suicide and religion has been disproved given that secular terrorist groups have employed the tactic.
- Tosini believes that rational choice and religion are secondary factors in suicide attacks.
- The major factor is the social structure and culture of the group engaged in suicide terrorism.
- Groups take actions inside social structures based on their understanding of reality – this can create the group dynamics that lead to suicide terrorism.
- The dynamic agents involved in a suicide bombing are the armed terrorist group, the group's supporters, and the bombers.
- These three entities operate in social network where decisions are made based on the interpretations of situations.
- The decision to engage in suicide bombing is based on the interactions of terrorists, supporters, and attackers within a surrounding social network.
- Moving beyond rational choice, Tosini argues that the social climate must readily accept suicide bombings.
- Supporters of a terrorist group have to embrace the idea, and create social rewards for bombers and their relatives.
- Beyond this, the entire community must accept violence as a normative response to social grievances and believe that suicide bombing is an acceptable expression of violence.
- Supporting groups need material and symbolic rewards, and attackers must have a deep attachment to idealized representations of their communities.
- When altruism enters the equation, it produces culture of martyrdom and this in turn, combines with two common military approaches to war – dehumanization and depersonalization of enemies.
- Tosini argues that suicide terrorism develops when a culture accepts it as an expression of altruistic martyrdom and terrorist groups with the culture embrace the tactic.
- Suicide bombing takes place through a social process that endorses self-sacrifice as a legitimate expression of normal behavior.

REF: p. 130 OBJ: 10

166

CHAPTER 6

Long-Term Separatist Terrorism

Learning Objectives

After reading this chapter, students should be able to:

1. Explain the nature and characteristics of nationalistic and ethnic separatist terrorism.
2. Describe the emergence of the modern IRA and terrorism in Northern Ireland.
3. Outline the basis for negotiating peace in Northern Ireland.
4. Summarize the nature of Basque culture and its separateness from Spain.
5. Explain the impact of the Spanish Civil War on the Basque region.
6. Summarize the birth and evolution of the ETA.
7. Explain the rise of the GAL.
8. Outline the Spanish government's approach to Basque separatism.
9. Describe the rise of the LTTE and the role of the Tamil Diaspora.
10. Summarize the unique aspect of LTTE suicide bombings.
11. Describe the end of the LTTE and the danger of possible reconstitution.

Chapter Key Terms

Provisionals, p. 140

Ulster Volunteer Force, p.144

Anglo-Irish Peace Accord, p. 144

Tony Blair, p. 145

Belfast Agreement, p. 145

Independent Monitoring Commission (IMC), p. 145

Police Service of Northern Ireland (PSIN), p. 145

War of the Spanish Succession (1702– 1714), p. 146

Spanish Civil War (1936–1939), p. 147

Francisco Franco, p. 147

Tamils, p. 151

Velupillai Pirapaharan, p. 151

Rajiv Gandhi, p. 151

Ranasinghe Premadasa, p. 151

Colombo, p. 153

Provisionals: The nickname for members of the Provisional Irish Republican Army. They are also known as Provos. The name applies to several different Republican paramilitary terrorist groups.

Ulster Volunteer Force: One of a number of militant Unionist organizations. Such groups wage terrorist campaigns against Catholics and militant Republican organizations.

Anglo-Irish Peace Accord: An agreement signed in 1985 that was the beginning of a long-term attempt to stop terrorist violence in Northern Ireland by devising a system of political autonomy and by protecting the rights of all citizens. Extremist Republicans rejected the accord because it did not unite Northern Ireland and the South. Unionists rejected it because it compromised with moderate Republicans.

Tony Blair: (1953–) The Labour Party prime minister of the United Kingdom from 1994 to 2007.

Belfast Agreement: Also known as the Good Friday Agreement, an agreement signed in April 1998 that revamped criminal justice services, established shared government in Northern Ireland, called for the early release of prisoners involved in paramilitary organizations, and created a Commission on Human Rights and Equity. Its provisions led to the decommissioning of paramilitary organizations.

Independent Monitoring Commission (IMC): A commission created in 2004 to investigate paramilitary actions and alleged governmental abuses during the Irish peace process.

Police Service of Northern Ireland (PSNI): The police force created in November 2001 to replace the Royal Ulster Constabulary.

War of the Spanish Succession (1702–1714): The first global war exported from Europe pitting the French and Austrians against each other for familial control of the Spanish throne. Although it involved myriad political factors, it set the stage for the evolution of modern Spain. There are several dates given for the end of the war due to the many peace treaties that ended military operations in Europe and around the world.

Spanish Civil War (1936–1939): A war that pitted pro-Communist Republicans against pro-Fascist Nationalists. The war ended with a Nationalist victory and a fascist dictatorship under Franco.

Francisco Franco: (1892– 1975) Leader of the nationalistic forces during the Spanish Civil War and the fascist dictator of Spain from 1939 to 1975.

Tamils: An ethnic minority in southern India and Sri Lanka. The Tamils in Sri Lanka are primarily Hindu, and the Sinhalese majority, mostly Buddhist. Ethnicity, however, not religion, defines most of the conflict between the two groups.

Velupillai Pirapaharan (1954–): Founder and current leader of the LTTE. Pirapaharan's terrorists have conducted more successful suicide bombings than any other terrorist group in the world.

Rajiv Gandhi (1944– 1991): Prime minister of India from 1984 until 1991, when he was assassinated by an LTTE suicide bomber.

Ranasinghe Premadasa (1924–1993): President of Sri Lanka from 1989 until 1993, when he was killed by an LTTE suicide bomber.

Colombo: The traditional capital of Sri Lanka and the country's largest city with a population of 5,500,500. The Sri Lankan government moved the capital to Sri Jayawardenapura Kotte five miles away in 1982. Colombo remains the economic center of Sri Lanka.

Chapter Outline

I.   **Ethnic and Nationalist Separation Movements**
      OBJ 1: Explain the nature and characteristics of nationalistic and ethnic separatist terrorism

      OBJ 2: Describe the emergence of the modern IRA and terrorism in Northern Ireland
      OBJ 4: Summarize the nature of the Basque culture and its separateness from Spain
      OBJ 9: Describe the rise of the LTTE and the role of the Tamil Diaspora

      A. While separatist movements have shaped modern terrorism, the focus on international terrorism has diverted attention from these movements.
        1. Separatist movements are asymmetrical, pitting small groups of separatists against larger government forces.
      B. Unlike religious terrorists, separatists usually have a clear cut achievable goal.
      C. Ethnic terrorists are usually more nationalistic than their religious counterparts. Ethnic terrorists try to forge national identity.
      D. Terrorism polarizes other ethnic groups, and forces them to either ally with terrorists or oppose.
      E. Within the last decade jihadist networks have come to play a significant role in European terrorism.
        1. North African groups operate in Spain and Italy.
        2. Middle Eastern networks are active in Germany, Belgium, the Netherlands, France, and the United Kingdom.
      F. Violence serves to undermine moderates who seek peaceful solutions, yet peaceful negotiated settlements have proved to be the most effective method for ending ethnic and nationalistic terrorism.

II. **Modern Terrorism in Northern Ireland**
OBJ 1: Explain the nature and characteristics of nationalistic and ethnic separatist terrorism
OBJ 2: Describe the emergence of the modern IRA and terrorism in Northern Ireland

A. In 1927, de Valera was elected as prime minister.
   1. The split in the IRA
      a. By the 1930s, some members of the IRA wanted to follow the lead of their political party, Sinn Féin.
      b. Another group of IRA members rejected this philosophy; they believed the purpose of the IRA was to fight for republicanism.
      c. The provisional wing of the IRA was formed in the 1930s.
   2. A Catholic civil rights campaign engulfed Northern Ireland in 1969, as the government in Northern Ireland systematically reduced the civil rights of Catholics living in the North.
   3. The IRA and the Modern "Troubles"
      a. The political and economic conditions in Northern Ireland provided the rationale for a major civil rights movement among the Catholics.
      b. The civil rights movement was supported by both Protestants and Catholics, but the actions of the Northern Ireland government began to polarize the issue.
      c. The government in Northern Ireland reacted with a heavy hand against the civil rights workers and demonstrators.
      d. Catholics were not allowed to demonstrate for better housing and education; if they attempted to do so, they were attacked by the RUC and its reserve force, known as B-Specials.
      e. In the summer of 1969, civil rights demonstrators planned a long, peaceful march from Londonderry to Belfast, but they were gassed and beaten by the RUC and B-Specials.
      f. During the Protestant Apprentice Boys parade, Protestants began taunting Catholics, and violence broke out. Three days later, Britain sent the British army in as a peacekeeping force.
   4. The Army and Overreactions
      a. According to most analysts and observers, the early policies and tactics of the British army played an important role in the rebirth of the IRA.
      b. The British army should have become a peaceful, neutral force, but it mistakenly allied itself with one of the extremist positions in the conflict.
      c. The Republicans believed the British army would protect them from the Unionists and the police.
      d. Feeling oppressed by all sides, Catholics and Republicans looked for help; they partly found it in the form of the new IRA, who sought to

rid the British soldiers from Irish soil, brushing aside internal political differences.

    f. Each time the British army overreacted, as it tended to do when faced with civil disobedience, the Republican cause was strengthened.

    g. Violence in Northern Ireland is a group process; socially constructed meanings evolved in three ways:

       i. Small-group interpretation within the IRA.

      ii. General interpretation of activities by the Catholic population

     iii. Meanings assigned from the interaction between the small and large groups.

5. Unionist Terrorism

    a. In addition to the Republican violence, Unionist organizations have a long history of terrorism.

6. Historically, Unionists have appeared in three forms:

    a. State repression

    b. Vengeance

    c. Revolutionary violence for political change.

III. Negotiating a Peace Settlement in Ireland

OBJ 1: Explain the nature and characteristics of nationalistic and ethnic separatist terrorism

OBJ 2: Describe the emergence of the modern IRA and terrorism in Northern Ireland.

OBJ 3: Outline the basis for negotiating peace in Northern Ireland

A. In 1985, the United Kingdom and the Republic of Ireland signed the *Anglo-Irish Peace Accord* regarding the governance of Northern Ireland, but the violence continued.

B. Negotiating with Terrorists

1. Unionist and Republican terrorists continued to fight the settlement and the government.

2. In 1990, the IRA signed a cease fire, the first in fifteen years.

3. In 1998, Britain and Ireland signed the *Belfast Agreement*, which called for independent human rights investigations, compensation for the victims of violence, and decommissioning of paramilitary groups.

4. The peace process resulted in two important new bureaucratic structures:

    a. *Independent Monitoring Commission*

    b. *Police Service of Northern Ireland*

5. Experiences in Ireland embody the nature of ethnic and nationalist separatist movements.

6. Terrorism in Northern Ireland no longer grabs attention as it did in the past; however, while the major campaigns are over and groups disbanded, the situation remains volatile.

VI. **The Basque Nation and Liberty**
   OBJ 1: Explain the nature and characteristics of nationalistic and ethnic separatist terrorism
   OBJ 4: Summarize the nature of the Basque culture and its separateness from Spain
   OBJ 5: Explain the impact of the Spanish Civil War on the Basque Region
   OBJ 6: Summarize the birth and evolution of the ETA
   OBJ 7: Explain the rise of GAL
   OBJ 8: Outline the Spanish government's approach to Basque separatism

   A. Euskadi ta Askatasuna (ETA or Basque Nation and Liberty).
   B. The ETA has waged a campaign of violence since 1959 that has killed more than 800 people.
   C. The ETA's goal is to establish an autonomous homeland in northern Spain and southern France.
   D. The Basque region of France and Spain has been a source for separatist terrorism for more than fifty years.
   E. The origins of the Basques, like the Irish, are shrouded in lore and legend, and these stories are engrained in ethnic narratives supporting separateness.
   F. The Basques have been a key factor in Spanish history, but they have had, and maintain, distinct literary, cultural, and linguistic separateness, producing a tradition centered in pride, ethnocentrism, and independence.
   G. Modern Spain emerged from the unification of several Hispanic kingdoms in 1479, and was solidified at the end of the *War of the Spanish Succession* (1702-1714).
   H. The new monarchy joined the independent kingdoms together in 1716, but it granted the Basque region semi-autonomy within the realm.
   I. Spain's search for national identity and a philosophy of government came to a head in the *Spanish Civil War* (1936–1939).
   J. Francisco Franco, the leader of fascist forces, forcibly campaigned against Basque national identity.
      1. Franco completely incorporated the Basque region into Spain, banning its language and expressions of national culture.
   K. After World War II, many Basques believed the Allies would assist their bid for independence, or greater autonomy, because Franco had supported Hitler, but the United States courted Franco's fascist government in return for American air bases in Spain.
   L. 20th Century Basque Nationalism

172

1. Composed of young, frustrated nationalists, who wanted regional autonomy, the ETA advocated neither violence nor terrorism.
2. Like most Basque nationalists, ETA sought to preserve their cultural and linguistic identity.
3. The ETA was primarily a working-class movement, as are many nationalistic terrorist groups; the overwhelming majority felt they represented all the members of their community.

M. The ETA Turns to Terrorism
1. Some members of the ETA decided that the time had come to actively strike Spain.
2. Their ideas were symbolic; the ETA's first "attacks" involved spraying walls with nationalistic graffiti.
3. In 1968, the group started a true terrorist campaign.
4. A more militant group, the ETA-M, broke away from the ETA in 1974; ETA-M described itself as the military wing of the ETA.
5. As avenues for regional, cultural, and political expressions opened, ETA violence slowly began to wane.

N. ETA Tactics and Spanish Death Squads
1. As Spanish repression increased in the 1970s, the ETA escalated its attacks.
   a. It began a Marighella-style campaign of assassination, robbery, and banditry.
2. Death squads, such as Warriors of Christ the King and the Basque Spanish Battalion, began to torture and murder suspected terrorists and their supporters.
   a. The death squads evolved into the Anti-Terrorist Liberation Groups (GAL).
3. Both the ETA and the government denounced the death squads, but violence continued.

O. Reframing the Conflict
1. By the late 1980s, the Spanish government had had enough; it tried to delegitimize the ETA by fostering democracy in the Basque region.
2. As Spanish authorities opened opportunities for democracy and national expression, the ETA transformed itself into a social movement.
3. As most Basques were interested in cultural identity, not class revolution, Spain found an effective weapon against the ETA by opening doors to political participation and cultural expression.
4. Even though violence had waned, sporadic ETA bombings began again in 2007.
5. The ETA is Europe's oldest active terrorist group, and its future is not clear.

VII.   **The Liberation Tigers of Tamil Eelam**

OBJ 1: **Explain the nature and characteristics of nationalistic and ethnic separatist terrorism**
OBJ 9: **Describe the rise of the LTTE and the role of the Tamil Diaspora**
OBJ 10: **Summarize the unique aspect of the LTTE suicide bombings**
OBJ 11: **Describe the end of the LTTE and the danger of possible reconstitution**

A. The Liberation Tigers of Tamil Eelam (LTTE, or Tamil Tigers) fought for an independent homeland for nearly 3 million *Tamils* in northern and eastern Sri Lanka.
B. Formed by *Velupillai Pirapaharan* in 1976, the Tamil Tigers used terrorism as both a prelude to guerrilla warfare, and a way to support uniformed guerrillas in the field.
C. The LTTE pioneered the use of secular suicide bombings beginning in 1987, and it created a special suicide squad known as the Black Tigers.
D. After killing the leader of the LTTE, the government declared victory in May 2009.
E. The Origins of Tamil Dissatisfaction
   1. Manoj Joshi traces the struggle's origins to the autonomy India gained at the end of World War II.
   2. In addition to religious differences, the Tamil minority in Sri Lanka was concerned about maintaining its ethnic identity among the Sinhalese majority.
   3. Claiming that Tamils dominated the Sri Lankan government, the Sinhalese majority forced the government to adopt a Sinhalese-only policy.
   4. Buoyed by religious differences and ethnic support, Tamil separatists could begin a guerrilla campaign by waging terrorist war, and their ethnic support base gave them the opportunity to do so.
F. Sri Lanka and the Tamil Tigers
   1. The LTTE eventually emerged as the leading revolutionary group, and launched Sri Lanka into a full-blown terrorist campaign.
   2. The Sinhalese majority reacted violently in 1983, in a series of anti-Tamil riots.
   3. Many Tamils fled to India, and the LTTE returned to terrorism.
   4. Reactions to the riots were a turning point for the LTTE. The group established contacts with the Popular Front for the Liberation of Palestine.
G. LTTE Tactics
   1. The LTTE incorporated a variety of tactics since 1984.
   2. In 1988 and 1992, they sought to control geographic areas, and they moved using standard guerrilla tactics, forming uniformed units.

3. Driven into the jungle, the Tamil Tigers practiced terrorism from jungle hideaways.
4. In 1990 the LTTE expanded its operations by converting a fishing fleet into a makeshift navy.
    a. Suicide boats and other seaborne operations threatened shipping between Sri Lanka and India.
5. From 1994 to 1995 the Tamil Tigers waged another bombing and assassination campaign.
6. Faced with open revolution, the Sri Lankan government signed a peace agreement in January 1995.

H. Fighting Renewed
1. In the spring of 1996, Sri Lankan security forces launched an all-out assault on Tamil strongholds on the northern portion of the island.
2. In the wake of new fighting, the LTTE followed the path of suicide bombing.
3. Although the guerrilla campaign subsided a bit in 1999, suicide bombings increased in 2000, and the LTTE became the secular masters of suicide attacks.
4. Faced with draining economic resources, the Tamil Tigers lost their striking power.
5. Sri Lankan security forces developed a new strategy for a final offensive; they created "no-fire zones", and moved into Tamil areas.
6. Fighting ended in May with the remaining Tamil Tigers surrendering.
7. The Tamil Diaspora has created a transitional government, and it serves as an incubator for radicalization.
8. A new version of the LTTE will be reconstituted in the Diaspora unless the Sri Lankan government takes steps to end the marginalization of the Tamil population.

Chapter Summary

- Both the United Kingdom and the Republic of Ireland began to support a serious peace process for Northern Ireland in 1995. Law enforcement policies had weakened the IRA, and the public was tired of violence. Prime Minister Blair also recognized that Sinn Fein was seeking rational political goals. This provided the basis for a long-term political settlement. Extremists in the IRA attempted to derail this process, but they were unsuccessful.

- Modern Spain was formed through the unification of several ethnic areas. The Basque region has existed for at least 3,000 years, and ethnic Basques have never totally embraced Spanish culture. Basques have their own national mythology, literary tradition, culture, and language.

- The Spanish Civil War brought Franco to power, and he violently sought to eradicate Basque culture. This caused a surge of nationalism, and resulted in the formation of a Basque shadow government in Paris in the 1950s.

- A group of working-class students formed the ETA in 1959 to express nationalism in the Basque homeland. It began with a campaign of advocacy, transforming into activism. This led to a splintering of the ETA and the formation of a terrorist group. It reached its zenith in 1980, but it remains Europe's oldest violent separatist group.

- Disgruntled Spanish police officers and government officials formed death squads to counter the ETA. These squads eventually merged into the GAL. The Spanish government began taking actions against the GAL in 1987.

- Sri Lanka gained its independence in 1948, giving the Sinhalese majority most of the political power in the country. As Tamils felt discrimination from the Sinhalese, they resorted to violence when peaceful methods failed to address their grievances.

- The LTTE was formed in 1976, obtaining arms and logistical support from the Tamil Diaspora. They developed several effective terrorist and guerrilla tactics and assassinated prominent political leaders. The secular Tamil Tigers mastered the art of suicide bombing, even creating a suicide unit.

- The LTTE was defeated when funds and supplies from the Diaspora were cut off. The Sri Lankan government still needs to negotiate an equitable political settlement with the Tamils lest the LTTE be reconstituted in the Diaspora.

DISCUSSION QUESTIONS

1. Discuss the issues surrounding *Home Rule* of Ireland. (OBJ 1, 2, and 3)

2. Do you believe that any British policies could have achieved harmony between the United Kingdom and Ireland? (OBJ 1, 2, and 3)

3. Compare the original ETA with the modern day ETA. Do you feel the current ceasefire offered by the ETA has genuine staying power? Why or why not? (OBJ 1, 4, 5, 6, and 7)

4. White indicates that the Tamil Diaspora has created a transitional government, and that it serves as an incubator for radicalization. In your view, what does he mean? Do you believe this to be a correct statement? Explain. (OBJ 1, 9, 10, and 11)

176

ASSIGNMENTS

1. Have students choose a topic from this chapter and write a study guide/handout to present and share with the class. For example, students may focus their study guide on describing the emergence of modern piracy. Allow time to discuss topics to eliminate duplication. (OBJ 1 – 11)

2. Have students conduct cases studies analysis on death squads from varying regions. (OBJ 7)

3. Have each student comb through http://www.mynewsreader.com/34287/ethnic+terrorism/ (or another website as approved by the instructor) for a current event, and select an article that relates to one or more of the chapter's core concepts. Have students provide a journalistic summary and a personal opinion/reaction to the article. Have students orally present the article to the class, field Q & As from their fellow students, and provide a copy of the original source article following the presentation. Optional: Have students complete peer assessments at the end of each presentation. (OBJ 1 - 11)

4. Have students conduct independent research on the Basque Culture. In small groups have them debate whether or not there should be a Basque homeland. (OBJ 1, 4, and 5)

5. As a review, play jeopardy using key terms and/or concepts from the chapter.

MEDIA TOOLS

1. *"Wikis"*
   7 Things you should know about Wikis. Retrieved from the Web Jun 29, 2012 at http://net.educause.edu/ir/library/pdf/ELI7004.pdf

   This document offers easy to understand instruction on the history, development, and potential uses of Wikis.

   Have students develop (or make additions to a previously created one) a *Webliography* (resource list) using a Blog or Wiki that provides a short description, and link to a scholarly resource pertaining to course concepts. For example, have students add two to three resources each, and ask them to add their assessment of at least one of their peers' contributions. If desired, allow time to discuss Blogs/Wikis. This activity can be reused throughout the course, by asking students to add/revise their contributions each week, bi-weekly, etc. (OBJ 1 – 11)

2. *"Irish Home Rule Mock Debate"*

    BBC. Irish home Rule: an imagined future. Retrieved from the Web Aug 20, 2012 at http://www.bbc.co.uk/history/british/victorians/home_rule_movement_01.shtml

    This information on Irish home rule, authored by Dr. James McConnel, offers an in-depth look at the salient issues surrounding the movement.

    Have the class comb through McConnel's coverage, and analyze the issues at play in the Irish home rule question. Divide class into two groups – one for the movement, one against. Have the groups debate the issue. (OBJ 1 – 3)

3. *"ETA Ceasefire PowerPoint presentation"*
    Council on Foreign Relations. Basque Fatherland and Liberty (ETA) (Spain, separatists, Euskadi ta Askatasuna). Retrieved from the Web Aug 20, 2012 at http://www.cfr.org/france/basque-fatherland-liberty-eta-spain-separatists-euskadi-ta-askatasuna/p9271

    The article provides an examination of terrorist violence in Spain with focus on the ETA.

    Have students read the article and discuss the current debate on ETA's "ceasefire". Ask the class to debate and work on a consensus as to whether or not the ceasefire is likely to have staying power. Have class synthesize their debate into a PowerPoint presentation. (OBJ 4 – 8)

4. *"Current Events Article Summary with Peer Assessment"*

    Use the Article Summary Template, which can be obtained on the instructor companion website, for this assignment. The template offers information on Internet research, outside resources, identification of credible sources, and detailed directions on completing an assessment of a news article. It also includes a peer evaluation tool.

    Have each student comb the Internet for terrorism related news and select an article that relates to one or more of the chapter's core concepts. Be sure selections are an article of interest from a credible source (*more on credibility can be found in the article summary template above*). Fill out an article summary template. The *template asks for generic info about the article, a journalistic summary, as well as a personal opinion/reaction to the article.* Have each student summarize the article and present it orally to the class and field Q & As from their fellow students. Have students complete peer assessments at the end of each presentation. Have students submit templates, original source article, and peer-reviews prior to the end of class. (OBJ 1-9)

Chapter 6—Long Term Separatist Terrorism

TEST BANK

TRUE/FALSE

1. The primary purpose of ethnic terrorists is to mobilize a community in effort to forge national identity.

    ANS: T   REF: p. 139   OBJ: 1

2. The current struggles in Ireland largely started in 1969 when riots broke out in Londonderry and Belfast after the annual Apprentice Boys parade.

    ANS: T   REF: p. 157   OBJ: 1 and 2

3. There is no difference between separatist violence, ideological terrorism, and religious terrorism

    ANS: T   REF: p. 139   OBJ: 1, 4, and 8

4. If calculated by the sheer number of attacks, separatists present more of a threat to Europe than any other form of terrorism

    ANS: T   REF: p. 139   OBJ: 1, 4, and 8

5. Ethnic terrorists are usually more nationalistic than their religious counterparts.

    ANS: T   REF: p. 139   OBJ: 1, 4, and 6

6. Most Basques were interested in cultural identity, not class revolution.

    ANS: T   REF: p. 150   OBJ: 4, 5, and 8

7. The ETA has ceased all activity throughout Europe.

    ANS: F   REF: p. 151   OBJ: 6

8. The Spanish Civil War pitted pro-communist Nationalists against pro-fascist Republicans.

    ANS: F   REF: p. 147   OBJ: 5

9. Modern Spain emerged from the unification of several Hispanic kingdoms in the late 1700s.

    ANS: F   REF: p. 146   OBJ: 4, 5, and 8

10. The ETA death squads evolved into the Anti-Terrorist Liberation Groups (GAL).

ANS: T   REF: p. 149   OBJ: 6 and 7

11. The Euskadi Ta Askatasuna (ETA), an organization that waged a campaign of terrorism against Spain for nearly a half century, released a declaration in October 2011 declaring that it was ending its campaign of violence.

ANS: T   REF: p. 137   OBJ: 4, 5, 6, 7 and 9

12. The Euskadi Ta Askatasuna (ETA) is Europe's longest surviving ethnic conflict.

ANS: T   REF: p. 139   OBJ: 1, 4, and 6

13. There are more Basques living outside Spain than within the country.

ANS: T   REF: p. 146   OBJ: 4 and 5

14. ETA terrorism was at its peak in the 1960s.

ANS: F   REF: p. 150   OBJ: 6

15. The Sri Lankan conflict involved dissention between Hindus and Muslims.

ANS: F   REF: p. 152   OBJ: 9

MULTIPLE CHOICE

1. Who granted Sri Lanka independence in 1948?
    a. British
    b. France
    c. Spain
    d. Russia

ANS: a   REF: p. 152   OBJ: 9

2. Ethnic terrorists try to forge a _____ identity.
    a. National
    b. Religious
    c. International
    d. Social

ANS: a   REF: p. 139   OBJ: 1, 4, and 9

3. The 1916 Easter Rising is associated with what group?
    a. IRA
    b. ETA
    c. LTTE
    d. GAL

ANS: a   REF: p. 139   OBJ: 2

4. The Spanish Civil War occurred in what decade?
   a. 1930s
   b. 1850s
   c. 1950s
   d. 1970s

ANS: a   REF: p. 147   OBJ: 4 and 5

5. According to the text, the ETA's first "attacks" involved _____.
   a. Grafitti
   b. Large non-violent demonstrations
   c. Cyber-terrorism
   d. Simple assaults

ANS: a   REF: p. 149   OBJ: 6

6. On August 15, 1969 fighting in Ireland was focused in which two cities?
   a. Belfast and Londonderry
   b. Belfast and Limerick
   c. Londonderry and Dublin
   d. Belfast and Dublin

ANS: d   REF: p. 142   OBJ: 2 and 3

7. The political party of the IRA was known as _____.
   a. The Provisionals
   b. Sinn Fein
   c. The Apprentice Boys
   d. The Unionists

ANS: b   REF: p. 145   OBJ: 2 and 3

8. As Spanish authorities opened opportunities for democracy and national expression, the ETA transformed itself into a(n) _____ movement.
   a. Social
   b. Religious
   c. Political
   d. Military

ANS: a   REF: p. 150   OBJ: 4 and 6

9. After_____, many Basques believed the Allies would assist their bid for independence
   a. World War I
   b. The Spanish Civil War
   c. World War II
   d. The Spanish War of Succession

ANS: c   REF: p. 147   OBJ: 1, 5, AND 8

10. The ETA was primarily a(n) _____ movement.
   a. Ethnic
   b. Lower-class
   c. Political
   d. Working-class

ANS: d   REF: p. 147   OBJ: 1, 4, and 5

11. Most ETA members engaged in terrorism for only about ___ year(s). After this, they returned
    to their full-time occupations.
   a. Four
   b. Three
   c. One
   d. Six

ANS: b   REF: p. 149   OBJ: 6

12. Irish Republicans, primarily _____, controlled the Southern region of the country.
   a. Catholic
   b. Protestant
   c. Jewish
   d. Muslim

ANS: a   REF: p. 192   OBJ: 2 and 3

13. The reserve force of the royal Ulster constabulary (RUC) was known as _____.
   a. The Sein Fenn
   b. B-specials
   c. The Provisionals
   d. The Irish Brotherhood

ANS: b   REF: p. 142   OBJ: 2 and 3

14. The December 1990 ceasefire agreement in Ireland, was primarily due to negotiations
    between the government and which group?
   a. The Provisionals
   b. B-specials
   c. Sinn Fein
   d. IRB

ANS: c   REF: p. 145   OBJ: 3

15. Over Easter in _____, Patrick Pearse and James Connolly led a revolt in Dublin.
   a. 1921
   b. 1816
   c. 1886
   d. 1916

ANS: d   REF: p. 139   OBJ: 2 and 3

182

16. Which organization is viewed as to have set the stage for modern separatist terrorism?
    a. ETA
    b. IRA
    c. LTTE
    d. PKK

ANS: b   REF: p. 139   OBJ: 1 and 2

17. _____ refers to the political party of republicanism.
    a. Sinn Féin
    b. Conservatives
    c. Capitalists
    d. Parliamentary

ANS: a   REF: p. 140   OBJ: 2 and 3

18. The split in the IRA ranks, one side seeking peaceful political idealism and the other fighting for independence, began to occur in which decade?
    a. 1970s
    b. 1910s
    c. 1930s
    d. 1950s

ANS: c   REF: p. 140   OBJ: 2 and 3

19. The British granted Sri Lanka independence in _____.
    a. 1949
    b. 1955
    c. 1948
    d. 1946

ANS: c   REF: p. 152   OBJ: 9

20. Disgruntled Spanish police officers and government officials comprised the death squads known as _____.
    a. Euskadi Ta Askatasuna (ETA)
    b. Anti-Terrorist Liberation Groups (GAL)
    c. The Liberation Tigers of Tamil Eelam (LTTE)
    d. Irish Republican Army (IRA)

ANS: b   REF: p. 157   OBJ: 7

21. _____ was the Prime Minister of India from 1984 until 1991, when he was assassinated by an LTTE suicide bomber.
    a. Rajiv Gandhi
    b. Manoj Joshi
    c. Velupillai Pirapaharan
    d. Ranasinghe Premadasa

ANS: a   REF: p. 151   OBJ: 9 and 11

22. When was the Provisional IRA formed?
    a. The 1960s
    b. The 1890s
    c. The 1980s
    d. The 1930s

ANS: d   REF: p. 140   OBJ: 2

23. The failure of the _____ in Northern Ireland can be directly linked to modern Irish terrorism and the rebirth of the IRA.
    a. Civil rights movement
    b. Women's movement
    c. Protestant Reformation
    d. British rule

ANS: a   REF: p. 140   OBJ: 2 and 3

24. The ETA, in its return to terrorism in 1999, targeted which of Spain's major industries?
    a. Tourism
    b. Energy
    c. Shipping
    d. Telecommunications

ANS: a   REF: p. 150   OBJ: 6

25. According to most analysts and observers, the early policies and tactics of the _____ played an important role in the rebirth of the IRA.
    a. The Irish Army
    b. The British police
    c. The British army
    d. The Irish police

ANS: c   REF: p. 142   OBJ: 2 and 3

26. The Black and Tan War is associated with which organization?
    a. The IRA
    b. The LTTE
    c. The PKK
    d. The ETA

ANS: a   REF: p. 139   OBJ: 1, 2 and 3

27. The Liberation tigers of Tamil Elam (LTTE) formed in what country?
    a. Cypress
    b. Greece
    c. Sri Lanka
    d. Ireland

ANS: c   REF: p. 140   OBJ: 1, 9, and 11

28. Though fear exists about potential resurgence, the LTTE was defeated in what year?
    a. 2009
    b. 1991
    c. 2001
    d. 1945

ANS: a   REF: p. 140   OBJ: 1, 9, and 11

29. The Provisionals were associated with which of the following?
    a. The IRA
    b. The LTTE
    c. The PKK
    d. The ETA

ANS: a   REF: p. 142   OBJ: 1, 2, and 3

30. The Royal Ulster Constabulary was replaced by what organization?
    a. The Irish Army
    b. The Police Service of Northern Ireland
    c. Sinn Fein
    d. The Provisionals

ANS: c   REF: p. 145   OBJ: 2 and 3

31. In 1972 British paratroopers opened fire on Catholic protesters in Londonderry – a day that
    has come to be known as _____.
    a. Black September
    b. Bloody Sunday
    c. Red October
    d. Orange and Green Day

ANS: b   REF: p. 145   OBJ: 1, 2, and 3

32. The Basque region incorporates land regions in both Spain and _____.
    a. Portugal
    b. Monaco
    c. France
    d. Algeria

ANS: c   REF: p. 146   OBJ: 1, 4, and 5

33. According to most analysts and observers, the early policies and tactics of the _____ played
    an important role in the rebirth of the IRA.
    a. The Irish Army
    b. The British police
    c. The British army
    d. The Irish police

ANS: c   REF: p. 42   OBJ: 2 and 3

34. The IRA fought from 1939-1944 and again from 1956-1962 in attempt to bring _____ under Irish control.
    a. Kilkenny
    b. Galway
    c. Limerick
    d. Ulster

ANS: d   REF: p. 157   OBJ: 1, 2, and 3

35. In what city was the 1950s Basque shadow government formed in response to the Spanish government repression of Basque culture?
    a. Lisbon
    b. London
    c. Paris
    d. Marseilles

ANS: c   REF: p. 157   OBJ: 5

36. The LTTE garnered the majority of its arms and logistical support from _____.
    a. Tamil diaspora
    b. The Taliban
    c. Sinahelese aristocrats
    d. The Irish police

ANS: c   REF: p. 157   OBJ: 1, 9, and 11

37. Following the Spanish Civil War (1936- 1939), France was ruled by fascist dictator,
_____.
    a. Fulgencio Batista
    b. Antonio Salazar
    c. Francisco Franco
    d. Rajiv Gandhi

ANS: c   REF: p. 147   OBJ: 5 and 8

38. The LTTE were pioneers in the secular use of _____bombings.
    a. Improvised explosive device (IED)
    b. Chemical
    c. Thermobaric
    d. Suicide

ANS: c   REF: p. 140   OBJ: 10

39. From 1922 to 1969, the government systematically reduced the civil rights of Catholics living in _____ Ireland.
    a. Northern
    b. Southern
    c. Eastern
    d. Western

ANS: a   REF: p. 141   OBJ: 1, 2, and 3

40. The Independent Monitoring commission (IMC) investigates claims of both terrorist and governmental abuses in what region?
    a. Spain
    b. Sri Lanka
    c. Ireland
    d. France

ANS: c   REF: p. 145   OBJ: 3

Case 6.0

The focus on international terrorism has diverted attention from some of the world's separatist movements; yet, these struggles have shaped modern terrorism. RAND shows that ethnic terrorism differs from terrorism carried out in the name of ideology, religion, or economic gain. Ethnic terrorists are usually more nationalistic than their religious counterparts. Ethnic terrorists try to forge national identity. Their primary purpose is to mobilize a community, and they do so by appealing to the nationalistic background of a particular ethnic group.

41. Which of the following would be most appropriately classed as ethnic terrorists?
    a. Al Qaeda
    b. Euskadi Ta Askatasuna (ETA)
    c. Hezzbollah
    d. The Taliban

ANS: b   REF: p. 138   OBJ: 1 and 6

42. Which of the following would be most appropriately classed as ethnic terrorists?
    a. Al Qaeda
    b. Hamas
    c. Irish Republican Army (IRA)
    d. Islamic Jihad Union

ANS: a   REF: p. 138   OBJ: 1 and 2

43. Which of the following would be most appropriately classed as ethnic terrorists?
    a. Muslim Brotherhood
    b. Palestine Liberation Front
    c. Shining Path
    d. The Liberation Tigers of Tamil Eelam (LTTE)

ANS: d   REF: p. 138   OBJ: 1 and 9

44. Which of the following would be most appropriately classed as ethnic terrorists?
    a. Red Hand Commando
    b. Hamas
    c. Hezzbollah
    d. Kurdistan Workers Party (PKK)

ANS: d   REF: p. 138   OBJ: 1

45. Which of the following would NOT be most appropriately classed as ethnic terrorists?
    a. Al Qaeda
    b. Anti-Terrorist Liberation Groups (GAL)
    c. The Liberation Tigers of Tamil Eelam (LTTE)
    d. Irish Republican Army (IRA)

ANS: a   REF: p. 138   OBJ: 1, 2, 6, 7, and 9

Case 6.1

The first decade of the twenty-first century brought seemingly peaceful solutions to three violent separatist movements: the renewed troubles in Ireland resulting from civil disturbances in 1969, the ETA's campaign for Basque autonomy, and a long campaign of savage guerilla warfare and terrorism among two ethnic groups on the island nation of Sri Lanka. All of the conflicts appeared to end.

46. The Irish, Basque, and Sri Lankan conflicts all have a central focus that is primarily
    _____ in nature.
    a. Ethnic
    b. Economic
    c. Religious
    d. Monetary

ANS: a   REF: p. 139   OBJ: 1, 2, 3, 4, 5, 6, 7, 8, and 11

47. The apparent end to the three noted violent separatist movements were achieved primarily in the form of a _____ solution.

    a. Military
    b. Educational
    c. Economic
    d. Political

ANS: d   REF: p. 139   OBJ: 1, 2, 3, 4, 5, 6, 7, 8, and 11

Case 6.2

Separatist violence differs from ideological and religious terrorism. Violence plays a special role in ethnic terrorism. Whereas political terrorists use violence in a symbolic manner and religious extremists use it to make a theological statement, violence is the raison d'être of ethnic terrorism. It keeps an idea alive. Some data even suggest that separatist terrorism is the most violent form of terrorism in the modern world (Masters, 2008). As long as a bomb goes off or a police officer is murdered, the identity and existence of ethnic differences cannot be denied. Violence sustains the conflict, even when political objectives are far out of reach. The fear created by violence serves ethnic interests. Violence also serves to undermine moderates who seek peaceful solutions; yet, peaceful negotiated settlements have proved to be the most effective method for ending ethnic and nationalistic terrorism.

48. The terrorist group LTTE was one of the first to begin using suicide bombers. Their main
purpose in such attacks was to create _____.
   a. Fear
   b. Sympathy
   c. Negotiations with the government
   d. Loyalty within the organization

ANS: a   REF: p. 140   OBJ: 1, 3, and 5

49. Which of the following would be the least likely target of an ethnic terrorist group?
   a. Foreign national
   b. Sympathetic student
   c. Politician
   d. Police officer

ANS: b   REF: p. 139   OBJ: 1

50. Which of the following would be the least desirable target of an ethnic terrorist group?
   a. Government office
   b. Residences of supporters
   c. School
   d. Charitable organization

ANS: a   REF: p. 139   OBJ: 1

COMPLETION

1. The _____ are the dominant ethnic group in Sri Lanka.

ANS: Sinhalese   REF: p.151   OBJ: 9 and 11

2. The modern troubles in Ireland started in 1969, when riots broke out in Londonderry and
Belfast after the _____ parade.

ANS: Apprentice Boys   REF: p.157   OBJ: 2 and 3

3. _____ refers to the political party of Republicans with historical connections to
extremism and violence.

ANS: Sinn Fein   REF: p.140   OBJ: 2 and 3

4. British Prime Minister _____ is credited with the 1998 signing of the Belfast
Agreement, following his negotiations with Sinn Fein.

ANS: Tony Blair   REF: p.157   OBJ: 3

5. _____ wanted a homeland completely independent of Spain.

ANS: Basque separatists   REF: p.148   OBJ: 4 and 5

189

6. In the late 1990s, ETA terrorists began targeting Spain's number-one industry, _____.

ANS: tourism   REF: p.146   OBJ: 6 and 8

7. The Basque region of _____ and Spain has been a source for separatist terrorism for more than fifty years.

ANS: France   REF: p.146   OBJ: 4

8. Ranasinghe Premadasa was the President of _____ from 1989 until 1993 when he was killed by an LTTE suicide bomber.

ANS: Sri Lanka   REF: p.151   OBJ: 9

9. The _____ emerged as the leading revolutionary group in Sri Lanka.

ANS: LTTE   REF: p.153   OBJ: 9, 10, and 11

10. The suicide squad of the LTTE was known as the _____.

ANS: Black Tigers   REF: p.151   OBJ: 9 and 10

11. The most common tactic in asymmetrical warfare is _____.

ANS: terrorism   REF: p. 138   OBJ: 1

12. According to a recent study by the RAND Corporation, _____ is the most effective method for ending a terrorist campaign,

ANS: Political accommodation   REF: p. 138   OBJ: 3

13. The ____ was formed in 1976, obtaining arms and logistical support from the Tamil Diaspora.

ANS: LTTE   REF: p. 157   OBJ: 9 and 11

14. Sri Lanka gained its independence in 1948, giving the _____ majority most of the political power in the country.

ANS: Sinhalese   REF: p. 157   OBJ: 9 and 11

15. A group of _____ formed the ETA in 1959 to express nationalism in the Basque homeland.

ANS: working-class students   REF: p. 157   OBJ: 6

16. Unionist terror in Ireland came in three forms: (1) repression, (2) vengeance, and (3) ____

ANS: revolutionary violence   REF: p. 157   OBJ: 1 and 2

190

17. The Basque region has existed for at least _____ thousand years.

ANS: three   REF: p. 157   OBJ: 4, 5, and 6

18. The Black Tigers, the suicide wing of the LTTE, were known for carrying _____ around their necks when they attack.

ANS: cyanide capsules   REF: p. 152   OBJ: 10

19. _____ is Sri Lanka's traditional and economic capital.

ANS: Colombo   REF: p. 153   OBJ: 3 and 11

20. During ETA's most violent year, _____ its members killed ninety-two people.

ANS: 1980   REF: p. 149   OBJ: 6

ESSAY

1. Summarize factors that led to the ultimate demise of the LTTE.

ANS:
- In December 2001, the LTTE agreed to a ceasefire with the government of Sri Lanka. Although the Tigers still threatened violence, their resources may have been depleting.
- The Council on Foreign Relations (Zissis, 2006) believes that the international community's efforts to thwart terrorism after September 11 were responsible for this situation.
- Arms shipments were virtually eliminated, and expatriate Tamil communities in Australia, Canada, and the United States were forbidden to gather and ship resources to Sri Lanka.
- Draining economic resources accomplished what Sri Lankan security forces could not do. The Tamil Tigers lost their striking power.
- Facing a weakened LTTE, Sri Lankan security forces developed a new strategy for a final offensive. They created "no-fire zones" and moved into Tamil areas. People in the area could stay and fight; stay and hope that they would not be killed or injured; flee, risking injury or death; or move into the no-fire zone.
- Police and military forces established order in the no-fire zones, interrogating and arresting suspects at will.
- The strategy worked. Every person who remained in the area was considered to be an enemy, and the army unleashed a conventional offensive.
- The LTTE had remained the aggressor through most of the campaign, and it had forced security forces onto the defensive.
- The role was now reversed, and the Tamil Tigers fought on the military's terms. Unable to use guerrilla or terrorist tactics, the Tamil Tigers fought a defensive battle against conventional assaults.
- With limited communications and no ability to resupply or use the airport, the LTTE lost ground in every encounter. Many of the commanders began blowing themselves up rather than surrender. Pirapaharan died in this manner. Fighting ended in May, with the remaining Tamil Tigers surrendering (Chamberlain and Tran, 2009).

REF: p. 155   OBJ: 1, 9, 10, and 11

2. Explain J. Bowyer Bell's belief that the reason for IRA impotence can be found in the second generation.

ANS:
- Wanting to follow in the footsteps of their forebears, the Provisionals began to wage a campaign against the RUC in Northern Ireland in the late 1950s.
- They established support bases in the republic and slipped across the border for terrorist activities.
- Although the Provisionals initially enjoyed support among Republican enclaves in the North, most Irish people, Unionists and Republicans alike, were appalled by IRA violence.
- Even the Official IRA —the segment embracing a socialist ideology—criticized the military attacks of the Provisionals.
- Faced with a lack of public support, the Provisional IRA called off its offensive in the North.
- By 1962 almost all of its activities had ceased.
- Some Provisionals joined the civil rights movement; others rejoined former colleagues in the Official wing.
- Most members, however, remained in a secret infrastructure and hoping events would restore their ranks and prestige.

REF: p. 140   OBJ: 1, 2, and 3

3. Explain how the early policies and tactics of the British army played an important role in the rebirth of the IRA.

ANS:
- According to Bell, the British army came to Ulster with little or no appreciation of the historical circumstances behind the conflict.
- When the army arrived its commanders believed they were in the midst of a colonial war, they evaluated the situation and concluded there were two "tribes."
- One tribe flew the Irish tricolor and spoke with deep-seated hatred of the British; the other flew the Union Jack and claimed to be ultrapatriotic subjects of the British Empire.
- Far from being a conflict to preserve British influence in a colony, the struggle in Northern Ireland was a fight between two groups of Irish citizens, neither side was British.
- The British army mistakenly allied itself with one of the extremist positions in the conflict.
- The Unionists greeted the army with open arms.
- Historically, the British army had rallied to the Unionist cause; however, the Republicans also welcomed the British army.
- In Republican eyes, it was a peacekeeping force. The Republicans believed the British army would protect them from the Unionists and the police.
- As the British army made its presence felt in Ulster, Republicans and Catholics were subjected to the increasing oppression of British army measures.

192

- Catholic neighborhoods were surrounded and gassed by military forces searching for subversives, and the soldiers began working as a direct extension of the RUC.
- Londonderry and Belfast were military targets, and rebels fighting against the government were to be subdued.
- As confrontations became more deadly, Republican support for the British army vanished.
- Feeling oppressed by all sides, Catholics and Republicans found help in the form of the IRA.
- The IRA pushed its internal squabbles aside, and the Officials and Provisionals focused on their new common enemy, the British army.
- The new IRA policy emphasized the elimination of British soldiers from Irish soil and brushed aside internal political differences.
- The British army found itself in the middle of a conflict.
- Alienated nationalists offered support for the growing ranks of the IRA.
- Each time the British army overreacted the Republican cause was strengthened.
- IRA ranks grew from a few dozen to nearly 2,000, and members adopted an elaborate justification of violence.
- When crackdowns by British army patrols and incidents of alleged torture by intelligence services increased the ranks of the IRA, Unionist paramilitary organizations grew in response.
- The British army also began taking action against Unionist organizations and then truly found itself in the midst of a terrorist conflict.
- In 1972 the British government issued a report on the violence in Northern Ireland concluding that tensions inside the community were so great, once they had been unleashed, that little could be done to alleviate them.
- The policies of the police and the British army had done much to set those hostile forces in motion.

REF: p. 142   OBJ: 1, 2, and 3

4.   Explain how Robert White explains violence in Northern Ireland as a group process.

ANS:
- Socially constructed meanings evolved in three ways: (1) small-group interpretation within the IRA, (2) general interpretation of activities by the Catholic population, and (3) meanings assigned from the interaction between the small and large groups.
- IRA operatives were recruited by different patterns, and each recruiting style affected tactics, such as bombings, shootings, or hunger strikes.
- When the people of Northern Ireland, at least the Catholic minority, felt repressed by the British, it legitimized IRA violence.
- The IRA could not move without popular support.
- Additionally, popular support came when peaceful actions appeared to produce no results.
- Finally, as the IRA in the republic and in Ulster grew closer together, they also identified with the Republicans of Ulster.
- The British were, and remain, outsiders to Republicans.

REF: p. 143   OBJ: 1, 2, and 3

5.   Describe the new peace seeking strategies employed by the government between the period of the Anglo-Irish Peace Accord through tot eh development of the IMC and the PSIN.

ANS:
- In 1985, the United Kingdom and the Republic of Ireland signed a peace accord regarding the governance of Northern Ireland, but the violence continued. The agreement was the beginning of a long-term attempt to stop terrorist violence in Northern Ireland by devising a system of political autonomy and by protecting the rights of all citizens.
- Extremist Republicans rejected the accord because it did not unite Northern Ireland and the South. Unionists rejected it because it compromised with moderate Republicans.
- While the Anglo-Irish Peace Accord sought to bring an end to terrorism by establishing a joint Irish-British system of government for the troubled area, many Protestant groups felt betrayed and the Republicans continued to view Britain as a colonial power benefiting from the occupation of Northern Ireland (Dunn and Morgan, 1995).
- Republican and Unionist narratives had lasted hundreds of years, and their mystical hold on both sets of extremists was hard to break.
- This discord forced the British government to take a radical step.
- Although the United Kingdom and the Republic of Ireland were in direct negotiations and had agreed to share power, Unionist and Republican terrorists continued to fight the settlement and the government.
- In 1990, the British decided to take another step. Realizing that they had no economic or political interest in controlling Northern Ireland, British intelligence contacted Sinn Fein and began negotiations with the political leadership of the IRA.
- Something remarkable happened. The IRA signed a ceasefire, the first in 15 years, in December 1990.
- British intelligence units and the IRA kept talking after the ceasefire, and in 1992 Sinn Fein produced a paper calling for peace in Northern Ireland and recognizing that both Unionists and Republicans had to be included in any future agreement.
- It seemed as if peace would finally develop, but negotiations began to break down.
- Terrorists took up their arms again, but a new British prime minister, Tony Blair, was determined to end the violence. He formally invited Sinn Fein to the negotiating table. Despite emphatic rhetorical statements to the contrary, counterterrorists and terrorists sat down together.
- On Good Friday 1998, Britain and Ireland signed the Belfast Agreement, which called for independent human rights investigations, compensation for the victims of violence, and decommissioning of paramilitary groups (Northern Ireland Office, 2007).
- More radical Republicans and Unionists tried to break away. These groups renewed a campaign of violence in 1998, hoping to destroy the Anglo-Irish peace initiatives (Bell, 1998); however, the peace talks gained momentum, and radicals on both sides found that they were losing public support. I
- People who were jailed for terrorism and violent political activity seemed to be more concerned with reintegrating into their families and communities after their incarceration than with carrying on the struggle (Monaghan, 2004; Hughes and Donnelly, 2004; Carmichael and Knox, 2004).

194

- The few remaining violent radicals resorted to criminal activities, and the leadership of the major terrorist groups began suppressing violent activities within their ranks (McGinn, 2006).
- The peace process resulted in two important new bureaucratic structures, the Independent Monitoring Commission (IMC) and the Police Service of Northern Ireland (PSIN).
- The IMC investigated claims of both terrorist and governmental abuses, and its actions have resulted in the arrests of Republican and Loyalist terrorists, as well as members of the security forces who acted beyond the law (Henderson, 2006).
- In 2005, the IRA officially disbanded and handed over its weapons. Its leader disavowed terrorism and urged his followers to cooperate with the police (BBC News, 2005a).
- The government followed suit by creating the PSNI to replace the RUC.

REF: p. 145   OBJ: 3

6.   Outline the Basque conflict: include the issue, group, campaign, and the situation.

ANS:
- The Issue.
- Basque separatists want a homeland completely independent of Spain.
- The nationalists control a semiautonomous Basque parliament, but they are divided in their desire for autonomy.
- A substantial minority of Basques want to remain united with Spain.
- The Group.
- Although the Basque region has never been independent, it has its own language and culture.
- Francisco Franco, the Spanish dictator, tried to crush Basque culture and force the Basques to become Spanish.
- The Campaign.
- The Basque Nation and Liberty (ETA) began a campaign against Spain in 1959.
- The group was responsible for assassinating Franco's probable successor and many other officials.
- They agreed to a cease-fire in 1998 but broke the treaty a year later.
- The Spanish government has given the Basques regional governing authority, and Basques use their own language and run their own schools.
- The majority of Spaniards believe the ETA to be the most important issue in Spain, and both Basques and Spaniards are tired of ETA violence.
- Spain also has a strong jihadist movement, but there is no connection between the jihadists and the ETA.
- The Situation.
- The ETA agreed to a second cease fire but resumed violence after 2006 ceasefire.
- Spanish and French police forces increased their intelligence operations resulting in a number of arrests in late 2009 and early 2010.
- By most estimates, the ETA had gone into decline.

REF: p. 146   OBJ: 1, 4, 5, 6, 7, and 8

195

7. Discuss the variety of tactics employed by the LTTE since 1984.

ANS:
- Their ability to operate is directly correlated to the amount of popular support they enjoy during any particular period.
- In 1988 and 1992 they sought to control geographic areas, and they moved using standard guerrilla tactics, forming uniformed units including an ad hoc navy.
- In times of weakness, they relied on bank robberies, bombings, and murder.
- In the weakest times, they have employed suicide bombers – they used suicide attacks in 1995 on land and at sea.
- When not attacking India, the LTTE launched operations in Sri Lanka.
- Although they had once struggled to be recognized as the leaders of the independence movement, the Tigers now ruthlessly wiped out their opponents and terrorized their own ethnic group into providing support.
- Driven into the jungle, the Tamil Tigers practiced terrorism from jungle hideaways.
- They increased contact with Tamil bases in India, using India for logistical support.
- Politically adept, the LTTE asked for a cease-fire in 1989, giving India a chance to withdraw from the joint security force.
- No sooner had the Indians left than the LTTE renewed its attack on the Sri Lankans.
- In 1990 the LTTE expanded its operations by converting a fishing fleet into a makeshift navy.
- Suicide boats and other seaborne operations threatened shipping between Sri Lanka and India.
- The LTTE fought small-scale sea battles with the Indians.
- They assassinated Prime Minister Gandhi in 1991.
- From 1994 to 1995 the Tamil Tigers waged another bombing and assassination campaign, and they did what no other terrorist group has been able to do.
- Supported by guerrilla strongholds, Tamil Tigers appeared in uniforms in 1994 and fought pitched battles with the Sri Lankan security forces.
- Suicide bombings increased during the same time.

REF: p. 153   OBJ: 9, 10, and 11

8. Summarize the birth and evolution of the ETA and the rise of GAL.

ANS:
- Modern Spain was formed through the unification of several ethnic areas. The Basque region has existed for at least 3,000 years, and ethnic Basques have never totally embraced Spanish culture. Basques have their own national mythology, literary tradition, culture, and language.
- The Spanish Civil War brought Franco to power, and he violently sought to eradicate Basque culture. This caused a surge of nationalism and resulted in the formation of a Basque shadow government in Paris in the 1950s.
- A group of working-class students formed the ETA in 1959 to express nationalism in the Basque homeland

196

- It began with a campaign of advocacy, transforming into activism. This led to a splintering of the ETA and the formation of a terrorist group
- As Spanish repression increased in the 1970s, the ETA escalated its attacks, beginning a Marighella-style campaign of assassination, robbery, and banditry.
- ETA targeted government officials, academic advisors to the government, and members of the police and military.
- It reached its zenith in 1980, but it remains Europe's oldest violent separatist group.
- Disgruntled Spanish police officers and government officials formed death squads to counter the ETA.
- Death squads, such as Warriors of Christ the King and the Basque Spanish Battalion, began to torture and murder suspected terrorists and their supporters
- These squads eventually evolved into the Anti-Terrorist Liberation Groups (GAL)
- GAL death squads had one common goal: ETA terrorists could strike from the Basque region of France and return beyond the reach of Spanish law.
- The Spanish government began taking actions against the GAL in 1987.

REF: p. 157   OBJ: 9, 10, and 11

9.   Who was Francisco Franco? Explain his campaign against Basque national identity.

ANS:
- Francisco Franco was the leader of the nationalistic forces during the Spanish Civil War and the fascist dictator of Spain from 1939–1975.
- After achieving victory in 1939, Franco forcibly campaigned against Basque national identity.
- Franco completely incorporated the Basque region into Spain, banning its language and expressions of national culture.
- Franco's repression made the Basque region seem like it was occupied by a foreign colonial power.
- Priests were forbidden to make references the Basque region in religious services, and parents were forced to give their children Spanish first names.
- The Basque language was banned.
- Franco applied these rules to the entire Basque region, even though only two of the four provinces opposed his forces in the civil war.
- After World War II, many Basques believed the Allies would assist their bid for independence or even greater autonomy because Franco had supported Hitler, but the United States courted Franco's fascist government in return for American air bases in Spain.
- This resulted in a resurgence of Basque nationalism during the 1950s and the formation of a government in exile in Paris.
- The exiled Basques became an idealized expression of nationalism and ethnic identity, and while it was virtually powerless, it attracted a following in the Basque states.

REF: p. 157   OBJ: 4 and 5

10. Outline the Sri Lankan conflict: include the issue, group, and campaign.

ANS:
- The Issue.
- In 1948 the British granted Sri Lanka independence.
- The island was inhabited by the dominant Sinhalese and the Tamils.
- Although the constitution granted Tamils representation in the government and civil service, by 1955 they felt they were being systematically excluded from Sri Lanka's economic life.
- The Group.
- As ethnic tensions increased, some Tamils turned to violence.
- The Liberation Tigers of Tamil Eelam or Tamil Tigers formed in 1976 to fight for the Tamil minority.
- The Campaign.
- The LTTE began a campaign against the Sri Lankan Army, and they targeted India when the Indian prime minister tried to bring peace by deploying security forces.
- The LTTE is known for kidnapping young children and socializing them in LTTE camps.
- The Tigers also became masters of assassination and suicide bombings; the LTTE was the first modern secular group to use suicide bombers.
- Many members live in a virtual death cult, and the Black Tigers, the suicide wing of the LTTE, are known for carrying cyanide capsules around their necks when they attack.
- The Cease-fire.
- The LTTE agreed to a cease-fire in December 2001 and began peace negotiations in 2002.
- Although occasional outbreaks of violence have occurred, many experts believed the LTTE was suffering from a lack of resources.
- Renewed Fighting.
- Hostilities renewed in late 2006.
- After four years of relative peace, the Sinhalese refused to recognize a Tamil homeland.
- Both sides began sporadic fighting and terrorism returned to Sri Lanka.
- Conflict Ends

REF: p. 152   OBJ: 9, 10, and 11

CHAPTER 7

Nationalistic and Endemic Terrorism

Learning Objectives

After reading this chapter, students should be able to:

1. Summarize the EOKA revolt on Cyprus, FLN in Algeria, and Mau Mau in Kenya.
2. Explain the danger posed by Russia's breakaway states.
3. Describe the political and security issues surrounding violence in Chechnya.
4. Summarize the terrorist issues facing Turkey.
5. Describe ethnic tensions in China's Xinjiang province.
6. Explain the rationale behind China's policy toward Uighar separatism.
7. Briefly summarize Sikh separatism in India.
8. Define the term *endemic terrorism*.
9. Explain the relative importance of terrorism in light of Africa's other issues.
10. Summarize political conditions in western and central Africa.

Chapter Key Terms

David Galula, p. 164

Blind terrorism (Algeria), p. 164

Panga, p. 166

Shamil Basayev, p. 171

Moscow Theater, 2002, p. 171

Beslan school, 2004, p. 171

ibn al Khattab, p. 171

Black Widows, p. 172

Habib Akdas, p. 175

Abdullah Ocalan, p. 177

Uighar nationalists, p. 179

Golden Temple, p. 181

Lord's Resistance Army, p. 182

David Galula (1919– 1967): French Captain who fought in Algeria in 1956–1958. He returned to Paris to analyze the Algerian campaign, producing a critique of the strategy used in the war. His work inspired the development of counterinsurgency doctrine in the U.S. military.

Blind terrorism: Tactic used by the FLN. It included indiscriminate attacks against French outposts, which involved bombing, sabotage, and random assassination.

Panga: A heavy bladed machete used in agricultural work. It was the weapon favored by people who took the Mau Mau oath.

Shamil Basayev (1965–2006): A jihadist leader in Chechnya, Basayev engineered several operations resulting in mass civilian casualties.

Moscow theatre (Theatrical Center, Dubrovka, Moscow, 2002): The site of a Chechen attack where approximately 40 terrorists took 850 hostages. Russian forces stormed the theatre on the third day of the siege, killing 39 terrorists and at least 129 hostages.

Beslan school: A Chechen terrorist attack on the first day of school in September 2004 in North Ossetia. The scene was chaotic and Russian forces were never able to establish a security perimeter. Although details remain unclear, the incident resulted in the murder of nearly 400 people, including more than 100 children.

ibn al Khattab (1969– 2002): Also known as Emir Khattab or the Black Wahhabi, an international Saudi jihadist who went to fight in Chechnya. He tried to move the Chechen revolt from a nationalistic platform to the philosophy of religious militancy. He was killed by the Russian secret service in 2002.

Black Widows: Chechen female suicide bombers. They are known as Islamic martyrs in the Chechen language.

Habib Akdas (birth date unknown): Also known as Abu Anas al Turki, the founder of al Qaeda in Turkey. Akdas left Turkey to fight in Iraq after the American invasion. He was killed in a U.S. air strike in 2004.

Abdullah Ocalan (1948–): The leader of the PKK. Ocalan was captured in 1999 and sentenced to death, but his sentence was commuted. He ordered the end of a suicide-bombing campaign while in Turkish custody and called for peace between Turkey and the Kurds in 2006.

Uighar nationalists: China's ethnic Turkmen. Some Uighars nationalists organized to revive an eighteenth-century Islamic state in China's Xinjiang province. Using Kyrgyzstan and Kazakhstan as a base, they operate in China.

Golden Temple: The most sacred shrine of Sikhism. Its official name is the Temple of God.

Lord's Resistance Army: Ugandan guerrilla force opposing the government since 1987. The LRA has conscripted thousands of children, forcing them into ranks or mutilating and killing them. Dropping all pretense of political activity, it roams through Uganda, southern Sudan, the Democratic Republic of the Congo, and the Central Africa Republic. Its primary tactics are mass murder, mass rape, theft, and enslavement of children. Uganda has referred the LRA to the International Criminal Court.

Joseph Kony: (1961-) The leader of the Lord's Resistance Army in Uganda, his group has branched out to several other nations in central Africa. He is wanted by the International Criminal Court for crimes against humanity.

AIDS pandemic: The number of people with HIV/AIDS (human immunodeficiency virus/ acquired immunodeficiency syndrome). In 2005, Africa had 25.8 million HIV-positive adults and children. Africa has 11.5 percent of the world's population but 64 percent of its AIDS cases. From 1982 to 2005, AIDS claimed 27.5 million African lives (Cook, 2006).

sweet crude: A type of oil with less than 0.5 percent sulphur content. Nigeria sits on a large sweet crude field, giving the country potential wealth. The people who live above the oil, however, are poverty stricken, and oil production has been harmful to the environment.

Liberian Civil War: Two episodes of conflict involving rebel armies and militias as well as neighboring countries. The First War, 1989– 1996, ended when a rebel army brought Charles Taylor to Monrovia, the capital. The Second War, 1999–2003, toppled Charles Taylor from power. Both wars were characterized by village massacres and conscription of child soldiers.

Charles Taylor (1948–): A warlord in the First War of the Liberian Civil War and president of Liberia from 1997 to 2003.

Liberians United for Reconciliation and Democracy (LURD): A revolutionary movement founded in 1999 in western Africa. LURD was instrumental in driving Charles Taylor from power in 2003.

Big Man: An anthropological term to describe an important person in a tribe or clan. *Big Man* is sometimes used by political scientists to describe a dictator in a totalitarian government.

201

African Cell: A French military unit stationed in Africa and France. It retains between 10,000 and 15,000 troops in various African countries and answers directly to the president of France.

Chapter Outline

I. **Post World War II Anti-Colonial Terrorism**

   OBJ 1: Summarize the EOKA revolt on Cyprus, FLN in Algeria, and Mau Mau in Kenya

   A. Background of conflict with Israel and Palestine; revolutionary theory as developed in Cyprus and Algeria.
   1. Terrorism is surrounded by sloganeering.
   2. Each side believed it had moral authority.
   3. Terrorists demonize their enemies, and governments publically degrade terrorists.

   B. Cypress (1955 – 1959)
   1. UK established military headquarters in Middle East at end of WW II.
      a. Cypriots of Greek descent deeply resented British control, and sought unification with Greece.
      b. Turkish Cypriots looked to Turkey.
      c. Tensions rose; facing a much stronger army, Greek Cypriots organized movement to overthrow Britain (EOKA).
      d. Their leader, Georgios Grivas, developed a two-fold strategy.
         i. Draw international sympathy to cause.
         ii. Tie up large numbers of troops in an urban environment.
   2. Grivas reasoned that small groups of EOKA terrorists could strike in Cypriot cities thwarting any potential military offensive against rebel forces. In the end, his strategy worked.
      a. Brought press coverage, sympathy, and international pressure.
      b. Cypress gains independence.

   C. The Battle for Algiers (1954 – 1962)
   1. France invaded and occupied Algeria in the mid 19th century using brutal, military force.
   2. Administered it as if it were a French state; angering Algerians who resented the loss of ethnic autonomy.
   3. Algerians began political associations to advocate for independence in 1920s, and increased activity with the fall of France to the Nazi's in WW II.
   4. When France rejected overtures for independence, the Algerian National Liberation Front (FLN) formed with the purpose of violent revolution.
      a. Formed a two-fold strategy.

      i.   Terrify the European population through brutal violence
     ii.   Sought publicity and sympathy.
   iii.   Began with "Blind Terrorism" aimed at showing that French could not control the social environment.
   iv.   Never had to move beyond first phase; women were used to carry weapons and communiqués.

5. Algeria gained independence in 1962, as counterterrorist tactics drove Algerian sympathy toward the FLN, and French citizens lost their taste for a dirty war.

    a. Counterinsurgency required more subtle form of strategy.
    b. Parallels appear between French experience in Algeria and American response to the Iraq insurgency.

D. The Mau Mau and Kenya (1950 – 1960)

1. The UK and Germany began vying for imperial control of East Africa in the late 19th century.

    a. Britain gradually pushed Germany out, established rule.
    b. Displaced tribes from ancestral lands, land given to white farmers.
    c. One tribe, the Kikuyu, forced to resettle deep in Kenya, in an area that threatened its ability to support all families in the tribe.

2. The Mau Mau movement represents several factors that bear no resemblance to the anti-colonial urban revolts in Cyprus and Algeria.

    a. Based in rural areas.
    b. Based on tribal rights and ceremonies – symbols solidified the group.
    c. Violence frequently typified by massacres.
    d. Brought overwhelming military and police response with massive detainment and torture.
    e. The Mau Mau insurgents suffered the brunt of casualties, losing militarily, but winning the political settlement, as British pubic grew disgusted with government's repressive violence.

3. Fueled by anger over the loss of land, they began burning fields of European farmers.

4. The British responded with force, and what they believed to be unbridled moral authority in the face of savagery – the colonial government declared a state of emergency.

5. Unlike urban terrorist campaigns in Cyprus and Algeria, the Mau Mau movement failed in the field.

    a. The demise of the Mau Mau movement can be explained by breaking the movement into three phases.

        1. 1952 – 1953 gathered in camps in the lower forest of western Kenya
        2. 1953 – 1954 devolved into forest gangs.
        3. 1954 – 1955 military and police units laid siege to the forest; recruitment dropped and the gangs were isolated from one another.

6. Kenya would gain its independence and a former suspected Mau Mau exile would become its president.

II. **The Russian Federation**

   OBJ 2: Explain the danger posed by Russia's breakaway states

   OBJ 3: Describe the political and security issues surrounding violence in Chechnya

   A. Since the fall of the Soviet Union, the Russian Federation has been seeking its place among the world powers.
      1. Weakened by growth of former eastern European holdings, Russia faces economic and political problems.
      2. Two issues dealing with terrorism surface in the federation:
         a. Problem of breakaway states.
         b. Status of Chechnya and the spread of violence to the entire North Caucasus region.
   B. Breakaway States and Crime
      1. After collapse of Soviet Union, Russia experienced widespread economic dislocation.
      2. Suffered 50% drop in GNP, environmental problems, decline in life expectancy, and organized crime and corruption.
      3. Rise in de facto states that refuse to accept Russian government and control from Moscow.
   C. Chechnya
      1. Guerrillas and terrorists called for nationalism in a struggle for autonomy, as Moscow cannot control the corruption and poverty.
      2. The current dispute can be traced directly to the communist era, when Joseph Stalin (ruled 1922–1953) imposed Soviet power in the region.
      3. Many jihadists have flocked to the region, including leaders of movement.
      4. Chechens are engaged in a legitimate war of independence, and are not like other jihadist terrorists.
      5. Vladimir Putin, the newly elected Russian prime minister, blamed the Chechens for both attacks, and sent overwhelming military force into the breakaway state.
      6. The jihadists sought a new weapon, female suicide bombers, called the Black Widows, who were women who had suffered at the hands of the Russians.
      7. Russia faced two major problems in trying to pacify Chechnya and the surrounding states.
         a. Local officials may be loyal to Moscow, but they also remain loyal to their local constituencies.
         b. Many local insurgents have targeted officials who seem to be little more than Russian surrogates.

8. Russian Federation President Dmitry Medvedev is aware that jihadists are not behind the unrest; violence is caused by corruption, unemployment, and poverty.

III. **Turkey**
OBJ 4: Summarize the terrorist issues facing Turkey
OBJ 5: Describe the ethnic tensions in China's Xinxiang province
OBJ 6: Explain the rationale behind China's policy toward Uighar separatism

A. Turkey is 99 percent Muslim, and was the home of the last caliphate.
B. Turkey was accepted as a partner in NATO, and sought close trade ties with Europe and the United States after World War II.
C. In the mid-1980s a group known as Turkish Hezbollah appeared in eastern Turkey.
   1. Hezbollah expanded its targets in the 1990s to businesses and other establishments that it deemed to be un-Islamic.
D. The Kurdistan Workers Party and its alter egos.
   1. Turkey is currently facing a wave of religious terrorism.
   2. The Kurdistan Workers Party (PKK) is a Marxist-Leninist terrorist organization composed of Turkish Kurds.
      a. Willing to fight for independence, but not willing to condone massacres and terrorist attacks.
      b. Limited attacks to security forces and economic targets.
      c. Modified Marxist-Leninist rhetoric and spoke of nationalism.
   3. The PKK represents the pejorative nature of terrorism: when the terrorist label is applied to a group like the PKK, the whole movement is questioned.
   4. The United States Supreme Court declared that PKK was a terrorist organization, upholding the State Department's designation, and ruled that it was a federal crime to support it.
E. China's problems in Xinjiang
   1. After September 11, China was eager to join America's "war on terror."
   2. Beijing claims that international jihadists, trained in Afghanistan and Pakistan, are attempting to overthrow Chinese rule in the Xinjiang province, and establish an Islamic state.
   3. Uighars are China's ethnic Turkmen.
      a. Mostly Sufi Muslims who want independence.
      b. Inspired by collapse of Soviet Union, not Bin Ladin
      c. China fights for Xin because of large oil and gas reserves.
   4. Beijing has asked Washington to list militant Uighar organizations as terrorist groups, and the United States has been sympathetic to Chinese demands.

5. There are two problems with that classification:
   a. Most Uighar terrorism is not part of the jihadist movement.
   b. Many of the separatists are not violent and they do not endorse terrorism; they only want independence.

IV. **Endemic Ethnic Terror in Sub-Saharan Africa**
OBJ 8: Define the term endemic terrorism
OBJ 9: Explain the relative importance of terrorism in light of Africa's other issues
OBJ 10: Summarize political conditions in western and central Africa

A. Endemic terrorism describes the state of terrorist violence in Africa; this form of terrorism is created by artificial divisions of tribes, families, and ethnic groups.
   1. War, famine, and disease are more pressing matters.
B. Ethnic cleansing, child armies, wars by self-appointed militias such as the Lord's Resistance Army, crime and corruption, and internal strife have evolved into sub-Saharan Africa's unique brand of nationalist terrorism.
C. Old colonization issues complicate relationships between tribes, and fuel internal hostilities.
D. Sources of African Terrorism
   1. It is difficult to single out terrorism because Africa is the source of conventional and guerrilla wars, several revolutions, and criminal violence.
   2. Health conditions in Africa are also the worst on the planet, and the AIDS pandemic is creating havoc.
   3. Child armies, slavery, and starvation are part of the social problems plaguing the region; terrorism is one problem among many in Africa.
   4. The continent is not completely awash in violence, some believe the long-term solution to most African violence, including terrorism, is to bring economic development and stabilization.
E. Oil regions.
   1. In sub-Saharan Africa most of the sweet crude oil resources are located in the west, and are attractive to the United States for several reasons.
      a. It has a lower concentration of sulfur, and it is easier and cheaper to refine into gasoline.
      b. The oil fields are closer to the U.S. East Coast than the Middle East, reducing transportation costs.
      c. Africa is increasing its oil production; it is estimated that by 2020 the United States will purchase one quarter of its oil imports from western Africa.
   2. In Nigeria this resulted in an internal struggle among the country's Muslims about the purity of Islam; however, there is no evidence that

206

terrorist cells have formed, however, all of the predictive signs are there.

3. The International Crisis Group (2005b) sees western Africa as a region that is delicately balanced between moderate Islam and an undercurrent of jihadism.
4. Another potential problem in central and western Africa is the Big Man.
    a. An autocratic ruler—a Big Man—may ally with other countries at crucial times, but he does so only at the expense of the people.
        i. Housing several U.S. governmental entities, and the use of its ports, Kenya is vital to the U.S. struggle against terrorism – the U.S. gained its foothold there by courting Kenyan Big Men, who tended to favor their own tribes.
5. France has maintained an African policy that sharply differs from either the United States or the United Kingdom.
    a. After World War II, France created a special military unit known as the African Cell; its purpose was to extend French influence in the oil- and mineral-rich areas of Africa.

Chapter Summary

- The EOKA used an urban strategy, employing a small number of terrorists to fight 40,000 British soldiers. Their efforts brought international attention to Cyprus, and aroused international support for independence. The struggle ended with a negotiated settlement. Like the EOKA, the FLN focused on urban areas, and used terrorism to attract international publicity. Unlike the situation in Cyprus, most French people believed northern Algeria to be a part of France, and they saw the separatist movement as an internal rebellion, instead of a revolt against a colonial power. As a result, both the FLN and French security forces employed terrorism against each other. The Mau Mau movement in Kenya represents another postwar colonial revolt, but it differed from urban terrorism in Cyprus and Algeria. It was a rural resistance movement from a tribe displaced by colonial agricultural policies. Mau Mau fighters were defeated by repression, but Kenya achieved independence when the British public rejected inhumane measures.

- Breakaway states present a number of problems caused by political instability. In the former Soviet states, the breakaway states represent criminal shell states where terrorism, black market arms deals, and continued ethnic violence can grow. The political instability even caused a brief war between Georgia and Russia in 2008. Violence in the Caucasus region threatens regional stability, and, at times, it has attracted foreign terrorists.

- Chechnya has resisted Russian oversight since the nineteenth century. After failing at bids for independence, violence spread throughout the North Caucasus. Russia has

207

responded by empowering local ethnic political bosses, but they are among the most corrupt political leaders in the federation. Violence spread to Dagestan, Ingushetia, and Kabardino-Balkaria.

- Turkey has experienced several forms of terrorism in the past three decades. Some forms are based on religion, others are political. In addition, Turkey has a major ethnic separatist movement. Turkey has lost 40,000 people to terrorism since 1980. The PKK is Turkey's largest terrorist threat. A Marxist group growing from Kurdish separatism, the PKK seeks a Marxist Kurdistan. After the capture of its leader, and the end of a brief secular suicide bombing campaign, it appeared that a peace settlement might be negotiated. The creation of a strong economic Kurdish region in northern Iraq, however, has reenergized the PKK.

- Ethnic tensions are prominent in China's Xinjiang province because the native Uighar population aspires for autonomy. The Uighars are ethnic Turkmen. China annexed the area in 1759, and the Uighars have resisted this move throughout history. They won independence two times, only to be subjugated by China again.

- China has introduced several ethnic Chinese to the Xinjiang province in an attempt to exert political control. Uighars operating from Central Asia have resisted this policy. After 9/11, China eagerly endorsed the United States' "War on Terrorism," claiming that the Uighar nationalists were part of an international jihadist movement.

- Some Sikhs embraced terrorism after a deadly clash with Indian forces. The most damaging attack was on an Indian airliner. They planned an international terror campaign, and it fizzled by the mid-1990s.

- *Endemic terrorism* is a term used by J. Bowyer Bell to describe violence in sub-Saharan Africa. It results from European imperialism, and the creation of artificial national boundaries that link unrelated tribal and ethnic groups.

- Sub-Saharan Africa's main problem is poverty. It also suffers from internal wars, child soldiers, slavery, crime, and tribal violence. Terrorism is a potential problem, but millions of Africans die from these other issues.

- Western Africa is beset by political divisions, and struggles over the control of wealth generated by oil. Several militia style armies battle one another, often employing children as soldiers. Central Africa is plagued by tribal and political violence, exacerbated by roving bands of private armies. Rape, kidnapping, and mass murder are among the common tactics of these groups.

DISCUSSION QUESTIONS

1. Do you agree or disagree that war, famine, and disease are more pressing issues than endemic terrorism? Explain. (OBJ 8, 9, and 10)

2. Who are the Uighars? Detail the rationale behind China's policy toward Uighar separatism. (OBJ 5 and 6)

3. Compare the EOKA to the FLN in Algeria. What similarities and differences exist? In what way were the FLN innovative? Explain. (OBJ 1)

4. Describe the current political conditions in western and central Africa. Do you foresee any changes in the situation in the next five years? Twenty years? Ever? (OBJ 8 -10)

ASSIGNMENTS

1. Assign different Russian breakaway states to groups of students to research. Have them create 'fact sheets' on their assigned state to provide to the fellow students, and orally report their findings to the class. Tell students to be sure to explain the danger posed by the breakaway state. Allow time for discussion. (OBJ 2, 3, and 8)

2. Have each student comb through http://news.blogs.cnn.com/2012/06/18/somalia-tops-failed-states-index-for-fifth-year/ (or another website as approved by the instructor) for a current event, and select an article that relates to one or more of the chapter's core concepts. Have students provide a journalistic summary and a personal opinion/reaction to the article. Have students orally present the article to the class, field Q & As from their fellow students, and provide a copy of the original source article following the presentation. Optional: Have students complete peer assessments at the end of each presentation. (OBJ 1 - 10)

3. Have students research the hostage taking at the Dubrovka theatre by Chechan rebels in Moscow, and the hostage taking of the Israeli Athletes at the 1972 Olympic games in Munich by Black September. Open the class to discussion, directing their focus to similarities and differences between the two incidents. (OBJ 2 and 3)

4. As a review, play jeopardy using key terms and/or concepts from the chapter. (OBJ 1 – 10)

MEDIA TOOLS

1. ***"Wikis"***
    7 Things you should know about Wikis. Retrieved from the Web Jun 29, 2012 at
    http://net.educause.edu/ir/library/pdf/ELI7004.pdf

    This document offers easy to understand instruction on the history, development, and potential uses of Wikis.

    Have students develop (or make additions to a previously created one) a *Webliography* (resource list) using a Blog or Wiki that provides a short description and link to a scholarly resource pertaining to course concepts. For example, have students add two to three resources each and ask them to add their assessment of at least one of their peers' contributions. If desired, allow time to discuss Blogs/Wikis. This activity can be reused throughout the course, by asking students to add/revise their contributions each week, bi-weekly, etc. (OBJ 1 – 10)

2. ***"Failed States class discussion"***
    Foreign Policy. 10 Reasons Countries Fall apart. Retrieved from the Web Aug 20, 2012 at http://www.foreignpolicy.com/articles/2012/06/18/10_ reasons_ countries_fall_apart

    This article examines the factors contributing to demise of countries – the reason for 'failed states'. It also provides links to the 2012 global ranking of failed states.

    Have the class comb through the article and identify those factors listed in the article, and compare them to the environment in the failed states of Russia and Africa, noting any similarities and differences. Have the class discuss and debate the factors and their weight upon the creation of a failed state. (OBJ 1, 2, 3, 7, 8, 9, and 10)

3. ***"African Warlords class discussion"***
    Kony 2012. Invisible Children. Retrieved from the Web Aug 01, 2012 at
    http://www.youtube.com/watch?v=Y4MnpzG5Sqc.

    This video is a documentary examination of the atrocities committed by the African Warlord Joseph Kony, and the impact of his actions upon humanity.

    Have students review the video and discuss the impact it has had upon global awareness of such crimes against children in Africa, and the actions against Kony by the International Criminal Court. (OBJ 8 – 10)

4.   ***"Current Events Article Summary with Peer Assessment"***

Use the Article Summary Template, which can be obtained on the instructor companion website, for this assignment. The template offers information on Internet research, outside resources, identification of credible sources, and detailed directions on completing an assessment of a news article. It also includes a peer evaluation tool.

Have each student comb the Internet for terrorism related news, and select an article that relates to one or more of the chapter's core concepts. Be sure selections are an article of interest from a credible source (*more on credibility can be found in the article summary template above*). Fill out an article summary template. The *template asks for generic info about the article, a journalistic summary, as well as a personal opinion/reaction to the article.* Have each student summarize the article, present it orally to the class, and field Q & As from their fellow students. Have students complete peer assessments at the end of each presentation. Have students submit templates, original source article, and peer-reviews prior to the end of class. (OBJ 1 - 10)

Chapter 7—Nationalistic and Endemic Terrorism

TEST BANK

TRUE/FALSE

1.   The primary victims of Boko Harma's November 2011 attacks were Muslims.

ANS: F   REF: p. 160   OBJ: 8 and 9

2.   Nigeria is plagued by poverty, political corruption, police brutality and violent religious fanaticism.

ANS: T   REF: p. 160   OBJ: 10

3.   The majority of Mau Mau violence occurred in urban areas.

ANS: F   REF: p. 165   OBJ: 9 and 10

4.   Chechnya thrives on support from jihadist groups and imports jihadist tactics.

ANS: T   REF: p. 171   OBJ: 2 and 3

5.   The Liberian Civil War fostered criminal networks, corrupt leaders, and local military adventurers.

ANS: T   REF: p. 184   OBJ: 8, 9, and 10

6.   The Turkish Hezbollah of Eastern Turkey is connected the Lebanese Shiite Hezbollah.

ANS: F   REF: p. 175   OBJ: 4

7.   The U.S. Department of State groups Chechen rebels with other jihadist movements.

ANS: F   REF: p. 170   OBJ: 2 and 3

8.   The capital of Turkey, Ankara, was moved from Istanbul in the 1920s.

ANS: T   REF: p. 176   OBJ: 4

9.   PKK leaders increased their efforts to build a terrorist organization by moving into Lebanon's Bekaa Valley in September, 1980.

ANS: T   REF: p. 176   OBJ: 2 and 3

10. Ethnic cleansing, slavery, and starvation outweigh the problems presented by terrorism in the Horn of Africa.

ANS: T   REF: p. 182   OBJ: 9 and 10

11. The United Kingdom claimed Cypress as a crown colony after World War II.

ANS: F   REF: p. 161   OBJ: 1

12. The United Kingdom established its Middle East military headquarters in Saudi Arabia at the end of World War II.

ANS: F   REF: p. 161   OBJ: 1

13. The majority of Algerians felt that a peaceful separation from France could be negotiated.

ANS: T   REF: p. 163   OBJ: 1

14. The Mau Mau movement bears much resemblance to the anti-colonial urban revolts in Cyprus and Algeria.

ANS: F   REF: p. 165   OBJ: 1

15. Moldova, Georgia, and Azerbaijan are all failed Russian states.

ANS: T   REF: p. 168   OBJ: 2

MULTIPLE CHOICE

1. The UK established its Middle Eastern military headquarters in _____ at the end of World War II.
   a. Cyprus
   b. Cape Town
   c. Algeria
   d. Tunisia

ANS: a   REF: p. 161   OBJ: 1

2. Involved in a long guerrilla war in Indochina, France faced revolts in _____ and Algeria.
   a. Morocco
   b. Tunisia
   c. Cypress
   d. Tunisia

ANS: b   REF: p. 163   OBJ: 1

3.   Algeria received independence from France in _____.
        a. 1962
        b. 1952
        c. 1942
        d. 1972

ANS: c   REF: p. 162   OBJ: 1

4.   The Mau Mau movement originated in _____.
        a. France
        b. Spain
        c. Chad
        d. Kenya

ANS: d   REF: p. 165   OBJ: 9 and 10

5.   The National Organization of Cypriot Fighters (EOKA) was focused on ____.
        a. Cypriot independence
        b. Partitioning Cypress into Greek and Turk populations
        c. Maintenance of Cypress under British rule
        d. Maintenance of Cypress under Turkish rule

ANS: a   REF: p.161   OBJ: 1

6.   The former Soviet Union broke into _____ new nations in the early 1990s.
        a. Seventeen
        b. Fifteen
        c. Twenty
        d. Nineteen

ANS: b   REF: p. 168   OBJ: 2 and 3

7.   Imperial Russia expanded into the Caucasia region in _____.
        a. 1859
        b. 1917
        c. 1830
        d. 1849

ANS: c   REF: p. 170   OBJ: 2 and 3

8.   Groups in _____ have made their presence felt in the ethnic struggle between the Russian
        Federation and the would-be breakaway state of Chechnya.
        a. Europe
        b. United States
        c. Japan
        d. Asia

ANS: d   REF: p. 170   OBJ: 2 and 8

9.   _____ was a French Captain who fought in Algeria in 1956-1958.
        a. David Galula
        b. Charles Taylor
        c. Nicolas Sarkozy
        d. Dov Lynch

ANS: a   REF: p. 164   OBJ: 1

214

10.   The current dispute over Chechnya can be traced directly to the communist era when
      _____ imposed Soviet power in the region.
         a.   Vladimir Putin
         b.   Joseph Stalin
         c.   Vladimir Lenin
         d.   Karl Marx

ANS: b   REF: p. 170   OBJ: 2 and 3

11.   A jihadist leader in _____, Shamil Basayev engineered several operations resulting in
      mass civilian casualties.
         a.   Kurdistan
         b.   Greece
         c.   Chechnya
         d.   Turkey

ANS: c   REF: p. 171   OBJ: 2 and 3

12.   _____ is 99 percent Muslim and was the home of the last caliphate.
         a.   Pakistan
         b.   Algeria
         c.   Kurdistan
         d.   Turkey

ANS: d   REF: p. 174   OBJ: 1 and 4

13.   Although most of the country is in Asia, _____ was accepted as a partner in NATO.
         a.   Turkey
         b.   Cypress
         c.   Greece
         d.   Belgium

ANS: a   REF: p. 174   OBJ: 4

14.   Habib Akdas established al Qaeda in _____.
         a.   Cypress
         b.   Turkey
         c.   Pakistan
         d.   Chechnya

ANS: b   REF: p. 175   OBJ: 4 and 8

15.   The PKK was founded in 1974 to fight for an independent _____.
         a.   Chechnya
         b.   Turkey
         c.   Kurdistan
         d.   Pakistan

ANS: c   REF: p. 176   OBJ: 4 and 8

16.   Kemal Ataturk, also known as Mustafa Kemal, dissolved Islamic government in 1923
        and created a _____.
        a. Dictatorship
        b. Theocracy
        c. Monarchy
        d. Secular republic

ANS: d   REF: p. 174   OBJ: 4 and 8

17.   While never implemented, the Treaty of Sevres created an independent _____.
        a. Kurdistan
        b. Pakistan
        c. Chechnya
        d. Cape Town

ANS: a   REF: p. 177   OBJ: 4

18.   The leader of the PKK ordered the end of a suicide-bombing campaign, calling for peace
        between _____ in 2006.
        a. Chechens and the Russian Federation
        b. Turkey and Kurds
        c. Turkey and the Gulf states
        d. Iraq and Iran

ANS: b   REF: p. 177   OBJ: 4 and 8

19.   Ethnic Uighars are mostly _____ who are inspired by the collapse of the Soviet Union.
        a. Religious dissidents
        b. Social elitists
        c. Islamic mystics
        d. Ethnic militants

ANS: c   REF: p. 179   OBJ: 5 and 6

20.   India is home to over 80% of the world's population of _____.
        a. Muslims
        b. Hindus
        c. Buddhists
        d. Sikhs

ANS: d   REF: p. 39   OBJ: 7 and 8

21.   The group known as _____ has conscripted thousands of Ugandan children forcing them
        into ranks or mutilating or killing them.
        a. Lord's Resistance Army
        b. Ugandan guerillas
        c. Ugandan Hezbollah
        d. Congo Army of the Lord

ANS: a   REF: p. 182   OBJ: 8, 9, and 10

22. Charles Taylor was the president of _____ from 1997 to 2003 and considered a warlord in the First War of the Liberian Civil War.
    a. Uganda
    b. Liberia
    c. Libya
    d. Turkey

ANS: b   REF: p.184   OBJ: 8, 9, and 10

23. According to Joe Barkan, _____ is vital to the U.S. struggle against terrorism.
    a. Kurdistan
    b. Turkey
    c. Kenya
    d. Liberia

ANS: c   REF: p. 184   OBJ: 9 and 10

24. Faced with anti-colonial revolts after World War II, _____ created a special military unit known as the African Cell.
    a. England
    b. Spain
    c. Germany
    d. France

ANS: d   REF: p. 185   OBJ: 1, 8, 9, and 10

25. The Mau Mau movement is based in which of the following countries?
    a. Kenya
    b. Somalia
    c. Uganda
    d. Rwanda

ANS: a   REF: p. 165   OBJ: 8, 9, and 10

26. Algeria achieved independence from _____ in 1962.
    a. Great Britain
    b. France
    c. Germany
    d. The Soviet Union

ANS: b   REF: p. 165   OBJ: 1

27. The work of David Galula inspired the development of the _____ doctrine in the U.S. military.
    a. Total National Defense
    b. 1-4-2-1
    c. Counterinsurgency
    d. Win-Hold-Win

ANS: c   REF: p. 164   OBJ: 8

28.   In October 2002, about 50 Chechen rebels took over a _____ in Moscow.
       a. Police station
       b. Post office
       c. School
       d. Theatre

ANS: d   REF: p. 172   OBJ: 2 and 3

29.   The failure to separate the population from the insurgents is an example of the parallel
       between the French experience in Algeria and the initial American response to_____
       insurgency.
       a. Iraq
       b. Afghanistan
       c. Kurdistan
       d. Iran

ANS: a   REF: p. 164   OBJ: 1

30.   The _____ is a Marxist-Leninist terrorist organization comprised of Turkish Kurds.
       a. Lord's Resistance Army
       b. PKK
       c. Shining Path
       d. FLN

ANS: b   REF: p. 176   OBJ: 4

31.   Which organization is viewed as to have set the stage for modern terrorism?
       a. ETA
       b. IRA
       c. LTTE
       d. PKK

ANS: b   REF: p. 182   OBJ: 1 and 2

32.   Georgios Grivas created what organization to overthrow British rule in Cypress?
       a. EOKA
       b. FLN
       c. PKK
       d. ETA

ANS: a   REF: p 161   OBJ: 1

33.   What warlord was the subject of much public outrage in the West following a YouTube
       video that went viral in 2012?
       a. Idi Amin
       a. Joseph Kony
       b. Muammar Qahafi
       d. Sylvestre Mudacumura

ANS: b   REF: p. 182   OBJ: 9 and 10

218

34. In sub-Saharan Africa, most of the oil resources are located in the ___.
    a. North
    a. South
    b. East
    c. West

ANS: c   REF: p. 182   OBJ: 9 and 10

35. What African country currently has the largest population of muslims?
    a. Egypt
    b. Rwanda
    c. Nigeria
    d. Libya

ANS: a   REF: p. 183   OBJ: 10

36. Beijing claims that _____ are attempting to overthrow Chinese rule in the Xinjiang (New Frontier) province and establish an Islamic state.
    a. Lord's Resistance Army
    b. International jihadists
    c. Shining Path
    d. FLN

ANS: b   REF: p. 179   OBJ: 5

37. In 1949, Xinjiang province was _____Uighar, but it may be less than fifty percent today.
    a. 100%
    b. 90 %
    c. 10%
    d. 50%

ANS: b   REF: p. 180   OBJ: 5 and 6

38. Sikhism embodies elements of _____and Hinduism.
    a. Islam
    b. Judaeism
    c. Shintoism
    d. Paganism

ANS: a   REF: p. 181   OBJ: 7

39. Britain's primary foreign policy efforts in Africa have been aimed at expanding economic development and increasing _____.
    a. Human rights
    b. Military presence
    c. Tourism
    d. AIDS awareness

ANS: a   REF: p. 185   OBJ: 10

40. Turkey has lost 40,000 people to _____ since 1980.
    a. Famine
    b. Terrorism
    c. Emigration
    d. Floods

ANS: b   REF: p. 187   OBJ: 4

Case 7.0

The EOKA used an urban strategy using a small amount of terrorists to fight 40,000 British soldiers. Their efforts brought international attention to Cyprus and aroused international support for independence. The struggle ended with a negotiated settlement. Like the EOKA, the FLN focused on urban areas and used terrorism to attract international publicity. Unlike the situation in Cyprus, most French people believed northern Algeria to be a part of France, and they saw the separatist movement as an internal rebellion. As a result, both the FLN and French security forces employed terrorism against each other. The Mau Mau movement in Kenya represents another postwar colonial revolt, but it differed from urban terrorism in Cyprus and Algeria. It was a rural resistance movement from a tribe displaced by colonial agricultural policies. Mau Mau fighters were defeated by repression, but Kenya achieved independence when the British public rejected inhumane measures.

41. The struggles noted in the aforementioned scenario all have major foundations in ____?
    a. Anti-imperialism
    b. Religious zealotry
    c. Jihadism
    d. Economics

ANS: a   REF: p. 161   OBJ: 1, 2, 3, 4, 8, 9, and 10

42. The conflict in Cyprus was primarily of what nature?
    a. Ethnic terrorism
    b. Narco-terrorism
    c. Jihadist terrorism
    d. Eco-terrorism

ANS: a   REF: p. 161   OBJ: 1 and 9

43. The conflict in Kenya is primarily of what nature?
    a. Endemic terrorism
    b. Narco-terrorism
    c. Jihadist terrorism
    d. Eco-terrorism

ANS: d   REF: p. 165   OBJ: 8, 9, and 10

44. The EOKA, FLN, and the Mau Mau movement tactics most closely resemble those of the _____?
    a. Hamas
    b. The Taliban
    c. Hezzbollah
    d. IRA

ANS: d   REF: p. 161   OBJ: 1, 4, and 9

220

45. The outcome of the EOKA's struggle with the British in Cyprus most closely resembled the outcome of which conflict?
    a. The IRA and British parliament
    b. The Chinese and the Uighars
    c. Sikh separatism in India
    d. Chechnya and Russia

ANS: a   REF: p. 162   OBJ: 1, 2, 3, 4, 5, 6, and 7

Case 7.1
The first decade of the twenty-first century brought seemingly peaceful solutions to three violent separatist movements: the EOKA on Cyprus, the ETA's campaign for Basque autonomy, and a long campaign of savage guerilla warfare and terrorism among two ethnic groups on the island nation of Sri Lanka. All of the conflicts appeared to end.

46. The Cypriot, Basque, and Sri Lankan conflicts all have a central focus that is primarily _____ in nature.
    a. Ethnic
    b. Economic
    c. Religious
    d. Monetary

ANS: a   REF: p. 161   OBJ: 1 and 7

47. The apparent end to the three noted violent separatist movements were achieved primarily in the form of a _____ solution.
    a. Military
    b. Educational
    c. Economic
    d. Political

ANS: d   REF: p. 161   OBJ: 1 and 7

Case 7.2

The United Kingdom and Germany began vying for imperial control of East Africa in the late nineteenth century with Britain gradually pushing the Germans out and solidifying control after World War I. After establishing British rule in Kenya, the colonial government gave Kenya's agricultural areas to European farmers displacing tribes from the ancestral lands. One tribe, the Kikuyu, was forced to resettle deep in western Kenya in an area that threatened its ability to support all of the families in the tribe. British commissions recommended the expansion of Kikuyu land in the 1930s and 1940s, but the expansion was far less than the land given to white settlers. Around 1950, rumors reached the government in Nairobi indicating that there was some type of violent movement taking place in the Kikuyu tribal area. The movement, according to the rumors, was called Mau Mau.

48.   The artificial boundaries imposed by imperialists fostered a new form of terrorist violence called _____.
       a.   Endemic terrorism
       b.   Narco-terrorism
       c.   Jihadist terrorism
       d.   Eco-terrorism

ANS: a   REF: p. 181   OBJ: 8 and 9

49.   The Mau Mau movement would be most appropriately classified as being a _____ movement.
       a. Socialistic
       b. Nationalistic
       c. Religious
       d. Political

ANS: b   REF: p. 186   OBJ: 1, 8, 9, and 10

50.   Imperial powers sought to control regions of Africa for what primary reason?
       a.   Access to mineral and energy resources
       b.   Access to shipping routes
       c.   Military advantage
       d.   Political advantage

ANS: a   REF: p. 182   OBJ: 1, 8, 9, and 10

COMPLETION

1.   Primary tactics of Uganda's LRA include mass murder, mass rape, theft, and _____.

ANS: enslavement of children   REF: p. 182   OBJ: 8, 9 , and 10

2.   The French Indochina War involved revolts in _____ and _____.

ANS: Tunisia, Morocco   REF: p. 163   OBJ: 1

3.   _____ is a heavy bladed machete used in agricultural work - the favored weapon of the Mau Mau.

ANS: Panga   REF: p. 166   OBJ: 1

4.   _____ is the leader of the Lord's Resistance Army in Uganda.

ANS: Jospeh Kony   REF: p. 182   OBJ: 9 and 10

5.   International jihadists enjoy the _____ region of the Russian Federation, viewing it as another Afghanistan.

ANS: Caucasus   REF: p. 170   OBJ: 2 and 3

222

6. _____ are female suicide bombers employed in the Caucasian region of the Russian Federation.

ANS: Black widows   REF: p. 172   OBJ: 2 and 3

7. An economic consortium of several European states formed in 1992, the _____ was designed to remove trade barriers and to create a unified European economy.

ANS: European Union   REF: p. 175   OBJ: 3, 8, and 10

8. The United States Supreme Court has declared PKK to be a _____ organization.

ANS: foreign terrorist   REF: p. 177   OBJ: 4

9. Some Uighar nationalists organized in hopes of reviving an 18th century Islamic state in China's _____ province.

ANS: Xinjiang   REF: p. 179   OBJ: 5 and 6

10. China fights for Xinjiang because it has China's largest _____ and _____ reserves.

ANS: oil, gas   REF: p.180   OBJ: 5 and 6

11. After India was partitioned in 1947, some Sikhs sought independence in _____, a state where they represented the majority of the population.

ANS: Punjab   REF: p.181   OBJ: 7

12. While terrorism is a horrendous problem, poverty and the _____ have been the cause of most of Africa's suffering.

ANS: AIDS crisis   REF: p.182   OBJ: 9

13. It is estimated that by 2020 the United States will purchase one quarter of its oil imports from _____.

ANS: western Africa   REF: p.183   OBJ: 10

14. _____ was the first Muslim-majority country to recognize the state of Israel.

ANS: Turkey   REF: p.174   OBJ: 1 and 4

15. The terrorist group Boko Haram are from the African nation ___.

ANS: Nigeria   REF: p.183   OBJ: 8, 9, and 10

223

16. PKK officially changed its name to _____ in 2002.

ANS: Kurdistan Freedom and Democracy (KADEK)   REF: p.176   OBJ: 4

17. Freedom and Democracy Congress of Kurdistan, Kurdistan Peoples' Congress, Peoples' Congress of Kurdistan, and Liberation Units of Kurdistan are all psuedonymns for _____.

ANS: PKK   REF: p.176   OBJ: 4

18. The majority of Uighars identify as _____ muslims.

ANS: sufi   REF: p.179   OBJ: 5 and 6

19. France created a special military unit known as the _____ to extend French influence in the oil- and mineral-rich areas of Africa.

ANS: African cell   REF: p.185   OBJ: 1

20. The most sacred site of the Sikh religion is the _____.

ANS: Golden Temple   REF: p. 181   OBJ: 7

ESSAY

1. Illustrate the moral authority belief of Cypriot, Algerian, and Mau Mau revolutionaries.

ANS:
- One of the important aspects of these revolts is that in every case each side believed it had moral authority.
- The British believed they were maintaining peace on Cyprus while Greek Cypriots waged a terrorist campaign for freedom and political domination of Turk Cypriots.
- In other words, they would seek to do the same thing to the Turks that the British were doing to them.
- Algerian rebels justified the murder of non-combatants in the name of independence.
- The French responded with suppression and torture telling the police officers and soldiers that Algerian terrorists were less than human.
- Mau Mau insurgents murdered fellow citizens while British and loyalists struck back ruthlessly believing they could create a multicultural society.
- The Mau Mau rebels were destroyed, yet the political settlement that followed achieved their overall goal partially because the British voters were appalled by counterterrorist tactics.
- Terrorists demonize their enemies and governments publically degrade terrorists.

REF: p. 168   OBJ: 1, 4, 8, 9, and 10

2. List the parallels between the French experience in Algeria and initial American response to the Iraq insurgency.

ANS:
- The absence of a clear doctrine to thwart an insurgency.
- Failure to recognize warning signs of an impending insurgency.
- Insurgent focus on urban areas.
- Failure to separate the population from the insurgents.
- The necessity to avoid alienating the indigenous population.
- Promoting women's rights to counteract support for the insurgency.
- The need to emphasize law enforcement over military tactics.
- Failure to realize the limited effect of neutralizing insurgent leaders.
- The critical importance of intelligence.
- The importance of sealing borders.
- The critical impact of the humane treatment of captured insurgents.

REF: p. 164   OBJ: 1

3. Explain how the Mau Mau rebellion in Kenya illustrates how counterterrorism measures often produce more violence and suffering than does the actions of terrorists.

ANS:
- After the state of emergency went into effect, thousands of British soldiers arrived in Kenya and were charged with ending the rebellion.
- The government recruited and trained a large local force to assist the army.
- The ensuing campaign was ruthless and violent.
- 90,000 suspected rebels were detained in special internment camps.
- The level of rebel violence dropped as government violence increased.
- Mau Mau units were forced to retreat deeper into the forest in the wake of British military offensives.
- They devolved into forest gangs.
- Military and police units laid siege to the forest.
- After the summer of 1955 the Mau Mau movement became a paper tiger and the Kiuya struggled to survive.
- This situation continued until the end of fighting in 1960.
- Governmental policy was ruthless.
- Over 90,000 Mau Mau suspects were interned during the state of emergency, and the conditions of custody were appalling.
- Thousands of suspects were tortured and a few were executed outside of the justice system.
- Beatings were routine until suspects confessed that they had taken the oath and renounced it.
- As group of Mau Mau detainees began to band together in prison, the government began to break up prison gangs by increasing individual torture.

225

- The military began employing two additional tactics in the forest.
- Separating rebels from food sources they began starving the Kikuya.
- In addition, they systematically singled out women after entering villages for rape and torture.

REF: p. 167   OBJ: 8, 9, and 10

4.   Summarize the potential dangers posed the Russian breakaway states.

ANS:
- Three nations – Moldova, Georgia, and Azerbaijan – have internal separatist movements creating areas where neither the government nor the separatists are in control.
- This has resulted in virtual shell states where crime flourishes and corruption rules.
- The breakaway regions are ripe for illegal arms trading, and they present a tempting location to headquarter internal criminal and terrorist groups.
- Ethnic tensions in these regions also add to the problem.
- For example, the Russian Federation launched a brief invasion of Georgia in 2008 to protect Russian nationals in South Ossetia.
- The separatist movement in Chechnya threatens regional stability, and it has resulted in two internal wars in the Russian Federation, one from 1994 to 1996 and the other from 1999 to 2009.
- It has also created a campaign of internal terrorism involving the deaths of hundreds of people.
- Fighting has spread throughout the North Caucasus region to Dagestan, Ingushetia, and Kabardino-Balkaria.
- Attacks in Moscow and other areas outside the region have accelerated Russia's drift away from democracy.
- Russia has responded by installing local regional political bosses, but they have introduced a culture of political corruption and repression.

REF: p. 168   OBJ: 2 and 3

5.   Provide the timeline for the Chechnya Nationalistic revolt.

ANS:
- 1830: Imperial Russia expands into the Caucasia region.
- 1859: Russia annexes Caucasia, including Dagestan and Chechnyna.
- 1917–1923:   Dagestan and Chechnya declare independence.
- 1923: The Communists conquer Caucasia, adding Dagestan and Checheno-Ingush to the USSR.
- 1944: Stalin purges the Caucasia area, fearing Chechens and others were influenced by Germany.
- 1991: The USSR falls; Chechens declare independence, but Russia rejects the claim.

- 1994–1996: Russia invades Chechnya; agrees to a cease-fire after severe casualties.
- 1997: Chechens launch bombing campaign in Russia; rebels enter Dagestan.
- 1999: Russia renews the war, takes Dagestan and launches devastating strikes on Chechnya.
- 2002: The Moscow theater takeover.
- 2003-2004: Suicide bombing campaign. Suicide bombers destroy two airliners in flight.
- 2004: The Beslan school takeover.
- 2009: April Kremlin announces the end of the 2nd Chechen War
- 2009: In November a high speed train between Moscow and St. Petersburg derailed killing 30 passengers
- 2010: Two female suicide bombers kill 40 on Moscow Metro during morning rush hour

REF: p. 170   OBJ: 2 and 3

6.   Discuss the three primary characters in the 1999 Dagestan rebellion according to   Paul Murphy.

ANS:
- The first was Shamil Basayev, a man who had gained fame by taking an entire hospital hostage in 1995 during the first Chechen war and whose 1999 actions in Dagestan started the second.
- Basayev is described as a Che Guevara–type figure who led by charisma and example.
- Basayev would increase his reputation by planning the takeover of a Moscow theater in 2002.
- An estimated 200 people—130 hostages and the remainder terrorists and security forces—were killed.
- Two years later, on the opening day of the Beslan school, Basayev masterminded another takeover.
- Using children as hostages, his terrorists killed an estimated 300 to 400 people, mostly children. Basayev was killed in the summer of 2006.
- The second international jihadist leader, a mysterious leader known by the nom de guerre ibn al Khattab, was a Saudi. Basayev brought Khattab to Chechnya in 1995.
- Described as the "Black Wahhabi," he became known for ruthlessness.
- He was assassinated by Russian agents in 2002.
- The third leader, Salman Raduyev, took more hostages than any other terrorist.
- Before he went mad, Raduyev threatened to attack Russian nuclear facilities.
- Khattab and Basayev were responsible for the Dagestan invasion.

REF: p. 171   OBJ: 2, 3, and 8

227

7. Summarize some of the *strategic errors* made by the terrorists during the Dubrovka Theatrical Center attack in 2002

ANS:
- *Moscow Dubrovka Theatrical Center: October 2002*
- What went wrong:
- Terrorists formed partial bonds and relationships with some hostages.
- Female terrorists took orders from males; therefore, when Russian special forces attacked, females waited for instructions to detonate bombs; however, but the males were busy fighting and could not give them.
- Some hostages kept and used cell phones.
- What the terrorists learned:
- Ruthlessness, including random executions, keeps human bonds from forming.
- Bombers should be readily prepared to detonate explosives at the first sign of an assault.
- Cell phones must be destroyed.
- *The Beslan Middle School Number 1 Attack: September 2004*
- To eliminate bonding and maintain control they did the following:
- Publicly executed hostages at the beginning of the incident.
- Destroyed cell phones.
- Executed a terrorist who stated he never intended to attack a school.
- Humiliated and intimidated the children taken hostage.
- Played psychological games to keep parents in fear.
- Denied food and water to hostages.
- Bayoneted a young boy when he cried for a drink of water.
- Gave selected females leading roles.
- Placed bombs to detonate upon any counterattack without orders.

REF: p. 173   OBJ: 2, 3, and 8

8. Outline the Kurdish Conflict – include the issue, group, campaign, and the future.

ANS:
- The Issue.
- The Kurds are an ethnic group inhabiting northern Iraq, southern Turkey, and northern Iran.
- When other groups received national sovereignty at the end of the World War I, the Kurds remained divided among the three nations.
- The Treaty of Sevres (1920) created an independent Kurdistan, but it was never implemented.
- About 12 million Kurds live in Turkey.
- The Group.
- The Kurdistan Workers Party (PKK) formed in 1978 as a Marxist-Leninist group. Its goal was to create an independent socialist Kurdistan.
- The Campaign. After training in Syria, the PKK launched a guerrilla campaign in Turkey.

- By the early 1990s, the PKK turned to urban terrorism, targeting Turks throughout Europe and in Turkey.
- After its leader, Abdullah Ocalan, was captured in 1999, the PKK pledged to work for a peaceful solution; however, it maintained various militant organizations operating under a variety of names.
- The PKK maintains links with other revolutionary groups in Turkey and with some international terrorist groups.
- The Campaign Renewed.
- Turkey is being considered for admission to the European Union.
- The EU, NATO, and the United States list the various entities of the PKK as terrorist organizations.
- In October 2003 the United States agreed to crack down on the PKK in northern Iraq, but the group remained.
- Turkey began clandestine incursions into the Kurdish area of Iraq around 2006.
- Open confrontation began in 2008, and by 2010 PKK units were crossing into Turkey attacking military outposts.
- The Future.
- After years of challenges the United States Supreme Court ruled that the PKK is a foreign terrorist group.
- Turkey conducts intelligence, military, and law enforcement operations against the PKK, and it is gradually moving further from Europe seeking closer ties with the Middle East.

REF: p. 177   OBJ: 1, 4, and 8

9.   Explain "endemic terrorism" to describe the state of terrorist violence in Africa.

ANS:
- Endemic terrorism describes the state of terrorist violence in Africa; it is defined as a form of terrorism created by artificial divisions of tribes, families, and ethnic groups.
- When moving south of the Sahara, it is possible to see the extent of endemic terrorism, but problems in sub-Saharan Africa extend beyond terrorism.
- War, famine, and disease are more pressing.
- Both children and women are exploited, and totalitarian governments control some countries.
- Africa is the poorest region on earth.
- Africa was colonized by European nations in the 19th and early 20th centuries, and they divided the continent based on European spheres of influence.
- Paying no attention to traditional regions or tribal boundaries in sub-Saharan Africa, various ethnic groups were placed in newly formed European countries.
- This was problematic as many times competing tribes or groups of deadly rivals were joined in the new countries.
- Post colonial revolts and political pressure slowly forced European countries out of the area after World War II leaving many countries seething with internal hostilities.
- Additionally, some countries were dominated by white colonists who refused to yield power to black majorities after the Europeans departed.

- Feelings of social animosity were exacerbated by extreme disparity in the unequal distribution of Africa's limited wealth and fierce economic exploitation of the continent's mineral and energy resources.
- Ethnic cleansing, child armies, wars by self-appointed militias such as the Lord's Resistance Army, crime and corruption, and internal strife have evolved into sub-Saharan Africa's unique brand of nationalist terrorism.
- It is endemic indeed. In western and central Africa, terrorism represents a potential problem.
- The Horn of Africa has active groups, including a jihadist movement, but even there ethnic cleansing, revolts, slavery, and starvation outweigh the problems presented by terrorism.
- Africa is suffering from a colonial past, poverty, and a modern epidemic.
- Some policy makers believe that these issues must be addressed but they are separate from terrorism.
- Others argue that a comprehensive approach to Africa's massive social problems is a more effective method of controlling terrorism.

REF: p. 182   OBJ: 8, 9, and 10

10.   Why do scholars claim that terrorism is one problem among many in Africa? Would you agree with this? Why or why not?

ANS:
- It is difficult to single out terrorism because Africa is the source of conventional and guerrilla wars, several revolutions, and criminal violence.
- One of the primary reasons for this is Africa's position in the world; it is the most poverty-stricken region on earth.
- The sub-Saharan portion of the continent has negative economic growth.
- In other words, the countries in the south produce less income year by year.
- Health conditions in Africa are also the worst on the planet, and the AIDS pandemic is creating havoc.
- There are hundreds of thousands of homeless orphans.
- Tribal violence has led to genocide and countless deaths.
- Child armies, slavery, and starvation are part of the social problems plaguing the region.
- Terrorism is one problem among many in Africa.
- View will vary.

REF: p. 182   OBJ: 8, 9, and 10

CHAPTER 8

Background to the Middle East

Learning Objectives

After reading this chapter, students should be able to:

1. Define the Middle East as a historical, geographical, and cultural metaphor.
2. Briefly sketch the origins of Islam.
3. Describe the difference between Shiites and Sunnis.
4. Explain the emergence of militant theology.
5. Discuss the historical significance in the decline of the Ottoman Empire and the birth of Zionism.
6. Summarize the impact of World War I on the Middle East.
7. Describe the formation of Israel and the Arab-Israeli wars.
8. Explain the emergence of terrorism after the 1967 Six Days' War.
9. Briefly sketch the history of modern Iran.

Chapter Key Terms

Gulf States, p 190

Ibn Taymiyya, p. 196

Mohammed ibn Abdul Wahhab, p. 196

Sayyid Qutb, p. 196

Muslim Brotherhood, p. 196

Hassan al Banna, p. 197

Ottoman Empire, p. 199

Balfour Declaration, p. 202

Mandate of Palestine, p. 202

Baathist, p. 204

Six Day War, p. 205

Yom Kippur War, p. 206

Camp David Peace Accord, p. 206

Iran-Iraq War, p. 207

Reza Shah Pahlavi, p. 208

SAVAK, p. 209

Gulf States: Small Arab kingdoms bordering the Persian Gulf. They include Bahrain, Qatar, the United Arab Emirates, and Oman.

Ibn Taymiyyah: (circa 1269–1328) also known as Taqi al Din ibn Taymiyya, a Muslim religious reformer in the time of the Crusades and a massive Mongol invasion.

Abdul Wahhab: (1703– 1792) Also known as Mohammed ibn Abdul Wahhab, a religious reformer who wanted to purge Islam of anything beyond the traditions accepted by Mohammed and the four Rightly Guided caliphs. He conducted campaigns against Sufis, Shiites, and Muslims who made pilgrimages or who invoked the names of saints.

Sayyid Qutb: (1906– 1966) An Egyptian educator who called for the overthrow of governments and the imposition of purified Islamic law, based on the principles of previous puritanical reformers. Qutb formed a militant wing of the Muslim Brotherhood.

Muslim Brotherhood: An organization founded by Hassan al Banna designed to recapture the spirit and religious purity during the period of Mohammed and the four Rightly Guided caliphs. The Brotherhood seeks to create a single Muslim nation through education and religious reform. A militant wing founded by Sayyid Qutb sought the same objective through violence. Hamas, a group that defines itself as the Palestinian branch of the Muslim Brotherhood, has rejected the multinational approach in favor of creating a Muslim Palestine.

Hassan al Banna: (1906– 1949) the founder of the Muslim Brotherhood. He was murdered by agents of the Egyptian government.

Iranian Revolution: The 1979 religious revolution that toppled Mohammed Pahlavi, the shah of Iran, and transformed Iran into an Islamic republic ruled by Shiite religious scholars.

Ottoman Empire: A Turkish empire that lasted for 600 years, until 1924. The empire spanned south-eastern Europe, North Africa, and southwest Asia, and it reached its zenith in the fourteenth and fifteenth centuries.

Balfour Declaration: A policy statement signed by the British government in November 1917 that promised a homeland for Jews in the geographical area of biblical Israel. Sir Arthur Balfour was the British foreign secretary.

Mandate of Palestine: The British Mandate of Palestine was in effect from 1920 to 1948. Created by the League of Nations, the mandate gave the United Kingdom the right to extend its influence in an area roughly equivalent to modern Jordan, Israel, and the Palestinian Authority.

Baathist: A member of the pan-national Arab Baath Party. Baathists were secular socialists seeking to unite Arabs in a single socialist state.

Six Day War: A war between Israel and its Arab neighbors fought in June 1967. Israel launched the pre-emptive war in the face of an Arab military build-up, and it overwhelmed all opposition. At the end of the war, Israel occupied the Sinai Peninsula, the Golan Heights, and the West Bank of the Jordan River. It also occupied the city of Jerusalem, or al Quds to Muslims.

Yom Kippur War: A war between Israel and its Arab neighbors fought in October 1973. Also known as the Ramadan War, hostilities began with a surprise attack on Israel. After initial setbacks, Israel counterattacked and regained its positions.

Camp David Peace Accord: A peace treaty between Egypt and Israel brokered by the United States in 1979.

Iran-Iraq War: A war fought after Iraq invaded Iran over a border dispute in 1980. Many experts predicted an Iraqi victory, but the Iranians stopped the Iraqi Army. The war produced an eight-year stalemate and more than a million casualties. The countries signed an armistice in 1988.

Chapter Outline

    I.   **Defining the Middle East**
          OBJ 1: Define the Middle East as a historical, geographical, and cultural metaphor

          A. Bernard Lewis implies that the Middle East is not a geographical region; it is a concept based on a Western orientation to the world.
          B. The Middle East is a region that witnessed the birth of three great monotheistic religions: Judaism, Christianity, and Islam.

C. The Middle East gave birth to modern nations in the twentieth century, including Lebanon, Syria, Jordan, Yemen, the independent *Gulf States*, Iraq, Saudi Arabia, Iran, and Israel.

D. Three issues help illustrate the importance of the region:
1. The birth and spread of Islam.
2. Historical confrontations between Christianity and Islam.
3. The expansion of conflict beyond the traditional geographical realm of the Middle East.

II. **Brief Introduction to Islam**
OBJ 2: Briefly sketch the origins of Islam
OBJ 3: Describe the difference between Shiites and Sunnis

A. The centrality of Mohammed's revelation
1. Mohammed was born about 570 C.E. in the Western calendar in the Arabian city of Mecca.
2. He was extremely spiritual, by most accounts, and exposed to three great monotheistic religions, Judaism, Christianity, and Zoroastrianism.
3. He was close to his cousin *Ali ibn Talib,* who looked upon Mohammed as an older brother.
4. Mohammed had a vision of the angel Gabriel (Jabril), who told him that God had chosen Mohammed to be a prophet to the Arabs. Mohammed's role as a prophet, as *the* Prophet, is crucial in Islam; he stands in a long line of Jewish prophets—the visionaries later adopted by Christians—and Jesus of Nazareth.
5. Muslims believe that Mohammed was given the direct revelation of God through Gabriel.
6. One of the greatest mistakes, according to Muslims, was the deification of Jesus.
7. God has given divine law through the Prophets and Mohammed was chosen to correct the errors of the past.

B. Creating the Muslim community at Medina.
1. Mohammed won early converts in Mecca, including, his cousin Ali, his wife Khadijah, and three influential friends: *Abu Bakr*, *Umar*, and *Uthman.*
2. Many of the wealthy merchants of Mecca were not impressed. They resented that Mohammed's emphasis of social egalitarianism called on them to share wealth; they asked Abu Talib to remove familial protection from the young Prophet, a request Abu Talib refused.
3. After Abu Talib's death, Mohammed's life was in jeopardy; legend says he left for Medina in 622 C.E. with 72 families.
4. Muslims believe Mohammed created the perfect Islamic community at Medina, combining a just government with religion.

5. Mohammed eventually conquered Mecca, and the new religion spread along trade routes.

6. Mohammed died in 632 C.E. leaving the community of believers to chart the path for the new religion.

C. The Shiite – Sunni split

1. The poetic utterances of Gabriel were eventually written down, and a single book, the Qur'an, was codified.

    a. All Muslims came to believe that it was necessary to confess the existence of one God and Mohammed as God's Prophet.

    b. They were also expected to pray as a community, to give to the poor, to fast during holy times, and to make a pilgrimage to Mecca when able.

2. Problems came in the question of leadership.

3. According to Arabic tradition, Mohammed's male heir should lead the community, but Mohammed claimed to have revealed a new law that said the importance of the community would take precedence over tribal rules of inheritance.

4. One group of people believed the community should select its own leaders, but another group believed that Mohammed had designated Ali, his cousin and son-in-law, as the Muslim leader.

5. While the community selected a political and religious leader, a caliph, Ali's followers encouraged him to exercise the leadership authority they believed God had provided.

6. Mohammed's friend, Abu Bakr, became the first caliph is 632 C.E.

7. The followers of Ali felt that the *Umayyads*, Uthman's family, had abandoned the principles of Islam in favor of worldly goods.

8. This split came to dominate the Muslim community.

9. Mainstream Muslims following the caliph were conventionally called Sunnis, while the followers of Ali became known as Shiites.

    a. Zaidi Shiites recognize a line of succession differing from Hussein.

    b. Ismalis believe there were seven Imams who followed Mohammed.

    c. Ithna Ashari or Twelver Shiites compose the majority of Shiite Muslims.

10. Initially, there were few theological differences between Sunnis, who compose an estimated 85 to 90 percent of all Muslims today, and Shiites.

11. The main difference focused on the line of succession to Mohammed.

12. The split between Sunnis and Shiites remains today.

D. The golden age of Arabs

1. Mohammed's followers spread Islam and Arabic culture through the Middle East in the years after his death.

2. Two dynasties of leaders, the Umayyads (661–750) and the *Abbasids* (750–1258), ruled the area in the years following Mohammed.

3. The purpose of Islam was to subject the world to God's will.

       a. Islam means "submission to the will of God," and a Muslim is "one who submits."

    4. About 1000 C.E. the Turks began to take the domains of the Abbasids. Struggles continued for the next hundred years, until a Mongol advance from East Asia brought the Abbasid dynasty to an end.

    5. The West began its first violent encounters with the European attempts to conquer the Middle East, known as the Crusades (1095 to about 1250).

    6. When the Turks were driven back from the gates of Vienna, nearly 200 years later, it symbolized the ascendancy and domination of the West.

E. Agrarian response to political crises

    1. Karen Armstrong:

       a. Islam went through a series of crises before and after 1492.

       b. When agrarian empires falter, religious zealots arise to call the faithful back to the true meaning of religion.

       c. This happened several times in the history of Islam; each instance brought a theologically-driven political reform movement.

          i. The invasion of Mongol and Crusader armies in the eleventh and twelfth centuries.

         ii. The stagnation of Arab thought and technological development after 1200.

         iv. The collapse of the Caliphate in 1924.

III. Militant Philosophy
OBJ 4: Explain the emergence of militant theology

A. As religions develop, various interpretations follow, and this is especially true in times of crisis.

B. *Taqi al Din ibn Taymiyya* introduced new ideas about militancy and the faith after Arab setbacks by Mongols and Crusaders.

C. Ibn Taymiyya

    1. Western Crusaders began waging war against the Muslims in the eleventh century, and Mongol invaders struck the Arab lands one hundred years later.

    2. Taqi al Din ibn Taymiyya, an Islamic scholar, was appalled by the slaughter and sought to find an answer in his faith.

    3. He called for the destruction of heretics and invaders, calling jihad (struggle or effort) the sixth pillar of Islam.

    4. His ideas deeply affected *Mohammed ibn Abdul Wahhab,* who led a purification movement in Saudi Arabia in the eighteenth century.

    5. Islam is frequently described as a monotheistic religion based on five tenets, or pillars:

       a. A confession of faith in God and acceptance of Mohammed as God's last and greatest Prophet.

      b. Ritual prayers with the community.

      c. Giving alms.

      d. Fasting, especially during holy periods.

      e. Making a pilgrimage to Mohammed's birthplace, Mecca.

6. Different Islamic scholars (*ulema*) interpret jihad in various ways.

      a. Most Muslims defined jihad as defending a community and waging an internal struggle against one's own tendency toward evil.

      b. Ibn Taymiyya expanded the meaning of jihad by advocating attacks on nonbelievers and impure Muslims.

D. Abdul Wahhab

  1. Two recent movements became important to the jihadists.

      a. In the late eighteenth century a purification movement started by Mohammed ibn Abdul Wahhab (1703–1792), who was influenced by ibn Taymiyyah, took root in Arabia.

        i. Wahhab preached a puritanical strain of Islam that sought to rid the religion of practices added after the first few decades following Mohammed's death.

  2. Militant application of Wahhab's puritanical principles spread to India and other parts of Asia.

      a. Strict Muslims who follow the practices of Wahhab argue that they are trying to rid the religion of superstition and return it to the state envisioned by Mohammed and his first followers.

E. Sayyid Qutb

  1. *Sayyid Qutb* was an Egyptian teacher and journalist.

  2. Qutb's experience in America soured his opinion of Western civilization upon his return to Egypt he became an active member of the *Muslim Brotherhood* – an organization that seeks to create a single Muslim nation through education and religious reform.

  3. He published his most famous work, *Milestones*, in 1965; the book outlines the theology and ideology of Jihadist revolution, and its militant tone led to Qutb's second arrest and subsequent hanging in 1966.

  4. He believed that the Islamic world descended into darkness (*jahaliyya*) shortly after the death of Mohammed.

  5. Qutb rejected the West and called on Muslims to overthrow their corrupt governments.

  6. Qutb called for the destruction of all enemies.

  7. Qutb's books and articles popularized many militant ideas, and they continue to influence jihadists today.

  8. Jihadists utilize ibn Taymiyya, Wahhab, and Qutb to justify violence.

  9. Two other factors, play into the rise of extremism:

      a. The birth of modern Israel.

  10. b. The collapse of Western imperialism.

IV. **Modern Israel**
   OBJ 5: Discuss the historical significance in the decline of the Ottoman Empire and the birth of Zionism
   OBJ 6: Summarize the impact of World War I on the Middle East
   OBJ 7: Describe the formation of Israel and the Arab-Israeli wars
   OBJ 8: Explain the emergence of terrorism after the Six Days' War

   A. Jihadist theology has come to dominate religious terrorism, but nationalism and secularism predated the late-twentieth-century movement.
   B. Ethnic violence can be traced to the founding of the modern state of Israel.
   C. The creation of Israel was the result of three events in the nineteenth century:
      1. The persecution of Jews in Eastern Europe.
      2. The founding of the Zionist movement and its desire for a Jewish state.
      3. The collapse of the Ottoman Empire.
   D. These Zionist settlers began to carve out the nucleus of the land that would become modern Israel in 1948.
   E. A synopsis of modern Middle Eastern issues.
      1. In the late 1800s, three critical events took place that helped to shape the modern Middle East:
         a. The *Ottoman Empire,* the Turk-based government that ruled much of the Middle East, was falling apart in the nineteenth century.
         b. The second critical event came from a political movement called Zionism.
         c. European armies engulfed the Middle East from 1914 to 1918, as they fought World War I.
   F. Three sources of violence in Mahan's Middle East.
      1. The situation at the end of World War I set the stage for developments over the next century, and it is the basis for terrorism in the traditional Middle East.
      2. Three factors became prominent in Middle Eastern violence:
         a. The Palestinian question (control of Palestine).
         b. Intra-Arab rivalries/struggles.
         c. The future of revolutionary Islam.
      2. The sources of terrorism in the Middle East are symbiotic.
      3. All forms of Middle Eastern terrorism exhibit certain common traits.
         a. Many Arab groups express dissatisfaction over the existence of Israel.
         b. Most Middle Eastern terrorist groups are anti-imperialist.
         c. Middle Eastern terrorism is united by kinship bonds.
      4. When the Israelis practice terrorism, they usually claim their activities are conventional military actions.
      5. It is perhaps more accurate to argue that all Middle Eastern violence, Arabic and non-Arabic, is locked into symbiosis; it is interdependent.

238

G. The early Zionist movement in Palestine
   1. The Zionist movement took place at the same time the Ottoman Empire was breaking up.
   2. Palestinians sold land to the Zionists, and the Zionists linked their holdings together. Their ultimate purpose was to create a Jewish state.
   3. The Zionists originally stated they had no desire to displace the Palestinians; they wanted to coexist with them.
   4. As Jewish settlers bought land, however, they purchased large parcels next to each other.
   5. They established governing councils for their farmland and refused to sell land back to Arabs.
H. World War I and contradictory promises
   1. Jewish immigration in Palestine played into the political issues of the First World War.
   2. In return for a general Arab revolt against the Turks, the British agreed to support the creation of a united, independent Arab state at the close of the war.
   3. The Arabs felt they had been promised the ancient Arab realm of Islam.
   4. The British promised the Zionists a Jewish homeland in Palestine.
   5. *The Balfour Declaration* of November 1917 promised to create the state of Israel.
   6. *Sir Mark Sykes,* a British Foreign Service officer, negotiated a treaty with the French to extend spheres of British and French influence in the states of the old Ottoman Empire.
   7. The British approached the Russians with another deal – Iran would be divided into three parts: a northern area controlled by Russia, a southern zone under British rule, and a neutral area in between.
   8. When the war ended in 1918, the entire Middle East was controlled by the British, French, and Russians.
   9. The Arabs could not counter the continuing British influence, and neither a pan-Arabic realm nor a Jewish national state could develop under the watchful eyes of the British.
   10. The *Mandate of Palestine* gave Britain control of Palestine and placed the British in the center of Middle Eastern affairs.
   11. The Arabs believed they had received a false promise, and the Jews avidly demanded their right to a homeland.
I. The birth of Israel.
   1. While the British established the Protectorate, in Palestine feelings of nationalism and anger increased.
   2. Sporadic violence against the Jews began in 1921, and the Jews formed a defense force known as the Haganah.
   3. Tensions increased throughout the decade culminating in a riot in 1929 when the Islamic mufti of Jerusalem inspired an attack against Jewish worshippers.

239

4. An Arab revolt in Palestine began in 1936 and lasted until 1939.
5. It was primarily aimed at the British, but the brewing hatred and distrust between the Arab and Jewish communities also came to the surface.
6. In late 1945 and 1946, thousands of Jews displaced by the Nazi holocaust flocked to Palestine.
7. Seeing the danger presented by this massive influx of Jews, Palestinian Arabs began to arm themselves.
8. The UN suggested that one part of Palestine be given to the Arabs and another part be given to the Jews.
9. On May 15, 1948, the United Nations recognized the partition of Palestine and the modern nation-state of Israel.
10. Both Arabs and Jews shifted to conventional warfare and would fight that way until 1967.

J. Arab power struggles and Arab-Israeli war.
1. Modern Middle Eastern terrorism is the result of continuing conflicts in the twentieth century.
2. Aside from the Palestinian issue, other Arabs felt slighted by various peace settlements, and their dissatisfaction continued through the end of World War II.
3. The French and British created a number of states that did not reflect the realistic divisions in the Middle East.
   a. Libya was divided into British and French sections, and it did not become independent until 1951.
   b. Egypt achieved its independence before World War II but did not fully break with Britain until Gamal Nasser took power in 1954.
   c. Syria was under French rule from 1922 to 1946.
   d. Lebanon has become one of the most violent regions in the area.
4. In an effort to secure the land route to India, the British established several states from the Mediterranean to the Persian Gulf in the 19th and 20th centuries.
   a. Jordan became a constitutional monarchy ruled by King Hussein from 1952 to 1999 and his son, King Abdullah, from 1999 to the present.
   b. Iraq's path was more turbulent – a 1958 coup eliminated the Iraqi Hashemites from power, another coup in 1968 brought *Baathist* rule, and Saddam Hussein, a Baathist, came to power in 1979.
5. Saudi Arabia and the Persian Gulf states fared somewhat better because of their immense wealth and independence from Europe.
6. From 1947 to 1967, the Middle East was dominated by a series of short conventional wars.
7. In 1967, the Israelis demonstrated their superiority over all their Arab neighbors – although better equipped and outnumbered, in six days Israel doubled its territory and soundly defeated its opponents.

8. After the 1967 *Six Days' War*, the Palestine Liberation Organization (PLO) began a series of terrorist attacks against civilian Israeli positions.
9. Arab states also split into several camps:
    a. One group, represented by King Hussein of Jordan, was anxious to find a way to coexist with Israel.
    b. A few nations, like Egypt, simply wanted to avenge the embarrassment of the Six Days' War.
    c. Represented by the Baath Party, groups of Arab socialists called for both Arab unity and the destruction of Israel.
    d. A group of wealthy oil states hoped for stability in the region.
10. Despite the myriad positions, the embarrassment of the Six Days' War proved to be the strongest catalyst to action.
11. The *Yom Kippur War* reversed the defeat of the Six Days' War; catching the Israelis by surprise, the Egyptians drove Israeli forces back into the Sinai.
12. Under the mediation of U.S. President Jimmy Carter, Anwar Sadat agreed to a separate peace with Israel, provided Israel would withdraw from the Sinai Peninsula.
    a. Menachim Begin agreed, and on May 26, 1979, Egypt and Israel signed the *Camp David Peace Accord*.
13. Sadat was assassinated by Muslim fundamentalists in 1981 for agreeing to peace.
K. The return of terrorism.
    1. The Arabs who rejected peace with Israel fell into two camps.
        a. The radicals rejected any peace or recognition of Israel.
        b. The more moderate group was concerned about the fate of the Palestinians.
    2. In the melee of the 1980s, Middle Eastern terrorism fell into several broad categories:
        a. Suicide bombings and other attacks on Israeli and Western positions in Lebanon.
        b. Various militias fighting other militias in Lebanon.
        c. State-sponsored terrorism from Libya, Syria, and Iran.
        d. Freelance terrorism to high-profile groups.
        e. Terrorism in support of Arab Palestinians.
        f. Attacks in Europe against Western targets.
        g. Israeli assassinations of alleged terrorists.
    3. Despite the appearance of terrorism, conventional war continued to dominate the Middle East, and Arabs struggled against Arabs.
    4. As the *Iran-Iraq War* neared its end, Saddam Hussein turned his attention to Kuwait.
    5. Saddam Hussein invaded the small country to gain control of its oil production.

6. As Iraq retreated in the Persian Gulf, terrorists began plotting new methods for striking the United States.

V. **Iran**
OBJ 9: Briefly sketch the history of modern Iran

A. Americans found it convenient in the 1980s to speak of Iranian terrorism; the Iranians had violated international law in the early stages of their revolution by taking the American embassy in Tehran.

B. Intelligence sources reported that the Iranians were allied with other terrorist states and supported a shadowy group known as Islamic Jihad— which turned out to be a cover name for an operational group of Hezbollah.

C. Far from being a rebirth of fundamentalism, it was more indicative of a religious split in Islam.

D. Uniquely Persian
1. Iranians are not Arabs; they are Persian and have strong ethno-national ties to the ancient Persian Empire.
2. Iranians resisted Turks and later European imperialists.
3. European imperialism cannot be overemphasized when considering the politics of modern Iran.
4. During the nineteenth century, Iranians developed a hierarchy of Shiite Islamic scholars, including local prayer leaders, masters of Islam, ayatollahs, and grand ayatollahs.
5. Leading scholars formed a theological advisory board to the government called the *majilis council.*

E. British influence and control
1. British imperialism came to Iran in the 1800s; after 1850, the British began to view Iran as the northern gate to India.
2. Oil production had a tremendous impact on the way the British used Iran.
3. *Reza Shah Pahlavi*, with British support, became shah of Iran in 1925.
4. For Iran to gain full independence, Reza Shah needed to develop an economic base that would support the country and consolidate his strength among the ethnic populations in Iran.
   a. He encouraged Western investment, primarily British and American, in the oil and banking industries.
   b. He courted various power groups inside Iran, including the Shiite fundamentalists.
5. Reza Shah's long-term failure was a result of his foreign policy.

F. The revolution
1. Khomeini's rise to power was a key to the revolution.
2. He was intolerant, not only of the shah's American infatuation, but of other Shiites who refused to accept his narrow interpretation of Islam. *Khomeini* headed a network of 180,000 Islamic revolutionaries in

addition to 90,000 mullahs (low-ranking prayer leaders), 5,000 hojatalislams (middle-ranking scholars), and 50 ayatollahs (recognized scholars with authoritative writings).

3. The Shiite scholars called for a holy revolution and the restoration of Islam; Khomeini led the way while in Iraqi exile.

4. Khomeini returned to Tehran in 1978; in February 1979, the shah fled from Iran.

5. The Iranian Revolution of 1979 caused another form of terrorism to spread from the Middle East; because the superpowers would win any war fought out in the open, the Ayatollah Khomeini chose to fight in the shadows.

6. In 1982, Israel invaded Lebanon, moving through the Shiite areas of the south.

7. The Iranian Revolutionary Guard arrived in the Bekaa Valley and established the nucleus of a new type of revolutionary force, Hezbollah.

G. The call to Karbala

1. Khomeini used a mixture of repressive tactics and political strategies to consolidate his power in Iran; he is best understood within the Shiite tradition of Islam.

2. The Ayatollah Khomeini was guided by the message of Karbala, and he removed Islamic scholars and political leaders who disagreed with his message.

3. He believed the Iranian Revolution was the first step in purifying the world.

4. After Khomeini's death in 1989, several competing schools of thought emerged in Iran.

5. Although opposed by some Islamic scholars and almost all political moderates, a Khomeini-influenced majilis council came to dominate Iranian politics.

Chapter Summary

- The Middle East is a cultural concept. It can refer to a geographical area, but the boundaries are not distinct. *The Middle East* means different things to different people.

- Islam is one of the world's great monotheistic religions. Believers contend that God is revealed through prophets and that Mohammed was the last and greatest Prophet. God's holy law is revealed in the Quran, and Islamic law can be interpreted by the sayings and actions of Mohammed.

- Islam has many different branches. The two main branches—the Shiites and the Sunnis—are initially split over the leadership of the Muslim community. Today, there are theological and structural differences.

- Militant interpretations of Islam developed as the Islamic world faced military, political, and economic crises. Some researchers believe that the disciples of ibn Taymiyyah and abdul Wahhab were violent, but that these Islamic scholars were nonviolent reformers. Most Islamic scholars blame violent interpretations of the religion on Qutb.

- When the Ottoman Empire collapsed, it led to the dissolution of the caliphate. British and French forces divided the Middle East into spheres of influence after World War I. Zionist activists had purchased land in Palestine, and they sought to create a Jewish state. European actions led to the creation of modern Israel within the British sphere of influence, and the first modern terrorists were Zionist separatists in Palestine.

- The Arabs and Israelis engaged in a series of conventional wars from 1948 to 1973, and the Israelis demonstrated their military superiority in each one. After the devastating defeat of June 1967, some Palestinians turned to terrorism as a method for confronting Israeli military superiority.

- Modern Iran formed within the context of European imperialism. The British were instrumental in placing Iranian leaders on the throne, and the United States took their place after World War II. Iran disavowed the United States after the 1979 Iranian Revolution.

DISCUSSION QUESTIONS

1. Militants have altered the social meaning of Islam, especially in the Western mind. Do you believe that there are any other religions that offer violent extremism through misinterpretation? If so, which ones? Did the events of 9/11 impact your view of Islam? In what way? (OBJ 1 – 4)

2. After reading this chapter, what do you believe is the recurring theme that emerges about the cause of religious and nationalist conflict? Can you think of any policy changes that might prevent the rise of these conflicts from occurring in the future? (OBJ 1 – 9)

3. White indicates that one can better begin to understand the Middle East by focusing on the late 1800s, during which time three critical events took place that facilitated in shaping the modern Middle East. Discuss these events. Which of the three do you believe to be most important or do you believe all three were equally important? Defend your position. (OBJ 1 – 5)

4. Who was Taqi al Din ibn Taymiyyah? Why is he important in understanding the emergence of militant theology? (OBJ 2, 3, and 4)

ASSIGNMENTS

1. Before having the students read this chapter, have them discuss their knowledge of Islam. Make sure that students address the beliefs, the leaders, the holy text, and the history of the religion. After the students discuss their understanding of the religion, include where this knowledge was obtained. Have them identify whether they basing their beliefs on media stereotypes, religious scholarship, or something else? (OBJ 1, 2, 3, and 4)

2. Have the students construct three maps of the Middle East: the social Middle East, the historical Middle East, and the geographical Middle East. Display the maps in the front of the class room and allow time to discuss the differences between them and examine the difficulty in defining the Middle East. (OBJ 1, 5, 6, 7, and 8)

3. Have students break into two groups. Have group A prepare a presentation about the rise of conflict involving Palestine and Israel. Assign group B the rise of conflict in Iran. Have the groups 'teach back' their presentation to the class. (OBJ 1 – 9)

4. As a review, play jeopardy using the key concepts and terms from the chapter. (OBJ 1 – 9)

5. Have each student comb through http://topics.cnn.com/topics/islam (or another website as approved by the instructor) for a current event and select an article that relates to one or more of the chapter's core concepts. Have students provide a journalistic summary and a personal opinion/reaction to the article. Have students orally present the article to the class, field Q & As from their fellow students, and provide a copy of the original source article following the presentation. Optional: Have students complete peer assessments at the end of each presentation. (OBJ 1 - 9)

MEDIA TOOLS

1. *"Wikis"*
   7 Things you should know about Wikis. Retrieved from the Web Jun 29, 2012 at http://net.educause.edu/ir/library/pdf/ELI7004.pdf

   This document offers easy to understand instruction on the history, development, and potential uses of Wikis.

   Have students develop (or make additions to a previously created one) a *Webliography* (resource list) using a Blog or Wiki that provides a short description and link to a scholarly resource pertaining to course concepts. For example, have students add two to three resources each and ask them to add their assessment of at least one of their peers' contributions. If desired, allow time to discuss Blogs/Wikis. This activity can be reused throughout the course, by asking students to add/revise their contributions each week, bi-weekly, etc. (LO 1 through 9)

2. ***"Current Events Article Summary with Peer Assessment"***
    Use the Article Summary Template, which can be obtained on the instructor companion website, for this assignment. The template offers information on Internet research, outside resources, identification of credible sources, and detailed directions on completing an assessment of a news article. It also includes a peer evaluation tool.

    Have each student comb the Internet for terrorism related news and select an article that relates to one or more of the chapter's core concepts. Be sure selections are an article of interest from a credible source (*more on credibility can be found in the article summary template above).* Fill out an article summary template. The *template asks for generic info about the article, a journalistic summary, as well as a personal opinion/reaction to the article.* Have each student summarize the article and present it orally to the class and field Q & As from their fellow students. Have students complete peer assessments at the end of each presentation. Have students submit templates, original source article, and peer-reviews prior to the end of class. (OBJ 1-9)

3. ***"Interactive Timeline of Middle Eastern Control"***
    Maps of War. Timeline of Middle Eastern control 3000 B.C.E. through 2006 C.E. Retrieved from the Web Aug 20, 2012 at http://www.mapsofwar.com/ind/imperial-history.html

    This website offers an interactive visual display of the varying entities that have controlled the Middle Eastern region over the millennia.

    Using a projector or other means to visually share the screen with the class, play the timeline stopping before each progression to give students a chance to reflect upon and guess who controlled the region at that given time. Supplement the timeline video, with commentary on important events at corresponding times during the timeline progression. (OBJ 1 – 9)

4. ***"Interactive Map of Middle East"***
    Rethinking Schools. Interactive Map of the Middle East. Retrieved from the Web Aug 20, 2012 at http://www.rethinkingschools.org/just_fun/games/mapgame.html

    The website offers a fun game via an interactive map of the Middle East wherein participants 'click' and drag' countries to their corresponding locations.

    Have students test their knowledge of the region by playing the game individually at their stations or compete as a class via a screen share projection. (OBJ 1 – 9)

Chapter 8—Background to the Middle East

TEST BANK

TRUE/FALSE

1. Muslims believe that Jews, Christians, and Zoroastrians worship the same deity.

ANS: T   REF: p. 191   OBJ: 2

2. The followers of Ali are known as Sunnis.

ANS: F   REF: p. 191   OBJ: 1, 2, and 3

3. Different Islamic scholars (*ulema*) interpret jihad the same way.

ANS: F   REF: p. 196   OBJ: 2, 3, and 4

4. Some Islamic countries refer to their legislative body as a majilis.

ANS: T   REF: p. 207   OBJ: 2, 3, and 4

5. The Zionist movement took place at the same time the Ottoman Empire was forming.

ANS: F   REF: p. 201   OBJ: 5 and 6

6. Leaders of the Irgun studied and incorporated the tactics of Marighella.

ANS: F   REF: p. 203   OBJ: 4, 5, and 6

7. Sayyid Qutb believed that the Islamic world descended into darkness shortly after the death of Mohammed.

ANS: T   REF: p. 197   OBJ: 1, 2, 3, and 4

8. Gulf States include only those Arab kingdoms bordering the Dead Sea.

ANS: F   REF: p. 190   OBJ: 1 and 6

9. In 1969, Colonel Muammar Gadhafi seized power in a military coup, claiming Libya as an anti-Western socialist state.

ANS: T   REF: p. 204   OBJ: 1, 6, 7, and 8

10. Mainstream Muslims following the caliph were conventionally called Sunnis, while the followers of Ali became known as Shiites.

ANS: T   REF: p. 193   OBJ: 1, 2, and 3

11.   Ismalis believe that there were twelve Imams who followed Mohammed.

ANS: F   REF: p. 193   OBJ: 1, 2, and 3

12.   Zaidi Shiites compose the majority of Shiite Muslims.

ANS: F   REF: p. 193   OBJ: 1, 2, and 3

13.   Although theological divisions with Sunnis would eventually arise and the Shiites themselves would split into competing sects, the first division in Islam was political.

ANS: T   REF: p. 194   OBJ: 1, 2, and 3

14.   Militant Muslims view jihad as the *sixth* pillar of Islam.

ANS: T   REF: p. 196   OBJ: 3

15.   The only persons to practice terrorism in the name of their religion are Muslim fanatics.

ANS: F   REF: p. 199   OBJ: 3

MULTIPLE CHOICE

1.   What country's leader proclaimed that, "Israel had no right to exist and that nuclear weapons could be used to eradicate the country"?
        a. Iran
        b. Iraq
        c. Saudi Arabia
        d. Russia

ANS: a   REF: p. 189   OBJ: 1, 5, and 8

2.   Which of the following religions were not founded in the Middle East: Judaism, Christianity, Hinduism, and Islam?
        a. Christianity
        b. Judaism
        c. Hinduism
        d. Islam

ANS: c   REF: p. 190   OBJ: 2

248

3. According to Islam, Mohammed was born in which city?
   a. Mecca
   b. Medina
   c. Badr
   d. Jerusalem

ANS: a   REF: p. 8   OBJ: 1, 2, and 3

4. Who are the four major Prophets of Islam?
   a. Abraham, Moses, Jesus, and Mohammed
   b. Moses, Jesus, Mohammed, and Ali
   c. Mohammed, Abu Bakr, Umar, and Uthman
   d. Mohammed, Ali, Hasan, and Hussein

ANS: a   REF: p. 191   OBJ: 2 and 3

5. According to the text, in what year was Mohammed born?
   a. 100 B.C.E
   b. 560 A.D.
   c. 580 A.D.
   d. 570 BCE

ANS: d   REF: p. 191   OBJ: 2

6. _____ is the site of a battle between the Muslims of Medina and the merchants of Mecca in 624.
   a. Jordan
   b. Iraq
   c. Badr
   e. Qutb

ANS: c   REF: p. 192   OBJ: 2, 3, and 4

7. The Quran is a codified version of the communication Mohammed received from the angel, _____.
   a. Gabriel (Jabril)
   b. Raphael (Israfil)
   c. Michael (Mikail)
   d. Azreal (Malak al-maut)

ANS: a   REF: p. 192   OBJ: 2

8. The initial split of the Islam faith into the Sunnis and Shiites was based on the issue of ____.
   a. Militarization
   b. Money
   c. Leadership
   d. Geography

ANS: c   REF: p. 192   OBJ: 2 and 4

9. Following the split of the Islamic faith, the family of _____ assumed control of the Islamic movement and ruled the first Arab empire.
   a. Bakr
   b. Talib
   c. Umar
   d. Uthman

ANS: d   REF: p. 193   OBJ: 2 and 4

10. The _____ was a Turkish based government that lasted for six hundred years until 1924.
   a. Persian Empire
   b. Arab Empire
   c. British Empire
   d. Ottoman Empire

ANS: d   REF: p. 199   OBJ: 1 and 5

11. The _____ Declaration signed by the United Kingdom in November 1917 promised a homeland for Jews in the geographical area of biblical Israel.
   a. Sykes-Picot
   b. Balfour
   c. Mawdudi
   d. Palestine

ANS: b   REF: p. 202   OBJ: 1, 6, 7, and 8

12. The _____ refers to a peace treaty between Egypt and Israel brokered by the United States in 1979.
   a. United Nations Peace Accord
   b. Amnesty Accord
   c. Camp David Peace Accord
   d. International Peace Accord

ANS: c   REF: p. 206   OBJ: 6 and 7

13. When forced to flee for his life, Ayatollah Khomeini received asylum in _____.
   a. Berlin
   b. Paris
   c. Tehran
   d. Cypress

ANS: b   REF: p. 210   OBJ: LO9

14. Sunnis compose an estimated _____ percent of all Muslims today.
   a. 40-45
   b. 10-15
   c. 85-90
   d. 70-75

ANS: c   REF: p. 193   OBJ: 2 and 3

15. Emphasizing _____, or the oneness of God, ibn Taymiyyah attacked anything that threatened to come between humanity and God.
    a. Rishidun
    b. Tawhid
    c. Islam
    d. Jahaliyya

ANS: b   REF: p. 196   OBJ: 2, 3, and 4

16. Muslims believe Mohammed created the perfect Islamic community at _____.
    a. Medina
    b. Mecca
    c. Badr
    d. Jerusalem

ANS: a   REF: p. 192   OBJ: 1 and 2

17. Islam is frequently described as a monotheistic religion based on _____ tenets, or pillars.
    a. Two
    b. Three
    c. Four
    d. Five

ANS: d   REF: p. 196   OBJ: 2

18. Which of the following is NOT a pillar of Islamic faith?
    a. Ritual prayers with the community
    b. Giving alms
    c. Tithing
    d. Fasting, especially during holy periods

ANS: c   REF: p. 196   OBJ: 2

19. Who penned the 1965 work, *Milestones*, which outlined the theology and ideology of jihadist revolution with militant tone?
    a. ibn Taymiyyah
    b. Sayyid Qutb
    c. Mohammed ibn Abdul Wahhab
    d. Mawlana Mawdudi

ANS: b   REF: p. 197   OBJ: 4

20. The Al Qaeda Manual cites _____ as a source of inspiration.
    a. Sayyid Qutb
    b. Abdul Wahhab
    c. Ayman al Zawahiri
    d. Mawlana Mawdudi

ANS: a   REF: p. 198   OBJ: 4

21. After _____, the British began to view Iran as the northern gate to India.
    a. 1800
    b. 1900
    c. 1850
    d. 1950

ANS: c   REF: p. 208   OBJ: 5 and 9

22. The British established the Anglo-Persian Oil Company in 1909 and started taking oil profits out of ____.
    a. Saudi Arabia
    b. Iraq
    c. Iran
    d. Turkey

ANS: c   REF: p. 208   OBJ: 9

23. The Crusades lasted from 1095 to about _____.
    a. 1500
    b. 1492
    c. 1600
    d. 1250

ANS: d   REF: p. 195   OBJ: 1 and 5

24. In 1922 Great Britain received permission from _____ to create the Mandate of Palestine.
    a. The League of Nations
    b. The United Nations
    c. The European Council
    d. The Shah of Iran

ANS: a   REF: p. 202   OBJ: 7

25. Taqi al Din ibn Taymiyyah, an Islamic scholar, called for jihad, the destruction of heretics and invaders, calling it the _____ of Islam.
    a. Fifth pillar
    b. Fourth pillar
    c. Sixth pillar
    d. Eighth pillar

ANS: c   REF: p. 196   OBJ: 3 and 4

26. Israel officially functions as a _____.
    a. Constitutional republic
    b. Theocracy
    c. Oligarchy
    d. Parliamentary democracy

ANS: d   REF: p. 199   OBJ: 1 and 5

27. The _____ gave Britain control of Palestine and placed the British in the center of Middle Eastern affairs.
    a. Mandate of the Middle East
    b. Treaty of the Middle East
    c. Mandate of Palestine
    d. Treaty of Palestine

ANS: c   REF: p. 202   OBJ: 6, 7, and 9

28. In _____ the United Nations recognized the partition of Palestine and the modern nation-state of Israel.
    a. 1948
    b. 1988
    c. 1990
    d. 1848

ANS: a   REF: p. 204   OBJ: 7

29. At the turn of the 19th Century, European Jews, separated from their ancient homeland for nearly 2,000 years lead a political movement called _____ in the hopes of creating their own nation.
    a. Catharism
    b. Mandaeism
    c. Zionism
    d. Zoroastrianism

ANS: c   REF: p. 199   OBJ: 6 and 7

30. U.S. President _____ was in attendance when Egypt and Israel signed the Camp David Peace Accord.
    a. Jimmy Carter
    b. George W. Bush
    c. Bill Clinton
    d. Ronald Regan

ANS: a   REF: p. 206   OBJ: 6, 7, 8, and 9

31. The _____ was a war between Israel and its Arab neighbors fought in June 1967.
    a. Yom Kippur War
    b. Four Days' War
    c. Zionist War
    d. Six Days' War

ANS: d   REF: p. 205   OBJ: 7, 8, and 9

32. _____ used a mixture of repressive tactics and political strategies to consolidate his power in Iran, and he is best understood within the Shi'ite tradition of Islam.
    a. Saddam Hussein
    b. Ayatollah Khomeini
    c. Mohammed Reza Pahlavi
    d. Gamal Nasser

ANS: b   REF: p. 211   OBJ: 7, 8, and 9

33. The Balfour Declaration of November 1917 promised to create the state of _____.
    a. Palestine
    b. Persia
    c. Israel
    d. Iran

ANS: c   REF: p. 202   OBJ: 1, 7, and 8

34.   The three most important cities in Sunni Islam are: _____.
    a. Badr, Mecca, and Medina
    b. Mecca, Medina, and Jerusalem (al Quds)
    c. Medina, Jerusalem (al Quds), and Cairo
    d. Mecca, Medina, and Karbala

ANS: b   REF: p. 202   OBJ: 1, 2, and 3

35.   Geographically, ancient Persia occupied the area known as _____.
    a. Iran
    b. Syria
    c. Egypt
    d. Turkey

ANS: a   REF: p. 202   OBJ: 1

36.   At the end of _____, the entire Middle East was controlled by the British, French, and Russians.
    a. WWII
    b. WWI
    c. The Six Days Way
    d. The 100 Years War

ANS: b   REF: p. 202   OBJ: 1, 6, 7, 8, and 9

37.   Syria was under _____ rule from 1922 to 1946.
    a. British
    b. French
    c. American
    d. German

ANS: b   REF: p. 204   OBJ: 6 and 7

38.   _____ became a constitutional monarchy ruled by King Hussein from 1952 to 1999.
    a. Jordan
    b. Iraq
    c. Iran
    d. Syria

ANS: a   REF: p. 205   OBJ: 8

39. What world leader was assassinated by Muslim fundamentalists in 1981 for agreeing to peace?
   a. Anwar Sadat
   b. Menachim Begin
   c. Gamal Nasser
   d. Muammar Gadhafi

ANS: a　　　　　　　REF: p. 206　　　　　　OBJ: 7 and 8

40. In 1978, Israel launched a minor invasion of _____, followed by a full-scale attack in 1982.
   a. Iran
   b. Lebanon
   c. Iraq
   d. Syria

ANS: b　　　　　　　REF: p. 206　　　　　　OBJ: 7 and 8

Case 8.0

The Muslims who followed Mohammed agreed on many aspects of the new faith. God's revelation to Mohammed was critical. The angelic utterances received by Mohammed were eventually codified in a single book, the Quran. The things Mohammed had said and done were recorded, and his actions became the basis for interpreting the Quran. All Muslims came to believe that it was necessary to confess the existence of one God and Mohammed as God's Prophet. They were also expected to pray as a community, to give to the poor, to fast during holy times, and to make a pilgrimage to Mecca when able to do so. Problems came, however, in the question of leadership. According to Arabic tradition, Mohammed's male heir should lead the community, but Mohammed claimed to have revealed a new law that said the importance of the community would take precedence over tribal rules of inheritance. One group of people believed the community should select its own leaders, but another group believed that Mohammed had designated Ali, his cousin and son-in-law, as the Muslim leader. The proponents of community selection carried the day, but Ali's followers came to believe that God had given a special inspiration to Mohammed's family.

41. What was the core reason for the Sunni-Shiite split in Islam?
   a. Questions over leadership
   b. Geographical conflicts
   c. Military conflicts
   d. Economic issues

ANS: a　　　　　　　REF: p. 192　　　OBJ: 1, 2, 3, and 4

42. The faith-based expectations of Muslims noted above are known as the five _____ of Islam.
   a. Pillars
   b. Corners
   c. Sacraments
   d. Rites

ANS: a　　　　　　　REF: p. 196　　　　　　OBJ: 1 and 2

43. Of the four Rightly Guided Caliphs, Shiites only recognize _____.
   a. Abu Bakr
   b. Umar
   c. Uthman
   d. Ali

ANS: d   REF: p. 193   OBJ: 1, 2, and 3

44. The angelic utterances referred to above came from the angel, _____.
   a. Gabriel (Jabril)
   b. Raphael (Israfil)
   c. Michael (Mikail)
   d. Azreal (Malak al-maut)

ANS: a   REF: p. 192   OBJ: 2

45. What was the official title of the community leader chosen by the Sunnis?
   a. Imam
   b. Caliph
   c. Sufi
   d. Allah

ANS: b   REF: p. 192   OBJ: 1, 2, and 3

Case 8.1
Islam is frequently described as a monotheistic religion based on five tenets, or pillars: (1) a confession of faith in God and acceptance of Mohammed as God's last and greatest Prophet, (2) ritual prayers with the community, (3) giving alms, (4) fasting, especially during holy periods, and (5) making a pilgrimage to Mohammed's birthplace, Mecca (Farah, 2000, pp. 132–148). Jihad has a place in this system, and different Islamic scholars (*ulema*) interpret jihad in various ways. There are many meanings, but most Muslims defined *jihad* as defending a community and waging an internal struggle against one's own tendency toward evil.

46. A Muslim offers a multitude of seed grain to his neighbor who lost all his crops due to a drought. This act is an example of what pillar of Islam?
   a. First
   b. Second
   c. Third
   d. Fourth

ANS: c   REF: p. 196   OBJ: 2

47. A Muslim completes ablutions (ritual bathing/cleansing) prior to entering a mosque. This act is an example of what pillar of Islam?
   a. First
   b. Second
   c. Third
   d. Fourth

ANS: b   REF: p. 196   OBJ: 2

48. A Muslim fanatic kidnaps his neighbor's wife, holding her hostage until the neighbor renounces his Jewish faith. This act is an example of what pillar of Islam?
   a. Third
   b. Fourth
   c. Fifth
   d. Sixth

ANS: d   REF: p. 196   OBJ: 2

Case 8.2

The Zionist movement took place at the same time the Ottoman Empire was breaking up, and this created opportunities for several groups interested in the region. For Arabs in general it signaled the possible recreation of the Arab empire shortly after the death of Mohammed. Palestinian Arabs, much more modest in their political views, sought to join with Syria to form a new country. Many Palestinians welcomed the Zionists, thinking that Jews would assist them in the formation of a new country. The Zionists held no such belief: the Jews had no intention of becoming part of Syria. Nasr (1997, pp. 6–7) argues that the Palestinian Arabs represented a cohesive mixture of Muslims and Christians and that they were leery of Jewish settlements. Regardless, Palestinians sold land to the Zionists, who linked their holdings with the ultimate purpose of creating a Jewish state.

49. The Zionist movement was ultimately successful in their desire to create a Jewish state (Israel) in what year?
   a. 1968
   b. 1948
   c. 1978
   d. 1958

ANS: b   REF: p. 199   OBJ: 1, 5, 6, 7, and 8

50. Both the Zionists and the Arabs in the Palestine region harbored anti-imperial sentiment against which nation which controlled the area?
   a. Britain
   b. America
   c. France
   d. Russia

ANS: a   REF: p. 201   OBJ: 1, 5, 6, 7, and 8

COMPLETION

1. Bernard Lewis implies that the Middle East is not a _____, it is a concept.

   ANS: geographical region   REF: p. 190   OBJ: 1

2. Sunni Muslims believe ___ is the fourth and last Rightly Guided caliph.

   ANS: Ali   REF: p. 191   OBJ: 2 and 3

3. In the late eighteenth century, a purification movement started by Mohammed ibn Abdul Wahhab (1703–1792), who was influenced by ibn Taymiyyah, took root in _____.

   ANS: Arabia   REF: p. 196   OBJ: 2, 3, and 4

4. The _____ refers to an organization founded by Hassan al Banna designed to recapture the spirit and religious purity during the period of Mohammed and the four Rightly Guided caliphs.

   ANS: Muslim Brotherhood   REF: p. 197   OBJ: 3 and 4

5. The _____ were the first Arab and Muslim dynasty, ruling Damascus from 661 to 750.

   ANS: Umayyads   REF: p. 193   OBJ: 2 and 3

6. When the Israelis practice terrorism, they usually claim their activities are _____ actions.

   ANS: conventional military   REF: p. 200   OBJ: 7 and 8

7. The things Mohammed had said and done were recorded and his actions became the basis for interpreting the _____.

   ANS: Quran   REF: p. 192   OBJ: 2

8. The two main branches of Islam are the _____ and the _____.

   ANS: Shiites, Sunnis   REF: p. 200   OBJ: 2 and 3

9. Most Islamic scholars blame violent interpretation of the religion on _____.

   ANS: Sayyid Qutb   REF: p. 212   OBJ: 4

10. The Arabs and _____ engaged in a series of conventional wars from 1948 to 1973.

    ANS: Israelis   REF: p. 212   OBJ: 5, 7, and 8

11. The Camp David Peace Accord brokered peace between _____ and Israel.

    ANS: Egypt   REF: p.206   OBJ: 7 and 8

12. Ottoman Turks conquered _____ in 1453, renaming it Istanbul.

    ANS: Constantinople   REF: p.195   OBJ: 1 and 5

13. The Zionists purchased land in _____ to create their new homeland.

    ANS: Palestine   REF: p.201   OBJ: 5 and 7

14. The Mandate of Palestine gave _____ control of Palestine.

    ANS: Britain   REF: p.202   OBJ: 6, 7, and 8

15. Sporadic violence against Palestinian Jews began in 1921, and the Jews formed a defense force known as the ___.

    ANS: Haganah   REF: p.203   OBJ: 7 and 8

16. A 1929 riot in Palestine pitted the Islamic mufti of Jerusalem against _____ worshippers.

    ANS: Jewish   REF: p. 203   OBJ: 7 and 8

17. The _____ Declaration of November 1917 promised to create the state of Israel.

    ANS: Balfour   REF: p.202   OBJ: 5 and 6

18. The United Nations post WWII solution to the Arab-Israeli conflict was for one part of Palestine to be given to the Arabs and another part to be given to the ____.

    ANS: the Jews   REF: p.204   OBJ: 7 and 8

19. Gamal Nasser took power over _____ in 1954.

    ANS: Egypt   REF: p.204   OBJ: 7 and 8

20. In an effort to secure the land route to _____, the British established several states from the Mediterranean Sea to the Persian Gulf in the nineteenth and early twentieth centuries.
    ANS: India   REF: p.205   OBJ: 5, 6, 7

ESSAY

1. Outline the four rightly guided Caliphs, following the Shiite-Sunni split.

ANS:
- Problems came in the question of leadership.

- According to Arabic tradition, Mohammed's male heir should lead the community, but Mohammed claimed to have revealed a new law that said the importance of the community would take precedence over tribal rules of inheritance.
- Questions that still affect the practice of Islam today, over leadership spawned a debate and eventually a civil war.
- The question of leadership focused on the community.
- One group of people believed the community should select its own leaders, but another group believed that Mohammed had designated Ali, his cousin and son-in-law, as the Muslim leader.
- The proponents of community selection carried the day, but Ali's followers came to believe that God had given a special inspiration to Mohammed's family.
- The community selected a political and religious leader, a caliph, but Ali's followers encouraged him to exercise the leadership authority they believed God had provided.
- When Ali's sons, Hasan and Hussein, were born, his followers believed they also carried special gifts based on their relationship with their grandfather Mohammed.
- The Muslim community eventually split over this question.
- Mohammed's friend Abu Bakr became the first caliph; after his death Umar became caliph.
- Umar was assassinated by a Persian captive, and another of Mohammed's friends, Uthman, was selected as caliph.
- As Uthman consolidated wealth, groups of Arab soldiers came to feel he favored his own family over the community.
- They broke into his house and assassinated him.
- The followers of Ali came forward, and proposed that he become caliph.
- Ali believed that Uthman's family and Muslims in general were forgetting the straight path that had been revealed to Mohammed.
- He led an army against Uthman's family but sought a negotiated peace between both factions of Muslims, he too was assassinated.
- The family of Uthman assumed control of the Islamic movement and ruled the first Arab empire.
- Sunnis believe that Four Rightly Guided Caliphs: Abu Bakr, Umar, Uthman, and Ali served as the true successors to Mohammed.
- Shiites only recognize Ali.

REF: p. 193   OBJ: 2 and 3

2. Discuss the critique of Western interpretations as presented in Haneef James Oliver's *The "Wahhabi" Myth*.

ANS:

- Haneef James Oliver reflects his position on the misinterpretations of Mohammed ibn Abdul Wahhab, in *The "Wahhabi" Myth*.
- There is no such thing as a Wahhabi, or follower of Wahhab.

- Orthodox Muslims in Saudi Arabia and other areas emphasize the oneness of God and the importance of Mohammed and the Rightly Guided caliphs, the salafiyya.
- To call them Wahhabis suggests that there is more than one correct interpretation of Islam, Oliver says.
- Mohammed ibn Abdul Wahhab was not a radical Muslim, his call for reform was based on the Quran.
- Osama bin Laden, Ayman al Zawahiri, and other members of al Qaeda do not follow the teachings of Wahhab, the Quran, or Islam.
- They are mystics who believe their personal experiences and theologies are superior to Mohammed.
- Oliver believes, as did Wahhab, that mystical Sufis corrupted Islam by emphasizing their own encounters with the holy and that al Qaeda follows this tradition.
- Mohammed provided the last revelation; there are no more Prophets despite Sufism and mystics in other religions.
- When terrorists are called Salafis, Wahhabis, or Salafi-Wahhabis, it completely miscasts and misinterprets Islam.
- Terrorists follow the teachings of Sayyid Qutb, who was neither an Islamic scholar nor a good Muslim.

REF: p. 198   OBJ: 2, 3, and 4

3. Explain Karen Armstrong's theory of the rise and fall of agrarian empires.

ANS:
- Karen Armstrong argues that Islam went through a series of crises before and after 1492, and describes both a theological and political response to events.
- Armstrong believes that when agrarian empires falter, religious zealots arise to call the faithful back to the true meaning of religion.
- As agrarian empires expand, winning victories in the name of their deity, all is going well.
- The chosen people prosper under the protection of a divine force.
- At some point, however, the empire eventually suffers a strategic military reverse.
- Because the empire grew under the favor of a deity, the only logical conclusion is that the deity is no longer with the people, n other words, they are no longer chosen.
- Inevitably, prophets call the people back to religious purity, to the golden age of the faith.
- Prophets obscure the past with an idealistic remembrance of the Golden Age, and they separate the pure from the impure.
- This happened several times in the history of Islam, including the invasion of Mongol and Crusader armies in the eleventh and twelfth centuries, the stagnation of Arab thought and technological development after 1200, and the collapse of the Ottoman caliphate in 1924.
- Each instance brought a theologically driven political reform movement.

REF: p. 195   OBJ: 1 and 5

4. Who was Taqi ibn Taymiyya? How did his teachings influence Muslim militancy?

ANS:

- Taqi al Din ibn Taymiyyah, an Islamic scholar, was appalled by the slaughter of the Crusades and sought to find an answer in his faith.
- He believed that Muslims had fallen away from the truth and must therefore internally purify themselves, calling for a jihad (struggle or effort), the destruction of heretics and invaders; he called this the sixth pillar of Islam.
- Ibn Taymiyyah fled Baghdad to escape invading Mongols.
- He believed that the Crusaders and Mongols defeated Islamic armies because Muslims had fallen away from the true practice of Islam.
- Emphasizing *tawhid*, or the oneness of God, ibn Taymiyyah attacked anything that threatened to come between humanity and God.
- He forbade prayers at gravesites, belief in saints, and other practices that had worked their way into Islam.
- He was especially harsh on the mystical Sufis, who believed that deep prayer revealed the will of God beyond the prophecy of Mohammed and the Quran.
- Individual Sufis pledged allegiance to various masters and followed their masters even when actions violated Islamic law.
- According to ibn Taymiyyah, any belief that went beyond Mohammed's revelation was to be subjected to a purifying jihad.
- He preached that holy war should be waged against all people who threatened the faith. His targets included Muslims and non-Muslims.
- Ibn Taymiyyah's shift is important. Islam is frequently described as a monotheistic religion based on five tenets, or pillars.
- Jihad has a place in this system, and different Islamic scholars interpret jihad in various ways.
- There are many meanings, but most Muslims defined jihad as defending a community and waging an internal struggle against one's own tendency toward evil.
- Ibn Taymiyyah expanded the meaning of jihad by advocating attacks on nonbelievers and impure Muslims; however, he preached toleration for Muslims who accepted one of the more rigid versions of Sunni Islam. He claimed that this was another pillar of Islam.

REF: p. 196   OBJ: 1, 2, 3, 4, 7, and 8

5. Explain the three factors prominent in Mahan's Middle Eastern violence, how are these factors interdependent?

ANS:

- The basis for terrorism in the traditional Middle East defined by the U.S. Navy's Captain Mahan as Israel, Lebanon, Jordan, Egypt, Syria, Iraq, and the Arabian Peninsula was the situation at the end of World War II.
- As events unfolded, three factors became prominent in Middle Eastern violence: (1) questions about the political control of Israel and Palestine or the Palestinian question, (2) questions of who would rule the Arab world or Intra-Arab rivalries and struggles, and (3)

questions concerning the relations between the two main branches of Islam: Sunnis and Shiites or the future of revolutionary Islam.

- These problems are all separate, but they are also interrelated.
- The sources of terrorism in the Middle East are symbiotic; that is, they are independent arenas of violence with a dynamic force of their own, but they are also related to and dependent on each other.
- All forms of Middle Eastern terrorism share certain traits.
- Primarily, many Arab groups express dissatisfaction over the existence of Israel.
- They are not necessarily pro-Palestinian, but they find the notion of a European-created, non-Arab state in their lands offensive.
- Most Middle Eastern terrorist groups are anti-imperialist.
- The intensity of their passion wavers according to the type of group, but terrorism has largely been dominated by anti-Western feelings.
- Another symbiotic factor is the pan-Arabic or pan-Islamic orientation of terrorist groups.
- Although they fight for local control, most wish to revive a united Arab realm of Islam.
- Finally, Middle Eastern terrorism is united by kinship bonds. In terrorism, as in Middle Eastern politics in general, familial links are often more important than national identification
- When the Israelis practice terrorism, they usually claim their activities are conventional military actions.
- At times, however, the Israelis have used the same tactics the PLO used in the 1960s and 1970s.
- It is perhaps more accurate to argue that all Middle Eastern violence, Arabic and non-Arabic, is locked into symbiosis; it is interdependent.

REF: p. 200   OBJ: 1, 3, 4, 5, 6, 7, 8, and 9

6. Who was Sayyid Qutb? How did his teachings influence al Qaeda?

ANS:
- Sayyid Qutb was an Egyptian teacher and journalist who was initially employed by the Ministry of Education. .
- He traveled to the United States and lived as an exchange professor in Greeley, Colorado, from 1948 to 1950.
- Qutb's experience in America soured his opinion of Western civilization; he returned to Egypt and became an active member of the Muslim Brotherhood, an organization that seeks to create a single Muslim nation through education and religious reform.
- Qutb was arrested in 1954 after the Brotherhood tried to overthrow the Egyptian government, but he was released in 1964 because of health problems.
- He published his most famous work, *Milestones*, in 1965.
- The book outlines the theology and ideology of jihadist revolution, and its militant tone led to Qutb's second arrest and subsequent hanging in 1966.

- Qutb's books and articles popularized many militant ideas, and they continue to influence jihadists today.
- He believed that the Islamic world descended into darkness (*jahaliyya*) shortly after the death of Mohammed.
- The so-called Islamic governments of the Arab empires were really corrupt nonreligious regimes.
- Qutb rejected the West and called on Muslims to overthrow their corrupt governments arguing that rulers should impose Islamic law on their subjects, and when pure Islamic states were created, they should confront the world.
- In *Milestones* Qutb argued that Muslims were in a cosmic battle with the forces of darkness and called for the destruction of all enemies.
- The forces of darkness could not be tolerated, he wrote and Muslims were called to fight it.
- Qutb's writings were banned in many Islamic countries, and they infuriated the Egyptian government under Gamal Nasser.
- The *Al Qaeda Manual* cites Qutb as a source of inspiration.

REF: p. 197   OBJ: 1, 2, 3, 4, 7, and 8

7.   Describe the assumptions White indicates should be kept in mind to understand the Middle East.

ANS:
- The current structure of Middle Eastern geography and political rule is a direct result of nineteenth-century European imperial influence in the region and the outcomes of World War I.
- Many of the Arab countries in the Middle East place more emphasis on the power of the family than on contemporary notions of government. However, Israel rules itself as a parliamentary democracy.
- The modern state of Israel is not the biblical Kingdom of David mentioned in the Hebrew and Christian Bibles or the Islamic Quran. It is a secular power dominated by people of European descent.
- Arabs and Palestinians in particular, do not hold a monopoly on terrorism.
- The religious differences in the region have developed over centuries, and fanaticism in any religion can spawn violence. Fanatical Jews, Christians, and Muslims in the Middle East practice terrorism in the name of religion.
- Although the Middle East has been volatile since 1948, the year Israel was recognized as a nation-state, modern terrorism grew after 1967. It increased after 1973 and became a standard method of military operations in the following two decades.
- In 1993, however, the Palestine Liberation Organization (PLO) renounced terrorism, but instead of decreasing tension, that has created tremendous tension. On the Arab side, some groups have denounced the PLO's actions whereas others have embraced it. The same reaction has occurred in Israel, where one set of political parties endorses peace plans and another prepares for war. Middle Eastern peace is a very fragile process, and

© 2014 Cengage Learning. All Rights Reserved. May not be copied, scanned, or duplicated, in whole or in part, except for use as permitted in a license distributed with a certain product or service or otherwise on a password-protected website for classroom use.

terrorism is a wild card. It can upset delicate negotiations at any time, even after a peace treaty has been signed and implemented (for an example, see Hoffman, 1995).

- All of these issues are complicated by a shortage of water and vast differences in social structure. The area contains some of the world's richest and some of the world's poorest people. Most of them are far from water sources.

REF: p. 199   OBJ: 1, 2, 3, 4, 5, 6, 7, 8, and 9

8.   List and discuss the major contradictory promises surrounding the Middle East made by the British during WWI?

ANS:

- Because the Turks were allied with the Germans, the British encouraged the Arabs to revolt against the Turks.
- If the Arabs would fight for the British, the British promised to move the caliphate from Istanbul to Mecca and to name an Arab as caliph.
- The military commander in Cairo, who promised to restore the caliphate, thought he was promising the Islamic equivalent of a pope and that secular, individual Arab states would continue to exist.
- He did not understand the nature of the caliphate.
- In return for a general Arab revolt against the Turks, the British agreed to support the creation of a united, independent Arab state at the close of the war.
- The British believed this to be sound foreign policy. They believed the nebulous understanding was not a promise of support to the Arabs.
- However, the Arabs felt they had received a promise for the ancient Arab realm of Islam.
- Although the British had gained an ally at little expense, the circumstances were ripe for resentments.
- The British made other promises.
- Partially in response to the Zionist movement and partially to keep the goodwill of American Jews, the British promised the Zionists a Jewish homeland in Palestine.
- The Balfour Declaration of November 1917 promised to create the state of Israel.
- It was backed by Protestant Christians who understood neither the nature of the caliphate nor the importance of Jerusalem (al Quds to Muslims) in Islam.
- Supporters of the Balfour Declaration were unaware that their promise directly contradicted the British commander's promise in Cairo, the promise to reestablish an Arab-dominated caliphate.
- All Arab Muslims would expect the caliphate to include the three most important cities in Sunni Islam: Mecca, Medina, and Jerusalem.
- The Balfour Declaration threatened to transfer Jerusalem to the new state of Israel.
- The British also made promises to their allies.
- On the other side of the region, in ancient Persia (modern Iran), the British approached the Russians with another deal. Iran would be divided into three parts, a northern area controlled by Russia, a southern zone under British rule, and a neutral area in between.
- When the war ended in 1918, the entire Middle East was controlled by the British, French, and Russians, but it was a powder keg.

- Explicable in a time when national survival was threatened, these contradictory promises were nothing more than an extension of prewar British imperial policies.
- They did not alleviate the tensions between the Palestinian Arabs and the newly arrived Palestinian Jews.
- At the end of the war, the British created a series of Arab countries dominated by strong, traditional family groups.
- Far from representing a united Arab realm of Islam, the British division was challenged internally by rival families and externally by other Arab states.
- Each family and each of the Arab leaders wished to unite Islam under their own banner. Major states eventually emerged from this scenario: Syria, Iraq, Saudi Arabia, Jordan, and the Gulf States.
- Some of the new nations dreamed of a pan-Islamic region, but none was willing to let another run it.
- Other ethnic groups, like the Kurds, wanted autonomy; Christian Assyrians and Jewish settlers in Palestine also wanted independence.
- The Arabs also could not counter the continuing British influence, and neither a pan-Arabic realm nor a Jewish national state could develop under the watchful eyes of the British.
- Great Britain received permission from the League of Nations to create the Mandate of Palestine which came with a cost.
- It left neither Arab nor Jew satisfied; the Arabs believed they had received a false promise, and the Jews avidly demanded their right to a homeland.

REF: p. 202   OBJ: 5, 6, 7, and 8

9. Name three states that the French and British created that did not reflect realistic divisions of the Middle East. Briefly explain what occurred because of these state creations.

ANS:
- North Africa was completely dominated by Britain and France.
- Libya was divided into British and French sections, and it did not become independent until 1951.
- In 1969 Colonel Muammar Gadhafi seized power in a military coup, claiming Libya as an anti-Western socialist state.
- Egypt achieved its independence before World War II but did not fully break with Britain until Gamal Nasser took power in 1954.
- Gadhafi sought to follow Nasser's footsteps but broke with Egypt after Nasser's death in 1970.
- Syria was under French rule from 1922 to 1946.

- After several military coups and a failed attempt to form a united republic with Egypt, a group of pan-Arabic socialists, the Baath Party, seized power in 1963.
- Aside from internal problems, Assad believed that Lebanon and Palestine were rightly part of Greater Syria.
- Lebanon has become one of the most violent regions in the area.
- Ruled by France until 1943, the government of Lebanon managed a delicate balance of people with many different national and religious loyalties.
- In 1948 when Palestinians displaced by Israel began flocking to the country, the delicate balance was destroyed.
- Lebanon has suffered internal conflict ever since including civil wars in 1958 and 1975–1976, continued fighting to 1978, an Israeli invasion in 1978, another Israeli invasion in 1982, Iranian revolutionary intervention from the 1982 Israeli invasion, a fragile peace in 1990, and the growth of a terrorist militia from 1983 to 1996.
- Several large militias still roam the countryside, despite their agreement to disarm by the terms of the 1990 peace plan.

REF: p. 204   OBJ: 6, 7, and 8

10.   Who were the SAVAK? Explain the role of SAVK in Ruhollah Khomeini's rise to power in Iran.

ANS:
- The SAVAK refers to Mohammed Pahlavi's secret police empowered after the 1953 downfall of the democratic government.
- The shah used a fairly effective strategy to employ SAVAK.
- Rather than taking on all his enemies at once, he became selective.
- He allied with one group to attack another group. SAVAK's enthusiasm for the torture and murder of political opponents complemented the policy.
- After 1953 the shah found it convenient to ally with the Shiite holy men, who welcomed the shah's support and turned a blind eye to SAVAK's activities.
- As the clergy organized demonstrations among theology students in Qom and marches of the faithful in Tehran, the shah unleashed his forces.
- SAVAK infiltrated Shiite opposition groups in Tehran, and the army attacked Qom.
- There were thousands of arrests, and demonstrators were ruthlessly beaten or, in some cases, shot in the streets.
- Khomeini was promoted to the rank of ayatollah and ran a campaign against the shah from Iraq.
- Under his leadership, the mosque came to be perceived as the only opposition to the shah and the hated SAVAK.
- Revolutionaries gained momentum after the election of Jimmy Carter as president of the United States in 1976.

- Carter pressured the shah to end SAVAK's human rights abuses.
- Fearful of a loss of American aid, the shah ordered SAVAK to ease off the opposition, increasing the ability of revolutionaries to operate inside Iran.

REF: p. 209   OBJ: 7, 8, and 9

CHAPTER 9

Terrorism in Israel and Palestine

Learning Objectives

After reading this chapter, students should be able to:

1. Describe the rise of Fatah and the Palestine Liberation Organization (PLO).
2. Identify factional groups that emerged from squabbles among the Palestinians.
3. Discuss the origins and growth of Hezbollah after the 1982 Israeli invasion of Lebanon.
4. Explain the current political and military aspects of Hezbollah.
5. Outline the impact of the first Intifada and the birth of Hamas.
6. Describe the current operational capabilities of Hamas.
7. Summarize the tactics of the al Aqsa Martyrs Brigades.
8. Summarize controversial Israeli counterterrorist policies.

Chapter Key Terms

Yasser Arafat, p. 454

Sabri al Banna, p. 219

Intifada, p. 219

Al Aqsa Intifada, p. 220

Revolutionary Guards, p. 224

Sheik Mohammed Hassan Fadlallah, p. 224

Abbas Musawi, p. 224

Hassan Nasrallah, p. 224

Imad Mugniyah, p. 227

Shaba farm region, p. 227

Ahmed Yassin, p. 231

Izz el Din al Qassam Brigades, p. 232

Musa Abu Marzuq, p. 232

Mahmud Abbas, p. 232

Khalid Meshal, p. 233

Yasser Arafat: (1929– 2004) the name assumed by Mohammed al Husseini. Born in Cairo, he was a founding member of Fatah and the PLO. He merged the PLO and Fatah in 1964 and ran a terrorist campaign against Israel. After renouncing terrorism and recognizing Israel's right to exist, Arafat was president of the Palestinian National Authority from 1993 to 2004.

Intifada: The first spontaneous uprising against Israel that lasted from 1987 to 1993. It began with youths throwing rocks and creating civil disorder. Some of the violence became more organized. Many people sided with religious organizations, abandoning the secular PLO during the Intifada.

Sabri al Banna: (1937– 2002) the real name of Abu Nidal. Al Banna was a founding member of Fatah but split with Arafat in 1974. He founded militias in southern Lebanon, and he attacked Western and Israeli targets in Europe during the 1980s. In the 1990s, he became a mercenary. He was murdered in Iraq, probably by the Iraqi government.

al Aqsa Intifada: An uprising sparked by Ariel Sharon's visit to the Temple Mount with a group of armed escorts in September 2000. The area is considered sacred to Jews, Christians, and Muslims. Muslims were incensed by the militant aspect of Sharon's visit because they felt his was invading their space with an armed group. Unlike the 1987 Intifada, the al Aqsa Intifada has been characterized by suicide bombings.

Musa al Sadr: (1928-circa 1978) a reforming Lebanese Shiite cleric and political leader. He created Amal, a private Shiite militia, in 1975.

He disappeared with two companions while travelling in Libya in August 1978. His supporters suspect the Libyan government murdered him.

Revolutionary Guards: The militarized quasi-police force of the revolutionary government during the Iranian Revolution.

Sheik Mohammed Hassan Fadlallah: (1935–2010) a grand ayatollah and leader of Shiites in Lebanon. The spiritual leader of Hezbollah. He was the target of a 1985 U.S.-sponsored assassination plot that killed seventy-five people.

Abbas Musawi: (1952– 1992) A leader of Hezbollah, who was killed with his family in an Israeli attack in 1992.

Hassan Nasrallah: (1960–) the secretary-general of Hezbollah. He took over the leadership of Hezbollah after Musawi's death in 1992. Nasrallah is a lively speaker and charismatic leader.

Imad Mugniyah: (1962– 2008) the leader of the international branch of Hezbollah. He has been implicated in many attacks, including the 1983 U.S. Marine and French paratrooper bombings. He is also believed to have been behind bombings of the U.S. embassy in Beirut and two bombings of Israeli targets in Argentina. He was assassinated in Damascus in February 2008.

Shaba farm region: A small farming region in southwest Lebanon annexed by Israel in 1981. When Israel withdrew from southern Lebanon in 2000, it remained in the Shaba farm region, creating a dispute with Lebanon, Hezbollah, and Syria.

Ahmed Yassin: (1937– 2004) One of the founders and leaders of Hamas. Yassin originally started the Palestinian Wing of the Muslim Brotherhood but merged it into Hamas during the Intifada. He was killed in an Israeli-targeted assassination.

Izz el Din al Qassam Brigades: The military wing of Hamas, named after the Arab revolutionary leader Sheik Izz el Din al Qassam (1882–1935), who led a revolt against British rule.

Musa Abu Marzuq: (1951–) the "outside" leader of Hamas, who is thought to be in Damascus, Syria. He is believed to have controlled the Holy Land Foundation.

Abdel Aziz Rantisi: (1947–2004) One of the founders of Hamas along with Ahmed Yassin. He took over Hamas after Israeli gunships assassinated Yassin. He, in turn, was assassinated by the Israelis a month after taking charge.

Mahmud Abbas: (1935–) the president of the Palestinian Authority since 2005, founding member of Fatah, and an executive in the PLO.

Khalid Meshal: (1956–) one of the "outside" leaders of Hamas, in Damascus, Syria, Mashal became the political leader of Hamas in 2004. After the 2006 election he continued to lead in exile.

Muqtada al Sadr: (1974–) An Iraqi ayatollah. Al Sadr leads the Shiite militia known as the Mahdi Army.

Marwan Barghouti: (1969–) A leader of Fatah and alleged leader of the al Aqsa Martyrs Brigades. A Brigades statement in 2002 claimed that Barghouti was their leader. He rose to prominence during the al Aqsa Intifada, but he is currently held in an Israeli prison.

Mossad: The Israeli intelligence agency was formed in 1951. It is responsible for gathering foreign intelligence. Shin Beth is responsible for internal security.

Chapter Outline

I.   **The PLO from the Six Days' War to the Al Aqsa Intifada**
      OBJ 1: Describe the rise of Fatah and the Palestine Liberation Organization (PLO)
      OBJ 7: Summarize the tactics of the al Aqsa Martyrs Brigades

      A. In 1968, Cuba hosted revolutionary groups in a training session outside Havana; individuals from around the world attended the event, including *Yasser Arafat*, leader of the Palestine Liberation Organization (PLO).

1. In 1957, Arafat gathered groups of disgruntled Palestinians in Jordan, and in 1964 he formed the PLO to form a multinational alliance against Israel.

B. Fatah and the Six Days' War.

   1. Arafat formed Fatah in 1959, a guerrilla organization, to wage a campaign against the Israelis. He merged it into the PLO in 1964.

   2. Using a group of Fatah warriors known as *fedayeen*, Arafat and *Kahlil Wazir* began to attack Israel.

   3. Arafat conducted Fatah operations from Jordan, despite protests from King Hussein.

C. Fatah after Karamah

   1. Israel, angered by a lack of action by King Hussein of Jordan, decided to take matters into its own hands, sending a combined tank and mechanized infantry unit to raid the Palestinians.

   2. Fedayeen fought back. Israelis and infantry units in Karamah pulled back, not wanting to provoke a war with Jordan.

   3. The legend of the battle told of Fatah's fedayeen standing at Karamah and defeating the IDF.

   4. Millions of donated dollars flowed into Arafat's coffers, making the PLO the most powerful Palestinian group. The PLO leadership was corrupted as a result.

   5. Black September and Munich.

      a. Arafat could not control terrorists in the many PLO splinter groups, so he created a new group after King Hussein's September attack; he called the group Black September.

      b. In 1972, at the Olympic Games, Black September struck the Olympic Village, and took most of the Israeli Olympic team hostage. Before the German police could take control, the Israelis and a German police officer were killed.

D. The 1982 invasion of Lebanon.

   1. In southern Lebanon the mainstream PLO, under Arafat, became a fairly autonomous and potent force.

   2. On June 6, a massive three-pronged IDF force invaded Lebanon in *Operation Peace for Galilee*.

   3. Syrians rallied all local militias, except the Christians, to their side, and turned their own aircraft and tanks on the Israeli invaders. Israel found itself in a new war, and Arafat found himself out of options.

II. **Factionalism in Palestinian Terrorism**

   OBJ 2: Identify factional groups that emerged from squabbles among the Palestinians

   OBJ 3: Discuss the origins and growth of Hezbollah after the 1982 Israeli invasion of Lebanon

   OBJ 4: Explain the current political and military aspects of Hezbollah

A. The October 1973 Yom Kippur War caused a shift in the structure of Middle Eastern terrorism, which eventually resulted in peace between Israel and Egypt, and brought a domestic campaign of terrorism to Egypt.
B. This brought another type of war; a war of internal battles for supremacy in the Palestinian movement.
C. The background of current factionalism
   1. Palestinian terrorism began to transform after the 1982 invasion of Lebanon.
   2. A shadowy, non-Palestinian group, Hezbollah, emerged from the fighting in Lebanon to conduct murderous bombings against American targets in Beirut. They utilized the new tactic of suicide bombing.
   3. A new movement developed in the Palestinian areas of Israel in 1987, the *Intifada*.
   4. In 2000, the Palestinians began a second intifada marked by terrorist violence and suicide bombings.
   5. Hamas won the Parliamentary elections in 2006.
   6. Three crucial events followed Hamas' electoral victory:
      a. Hezbollah, not part of the Palestinian malaise, but still opposed to Israel, continued operations from Lebanon.
      b. Fatah and Hamas fought their own war.
      c. A blockade of Gaza and a twenty-two day attack against Hamas that killed hundreds of Palestinian civilians.
   7. From 1967 to 1973, the PLO was characterized by internal splintering.
   8. Some of the groups included:
      a. The Democratic Front for the Liberation of Palestine
      b. The Popular Front for the Liberation of Palestine
      c. The Popular Front for the Liberation of Palestine, General Command.
   9. The dominant groups within the context of the Israeli-Palestinian struggle:
      a. Al Aqsa Martyrs Brigades
      b. Black September
      c. Democratic Front for the Liberation of Palestine (DFLP) – Naiaf Hawatmeh
      d. Fatah – Fatah began as the military wing of the former PLO. Formed in the early stages of the PLO.
      e. Force 17 – Officially known as Presidential Security, Force 17 is an arm of Fatah.
      f. Hamas –the Islamic Resistance Movement
      g. Hezbollah
      h. Palestinian Islamic Jihad (PIJ
      i. Palestine Liberation Front (PLF) -- Three different groups call themselves the Palestine Liberation Front: The Abu Abbas faction based in Iran, the Abdal Fatah Ghanem faction which received

support from Libya, and the Talat Yaqub faction which sought favor with Syria.

    j.   Popular Democratic Front for the Liberation of Palestine (PDFLP) – The PDFLP is the military wing of the DFLP.

    k.   Popular Front for the Liberation of Palestine (PFLP)

    m.   Tanzim Bridage – Claiming not to be directly involved in terrorism, the Tanzim Brigade is the militia wing of Fatah.

III.   The Abu Nidal Organization

    OBJ 2: Identify factional groups that emerged from squabbles among the Palestinians

    OBJ 7: Identify factional groups that emerged from squabbles among the Palestinians

A. Arafat, trying to hold a diverse coalition of groups together, hinted that he would recognize the state of Israel, if the world would recognize a Palestinian state.

B. Sabri al Banna (whose code name was Abu Nidal) and Yasser Arafat were once comrades-in-arms in the struggle for Palestine, but as others broke from Arafat, so too did Abu Nidal's rebel organization, called *Black June.*

C. *Muammar Gadhafi* brought Abu Nidal to Libya, offered financial help, and gave Abu Nidal space for recruiting and training terrorists

D. Abu Nidal changed the face of Middle Eastern terrorism:

    1. First, he increased activities in Europe, resulting in spectacular attacks in Rome and Vienna.

    2. Second, he created a large terrorist group, defying the trend to split, by maintaining a ruthless internal enforcement mechanism.

    3. Third, he threw himself into the *Lebanese Civil War*, maintaining militias in southern Lebanon.

    4. Finally, terrorism became the reason for existence.

IV.   The Palestinian Islamic Jihad

    OBJ 2: Identify factional groups that emerged from squabbles among the Palestinians

A. The emergence of PIJ.

    1. The PIJ emerged from Egypt. Its founders— *Fathi Shekaki*, *Abdul Aziz*, and *Bashir Musa*—were influenced by militant Salafism, and were disillusioned with the Muslim Brotherhood.

    2. The PIJ's first leader, Fathi Shekaki, fell under the influence of the Muslim Brotherhood in Egypt, but he longed to take direct action against corrupt Muslim governments and the infidels who influenced them.

B. The PIJ and the invasion of Lebanon.
   1. Shekaki was impressed with two of Hezbollah's innovations: the umbrella-style organization and the suicide bomber.
   2. Shekaki found that by letting his group split, he became virtually invisible to his enemies.
C. PIJ operations.
   1. When the first Intifada broke out in 1987, the PIJ increased political action and joined the battle in the streets.
   2. Shekaki was captured and deported from Gaza in 1988, but he returned in short order.
   3. The PIJ struck Israeli targets, assassinated soldiers, and perfected the tactic they copied from Hezbollah: suicide bombing.
   4. The PIJ remained active, especially in suicide bombings. The September 2000 *al Aqsa Intifada* sent the PIJ into a frenzy of activity, as the group launched a suicide bombing campaign,
   5. The U.S. government continues to view the PIJ as an active threat, and sees the group's strength flowing from its networked structure.
   6. In 2003, the U.S. Department of Justice (2003) took actions against the PIJ in Florida.

V. **Hezbollah: Local and International**
   OBJ 3: Discuss the origins and growth of Hezbollah after the 1982 Israeli invasion of Lebanon
   OBJ 4: Explain the current political and military aspects of Hezbollah

A. Hezbollah is one of the more enigmatic organizations in the Middle East due to the manner in which it was formed, its historical metamorphosis, and its desire to play a leading role in Lebanon's politics.
B. Hezbollah has an international wing believed to be based in Damascus.
C. It also created the organizational style that jihadist groups like the Egyptian Islamic Group, the Egyptian Islamic Jihad, the Armed Islamic Group in Algeria, and al Qaeda would use.
D. The origins of Hezbollah.
   1. Hezbollah is a product of political actors from the 1979 Iranian Revolution and the Shiite community of southern Lebanon.
   2. It roots can be traced to a desire to export revolutionary ideals from Iran, and Shiite emancipation in Lebanon.
   3. Shiite scholars, known as *ayatollahs*, gained control of the Iranian Revolution through the *Revolutionary Guards*, a group of young fanatic Shiites, who evolved into a paramilitary arm of the revolution.
   4. The Iranian Revolution made many Sunni Muslims nervous because the Revolutionary Guards vowed to create revolutionary Shiite governments throughout the Muslim world.

5. The situation changed in 1982, when Israel invaded Lebanon.
6. Iran's foreign policy under the Ayatollah Khomeini's Revolutionary Guards was designed to spread religious revolutionary thought throughout the Muslim world.
7. Hezbollah grew from a council of Shiite scholars, who claimed to be part of a spiritual movement.
   a. Its structure – really lack of structure – simply developed because no one was in charge.
8. During the first few years of its existence, Hezbollah acted more or less like a terrorist clearinghouse.
9. Hezbollah developed under the leadership of three central figures:
   a. *Sheik Mohammed Hassan Fadlallah,*
   b. *Abbas Musawi,*
   c. *Hassan Nasrallah*
10. After introducing suicide bombers in its initial phase, Hezbollah struck U.S. Marines and the French army in October 1983.
11. In its second phase, Hezbollah's leadership launched a kidnapping campaign in Beirut.
12. The third phase of Hezbollah's metamorphosis came in 1990, when Nasrallah created a regional militia, after the death of Musawi

E. Hezbollah's operational capabilities.
   1. By the end of the 20th century Hezbollah became one of the strongest non-state groups in the Middle East.
   2. It became the most technologically sophisticated non-state actor in the first decade of the 21st century.
   3. Hezbollah is organized in three directorates:
      a. A political wing.
      b. A social services wing.
      c. A security wing.
   4. A weak Lebanese government allows Hezbollah to maintain strongholds in southern Lebanon, the Bekaa Valley, and central pockets in Beirut.
   5. The primary terrorist tactic is bombing, and Hezbollah has mastered two forms:
      a. Suicide bombing.
      b. Radio-controlled bombs for ambushes.

F. Hezbollah's international branch appears to have three major functions:
   1. In Europe and in the United States, Hezbollah raises money to support operations.
   2. Iran uses Hezbollah as an extension of its own power.
   3. Hezbollah has established a strong presence in South America; it uses this base to raise funds through legitimate and illegitimate methods, conduct propaganda, and launch terrorist operations.

G. Anthony Cordesman says the Israelis entered Lebanon with several specific goals:
   1. Neutralize Hezbollah's effectiveness before Iran could develop nuclear weapons.
   2. Counter the IDF's image after the 2000 Lebanon and 2005 Gaza withdrawals.
   3. Force Lebanon to control Hezbollah.
   4. Rescuing two Israeli soldiers without a prisoner exchange.
F. A sympathetic view of Hezbollah.
   1. Many voices in Lebanon, and elsewhere, claim that Hezbollah is a legitimate self-defense force.
   2. Far from being viewed as a terrorist organization, Hezbollah has achieved heroic status in the eyes of many Arabs.
   3. Hezbollah's entry into politics further legitimized its activities.
   4. Most Hezbollah members share *Mohammed Fneish's* perspective, which points to Hezbollah's large-scale health care and education systems as evidence that their emphasis is primarily humanitarian.

VI. **A Critical View of Hezbollah**
OBJ 3: Discuss the origins and growth of Hezbollah after the 1982 Israeli invasion of Lebanon
OBJ 4: Explain the current political and military aspects of Hezbollah

A. Many people in the world consider Hezbollah to be a terrorist organization.
B. The U.S. Department of State: Hezbollah is a deadly international terrorist organization that has developed international links, and uses international crime to finance operations.
C. Its primary sponsor is Iran, and it receives secondary support from Syria, nations that are listed as state sponsors of terrorism.
D. The Council on Foreign Relations: Hezbollah is a terrorist organization because of the suicide attacks it carried out against civilian and peacekeeping forces, and because of its kidnapping rampage from 1983 to 1990.
E. It was also involved in the *1985 hijacking of a TWA flight*.
F. Critics also point to Hezbollah's uncompromising political stand, saying that it exists for only two reasons:
   1. To impose a Shiite government on Lebanon.
   2. To destroy the state of Israel.

VII. **Hamas and the Rise of Religious Organizations**
OBJ 5: Outline the impact of the first Intifada and the birth of Hamas
OBJ 6: Describe the current operational capabilities of Hamas

A. *Arab nationalism* grew through the early part of the twentieth century, and flourished until the June 1967 Six Days' War.
B. As nationalism waned, religious fervor took its place.
C. An overview of Hamas.
   1. The story of Hamas is tied to the late Sheik *Ahmed Yassin*.
   2. Hamas was formed in December 1987, at the beginning of the first Intifada.
   3. Several technically trained university graduates, engineers, teachers, and Islamic scholars joined the movement.
      a. They published the Hamas Charter in 1988, declaring that Palestine was God-given land, from the Jordan River to the Mediterranean.
   4. Hamas's organization reflects this original charter, maintaining a political wing to oversee internal and foreign relations. Its largest unit, especially in Gaza, is its social wing.
D. Struggles for leadership.
   1. After the first Intifada, Hamas faced an internal power struggle.
   2. *Musa Abu Marzuq* took over Hamas; his strategy was much more violent than Yassin's.
   3. He assembled a new leadership core and based it in Jordan, leading others to call it the "outside" leadership, in contrast to the "inside" leadership group of Yassin, who believed the struggle should remain inside Palestine.
   4. In 1996, Marzuq authorized a campaign of suicide bombing inside Israel.
   5. After Yassin was released from prison in 1997, he gradually reasserted control over Hamas, even though he remained under house arrest.
E. The al Aqsa Intifada.
   1. In the summer of 2003, Palestinian Prime Minister Mahmud Abbas brokered a limited cease-fire, asking Hamas, the PIJ, and related groups to end their campaigns.
   2. Hamas passed another milestone in the campaign against Israel: it used a female suicide bomber in a joint operation with a newer group, the al Aqsa Martyrs Brigades.
F. Hamas v. Fatah.
   1. Hamas controlled the majority of seats in the Palestinian Parliament, while Mahmud Abbas retained the presidency, thus setting the stage for a confrontation between Hamas and Fatah.
   2. The United States and the European Union refused to recognize Hamas' victory, stating that they would neither support nor discuss settlements with a terrorist organization.
   3. Disheartened by the split in Palestinian leadership, Saudi Arabia brokered a power sharing arrangement between Hamas and Fatah.

4. All pretense of power sharing broke down in June, when Hamas openly attacked Fatah strong points in Gaza.

G. Rockets and Operations Cast Lead.

1. On December 27, 2008, Israel kicked off Operation Cast Lead, a devastating air and artillery assault on Gaza, which was followed by a ground invasion on January 3.

2. Controversy over the invasion centered on proportionality; faced with rocket attacks, Israel responded with overwhelming military force.

3. George Bisharat argues that the Israeli response was illegal under international law.

4. Two primary factors weigh against Israel:

   a. The massive response produced hundreds of civilian casualties.

   b. Israel effectively occupied the Gaza Strip, making Israel legally responsible for protecting all the residents of Gaza.

H. Hamas and the United States.

1. After September 11, the American intelligence community assessed Hamas' ability and desire to strike the United States. They concluded that Hamas routinely engaged in anti-American rhetoric, but it had several disincentives for attacking the West in general, and the United States in particular.

2. Hamas used the United States and other Western countries as a financial resource.

   a. Some officials believed Hamas raised quite a bit of money through charities, such as the *Holy Land Foundation*.

3. Hamas could target the West; the militant theology behind Hamas might also encourage individual terrorists to take action.

VIII. **Fatah Restructured – The al Aqsa Martyrs Brigades**
   OBJ 1: Describe the rise of Fatah and the Palestine Liberation
   Organization (PLO)
   OBJ 7: Summarize the tactics of the al Aqsa Martyrs Brigades

A. Suicide bombing became the most important tactic of all the Palestinian terrorist groups at the beginning of the *al Aqsa Intifada*.

B. The al Aqsa Brigades were formed to put Fatah at the center of the new Intifada.

C. The Brigades began as a secular group, but they increasingly used jihadist rhetoric.

D. They were also the first secular Palestinian group to use suicide tactics.

E. The Brigades have become the most potent Palestinian force in the al Aqsa Intifada.

F. Effective tactics.

1. The tactics of the al Aqsa Martyrs Brigades have made them particularly deadly against the Israelis.

279

2. The Brigades' primary tactics have been drive-by shootings, snipers, ambushes, and kidnap-murders.
    a. Yet, as with so many other terrorist groups, their most devastating tactic has been the use of suicide bombers.
3. The al Aqsa Martyrs Brigades suicide bombers were frightening for two reasons:
    a. They were secular
    b. They sought out crowded civilian targets.
G. Leadership in the Martyrs Brigade
    1. Leadership of the Brigades is a controversial topic.
    2. One school of thought maintains that Arafat led and paid for the Brigades.
    3. A BBC News investigation points to *Marwan Barghouti* as the commander.
    4. Whether Arafat had direct control of the Brigades remains a subject of debate, partly because of the way the Brigades are organized; the Brigades have little centralized structure.
H. Beginning a network.
    1. No matter where leadership authority lies, the managerial relations within the Brigades remain a paradox.
    2. Their strength comes from the ability of small cells to operate without a strong leader.
    3. The Brigades have been effective because they operate in a network.

X. **Controversial Counterterrorist Policies**
OBJ 8: Summarize controversial Israeli counterterrorist policies

A. Many Israeli police and military units have established excellent reputations in counterterrorist operations:
    1. *Mossad,* the Israeli intelligence service.
    2. Shin Beth, the domestic Israeli security service.
    3. The IDF.
    4. The Israeli police.
B. Unlike Israel's excellent tactical record, its counterterrorist policies have stirred international controversy.
C. Bulldozing.
    1. When Israel first faced suicide bombings, the government implemented a controversial policy called "bulldozing", whose purpose was to destroy the family homes of suicide bombers.
    2. The policy expanded to include clearing ground for military reasons, and clearing space to build a security fence, which is a wall separating Israel from Palestinian areas.

D. Invading Lebanon.
1. Israel launched its first invasion of Lebanon in order to rid the south of the PLO.
2. In 1996, Israel launched a limited offensive in Lebanon to disrupt Hezbollah operations.
3. The Israelis responded with force again in July of 2006.
5. Israel was surprised when Hezbollah launched *Katyusha rockets* into Israel, while sending ground forces across the border to ambush an Israeli patrol.
6. Israel announced that it planned to destroy Hezbollah, and it launched a number of air strikes, and a naval blockade of Lebanon.
7. The IDF followed with a ground invasion a few days later, but Hezbollah fought the Israeli soldiers to a standstill.
8. Israel defended its action, with support from the United States, by stating that the massive strike was necessary because the Lebanese government was not able to confront and disarm Hezbollah's militia.
E The wall.
1. In an effort to stop Palestinian attacks, the Israelis began constructing a massive wall that snaked through Palestinian areas, separating people from services, jobs, and their families.
F Selective assassination.
1. The most controversial aspect of Israel's counterterrorism policy is selective assassination.
2. The United States has repeatedly taken the position that Israel cannot be condemned for harsh measures until the international community also denounces Palestinian terrorism.

Chapter Summary

- The PLO emerged in 1964, and took center stage after the June 1967 Six Days' War. Fatah was its main military wing, but groups kept splitting off. After the 1982 invasion of Lebanon, the PLO retreated to North Africa and the occupied territories. Still sponsoring terrorism, Fatah's activities were eclipsed by other groups.

- A number of groups emerged from the Israeli-Palestinian conflict. The Abu Nidal Organization was one of the deadliest groups, but now it appears to be dormant. Other main groups are the PFLP, Black September, the PFLP-GC, and the al Aqsa Martyrs Brigades. Related groups such as the PIJ, Hezbollah, and Hamas developed independently.

- The Abu Nidal Organization began as a member of the Rejectionist Front. It then worked for various countries, and finally became a mercenary group. Its leader, Sabri al Banna, was murdered in Iraq in August 2002.

- The PIJ emerged from Egypt in the 1970s. It evolved into a religious organization with the philosophy that religious law would be implemented after victory, but the more immediate objective was the destruction of Israel. By 1995, most of its founding leaders had been killed. New leaders purposely maintain a small group of operatives in a rigid hierarchy.

- Several groups use *Islamic Jihad* in their names. There are even factions in the PIJ.

- Hezbollah grew when Revolutionary Guards joined Shiites in Lebanon after the 1982 Israeli invasion. Beginning as a social movement, it evolved into an umbrella group, covering independent operators and its own military wing. It utilized suicide bombings and other attacks against Israeli targets.

- Hezbollah has undergone distinct phases, moving from small terrorist operations in Beirut, to political and social action. It also created a defense force which successfully fought Israel in the 2006 war.

- The status of Hezbollah is hotly debated. Supporters see it as a legitimate militia defending Lebanese Shiites from Israelis and other threats. Critiques maintain that it is an international terrorist organization representing Iranian foreign policy.

- Hamas emerged from the first Intifada. It embraced the principles of religious law, and it expressed disgust for the secular policies and corruption of the PLO. It formed a large organization, and mastered the art of suicide attacks. It opposes any peace with Israel, and its charter calls for the destruction of Israel. Hamas won control of the Palestinian government in 2006. Although the United States has refused to negotiate with Hamas, many people believe Hamas will target neither the United States nor other Western countries.

- The al Aqsa Martyrs Brigades formed from Fatah, embracing religion and suicide attacks. There are many questions about its leadership. Currently, it operates in a network of independent cells with no central command structure.

- Israel has responded to terrorism with controversial policies. These include bulldozing, invasions of Lebanon, constructing a wall to separate Palestinians from Israelis, and targeted assassinations.

DISCUSSION QUESTIONS

1. Looking at some of the prominent Middle Eastern terrorist groups discussed in this chapter, what are some of the techniques used by terrorist organizations to increase recognition, support, and power? What external forces discussed in previous chapters multiplied the strength of these terrorist organizations? (OBJ 1 – 8)

2. According to Moshe Amon, in order to create the opportunity for a peaceful settlement, all religious extremism must come to an end. Discuss if and how it is possible to bring religious extremism to an end. (OBJ 2)

3. Summarize the critical and sympathetic views regarding Hezbollah. What are your views on Hezbollah? Explain. (OBJ 3 and 4)

4. Summarize the history of the Abu Nidal Organization.(OBJ 2 and 7)

ASSIGNMENTS

1. "Guess who". Using a flip chart or whiteboard, describe the terrorist organizations mentioned in this chapter, using a series of bullet points. Start with generalities and move to specifics. Cover the bullet points with paper, exposing only one bullet point at a time. Encourage students to uncover the identity of the organization in as few bullet points as possible. (OBJ 1 – 8)

2. Give students time to research and discuss Israel's counterterrorism policies. Provide students with flipchart paper and have them identify 3 - 5 of the most controversial policies. Poll the class offerings, and then have them reduce their list to what they feel is the single most controversial one. Have them discuss the reasoning for their selection. Time permitting; segue into a comparison of counterterrorism policies across the globe. (OBJ 8)

3. Have students choose a topic from this chapter and write a study guide/handout to present and share with the class. For example, students may focus their study guide on describing the emergence of modern piracy. Allow time to discuss topics to eliminate duplication. (OBJ 1 – 8)

4. As a review, play jeopardy using key concepts and terms from the chapter. (OBJ 1 -8)

5. Have each student comb through http://articles.businessinsider.com/2011-04-28/politics/29991479_1_hamas-fatah-past-peace-accords-abbas (or another website as approved by the instructor) for a current event and select an article that relates to one or more of the chapter's core concepts. Have students provide a journalistic summary and a personal opinion/reaction to the article. Have students orally present the article to the class, field Q & As from their fellow students, and provide a copy of the original source article following the presentation. Optional: Have students complete peer assessments at the end of each presentation. (OBJ 1 - 8)

MEDIA TOOLS

1. *"Wikis"*
7 Things you should know about Wikis. Retrieved from the Web Jun 29, 2012 at http://net.educause.edu/ir/library/pdf/ELI7004.pdf

This document offers easy to understand instruction on the history, development, and potential uses of Wikis.

Have students develop (or make additions to a previously created one) a *Webliography* (resource list) using a Blog or Wiki that provides a short description and link to a scholarly resource pertaining to course concepts. For example, have students add two to three resources each, and ask them to add their assessment of at least one of their peers' contributions. If desired, allow time to discuss Blogs/Wikis. This activity can be reused throughout the course, by asking students to add/revise their contributions each week, bi-weekly, etc. (OBJ 1 – 8)

2.   *"Video on militant Islam…structured Q & A"*

PBS. "Looking for Answers". Retrieved Aug 16, 2012 at
http://www.pbs.org/wgbh/pages/frontline/shows/target/etc/modern.html
http://www.pbs.org/wgbh/pages/frontline/shows/terrorism/etc/video.html

The website offers a variety of activities that can be used with any of PBS's FRONTLINE programs on terrorism, except where otherwise noted, as well as links to related web materials and curriculum standards. The bottom link takes you directly to a short video clip of PBS's "Looking for answers" focuses on the rise of militant Islam in Egypt, and probes the Abu Nidal Organization.

Play the clip, then prompt students with questions, either from the instructor or derived from the activity links from the website. (OBJ 1 – 8)

3.   *"Current Events Article Summary with Peer Assessment"*

Use the Article Summary Template, which can be obtained on the instructor companion website, for this assignment. The template offers information on Internet research, outside resources, identification of credible sources, and detailed directions on completing an assessment of a news article. It also includes a peer evaluation tool.

Have each student comb the Internet for terrorism related news, and select an article that relates to one or more of the chapter's core concepts. Be sure selections are an article of interest from a credible source (*more on credibility can be found in the article summary template above*). Fill out an article summary template. *Your template asks for generic info about the article, a journalistic summary, as well as a personal opinion/reaction to the article.* Have each student summarize the article, present it orally to the class, and field Q & As from their fellow students. Have students complete peer assessments at the end of each presentation. Have students submit templates, original source article, and peer-reviews prior to the end of class. (OBJ 1 – 8)

Chapter 9—Terrorism in Israel and Palestine

TEST BANK

TRUE/FALSE

1. Arab Fall was the name given to the populist uprisings that occurred in Tunisia, Egypt, Libya, and Syria in 2011.

    ANS: F   REF: p. 214   OBJ: 4 and 5

2. The PLO was financially backed by King Hussein of Jordan.

    ANS: F   REF: p. 215   OBJ: 1 and 2

3. Yasser Arafat's primary purpose in the creation of the PLO was to help form a multinational alliance against Israel.

    ANS: T   REF: p. 215   OBJ: 1

4. The October 1973 Yom Kippur (Ramadan) War caused a shift in the structure of Middle Eastern terrorism.

    ANS: T   REF: p. 216   OBJ: 2

5. Hamas runs charities, schools, hospitals, and other social service organizations in Gaza where unemployment is sometimes as high as eighty-five percent.

    ANS: T   REF: p. 232   OBJ: 5 and 6

6. Hezbollah International has cells in the United States.

    ANS: T   REF: p. 227   OBJ: 3 and 4

7. Hezbollah International maintains an extensive international finance ring partially based on smuggling, drugs, and other criminal activity.

    ANS: T   REF: p. 228   OBJ: 3 and 4

8. Hezbollah is believed to be responsible for the 1985 hijacking of TWA Flight 847.

    ANS: T   REF: p. 230   OBJ: 3 and 4

9. The Revolutionary Guards were the militarized quasi-police force of the revolutionary government during the Iranian Revolution.

ANS: T   REF: p. 223   OBJ: 3

10. Unlike Israel's excellent tactical record, its counterterrorist policies have stirred international controversy.

ANS: T   REF: p. 237   OBJ: 8

11. The domestic intelligence service Shin Beth does not operate within Israeli borders.

ANS: F   REF: p. 237   OBJ: 8

12. The expertise of Mossad, the Israeli intelligence service, is not highly respected in international intelligence circles.

ANS: F   REF: p. 237   OBJ: 8

13. When Israel first faced suicide bombings, the government implemented a controversial policy called *bulldozing,* whose purpose was to destroy the family homes of suicide bombers.

ANS: T   REF: p. 237   OBJ: 8

14. In 1959, Arafat formed Fatah, a guerrilla organization, to wage a campaign against Lebanon.

ANS: F   REF: p. 215   OBJ: 1, 2, 3, 4, and 5

15. The West Bank of the Jordan River was seized by Israel prior to WWII.

ANS: F   REF: p. 217   OBJ: 2 and 5

MULTIPLE CHOICE

1. In 1959, Arafat formed _____, a guerrilla organization to wage a campaign against the Israelis.
   a. Fatah
   b. Hamas
   c. Abu Nidal
   d. PLF

ANS: a   REF: p. 215   OBJ: 1 and 2

286

2. _____ was the name assumed by Mohammed al Husseini. Born in Cairo, he was a founding member of Fatah and the PLO.
   a. Kahil Wazir
   b. Yasser Arafat
   c. Sabri al Banna
   d. Hafez Assad

ANS: b   REF: p. 215   OBJ: 1

3. The first spontaneous uprising against Israel, which lasted from 1987 to 1993, is referred to as the _____.
   a. Six Days' War
   b. Operation Peace for Galilee
   c. Intifada
   d. Yom Kippur War

ANS: c   REF: p. 219   OBJ: 5, 6, 7, and 8

4. The president of the Palestinian Authority since 2005, _____, was a founding member of Fatach and an executive of the PLO.
   a. Hafez Assad
   b. Yasser Arafat
   c. Sabri al Banna
   d. Mahmud Abbas

ANS: d   REF: p. 232   OBJ: 1 and 2

5. The Marxist-Leninist group, _____, seeks a socialist Palestine and was closely associated with the former Soviet Union.
   a. Democratic Front for the Liberation of Palestine
   b. Fatah
   c. Al Aqua Martyrs Brigade
   d. Force 17

ANS: a   REF: p. 220   OBJ: 1,3, and 8

6. The groups Abu Abbas, Abdal Fatah Ghanem, and Talat Yaqub all call themselves the
   _____.
   a. Fatah
   b. PIJ
   c. PLF
   d. Hamas

ANS: c   REF: p. 221   OBJ: 1 and 2

7.   _____ refers to the rebel organization created by Abu Nidal in 1976. The name was later changed to the Fatah Revolutionary Council.
   a.   PIJ
   b.   Black June
   c.   Hamas
   d.   PLF

ANS: b   REF: p. 219   OBJ: 1, 2, and 5

8.   _____ was responsible for the murder of Jordanian ambassadors in Spain, Italy, and India in the 1980s.
   a.   PLO
   b.   Hamas
   c.   Black June
   d.   Palestinian Islamic Jihad (PIJ)

ANS: c   REF: p. 219   OBJ: 1 and 2

9.   The al Aqsa Martyrs Brigades are based in _____ refugee camps.
   a.   Iranian
   b.   Iraqi
   c.   Syrian
   d.   West Bank

ANS: d   REF: p. 220   OBJ: 7

10.   The al Aqsa Martyrs Brigades were organized along military lines and became one of the first secular groups in the Middle East to use _____.
   a.   Nuclear weapons
   b.   Suicide bombers
   c.   Cyberterrorism
   d.   Dirty bombs

ANS: b   REF: p. 220   OBJ: 7

11.   Hezzbollah is centered within what nation?
   a.   Lebanon
   b.   Iran
   c.   Israel
   d.   Syria

ANS: a   REF: p. 219   OBJ: 2, 3, and 4

12.   The Israeli intelligence agency, Mossad, was formed in what year?
   a.   1948
   b.   1971
   c.   1942
   d.   1951

ANS: d   REF: p. 237   OBJ: 5 and 6

13. In 2003 the U.S. Department of Justice took actions against what _____ Florida, arguing that the group had an organized network of financial supporters around the world, including the United States.
    a. The PIJ
    b. Hamas
    c. Hezzbollah
    d. al Aqsa Martyrs Brigades

ANS: a   REF: p. 221   OBJ: 2

14. Many analysts believe that the majority of funding for Palestinian Islamic Jihad (PIJ) activities comes from _____.
    a. Syria
    b. Iraq
    c. Iran
    d. Afghanistan

ANS: c   REF: p. 221   OBJ: 1 and 2

15. One of the largest militias in the Lebanese Civil War, _____, was a Shiite militia started by an Iranian Shiite scholar.
    a. Islamic Jihad
    b. Al Dawa
    c. Revolutionary Guards
    d. Amal

ANS: d   REF: p. 225   OBJ: 2

16. Most of Hezbollah's activities deal with the politics of _____ and the vast social service network it maintains in the south.
    a. Lebanon
    b. Iraq
    c. Syria
    d. Iran

ANS: a   REF: p. 222   OBJ: 2, 3, and 4

17. Hamas won control of the Palestinian government in _____.
    a. 2012
    b. 2006
    c. 1948
    d. 1990

ANS: b   REF: p. 240   OBJ: 5 and 6

18. The PIJ's first leader, _____, fell under the influence of the Muslim Brotherhood.
   a. Fathi Shekaki
   b. Yasser Arafat
   c. King Hussein
   d. Ariel Sharon

ANS: a   REF: p. 238   OBJ: 1 and 2

19. Arab nationalism grew through the early part of the 20th century and flourished until the _____.
   a. Yom Kippur War
   b. Six Day's War
   c. al Aqsa Intifada
   d. Lebanese Civil War

ANS: b   REF: p. 231   OBJ: 1, 2, 3, 4, 5, 6, 7, and 8

20. The Palestinian Muslim Brothers became the nucleus of _____.
   a. PLO
   b. Arab Nationalism
   c. Hamas
   d. Arab Socialism

ANS: c   REF: p. 231   OBJ: 2, 5, and 6

21. The transformation of Hamas began after the _____ and growing disillusionment with Fatah.
   a. Six Days' War
   b. Palestinian Peace Talks
   c. Yom Kippur War
   d. Oslo Accords

ANS: d   REF: p. 233   OBJ: 5 and 6

22. _____ became the most important tactic of all the Palestinian terrorist groups at the beginning of the al Aqsa Intifada.
   a. Kidnapping
   b. Suicide bombing
   c. Hijacking
   d. Arson

ANS: b   REF: p. 227   OBJ: 1, 2, 3, 4, 5, 6, 7, and 8

23. The politically oriented Force 17 and the Tanzim Brigade were the two main forces of ___.
   a. Hamas
   b. Fatah
   c. Hezbollah
   d. PIJ

ANS: b   REF: p. 220   OBJ: 1 and 2

24.   All three factions of the PLF seek to destroy what nation?
        a. Jordan
        b. Syria
        c. Israel
        d. Lebanon

ANS: c   REF: p. 221   OBJ: 1, 2, 3, 4, 5, 6, 7, and 8

25.   Gush Emunim is a fundamentalist Israeli settlement in _____.
        a. Palestine
        b. Lebanon
        c. Jordan
        d. Egypt

ANS: a   REF: p. 216   OBJ: 2 and 8

26.   According to the text, the domestic Israeli security service, _____, is one of the most
        effective secret police forces in the world.
        a. Kahane
        b. Mossad
        c. Shin Beth
        d. Kach

ANS: c   REF: p. 237   OBJ: 8

27.   Black September was a splinter group formed from which terrorist organization?
        a. The PLO
        b. Hamas
        c. Hezbollah
        d. The PIJ

ANS: a   REF: p. 218   OBJ: 1, and 2

28.   _____ almost always supports Israel, frequently using its veto power in the UN
        Security Council to keep the United Nations from condemning Israeli actions.
        a. Iran
        b. Great Britain
        c. The United States
        d. France

ANS: c   REF: p. 237   OBJ: 8

29.   The massive wall that ran through Palestinian areas in effort to thwart Palestinian attacks,
        was sanctioned by which Israeli leader?
        a. Shimon Peres
        b. Yitzhak Rabin
        c. Ariel Sharon
        d. Benjamin Netanyahu

ANS: c   REF: p. 238   OBJ: 8

30. The Islamic Resistance Movement, created in 1987, has come to be known as ____.
a. Hezbollah
b. The IDF
c. The PLO
d. Hamas

ANS: d   REF: p. 220   OBJ: 5 and 6

31. The _____ was a war between Israel and its Arab neighbors fought in June 1967.
a. Yom Kippur War
b. Four Days' War
c. Zionist War
d. Six Days' War

ANS: d   REF: p. 221   OBJ: 7, 8, and 9

32. The Party of God is also known as _____.
a. Hezbollah
b. The IDF
c. The PLO
d. Hamas

ANS: a   REF: p. 221   OBJ: 2, 3, and 4

33. _____ developed under the leadership of three central figures: Sheik Mohammed Hassan Fadlallah, Abbas Musawi, and Hassan Nasrallah.
a. Hezbollah
b. The IDF
c. The PLO
d. Hamas

ANS: a   REF: p. 224   OBJ: 2, 3, and 4

34. The shadowy organization known as Islamic Jihad is connected to which terrorist organization?
a. Al Qaeda
b. Hezzbollah
c. PLO
d. Hamas

ANS: b   REF: p. 225   OBJ: 2, 3, and 4

35. Hezbollah struck U.S. Marines and the _____ army in October 1983, forcing a withdrawal of a multinational peacekeeping force.
a. French
b. British
c. Russian
d. Italian

ANS: a   REF: p. 225   OBJ: 2, 3, and 4

36.	Who was the founding father of Hamas?
	a.	Fathi Shekaki
	b.	Sheik Ahmed Yassin
	c.	Yasser Arafat
	d.	Ayman al Zawahiri

ANS: b			REF: p. 231			OBJ: 5 and 6

37.	The Hamas Charter of 1988, declared that _____ was a God-given land.
	a.	Israel
	b.	Palestine
	c.	Jordan
	d.	Egypt

ANS: b			REF: p. 231			OBJ: 5 and 6

38.	Which of the following organizations is not one of the current major operational groups surrounding the Israeli-Palestinian conflict?
	a.	Hezbollah
	b.	Hamas
	c.	the al Aqsa Martyrs Brigades
	d.	the PLO

ANS: d			REF: p. 239			OBJ: 1, 2, 3, 4, 5, 6, 7, and 8

39.	The al Aqsa Intifada was sparked by Ariel Sharon's visit to _____ with a group of armed escorts in September 2000.
	a.	the Temple Mount
	b.	Medina
	c.	Mecca
	d.	Bethlehem

ANS: a			REF: p. 220			OBJ: 5

40.	Shin Beth is the domestic intelligence service of which nation?
	a.	Iran
	b.	Israel
	c.	Iraq
	d.	Ireland

ANS: b			REF: p. 237			OBJ: 8

Case 9.0

During the first few years of its existence, Hezbollah acted more or less like a terrorist clearinghouse. Influenced by Iran, Hezbollah met as an independent organization, always willing to deny its Iranian connections. Hezbollah grew from a council of Shiite scholars who claimed to be part of a spiritual movement to an international terrorist organization. Its structure—really, lack of structure—simply developed because no one was in charge. In essence, the council interconnected semiautonomous groups that were buoyed by the

council's charisma and sheltered by its protection. Syrian and Iranian money and supplies poured into the council, and Hezbollah denied any direct connection with the network gathering under its auspices. Beneath Hezbollah, several Shiite cells operated autonomously and received money, weapons, and ideas through hidden channels linked with the spiritual leaders.

41. What term best describes Hezzbollah's organizational structure?
     a. Umbrella
     b. Hierarchy
     c. Para-military
     d. Bureaucratic

ANS: a   REF: p. 224   OBJ: 1, 2, 3, and 4

42. Hezzbollah subscribes, though in a militarized fashion, to which faith?

     a. Islam
     b. Judaeism
     c. Sufisim
     d. Kabbalism

ANS: a   REF: p. 222   OBJ: 3 and 4

43. What group uses Hezzbollah as a model for the structure of its organization?
     a. Al Qaeda
     b. The PLO
     c. The LTTE
     d. The IDF

ANS: d   REF: p. 227   OBJ: 3 and 4

44. What force multiplier is NOT mentioned in the above scenario?
     a. Transnational support
     b. Technology
     c. Media coverage
     d. Religion

ANS: c   REF: p. 224   OBJ: 3 and 4

45. Who as *not* one of the original founders of Hezbollah?
     a. Sheik Mohammed Hassan Fadlallah
     b. Abbas Musawi
     c. Mahmud Abbas
     d. Hassan Nasrallah

ANS: c   REF: p. 224   OBJ: 3

Case 9.1

Hamas was formed in December 1987 at the beginning of the first Intifada. Several technically trained university graduates—engineers, teachers, and Islamic scholars joined the movement. They published the Hamas Charter in 1988, declaring that Palestine was a God-given land, from the Jordan River to the Mediterranean. Unlike the PIJ, Hamas would be much more than a military organization - it would be a Muslim government, the forerunner of a Palestinian Muslim state.

Hamas's organization reflects this original charter (Hamas, 1988), maintaining a political wing to oversee internal and foreign relations. Its largest unit, especially in Gaza, is its social wing. Hamas runs charities, schools, hospitals, and other social service organizations in Gaza where unemployment is sometimes as high as eighty-five percent. These social services have made Hamas popular among the Palestinians.

46.   What pillar of Islam is Hamas demonstrating by running charities, schools, hospitals, and other social service organizations?
a. First (Shahada)
b. Second (Salat)
c. Third (Saum)
d. Fourth (Zakat)

ANS: d   REF: p. 226   OBJ: 5 and 6

47.   What Nation faces the greatest threat according to the Hamas charter?
a. Lebanon
b. Israel
c. Jordan
d. Syria

ANS: b   REF: p. 240   OBJ: 5 and 6

Case 9.2

Many Israeli police and military units have established excellent reputations in counterterrorist operations. Mossad, the Israeli intelligence service, is known for its expertise. Shin Beth, the domestic Israeli security service, is one of the most effective secret police forces in the world. The IDF is an excellent fighting machine. The Israeli police know how to handle bombs, snipers, kidnappings, and everyday crime. The tactical operations of these units are second to none.

48.   What is the closest American equivalent to the Mossad?
a. CIA
b. FBI
c. NSA
d. ATF

ANS: a   REF: p. 237   OBJ: 5 and 6

49.   What is the closest British equivalent to the Mossad?
      a. MI3
      b. MI4
      c. MI5
      d. MI6

ANS: c   REF: p. 237   OBJ: 5 and 6

50.   What is the closest British equivalent to the Shin Beth?
      a. MI3
      b. MI4
      c. MI5
      d. MI6

ANS: d   REF: p. 237   OBJ: 5 and 6

COMPLETION

1.   _____ refers to the code name for the 2008 Israeli assault on Gaza.

ANS: Operation Cast Lead   REF: p. 234   OBJ: 5, 6, and 8

2.   Israel added the West Bank and _____ after the Six Days' War.

ANS: Gaza Strip   REF: p. 236   OBJ: 3, 4, 5, 6, 7, and 8

3.   The general secretary and founder of the PIJ, _____, was a Palestinian physician who was
     killed in a targeted assassination.

ANS: Fathi Shekaki   REF: p. 238   OBJ: 1, 2, and 5

4.   In January 2006, _____ stunned the world by winning the majority of seats in the
     Palestinian Parliament.

ANS: Hamas   REF: p. 233   OBJ: 5 and 6

5.   When Israel first faced suicide bombings, the government implemented a controversial
     policy called _____, the purpose of which was to destroy the family homes of suicide
     bombers.

ANS: bulldozing   REF: p. 237   OBJ: 8

6.   Born in Cairo, _____ was a founding member of Fatah and the PLO.

ANS: Yasser Arafat   REF: p. 215   OBJ: 1

7. Disheartened by the split in Palestinian leadership in 2006, Saudi Arabia brokered a power- sharing arrangement between Hamas and _____ .

ANS: Fatah   REF: p. 233   OBJ: 1, 2, 5, and 6

8. Known for its expertise, _____ is the Israeli intelligence agency formed in 1951 responsible for gathering foreign intelligence.

ANS: Mossad   REF: p. 237   OBJ: 8

9. The _____ is an Islamic charity based in the U.S. The charity was closed in 2001 by the U.S. on allegations that it sponsored terrorist activities.

ANS: Holy Land Foundation   REF: p. 232   OBJ: 5 and 6

10. In 1972, _____ struck the Olympic Village and took most of the Israeli Olympic team hostage, killing those who tried to escape.

ANS: Black September   REF: p. 218   OBJ: 1 and 2

11. The 1978 Camp David Peace Accord brokered peace between _____ and Israel.

ANS: Egypt   REF: p.216   OBJ: 7 and 8

12. The series of populist uprisings that occurred in Tunisia, Egypt, Libya, and Syria in 2011 came to be known as _____ .

ANS: Arab spring   REF: p.214   OBJ: 2, 3, 4, 6, and 7

13. Baalbek, a Lebanese city in the Bekaa Valley, is the original headquarters of _____ .

ANS: Hezzbollah   REF: p.216   OBJ: 3 and 4

14. Palestinian diaspora refers to the displacement in 1948 of Palestinians living in _____ .

   ANS: Israel   REF: p.216   OBJ: 5 and 6

15. Road Map for Peace was the term used by President _____ while trying to bring peace to the Middle East, starting in 2002.

ANS: George W. Bush   REF: p.217   OBJ: 8

16. The group Black September took most of the Israeli Olympic team hostage, ultimately killing them and a German police officer, during what the 1972 Olympic games in what city?

ANS: Munich   REF: p. 218   OBJ: 1 and 2

17. The most controversial aspect of Israel's counterterrorist policy is _____.

ANS: selective assassination   REF: p.238   OBJ: 8

18. The 2006 Palestian Parliamentary election was won by _____.

ANS: Hamas   REF: p. 233   OBJ: 5

19. As Hamas challenged the PLO for power, _____ disavowed terrorism in 1988 and called for peace.

ANS: Yasser Arafat   REF: p.219   OBJ: 1 and 2

20. ____began as the military wing of the former PLO and was Yasser Arafat's strongest military muscle.

ANS: Fatah   REF: p.220   OBJ: 1

ESSAY

1. Who was Black September? Discuss the Munich attack.

ANS:
- Arafat could not control terrorists in the many PLO splinter groups, so he created a new group after King Hussein's September attack, calling the group Black September.
- Using German leftist allies, Black September began planning a strike against the Israelis.
- It came, with German terrorist help, in Munich at the 1972 Olympic Games.
- Black September struck the Olympic Village and took most of the Israeli Olympic team hostage, killing those who tried to escape.
- German police moved in, and the world watched a drawn-out siege.
- Black September terrorists negotiated transportation to Libya, but while moving to the aircraft designated to fly them from Germany, the German police launched a rescue operation.

- Plans immediately went awry.
- Reacting quickly, terrorists machine-gunned their hostages before the German police could take control.
- The Israelis and a German police officer were killed.
- It was a terrorist victory, and European leftists and nationalists saw it as partially their triumph.

REF: p. 220   OBJ: 1

2. Discuss the Oslo Accords; what was the outcome?

ANS:

- The Oslo Accords refer to a 1993 agreement between Palestinians and Israel resulting the Palestinian Authority and limited self-rule.
- Arafat, wishing to regain political control, announced that the PLO was the international voice of the Palestinians and he disavowed terrorism in 1988.
- This caused the United States to begin a dialogue with the PLO resulting in an agreement to negotiate and finally the discussion of the formation of a Palestinian state in the 1993 Oslo Accords.
- On the surface it appeared that peace might actually be in the offing, but Arafat could not control the multitude of Palestinian groups.
- Several groups rejected the Oslo agreement and continued the fight.
- These included Hamas, the Palestine Popular Struggle Front, the Palestinian Islamic Jihad, Palestine Liberation Front, the Democratic Front for the Liberation of Palestine, and the Popular Front for the Liberation of Palestine, General Command.
- Arafat and Fatah took immediate control of the Palestinian Authority (PA), but opposition groups remained active for the remainder of the decade.
- The Clinton Administration brought the PA and the Israeli government together to work for a new agreement in 1998.
- The purpose of the negotiation was to surrender Israeli land to the Palestinians for a guarantee of Israeli security.
- President Clinton tried to keep the dialogue going, but Arafat would not – possibly could not – seal the deal and Israeli opponents of "land for peace" were incensed.
- Everything fell apart in September 2000 when the opposition leader, Ariel Sharon, visited the Temple Mount, a site sacred to Jews, Christians, and Muslims.
- The Palestinians were incensed, and they began a second intifada marked by terrorist violence and suicide bombings.

REF: p. 233   OBJ: 1, 2, 3, 4, 5, 6, 7, and 8

3.   Describe how the Abu Nidal Organization reinforced the international spread of Palestinian terrorism.

ANS:

- The Abu Nidal Organization reinforced the international spread of Palestinian terrorism.
- It targeted Israelis outside the Middle East and set up branches in several countries.

- The 1980s proved to be its most successful year and attacks which included:
- The murder of Jordanian ambassadors in Spain, Italy, and India.
- Raids on Jewish schools in Antwerp, Paris, Istanbul, and Paris.
- Airport attacks in Rome and Vienna.
- Assassinations of PLO leaders in Tunis.
- The attempted assassination of the Israeli ambassador to the United Kingdom.
- An attack on a synagogue in Istanbul.
- The Abu Nidal Organization evolved into an international group operating in more than twenty countries.
- Although the group became dormant in the 1990s and faded from activity in the years after Abu Nidal's death, it came to symbolize international Palestinian terrorism.

REF: p. 219 OBJ: 1 and 2

4. Provide a timeline of the phases of Hezbollah.

ANS:
- 1982 Organizing: Different groups carry out attacks under a variety of names.
- 1985-1990 Kidnapping & bombing: A terrorist organization is created.
- 1990-2000 Legitimacy: The group organizes social services, a political party, and a military wing.
- 2000-2004 Coalition: Hezbollah forms temporary alliances with others in the September 2000 Palestinian uprising against Israel (the al Aqsa Intifada).
- 2006 (July): Israel launches offensive in Lebanon.
- 2006 (August): Israel withdraws and Hezbollah claims victory.
- 2006 (September): Iran begins to rebuild Lebanese infrastructure.

REF: p. 225 OBJ: 3, 4, 7, and 8

5. Describe David's Kingdom and Israeli settlements as indicated by Moshe Amon. Do you agree or disagree with Moshe Amon? Why or why not?

ANS:
- Many supporters of Israel and a good number of Israeli peace activists do not favor expansion into Palestinian areas.
- Moshe Amon writes that although Israel is a secular democracy, it is being influenced by religious extremists.
- Ultraorthodox rabbis, he maintains, seek to conquer the biblical Kingdom of David.
- Jewish extremists, with the support of the state, have moved into Palestinian areas to establish permanent settlements.
- Many militants believe that when David's kingdom is restored every person on earth will follow the teachings of the God of Israel.
- Amon says some of the militants fight Israeli soldiers, and some of their leaders call for the murder of non-Jews.

- Amon believes this behavior threatens not only Israel's moral character but its very survival.
- Views will vary.

REF: p. 236   OBJ: 1, 2, 3, 4, 5, 6, 7, and 8

6.   List the controversial tactics utilized by Israel. What do the critics and defenders say? What do you say about the tactics? Why?

ANS:

- Israel has engaged in tactics that have enraged the Palestinians and many others.
- Critics call these tactics Israeli terrorism.
- Defenders say that Israel has a right to protect itself.
- The United States almost always supports Israel, frequently using its veto power in the UN Security Council to keep the United Nations from condemning Israeli actions.
- Controversial tactics include:
- Destroying the homes of suicide-bomber families (bulldozing).
- Selective assassination of Palestinian leaders.
- Killing innocents when striking militants.
- Excessive use of force.
- Commando raids in neighboring countries.
- June 2006 invasion of Lebanon.
- December 2008 invasion of Gaza.
- Blockade of Gaza.
- May 2010 violent interception of ships during Gaza blockade.
- Views will vary.

REF: p. 237   OBJ: 3, 5, 7, and 8

7.   Describe the four phases of the structural change of Hezbollah. What was the outcome of the last phase?

ANS:

- After introducing suicide bombers in its initial phase, Hezbollah struck U.S. Marines and the French army in October 1983, forcing a withdrawal of a multinational peacekeeping force.
- The marine barracks bombing resulted in the deaths of 200 marines, and a second suicide bomber killed 50 French soldiers.
- In its second phase, Hezbollah's leadership launched a kidnapping campaign in Beirut.
- Westerners, especially Americans, were taken hostage, but Hezbollah always denied any affiliation with the group conducting the operation.
- Tactics were extremely effective in the first two phases.
- Suicide actions and other bombings disrupted Lebanon. The U.S. embassy was targeted for a bomb attack, and Hezbollah managed to kill the top six CIA operatives in the Middle East.

- Two of Hezbollah's kidnappings were simply designed to murder the victims.
- Hezbollah kidnapped, tortured, and murdered the CIA station chief in Beirut, as well as a marine colonel working for the United Nations.
- This strategy made the group extremely effective.
- The third phase of Hezbollah's metamorphosis came in 1990.
- Taking over the organization after the death of Musawi, Nasrallah created a regional militia by 1990. In 1991 many of Lebanon's roving paramilitary groups signed a peace treaty, but Hezbollah retained its weapons and revolutionary philosophy and became the primary paramilitary force in southern Lebanon.
- It claimed to be a legitimate guerrilla force, resisting the Israeli occupation of the area.
- Hezbollah's militia, however, soon found itself in trouble. Squabbling broke out among various groups, and Hezbollah was forced to fight Syria and Islamic Amal. Diplomatic pressure increased for the release of hostages.
- Nasrallah took bold steps in response. He sought peace with the Syrians, and with Syrian approval, Western hostages were gradually released.
- Hezbollah's militia began to operate in the open, and it stepped up its campaign against the Israelis in Lebanon.
- Hezbollah joined the Lebanese political process.
- Hezbollah's fourth phase brought the organization from the shadows.
- Its militia, while operating as a guerrilla force, repeatedly struck the Israelis in Lebanon.
- The success of this action brought political payoffs, and by 1995 Hezbollah developed strong political bases of support in parts of Beirut, the Bekaa Valley, and its stronghold in southern Lebanon.
- It created a vast organization of social services, including schools, hospitals, and public works.
- This final change worked; in 1998 Hezbollah won a number of seats in Beirut while maintaining control of the south.

REF: p. 226   OBJ: 3, 4, 7, and 8

8.   Explain the three major functions of Hezbollah's international branch.

ANS:
- Hezbollah's international branch appears to have three major functions.
- In Europe and in the United States, Hezbollah raises money to support operations
- Iran uses Hezbollah as an extension of its own power.
- It protects Iranian interests in Lebanon, and projects an Iranian-influenced military presence in other parts of the Middle East.
- It also acts as a buffer between Iran and Israel.
- Finally, Hezbollah has established a strong presence in South America.
- It uses this base to raise funds through legitimate and illegitimate methods, conduct propaganda, and launch terrorist operations.

REF: p. 227   OBJ: 3, 4, 7, and 8

9.   What was Operation Cast Lead; explain the controversy over the invasion. What is your opinion? Explain.

ANS:
- On December 27, 2008 Israel kicked off Operation Cast Lead, a devastating air and artillery assault on Gaza followed by a ground invasion on January 3.
- According to news reports, several nations condemned the Israeli incursion and the United States urged Israel to show restraint.
- Supporters of Israel were infuriated stating that Israel had a right to defend itself.
- They asked why had there been no international outcry against Hamas' rocket attacks.
- Critics only emerged, the supporters argued, when Israel took steps to defend its borders.
- Israel maintained the attack for twenty-two days destroying munitions and supplies.
- They also targeted underground tunnels Hamas used to bring in military stores; fighting caused hundreds of casualties.
- Controversy over the invasion centered on proportionality.
- Strategic results might eventually be questionable, but the tactical results were clear.
- Faced with rocket attacks, Israel responded with overwhelming military force.
- This temporarily eradicated Hamas' military capability while ensuring that Israeli troops would suffer minimal casualties during the fighting.
- This exacts a high humanitarian toll but it reflects legitimate military action and it was a tactical success.

REF: p. 234   OBJ: 5, 6, 7, and 8

10.   Describe the operations of the Abu Nidal Organization in the 1980s.

ANS:
- *Abu Nidal Organization (Black June)*
- Sabri al Banna (whose code name was Abu Nidal) and Yasser Arafat were once comrades in arms in the struggle for Palestine, but as others broke from Arafat, so too did Abu Nidal's rebel organization, called Black June.

- In the end, Abu Nidal and his organization became a mercenary group, not only abandoning Arafat but also completely forsaking the Palestinian cause.

- The group's international exploits drew more attention than did those of its rival terrorist organizations as Nidal conducted ruthless operations in the 1980s, including:
  - The murder of Jordanian ambassadors in Spain, Italy, and India
  - Raids on Jewish schools in Antwerp, Istanbul, and Paris
  - Attacks on airports in Rome and Vienna
  - Assassinations of PLO leaders in Tunis
  - The attempted assassination of the Israeli ambassador to the United Kingdom
  - An attack on a synagogue in Istanbul

- The Abu Nidal Organization evolved into an international group operating in more than 20 countries. It faded from significance by the 1990s, and Abu Nidal was murdered in Iraq in 2003.

REF: p. 219   OBJ: 2

Chapter 10

Revolutionary and Counter Revolutionary Terrorism

Learning Objectives

After reading this chapter, students should be able to:

1. Define revolutionary and counter revolutionary terrorism.
2. Outline the history, philosophy, and influence of the Tupamaros.
3. Summarize the emergence and current status of FARC and the ELN.
4. Describe the function and purpose of the MeK.
5. Describe the rise, fall, and resurgence of the Shining Path.
6. Explain the Maoist rebellion in Nepal.
7. Outline the issues surrounding Naxilite terrorism.
8. Explain the operations and tactics of the New Peoples Army.
9. Describe the rise, fall, and transformation of revolutionary terrorism in Europe.
10. Explain the rise of death squads as a reaction to revolutionary terrorism.

Chapter Key Terms

Raul Sendic, p. 248

National Liberation Movement, p. 248

Red Brigades, p. 253

Plan Colombia, p. 255

Alvaro Uribe, p. 255

American embassy takeover, p. 256

Tupac Amaru, p. 257

Abimael Guzman, p. 257

Cultural Revolution, p. 257

Alberto Fujimori, p. 258

King Gyanendra, p. 260

Red Corridor, p. 262

No-go areas, p. 264

People Power Revolution, p. 264

Red Army Faction, p. 266

Renato Curcio, p. 267

Raul Sendic: (1926– 1989) A Uruguayan revolutionary leader. Sendic founded the National Liberation Movement (MLN), popularly known as the Tupamaros. Following governmental repression in 1973, he fled the country. Sendic died in Paris in 1989.

National Liberation Movement: the Tupamaro's official name.

Red Brigades: an Italian Marxist terrorist group that had its most effective operations from 1975 to 1990. It amended the centralized Tupamaro model by creating semi-autonomous cells.

Plan Colombia: A joint effort by the United States and Colombia to reduce violence and illegal drugs. It began in 1999.

Alvaro Uribe: (1952–) the President of Colombia, 2002–2010. He was known for his tough stance against FARC and other revolutionary movements.

American embassy takeover–The Iranian Hostage Crisis: Revolutionary students stormed the U.S. embassy in Tehran with the support of the Iranian government. They held 54 American hostages from November 1979 to January 1981.

Tupac Amaru: (? – 1572) An Inca chieftain who led a revolt against Spain in the sixteenth century. His story has inspired many liberation and democratic movements in South America.

Abimael Guzman :(1934–) A philosophy professor who led the Shining Path from 1980 until his arrest in 1992. Guzman is serving a life sentence in Peru.

Cultural Revolution: A violent movement in China from 1966 to 1976. Its main purpose was to rid China of its middle class and growing capitalist interests. The Cultural Revolution ended with the death of Mao Zedong.

Alberto Fujimori: (1938–) President of Peru from 1990 to 2000. He fled to Japan in 2000 and was extradited to Peru in 2007. He was convicted of human rights violations and sentenced to prison.

King Gyanendra: (1947–) the king of Nepal from 2001 to 2008. After the attack and murder of several members of the royal family, Gyanendra became king of Nepal in 2001. Gyanendra took complete power in 2005 to fight the Maoist rebellion. In the spring of 2006, he was forced to return power to parliament, and he was removed from power in 2008.

Red Corridor: The area of Naxalite violence in India. The length of the corridor runs from Nepal through southern India, and the width extends from India's east coast to the central regions.

No-Go areas: An informal term to describe geographical areas that the duly empowered government cannot control. Security forces cannot routinely patrol these places.

People Power Revolution: A mass Philippine protest movement that toppled Ferdinand Marcos in 1986. Marcos ruled as a dictator after being elected as president in 1965 and declaring martial law in 1972. When Gloria Macapagal-Arroyo (president 2001–2010)

assumed the presidency in January 2001, her government proclaimed a second People Power Revolution.

Red Army Faction: a West German Marxist group modelled as Marighella-style urban guerrillas. They were the most violent and active revolutionary group during the heyday of left-wing European terrorism. After German reunification, the records of former East German secret police led to the demise of the RAF. It was also known as the Baader-Meinhof Gang when it first formed.

Renato Curcio: (1941–) the founder and leader of the Red Brigades in Italy.

Margherita Cagol: (1945–1975) Also known as Mara Cagol, the wife of Renato Curcio and a member of the Red Brigades. She was killed in a shoot-out with Italian police a few weeks after freeing her husband from prison.

Anders Breivik: (1979-) A violent right-wing extremist who went on a one-day killing spree in Norway in July 2011. He detonated a bomb in Oslo and went on a shooting spree at a Labour Party youth camp for political reasons.

Chapter Outline

I.   **Modeling Revolutionary Terrorism – Uruguay's Tupamaros**
     OBJ 1: Define revolutionary and counter revolutionary terrorism
     OBJ 2: Outline the history, philosophy, and influence of the Tupamaros

   A. In the early 1960s, a group of revolutionaries called the Tupamaros surfaced in Uruguay.
   B. The Tupamaros epitomized urban terrorism.
   C. By 1959 Uruguay had undergone a devastating economic reversal, and workers were restless.
   D. Several militant radicals injected themselves into the union movement, and when the sugar workers organized in 1959, the militants dominated the union and called for confrontation with the government.
   E. By 1962 the union organizers believed they should move their organization from the rural north to Montevideo, the capital, to make its presence felt.
   F. *Raul Sendic* founded the National Liberation Movement (MLN), popularly known as the Tupamaros.
       1. Sendic believed violence was the only appropriate tool to change the political order.
   G. The urban philosophy
       1. According to Arturo Porzecanski, the group was not willing to move outside Montevideo to begin a guerrilla war for several reasons.
           a. First, the group was not large enough to begin a guerrilla campaign because it represented radical middle-class students.
           b. Second, the countryside of Uruguay did not readily lend itself to a guerrilla war because unrest grew from the urban center of Uruguay.
           c. Third, the peasants were unwilling to provide popular support for guerrilla forces.

307

      d.   Fourth, Montevideo was the nerve center of Uruguay.

  2. In 1963 the group adopted its official name, the National Liberation Movement (MLN).

  3. The Tupamaros organized to do battle inside the city, following the recent guidelines of Carlos Marighella – terrorism would become the prime strategy for assaulting the enemy.

  4. In 1968 the Tupamaros launched a massive campaign of decentralized terrorism, and began a campaign of kidnapping at will.

  5. Frustrated, the police turned to an old Latin American tactic – torture.

  6. Torturing prisoners served several purposes:

      a.   First, it provided a ready source of information.

      b.   Second, torture was believed to serve as a deterrent to other would-be revolutionaries.

  7. Although the Tupamaros waged an effective campaign of terrorism, they were never able to capture the hearts of the working class.

  8. In 1972 the Tupamaros were finished; their violence helped bring about a revolution, but not the type they had intended.

H. Creating the urban organization.

  1. The Tupamaros were one of the most highly organized yet least structured terrorist groups in modern history.

  2. The Tupamaros believed in strong internal discipline.

  3. Operational power in the Tupamaros was vested in the lower- echelon units.

  4. Peter Waldmann believes that in terms of striking power, organization, and the ability to control a city, no group has ever surpassed the Tupamaros – they epitomized the terrorist role.

II.   The Urban Philosophy
OBJ 2: Outline the history, philosophy, and influence of the Tupamaros

A. The grand strategy centered on winning support from the middle and working classes.

B. Because of the state of the economy and the lack of opportunity for educated people, the Tupamaros began their campaign with a good deal of sympathy in the middle class.

C. Because the physical situation of Uruguay was not suitable for guerrilla war, the Tupamaros turned to the city.

D. Tupamaro-style terrorism involved extremely small units engaging in individual acts of violence.

E. They believed they could obtain power only at a critical juncture, when the political, social, and economic conditions were conducive to revolution.

  1. They called this juncture the *coyuntura*, and they aimed all revolutionary activities at this point.

F. John Wolf says the Tupamaros saw violence as the only method to bring about social change.

G. Food distribution and appeals to the working class could not neutralize violence and murder.

      1. Tupamaro humanitarian gestures were viewed with contempt because of the concurrent, violent terrorist campaign.

   H. According to Peter Waldmann, the major mistake of the Tupamaros was that they alienated their supporters.

   I. In the final analysis, Tupamaro tactics failed.

   J. Many revolutionary manuals and proposed terrorist organizations are based on Tupamaro experiences.

III.   **Death Squads and Counter Revolutionaries**
OBJ 10: Explain the rise of death squads as a reaction to revolutionary terrorism

   A. Death squads come into being when people who hold economic and political power believe their position is being threatened and the threat is beyond the control of law and order.

   B. The purpose of a death squad is to eliminate opposition when a government is either unable or unwilling to do so.

   C. The tactics of death squads range from semi-official raids on governmental opponents to torture and secret murder

   D. Paramilitary death squads come into play only when power elites feel that social changes are undermining their societies and nothing can be done to stop it.

   E. Julie Mazzei argues that the conditions giving rise to death squads develop when several factors come together to form a favorable environment:

      1. First, political elites must be entrenched in a society with a vested interest in maintaining societal structures, and these elites have a history of employing armed force to protect their positions.

      2. Second, a reform movement threatens to break up elitist power structures with the redistribution of wealth of power.

      3. Third, the government must be either unwilling or unable to stop the reform movement.

      4. Finally, hardliners among the political elites break away from their mainstream counterparts, based on the belief that moderate political elites are too soft and are unable to stop the reform movement.

   F. A group creating a death squad believes that its place in society is natural and legitimate.

IV.   **Revolutionary Terrorism**
OBJ 1: Define revolutionary and counter-revolutionary terrorism
OBJ 3: Summarize the emergence and current status of FARC and the ELN

   A. A common misconception is that the American Revolution was based on terrorism.

   B. Martha Crenshaw says revolutionary terrorism can be defined as an insurgent strategy in the context of internal warfare or revolution.

1. It is an attempt to seize power from a legitimate state for the purpose of creating political and social change.
C. Modern revolutionary terrorism is embodied by the Tupamaro philosophy, and it emerged in North and South America in the 1960s and 1970s.
   1. It was the dominant form of terrorism in Europe until about 1990, and it still guides some terrorist campaigns today.
D. FARC, ELN, and Narcoterrorism
   1. Illegal drugs are also part of Colombia's problem with terrorism.
   2. Originally liberated by Simon Bolivar in 1812, Colombia became part of a large nation known as Grand Colombia.
   3. The Revolutionary Armed Forces of Colombia (FARC) is Latin America's oldest and largest terrorist group.
   4. Formed as a military wing of the Colombian Communist Party in 1964, it is probably the most capable terrorist group in South America.
   5. The United States had long been involved in Colombian affairs, and it stepped up measures in 1999 with a new project *Plan Colombia*.
   6. The purpose was to move against three different groups: FARC, the National Liberation Army (ELN), and the United Self-Defense Forces of Colombia (AUC).
   7. Modern Colombian violence cannot be separated from the production of cocaine.
   8. In 2008 *Alvaro Uribe*'s aggressive counterterrorism policy struck deeply into FARC, and some of its key leaders were killed in military operations.
   FARC and ELN are linked by a radical socialist ideology, but they are torn over control of drug profits.

V. **The Demise of the Left in Europe**
   OBJ 4: Describe the function and purpose of the MeK

A. Europe has experienced a pattern of declining left-wing revolutionary terrorism and its reemergence into single-issue violence.
B. The ideological terrorists of the 1960s, on both the left and the right, were expressing their frustration with the social structures imposed by a modern industrial society.
C. Ideological terrorists in Europe reject the economic and social structure of industrial capitalism; they want a new order.
D. Three key events that changed the political landscape of Europe and the world:
   1. In 1989 the Berlin Wall came down, leading to the reunification of Germany.
   2. To the south, new nations emerging from the former Yugoslavia took up arms and resumed a centuries-old struggle.
   3. The Soviet Union dissolved, along with the authoritarian rule of the Communist Party in the republics of the former Soviet Union and Eastern Europe.

E. As the structure of Europe and the world changed from 1989 to 1992, European terrorism also changed.

F. Nationalistic terrorism remained, but conflict rose in the form of ethnic violence.

G. The threat of jihadist terrorism replaced threats from the left, and Europe experienced new strains of terrorism.

H. Fueled by the Vietnam War, European leftists were influenced by events in Latin America, as well as by revolutionary leaders such as Carlos Marighella.

I. Currently, left-wing terrorism in Europe is out of vogue.

J. The bigger threat comes from international jihadists, who have targeted Germany, Belgium, the Netherlands, France, Spain, and the United Kingdom.

K. The Mujahedin-eKahlq.

   1. The Mujahedin-e Kahlq (MeK) was founded in 1965, fourteen years before the Iranian revolution, for the purpose of overthrowing the Iranian government.

   4. It is the largest and most militant group opposed to the Islamic Republic of Iran.

   5. Mujahedin-e Khalq presents a conundrum for the United States.

   6. In 2007 President George Bush received a budget of $400,000,000 from Congress to support groups violently opposed to Iran's Islamic regime – one of the groups included on the list was the MeK

   8. The group has been removed from British and European Union list of terrorist organizations, and it has shared information with clustered intelligence agencies.

L. The Revolutionary Struggle (EA) in Greece.

   1. Greece was ruled by military junta from 1967 to 1974, and the roots to Greek revolutionary terrorism can be traced to this time.

   2. Two terrorist groups appeared shortly after democracy returned to Greece: the Revolutionary People's Struggle (ELA) and November 17 (N17).

   3. Karyotis explains Greek counterterrorism policy by examining three phases of recent history:

      a. In the first phase Greek security forces simply did not consider terrorism to be a problem.

      b. At that point the Greek political system deemed terrorism to be a problem, but instead of developing strong security policy, Greek politicians debated the issue of terrorism until 1999.

      c. The third phase of the Greek response came in 1999 when authorities accepted the reality of the threat and developed security mechanisms to deal with it.

   4. Despite these efforts, a new group emerged in 2003: Revolutionary Struggle (EA).

   5. In 2009, during a worldwide recession, the Greek economy took a turn for the worse; by 2010, Greece was in an economic meltdown.

311

6. While revolutionary terrorism faded in Europe from its heyday in the 1970s to its demise in the 1990s, the concept remains alive in Greece.

VI. **Maoist Revolutionary Terrorism.**
   OBJ 5: Describe the rise, fall, and restructuring of the Shining Path
   OBJ 6: Explain the Maoist rebellion in Nepal
   OBJ 7: Outline the issues surrounding Naxalite terrorism
   OBJ 8: Explain the operations and tactics of the New Peoples Army
   OBJ 9: Describe the rise, fall, and transformation of revolutionary terrorism in Europe

   A. Maoist terrorism is a form of revolutionary terrorism.
   B. In practice, Maoist groups tend to be more violent than other revolutionary groups.
   C. Maoist groups exhibit three striking differences from most other revolutionary terrorists:
      1. First, they practice ruthless domination in the areas they control, and they rule by terrorism.
      2. Second, Maoist groups have a reputation for maintaining internal discipline.
      3. Finally, Maoist groups follow the revolutionary philosophy of Chinese communist leader Mao Zedong.
   D. Maoist groups are based in rural peasant movements.
   E. Peru's Shining Path
      1. A Maoist group known as the Shining Path launched a campaign in rural Peru that began in 1980, and lasted for the following two decades.
      2. Peru's revolutionary past was grounded in anti-colonialism as the indigenous people sought to free themselves from European rule.
         a. *Tupac Amaru* led a revolt against Spain from 1581 to 1582.
      4. The Shining Path's Maoist campaign of terrorism utilized his name.
      5. Led by *Abimael Guzman,* the group was deeply influenced by China and its Cultural Revolution.
      6. Guzman led the Shining Path in a twofold strategy.
         a. First, the guerrillas operated in rural areas trying to create regional military forces.
         b. Second, Guzman attempted to combine Mao Zedong's ruthless revolutionary zeal with the guerrilla philosophy of Che Guevara.
      9. The Shining Path reemerged around 2007 by reinventing itself as a drug trafficking organization.
   F. The New Peoples' Army
      1. The Philippines have differing cultures, radical gaps in income, different religious traditions, and divisive politics.

312

2. In addition to foreign occupation by three different countries in the 19th and 20th centuries, Philippine politics have been characterized as a struggle for democracy in the midst of local revolts.

3. The New People's Army (NPA) is the longest running communist insurgency in the world.

4. It is a rural movement that began in 1969 as a response to a Philippine dictatorship.

5. The group eventually adopted a Maoist revolutionary philosophy, targeting security forces, politicians, judges, and U.S. military personnel assigned to the Philippines.

7. Underground death squads began eliminating suspected enemies in Mafia-style executions in 2001, and murders increased with the campaign against terrorism in 2006.

9. The Philippines have been plagued by terrorism since the mid-1970s.

10. Two of the issues that keep the NPA in the field: the structure of political power and the distribution of wealth.

11. Poverty does not cause terrorism, but social inequities can draw people to revolutionary causes.

G. The Maoist rebellion in Nepal.

1. The small Himalayan nation of Nepal experienced a ruthless Maoist rebellion from 1995 to 2005.

2. The Maoist rebels were unique; they had international connections through their leftist positions, yet their specific objectives were aimed only at the national level.

3. Nepal appeared to be on its way to becoming a constitutional monarchy in the 1950s.

   a. The king suspended parliament in 1960 and ended party politics in 1962.

   b. The king saw democracy as a threat, and moved to stop it. These actions frustrated many people, especially a small communist party.

4. In 1990 the king agreed to a new constitution, and the NCP won elections in 1991.

5. The king dissolved the parliament in 1995, and the Nepal Communist Party began a rural rebellion.

6. The government and the Maoists signed a peace agreement in late 2006, with both sides promising to agree to a power-sharing arrangement and to write a new constitution.

7. The Maoist coalition, however, fell apart and a new government excluded the Nepalese Communist Party. The constitution remained in limbo.

H. Naxalites

1. India has a variety of terrorist problems arising from political, religious, and ethnic strife.

2. India's agrarian system is based on large wealthy landholders and un-landed peasants, formerly of the lower caste, who are alienated from the current economic structure.

3. Great economic disparities have caused the growth of left-wing movements that demand a more equal distribution of resources. One of these movements has turned violent.
4. The Naxalites emerged in a 1967 uprising in West Bengal.
5. When tensions between the Soviet Union and China led to a breakup of the Sino-Soviet alliance, the Naxalites chose a Maoist path.
6. The Naxalites began to emerge again in the 1990s in a variety of smaller movements.
7. Their goals evolved into a movement with three promises:
   a. Land to the tiller.
   b. Higher wages for agricultural work.
   c. Ending the *de facto* caste system.

Chapter Summary

- Revolutionary terrorism involves violent activity for the purpose of changing the political structure of government, or the social orientation of a country or region. Maoist terrorism is a form of revolutionary terrorism. Its goal is to establish a communist society similar to revolutionary China. Counterterrorism involves the legitimate legal activities of security forces, but some unofficial groups operate outside the law. When these groups engage in violence, it can be described as counter revolutionary terrorism.

- The Tupamaros established an urban organization. The active cadre conducted terrorism (robbery, kidnapping, attacking symbolic targets) while waiting on sympathizers to create a revolutionary climate. The organizational structure included firing teams (small units described in Marighella's mini manual which were separated from one another in secretive cells), a command structure, and logistical support. The Tupamaros thwarted efforts by Montevideo police and security forces to suppress them, and they gained limited support from the urban poor. . Modern network and cellular concepts are rooted in the Tupamaro structure.

- FARC and the ELN emerged as revolutionary groups in Colombia. They formed alliances with drug cartels, and their influence spread beyond Colombia. They remain operational, but their effectiveness is believed to have been reduced.

- The MeK fought against the revolutionary government of Iran. Its operations and finances were influenced, and at times, controlled by Iraq.

- The Shining Path launched a twenty-year terrorist campaign in Peru in 1980. It was a rural Maoist movement that prompted a harsh governmental response. Peasants were caught in the middle. It reemerged around 2007, but its major goal was control of the drug trade. The Shining Path broke into two major factions centered on drug trafficking. It gained a strong foothold in the coca producing regions in southern Peru after 2012.

314

- The Naxalite rebellion began in 1967 in west Bengal. It started as several communist movements agitating for agrarian reform and peasants rights. The first rebellion was repressed with military and police power. In the second phase, Naxalites began to spread and organize in central India, creating a Red Corridor. The third phase began in 2004 when two major groups united and launched an open rebellion. It's most deadly year was 2010, but the group suffered setbacks in 2011 after one of its main leaders was killed. It remains active, although the level of violence dropped in early 2012.

- The Maoist rebellion in Nepal began in 1995 and grew into a major insurrection. A peace treaty in 1995 temporarily brought the Nepali Communist Party into the government, and resulted in limitations on the power of the monarchy. However, Maoist rebels launched attacks in 1996 which caused a civil war that lasted until a ceasefire was declared in 2006. UN monitoring began in 2007. The Maoist threatened to renew violence in 2012.

- Europe embodied revolutionary terrorism from about 1965 to 1990. Most groups waned after the demise of the former Soviet Union. Ethnic terrorism has now emerged as the most likely threat, although single-issue groups may emerge to replace the left. N17 followed the path of most revolutionary groups in Europe, and it lasted into the twenty-first century. The Revolutionary Struggle emerged after the demise of N17, and remains operational in Greece. Anarchist violence has increased recently as a result of an economic crisis in Europe.

- Death squads developed as a reaction to revolutionary terrorism. The premise behind extrajudicial arrest, torture, and murder is that normative law cannot cope with terrorist violence. People supporting death squads believe that their existence is threatened; therefore, it is necessary to operate outside the law and terrorize the terrorists.

DISCUSSION QUESTIONS

1. Julie Mazzei argues that the conditions giving rise to death squads develop when several factors come together to form a favorable environment. What are these factors? Do you agree or disagree with her argument? Explain. (OBJ 1, 9, and 10)

2. Discuss the rise and fall of revolutionary terrorism in Europe; does it align with Latin America? Explain. (OBJ 1 – 10)

3. Why does White say the Mujahedin-e Khalq presents a conundrum for the United States? (OBJ 4)

4. What are the major issues surrounding Naxilite terrorism? How does this compare to the issues that gave rise to the Tupamaros? Be specific in your response. Provide examples to illustrate your points. (OBJ 1, 2, 7, and 10)

ASSIGNMENTS

1. Set up 5 - 8 pieces of flipchart paper in different areas of the classroom. Put a different terrorist organization, which is mentioned in the chapter, as a heading on the paper. Provide markers at each station and have each student add an informative bullet point at each station that correctly describes or relates to the respective terrorist group. Once they have had time to finish their rounds, have the students review the completed charts and discuss the results. (OBJ 1 – 10)

2. Have students choose a topic from this chapter and write a study guide/handout to present and share with the class. For example, students may focus their study guide on describing the emergence of modern piracy. Allow time to discuss topics to eliminate duplication. (OBJ 1 – 10)

3. Have students research the history of death squads. Provide guiding questions such as, "How often throughout history have death squads been utilized as a means of control? Where? In modern times, what was the response of the media? Have students discuss and debate their discoveries. (OBJ 1, 5, and 8)

4. As a review, play jeopardy using key concepts and terms from the chapter. (OBJ 1 – 10)

5. Have each student comb through http://www.strategycenter.net/research/pubID.149/pub_detail.asp (or another website as approved by the instructor) for a current event and select an article that relates to one or more of the chapter's core concepts. Have students provide a journalistic summary and a personal opinion/reaction to the article. Have students orally present the article to the class, field Q & A's from their fellow students, and provide a copy of the original source article following the presentation. Optional: Have students complete peer assessments at the end of each presentation. (OBJ 1 - 10)

MEDIA TOOLS

1. ***"Wikis"***
    7 Things you should know about Wikis. Retrieved from the Web Jun 29, 2012 at http://net.educause.edu/ir/library/pdf/ELI7004.pdf

    This document offers easy to understand instruction on the history, development, and potential uses of Wikis.

Have students develop (or make additions to a previously created one) a *Webliography* (resource list) using a Blog or Wiki that provides a short description and link to a scholarly resource pertaining to course concepts. For example, have students add two to three resources each and ask them to add their assessment of at least one of their peers' contributions. If desired, allow time to discuss Blogs/Wikis. This activity can be reused throughout the course, by asking students to add/revise their contributions each week, bi-weekly, etc. (OBJ 1 – 10)

2. ***"Current Events Article Summary with Peer Assessment"***

Use the Article Summary Template, which can be obtained on the instructor companion website, for this assignment. The template offers information on Internet research, outside resources, identification of credible sources, and detailed directions on completing an assessment of a news article. It also includes a peer evaluation tool.

Have each student comb the Internet for terrorism related news, and select an article that relates to one or more of the chapter's core concepts. Be sure selections are an article of interest from a credible source (*more on credibility can be found in the article summary template above*). Fill out an article summary template. *Your template asks for generic info about the article, a journalistic summary, as well as a personal opinion/reaction to the article.* Have each student summarize the article and present it orally to the class and field Q & A's from their fellow students. Have students complete peer assessments at the end of each presentation. Have students submit templates, original source article, and peer-reviews prior to the end of class. (OBJ 1 - 10)

3. ***"Terrorist Organization Portfolio or PowerPoint"***
The FBI's Terrorism Screening Center. Retrieved from the Web Jun 29, 2012 at http://www.fbi.gov/about-us/nsb/tsc.

This site offers a substantial array of information on terrorism related topics including: postings of fugitives; terrorists; and terrorist organizations. It also provides several links to related agencies in the War on Terror. In addition, the site also offers information on careers with the FBI, virtual tours, as well as a fun & games page.

Have students visit the various pages on the site, gathering information on one of the terrorist organizations (either assigned or self-selected) mentioned in the chapter. Have students, either individually or in groups, synthesize their findings into a single, organized portfolio or PowerPoint presentation that provides detailed information about he organization. Students may supplement their research using additional resources. (OBJ 1 – 10)

317

4.   ***"Interactive Map of Latin America"***
     Sheppard's Software. Interactive Map of South and Central America. Retrieved
     from the Web Aug 20, 2012 at
     http://www.sheppardsoftware.com/country_SoAmCA_G1_drag_drop.html

     The website offers a fun game via an interactive map of Latin America, wherein
     participants 'click' and drag' countries to their corresponding locations.

     Have students test their knowledge of the region by playing the game individually
     at their stations, or compete as a class via a screen share projection. (OBJ 1 – 9)

TEST BANK

Chapter 10—International Terrorism: Ideological and Religious Movements

TRUE/FALSE

1. The Shining Path subscribed to Maoist ideology.

ANS: T   REF: p. 257   OBJ: 1 and 2

2. Death squads have been associated primarily with left-wing activities.

ANS: F   REF: p. 269   OBJ: 1, 9, and 10

3. A common misconception is that the American Revolution was based on terrorism.

ANS: T   REF: p. 246   OBJ: 1

4. In the Tupamaro organization, the Executive Committee was in charge, but it ran a highly decentralized operation.

ANS: T   REF: p. 252   OBJ: 1 and 2

5. Ethnic strife is the sole cause of India's terrorist problems.

ANS: F   REF: p. 261   OBJ: 1, 7, and 9

6. The FARC and ELN, originally inspired by the Tupamaros, have turned to drug trafficking to survive.

ANS: T   REF: p. 271   OBJ: 3

7. When revolutionary terrorism appeared in 1974, the Greek government did not view it as a security threat.

ANS: T   REF: p. 268   OBJ: 1, 3, and 9

8. As champions of revolutionary terrorism, the Tupamaros were copied around the world, especially by groups in the U.S. and western Europe.

ANS: T   REF: p. 253   OBJ: 1, 2, and 9

9. After World War II, revolutionary terrorism was mainly composed of left-wing and Marxist movements.

ANS: T   REF: p. 246   OBJ: 1 and 9

10.   A Naxalite group known as the Shining Path launched terrorist campaigns in rural Peru.

ANS: F   REF: p. 245   OBJ: 1, 7, and 9

11.   Though formally abandoned by India's Constitution, Indian society was governed by a rigid caste system for centuries.

ANS: T   REF: p. 261   OBJ: 7 and 9

12.   Mahatma Gandhi was assassinated by an Islamic extremist.

ANS: F   REF: p. 262   OBJ: 1, 7, and 9

13.   India is one of the most under policed countries of the world.

ANS: T   REF: p. 264   OBJ: 1, 7, and 9

14.   The New People's Army (NPA) is the longest-running communist insurgency in the world.

ANS: T   REF: p. 264   OBJ: 1, 8, and 9

15.   FARC and the ELN emerged as revolutionary groups in 1960s France.

ANS: F   REF: p. 254   OBJ: 1 and 3

MULTIPLE CHOICE

1.   In the early 1960s, a group of revolutionaries called the Tupamaros surfaced in ____.
      a. Uruguay
      b. Columbia
      c. Argentina
      d. Paraguay

ANS: a   REF: p. 247   OBJ: 1 and 2

2.   As Nepal's rebellion grew, the role of women in the _____ movement expanded.
      a. Naxalite
      b. Maoist
      c. Hamas
      d. FARC

ANS: b   REF: p. 260   OBJ: 1, 6, and 9

3.   Maoist terrorism is most appropriately classed as _____ in nature.
      a. Religious
      b. Political
      c. Revolutionary
      d. Criminal

ANS: c   REF: p. 246   OBJ: 1, 6, and 9

4.   The Naxalites emerged in an uprising in West Bengal in what year?
     a. 1967
     b. 1860
     c. 1948
     d. 1990

ANS: a   REF: p. 261   OBJ: 1, 6, and 9

5.   Prime Minister Indira Gandhi was assassinated by _____ bodyguards in 1984.
     a. Hindi
     b. Muslim
     c. Neonazi
     d. Sikh

ANS: d   REF: p. 262   OBJ: 1, 7, 9, and 10

6.   Prime Minister Rajiv Gandhi was assassinated by_____ in Tamil Nadu, India in 1991.
     a. Maoists
     b. Naxalites
     c. The LTTE
     d. Tuparamos

ANS: c   REF: p. 262   OBJ: 1,7, 9, and 10

7.   In 2006, terrorists killed 185 people in a series of seven explosions in what city?
     a. Mumbai
     b. London
     c. Tokyo
     d. Munich

ANS: a   REF: p. 262   OBJ: 1, 7, and 9

8.   _____ is Latin America's oldest and largest terrorist group.
     a. FARC
     b. Shining Path
     c. RAF
     d. ELN

ANS: a   REF: p. 254   OBJ: 1 and 3

9.   In the 1950s, Nepal appeared to be on its way to creating what form of government?
     a. Communist state
     b. Democracy
     c. Dictatorship
     d. Constitutional monarchy

ANS: d   REF: p. 259   OBJ: 1, 6, and 9

10. Straying from the tactics of counterparts in the region, the Tupamaros opted to battle urban centers instead of rural regions, aligning with the operational guidelines of what revolutionary leader?
   a. Fidel Castro
   b. Carlos Marighella
   c. Tupac Amaru
   d. Renato Curcio

ANS: b   REF: p. 249   OBJ: 1 and 2

11. Revolutionary terrorism is currently most active in which of the following countries?
   a. Greece
   b. The U.S.
   c. Canada
   d. Norway

ANS: a   REF: p. 268   OBJ: 1 and 9

12. Between 1975 and 2000, no less than ___ revolutionary terrorist groups operated in Greece.
   a. 100
   b. 200
   c. 50
   d. 250

ANS: d   REF: p. 268   OBJ: 1 and 9

13. In the midst of revolution and torture of the 60s and 70s, the Tupamaros blamed _____ for supporting the brutal Uruguayan government.
   a. The British
   b. The U.S.
   c. The French
   d. The Greeks

ANS: b   REF: p. 250   OBJ: 1, 2, and 10

14. _____ founded the Movement of National Liberation (MLN), popularly known as the Tupamaros.
   a. Fidel Casatro
   b. Raul Sendic
   c. Carlos Marighella
   d. Tupac Amaru

ANS: b   REF: p. 248   OBJ: 1, 2, and 10

15. The Philippines have been plagued by terrorism since the _____.
   a. mid-1800s
   b. early-1920s
   c. mid-1970s
   d. late 1940s

ANS: c   REF: p. 265   OBJ: 1 and 8

16. The United States granted the Philippines independence in what year?
    a. 1997
    b. 1982
    c. 2001
    d. 1946

ANS: d   REF: p. 265   OBJ: 1 and 8

17. The Baader-Meinhof Gang evolved into what organization?
    a. The Red Army Faction (RAF)
    b. The New Peoples' Army (NPA)
    c. The Revolutionary Armed Forces of Colombia (FARC)
    d. The National Liberation Army (ELN)

ANS: a   REF: p. 266   OBJ: 1 and 9

18. Beginning in 1980, the Maoist group _____ launched a terrorist campaign in rural Peru.
    a. The New Peoples' Army (NPA)
    b. The Shining Path
    c. The National Liberation Army (ELN)
    d. The Tupamaros

ANS: b   REF: p. 257   OBJ: 1 and 5

19. The Mujahedin-e Kahlq (MeK) was established in which of the following countries?
    a. Iran
    b. Israel
    c. Pakistan
    d. Peru

ANS: a   REF: p. 256   OBJ: 1 and 4

20. The ELN is composed of determined revolutionaries primarily funded by _____.
    a. The slave trade
    b. Charities
    c. Corrupt politicians
    d. The drug trade

ANS: d   REF: p. 256   OBJ: 1 and 3

21. Former Columbian President _____ was internationally recognized for his tough stance against FARC and other revolutionary movements.
    a. Raul Sendic
    b. Alvaro Uribe
    c. Renato Curcio
    d. Felipe Calderón

ANS: b   REF: p. 255   OBJ: 1 and 3

22. What is the name applied to the region of Naxalite violence in India.
   a. Red Corridor
   b. Nasalbari
   c. West Bengal
   d. Northern region

ANS: a   REF: p. 262   OBJ: 1 and 7

23. Which of the following organizations is viewed as the longest running communist insurgency in the world?
   a. FARC
   b. ELN
   c. MeK
   d. NPA

ANS: d   REF: p. 264   OBJ: 1 and 8

24. Renato Curcio is the founder and leader of the Red Brigades in what country?
   a. Russia
   b. Abimael Guzman
   c. Italy
   d. Argentina

ANS: c   REF: p. 267   OBJ: 1 and 9

25. The Tupamaros operated solely in what Latin American city?
   a. Lima
   b. Asuncion
   c. Montevideo
   d. Rio de Janeiro

ANS: c   REF: p. 267   OBJ: 1, 2, and 10

26. The terrorist groups Revolutionary People's Struggle (ELA) and November 17 (N17) appeared shortly after democracy returned to what country?
   a. Spain
   b. The Phillipines
   c. France
   d. Greece

ANS: d   REF: p. 272   OBJ: 1 and 9

27. The FARC and ELN, originally inspired by the Tupamaros, have turned to drug trafficking to survive.
   a. Greece
   b. Spain
   c. Ireland
   d. Austria

ANS: a   REF: p. 271   OBJ: 9

324

28.   What country was home to the 1979 Sandinista revolution?
          a. Venezuela
          b. Uraguay
          c. Nicaragua
          d. Brazil

ANS: c   REF: p. 269   OBJ: 1 and 10

29.   The *stated* goal of the Mujahedeen-e Khalq (MeK) is to bring a secular government, a
       democracy, and _____ to Iran.
          a. Women's rights
          b. Economic stability
          c. Peace
          d. International military supremacy

ANS: a   REF: p. 272   OBJ: 1 and 4

30.   After taking control of MeK during Operation Iraqi Freedom, the U.S. treated MeK as an
       ally for what purpose(s)?
          a. Intelligence-gathering
          a. Economic
          b. Diplomatic peace talks
          c. Humanitarian

ANS: a   REF: p. 272   OBJ: 1 and 4

31. The Tupamaros have a history with union workers in what Uruguayan industry?
          a. Sugar
          b. Coal
          c. Gold
          d. Salt

ANS: a   REF: p. 248   OBJ: 1 and 2

32. What did the Uraguayan government primarily target in their 1972 attack upon the
     Tupamaros?
          a. the group's logistical network
          b. the group's family members
          c. the group's leaders
          d. the groups weapons caches

ANS: a   REF: p. 252   OBJ: 1 and 2

33. Although criminal syndicates in Mexico assumed control of the drug routes to the United
     States after 2000, what country still accounts for the lion's share of cocaine production?
          a. Nicaragua
          b. Columbia
          c. Venezuela
          d. Costa Rica

ANS: b   REF: p. 255   OBJ: 1, 3, and 10

34.   The United States' 1999 project "Plan Colombia" was intended to move against which three Columbia groups?
        a. Mek, ELN, and RAF
        b. FARC, ELN, and AUC
        c. ELN, RAF, and LTTE
        d. FARC, ELA, and ELN

ANS: b   REF: p. 255   OBJ: 1, 3, and 10

35.   In 2009, government forces in Columbia captured military hardware from _____ that had been sold to Venezuela in 1980.
        a. Sweden
        b. Russia
        c. the U.S.
        d. Iran

ANS: a   REF: p. 255   OBJ: 1, 3, and 10

36.   In 2008, the ELN began intermittent fighting with the FARC for control of _____.
        a. Drug routes leading into Colombia
        b. Television networks
        c. Farmland
        d. Cocaine processing factories

ANS: a   REF: p. 256   OBJ: 1, 3, and 10

37.   What group is responsible for the assassinations of six Americans in Tehran during the 1970s?
        a. The Mujahedin-e Kahlq (MeK)
        b. The Red Army Faction (RAF)
        c. The Shining Path
        d. The New Peoples' Army

ANS: a   REF: p. 256   OBJ: 1 and 4

38.   Illegal military and police units who torture and kill suspected terrorists and their supporters are commonly referred to as _____.
        a. Brigades
        b. Feyadeen
        c. Death squads
        d. Mujahedeen

ANS: c   REF: p. 271   OBJ: 10

39.   The Shining Path was influenced by the revolutionary philosophy of which Chinese communist leader?
        a. Zhou Enlai
        b. LinBiao
        c. Mao Zedong
        d. Peng Chen

ANS: c   REF: p. 257   OBJ: 1 and 5

40.   The *New York Times* (2009) reports that the Shining Path reemerged around 2007, by reinventing itself as a _____ organization.
    a. Non-violent political
    b. Sex trafficking
    c. Drug trafficking
    d. Human trafficking

ANS: c   REF: p. 259   OBJ: 1, 5, and 10

Case 10.0

Modern Colombian violence cannot be separated from the production of cocaine. Although criminal syndicates in Mexico assumed control of the drug routes to the United States after 2000, Colombia still accounts for the lion's share of cocaine production. Opinions about the success of antidrug efforts are mixed. Officially, the U.S. Department of State (2008) claims that U.S. strategy, such as "Plan Columbia" has been a success. The purpose of the plan was to move against three different groups: FARC, the National Liberation Army (ELN), and the United Self-Defense Forces of Colombia (AUC). Not only have groups been disarmed, but drug production has decreased. Violence has been reduced, but the drug problem remains.

41.   What form of terrorism appears to be the primary concern of "Plan Columbia"?
    a. Religious terrorism
    b. Cyber-terrorism
    c. Narco-terrorism
    d. Revolutionary terrorism

ANS: c   REF: p. 255   OBJ: 1 and 3

42.   What reason do scholars point to as the major reason for the difficulty in eliminating the drug problem in the region?
    a. Demand for cocaine in the United States
    b. Government corruption in Columbia
    c. Inexperience of U.S. operatives in the region
    d. Apathy on part of the American public

ANS: a   REF: p. 255   OBJ: 1 and 3

43.   "Plan Columbia" would be best classed as a(n) _____ ?
    a. Global economic policy
    b. American counterterrorism strategy
    c. Foreign relief program
    d. U.N. intervention

ANS: b   REF: p. 255   OBJ: 1 and 3

Case 10.1

Maoist groups exhibit three striking differences from most other revolutionary terrorists. First, they practice ruthless domination in the areas that they control, and they rule by terrorism. Second, Maoist groups have a reputation for maintaining internal discipline. They

327

purge and control their own members. Finally, and most important, Maoist groups follow the revolutionary philosophy of Chinese communist leader Mao Zedong. Maoist groups are based in rural peasant movements.

The chart below outlines a number of mythical terrorist groups. Use the chart as a reference to answer the following questions:

Group	Descriptions
Alpacas	A group of peanut farmers in the remote hills of Italy who charge businesses in the nearby towns a "safety tax" to ensure that business owners are "protected". Those who refuse to pay the tax are brutally assaulted and their operations burned to the ground. Alpha members offended by the arsons may excuse themselves from action without fear of penalty from the group's leaders.
Bears	A group of urban youth who gather regularly to discuss and debate the advantages of communism. Leaders of the group seek out opponents to such philosophy and target them for intimidation. Family member of targets are taken hostage and held for ransom - targets routinely killed after paying the ransom demand. Bravo leaders use new members to conduct the murders, killing any member who display disdain for such tactics.
Coyotes	A hierarchal communist organization centered in a rural Arkansas community. They militantly target a small group of American-Muslim students, a small minority in the neighborhood through theft of business goods and 'tagging' business fronts with racial slurs as they feel that the group is too flush on capitalist American philosophy in the hopes of getting the neighborhood and greater America on board to make change and adopt communism. Corporal and , in many cases, capital punishment is a common form of discipline within its ranks.
Dingos	A pro-communist group places IEDs along the roadside entrance to its neighborhood whenever non-communist members of the neighborhood enter or leave the area, causing numerous deaths each day. Photos of the victims are circulated throughout the community with slogans, "Communist or die!" Delta leadership forces its own members to walk through the IED gauntlet as punishment for any mistakes.
Elks	An ethnic group from Iraq, displaced by the government - moving from country to country awaiting vengeance for the displacement from and ultimate return to their homeland. Followers of Mao philosophy, they bomb Iraqi embassies on days of special significance for media attention and sympathy for their cause in the hopes of forcing Iraq to permit them to return home. Membership is quite fluid, with members selecting which activities they wish to or not to participate in, without fear of consequence from the group's leadership.

44. Given what you learned from your text and the outline above, which of the mythical organization(s) from the chart above is more akin to Maoist style terrorists than most other revolutionary terrorists?
   a. Alpacas and Coyotes
   b. Alpacas, Bears, Coyotes, and Dingos
   c. Bears, Coyotes, and Dingos
   d. Alpacas, Coyotes, and Elks

ANS: c   REF: p. 257   OBJ: 1, 2, 3, 4, 5, 6, 7, 8, 9, and 10

45. Given what you learned from the above scenario, which of the mythical organization(s) from the chart above is LEAST like the Maoist style terrorists?
   a. Bears, Coyotes, and Dingos
   b. Alpacas and Elks
   c. Alpacas and Coyotes
   d. Alpacas, Coyotes, and Elks

ANS: b   REF: p. 257   OBJ: 1, 2, 3, 4, 5, 6, 7, 8, 9, and 10

46. Which of the mythical organization(s) from the chart DO NOT employ a force multiplier as part of its terrorist strategy?
   a. Alpacas
   b. Elks
   c. Bears
   d. Dingos

ANS: a   REF: p. 257   OBJ: 1, 2, 3, 4, 5, 6, 7, 8, 9, and 10

47. Which of the mythical organization(s) from the chart appears most similar to the Zionist movement explored in previous chapters?
   a. Alpacas
   b. Elks
   c. Bears
   d. Dingos

ANS: b   REF: p. 257   OBJ: 1, 2, 3, 4, 5, 6, 7, 8, 9, and 10

48. What element is missing from the description of the Echoes that make the group unlike a Maoist-style one?
   a. They practice ruthless domination in the areas that they control
   b. They rule by terrorism
   c. Internal discipline is severe - they purge and control their own members
   d. They follow the revolutionary philosophy of Chinese communist leader Mao Dong

ANS: d   REF: p. 257   OBJ: 1, 2, 3, 4, 5, 6, 7, 8, 9, and 10

Case 10.2

In looking at the organizational structure of the Tupamaros, the Executive Committee was in charge, but it ran a highly decentralized operation. Its main power came from the internal rule enforcement provided by the Committee for Revolutionary Justice. Columns were the major units, but they tended to be tactical formations. The real operational power came from the cells, which joined for column-style operations on rare occasions. The combat striking power of the Tupamaros came from the four- to six-person groups in the cells.

49.   Which terrorist organization is the LEAST similar in structure to the Tupamaros?
      a. IRA
      b. PLO
      c. the Taliban
      d. RAF

ANS: c   REF: p. 251   OBJ: 1, 2, 3, 4, 5, 6, 7, 8, 9, and 10

50.   What term best describes the organizational structure of the Tupamaros?
      a. Bureaucratic
      b. Functional
      c. Hierarchy
      d. Team-based

ANS: c   REF: p. 251   OBJ: 1, 2, 3, 4, 5,6, 7, 8, 9, and 10

COMPLETION

1.   The National Liberation Movement (MLN) renamed themselves the _____.

ANS: Tupamaros   REF: p. 249   OBJ: 1 and 2

2.   The Tupamaros, unlike Castro, were not interested in building a _____to strike at the government.

ANS: conventional military force   REF: p. 249   OBJ: 1 and 2

3.   FARC and ELN are linked by a radical socialist ideology, but torn over control of _____.

ANS: drug profits   REF: p. 256   OBJ: 1 and 3

4.   As the structure of Europe and the world changed during the late 1980s and early 1990s, ethnic violence grew into open warfare in the _____.

ANS: Balkans   REF: p. 266   OBJ: 1 and 9

5.   _____ refers to a mass Philippine protest movement that toppled Ferdinand Marcos in 1986.

ANS: People Power Revolution   REF: p. 264   OBJ: 1

6. The MeK was founded in 1965 for the purpose of overthrowing the _____ government.

ANS: Iranian   REF: p. 256   OBJ: 1 and 4

7. The Iranian Hostage Crisis lasted _____ months.

ANS: three   REF: p. 256   OBJ: 1 and 4

8. The _____ of Uruguay embodied the concept of urban revolution.

ANS: Tupamaros   REF: p. 247   OBJ: 1 and 2

9. The Cultural Revolution in China ended with the death of _____.

ANS: Mao Zedong   REF: p. 258   OBJ: LO13

10. _____ ruled the Phillipines as a dictator after being elected as president in 1965.

ANS: Ferdinand Marcos   REF: p. 264   OBJ: 1

11. The Red Army Faction was a West German Marxist group who modeled their urban guerilla style after _____.

ANS: Marighella   REF: p. 266   OBJ: 1 and 9

12. Anders Breivik was a violent right-wing extremist who went on a one-day killing spree in in _____ in July 2011.

ANS: Norway   REF: p. 269   OBJ: 1 and 9

13. Right-wing terrorism is often a response to _____ violence.

ANS: left-wing   REF: 269   OBJ: 1, 9, and 10

14. Illegal military and police units who torture and kill suspected terrorists and their supporters are known as _____.

ANS: Death Squads   REF: p. 271   OBJ: 1 and 10

15. The most notorious revolutionary groups in Columbia include _____, the ELN, and the AUC.

ANS: FARC   REF: p. 255   OBJ: 1 and 3

16. The NPA's income averages about $ ____ per year.

ANS: 30 million   REF: p. 264   OBJ: 1 and 8

331

17. Greece was ruled by a _____ from 1967 to 1974.

ANS: military junta   REF: p. 268   OBJ: 1 and 9

18. _____ produces the lion's share of cocaine entering the U.S.

ANS: Columbia   REF: p. 255   OBJ: 1 and 3

19. The Secretary of Defense Donald Rumsfeld changed the MeK members' status in 2004 with the new label, civilian "_____."

ANS: protected persons   REF: p. 256   OBJ: 1 and 4

20. King Gyanendra took control of _____'s government in 2001, and he ordered the military to wage a brutal campaign of counterterrorism.

ANS: Nepal   REF: p. 260   OBJ: 1 and 6

ESSAY

1. Summarize the environment in which death squads emerge and describe the tactics they employ.

ANS:
- Death squads come into being when people who hold economic and political power believe their position is being threatened and the threat is beyond the control of law and order.
- The purpose of a death squad is to eliminate opposition when a government is either unable or unwilling to do so.
- The tactics of death squads vary; they range from semi-official raids on governmental opponents to torture and secret murder.
- In a common scenario, uniformed members of a death squad will "arrest" a victim. The victim is carried away and there are no records. The arresting officers frighten lucky victims and torture and murder the unlucky ones.
- First, political elites must be entrenched in a society with a vested interest in maintaining societal structures, and these elites have a history of employing armed force to protect their positions.
- This combines with a second factor, a reform movement which threatens to break up elitist power structures with the redistribution of wealth of power.
- Third, the government must be either unwilling or unable to stop the reform movement.
- Finally, hardliners among the political elites breakaway from their mainstream counterparts based on the belief that moderate political elites are too soft and unable to stop the reform movement.
- One common base for death squads is to "protect the established order"
- The only action that will maintain social order, the hardliners believe, is physically eliminating opponents and destroying the mentality seeking reform.

REF: p. 269   OBJ: 1 and 10

2. Discuss project "Plan Colombia"; who was involved and what was the outcome?

ANS:
- Plan Colombia is a joint effort by the United States and Colombia to reduce violence and illegal drugs. It began in 1999.
- The United States had long been involved in Colombian affairs, and it stepped up measures in 1999 with a new project "Plan Colombia."
- The purpose was to move against three different groups: FARC, the National Liberation Army (ELN), and the United Self-Defense Forces of Colombia (AUC).
- Like FARC the ELN is a revolutionary group that extends into surrounding countries, and the AUC is composed of underground government officials who terrorize in the name of security.
- The goal of Plan Colombia was to disarm all the groups and to deal with endemic cocaine trade.
- Modern Colombian violence cannot be separated from the production of cocaine.
- Although criminal syndicates in Mexico assumed control of the drug routes to the United States after 2000, Colombia still accounts for the lion's share of cocaine production.
- Opinions about the success of anti-drug efforts are mixed. Officially, the U.S. Department of State (2008) claims that Plan Colombia has been a success.
- Not only have groups been disarmed, but drug production has decreased. Other assessments are not so optimistic.
- Michael Bustamante and Sebastian, argue that Plan Colombia has been a dismal failure.
- Violence has been reduced, but the drug problem remains. It has more to do with demand for cocaine in the United States than internal issues in Colombia.

REF: p. 255   OBJ: 1, 3,and 10

3. Discuss the three key elements that changed the political landscape of Europe and the world during the late 1980s and the early 1990s.

ANS:
- In 1989 the Berlin Wall came down, leading to the reunification of Germany.
- To the south, new nations emerging from the former Yugoslavia took up arms and resumed a centuries-old struggle.
- But the greatest change of all came in the East.
- The Soviet Union dissolved, along with the authoritarian rule of the Communist Party in the republics of the former Soviet Union and Eastern Europe.
- These three changes occurred at a time when Western Europeans were taking bold steps toward economic and political unity.
- As the structure of Europe and the world changed from 1989 to 1992, European terrorism also changed.
- Ideological terrorism swung from left to right, changing its structure as it moved.
- Nationalistic terrorism remained, but conflict rose in the form of ethnic violence.
- Ethnic violence grew into open warfare in the Balkans.
- New criminal organizations appeared, and old ones were revitalized.

333

- The threat of jihadist terrorism replaced threats from the left, and Europe experienced new strains of terrorism.
- After growth unprecedented since 1968, left-wing terrorism began to decline by 1986.

REF: p. 266   OBJ: 1, 2, 3, 4, 5, 6, 7, 8, 9, and 10

4. Scholars argue that the Mujahedin-e Khalq presents a conundrum for the United States. Illustrate their argument.

ANS:
- Officially listed as a terrorist group since 1997, the MeK had settled in a camp about 40 miles north of Baghdad in 2003.
- As soon as the invading United States military forces negotiated a peace settlement with the MEK, they found that they could not fit its members into a neat package.
- American military planners had not prepared for MeK prisoners.
- At first American forces sought to treat the group's members as prisoners of war, but according to the Geneva Convention each member was entitled to a separate hearing to determine the status.
- In addition, a significant portion of the membership had been duped into joining during the Iran Iraq war.
- The Secretary of Defense Donald Rumsfeld changed their status in 2004 without a legal review stating that all members were civilian "protected persons"; this was the result of improper planning.
- It placed the United States in a hypocritical position of having a relationship with the designated terrorist group.
- In 2007 President George Bush received a budget of $400,000,000 from Congress to support groups violently opposed to Iran's Islamic regime.
- One of the groups included on the list was the MeK.
- Prominent advisors to the Bush administration were advocating that the United States form a link with the MeK.
- It was the best hope for destabilizing Iran, the advisors argued.

REF: p. 256   OBJ: LO9

5. Briefly explain the history behind the Shining Path and its twenty-year terrorist campaign in Peru in 1980. Why is the group's political orientation debated?

ANS:
- A Maoist group, the Shining Path launched a campaign in rural Peru that began in 1980 and lasted for the following two decades.
- Peru's revolutionary past was grounded in anti-colonialism as the indigenous people sought to free themselves from European rule.
- Tupac Amaru led a revolt against Spain from 1581 to 1582.
- Scholars have debated the political orientation of the Shining Path almost from its inception.

334

- Led by a philosophy professor, Abimael Guzman, the group was deeply influenced by China and its Cultural Revolution.
- Guzman believed that the leftist politics of Peru's Communist Party were too tame, and he embraced the radical violence espoused by Maoist revolutionaries.
- In addition, the Maoist approach matched Peru's economic structure.
- Guzman moved to build a rural power base, and most scholars view the organization as a violent Maoist movement.
- Other scholars do not accept the view that the Shining Path was based in Maoism.
- Paul Navarro believes the entire Peruvian left was influenced by Mao, but the influence was rhetorical.
- Most Peruvian leftists were main stream Marxists.
- While they called for violent revolution, the starting point was decades away.
- Peru's Communists were not inherently violent.
- The Shining Path was a typical Marxist group as it embraced orthodoxy and its violence was caused by the internal contradictions of Marxism.

REF: p. 257   OBJ: 1 and 4

6. Explain the Uruguayan political structure of the 1950s and 1960s that gave rise to revolution.

ANS:
- In the years immediately after World War II, Uruguay appeared to be a model Latin American government.
- Democratic principles and freedoms were the accepted basis of Uruguay's political structures.
- Democratic rule was complemented by a sound economy and an exemplary educational system.
- Although it could not be described as a land of wealth, by the early 1950s Uruguay could be called a land of promise.
- All factors seemed to point to peace and prosperity.
- Unfortunately, Uruguay's promise started to fade in 1954.
- The export economy that had proved so prosperous for the country began to crumble.
- Falling prices on exported goods brought inflation and unemployment, and economic dissatisfaction grew.
- By 1959 many workers and members of the middle class faced a bleak future.
- Uruguay had undergone a devastating economic reversal, and workers were restless.
- In the northern section of Uruguay, sugar workers were particularly hard hit.
- Sugar exports had decreased in the 1950s, and sugar workers suffered all of Uruguay's economic woes.
- As a result, the workers took steps to form a national union.
- Several militant radicals injected themselves into the union movement, and when the sugar workers organized in 1959, the militants dominated the union and called for confrontation with the government.

REF: p. 247   OBJ: 1, 2, and 10

7. Explain why a common misassumption is that the American Revolution was based on terrorism. What is revolutionary terrorism?

ANS:
- If this were true, rebels would have indiscriminately murdered British citizens and clandestinely destroyed symbolic targets.
- General George Washington would not have fought to destroy the British Army; he would have waged a campaign of symbolic murder in the hope that the horror of it all would change British political behavior.
- Instead, many Americans operated as guerrillas while the majority joined a conventional army and fought within the accepted norms of conventional warfare.
- Revolutions cannot be equated with terrorism, although terrorism is sometimes used during the course of the revolution.
- When examining ideological terrorism, it is possible to broadly categorize a revolutionary style.
- Martha Crenshaw says revolutionary terrorism can be defined as an insurgent strategy in the context of internal warfare or revolution.
- It is an attempt to seize power from a legitimate state for the purpose of creating political and social change.
- It involves the systematic use of terrorism to achieve this goal.
- Violence is neither isolated nor a series of random acts, and it is far from guerrilla or conventional warfare.
- Revolutionary terrorism differs from other forms of violence because it occurs outside the normal realm of violent political action.
- It involves acts of violence that are particularly atrocious, and it usually occurs within a civilian population.
- The violence is symbolic and is designed to have a devastating psychological impact on established power.

REF: p. 246   OBJ: 1 and 9

8. Explain why Maoist terrorism is a form of revolutionary terrorism.

ANS:
- In practice, Maoist groups tend to be more violent than other revolutionary groups.
- Critical scholars debate the differences among various Marxist schools of thought, yet in terrorism Maoist groups exhibit three striking differences from most other revolutionary terrorists.
- First, they practice ruthless domination in the areas they control, and they rule by terrorism.
- Second, Maoist groups have a reputation for maintaining internal discipline.
- They purge and control their own members.
- Finally and most importantly, Maoist groups follow the revolutionary philosophy of Chinese communist leader Mao Zedong.
- Maoist groups are based in rural peasant movements.

REF: p. 246   OBJ: 1, 6, and 10

9. How has India dealt with the issues presented by the Naxalite? Has the response been effective, what could the government do to effectively deal with the problem?

ANS:
- The Indian government believes the Naxalite rebellion has become its number one internal security problem.
- In the summer of 2010 the prime minister was considering calling on the military to deal with problem.
- Other research suggests that violence has grown because of an ineffective response.
- The police launched a campaign of brutality, although they have suffered hundreds of casualties themselves.
- There is some speculation that they have authorized death squads.
- One of more controversial moves has been the establishment of a Special Police force composed of local peasants.
- With no training and little regard for human rights, the Special Police frequently operate outside the law.
- The Naxalites have responded in kind, and more than half the states in India are involved in the dirty war.
- Shameul Tharu argues that the rebellion cannot be stopped by either police were military power; it is simplistic to classify the Naxalite rebellion as a criminal problem.
- The Indian government needs to address several structural issues, including land reform, political reform, and ending bureaucratic corruption.
- The government reform would rectify the peasants' alienation from the land.
- Naxalite violence and human rights violations against peasants had alienated their potential supporters.

REF: p. 261   OBJ: 1 and 7

10.   Examine the role of the executive committee of the Tupamaros - what was its structure, function, and day-to-day activities. How did it differ from the rest of the organization?

ANS:
- John Wolf believes an executive committee controlled all activities in Montevideo and Arturo Porzecanski makes several references to this same executive committee.
- For all practical purposes, it seems to have controlled the Tupamaros; the executive committee was responsible for two major operations.
- It ran the columns that supervised the terrorist operations, and it also administered a special Committee for Revolutionary Justice.
- The power of the executive committee derived from internal enforcement.
- The job of the committee was to terrorize the terrorists into obedience.
- If an operative refused to obey an order or tried to leave the organization, a delegation from the committee would usually deal with the matter.
- It was not uncommon to murder the family of the offending party, along with the errant member.
- The Tupamaros believed in strong internal discipline.

- In day-to-day operations, however, the executive committee exercised very little authority.
- The Tupamaros lacked a unified command structure for routine functions.
- The reason can be found in the nature of the organization.
- Because secrecy dominated every facet of its operations, it could not afford open communications.
- Therefore, each subunit evolved into a highly autonomous operation.
- There was little the executive committee could do about this situation, and the command structure became highly decentralized.
- The Tupamaros existed as a confederacy.

REF: p. 251   OBJ: 1, 2, and 10

CHAPTER 11
Al Qaeda and Jihadist Networks

Learning Objectives

After reading this chapter, students should be able to:

1. Describe the rise of religious terrorism and its relationship to the Soviet-Afghan War.
2. Summarize the important roles of Osama bin Laden and Ayman al Zawahiri.
3. Outline the early history of al Qaeda.
4. Explain the structure and operations of al Qaeda until September 11, 2001.
5. Describe al Qaeda's current franchise-style structure and current operational capabilities.
6. Outline the operations of franchises including AQAP, AQIM, and al Shabab.
7. Summarize al Qaeda's political theology.
8. Describe other forms of terrorism in Pakistan.
9. Summarize operations in other parts of Asia and the Pacific.

Chapter Key Terms

Interservice Intelligence Agency (ISI), p. 276

Abdullah Azzam, p. 277

Sayyid Imam al Sharif, p. 278

Taliban, p. 280

Mullah Omar, p. 280

Sheik Omar Abdel Rahman, p. 280

near enemy, p. 581 (p. 384)

far enemy, p. 281

Hassan al Turab, p. 282

World Islamic Front against Jews and Crusaders, p. 283

Haqqani network, p. 286

Nasir al Wuhayshi, p. 289

USS *Cole,* p. 289

Anwar al Awlaki, p. 290

Islamic Courts Union (ICU), p. 292

Mohammed Ali Jinnah, p. 296

Ayub Khan, p. 297

Interservice Intelligence Agency (ISI): The Pakistani domestic and foreign intelligence service created by the British in 1948. Supporters claim that it centralizes Pakistan's intelligence. Critics maintain that it operates like an independent state and supports terrorist groups.

Abdullah Azzam: (1941– 1989) The Palestinian leader of Hizb ul Tahrir and the spiritual mentor of bin Laden.

Sayyid Imam al Sharif: (1951–) Also known as Dr. Fadl, one of Egypt's leading militants in the 1970s. While jailed, he embraced Islam and renounced the violence of al Qaeda-style militancy. He is viewed as a traitor by violent jihadists. He has provided much of the information about religious militancy, and he continues to publish works denouncing it. Still maintaining anti-Western and anti-government views, he sees jihad as a necessary part of Islam. Al Qaeda's version, he claims, violates the morality of Islamic law.

Taliban: The Islamicist group that governed Afghanistan from 1996 to 2001.

Mullah Omar: (1959–) the leader of the Taliban. After the collapse of the Taliban government in 2001, Omar went into hiding.

Sheik Omar Abdel Rahman: (1938–) A Sunni Islamic scholar linked to the Egyptian IG. He came to the United States in 1990 even though his name was on a State Department watch list. He was arrested and convicted of conspiracy after the 1993 World Trade Center bombing. He is currently serving a life sentence in the American federal prison system.

near enemy: A jihadist term referring to forms of Muslim governments and Islamic law (*sharia*) that do not embrace the narrow-minded philosophy of Sayyid Qutb.

far enemy: A jihadist term referring to non-Islamic powers or countries outside the realm of Islam

Hassan al Turabi: (1932–) A Sudanese intellectual and Islamic scholar. He served in the Sudanese government during the time bin Laden was in exile in Sudan.

World Islamic Front against Jews and Crusaders: An organization created in 1998 by Osama bin Laden and Ayman al Zawahiri. It represents a variety of jihadist groups that issued a united front against Jews and the West. It is commonly called al Qaeda.

Haqqani network: a family in the tribal area of Pakistan that has relations with several militant groups and the ISI. The Haqqani family is involved in organized crime, legitimate businesses, the ISI, and terrorism groups. It is the major power broker in the tribal region.

Nasir al Wuhayshi: (age unknown) the spiritual leader of AQAP and a former aid to Osama bin Laden. Wuhayshi escaped from a Yemeni prison in 2006 to form AQY. In 2009, he joined his group with dissidents in Saudi Arabia to form AQAP.

USS *Cole*: A U.S. Navy destroyer attacked by two suicide bombers in the port of Aden, Yemen, on October 12, 2000. Seventeen American sailors were killed in the attack.

Anwar al Awlaki: (1971–) An American-born Muslim cleric who worked to build U.S.-Muslim relations after 9/11. He became increasingly militant and called for attacks on America. He was arrested in Yemen in 2006 and released in 2007. In 2009, he swore allegiance to AQAP.

Islamic Courts Union (ICU): A confederation of tribes and clans seeking to end violence and bring Islamic law to Somalia. It is opposed by several neighboring countries and internal warlords. Some people feel that it is a jihadist organization, but others see it as a grouping of clans with several different interpretations of Islamic law.

Mohammed Ali Jinnah: (1876–1948) the leader of the Muslim League and the founder of modern Pakistan. He served as Governor-General until his death in 1948.

Ayub Khan: (1907–1974) the second president of Pakistan from 1958 to 1974. Khan seized control of the government in 1958 and then staged elections. He was the first of Pakistan's many military leaders.

Asif Ali Zardari: (1955–) the husband of Benazir Bhutto, Zardari, inherited control of the Pakistan Peoples Party after Bhutto's assassination in December 2007. He was elected president in 2008.

Jammu and Kashmir: A mountainous region in northern India claimed by India and Pakistan. It has been the site of heavy fighting during three wars between India and Pakistan in 1947–1948, 1971, and 1999. Kashmir is artificially divided by a line of control (LOC), with Pakistani forces to the north and India's to the south. India and Pakistan made strides toward peace after 2003, but many observers believe that the ISI supports jihadist operations in the area.

Red Mosque: *Lal masjid*, located in Islamabad, with a madrassa and a school for women. It taught militant theology. The government ordered the mosque closed in 2007. This resulted in a shootout and a standoff. Government forces stormed the mosque on July 2007, killing more than one hundred students. One of the leaders, Abdul Rashid Ghazi, was killed. His brother Maulana Abdul Aziz, the mosque's other leader was captured while trying to escape in women's clothing.

Chapter Outline

I.   **The Rise of Religious Terrorism and the Soviet Afghan War**
      OBJ 1: Describe the rise of religious terrorism and its relationship to the Soviet Afghan War

      A. Before 2001 al Qaeda maintained a command hierarchy; after 2001 its leaders ran virtual networks, and inspired autonomous jihadists around the globe.
      B. Cold War origins.
          1. Al Qaeda's origins can be traced to the Cold War.

341

2. The world was divided into two camps, communist and non-communist nations, and each side formed alliances with any government willing to offer its assistance.

3. The United States formed alliances, not only with the democracies of Western Europe, but also with some of the most brutal dictatorships in the late 20th century; all in the name of anti-communism.

C. The Soviet Afghan War 1979 – 1989
1. Western efforts to support Islamic reformers came to fruition in 1979.
2. President Jimmy Carter's State Department encouraged Arab and other Islamic allies to send money and religious puritans to fight the Soviets in a guerrilla war.
3. The United States formed an alliance with Pakistan, and the Pakistani *Interservice Intelligence Agency (ISI)* began to train and equip the mujahedeen. When Ronald Reagan became president in 1980, American efforts against the Soviets increased.
4. Several researchers have looked at the relationship between the United States and the mujahedeen during the Soviet-Afghan War; their research points to several important conclusions:
   a. The United States helped Saudi Arabia develop a funding mechanism and underground arms network to supply the mujahedeen.
   b. The United States agreed to give most of the weapons and supplies to the ISI, which built mujahedeen groups with little American participation.
   c. Islamic charities flourished in the United States, and their donations supported the mujahedeen. Finally, when the Soviets left Afghanistan in 1989, the United States rejoiced and abandoned war-torn Afghanistan.
5. Virtually ignored by the United States, the jihadist movement grew, and terrorism grew with it.

II. **Bin Laden, Zawahiri, and al Qaeda**
OBJ 2: Summarize the important roles of Osama bin Laden and Ayman al Zawahiri
OBJ 3: Outline the early history of al Qaeda

A. As the Soviets began leaving Afghanistan in April 1988, the United States celebrated a vicarious victory.
B. The Soviets were on the run, the defeat was another blow to a crumbling empire, and by 1991 the Soviet Union had dissolved.
C. American oil companies sought alliances with some groups in hopes of building an oil pipeline from central Asia to the Indian Ocean.
D. Bin Laden emerged as a spokesman for the discontented, and his own movement began to take form.
E. Bin Laden and Abdullah Azzam

1. While in Afghanistan, bin Laden fell under the influence of *Abdullah Azzam.*
2. Azzam came to believe that a purified form of Islam was the answer to questions of poverty and the loss of political power; he later joined the Afghan jihad.
3. According to the 9/11 Commission Report, bin Laden and Azzam, toward the end of the Soviet-Afghan War, "established what they called a base or foundation (al Qaeda) as a potential general headquarters for future jihad" The ISI developed the structure that would support al Qaeda with U.S. and Saudi funds during the Soviet-Afghan War.
4. Training in Pakistan and Afghanistan under Azzam's spiritual mentoring, bin Laden financed mujahedeen operations, and taught the guerrillas how to build field fortifications.

F. Ayman al Zawahiri and the path from Egypt.
   1. Zawahiri fell under the influence of a violent religious philosophy in high school, and his passion and intolerance grew in college.
   2. Zawahiri opposed the government of Anwar Sadat.
      a. Egyptian police arrested dissidents from all over Egypt after Sadat's assassination in 1981.
      b. Zawahiri was arrested and charged with weapons violations, although he was not officially charged in the assassination.

G. The early history of al Qaeda.
   1. When the Soviets prepared to withdraw from Afghanistan in 1988, the ISI created its own Afghan guerrilla force and used it to take control of major areas of the country.
   2. Zawahiri began sketching out a grand model for al Qaeda, proposing an umbrella structure with multiple independent groups gathered under the loosely guiding hand of al Qaeda.
   3. Bin Laden began to recruit into al Qaeda the mujahedeen registered in his computer database, while al Zawahiri organized training camps and cells.
   4. In November 1989, Azzam was killed by a remote-controlled car bomb; the result was that bin Laden and Zawahiri became the undisputed leaders of al Qaeda.
   5. Bin Laden's first cause was the Saudi government and its "corrupt" royal family.
   6. While the Saudis looked on, bin Laden became independently wealthy, and his agents began making real estate purchases in Sudan.
   7. The situation changed in 1990, when Iraq invaded Kuwait.
      a. The U.S.-led coalition called this military buildup *Desert Shield*, and it became *Desert Storm* in February 1991, when American, British, and other allied forces poured into Iraq and Kuwait. For bin Laden, however, it was a desert apostasy.
   8. After Desert Storm, the Saudi government allowed U.S. troops to be stationed in Saudi Arabia, the site of the cities of Mecca and Medina.

9. Bin Laden now thought of declaring his own war on the Saudi royal family and the United States.

III. **The Evolution of al Qaeda**

OBJ 3: Outline the early history of al Qaeda

OBJ 4: Explain the structure and operations of al Qaeda until September 11, 2001

OBJ 7: Summarize al Qaeda's political theology

A. Al Qaeda was born in the last stages of the Soviet-Afghan War, and it grew until the U.S. offensive in Afghanistan in October 2001, when U.S. forces struck the al Qaeda and *Taliban* forces there.
  1. Led by *Mullah Omar*, the Taliban was composed of Islamic students who wanted to bring order to Afghanistan through the forced imposition of Islamic law.
B. Al Qaeda transformed after 2001, becoming a decentralized alliance of al Qaeda terrorists spread throughout the world.
  1. The movement never had mass appeal as its theology was deemed unsound in spite of its constant Islamic references.
C. After Azzam's assassination and the breakup of the mujahedeen confederation in Afghanistan, Zawahiri returned to Egypt with the hope of creating an Islamic state.
D. Egyptian Islamic Jihad
  1. Ayman al Zawahiri was the driving force behind another terrorist group in Egypt, the Egyptian Islamic Jihad (EIJ).
  2. Zawahiri believed the government represented the *near enemy*.
  3. Using Egyptians trained in camps in Afghanistan, EIJ focused on governmental targets.
     a. Terrorists tried to assassinate Egypt's interior minister.
E. Bin Laden returns to Afghanistan.
  1. Bin Laden had returned to Afghanistan by a separate path.
  2. Bin Laden found friends in Sudan's radical government which was formed under the influence of *Hasan al Turabi*.
  3. By the end of 1992 bin Laden employed Afghan-hardened mujahedeen in Sudan.
     a. He also began to internationalize, creating multinational corporations, false charities, and front companies.
  4. President George H. W. Bush sent U.S. forces to *Mogadishu* to end a humanitarian crisis there, and they were joined by other armies, including Muslim forces.
  5. Most of the world saw the multinational peacekeeping force as a method for feeding the starving Somalis, but this was not the view of bin Laden.
  6. In December 1992, a bomb exploded in a hotel in Yemen that had been housing American troops.

7. Regardless of its source, bin Laden had financing and did not need the support of a rogue nation.
8. In October 1993, a U.S. Army Black Hawk helicopter was downed while on patrol in Mogadishu.
   a. Bin Laden claimed he trained and supported the troops that struck the Americans.

F. Declaring war on the United States.
1. Bin Laden declared war on the United States in 1996.
2. He followed this by having his religious council issue two religious rulings, called fatwas, in 1998, even though few Muslims recognized the validity of the council's religious scholars, and bin Laden has no theological credentials.
3. In 1998, EIJ was absorbed into al Qaeda when Osama bin Laden announced that he was forming the *World Islamic Front against Jews and Crusaders*.
4. In his fatwas of February 1998, he calls for the killing of any American anywhere in the world.
5. In August 1998, bin Laden's terrorists bombed the U.S. embassies in Nairobi, Kenya, and Dar es Salaam, Tanzania.
6. Then came the attack on the *USS Cole* in 2000, a failed millennium plot, and the attacks of September 11, 2001.
7. After the United States and allied forces struck al Qaeda bases in Afghanistan in October 2001, the structured operations gave way to the loose network.
8. Bin Laden and Zawahiri became symbols of religious violence, and this also had an adverse effect – their theology was so poor that Muslims vehemently began to reject it.

IV. **Al Qaeda's Political Theology**
   OBJ 7: Summarize al Qaeda's political theology

A. Because jihadists make religious claims, many Muslims become upset when their faith is portrayed in terms of violent terrorism.
B. Magnus Ranstorp says the jihadists are doomed to failure within their own culture because their theology of violence does not convey the meaning of Islam.
1. Islam is a religion that values peace and toleration.
C. Confusion about mainstream Islam complicates attempts to understand jihadists, and misunderstandings increase when jihadists use religious rhetoric.
D. Some *madrassas* (Islamic schools) in many areas of the world glamorize violence, and inspire young people to join terrorist organizations.
E. Samuel Huntington points out that Christians, Hindus, and Buddhists do not create international associations of nation-states that are based on religion, Muslims do.

345

1. Such religious and cultural issues are factors that complicate attempts to understand the nature of jihadist networks.
F. Al Qaeda continued to operate while on the run in Pakistan, inspiring bombings around the world, and bin Laden and Zawahiri remained the symbols of violent religion.
G. Martin Hart believes that the Taliban represent another matter, and they should not be equated with al Qaeda; they are a religious organization with a grassroots following.
    1. The Internet and al Qaeda-controlled media glorify religion, but this does not build local organizations.

V. **Al Qaeda's Operational Capabilities**
    OBJ 5: Describe al Qaeda's current franchise-style structure and current operational capabilities
    OBJ 6: Outline the operations of franchises including AQAP, AQIM, and al Shabab

A. Al Qaeda's ability to attack changed after September 11, 2001.
B. The operational capabilities of al Qaeda have stirred debate in the counterterrorism community.
C. The Sageman-Hoffman Debate.
    1. Marc Sageman believes that al Qaeda is no longer the main threat to the West.
        a. The more immediate threat comes from marginalized Western Muslim immigrants, and citizens who feel disenfranchised.
    2. Bruce Hoffman states that al Qaeda has regrouped in the border area between Afghanistan and Pakistan, and that it has reemerged as a central threat to the United States.
        a. It will not be destroyed by focusing on networks; Al Qaeda must be defeated by eliminating leadership and debasing its ideology.
D. Degraded Leadership
    1. The Sageman-Hoffman debate is important because it represents the fundamental thrust of counterterrorism policy.
    2. According to Peter Bergen: although al Qaeda's central leadership remains active it has been significantly degraded due to U.S. drone attacks in Pakistan.
        a. Bergen also notes that al Qaeda has lost support among most Muslims because of its murders of Muslim civilians.
E. The Role of women.
    1. Katharina von Knopp notes that the role of women in terrorism is frequently overlooked, and that this has been true in studies of al Qaeda.
    2. The female jihad involves supporting male relatives, educating children in the ideology, providing support for operations, and assisting with financing.

346

3. Al Qaeda's women tend to be better educated than its men, and they are more interested in fulfilling traditional roles than assuming an operative position.
4. Al Qaeda had already created a women's suicide division in 2003.
F. Virtual war.
   1. Despite its physical presence in Pakistan, al Qaeda is oriented toward the electronic media.
   2. Communications are central to the al Qaeda strategy.
   3. The Internet has also become a forum for spreading tactical advice, bomb-making instructions, and theological debates.
   4. Al Qaeda runs its own media outlet, As Sahab (the Cloud); it continually streams video to the internet, and it is managed in a production studio in Pakistan.
G. Jihadist networks.
   1. Jihadist networks do not represent a single organization, nor do they espouse a unified religious message.
   2. Jihadist networks are fragmented, and they have separate command structures.
   3. In the most ironic twist of their ranting religious rhetoric, their most frequent victims are neither Westerners nor Jews.
      a. Jihadists kill far more Muslims than any other group.

VI. **Networks in the Horn of Africa**
    OBJ 6: Outline the operations of franchises including AQAP, AQIM, and al Shabab

A. Terrorists are currently active in the Horn of Africa.
B. After 9/11 the United States worked with governments in the region to create the *Combined Joint Task Force, Horn of Africa (CJTF-HOA)*.
   1. Its purpose was similar to the domestic Joint Terrorism Task Forces (JTTFs) in the United States.
   2. Unlike a JTTF, CJTF-HOA relies heavily on military force and national security intelligence.
C. United States activities in the Horn have ranged from targeted killings to intelligence-gathering.
D. Kenya is the only sub-Saharan country with known al Qaeda cells, but there are many other known jihadist organizations in the Horn.
   1. Jihadist activities bleed across Kenya's borders into Somalia.
E. Debra West says the United States faces differing terrorist threats in the Horn of Africa:
   1. The most obvious threat comes from the ability of terrorist groups to take immediate action.
   2. Another threat is the ability of terrorist groups, especially jihadists, to organize in the region.
   3. They are able to do this because of two other threats:
      a. Unstable political environments.

347

b. A population that supports terrorism against the United States and its allies.

F. John Prendergast and Colin Thomas-Jensen argue that the Horn represents the hottest war zone in the world, and it is a region of massive humanitarian crises and ethnic conflicts.

1. By approaching the Horn as a military problem, the United States has actually made the situation worse.

G. Two clusters of conflicts lay at the heart of the matter:

1. The first involves rebellions in Sudan, particularly Darfur.
2. The second cluster of conflicts involves a dispute between Ethiopia and Eritrea over complicated fighting in Somalia.

H. During the Cold War, the United States used Somalia as a base against communism in Africa.

1. This resulted in a fragmented system, where a central government tried to control policy from Mogadishu, but political power was exercised by local tribes and clans.
2. The country served as a base for some of the al Qaeda operatives who attacked the United States' embassy in Dar es Salaam and Nairobi in 1998, and known al Qaeda suspects were present after the 9-11 attacks.
3. The Harakat Shabab al-Mujahedeen, better known as al Shabab or the Youth, emerged from the retreat of the ICU.
   a. Al Shabab has sparked a policy debate in America concerning the Somalian diaspora in the United States.

VII. Pakistan
OBJ 8: Describe other forms of terrorism in Pakistan

A. Pakistan became a country in 1947, as part of a political settlement when the British departed India.
B. According to Tariq Ali, it was to be a Muslim country, but unofficially its first leader, *Mohammed Ali Jinnah*, was quite happy to have an independent democracy of landed elites,
C. The country is composed of five major states (four provinces and one territory) divided primarily along ethnic lines.
D. Control of Jammu and Kashmir is disputed with India.
E. Two international issues dominate Pakistan: nuclear weapons and relations with the United States, and both of these issues are ultimately tied to terrorism.
F. Pakistan formed in 1947, when British rule in India and the region ended. It was divided into East and West, East Pakistan revolted in 1971, and formed the new country of Bangladesh.
G. Pakistan has two groups associated with jihadist networks:
1. The Lashkar-e-Tayibba (LeT)
2. The Pakistani Taliban
H. The Lashkar-e-Tayibba (LeT) was created in 1993 under the watchful eye of the ISI to strike at Indian targets in Jammu and Kashmir.

348

I. The Pakistani Taliban.
   1. Although the Taliban is most closely associated with Afghanistan, its core emerged from Pakistan after the Soviet-Afghan War.
   2. The Taliban seized control of Kandahar in 1994, and controlled 95% of the country by 1997.
   3. After the American offensive in Afghanistan in October 2001, many members of the Taliban retreated into the Federal Administered Tribal Area (FATA) of Pakistan, using this area for two primary purposes:
      a. As a base for launching anti-NATO attacks into Afghanistan.
      b. To form a new Pakistani movement, the Tehrik-e-Taliban, or Pakistani Taliban.
   4. More important than military aid, is the need to assist average Pakistanis in building an infrastructure; military aid will not solve the problem of terrorism.

VIII. **Other Networks**
   OBJ 6: Outline the operations of franchises including AQAP, AQIM, and al Shabab
   OBJ 9: Summarize operations in other parts of Asia and the Pacific

A. Jihadist networks are fragmented, and they have separate command structures. Their leaders tend to be theologically unsophisticated or ideologically intolerant fanatics.
B. AQAP
   1. One of the newest jihadist groups grew from the tangled political situation in Yemen, and it maintains cross border ties with radicals in Saudi Arabia.
   2. Andrew McGregor says that al Qaeda in the Arabian Peninsula (AQAP) is the most active group in the jihadist network outside Pakistan.
   3. Yemen suffers from three differing conflicts:
      a. A struggle for control of the central government.
      b. A rebellious southern region.
      c. A growing presence of AQAP in the Marib.
   4. Yemen did not become a unified country until 1990, and its internal divisions have created an environment where AQAP can grow.
   5. According to the National Counterterrorism Center, AQAP evolved from previous organizations in the Arabian Peninsula.
   6. Al Qaeda was active in Yemen in October 2000, when it launched a suicide attack on the *USS Cole*.
   7. The NCTC says that attacks continued through 2007 and 2008, and they became more intense, targeting embassies, the presidential compound in Sanna, and Yemeni military bases.
   8. AQAP claimed responsibility for the attempted downing of a Northwest airliner outside Detroit on Christmas 2009.

349

C. AQIM
1. Algeria's jihadist civil war in the 1990s spawned the Salafi Group for Preaching and Combat (GSPC) in 1998, and the GSPC gave rise to a new group, al Qaeda in the Maghreb (AQIM), in 2006.
2. In 2006 the GSPC announced its unity with al Qaeda, and changed its name to the AQIM.
3. AQIM's allegiance to al Qaeda is confusing.
   a. It claims loyalty and unity, yet in practice it does not take direction from Afghanistan or Pakistan.
4. A three part debate about the true nature of AQIM has unfolded among counterterrorism experts:
   a. One set of analysts believes that the AQIM is emerging as a regional force in West Africa.
   b. A second opinion is that it is nothing more than an Algerian group, and that its effectiveness is questionable.
   c. A third group classifies AQIM in the same way they do the Abu Sayuff Group in the Philippines.

D. Thailand
1. Thailand is experiencing a rebellion in its southern provinces.
2. The Pattani United Liberation Organization (PULO) formed in India in 1968 to create a Muslim state through armed struggle.
3. Radicals in the Philippines and Indonesia see the revolt as part of the international jihad.

E. Indonesia
1. Jihadist groups began forming in Indonesia in the early 1990s.
3. In 1999 fighting broke out between Christians and Muslims in the eastern islands, and militant Islamic groups grew.
4. Lashkar Jihad formed to fight Christians in the east.

F. The Philippines.
1. Zachary Abuza says three recent terrorist groups have formed in the Philippines:
   a. The Moro National Liberation Front (MNLF) is a continuation of the old religious struggle.
   b. Breaking away from the MNLF is the more radical Moro Islamic Liberation Front (MILF).
   c. A third group, Abu Sayyuf, claims to be part of the jihadist movement, but it is most closely associated with criminal activity, and seems more interested in money than religion.

G. Islam in Southeast Asia.
1. Christopher Bond and Lewis Simmons believe that Southeast Asia is critical to the war on terrorism.
2. They suggest that American foreign policy should be aimed at religious and cultural engagement in these areas, and it should reduce the projection of military force.

Chapter Summary

- During the Cold War the United States allied with any form of government that opposed communism, including conservative Muslims who detested Soviet atheism. It found its greatest expression in Afghanistan, and it took root there after the Soviet Afghan War.

- Osama bin Laden was born into a wealthy Saudi construction family. He was strongly influenced by the ideas of Sayyid Qutb. Bin Laden left Saudi Arabia to fight in the Soviet Afghan War, and joined a group of Arab mujahedeen.

- Bin Laden organized a base to service mujahedeen during the Soviet Afghan War, and it evolved into al Qaeda. He returned to Saudi Arabia, but was exiled to Sudan for his resistance to the Saudi alliance with the West against Iraq. He returned to Afghanistan in 1996, and formed an alliance with Egyptian mujahedeen. He "declared war" on the United States.

- Ayaman al Zawahiri trained in medicine, but accepted Qutb's theory of religious revolution. Jailed after the assassination of Anwar Sadat, Zawahiri went to Afghanistan and met bin Laden.

- Zawahiri returned to Egypt after the Soviet Afghan War to lead Egyptian Islamic Jihad, only to flee after its defeat. He eventually joined bin Laden, leading his Egyptians into an alliance with the Saudis. The resulting group was popularly known as al Qaeda.

- Zawahiri and bin Laden formed a partnership in 1996. Deciding that internal revolutions had failed, they expanded al Qaeda, and focused on the far enemy. By 1998, the year of a second declaration of war, al Qaeda had become a loose conglomeration of ideological cells with a hierarchy in Afghanistan.

- Al Qaeda's theology is based on a militarized version of Islam, an interpretation rejected by the vast majority of Muslims and Islamic scholars. The theology derives from the political-religious writings of Sayyid Qutb.

- Al Qaeda was an umbrella-style organization. Its central command reigned over a loose conglomeration of semi-autonomous groups. This network was able to launch high profile attacks from 1998 to 2001. Its most spectacular attack came on September 11, 2001.

- The 9-11 Commission summarized the events that led to the September 11 attacks and recommended a response. These recommendations included sweeping reforms in the intelligence community, the creation of a national director of intelligence, new roles for the FBI, greater cooperation among law enforcement agencies, increased domestic security safeguards, and reformed Congressional oversight.

- The United States responded to September 11 by moving into Afghanistan and toppling the government. Unable to capture or kill bin Laden or Zawahiri, it attempted to stabilize a new Afghani government, and to attack militant positions in Pakistan. The United States also led an invasion of Iraq in 2003. This devolved into an insurgency, and the formation of new jihadist networks.

- Radical opponents of the 9-11 report believe the attacks were part of a secret government conspiracy. More rational criticism is focused on the failure to criticize the manner in which local, state, and federal government responded to the attack. Organizational critics are concerned with the commission's recommendations. Although the commission was charged to investigate the circumstance of the 9-11 attacks, it recommended restricting law enforcement and intelligence operations.

- Al Qaeda's role changed after September 11. Driven into Pakistan, it was able to launch a few operations, but it gradually became a symbol inspiring religious violence. Most of its leaders had been killed or captured within a decade of September 11. Al Qaeda's demise resulted in a new international confederation of jihadist networks.

- Failed states combine with governmental corruption and organized crime to create a potential haven for terrorist groups. Jihadist groups are present in the Horn of Africa. Al Shabab is fighting in Somalia, and it seeks to join the al Qaeda movement.

- Tribal areas in Pakistan harbor militants and international jihadists. This creates problems for all of central Asia. Religious militants spread throughout the region from Bangladesh to Kazakhstan. The ISI has supported jihadist groups in Jammu and Kashmir, further fanning the flames of religious violence.

- AQIM is the most active jihadist movement in North Africa. Southeast Asia has a variety of jihadist movements, but groups generally operate within nationalistic contexts. Thailand has a rebellion in its southern provinces, and Indonesia's groups can be tied to madrassas. The Philippines has three active groups, but one of them behaves more like a criminal gang.

DISCUSSION QUESTIONS

1. Discuss the evolution of al Qaeda. Do you think the U.S. should have been more cognizant of the beginnings of al Qaeda, why or why not? (OBJ 2, 3, 4, 5, and 7)

2. Explain the issues surrounding terrorism in the Horn of Africa. (OBJ 6, 8, and 9)

3. Summarize the political issues surrounding terrorism in Pakistan. What is your opinion on these political issues? Do you believe the U.S. should be involved? Why or why not? Expand on your answers. (OBJ 8)

4.   Lt Colonel F.G. Hoffman presented an argument regarding al Qaeda. What was his analysis? What argument did Reid Sawyer and Michael Foster present to reinforce Lt. Colonel's point? (OBJ 1 – 9)

ASSIGNMENTS

1.   Divide the class into two groups to discuss the involvement of the U.S. in the Soviet-Afghan War. Have one group present arguments in favor of the U.S. Involvement, and one group argue the opposite. (OBJ 1)

2.   Using the whiteboard, have the class draw a map delineating the various tribal regions of Pakistan. Assign individual students, or small groups of students, to briefly describe each tribe to the class. ((OBJ 5, 6, and 8)

3.   Have students choose a topic from this chapter and write a study guide/handout to present and share with the class. For example, students may focus their study guide on describing the emergence of modern piracy. Allow time to discuss topics to eliminate duplication. (OBJ 1 – 9)

4.   Assign students to read Pakistan Jihad: The Making of Religious Terrorism found at http://ipripak.org/journal/summer2009/Article2.pdf . Have them investigate online other sources of information regarding this subject. In groups have students prepare a presentation on what they found. (OBJ 5, 6, and 8)

5.   As a review, play jeopardy using key concepts and/or terms from the chapter. (OBJ 1 – 9)

MEDIA TOOLS

1.   *"Wikis"*
    7 Things you should know about Wikis. Retrieved from the Web Jun 29, 2012 at http://net.educause.edu/ir/library/pdf/ELI7004.pdf

    This document offers easy to understand instruction on the history, development, and potential uses of Wikis.

    Have students develop (or make additions to a previously created one) a *Webliography* (resource list) using a Blog or Wiki that provides a short description, and link to a scholarly resource pertaining to course concepts. For example, have students add two to three resources each, and ask them to add their assessment of at least one of their peers' contributions. If desired, allow time to discuss Blogs/Wikis. This activity can be reused throughout the course, by asking students to add/revise their contributions each week, bi-weekly, etc. (OBJ 1 – 9)

2. Global Issues. Social, Political, Economic and Environmental Issues That Affect Us All. Full List in War on Terror Section. Retrieved from the Web Jun 29, 2012 at http://www.globalissues.org/article/358/war-on-terror-articles.

This document offers an exhaustive list of links to articles reposted from other sites that detail numerous terrorism related events that have occurred during America's "War on Terror". This resource can additionally serve as an example for media tool sample #1. (LO 2, 4, 5, and 9)

Have the class comb through the news section and select a current event related to course concepts. Divide class into two or more groups. Have each group discuss their articles, and present a summary of their discussions to the other group(s). Once completed, have the entire class compare and contrast their combined discoveries. (OBJ 1 - 9)

3. *"Current Events Article Summary with Peer Assessment"*

Use the Article Summary Template, which can be obtained on the instructor companion website, for this assignment. The template offers information on Internet research, outside resources, identification of credible sources, and detailed directions on completing an assessment of a news article. It also includes a peer evaluation tool.

Have each student comb the Internet for terrorism related news and select an article that relates to one or more of the chapter's core concepts. Be sure selections are an article of interest from a credible source (*more on credibility can be found in the article summary template above*). Fill out an article summary template. *Your template asks for generic info about the article, a journalistic summary, as well as a personal opinion/reaction to the article.* Have each student summarize the article, present it orally to the class, and field Q & As from their fellow students. Have students complete peer assessments at the end of each presentation. Have students submit templates, original source article, and peer-reviews prior to the end of class. (OBJ 1-9)

4. *"Interactive Timeline of Pakistani Control"*
PBS Frontline world. Tribal Pakistan: Who's in Control? Retrieved from the Web Aug 20, 2012 at http://www.pbs.org/frontlineworld/stories/pakistan703/history/map.html

The website offers a fun interactive experience for users to explore Pakistan's many tribal regions and terrorist influences in the area. Users's 'click' and learn which tribe is in control of which region as they scroll over the map.

Have students test their knowledge of geography, while learning about the many tribal regions and terrorist influences in the area, by exploring the site, either individually at their stations, or as a class via a screen share projection. (OBJ 8)

TEST BANK

Chapter 11—Al Qaeda and Jihadist Networks

TRUE/FALSE

1.   After 2001, al Qaeda leaders inspired autonomous jihadists around the globe.

ANS: T   REF: p. 275   OBJ: 1, 3, 4, 5, and 7

2.   Terrorism in the Horn of Africa will likely cease to be problem in the near future.

ANS: T   REF: p. 292   OBJ: 1, 6, and 8

3.   Al Qaeda's origins can be traced to the Cold War.

ANS: T   REF: p. 275   OBJ: 1, 2, 3, 4, and 7

4.   The United States formed alliances not only with the democracies of Western Europe but with some of the most brutal dictatorships in the late twentieth century, all in the name of anticommunism.

ANS: T   REF: p. 275   OBJ: 1

5.   The U.S. and Saudi Arabia backed Afghanistan when the Soviet Union invaded Afghanistan in 1979.

ANS: T   REF: p. 275   OBJ: 1

6.   The Soviet Union ceased to be a consolidated country in 1991.

ANS: T   REF: p. 275   OBJ: 1

7.   The United States helped Saudi Arabia develop a funding mechanism and underground arms network to supply the mujahedeen during the Soviet-Afghan War.

ANS: T   REF: p. 276   OBJ: 1, 3, 4, and 7

8.   Americans paid more attention to potential profits than to the political problems brewing in Afghanistan.

ANS: T   REF: p. 277   OBJ: 1, 3, 4, and 7

9.   Bin Laden was raised in the Saudi royal court.

ANS: T   REF: p. 277   OBJ: 2

10. Saudi Royal family members are followers of Wahhabism.

ANS: T   REF: p. 277   OBJ: 2 and 3

11. Al Qaeda's initial structure included an intelligence component, a military committee, a financial committee, a political committee, and a committee in charge of media affairs and propaganda.

ANS: T   REF: p. 278   OBJ: 3, 4, and 7

12. From 1945 through 1991, the world was essentially divided into two camps- the communist and noncommunist nations.

ANS: T   REF: p. 275   OBJ: 1, 2, and 3

13. The Soviets used poison gas as a weapon during the Soviet-Afghan War.

ANS: T   REF: p. 278   OBJ: 1

14. Following the Soviet-Afghan War, bin Laden sought to register all the foreign jihadists in a single computer database.

ANS: T   REF: p. 278   OBJ: 1, 2,3, and 4

15. Dr. Ayman al Zawahiri was born into a prominent Egyptian family in 1951.

ANS: T   REF: p. 278   OBJ: 2

MULTIPLE CHOICE

1. _____, also known as Dr. Fadl, was one of Egypt's leading militants in the 1970s.
   a. Mullah Omar
   b. Sayyid Imam al Sharif
   c. Abdullah Azzam
   d. Ayman al Zawahiri

ANS: b   REF: p. 278   OBJ: 3, 4, and 7

2. Pakistan became a country in _____ as part of a political settlement when the British departed India.
   a. 1953
   b. 1951
   c. 1948
   d. 1947

ANS: d   REF: p. 296   OBJ: 8

3.   The ethnic Bengals left Pakistan in 1971 to form the country of _____.
     a. Abyssinia
     b. Ethiopia
     c. Ceylon
     d. Bangladesh

ANS: d   REF: p. 296   OBJ: 8

4.   Pakistan is composed of _____ major states divided primarily along ethnic lines.
     a. Five
     b. Four
     c. Six
     d. Ten

ANS: a   REF: p. 297   OBJ: 8

5.   The _____ detects and disrupts terrorist activities before they occur and relies heavily
     on military force and national security intelligence.
     a. CJTF-HOA
     b. JTTF
     c. CIA
     d. FBI

ANS: a   REF: p. 291   OBJ: 5, 6, 7, and 8

6.   Al Qaeda's origins can be traced to the _____.
     a. World War II
     b. Korean War
     c. Cold War
     d. Lebanese Civil War

ANS: c   REF: p. 275   OBJ: LO1

7.   In 2001, an American-led coalition struck Afghanistan for the purpose of destroying
     which group?
     a. LTTE
     b. Al Qaeda
     c. PIJ
     d. PLO

ANS: b   REF: p. 280   OBJ: 5

8.   President George H. W. Bush sent U.S. forces to Mogadishu to deal with what type of
     crisis?
     a. Economic
     b. Military
     c. Humanitarian
     d. Agricultural

ANS: c   REF: p. 282   OBJ: 6 and 8

358

9. The International coalition known as Desert Shield became Desert Storm after allied forces entered Iraq and Kuwait in February of what year?
   a. 2001
   b. 1991
   c. 1945
   d. 1967

ANS: b   REF: p. 279   OBJ: OBJ 1, 3, and 4

10. In October 1993, a U.S. Army Black Hawk helicopter was downed while on patrol in what city?
    a. Tel Aviv
    b. Kabul
    c. Mogadishu
    d. Tehran

ANS: c   REF: p. 282   OBJ: 5

11. Bin Laden officially declared war on the United States in what year?
    a. 1996
    b. 2001
    c. 1982
    d. 1990

ANS: a   REF: p. 283   OBJ: 2, 3, 4, 5, and 7

12. What was the name of the U.S warship attacked while in a Yemeni port in 2000?
    a. USS *Washington*
    b. USS *Reagan*
    c. USS *Cole*
    d. USS *Freedom*

ANS: c   REF: p. 289   OBJ: 5

13. _____ has become the prime source of radicalization, and it is spreading the al Qaeda ideology to a growing network.
    a. Television
    b. The Internet
    c. Madrassas
    d. The prison system

ANS: b   REF: p. 285   OBJ: 5, 6, and 7

14. Central leadership of al Qaeda currently operates in the tribal areas of ___?
    a. Afghanistan
    b. Sudan
    c. Saudi Arabia
    d. Pakistan

ANS: d   REF: p. 286   OBJ: 3, 5, 7, and 8

15. _____ is one of the newest jihadist groups grown from the tangled political situation in Yemen, and it maintains cross border ties with radicals in Saudi Arabia.
     a. AQIM
     b. FATA
     c. AQAP
     d. ISI

ANS: c   REF: p. 289   OBJ: 6 and 7

16. Al Qaeda in the Islamic Maghreb (AQIM) began as an offshoot of what war?
     a. The Algerian Civil War.
     b. The Soviet-Afghan War
     c. The Iraq-Iran War
     d. The Six Days' War

ANS: a   REF: p. 290   OBJ: 6

17. After the collapse of the Taliban government in 2001 its leader, _____, went into hiding.
     a. Mullah Omar
     b. Osama bin Laden
     c. Abdullah Azzam
     d. Sayyid Imam al Sharif

ANS: a   REF: p. 280   OBJ: 5 and 7

18. What is the jihadist term referring to non-Islamic powers or countries outside the realm of Islam?
     a. Far enemy
     b. Near enemy
     c. New enemy
     d. Old enemy

ANS: a   REF: p. 281   OBJ: 2, 3, 4, 5, 6, 7, and 8

19. Asif Ali Zardari inherited control of _____ after Benazir Bhutto's assassination in 2007.
     a. Pakistan Peoples Party
     b. World Islamic Front against Jews and Crusaders
     c. The Lashkar-e-Tayibba (LeT)
     d.   The Tehrik-e-Taliban

ANS: a   REF: p. 297   OBJ: 6 and 8

20. The Ghazi Brigades are more closely allied with _____ than any of Pakistan's other terrorist groups.
     a. The Pakistani Taliban
     b. The Lashkar-e-Tayibba (LeT)
     c. Pakistan Peoples Party
     d. The Asian Tigers

ANS: a   REF: p. 299   OBJ: 6 and 8

21.   Although Thailand is dominated by Buddhism, _____ is the primary religion of the three most southern states.
       a. Hinduism
       b. Islam
       c. Shinto
       d. Christianity

ANS: b   REF: p. 300   OBJ: 6 and 7

22.   There is tension between Pakistan and India all along their border, especially in the areas of Jammu and _____ where both countries claim sovereignty.
       a. Dublin
       b. Punjab
       c. Kashmir
       d. Karachi

ANS: c   REF: p. 297   OBJ: 8

23.   The Pattani United Liberation Organization (PULO) was formed 1968 to create a Muslim state through armed struggle in what country?
       a. India
       b. Pakistan
       c. Sri Lanka
       d. Thailand

ANS: a   REF: p. 301   OBJ: 8

24.   The militant theology of al Qaeda derives from the political-religious writings of ____?
       a. Marighelli
       b. Marx
       c. Mao Zedong
       d. Qutb

ANS: d   REF: p. 280   OBJ: 2, 3, 4, 5, 6, and 7

25.   The Islamic Courts Union (ICU) is a confederation of tribes and clans seeking to end violence and bring Islamic law to what country?
       a. Thailand
       b. The Philippines
       c. Somalia
       d. India

ANS: c   REF: p 292   OBJ: 6 and 8

26.   During the Cold War era, the United States supported any form of Islam as a stand against _____.
       a. Anarchism
       b. Socialism
       c. Communism
       d. Capitalism

ANS: c   REF: p 275   OBJ: 1

27. The Soviet Union invaded _____ in 1979.
    a. Afghanistan
    b. China
    c. Somalia
    d. Iran

ANS: a   REF: p 275   OBJ: 1

28. In August 1998, bin Laden's terrorists bombed the U.S. embassies in _____ and Tanzania.
    a. Kuwait
    b. Sudan
    c. Kenya
    d. Saudi Arabia

ANS: c   REF: p 283   OBJ: 4 and 5

29. Which of the following is NOT part of Sawyer and Reid's four-fold strategy on combating al Qaeda?
    a. Understanding the nature of the network threat
    b. disrupting al Qaeda communications
    c. Neutralizing sanctuaries for leadership
    d. Freezing financial assets

ANS: d   REF: p 286   OBJ: 4 and 5

30. What important scholarly debate does the text label as "the fundamental thrust of counterterrorism policy"?
    a. Sawyer-Foster
    b. Bronson-Cooley
    c. Sageman-Hoffman
    d. Cooley-Napoleoni

ANS: c   REF: p 286   OBJ: 1 - 9

31. _____ is the only sub-Saharan country with known al Qaeda cells.
    a. Eritrea
    b. Kenya
    c. Sudan
    d. Liberia

ANS: b   REF: p 292   OBJ: 6 and 8

32. Ethnic Bengals left which country in 1971 to form the country of Bangladesh?
    a. Sudan
    b. Pakistan
    c. Somalia
    d. Afghanistan

ANS: b   REF: p 296   OBJ: 8

33. Which of the following groups is responsible for the 2008 terrorist attacks in Mumbai?
    a. Al Qaeda
    b. AQAP
    c. LeT
    d. Al Shabab

ANS: c   REF: p 298   OBJ: 8

34. The primary religion of Thailand's southern states is _____.
    a. Buddhism
    b. Hinduism
    c. Christianity
    d. Islam

ANS: d   REF: p 300   OBJ: 9

35. The Pattani United Liberation Organization (PULO) is focused within which country?
    a. Ireland
    b. Sudan
    c. Somalia
    d. India

ANS: d   REF: p 301   OBJ: 9

36. Indonesia gained its independence from _____ after World War II.
    a. France
    b. The U.S.
    c. The Netherlands
    d. Great Britian

ANS: c   REF: p 301   OBJ: 9

37. Egyptian police arrested dissidents from all over Egypt after the assassination of _____ in 1981.
    a. Anwar Sadat
    b. Gamal Abdel Nasser
    c. Hosni Mubarak
    d. Muhammad Naguib

ANS: a   REF: p 280   OBJ: 3, 6, and 7

38. Afgan, Kasmir, and Bengal are just a few of the various ethnic tribes of what country?
    a. Afghanistan
    b. Iraq
    c. Pakistan
    d. Iran

ANS: c   REF: p 296   OBJ: 4, 6, 8, and 9

39. The AQAP is a splinter group of what terrorist organization?
   a. Al Qaeda
   b. Hezzbollah
   c. Hamas
   d. LeT

ANS: a   REF: p 286   OBJ: 3, 4, 5, 6, 8, and 9

40. AQIM formed from disaffected jihadists from a long civil war in what country?
   a. Algeria
   b. The Philippines
   c. Somalia
   d. India

ANS: a   REF: p 290   OBJ: 6

Case 11.0

Reid Sawyer and Michael Foster (2008) argue that American policy has not taken into account that Al Qaeda has survived and it is waging a battle of ideas – any strategy based on eliminating a hierarchy is the wrong approach. U.S. policy should be aimed at striking at a network. They suggest a four-fold strategy: (1) understand the nature of the network threat, (2) disrupt al Qaeda communications, (3) neutralize sanctuaries for leadership, and (4) deny opportunities to link networks. These procedures need to be accomplished within a framework that counters al Qaeda's central message.

41. The U.S. has negotiated agreements with a number of Middle Eastern states that agree to not provide asylum for terrorists. Such acts best demonstrate which of Sawyer and Foster's four-fold strategy?
   a. Understand the nature of the network threat
   b. Disrupt al Qaeda communications
   c. Neutralize sanctuaries
   d. Deny opportunities to link networks

ANS: c   REF: p. 286   OBJ: 4, 5, and 7

42. If the U.S. intelligence community was to successfully take over and block al Qaeda's underground video network, As Sahab (the Cloud). The takeover would best demonstrate which of Sawyer and Foster's four-fold strategy?
   a. Understand the nature of the network threat
   b. Disrupt al Qaeda communications
   c. Neutralize sanctuaries
   d. Deny opportunities to link networks

ANS: b   REF: p. 286   OBJ: 4, 5, and 7

43. U.S. forces have captured a large number of al Qaeda's couriers. Such acts best demonstrate which of Sawyer and Foster's four-fold strategy?
a. Understand the nature of the network threat
b. Disrupt al Qaeda communications
c. Neutralize sanctuaries for leadership
d. Deny opportunities to link networks

ANS: b   REF: p. 286   OBJ: 4, 5, and 7

44. The U.S. government has utilized a number of think tanks to comb over and analyze Al Qaeda's literature, media, and recent cases of insurgency on a global scale. Such strategies best demonstrate which of Sawyer and Foster's four-fold strategy?
a. Understand the nature of the network threat
b. Disrupt al Qaeda communications
c. Neutralize sanctuaries for leadership
d. Deny opportunities to link networks

ANS: a   REF: p. 286   OBJ: 4, 5, and 7

45. If the U.S. government was to threaten severe economic sanctions on any countries that support al Qaeda. Such an act would demonstrate which of Sawyer and Foster's four-fold strategy?
a. Understand the nature of the network threat
b. Disrupt al Qaeda communications
c. Neutralize sanctuaries for leadership
d. Deny opportunities to link networks

ANS: c   REF: p. 286   OBJ: 4, 5, and 7

46. If U.S. intelligence forces were able to successfully breaks an al Qaeda code that it routinely uses to coordinate its transnational activities. Such an act would demonstrate which of Sawyer and Foster's four-fold strategy?

a. Understand the nature of the network threat
b. Disrupt al Qaeda communications
c. Neutralize sanctuaries for leadership
d. Deny opportunities to link networks

ANS: b   REF: p. 286   OBJ: 4, 5, and 7

Case 11.1

Al Qaeda's women tend to be better educated than its men, and they are more interested in fulfilling traditional roles rather than assuming an operative position. Al Qaeda members prior to 9/11 would have been offended if one of their female relatives had been recruited as an operative. Both of these premises are changing according to researcher Von Knopp. Women have a strong influence on family cohesion and provide the familial network to

365

support operatives. Bin Laden stated in his 1996 declaration of war that the role of al Qaeda women was to motivate sons, brothers, and husbands. They are to encourage jihad. In the 1998 declaration against Jews and crusaders, bin Laden portrayed women as the victims of Western imperialism. Bin Laden's latest documents have called for women to actively join the jihad. Their operative role is in the formative stage and growing. Al Qaeda created a women's suicide division in 2003.

47. Through its creation of a women's suicide division, al Qaeda followed in the footsteps of what terrorist organization?
    a. The IRA
    b. The LTTE
    c. The MeK
    d. The PULO

ANS: b   REF: p. 286   OBJ: 1, 3, 4, 5, and 7

48. What position in the al Qaeda organization would women NOT likely to have held prior to 1996?
    a. Suicide bomber
    b. Courier
    c. Senior leader
    d. Weapons expert

ANS: b   REF: p. 287   OBJ: 1, 3, 4, 5, and 7

Case 11.2

Abuza (2003b, pp. 89–120) outlines the formation of three recent terrorist groups in the Philippines. The Moro National Liberation Front (MNLF) is a continuation of the old religious struggle. Having proposed negotiations with the Philippine government, the MNLF seeks an independent Islamic state. Breaking away from the MNLF is the more radical Moro Islamic Liberation Front (MILF). It has ties with jihadist movements and seeks to create an Islamic state under strict interpretations of Islamic law. A third group, Abu Sayyuf, claims to be part of the jihadist movement, but it is most closely associated with criminal activity and seems more interested in money than religion.

49. The Moro National Liberation Front (MNLF) most closely mirrors which of the following?
    a. Maoist rebellion
    b. The Zionist movement
    c. The Taliban
    d. The Islamic Group (IG)

ANS: b   REF: p. 303   OBJ: 6

50. The Abu Sayyuf most closely mirrors which of the following?
    a. Shining Path
    b. Al Qaeda
    c. Maoist rebellion in Nepal
    d. The Egyptian Islamic Jihad (EIJ)

ANS: a   REF: p. 303   OBJ: 6

COMPLETION

1. _____ refers to a term used during Clinton's administration to describe reducing defense spending at the end of the cold war.

ANS: Peace dividend   REF: p. 277   OBJ: 1, 4, and 7

2. Training in Pakistan and Afghanistan under _____'s spiritual mentoring, Osama bin Laden financed mujahedeen operations and taught the guerrillas how to build field fortifications.

ANS: Abdullah Azzam   REF: p. 278   OBJ: 1, 2, 3, 4, 5 and 7

3. Waziristan is a tribal region between the North-West Frontier Province and Baluchistan of _____.

ANS: Pakistan   REF: p. 297   OBJ: 8

4. Peter Bergen notes that al Qaeda has lost support among _____ because of its numerous murders of Muslim civilians.

ANS: Muslim   REF: p. 288   OBJ: 1, 3, 4, 5, 6, 8, and 10

5. The _____ is a group established to govern Somalia in 2004 until a permanent government could be established.

ANS: Transitional Federal Government REF: p 293   OBJ: 6, 8, and 10

6. The United States, fearing a takeover by jihadists, supported an Ethiopian invasion of _____ in December 2006.

ANS: Somalia   REF: p. 293   OBJ: 6, 8, and 10

7. Two international issues dominate Pakistan: _____ and relations with the United States.

ANS: nuclear weapons   REF: p. 297   OBJ: 8

8. Pakistan and _____ dispute control of the areas of Jammu and Kashmir.

ANS: India   REF: p. 297   OBJ: 8

9. The _____ governed Afghanistan from 1996 to 2001.

ANS: Taliban   REF: p 280   OBJ: 3, 4, 5, 6, and 7

10.   A madsrassas is a school based in the _____ faith.

ANS: Islamic   REF: p. 295   OBJ: 4 and 7

11.   The _____Mosque in Islamabad focused teachings on militant Islam.

ANS: Red   REF: p. 298   OBJ: 3, 4, 5, and 7

12.   Although the Taliban is most closely associated with Afghanistan, its core emerged from Pakistan after the _____War.

ANS: Soviet-Afghan   REF: p. 298   OBJ: 3, 4, 6, and 9

13.   The _____ network is the major power broker in Pakistan.

 ANS: Haqqani   REF: p. 286   OBJ: 8

14.   During the Cold War, the United States formed an alliance with any form of government that opposed _____.

ANS: communism   REF: p. 275   OBJ: 1

15.   Three recent terrorist groups have surfaced in the Philippines, the Moro National Liberation Front (MNLF), _____, and the Abu Sayyuf.

ANS: Moro Islamic Liberation Front (MILF)   REF: p. 302   OBJ: 6

16.   The Soviets began leaving Afghanistan in _____.

ANS: 1998   REF: p. 276   OBJ: 1

17. Jihadists refer to Israel, the United States, and the West as the _____ *enemy*.

ANS: *far*   REF: p. 281   OBJ: 1, 3, 4, 5, 6, 7, and 8

18.   _____ is the only sub-Saharan country with known al Qaeda cells.

ANS: Kenya   REF: p. 292   OBJ: 3, 4, and 5

19.   The radical terrorist organization, the Asian Tigers, focus their fight against the government of _____.

ANS: Pakistan   REF: p. 299   OBJ: 8

20.   _____is the only Islamic country with nuclear capabilities

ANS: Pakistan   REF: p. 297   OBJ: 8

ESSAY

1.   Discuss why Martin Hart argues that al Qaeda has lost its appeal in the Muslim world.

ANS:
- Hart argues that al Qaeda has lost its appeal in the Muslim world because of its basic mission.
- Far from being a religious movement, it pictures itself as the vanguard of a popular uprising that will destroy Western influence and reestablish the caliphate.
- Many Muslims viewed al Qaeda's early attacks as the heroic resistance to unjust colonialism, but al Qaeda's central message failed to invoke a resurgence of religion.
- This is primarily due to its emphasis on violence over the message of Islam.
- Hart believes the overreliance on violence ultimately isolates al Qaeda from Islam.
- Their weakness is exacerbated because they have no organizational structure.
- Their most effective tactic is inspiration, and this does not move them beyond their small cell structures.
- Al Qaeda cannot expand, and it has weak support from any potential sponsor as well as insufficient areas to regroup in safe havens.
- There is no practical strategy and no solid theological foundation.
- Aside from its emphasis on violence, it cannot generate grassroots appeal.
- Its focus is on an idealized golden age that neither recognizes nor accepts local needs.
- The internet and al Qaeda-controlled media glorify religion, but this does not build local organizations.

REF: p. 295   OBJ: 1, 2, 3, 4, 5, 6, 7, and 8

2.   What is the CJTF-HOA and why was it formed?

ANS:
- The CJTF-HOA is an American-led counterterrorist unit combining military, intelligence, and law enforcement assets of several nations in the Horn.
- Its purpose was similar to the domestic Joint Terrorism Task Forces (JTTFs) in the United States.
- The CJTF-HOA detects and disrupts terrorist activities before the terrorists can commit violence.
- Unlike a JTTF, CJTF-HOA relies heavily on military force and national security intelligence. It is not limited to law enforcement activities.
- West points to the success of the CJTF-HOA as a measure of tactical effectiveness.
- When the CJTF-HOA first began to operate in 2002 it sought three terrorist organizations and 25 supporters.
- By 2004 it had killed or captured 65 terrorists and had identified 550 probable supporters.
- Working with other military forces, the CJTF-HOA has successfully struck numerous targets.
- Feickert says that the CJTF-HOA has been so successful that some observers believe it should be used as a model for the war on terrorism.

- The struggle against terrorism cannot be measured in conventional military terms, according to this logic, but success comes when American military and intelligence units are able to work hand in hand with local military and police forces.
- The CJTF-HOA's close relationship with indigenous forces will build a long-term partnership with governments in the Horn; security forces from local governments can operate in places where American troops cannot go.
- In a report for Congress, Feickert says that champions of this policy point to the number of terrorists that the CJTF-HOA approach has identified, captured, or killed.

REF: p. 291   OBJ: 5, 6, 7, and 8

3.   Do you agree with Francis Miko's assessment that terrorism in the Horn of Africa will remain a problem? Explain your reasons.

ANS:

- Terrorists are currently active in the Horn of Africa

- After 9/11, the United States worked with governments in the region to create the Combined Joint Task Force, Horn of Africa (CJTF-HOA). Its purpose was similar to the domestic Joint Terrorism Task Forces (JTTFs) in the United States.

- The CJTF-HOA detects and disrupts terrorist activities before the terrorists can commit violence. Unlike a JTTF, CJTF-HOA relies heavily on military force and national security intelligence. It is not limited to law enforcement activities. Francis Miko (2004) states that although the CJTF-HOA has been effective, terrorism in the Horn will remain a problem because of porous borders, lax security, and political instability.

- United States activities in the Horn have ranged from targeted killings to intelligence gathering.

- As in the Cold War, the U.S. foreign policy has favored repressive governments when it benefits American interests. Miko (2004) says that America justifies its actions by the regional presence of al Qaeda and other jihadist groups.

- Kenya is the only sub-Saharan country with known al Qaeda cells, but there are many other known jihadist organizations in the Horn.

- Jihadist activities bleed across Kenya's borders into Somalia.

- The Islamic Courts Union (ICU), for example, represented a coalition of groups wanting to rule Somalia with Islamic law.

- An Ethiopian offensive in 2006 displaced the ICU, but left militant in its wake. Opponents contentiously debate the relationship with these groups to the jihadist network, and they dispute Miko's claim about the presence of al Qaeda, believing that it has had cells in Somalia since 1998 (Bruton, 2009; Rothmyer, 2009).

REF: p. 292   OBJ: 3, 4, 5, 6, 7, and 8

4. Compare and contrast the varied opinions on Pakistan's efforts to curb terrorism.

ANS:
- Some Pakistani leaders support terrorism, some want to establish the caliphate while rejecting terrorism, and some want to fight the jihadists.
- Musharraf allowed Coalition forces fighting in Afghanistan to enter Pakistani airspace, allowed American personnel to operate within its borders, and had its military conduct counterterrorist operations, especially in the northwest where al Qaeda, Taliban, and other jihadist forces are housed.
- Musharraf does not have the support of his people for allowing these measures; he walks a fine line every time he takes actions against terrorism.
- The International Crisis Group points to another internal problem – Pakistan is not so much a modern country as it is a modern series of tribal confederations.
- Pakistan formed in 1947 when British rule in India and the region ended.
- Divided into East and West, East Pakistan revolted in 1971 and formed the new country of Bangladesh.
- The Pakistan Army is the power behind the president's office.
- The jihadist movement is strong in the North-West Frontier Province and strongest in the province's tribal area Waziristan.
- Baluchs are staging a revolt in Baluchistan, and two major religious parties resent Musharraf's relationship with the United States.
- Bombings, kidnappings, and terrorist assaults from multiple groups are commonplace.

REF: p. 297   OBJ: 8

5. Discuss the role of women in terrorism generally and in al Qaeda specifically.

ANS:
- Katharnia von Knop notes that the role of women in terrorism is frequently overlooked and that this has been true of studies of al Qaeda.
- Suicide bombers capture the public imagination, but females in al Qaeda tend to follow traditional gender roles within the radical ideology.
- The female jihad involves supporting male relatives, educating children in the ideology, providing support for operations, and assisting with financing.
- The female role is mollified when women assume the male role of suicide bomber; women are not as effective when used in this manner.
- Al Qaeda's women tend to be better educated than its men, and they are more interested in fulfilling traditional roles rather than assuming an operative position.
- They have a strong influence on family cohesion and provide the familial network to support operatives.
- Bin Laden stated in his 1996 declaration of war that the role of al Qaeda women was to motivate sons, brothers, and husbands – they are to encourage jihad.
- In the 1998 declaration against Jews and crusaders bin Laden portrayed women as the victims of Western imperialism.

371

- Women are typically recruited in sisterhoods, an off shoot of Hasan al Banna's Muslim Brotherhood, and radical sisterhoods are prevalent in Europe.
- Al Qaeda members prior to 9-11 would have been offended if one of their female relatives were to be recruited as an operative.
- Von Knop believes that attitude is changing. Bin Laden's latest documents have called for women to actively join the jihad.
- Their operative role is in the formative stage and growing; between 1985 and 2006, 225 women were involved in suicide bombings.
- Al Qaeda had already created a women's suicide division in 2003.

REF: p. 286   OBJ: 3, 4, 5, 6, and 7

6.   Discuss al Qaeda's strategy surrounding electronic media.

ANS:
- Ayman al Zawahiri has stated that over half the battle is being waged in the media.
- Communications are central to the al Qaeda strategy.
- The media are used to recruit followers, for propaganda, and to get Muslims to accept the idea of a clash of civilizations.
- The internet has also become a forum for spreading tactical advice, bomb-making instructions, and theological debates.
- Many people believe that bin Laden's video releases are associated with an increased threat, but a review of the release dates and al Qaeda attacks reveal no pattern.
- Al Qaeda runs a global marketing campaign in an attempt to capture the imagination and support of Muslims.
- Carl Ciovacco collected a sample of 64 al Qaeda media releases from 2001 to 2008 from the holdings of the Combating Terrorism Center at West Point and found that al Qaeda is quick to exploit local issues and surround them with its own theology.
- Anniversaries are used as propaganda platforms, and most releases use carefully redacted passages of the Qur'an and selective history to tailor the message.
- Civacco says the following seven themes are present in most media releases:
- A call to jihad.
- The clash of civilizations.
- Apostate (takfiri) Muslims regimes.
- U.S.-Israeli friendship.
- Muslim unity.
- American strategic weakness.
- American exploitation of Muslim oil.

REF: p. 287   OBJ: 3, 4, 5, and 7

7.   Explain how the Cold War influenced American international alliances.

ANS:
- The United States formed alliances with the democracies of Western Europe and some of the most brutal dictatorships in the late 20th century, all in the name of anti-communism.
- Saudi Arabia was one of many countries that stood for a form of government that violated expressed American ideals.
- American foreign policy makers also embraced the conservative religious views of the Saudi upper classes.
- The United States supported any form of Islam as a stand against communism.
- Rachel Bronson says the religious nature of Saudi Arabia was an asset during the Cold War.
- For nearly half century the kingdom's antisocial stance kept the country in the U.S. political orbit; the Soviet Union, on the other hand, supported the emergence of revolutionary socialism in the Islamic world driving the Saudis deeper into the U.S. camp.
- When the Soviet Union invaded Afghanistan in 1979, both the Saudis and the United States saw an opportunity to strike back – they would support Muslim resistance to the atheist invader.
- John Cooley believes the foundation of modern jihadist power grew from the cold war, and he blames the West for incubating the network.
- The French intelligence community knew that Islamic militants hated the communists for several reasons and therefore suggested to intelligence counterparts in Washington and London that militant Islamic reformers might be used against communist countries.
- Using ties with oil-rich Muslim states, especially Saudi Arabia and Kuwait, the Western allies channeled support to both militant and nonviolent purification movements within Islam.

REF: p. 275   OBJ: 1, 3, 4, and 5

8.   Trace the path of expansion of Jihadist groups into Southeast Asia.

ANS:
- Zachary Abuza, in an analysis of terrorism in that region, says that jihadist groups began forming in Indonesia in the early 1990s.
- The International Crisis Group says these movements had their origins after World War II when Indonesia gained its independence from the Netherlands.
- Islamic associations became part of the political process, but they were suppressed by the government and the army in the name of nationalism.
- Abuza notes that new leadership gained power in 1998, and Islamic groups blossomed, asserting their independence.
- In 1999 fighting broke out between Christians and Muslims in the eastern islands, and militant Islamic groups grew .
- The political situation in Indonesia provided a climate for the growth of jihadist groups.

- According to Abuza, many of the members of jihadist movements had been trained in the mujahideen camps of Afghanistan.
- Lashkar Jihad formed to fight Christians in the east. A more sinister group, Jamaat Islamiyya, formed with the purpose of placing Indonesia under strict Islamic law.

REF: p. 301   OBJ: 3, 4, 5, 6, 7, and 8

9.   Discuss the evolution of Lashkar-e-Tayibba (LeT) in Pakistan.

ANS:
- The LeT seems to be emerging as a new global jihadist organization working in conjunction with al Qaeda.
- It is best known for its attacks in India, including a deadly series of attacks in Mumbai in November 2008, and its rejects all forms of Islam except its own interpretation.
- Pakistan officially banned the LeT in 2002, so it operates under a series of differing names.
- The LeT traditionally defined its operations around the Jammu and Kashmir conflict.
- The group has engaged in a series of terrorist operations beginning in 1993.
- The LeT has also launched numerous attacks in Jammu and Kashmir.
- LeT began to expand operations in Asia and the West in 2003.
- The LeT may be operating with al Qaeda, and the two groups share many ideological concepts.
- This relationship protects the LeT from crackdowns when the Pakistani government moves against terrorist groups, and it allows LeT planners to have access to intelligence data.
- The LeT is well entrenched and in a position to launch further attacks; the LeT was a part of Pakistan's original regional strategy and an arm of the ISI.
- The growth of militancy in the tribal regions, however, has spawned a growth in the LeT.
- It has moved far beyond the ISI's ability to control the organization.
- There is fear the LeT will not only continue to execute Mumbai style attacks, it will continue to evolve as part of the international jihadist network.

REF: p. 297   OBJ: 6, 7, and 8

10.   Describe the three recent terrorist groups in the Philippines as presented in the text.

ANS:
- The Moro National Liberation Front (MNLF) is a continuation of the old religious struggle.
- Having proposed negotiations with the Philippine government, the MNLF seeks an independent Islamic state.
- Breaking away from the MNLF is the more radical Moro Islamic Liberation Front (MILF).
- It has ties with jihadist movements and seeks to create an Islamic state under strict interpretations of Islamic law.

- ·A third group, Abu Sayyuf, claims to be part of the jihadist movement, but it is most closely associated with criminal activity and seems more interested in money than religion.
- Senator Christopher Bond and Lewis Simmons believe that Southeast Asia is critical to the war on terrorism.
- They do not see Thailand, Indonesia, and the southern Philippines as a hotbed for jihadist networks.
- Rather, they believe these nations represent the future direction of Islam.
- Southeast Asia has a long tradition of toleration and respect for other religions.
- They suggest that American foreign policy should be aimed at religious and cultural engagement in these areas, and it should reduce the projection of military force.
- Southeast Asia is not part of a global jihadist network, they argue. It presents an opportunity to engage the majority of the world's peaceful Muslims.
- Views will vary.

REF: p. 302   OBJ: 6, 7, and 8

CHAPTER 12
Domestic Terrorism

Learning Objectives

After reading this chapter, students should be able to:

1. List the factors that improve and inhibit our understanding of domestic terrorism.
2. Utilize a typology of criminal extremism to classify domestic terrorism.
3. Describe anti-government criminal extremism from right-wing activities.
4. Explain the fluctuations in left-wing criminal extremism.
5. Summarize extremist crimes motivated by racism.
6. Describe threats from homegrown radicalization.
7. Define single-issue terrorism.
8. Summarize criminal activities supporting ecological extremism.
9. Describe the criminal activities involving Puerto Rican nationalism.
10. Summarize criminal activities conducted against abortion providers.

Chapter Key Terms

John Walker Lindh, p. 323

Adam Gadahn, p. 323

Eric Rudolph, p. 328

Whiskey Rebellion: The uprising that took place in 1791 when a group of Pennsylvania farmers refused to pay a federal tax on corn used to make alcohol. The rebellion ended when President George Washington sent troops to stop the rebellion.

Know-Nothings: Different groups of American nationalists in the early nineteenth century who championed native-born whites over immigrants.

Moorish Nation: An African American group that does not recognize the validity of the United States government.

Paper terrorism: Utilizing false documents to clog legal, financial, or bureaucratic processes

Ruby Ridge: The location of a 1992 standoff between alleged survivalists and U.S. federal law enforcement officers in Idaho during which a U.S. marshal and survivalist Randy Weaver's wife and son were killed.

Branch Davidians: Followers of Vernon Wayne Howell, also known as David Koresh. They lived in a compound outside Waco, Texas.

Vernon Wayne Howell: (or David Koresh, 1959– 1993) the charismatic leader of the Branch Davidian cult.

Anglo-Israelism: The belief that the lost tribes of Israel settled in Western Europe. God's ancient promises to the Hebrews became promises to the United Kingdom, according to this belief. Anglo-Israelism predated Christian Identity and is the basis for most Christian Identity

beliefs.

Christian Identity: An American extremist religion proclaiming white supremacy. Adherents believe that white Protestants of western European origin are the true descendants of the ancient Israelites. Believers contend that Jews were spawned by Satan and that nonwhites evolved from animals. According to this belief, white men and women are the only people created in the image of God.

Nordic Christianity: A religion that incorporates the ancient Norse gods in a hierarchy under the Christian triune deity. It is similar to Odinism, but it does not completely abandon Christianity.

Creativity: The deistic religion of the Creativity Movement. It claims that white people must struggle to defeat Jews and non-white races.

New World Order: A phrase used by President George H. W. Bush to describe the world after the fall of the Soviet Union. Conspiracy theorists use the phrase to describe what they believe to be Jewish attempts to gain control of the international monetary system and, subsequently, to take over the U.S. government.

free-wheeling fundamentalists: White supremacists or Christian patriots who either selectively use Bible passages or create their own religion to protect the patriot agenda.

Protocols of Zion: A forged document written in czarist Russia allegedly explaining a Jewish plot to control the world. It was popularized in the United States by Henry Ford. It is frequently cited by the patriot and white supremacy movements. Jihadists also use it as evidence against Jews.

Third Position: A movement started after the Branch Davidian standoff at Waco. It attempts to unite left-wing, right-wing, and single-issue extremists in a single movement.

Bruder Schweigen: German for *silent brothers*, the name used by two violent right-wing extremist groups, Bruder Schweigen and Bruder Schweigen Strike Force II. The late Robert Miles, leader of the Mountain Church of Jesus in Michigan, penned an article about the struggle for white supremacy, "When All of the Brothers Struggle."

John Walker Lindh: (1981–) An American captured while fighting for the Taliban in 2001 and sentenced to twenty years in prison.

Adam Gadahn: (1958–) The American spokesperson for al Qaeda. His nom de guerre is Azzam the American.

Eric Rudolph: (1966–) A right-wing extremist known for bombing the Atlanta Olympics, a gay night club, and an abortion clinic. Rudolph hid from authorities and became a survivalist hero. He was arrested in 2003 and received five life sentences in 2005.

Chapter Outline

I.   **Understanding Domestic Terrorism**
       OBJ 1: List the factors that improve and inhibit our understanding of domestic terrorism

       A. The United States has a long history of political violence, but until recently, few scholars characterized it as "terrorism."
       B.   Three exceptions were H. H. A. Cooper, J. Bowyer Bell, and Ted Robert Gurr, all three of whom initiated work in this area before it was popular to speak of domestic terrorism.
       C. Nixon's national advisory commission
           1. H.H.A. Cooper— Task Force on Disorders and Terrorism: The report focused on the police role in responding to terrorism; outlining the differences between criminal investigations and counterterrorist operations.
       D. Bell and Gurr: Examining the history of domestic terrorism
           1. Gurr argues that terrorism is a tactic used by the weak to intimidate the strong and, in turn, used by the strong to repress the weak.
           2. Terrorism in the nineteenth century was primarily aimed at protecting the status quo and the economic environment.
           3. The frontier had its own special form of violence. Some vigilante actions equaled terrorism.

4. In the 1960s the character of domestic terrorism began to change, becoming rooted in radical politics, nationalism, and the international community's experience with terrorism.
5. The shift toward left-wing violence was derived from foreign models.
6. The American public rejected the violence of revolutionary groups and popularity was never fully achieved.
7. Gurr outlines three types of terrorism: vigilante terrorism, insurgent terrorism, and transnational terrorism.
   a. The growth of right-wing extremists is indicative of vigilante terrorism. The purpose of vigilantes is to defend the status quo or return to the status quo of an earlier period.
   b. Insurgent terrorism aims to change political policies through direct threats or action against the government
   c. Transnational terrorism occurs when non-indigenous terrorists cross national borders

II. **The Problem of Understanding Terrorism in Law Enforcement**
OBJ 1: List the factors that improve and inhibit our understanding of domestic terrorism
OBJ 2: Utilize a typology of criminal extremism to classify domestic terrorism

A. Terrorism happens in other places.
   1. One of the reasons that it is difficult for law enforcement to understand terrorism is that it does not occur in most jurisdictions.
   2. American police officers are faced with a host of tasks dealing with social order.
B. Classifying terrorism as a normal crime.
   1. Another problem is that although U.S. law enforcement officers routinely deal with terrorism, they call it something else.
   2. The FBI's reports on domestic terrorism do not classify many terrorists' acts as "terrorism"; they are excluded from the terrorism report, and classified as regular crimes in the FBI's annual UCR.
C. Confusing hate crime and terrorism.
   1. Hate groups include certain violent right-wing extremists, the Ku Klux Klan, paramilitary organizations (or militias), abortion clinic bombers, violent anti-immigrant groups, and others who are violent in the name of race or ethnicity.
   2. The term *hate crime* is frequently used in conjunction with domestic terrorism.

III. **Classifying Terrorism in Criminal Justice**
OBJ 2: Utilize a typology of criminal extremism to classify domestic terrorism

OBJ 3: Describe anti-government criminal extremism from right-wing activities

OBJ 4: Explain the fluctuations in left-wing criminal extremism

OBJ 5: Summarize extremist crimes motivated by racism

A. A label appropriate for theoretical criminology will not always lead to a response that solves an immediate problem, such as terrorism.

B. Terrorism investigations also differ from routine crime scenes because terrorists behave differently.

C. The FBI Classification System.
   1. Five types of groups responsible for domestic terrorism in the 1980s
      a. White leftists
      b. Puerto Rican leftists
      c. Black militants
      d. Right-wing extremists
      e. Jewish extremists
   2. All domestic terrorist groups, with the exception of Puerto Rican nationalists, lacked an indigenous base, and they tended to have localized ideological bases.
   3. Domestic Terrorism (DT) and International Terrorism (IT).
      a. DT involves violent political extremism, single-issue terrorism, and lone wolf activities.
      b. IT is defined as threats that originate outside the United States.
      c. For DT, political extremism involves violent left and right-wing extremists.
   4. Single issue terrorism includes violent activities associated with debates over abortion, *eco-terrorism*, *animal rights*, and *genetic engineering.*
   5. Lone wolves are included in the category when their actions are politically motivated.
   6. IT is composed of three subsets: state-sponsored terrorism, clearly defined autonomous groups, and jihadists.

D. Using the classification system.
   1. Brent Smith places terrorist groups into three broad categories.
      a. Right-wing extremists
      b. Left-wing and single-issue terrorists
      c. International terrorists

E. Brent Smith says the factor separating the average criminal from the average terrorist is motivation.
   1. According to Smith, terrorists are criminals, but in addition, they are motivated by ideology, religion, or a political cause.
   2. Terrorists engage in another activity avoided by most criminals; they plan.
   3. Smith compares left- and right-wing terrorists in five categories:
      a. Ideology and beliefs about human nature
      b. Economic views

  c. Geographical bases of support

  d. Tactics

  e. Selection of targets

 4. Left-wing terrorists favor Marxism, target the economic status quo, base themselves in urban environments, and select symbolic targets of capitalism.

 5. Right-wing terrorists are vehemently anti-Marxist and very religious.

  i.In addition, they support the economic system without supporting the distribution of wealth, base themselves in rural areas, and focus attacks on symbols of governmental authority.

 6. Left-wing terrorists have undergone no major transformation, remaining essentially the same from the 1960s to the present.

 7. Ecological terrorists represent a trend similar to the actions of the older left-wing groups.

  a. Evan Mecham Eco-Terrorist International Conspiracy

  b. Animal Liberation Front

 8. Since 1985, the United States has experienced foreign terrorism as surrogate warfare.

 9. Laws regarding terrorism in the United States are exceptionally vague.

  a. International terrorists tend to plead guilty more frequently than right-wing and left-wing terrorists.

  b. Left-wing terrorists fare the best in court, whereas few right-wing cases are dismissed.

F. Leaderless resistance and geo-spacial findings.

 1. Data from the *American Terrorism Study* found common behavioral characteristics surrounding terrorist events.

 2. During the 1990s, several domestic extremists advocated the use of *leaderless resistance.*

  a. While this tactic seemed to be an American invention, it can be loosely related to the first phase of Marighella's revolutionary model.

  b. It was incorporated in umbrella organizations like Hezbollah, Egyptian Islamic Jihad, the Egyptian Islamic Group, and by fifth-generation jihadists after the breakup of the al Qaeda hub in October 2001.

 3. The purpose of leaderless resistance is to fight independently of other groups.

 4. Research results indicate that the size of domestic terrorist groups has been decreasing since 1992.

 5. Most domestic terrorists are also recruited close to home.

IV. **Right-Wing Violence**

  OBJ 3: Describe anti-government criminal extremism from right-wing activities

  OBJ 4: Explain the fluctuations in left-wing criminal extremism

  OBJ 5: Summarize extremist crimes motivated by racism

A. The development of right-wing violence.
   1. The first incident of anti-federal behavior came shortly after the American Revolutionary War.
      a. The *Whiskey Rebellion.*
   2. The so-called *Know-Nothings* operated in the eastern United States before the Civil War.
      a. Organizing under such names as the Order of the Sons of America and the Sons of the Star Spangled Banner, these groups were anti-Catholic, anti-Irish, and anti-immigration.
   3. Agrarian failures and depressions spawned radical economic theories during the 1870s and 1880s.
   4. After the turn of the century, mainstream Americans came to believe that the left posed a greater threat to democracy; this attitude increased after 1919, when a wave of left-wing terrorism swept the country.
   5. Right-wing extremists also turned to an organization that had been created in the wake of the Civil War, the Ku Klux Klan (KKK).
      a. The KKK had been the brainchild of Confederate cavalry General *Nathan Bedford Forrest.*
      b. The KKK has operated in three distinct phases through history.
         i. Shortly after the Civil War, hooded *Knight Riders,* as they were called, terrorized African Americans to frighten them into political and social submission.
         ii. The second phase of the Klan came in the 1920s as it sought political legitimacy.
         iii. The modern KKK grew after World War II. It is now fragmented, decentralized, and dominated by hate-filled rhetoric.
   6. The development of the modern Klan parallels the growth of right-wing extremism from the 1930s to the present.
B. The Christian Identity.
   1. *Christian Identity* is a strange blend of Jewish and Christian biblical passages, and is based on the premise that God was white.
   2. Identity theology is based on a story of conflict and hate. According to this theology, Jews have gained control of the United States by conspiring to create the Federal Reserve System.
   3. Christian Identity provided a theological base for stating that white people originated with God, and Jews came from the devil.
C. Contemporary right-wing behavior, beliefs, and tactics.
   1. The appearance of modern right-wing extremism came to fruition around 1984, and has remained active since that time.
   2. Several issues hold the movement together:
      a. First, the right-wing tends to follow one of the forms of extremist religions.
      b. Second, the movement is dominated by a belief in international conspiracy and other conspiracy theories.

     c.   Finally, right-wing extremists continue to embrace patriotism and guns; they want to arm themselves for a holy war.

3.   Three issues rejuvenated the extremist right.
    a. The Brady Bill
    b. Ruby Ridge
    c. Branch Davidians

4.   The Brady Bill and Ruby Ridge gave new life to the fading right-wing movement, and a shift in the religious orientation of the extremist right helped to rejuvenate their ranks.

5.   Militias tended to turn to patriotism and more normative behavior after September 11, however, the path of the violent offshoot groups remains undetermined.

6.   Small groups dominated by Christian Identify theology and Christian patriotism engage in localized violence.

D. Right-wing conspiracies, militias, and the call to arms.

1.   Christianity has undergone some strange transformations in the violent circles of right-wing extremism, sometimes known as the hate movement.

    a. Extremists began preaching *Nordic Christianity* in northern Germany.

    b. Another religious derivation, *Creatorism* rejects Judaism and Christianity altogether.

    c. The majority of right-wing extremists retreated to more conservative churches, and relied on individual interpretations of scripture to justify antigovernment actions. This group can loosely be described as *free-wheeling fundamentalists*.

       i.   Free-wheeling fundamentalists do not believe the American government is part of a satanic conspiracy.

       ii. They do believe, however, that the federal government and local governments are their enemies, and that God will assist them in their confrontation with evil.

       iii. As survivalist ideology grew in the 1980s, the Free-Wheeling Fundamentalists turned to a new idea—the *militia movement*.

       iv. ATF analysts believe militias tend to be issue oriented – groups gather around taxes, abortion, gun control, or Christian Identity.

E. One philosophy, the *Third Position*, tried to unite both extremes.

    a. The Third Position serves to blur the line between left and right by uniting former enemies around common themes.

F. The <u>Turner Diaries</u> and <u>Hunter</u>: Blueprints for revolution.

1.   William Pierce, a white supremacist, with headquarters in rural West Virginia, formed an organization called the *National Alliance.*

2.   Pierce's most noted novel, <u>The Turner Diaries,</u> is a fictionalized account of an international white revolution.

    a. The danger of the work is that from a technical standpoint, it is a how-to manual for low-level terrorism.

      b.   The book could serve as a psychological inspiration for violence; that is, it could inspire copycat crimes.

      c.   <u>Hunter</u> is another Pierce novel that tells the story of a lone wolf named Hunter, who decides to launch a one-person revolution.

F. Resurgent violent right-wing extremism.

    1. The election of President Barrack Obama had an impact on right-wing and anti-government extremism, although the government was reluctant to release the evidence of increased activity.

V.   Homegrown Violent Extremists
OBJ 6: Describe threats from homegrown radicalization

A. Jihadists appeared in the United States before the 9/11 attacks, and they remain active today.

    1. Well-known terrorist groups have established bases in the United States.

    2. The network involves covert autonomous cells linked to the al Qaeda philosophy. They do not limit their activities to America; they are part of an international Jihad.

B. Homegrown jihadists.

    1. One of the incubators for homegrown jihadists is the American prison system.

    2. In June 2006, JTTF officers arrested a group of jihadists in Miami and Atlanta who were not involved in any network.

    3. Such groups might become the greatest domestic threat.

      a.   They are self-recruited, self-motivated, and self-trained.

      b.   Their only direct contact with the jihadists is the internet.

    4. Homegrown terrorists are produced in a number of ways:

      a. Some are born in the United States, and prepare to wage the jihad, even though they have little contact with jihadists.

      b. Others immigrate, and they find themselves alone.

      c. Others, like *John Walker Lindh* and *Adam Gadahn,* leave the United States to join the jihad overseas.

      d. A third type threatens to become a hybrid form.

    5. The potential hybrid jihadist comes in several varieties.

    6. The United States experienced more domestic terrorism in the 1970s than it has in the first decade of the 21st century.

VI.   Single-Issue Criminal Extremists

OBJ 7: Define single-issue terrorism

OBJ 8: Summarize criminal activities supporting ecological extremism

OBJ 9: Describe the criminal activities involving Puerto Rican nationalism

OBJ 10: Summarize criminal activities conducted against abortion
providers

A. Left-wing terrorist groups dominated terrorism in the United States from about 1967 to 1985.
B. Several things contributed to the demise of left-wing terrorism in the United States.
  1. One of the major problems was that intellectual elites controlled the movement.
  2. The collapse of the Soviet Union did not help left-wing popularity.
  3. Guilt was a factor as left-wing terror faded in Europe.
C. Transformation to single issues.
  1. Left-wing terrorism did not disappear, it was transformed.
  2. Leftist movements became more specific, focusing not only on certain political behavior, but on particular causes.
D. Eco-terrorism, Animal Rights, and Genetic Engineering
  1. Supporters of eco-terrorism, animal rights, and anti-genetic engineering came together in the United Kingdom in 1992.
  2. The new group called itself the Earth Liberation Front (ELF).
    i. Composed of radicals from Earth First! the Animal Liberation Front (ALF), and other disaffected environmentalists, the group migrated from Europe to the United States.
  3. As was the case with the right wing, a novel, <u>The Monkey Wrench Gang</u>, inspired the eco-terrorists.
  4. ELF had no hierarchy and was not associated with any particular location.
    a. ELF targeted its victims with arson.
  5. In the past decade, ecological and animal-rights extremists have united, and are known by different names with various extremist causes.
  6. Most violence associated with eco-terrorism has taken place in the American West.
  7. Eco-terrorists are uncompromising, illogical extremists, just like their right-wing counterparts.
E. Puerto Rican Nationalism
  1. Puerto Rico was colonized by the Spanish shortly after the European discovery of America, and the Spanish ruled the island for nearly three centuries.
    a. This changed in 1898, when the United States captured Puerto Rico in the Spanish-American War.
    b. Currently, the population is of three opinions:
      i. Some desire Puerto Rican statehood.
      ii. Others want to create an independent country.
      iii. A third constituency wants to maintain commonwealth status.
  2. The Evolution of revolutionary groups.
    a. Violent revolutionaries in Puerto Rico appeared more than fifty years ago.
    b. The Armed Forces of National Liberation (FALN) began operating in the United States after 1945, and they were joined by other Puerto Rican terrorists in the following decades.

      c. Forces of Liberation (FARP), the Guerrilla Forces of Liberation (GEL), and the Pedro Albizu Campos Revolutionary Forces (PACRF).

      d. Antiabortion Violence

F. For the past three decades, the amount of violence against abortion clinics and personnel has risen.

G. Paul Hill and *Eric Rudolph*

H. Violent antiabortion advocates justify their actions in the same manner as other political extremists.

    1. Violence is not the only illegal action among those who break the law.

    2. The manual of the Army of God includes "99 Ways to Stop an Abortionist"; it discusses low-level tactics such as gluing locks, shutting off water, and slashing tires.

I. David Nice's explanations for violent political behavior:

    1. Social controls break down under stress and urbanization.

    2. Violence increases when people are not satisfied with political outcomes.

    3. Violence can also be reinforced by social and cultural values.

    4. Violence can stem from a group's strength or weakness, its lack of faith in the political system, or its frustration with economic conditions.

J. Clinic bombings are related to several social factors.

    1. Most of the bombings occurred in areas of rapidly expanding population and declining social controls.

    2. Bombings also reflected a method of communicating frustration with political processes and outcomes.

    3. Most bombings took place where the ratio of abortions to live deliveries is relatively high.

    4. Bombings predictably occur more frequently in states that have a highly active militant antiabortion constituency.

    5. States that experience bombings also exhibit a greater toleration for crimes against women.

    6. Bombings are also a sign of weakness. Although seemingly paradoxical, areas having strong concentrations of antiabortion sentiment do not experience as much bombing.

    7. When high populations of Roman Catholics, Baptists, or Mormons are present, the number of bombings declines.

    8. Nice found that abortion clinic bombings were positively correlated with every theory of violence, except the theory of economic deprivation.

    9. Nice concludes that antiabortion violence appears in areas of rapid population growth where the abortion rate is high. As social controls decrease, and the desire to substitute political controls increases, bombings develop into a form of political action.

K. Deana Rohlinger argues that current media coverage of abortion issues differs from the 1980s and early 1990s.

386

Chapter Summary

- As the level of domestic terrorism increased in recent years, Americans have gained a better understanding of it. State, local, and tribal law enforcement agencies have received training in recognizing indicators of terrorism. Improved intelligence analysis can be used to identify possible cases. Difficulties still arise because definitions change in shifting political environments, interest groups attempt to influence the social definition of terrorism, and some agencies still refuse to share information.

- There are several typologies for classifying domestic terrorism. One effective method is to substitute the phrase "violent criminal extremism" when describing politically motivated violence. This avoids the pejorative nature of "domestic terrorism." It also allows politically motivated crimes to be classified as anti-government extremism, racist extremism, homegrown jihadist extremism, and single issue extremism. It is important to remember that holding extremist beliefs is not a crime, but violating the law when acting out extremist beliefs is. Smith finds declining levels of ideological terrorism, and increasing threats from single-issue terrorists. Groups may be moving toward the network structure of international terrorists.

- Right-wing extremism can be traced to the Whiskey Rebellion of 1794. It continued through the next two centuries. Contemporary right-wing extremism is based on the Sovereign Citizen Movement, Christian patriotism, various militia movements, and various types of survivalism. Frequently, an individual extremist belongs to more than one phase of the movement.

- Left-wing terrorism dwindled much in the way it did in Europe. Single-issue violent extremists dominate the left-wing movement today. Radical ecologists and animal-rights activists primarily engage in property destruction in the name of their causes. Their goal is economic disruption. There are alliances among the groups today.

- The homegrown jihadist movement involves religious radicals taking criminal action in the name of Islam. There is no standard pattern of radicalization, and it may range from individual unorganized attacks to highly complex operations supported by an international infrastructure. Research shows that this is not an Islamic problem, and that most American Muslims do not support criminal violence.

- Single-issue terrorism involves criminal activity in support of one all-consuming ideology. Single-issue terrorism dominates left-wing criminal activities today, and it is exemplified by the anarchist movement.

- Criminal activities in support of ecology movements include eco-terrorism, animal rights, and anti-genetic engineering. Most of the attacks are aimed at property damage, and the most active groups are ELF and ALF. SHAC, an off shoot of ALF, has committed crimes of intimidation and violence.

- Puerto Rican nationalistic groups seek independence from the United States. However, many Puerto Ricans want to either keep commonwealth status or seek statehood.

- Antiabortion violence began with bombing and arson, but moved into assault and murder. A number of abortion providers have closed operations in response to violent extremism.

DISCUSSION QUESTIONS

1. Do you believe that domestic terrorism is still a threat in the United States? Why or why not? Which do you believe is more dangerous to the American public, domestic terrorism or international terrorism? Explain. (OBJ 1 – 10)

2. Compare and contrast international terrorist organizations (such as al Qaeda and LTTE) with domestic terrorist organizations (such as the KKK and ELF) How are they different in terms of membership, location, motivation, and life expectancy. How are they alike? (OBJ 1 – 10)

3. In regard to the First Amendment and freedom of religion, do you think that the government should investigate and/or monitor Black Hebrew Israelism? Why or why not? (OBJ 2 and 5)

4. You are tasked with developing a definition that would differentiate the difference between hate crimes and terrorist acts. What would your definition look like? (OBJ 1 and 2)

CLASS ACTIVITIES

1. Have students choose a topic from this chapter and write a study guide/handout to present and share with the class. For example, students may focus their study guide on describing the emergence of modern piracy. Allow time to discuss topics to eliminate duplication. (OBJ 1 – 10)

2. Bring in full reports of the Brady Bill, the Ruby Ridge incident, and the Waco siege. Divide the students into groups and assign each group one of the three reports. Have each group summarize their report for the class. You may also have students conduct further research into their assigned subjects. (OBJ 1, 2, 3, 5, and 6)

4. Have each student comb through http://news.google.com/nwshp?hl=en&tab=wn (or another website as approved by the instructor) for a current event, and select an article from a credible source that relates to one or more of the chapter's core concepts. Have students provide a journalistic summary and a personal

opinion/reaction to the article. Have students orally present the article to the class, field Q & As from their fellow students, and provide a copy of the original source article following the presentation. Optional: Have students complete peer assessments at the end of each presentation. (OBJ 1 - 10)

5.   As a review, play jeopardy using key concepts and terms from the chapter.
       (OBJ 1 - 10)

MEDIA TOOLS

1.   *"Wikis"*
       7 Things you should know about Wikis. Retrieved from the Web Jun 29, 2012 at
       http://net.educause.edu/ir/library/pdf/ELI7004.pdf

       This document offers easy to understand instruction on the history, development,
       and potential uses of Wikis.

       Have students develop (or make additions to a previously created one) a
       Webliography (resource list) using a Blog or Wiki that provides a short
       description, and link to a scholarly resource pertaining to course concepts. For
       example, have students add two to three resources each and ask them to add their
       assessment of at least one of their peers' contributions. If desired, allow time to
       discuss Blogs/Wikis. This activity can be reused throughout the course, by asking
       students to add/revise their contributions each week, bi-weekly, etc. (OBJ 1 – 10)

2.   *"Video Domestic Terrorists…Discussion & Debate"*
       CBS News. (Jul 25, 2011). Who are most likely U.S. domestic terrorists?
       Retrieved from the Web Jun 29, 2012 at http://www.cbsnews.com/8301-
       18563_162-20083189.html

       This video examines homegrown terrorism in the U.S., offering a profile of the
       'most likely suspects' to be involved in domestic terrorism.

       Play the video in class. Follow with an open forum discussion and debate on the
       profile offered by CBS as to who are most likely to be U.S. domestic terrorists.
       (OBJ 1 – 10)

3.   *"Current Events Article Summary with Peer Assessment"*
       CNN. Domestic Terrorism. Retrieved from the Web on Aug 25, 2012 at
       http://articles.cnn.com/keyword/domestic-terrorism.
       This website offers an exhaustive list of news articles related to domestic
       terrorism. This resource can additionally serve as an example for media tool
       sample #1.

Use the Article Summary Template, which can be obtained on the instructor companion website, for this assignment. The template offers information on Internet research, outside resources, identification of credible sources, and detailed directions on completing an assessment of a news article. It also includes a peer evaluation tool.

Have each student comb the CNN website above and select an article of interest. Fill out an article summary template. The *template asks for generic info about the article, a journalistic summary, as well as a personal opinion/reaction to the article.* Have each student summarize the article, present it orally to the class, and field Q & As from their fellow students. Have students complete peer assessments at the end of each presentation. Have students submit templates, original source article, and peer-reviews prior to the end of class. (OBJ 1- 10)

4.   *"Video Weather Underground…Discussion & Debate"*
"The Weather Underground "(2002). Hulu. Retrieved from the Web on Aug 25, 2012 at <object width="512" height="288"><param name="movie" value="http://www.hulu.com/embed/bh8qe1r68ioe7fibl1ap8w"></param><param name="allowFullScreen" value="true"></param><embed src="http://www.hulu.com/embed/bh8qe1r68ioe7fibl1ap8w" type="application/x-shockwave-flash" width="512" height="288" allowFullScreen="true"></embed></object>

Show clips from the film "The Weather Underground" (2002). Have students discuss the definitions of domestic terrorists and the aspects of the Weathermen that are unique to the study of terrorism. (OBJ 2, 4, and 7)

5.   *"Audio Book <u>Turner Diaries</u> …Discussion & Debate"*
Pierce, D. (1978). *Turner diaries.* Fort Lee, NJ: Barricade Books. Retrieved from the Web on Aug 25, 2012 at http://archive.org/details/TheTurnerDiariesAudiobook1978

Downloadable audio files of the <u>Turner Diaries</u> and <u>Hunter</u> as well as numerous radio broadcasts of Dr. Pierce.

Assign students to read the <u>Turner Diaries</u> or read excerpts in class. Have students discuss the implications of the book's message. (OBJ 1, 2, 3, 5, and 6)

6.   *"eBook **Hunter** ...Discussion & Debate"*
Pierce, D. (1989). *Hunter*. Fort Lee, NJ: National Vanguard Press. Retrieved from the Web on Aug 25, 2012 at
http://archive.org/details/TheHunterByAndrewMacdonaldWilliamLutherPierce
(for pdf version)
http://www.barnesandnoble.com/w/hunter-andrew-macdonald/1006081568
(for eReader, Nook, Kindle download)

Downloadable digital files of <u>Hunter</u> in PDF or eReader format.

Assign students to read <u>Hunter</u> or read excerpts in class. Have students discuss the implications of the book's message. (OBJ 1, 2, 3, 5, and 6)

TEST BANK

Chapter 12—Domestic Terrorism

TRUE/FALSE

1. Homegrown terrorists present a low risk of potential terrorist attacks.

ANS: F   REF: p. 323   OBJ: 1 - 10

2. Violent right-wing extremists, abortion clinic bombers, and non-violent ecological groups are all classed as domestic terrorists.

ANS: F   REF: p. 310   OBJ: 1 -10

3. Right-wing terrorist groups dominated terrorism in the U.S. from 1967 to 1985.

ANS: F   REF: p. 322   OBJ: 2, 3, 7, and 10

4. H. H. A. Cooper, J. Bowyer Bell, and Ted Robert Gurr were pioneering scholars in domestic terrorism.

ANS: T   REF: p. 310   OBJ: 1 - 10

5. *Vigilante terrorism* stems from the extremist right-wing views.

ANS: T   REF: p. 310   OBJ: 1 – 10

6. Christian Identity is based on the premise that God was white.

ANS: T   REF: p. 318   OBJ: 5

7. One of the main factors that serves to inhibit American understanding of domestic terrorism is the continual shifting political environment

ANS: T   REF: p. 311   OBJ: 1

8. The United States experienced more domestic terrorism in the 1970s than it has in the first decade of the twenty-first century.

ANS: T   REF: p. 325   OBJ: 1 and 2

9. The American prison system is a prime area of recruitment of homegrown jihadists.

ANS: T   REF: p. 324   OBJ: 6

10. Leftist movements have largely given way to single-issue groups.

ANS: T   REF: p. 317   OBJ: 4 and 8

11. The Earth Liberation Front (ELF) migrated from the U.S. to Europe.

ANS: F   REF: p. 325   OBJ: 7 and 8

12. The FBI labels the majority of domestic terrorist activities using the common crime designations in the Uniform Crime Report.

ANS: T   REF: p. 310   OBJ: 1 and 2

13. The Earth Liberation Front (ELF), Band of Mercy, and Paint Panthers all champion human rights.

ANS: F   REF: p. 326   OBJ: 6 and 7

14. The Earth Liberation Front (ELF) and the Animal Liberation Front (ALF) do not advocate nor engage in violent activity.

ANS: F   REF: p. 325   OBJ: 6, 7, and 8

15. Puerto Rican nationalists tried to assassinate President Harry S. Truman in 1950.

ANS: T   REF: p. 327   OBJ: 6 and 9

MULTIPLE CHOICE

1. Which terrorist organization is associated with Puerto Rico?
   a. The Armed Forces of National Liberation (FALN)
   b. LeT
   c. The Armed Forces of Liberation (FARP)
   d. Hezzbollah

ANS: c   REF: p. 327   OBJ: 6 and 9

2. Which of the following is NOT a type of terrorism outlined by Ted Robert Gurr?
   a. Vigilante terrorism
   b. Insurgent terrorism
   c. State sponsored terrorism
   d. Transnational terrorism

ANS: c   REF: p. 310   OBJ: 1 and 2

393

3. The first responder to domestic terrorism is generally _____.
   a. A CIA agent
   b. A FBI agent
   c. A homicide detective
   d. A patrol officer

ANS: d   REF: p. 312   OBJ: 1, 2, and 6

4. The Ku Klux Klan was created in the wake of what war?
   a. American Civil War
   b. Spanish-American War
   c. War of 1812
   d. WWI

ANS: a   REF: p. 314   OBJ: 5, 6, and 7

5. Domestic terrorists did not routinely target the United States until the _____.
   a. 1920s
   b. 1980s
   c. 2000s
   d. 1960s

ANS: b   REF: p. 327   OBJ: 1-10

6. A report issued by the _____ indicated that right-wing extremists would be anxious to recruit military veterans coming from Iraq and Afghanistan.
   a. DHS
   b. FBI
   c. CIA
   d. NSA

ANS: a   REF: p. 327   OBJ: 3 and 6

7. According to Brent Smith (1994), what is the factor separating the average criminal from the average terrorist?
   a. Financial support
   b. Motivation
   c. Self-esteem
   d. Intelligence

ANS: b   REF: p. 312   OBJ: 2

8. _____ terrorists, according to Smith, have the greater potential for violence in the future.
   a. Ecological
   b. Religious
   c. Vigilante
   d. International

ANS: a   REF: p. 316   OBJ: 2

9. According to Smith's typologies, which group would NOT be classed as left-wing criminal extremism?
   a. ALF
   b. KKK
   c. ELF
   d. Paint Panthers

ANS: b   REF: p. 316   OBJ: 1 - 10

10. According to the Southern Poverty Law Center (2011), more than ____ police officers have been killed in confrontations with members of Sovereign Citizen Movements.
    a. 80
    b. 10
    c. 30
    d. 50

ANS: c   REF: p. 315   OBJ: 3 and 6

11. In a survey of U.S. law enforcement in the 1990s, more than _____ of the urban agencies reported left-wing activity.
    a. Ten percent
    b. Fifty percent
    c. Twenty-five percent
    d. Ninety percent

ANS: c   REF: p. 322   OBJ: 4

12. Puerto Rican revolutionaries receive support primarily from what country?
    a. Cuba
    b. The United States
    c. Mexico
    d. Colombia

ANS: a   REF: p. 327   OBJ: 9

13. The _____ operated in the eastern United States before the Civil War and felt that Catholic immigrants were destroying American democracy.
    a. Know-Nothings
    b. Whiskey Rebellion
    c. Ku Klux Klan
    d. Aryan Nations

ANS: a   REF: p. 313   OBJ: 2 and 3

14. The election of _____ had an impact on right-wing and anti-government extremism.
    a. George Bush
    b. Bill Clinton
    c. Barack Obama
    d. Ronald Regan

ANS: c   REF: p. 321   OBJ: 3

15. _____ was the founder of the Ku Klux Klan.
    a. William Pierce
    b. William Potter Gale
    c. Nathan Bedford Forrest
    d. Richard Butler

ANS: c   REF: p. 314   OBJ: 5

16. Who founded the Aryan Nations?
    a. Nathan Bedford Forrest
    b. William Potter Gale
    c. Richard Butler
    d. Wesley Swift

ANS: c   REF: p. 316   OBJ: 5

17. Terrorism in the _____ century was primarily aimed at protecting the status quo and the economic environment.
    a. Nineteenth
    b. Eighteenth
    c. Early Twentieth
    d. Late Twentieth

ANS: a   REF: p. 328   OBJ: 1 and 2

18. The Ku Klux Klan was spawned from the ideas of _____.
    a. William Potter Gale
    b. Bedford Forrest
    c. Louis Beam
    d. William Pierce

ANS: c   REF: p. 314   OBJ: 3 and 5

19. Which religious derivation rejects Judaism and Christianity altogether?
    a. Creatorism
    b. Free-Wheeling Fundamentalism
    c. The New World Order
    d. Nordic Christianity

ANS: a   REF: p. 318   OBJ: 2

20. Vigilante terrorism, insurgent terrorism, and transnational (foreigners fighting on American soil) are typologies of _____ terrorism.
    a. Domestic
    b. International
    c. Narco
    d. Jihadist

ANS: a   REF: p. 309   OBJ: 1 and 3

21. Which philosophy tried to unite both left- and right-wing extremists?
    a. The New Order
    b. The National Alliance
    c. The Third Position
    d. The New Unity

ANS: c   REF: p. 320   OBJ: 2, 3, and 4

22. David Nice (1988) found that that there was no relationship between abortion clinic bombings and _____.
    a. Social standing
    b. Religious ideology
    c. Economic conditions
    d. Cultural beliefs

ANS: c   REF: p. 328   OBJ: 7 and 10

23. What novel inspired eco-terrorists?
    a. *The Monkey Wrench Gang*
    b. *The Turner Diaries*
    c. *The Anarchist Cookbook*
    d. *Hunter*

ANS: a   REF: p. 326   OBJ: 8

24. According to FBI classification, domestic terrorism involves violent political extremism, _____, and one-wolf activities.
    a. Single-issue terrorism
    b. Religious ideology
    c. Insurgency
    d. Radicaliztion

ANS: a   REF: p. 312   OBJ: 1 and 2

25. According to the text, the first incident of anti-federal behavior in the U.S. came to be known as the _____.
    a. Boston Tea Party
    b. Whiskey Rebellion
    c. Haymarket Riot
    d. Zoot Suit Riots

ANS: b   REF: p. 314   OBJ: 6

26. What factor dominates the left-wing movement today?
    a. Single-issue violence
    b. Political violence
    c. Religious violence
    d. Economic violence

ANS: a   REF: p. 317   OBJ: 4 and 7

27.   In June 2006, Joint Terrorism Task Force (JTTF) officers arrested a group of jihadists in Miami and Atlanta who were plotting to blow up the _____.
a. JFK Airport
b. Pentagon
c. New York Subway system
d. Sears Tower

ANS: d   REF: p. 324   OBJ: 6

28.   The African American group, Moorish Nation, is most closely aligned with _____.
a. Jihadist ideology
b. Eco-terrorist groups
c. The Sovereign citizen movement
d. Lone-wolf activities

ANS: c   REF: p. 314   OBJ: 1, 2, and 3

29.   The _____ developed a general classification system of domestic terrorism in the 1980s.
a. CIA
b. JTTF
c. FBI
d. NSA

ANS: c   REF: p. 312   OBJ: 2

30.   Monkey wrenching has become a key tactic of _____.
a. Eco-terrorists
b. Jihadist Terrorists
c. Narco-terrorists
d. Cyber-terrorists

ANS: a   REF: p. 326   OBJ: 2, 4, 6, 7, and 8

31.   Most violence associated with eco-terrorism has taken place in the American _____.
a. West
b. North
c. South
d. East

ANS: a   REF: p. 326   OBJ: 8

32.   The United States captured Puerto Rico in what war?
a. WWI
b. The Spanish-American War
c. WWII
d. The Bay of Pigs

ANS: b   REF: p. 327   OBJ: 9

33. According to K. Stern (1996), a shift in the _____ orientation of the extremist right helped to rejuvenate their ranks.
    a. Political
    b. Religious
    c. Revolutionary
    d. Social

ANS: b   REF: p. 317   OBJ: 3

34. ATF analysts believe that militias tend to be issue oriented. Groups gather around taxes, abortion, gun control, or _____Identity.
    a. Christian
    b. Jewish
    c. Islamic
    d. Atheistic

ANS: a   REF: p. 319   OBJ: 3, 5, and 6

35. In October 2003, law enforcement officers found small Cincinnati grocery stores raising millions of dollars for Hamas through _____.

    a. Price fraud
    b. Money laundering
    c. Credit card skimming
    d. Counterfeiting

ANS: a   REF: p. 323   OBJ: 3 and 6

36. One of the largest armored car robberies in the history of United States occurred in Connecticut in 1983. Where region were the robbers from?
    a. Arkansas
    b. The Middle East
    c. Michigan
    d. Puerto Rico

ANS: d   REF: p. 327   OBJ: 9

37. In a binding vote to determine Puerto Rico's status, what percentage of Puerto Rican voters wanted independence?
    a. 85
    b. 45
    c. 3
    d. 20

ANS: c   REF: p. 327   OBJ: 1 and 9

38.   Violent antiabortionists began with bombing and arson attacks more than ____ years ago, and
        they have enhanced their tactics since then.
        a. 40
        b. 30
        c. 20
        d. 10

ANS: c   REF: p. 327   OBJ: 3, 7, and 10

39.   Researchers found that about ___% of the clinics in the United States had experienced
        some form of attack, vandalism, or harassment.
        a. 10
        b. 40
        c. 85
        d. 60

ANS: b   REF: p. 329   OBJ: 3, 7, and 10

40.   The FBI classes white leftists, black militants, right-wing extremists, and Jewish extremists
        as what kind of terrorists?
        a. rural
        b. domestic
        c. international
        d. cyber
ANS: b   REF: 316   OBJ: 3

Case 12.0

        Leftist ideology is rooted in the liberal ideas of such concepts as communism, socialism,
        anarchism, and also includes some branches of feminism, animal rights, as well as
        environmentalism or green movements. Those who radicalize issues with violent activity
        are known as left-wing extremists.

        Right-wing ideology takes a more conservative approach with roots in nationalism and
        racism. It includes concepts of anti-federalism, survivalism, religious, ethnic, and racial
        Puritanism. Those who radicalize issues with violent activity are known as right-wing
        extremists.NARREND

41.   Which of the following is NOT classed as right-wing extremists?
        a. The KKK
        b. Posse Comitas
        c. The Earth Liberation Front (ELF)
        d. Sovereign Citizen movement

ANS: c   REF: p. 326   OBJ: 1 – 10

42. Which of the following is NOT classed as left-wing extremists?
    a. Vigilantes
    b. Band of Mercy
    c. The Animal Rights Militia
    d. The Paint Panthers

ANS: a   REF: p. 310   OBJ: 1 – 10

43. Which of the following is NOT classed as left-wing extremists?
    a. SHAC
    b. Violent anti-abortionists
    c. Earth First!
    d. The Earth Liberation Front (ELF)

ANS: b   REF: p. 322   OBJ: 1 - 10

44. Which of the following is NOT classed as right-wing extremists?
    a. Moorish Nation
    b. SPIKE groups
    c. Paint Panthers
    d. The Christian Identity

ANS: c   REF: p. 326   OBJ: 1 – 10

45. Which of the following is NOT classed as right-wing extremists?
    a. Know-nothings
    b. Animal Rights Militia
    c. The Aryan Nations
    d. The Christian Identity

ANS: b   REF: p. 326   OBJ: 1 – 10

46. Which of the following groups is classed as left-wing extremists?
    a. The Band of Mercy
    b. Sovereign Citizen movement
    c. The Creativity Movement
    d. Militant survivalists

ANS: a   REF: p. 326   OBJ: 1 – 10

Case 12.1

Although the Civil War had many causes—slavery, farming versus industry, and sectionalism—one of the greatest causes was disagreement over the power of the federal government. Southerners questioned the legitimacy of the federal government, and they believed that Congress was taking the powers reserved for the states. Most Southerners were not fighting to preserve slavery; they were fighting to keep the power of local governments. When the Confederacy was defeated in 1865, the issue did not die (McPherson, 1988, pp. 858–859; Foote, 1986a, pp. 35–40; 1986b, p. 1042).

47. Given the feeling of the Southerners during the Civil War, which of the following groups would those wishing to radicalize most likely gravitate to?
    a. The Moorish Nation
    b. The Ku Klux Klan
    c. Earth First!
    d. Sovereign Citizen movement

ANS: b   REF: p. 314   OBJ: 1, 2, 3, 4, 5, 6, 7, 8, 9, and 10

48. The Ku Klux Klan formed in the aftermath of the American Civil War. It quickly evolved to focus its extremism in which area?
    a. Land rights
    b. Religion
    c. Economics
    d. Racial purity

ANS: d   REF: p. 315   OBJ: 1, 2, 3, 4, 5, 6, 7, 8, 9, and 10

Case 12.2

The appearance of modern right-wing extremism came to fruition around 1984 and has remained active since that time. According to this author's research (J. White, 1997, 2000, 2002), several issues hold the movement together. First, the right wing tends to follow one of the forms of extremist religions. The name of God is universally invoked, even by leaders who dis-avow theism (a belief in God). Second, the movement is dominated by a belief in international conspiracy and other conspiracy theories. Followers feel that sinister forces are conspiring to take away their economic status and swindle them out of the American dream. The primary conspiratorial force was communism, but after the fall of the Soviet Union, it became the United Nations. The extremist right believes that a conspiracy of Jewish bankers works with the United Nations to create a New World Order in which Jews control the international monetary system. Finally, right-wing extremists continue to embrace patriotism and guns. They want to arm themselves for a holy war (see Barkun, 1997; Berlet and Lyons, 2000, pp. 345–352).NARREND

49. Which of the following incidents is an example of right-wing extremism?
    a. 1992 Ruby Ridge Siege
    b. 1987 destruction of animal research labs at UC Davis
    c. The 1950 assassination attempt of Truman by Puerto Rican nationalists
    d. The 1984 Rajneeshee bio-terror attack

ANS: a   REF: p. 316   OBJ: 2, 3, 5, 6, and 7

50. Which of the following incidents is an example of left-wing extremism?
    a. 1992 Ruby Ridge Siege
    b. 1995 Oklahoma City bombing
    c. 1983 rocket attack against FBI headquarters in San Juan
    d. 2010 shooting of two West Memphis by Sovereign citizens

ANS: c   REF: p. 327   OBJ: 2, 4, 6, 7, 8, and 10

COMPLETION

1. _____ is based on the premise that God is white.

ANS: Christian Identity   REF: p. 318   OBJ: 5

2. The KKK was the brainchild of Confederate cavalry genius, _____.

ANS: General Nathan Bedford Forrest   REF: p. 314   OBJ: 5

3. The sovereign citizen movement is not new, and it is not limited to any racial group or political orientation. The movement was traditionally linked to _____.

ANS: white supremacists   REF: p. 314   OBJ: 3, 5, and 6

4. The most common activity of sovereign citizens is _____.

ANS: paper terrorism   REF: p. 315   OBJ: 3 and 6

5. The extremist right believes that a conspiracy of Jewish bankers works with the _____ to create a New World Order in which Jews control the international monetary system.

ANS: United Nations   REF: p. 315   OBJ: 3, 5, and 6

6. Posse Comitatus subscribes to _____ extremism.

ANS: right-wing   REF: p. 316   OBJ: 3 and 6

7. Richard Butler was the former leader of the white supremacy group, _____.

ANS: the Aryan Nations   REF: p. 316   OBJ: 3 and 5

8. Ruby Ridge was the location of a 1992 standoff between alleged _____ and U.S. federal law enforcement officers in Idaho.

ANS: survivalists   REF: p. 316   OBJ: 3 and 6

9. One of the incubators for homegrown Jihadists is the _____.

ANS: American prison system   REF: p. 324   OBJ: 6

10. _____ penned the fictional novel *The Monkey Wrench Gang*.

ANS: Edward Abbey   REF: p. 326   OBJ: 4 and 8

11. The FBI labels the majority of domestic terrorist activities according to the common crime designations in the _____.

ANS: Uniform Crime Report   REF: p. 310   OBJ: 1 and 2

12.   The 1985 novel, T*he Turner Diaries*, was written by _____under the pseudonym
       Andrew MacDonald.

ANS: William Pierce   REF: p. 320   OBJ: 3, 5, and 6

13.   The United States has experienced two styles of homegrown attacks or attempted attacks
       – one involves individuals who become radicalized from personal experiences and the
       other involves some type of _____.

ANS: foreign connection   REF: 323   OBJ: 1, 2, and 6

14.   The U.S. Marshal's office botched an attempt to arrest _____on a bench warrant at Ruby
       Ridge in the mountains of Idaho.

ANS: Randy Weaver   REF: p. 316   OBJ: 1, 3, and 6

15.   _____evaded federal authorities for years after bombings at the 1996 Olympics, a gay
       night club, and an abortion clinic in Birmingham, Alabama.

ANS: Eric Rudolph   REF: p. 328   OBJ: 3, 7, and 10

16.   David Nice (1988) found that abortion clinic bombings were positively correlated with
       every theory of violence, except the theory of _____.

ANS: economic deprivation   REF: p. 328   OBJ: 3, 7, and 10

17. Greece Right-wing extremism can be traced to the _____.

ANS: Whiskey Rebellion of 1794   REF: p. 331   OBJ: 1 and 9

18.   As Donald Black (2004) states, the three main ingredients of modern terrorism are: an
       angry group of people or sometimes even a single enraged individual, _____, and who
       has access to technology that can cause massive casualties.

ANS: who has the ability to travel   REF: p. 311   OBJ: 2

19.   Right-wing extremists claimed communism to be *the* primary conspiratorial force, but
       after the fall of the Soviet Union, it became the_____.

ANS: United Nations   REF: p. 315   OBJ: 1 and 4

20. "_____" referred to small acts of sabotage against companies undertaking projects
       in undeveloped areas.

ANS: monkey wrenching   REF: p. 326   OBJ: 4, 6, 7, and 8

ESSAY

1.   List and define Ted Robert Gurr's three types of domestic terrorists. Provide an example
        of each to support your answer.

ANS:

- The growth of right-wing extremists is indicative of vigilante terrorism.
- The purpose of vigilantes is to defend the status quo or return to the status quo of an
  earlier period.
- Gurr points to the Ku Klux Klan, the Christian Identity movement, and other white
  supremacy organizations as examples of vigilante terrorism that rely on right-wing
  rhetorical traditions.
- Gurr describes insurgent terrorists in revolutionary terms.
- Black militants, white revolutionaries, and Puerto Rican nationalists fall into this
  category.
- Insurgent terrorism aims to change political policies through direct threats or action
  against the government.
- It is the political antithesis of vigilante terrorism because it attacks the status quo.
- Transnational terrorism occurs when non-indigenous terrorists cross national borders.
- Gurr identifies several sources of transnational terror in the United States.
- Some foreign nationals have carried their fights onto U.S. soil, and some domestic groups
  have been inspired by foreign events.
- In other cases, foreign countries may have begun to target Americans at home.

REF: p. 310   OBJ: 1 - 10

2. Explain the major problems impeding law enforcement's understanding of terrorism.

ANS:

- One of the reasons law enforcement has difficulty understanding terrorism is that it does
  not occur in most jurisdictions.
- American police officers do not spend a lot of time thinking about terrorism.
- They are faced with traffic accidents, gang problems, domestic disputes, and a host of
  tasks dealing with social order.
- Another problem is that, although U.S. law enforcement officers routinely deal with
  terrorism, they call it something else.
- Even the FBI labels the majority of domestic terrorist activities with common crime
  designations in the Uniform Crime Report.
- Closely related to this problem is that even after September 11 most domestic terrorism
  goes unnoticed.
- Another reason for the lack of concern is that recent terrorism developed slowly in
  America.
- Terrorism grew with radical groups beginning about 1965, and although there were some
  sensational activities, terrorists did not routinely target the United States until 1982.
- Views will vary.

REF: p. 310   OBJ: 1-10

3. Discuss David Nice's theory of violence and abortion clinic bombings.

ANS:
- David Nice attempts to build a theory of violence by examining trends in abortion clinic bombings; he notes that the literature reveals several explanations for violent political behavior.
- One theory suggests that social controls break down under stress and urbanization.
- Another theory says that violence increases when people are not satisfied with political outcomes.
- Violence can also be reinforced by social and cultural values.
- Finally, violence can stem from a group's strength or weakness, its lack of faith in the political system, or its frustration with economic conditions.
- Nice matches trends in abortion clinic bombings against these theories of violence and found that abortion clinic bombings are related to several social factors.
- Most of the bombings occurred in areas of rapidly expanding population and declining social controls meaning that bombings tended to occur in urban areas.
- The slowest-growing states in the United States did not experience bombings, whereas half of the fastest-growing states did.
- Bombings also reflected a method of communicating frustration with political processes and outcomes.
- Bombing is a means of taking direct action; abortion bombers believe they are making a positive impact on the political situation.
- States that experience bombings also exhibit a greater tolerance for crimes against women.
- Bombings are also a sign of weakness. When potential bombers feel outnumbered, however, they may take action because they feel weak.
- Nice found that abortion clinic bombings were positively correlated with every theory of violence, except the theory of economic deprivation.

REF: p. 328   OBJ: 1, 2, 3, 6, 7, and 10

4. *The Turner Diaries*, a book written by William Pierce, has been controversial. What does White indicate as the potential dangers of this book? Would you agree or disagree with White, why or why not?

ANS:
- For the most part, *The Turner Diaries* is a diatribe against minorities and Jews; it is a fictionalized account of an international white revolution.
- The danger of the work is that from a technical standpoint, it is a how-to manual for low-level terrorism.
- Using a narrative, or storytelling, format, Pierce describes the proper methods for making bombs, constructing mortars, attacking targets, and launching other acts of terrorism.
- Anyone of average intelligence who reads *The Turner Diaries* will come away with an elementary idea of how to become a terrorist.
- The second potential danger of *The Turner Diaries* is more subtle.

- The book could serve as a psychological inspiration for violence; that is, it could inspire copycat crimes.
- The frequent diatribes in and the philosophy behind the book justify murder and mayhem.
- Pierce presents the destruction of nonwhite races, minorities, and Jews as the only logical solution to social problems.
- Although Pierce himself was not religious, he used a general cosmic theology, presented in a "holy" work called The Book, to place Earl Turner on the side of an unknown deity.
- Views will vary. Students may include The Silent Brotherhood or Oklahoma City bomber Timothy McVeigh as examples.

REF: p. 320   OBJ: 1, 2, 5, and 7

5.   Compare and contrast criminal behavior of left-wing and right-wing extremists.

ANS:
- Leftist ideology is rooted in liberal ideas of concepts of communism, socialism, anarchism, and also includes some branches of feminism, animal rights, as well as environmentalism or green movements. Those who radicalize issues with violent activity are known as left-wing extremists.

- Right-wing ideology takes a more conservative approach with roots in nationalism and racism. It includes concepts of anti-federalism, survivalism, religious, ethnic, and racial Puritanism. Those who radicalize issues with violent activity are known as right-wing extremists.

Right-wing extremists

- *Nonviolent offenders.* Tend to be high school dropouts, engage in rhetoric or publication, disrupt public meetings, use "constitutional" driver's licenses and permits, use "common law" court documents that they print on their own. Such documents are not valid. Common criminal behavior: fraud schemes.

- *Violent defenders.* Stockpile survivalist materials and weapons, wait for the U.S. government to attack. Violent defenders call the government the Zionist Occupation Government (ZOG) or the Jewish Occupation Government (JOG) because they believe that it is controlled by an international conspiracy of Jewish financial interests. Common criminal behavior: violent standoffs.

- *Violent attackers.* Use standard terrorist tactics such as weapons violations, assaults, bombings, arsons, ambushes, and murders. Common criminal behavior: shooting sprees.

- Sample right-wing extremists include: the KKK, sovereign citizens, religious and race based groups, paramilitants (militias)

- Left-wing terrorist groups dominated terrorism in the United States from about 1967 to 1985.

- Fueled by dissatisfaction with the Vietnam War, violent radicals broke away from student protest movements.

- Soon, various groups emerged, and they separated from the student movement to join ranks with nationalist terrorists.
- Their favorite tactic was bombing, but unlike right-wing groups, they tried to avoid causing casualties.
- Sample left-wing extremists include: the Earth Liberation Front (ELF). Composed of radicals from Earth First! the Animal Liberation Front (ALF)

REF: p. 330   OBJ: 1, 2, 6, and 7

6.   How did revolutionary ideas emerge and evolve in Puerto Rico? What major nationalist groups have in the region in recent years?

ANS:
- Violent revolutionaries in Puerto Rico appeared more than fifty years ago.
- Puerto Rican nationalists tried to assassinate President Harry Truman in 1950 and entered the chambers of the House of Representatives in 1954, shooting at members of Congress on the floor.
- Like their nationalist counterparts in Europe, revolutionary groups merged with left-wing organizations around 1970 through roughly 1980.
- The Armed Forces of National Liberation (FALN) began operating in the United States after 1945, and they were joined by other Puerto Rican terrorists in following decades.
- One of the most notorious groups was the Macheteros; other groups included the Volunteers for the Puerto Rican Revolution (OVRP), the Armed Forces of Liberation (FARP), the Guerrilla Forces of Liberation (GEL), and the Pedro Albizu Campos Revolutionary Forces (PACRF).
- Before the decline of the left, Puerto Rican terrorists routinely joined left-wing operations.
- Currently, the population is divided by three opinions.
- Some desire Puerto Rican statehood. Others want to create an independent country, and some of these people favor a Marxist government.
- A third constituency wants to maintain commonwealth status.
- The problem of Puerto Rican violence will not simply evaporate.
- Law enforcement officers must continue to respond to Puerto Rican terrorism, but at some point, American policy makers need to resolve the status of Puerto Rico to the satisfaction of its people.
- Currently, Puerto Rico is economically dependent on the United States.

REF: p. 327   OBJ: 1, 2, 6, and 9

7.   Describe how the United States has been affected by homegrown terrorists.

ANS:
- In 1977 a group of ten homegrown religious radicals stormed three sites in Washington, DC and took more than 150 hostages.
- In May 2007 a group in New Jersey planned to enter Fort Dix and murder American soldiers.

- In 2009 FBI agents arrested an Afghan-born permanent legal resident of the United States and two friends for planning suicide attacks in New York City.
- Brian Jenkins found that 46 publically recorded attacks or attempted attacks came from homegrown jihadist terrorists between September 11, 2001 and December 2009.
- Homegrown terrorists are produced a number of ways.
- Some are born in the United States and prepare to wage the jihad even though they have little contact with jihadists.
- Others, like John Walker Lindh and Adam Gadahn, leave the United States to join the jihad overseas.
- A third type threatens to become a hybrid form – American citizens may join experienced international sleeper cells hiding in America.
- One of the incubators for homegrown jihadists is the American prison system. America's prisons have many variations of Islam, and Wahhabi missionaries covertly preach religious militancy in them.
- Although prisons and jails are recruiting grounds, homegrown jihadists appear in different areas.
- In June 2006 JTTF officers arrested a group of jihadists in Miami and Atlanta who were not involved in any network, but authorities claimed they were plotting to blow up the Sears Tower in Chicago.
- The group did not even follow Islam. Its leader made up a religion combining Islam and other beliefs.
- The suspects were amateurs who had no real understanding of explosives, Islam, or the jihadist movement – such groups might become the greatest domestic threat. They are self-recruited, self-motivated, and self-trained.

REF: p. 325   OBJ: 1-10

8.   What is Christian Identity and how has it helped to provide the basis for violence among the extremists?

ANS:
- An American extremist religion proclaiming white supremacy.
- Adherents believe that white Protestants of western European origin are the true descendants of the ancient Israelites.
- Believers contend that Jews were spawned by Satan and that nonwhites evolved from animals.
- According to this belief, white men and women are the only people created in the image of God.
- Christian Identity theology is based on a story of conflict and hate.
- According to this theology, Jews have gained control of the United States by conspiring to create the Federal Reserve System.
- The struggle between whites and Jews will continue until whites ultimately achieve victory with God's help.
- At that point, the purpose of creation will be fulfilled. Such theological perversions are necessary when converting a religion of love into a doctrine of hate.

- Barkun points out that Christian Identity helped to provide the basis for violence among the extremists.
- Before the Christian Identity movement, American extremism was characterized by ethnocentrism and localized violence.
- Christian Identity gave a new twist to the extremist movement: it was used to demonize Jews.
- Christian Identity provided a theological base for stating that white people originated with God and Jews came from the devil. Such eschatological presumptions are deadly.

REF: p. 318   OBJ: 1, 2, 3, 5, 6, and 7

9.   Describe the three events that gave rise to the new extremist right in the 1990s. How did the extremist right mutate after 9/11?

ANS:
- First, the Brady Bill caused many conservatives to fear federal gun-control legislation.
- The extremist right played on these fears, toning down issues like white supremacy and Christian Identity and claiming that the intrusive federal government was out to eliminate gun ownership.
- The second issue dealt with U.S. Marshal's office attempt to arrest Randy Weaver on a bench warrant at Ruby Ridge in the mountains of Idaho.
- A white supremacist and adherent of Christian Identity, Weaver was charged with selling illegal firearms to undercover agents from the Bureau of Alcohol, Tobacco, and Firearms (ATF).
- Weaver was arrested and released on bail.
- When he refused to appear for the assigned court date, U.S. marshals tried to bring him in; U.S. Marshal William Degan and Weaver's young son, Sammy, were killed in the ensuing shootout.
- The FBI responded by laying siege to Weaver's mountain cabin, an FBI sniper shot and killed Weaver's pregnant wife before Weaver surrendered.
- The third event: the federal siege of the Branch Davidian compound near Waco, Texas.
- In 1993 ATF agents attempted to serve a search warrant on the compound, but they were met with a hail of gunfire, four agents were killed, and several were wounded.
- When the FBI moved in, after a three month siege, the Branch Davidians burned their fortress, killing eighty-two people, including several young children, inside the compound.
- After being revitalized in the 1990s, the movement mutated after September 11, 2001.
- Violent members of the right-wing movement melted away from large organizations and began to congregate in small groups.
- Following the pattern of international terrorist groups, they organized chains or hubs, small groups operating autonomously; the movement in the Pacific Northwest looks more like a conglomeration of terrorist cells.
- They remain violent and anticipate that white Christians will experience an anti-Jewish awakening.

REF: p. 316   OBJ: 1, 2, 5, 6, and 7

10. Discuss the confusion between hate crimes and terrorism. What does White suggest as the best way to approach the definitional problem?

ANS:
- According to Levitas, hate crimes include certain violent right-wing extremists, the Ku Klux Klan, paramilitary organizations (or militias), abortion clinic bombers, violent anti-immigrant groups, and others who are violent in the name of race or ethnicity.
- Many police officers would agree with this analysis, but it confuses the issue of domestic terrorism.
- Specifically, it brings up the problem of differentiating between hate groups and terrorist groups, and hate crime and terrorism.
- The term hate crime is frequently used in conjunction with domestic terrorism.
- Hate crime is a relatively new term defined by federal law and dozens of state statutes; it is a legal definition, not a manifestation of terrorism.
- Mark Hamm says that a hate crime is an illegal act designed to target a particular social group.
- The issue of hate crime complicates the understanding of domestic terrorism.
- Perhaps the best way to approach the definitional problem is to remember that terrorists commit crimes when they conduct operations.
- They are armed robbers, bombers, kidnappers, and murderers, but most armed robbers, kidnappers, and murderers are not terrorists.
- The same applies to hate crime – hate crimes involve specific violations of criminal law, it may or may not be terrorism.
- Terrorists always commit crimes; criminals rarely commit terrorism.

REF: p. 310   OBJ: 1, 2, 3, 4, 5, 6, 7, 9, and 10

CHAPTER 13
An Introduction to Homeland Security

Learning Objectives

After reading this chapter, students should be able to:

1. Define *homeland security* and explain why confusion surrounds the term.
2. List the agencies responsible for homeland security and describe their functions.
3. Describe the intelligence process.
4. Differentiate between criminal and national security intelligence.
5. Explain the importance of the National Criminal Intelligence Sharing Plan.
6. Describe the functions of fusion centers.
7. List some of the organizations responsible for processing intelligence.
8. Summarize some of the major issues in homeland security.
9. List perceived weaknesses in the homeland security from 9-11 to the present.
10. Discuss the aspects of intelligence reform.

Chapter Key Terms

Department of Homeland Security (DHS), p. 334

Civil defense, p. 335

Federal Law Enforcement Training Center (FLETC), p. 338

National security intelligence, p. 339

Criminal intelligence, p. 341

COINTELPRO, p. 342

National Criminal Intelligence Sharing Plan (NCISP), p. 344

Regional Information Sharing System (RISS), p. 344

Fusion centers, p. 344

Regional Intelligence Centers, p. 345

High Intensity Drug Trafficking Area, p. 345

Department of Homeland Security (DHS): A federal agency created in 2003 by Congress from the Office of Homeland Security after the attacks of September 11, 2001.

civil defense: Citizens engaged in homeland security.

Federal Law Enforcement Training Center (FLETC) A law enforcement training academy for federal agencies. Operating in Glencoe, Georgia, FLETC trains agents and police officers for agencies that do not operate their own academy.

national security intelligence: A system of agencies and networks that gather information about threats to the country. Any threat or potential threat is examined under the auspices of national defense intelligence. Unlike criminal intelligence, people and agencies gathering defense information do not need to suspect any criminal activity. The FBI is empowered to gather defense intelligence.

criminal intelligence: Information gathered on the reasonable suspicion that a criminal activity is occurring or about to occur. It is collected by law enforcement agencies in the course of their preventive and investigative functions. It is shared on information networks such as the Regional Information Sharing System (RISS). Unlike national defense intelligence, criminal intelligence applies only in criminal law. Agencies must suspect some violation of criminal law before they can collect intelligence.

COINTELPRO: An infamous FBI counterintelligence program started in 1956. Agents involved in COINTELPRO violated constitutional limitations on domestic intelligence gathering, and the program came under congressional criticism in the early 1970s. The FBI's abuse of power eventually resulted in restrictions on the FBI.

National Criminal Intelligence Sharing Plan (NCISP): A plan to share criminal intelligence among the nation's law enforcement agencies. It suggests minimum standards for establishing and managing intelligence operations within police agencies.

Regional Informational Sharing System (RISS): A law enforcement network that allows law enforcement agencies to share information about criminal investigations.

Fusion centers: Operations set up to fuse information from multiple sources, analyze the data, turn it into usable intelligence, and distribute intelligence to agencies needing the information.

Regional Intelligence Centers: Originally established to gather drug tracking intelligence, RICs helped provide the basis for fusion centers.

High Intensity Drug Trafficking Area: Specialized RICs in regions experiencing a high level of drug trafficking and drug-related crimes. They evolved from RICs and were the direct predecessor to fusion centers. Some HIDTAs simply expanded to become a full fusion center.

Regional Crime Gun Centers: ATF intelligence centers similar to RICs but focused on the illegal use of firearms

Intelligence product: The output of information analysis. Information is analyzed and turned into intelligence. This product is distributed to users.

Total Criminal Intelligence (TCI): An "all crimes" approach to the intelligence process. The same type of intelligence that thwarts terrorism works against other crimes and community problems **symbolic targets:** Terrorist targets that may have limited military or security value but represent the power of the state under attack. Terrorists seek symbolic targets to strike fear into society and to give a sense of power to the terrorist group. The power of the symbol also multiplies the effect of the attack.

intelligence-led policing: A type of law enforcement in which resources are deployed based on information gathered and analyzed from criminal intelligence.

total criminal intelligence (TCI): All criminal intelligence gathered and analyzed for intelligence-led policing. Rather than focusing on one type of issue, such as terrorism, agencies focus on gathering information about all potential crimes and social problems.

group think: Refers to a bureaucratic process where members of a group work together to solve a problem; however, innovation and deviant ideas are discouraged as the group tries to seek consensus about a conclusion. Powerful members of the group may quash alternative voices. Intelligence groups tend to resist making any risky conclusion lest they jeopardize their individual careers. Peer pressure creates an atmosphere where every individual comes to the same conclusion.

Chapter Outline

I.   **Defining Homeland Security**
        OBJ 1: Define homeland security and explain why confusion surrounds The term

        A. It is necessary for the Department of Homeland Security (DHS) to operate as a multifaceted team of differing organizations to stop terrorism before it occurs.
        B. Searching for Defined Roles
           1. Agencies have made progress over the last few years, especially in the area of information sharing and cooperation.
           2. The reason for the initial confusion about policy is that America had no common definition of homeland security.

414

3. Another reason for confusion lies in the fact that the new Department of Homeland Security (DHS) was responsible for protecting the borders and the country's interior.
4. A host of private businesses, nonprofit organizations, and health care systems were involved in security efforts.
5. Roles are divided into three functions:
   a. Preventing terrorism.
   b. Responding to attacks.
   c. Providing technical support to local agencies.
6. Agencies are coming to grips with the concept of homeland security because, in its most rudimentary form, the term means keeping the country safe.
7. Homeland security protects lives, property, and infrastructure.
C. Security Missions.
1. The policy guiding homeland security in the United States has not been fully developed, and agency leaders are not quite sure of the way that all the missions of various agencies fit together.
2. Homeland security also involves *civil defense*, that is, citizens engaged in homeland security.
   a. Civil defense emerged slowly from civilian functions during World War II.
3. A major portion of homeland security is a civic responsibility.

II. **Agencies Charged with Preventing and Interdicting Terrorism**
   OBJ 2: List the agencies responsible for homeland security and describe their functions

A. Congress approved the creation of the Department of Homeland Security by uniting twenty-two agencies in 2002. There are many other governmental organizations also focused on homeland security.
B. Two types of private-sector organizations participate in homeland security: businesses providing critical infrastructure, and businesses centered on security technology and service.
C. The Department of Homeland Security.
1. The *Department of Homeland Security* was created from the Office of Homeland Security in 2003 as a direct result of the 9/11 attacks; it has several different missions.
2. The U.S. Coast Guard, formerly under the Department of Transportation, was the first agency to be assigned to the DHS.
3. Many DHS agencies are involved in intelligence, and the Office of Intelligence and Analysis coordinates these efforts as well as coordinating intelligence with other agencies.
4. Many DHS employees are employed in law enforcement tasks, and they have arrest powers. These special agents and federal police

415

officers are trained in the Federal Law Enforcement Training Center (FLETC).

D. The Department of Justice.
   1. The Department of Justice (DOJ) maintains several functions in the realm of terrorism. The most noted DOJ agency is the FBI.
   2. The Department of Justice is involved in other areas.
      a. The U.S. Marshall's Service
      b. The Bureau of Alcohol, Tobacco, and Firearms (ATF)
         i. Although the FBI is the lead agency in domestic terrorism, ATF's role in explosives and firearms enforcement is crucial.
E. The Department of Defense.
   1. In time of war, the military organizations in the Department of Defense (DOD) play the leading role.
   2. The DOD has assumed counterterrorist functions in two ways:
      a. First, DOD operates the United States Northern Command to ensure homeland security.
      b. Second, in times of emergency military forces can provide much needed assistance to local units of government.
F. The Intelligence Community.
   1. The federal intelligence community underwent massive changes after 9/11 and the failure to find WMD after the invasion of Iraq.
   2. The purpose of the ODNI is to unite America's national security intelligence under one umbrella.
      a. It coordinates information from national security and military intelligence.
      b. It also includes intelligence operations from the Department of State.
      c. Based on the recommendations of the 9/11 Commission, the ODNI has incorporated federal law enforcement intelligence under its umbrella.
G. State, Local, and Tribal Enforcement.
   1. The federal government also envisions three intelligence roles for local governments.
      a. State, local, and tribal law enforcement agencies need to collect tactical intelligence for the prevention of terrorism and other crimes.
      b. They must also utilize intelligence for planning and the deployment of resources.
      c. Information sharing is at the heart of local intelligence systems.
   2. When it comes to terrorism, state, local, and tribal agencies are crucial to homeland security.

III. **Building Intelligence Systems**
   OBJ 3: Describe the intelligence process

A. Redirecting military and police forces is an essential part of developing a system to protect the nation.

B. The Intelligence Process.
   1. Police intelligence systems can be modeled after academic research.
   2. Basic intelligence involves general information about a subject and its sub-disciplines.
   3. Applied intelligence involves gathering basic information about a target and real-time information about current activities.
   4. All levels of law enforcement should be involved in collecting, analyzing, and forwarding information.

C. National Security and Criminal Intelligence.
   1. In network-to-network conflict, bureaucracies should not change their role.
   2. Each organization in a network has its own function, and the key to success in a network is sharing information.
   3. *National security intelligence* is gathered to defend the nation.
      a. People and agencies gathering defense information do not need to suspect any criminal activity.
   4. *Criminal intelligence* is information gathered on the reasonable suspicion that a criminal activity is occurring or about to occur.
      a. It is collected by law enforcement agencies in the course of their preventive and investigative functions.

D. Checkered Past.
   1. The CIA had tested drugs and biological agents on unknowing citizens, and the FBI's counterintelligence program, *cointelpro,* had exceeded the authority of law enforcement.
   2. Law enforcement and national defense intelligence came under difficult times during the administration of President Jimmy Carter.
      a. The president tried to correct the abuse of power and end the scandal of using covert operations against American citizens.
   3. The USA Patriot Act increases the ability of law enforcement and intelligence agencies to share information.

E. The New Jersey Intelligence System.
   1. The New Jersey State Police (NJSP) have an extensive intelligence-gathering apparatus.
   2. The NJSP Intelligence Service Section is made up of three main divisions.
      a. The Intelligence Bureau, the Central Security Unit, and the Solid Waste Unit

D. The California Intelligence System.

417

1. Formed after 9/11, the California Anti-Terrorism Information Center (CATIC) was designed to combat terrorism.
2. The center linked federal, state, and local information services in one system, and divided operational zones into five administrative areas.
3. Trained intelligence analysts operated within civil rights guidelines, and utilized information in a secure communications system.
4. It combined both machine intelligence, that is, the type of information that can be gathered by computers and other automated devices, with information coming from a variety of police agencies.
5. California created new systems under the tight control of regional law enforcement agencies, and in partnership with four regional Joint Terrorism Task Forces.
6. The State Terrorism Threat Assessment Center now coordinates the activities of regional threat assessment centers.

E. The NYPD Intelligence System.
1. Police Commissioner Raymond Kelly created two new units, one for counterterrorism and one for intelligence.
2. Kelly stated that he wanted the NYPD to do a better job of intelligence analysis, and to work more closely with the federal government.

F. US Attorneys and the JTTFs.
1. The Department of Justice has created two intelligence systems, one in federal prosecutors' offices and the other in law enforcement.
2. There are 93 United States Attorneys stationed throughout the United States, Puerto Rico, the Virgin Islands, Guam, and the Northern Mariana Islands.
3. Each U.S. Attorney's office has an Anti-Terrorist Assistance Coordinator (ATAC).
4. Each JTTF is made up of officers from all levels of American law enforcement, and from a variety of different types of agencies.

G. Plans, Networks, and Fusion Centers.
1. Shortly after 9/11, the International Association of Chiefs of Police (IACP) joined with the Department of Justice to create the *National Criminal Intelligence Sharing Plan (NCISP)*.
2. The plan was to establish norms for collecting, analyzing, and storing criminal intelligence within legal guidelines.
3. Criminal intelligence networks in operation after 9/11:
   a. *The Regional Information Sharing System* (RISS)
   b. The Anti-Terrorism Information Exchange (ATIX)
   c. FBI's Law Enforcement Online (LEO)
   d. The Law Enforcement Intelligence Unit (LEIU)
   e. The Homeland Security Information Network (HSIN)
5. The Homeland Security Information Network (HSIN) is set up to connect all jurisdictions with real-time communication. It includes state

418

homeland security officials, the National Guard, emergency operations centers, and local emergency service providers.

6. Despite the systems and networks that were developed to share information, many agencies still were not part of the information-sharing process; fusion centers came about to correct this.

IV.   **Issues in Homeland Security**
       OBJ 8: List and discuss some of the major issues in homeland security
       OBJ 9: List perceived weaknesses in the homeland security from 9-11 to the present

A. Law Enforcement's Special Role.
   1. Whether terrorists are homegrown or imported from foreign lands, police agencies are responsible for breaking some of America's most formidable terrorist cells.
   2. American law enforcement has a long tradition of reactive patrol, that is, responding to crimes and calls for assistance.
   3. The problem of terrorism brings the need for preemptive, offensive policing to a new level.
   4. If state and local agencies shift to offensive thinking and action, two results will inevitably develop.
      a. First, police contact with potential terrorists will increase.
      b. Second, proactive measures demand increased intelligence gathering, and much of the information will have no relation to criminal activity.
   5. Another issue is in the private sector; offensive action begins in the local community.
   6. One of the greatest potential allies is private security.
   7. Police intelligence operations and drug enforcement units can add counterterrorism to their agendas, and patrol and investigative units can be trained to look for terrorist activities in the course of their normal duties.
B. The Role of Symbols and Structures.
   1. Asymmetrical war is waged against *symbolic targets*, and homeland security is designed to secure symbols.
   2. Symbolic attacks may simply be designed to inflict massive casualties; that is, killing people has a symbolic value.
   3. It is more productive to understand that Americans represent symbolic targets of military value.
   4. Ian Lesser outlines three forms of terrorism:
      a. Symbolic terrorism is a dramatic attack to show vulnerability.
      b. Pragmatic terrorism involves a practical attempt to destroy political power.

© 2014 Cengage Learning. All Rights Reserved. May not be copied, scanned, or duplicated, in whole or in part, except for use as permitted in a license distributed with a certain product or service or otherwise on a password-protected website for classroom use.

      c. Systematic terrorism is waged over a period of time to change social conditions.

    5. Terrorists use symbolic attacks, or attacks on symbols, to achieve pragmatic or systematic results.

    6. In a time of asymmetrical war, American symbols demand protection.

    7. The key is to make symbolic targets as secure as possible, while giving the illusion that very few security precautions need to be taken.

C. Planning for Homeland Security.

    1. Effective police planning incorporates a description of a goal and methods for achieving it.

    2. The complexities of terrorism can seem overwhelming, so planning is essential.

    3. Planning can be guided by looking for threats inside local communities.

D. Creating a Culture of Information Sharing.

    1. The National Strategy for Homeland Security calls for increased information sharing among law enforcement agencies, by building a cooperative environment that enables sharing of essential information.

    2. Many of these systems are already in place:

        a. RISS information network is ideal for sharing intelligence.

        b. The High Intensity Drug Trafficking Areas system and the El Paso Intelligence Center are also sources for information sharing.

        c. International Association of Law Enforcement Intelligence Analysts routinely shares information with member agencies.

    3. Robert Taylor found two primary weaknesses in the U.S. systems:

        a. Intelligence is not properly analyzed.

        b. Agencies do not coordinate information.

    4. *Intelligence-led policing* is a continuation of community policing, where police officers anticipate and solve community problems, with citizens, before crime and social disorder increase.

    5. Intelligence-led policing not only prevents terrorism, but it becomes total criminal intelligence, and it serves to prevent and address all problems in a community.

    6. Critics say intelligence-led policing may work in conjunction with national security intelligence gathering, and there will be no oversight of the collection, analysis, and storage of information.

V.   **The 9-11 Commission and Intelligence**
    OBJ 8: List and discuss some of the major issues in homeland security
    OBJ 9: List perceived weaknesses in the homeland security from 9-11 to the present

A. The 9-11 Commission Report findings.

    1. The 9/11 Commission Report summarized some of the mistakes government agencies made as al Qaeda was growing.

2. The FBI did not emphasize the role of intelligence gathering and analysis.
3. Several misinterpretations of the Foreign Intelligence Surveillance Act of 1978 prevented intelligence agencies from sharing relevant information with FBI criminal investigators.
4. The Commission believed that America's multiple intelligence agencies did not see the attack coming because of the way the intelligence bureaucracy was structured.
5. The Commission criticized the executive branch of government because there was no overall director of intelligence; in addition, intelligence operations were hampered by reduced resources.
6. The findings also pointed to the Department of State.
7. The DOD needed more intelligence resources and greater flexibility in unconventional operations.
8. The Commission said that Congress bore much of the responsibility for the state of affairs in government – it had failed to create an effective mechanism for protecting the country.
9. American institutions and, more importantly, the American people were not overly concerned with jihadist terrorism.
B. The 9-11 Commission Report intelligence recommendations.
1. The recommendations focused on defense, intelligence, information sharing, homeland security, and law enforcement.
2. The most sweeping recommendation came with the creation of a national intelligence director.
3. Judge Richard A. Posner argues that the 9/11 Commission Report presents two competing parts.
a. First, an excellent step-by-step analysis of the events that led up to the attacks on September 11, and an explanation of actions after the terrorists struck.
b. The second part of the report is a series of recommendations.
4. In the aftermath of September 11, governmental agencies have an incentive to work together, but restructuring bureaucracy will not automatically make the United States safer.
5. Balancing security with freedom is a delicate matter, and the new intelligence infrastructure has not dealt with all the issues.
C. Responses to the 9-11 Commission.
1. Most of the support came from government agencies, and there was a range of responses among the general public.
2. Responses included:
a. Support: Government agencies responded with massive actions.
b. Conspiracy: Some critical scholars believe that the 9-11 Commission did not reveal the truth about the attacks.
i. Jay Kolar believes that the investigation of 9-11 was a cover up to protect people with political connections.

421

       ii. Diana Ralph believes the attacks were designed to inspire an American war of conquest.

    c. Covering Mistakes: A variation of conspiracy theories suggests that political actors and bureaucrats manipulate evidence to cover their mistakes or protect their interests.

    d. Unanswered Questions and Personal Bereavement: Families suffering from loss that can never be replaced, and other people who are not satisfied with the answers are critical of the 9-11 Commission report.

  3. Two of the most pressing issues deal with the decision to deploy U.S. military forces, and the nature of their mission.

VI. Intelligence Reform
OBJ 10: Discuss the aspects of intelligence reform

A. The number of people involved in intelligence, and the number of agencies doing the same work, was also unknown.

B. Over 50,000 intelligence reports were published each year, and not one agency had the authority to manage the overall operation.

  1. A panel of experts concluded that the massive endeavor was unmanaged, ineffective, and operated with no clear lines of authority.

C. Moving in the right direction?

  1. The failure of intelligence analysis is evidenced by two factors:

    a. The surprise attacks of September 11.

    b. The prediction of the WMD program in Iraq.

  2. The massive restructuring met with resistance:

    a. First, many people believed that the efficiency and methods of the intelligence community needed to be improved.

    b. Second, the new organization confused traditional lines of authority.

  3. The reorganization of intelligence under the ODNI has signaled the beginning of improvement, as the ODNI is able to balance the needs of information of all the intelligence agencies.

  4. The ODNI has also been able to attack the problem of *group think* by placing analysts in critical thinking training during the first stages of their careers.

  5. A single National Intelligence University should be created to train all analysts from every agency.

  6. The system of classifying information can be unreasonable. This happens in two primary manners:

    a. First, political actors may classify information to defend their political position.

    b. Second, bureaucracies hold classified information for power.

  7. Classification should be designed to protect sources, not information.

D. Redirecting the focus of reform.
  1. The problem in intelligence is not the structure of the system; the problem can be found with individual analysts.
  2. Personality assessment tests are able to screen people for these tendencies, and intelligence agencies should spend more time examining and selecting analysts.
  3. It is important to identify biases that an analyst brings to the job, in order to ensure that internal prejudices do not filter the information under review.
  4. Group think leads to a three-part pattern:
     a. There is sufficient new information about a surprise activity before a terrorist attack develops.
     b. Analysts ignore new information, and focus on their previous experiences with terrorism.
     c. The real life outcome is a surprise.
  5. There was tremendous pressure to reform the intelligence community after 9-11, and these calls for reform fell into two broad categories:
     a. One approach called for the comprehensive reform of the intelligence system.
     b. The second part of the debate focused on reforming the specific components of the system.
  6. The key to reform is to shift the unit of analysis away from organizational structures and consumer driven intelligence.
E. Target based analysis.
  1. The bureaucracies in the intelligence community have a tremendous stake in preserving the status quo, and protecting employees in each organization from blame for misinterpreting information.
  2. Intelligence works best when information is based on potential threats, and is shared among different levels of government.

Chapter Summary

- Americans define *homeland security* in several different ways. It has a variety of meanings to different government agencies, private organizations, and interest groups. The best way to define it is to look at the mission of the particular agency dealing with homeland security.

- After 9/11, several federal agencies were tasked with homeland security. The Departments of Homeland Security, Justice, and Defense have major roles in preventing terrorism. The intelligence community contributes to counterterrorism, and there is a major role for state, local, and tribal law enforcement to play.

- The intelligence process is very close to basic and applied academic research. It involves the legal recognition, collection, analysis, and distribution of information. *Intelligence* is "analyzed information."

- It is important to understand the legal differences between criminal intelligence and national security intelligence when using the information. National security intelligence is not meant to be used in criminal prosecutions.

- The Internal Association of Chiefs of Police (IACP) created a committee to develop national standards for criminal intelligence. This resulted in the National Criminal Intelligence Sharing Plan (NCISP). The Department of Justice created the Global Justice Information Sharing Coordinating Council (Global) to address the problems inherent in sharing information among multiple levels of law enforcement.

- Fusion centers developed from Regional Intelligence Centers. The Department of Homeland Security expanded their operations after the 9-11 attacks. Fusion centers take criminal intelligence from multiple sources and blend or "fuse" it together to create a real time picture of criminal activity. They can also forward national security intelligence without using it in criminal prosecutions.

- Law enforcement has a leading role in homeland security because of its presence in communities, and its ability to gather information. Model systems for information gathering can be found in the NJSP and the NYPD. There are several excellent federal networks such as RISS and HSIN. The HIDTA system and EPIC assist in distributing anti-terrorism intelligence, even though they were designed for drug interdiction. Federal law enforcement agencies, and several units in the Department of Homeland Security, also gather and analyze information.

- There are several important issues for homeland security. Law enforcement has a special role in terms of recognizing possible terrorist activity, and coordinating preventative measures from multiple community partnerships. Planning is a crucial part of the process. While the infrastructure is critical, symbolic targets also have a special significance. Finally, all partners responsible for homeland security must create a culture of information sharing.

- The 9/11 Commission summarized the events that led to the September 11 attacks, and recommended a response. Its recommendations included sweeping reforms in the intelligence community, the creation of a national director of intelligence, new roles for the FBI, greater cooperation among law enforcement agencies, increased domestic security safeguards, and reformed Congressional oversight. Both governmental and academic critiques question whether this has happened or not.

- While intelligence has received quite a bit of attention since 9-11, there are areas where it can be improved. The goal of creating a safe homeland should guide

intelligence efforts. Analysts must be trained to recognize broad patterns. Finally, intelligence must be based on threats to known or suspected targets.

DISCUSSION QUESTIONS

1. List the agencies responsible for homeland security and describe their functions. What could the government do to ensure cooperation between agencies? (OBJ 1 – 10)

2. List and discuss some of the major issues in homeland security. If you were to rank these issues in order , what would that look like? Explain. (OBJ 1 – 10)

3. Discuss the role of role of symbols and structures in regard to terrorism. Why does White say that symbols are important? Do you agree or disagree? Explain. (OBJ 3, 8, and 9)

4. Describe the intelligence process. How is this similar or different from academic research? (OBJ 3, 4, and 6)

CLASS ACTIVITIES

1. Have students investigate how law enforcement in their state is handling counterterrorism. If there is not a variance in regions, assign different states to individuals or groups. Do various state law enforcement agencies share information? How so? If various states are researched, what are the similarities and differences? After researching the topic, have the students discuss what they found. (OBJ 2, 3, 4, 5, 6, 7, 8, 9, and 10)

2. Have students debate the pros and cons of the "group think" concept. You may have students divided into groups or have an open debate. (OBJ 2, 3, 5, 8, 9, and 10)

3. Have the class create an organizational chart for the DHS. (OBJ 1, 2, 6, 7, 8, and 9)

4. Have students choose a topic from this chapter and write a study guide/handout to present and share with the class. For example, students may focus their study guide on describing the emergence of modern piracy. Allow time to discuss topics to eliminate duplication. (OBJ 1 – 10)

5. Have each student comb through http://www.msnbc.msn.com/id/11881780/q/homeland%20security%20public%20private%20partnerships/search//p/1/st/1/sm/user/ (or another website as approved by the instructor) for a current event, and select an article that relates to one or

more of the chapter's core concepts. Have students provide a journalistic summary and a personal opinion/reaction to the article. Have students orally present the article to the class, field Q & As from their fellow students, and provide a copy of the original source article following the presentation. Optional: Have students complete peer assessments at the end of each presentation. (OBJ 1 - 10)

MEDIA TOOLS

1. *"Wikis"*
   7 Things you should know about Wikis. Retrieved from the Web Jun 29, 2012 at http://net.educause.edu/ir/library/pdf/ELI7004.pdf

   This document offers easy to understand instruction on the history, development, and potential uses of Wikis.

   Have students develop (or make additions to a previously created one) a *Webliography* (resource list) using a Blog or Wiki that provides a short description and link to a scholarly resource pertaining to course concepts. For example, have students add two to three resources each, and ask them to add their assessment of at least one of their peers' contributions. If desired, allow time to discuss Blogs/Wikis. This activity can be reused throughout the course, by asking students to add/revise their contributions each week, bi-weekly, etc. (OBJ 1 – 10)

2. *"DHS examination….student prepared handouts"*
   "Exploring the Department of Homeland Security".
   http://www.dhs.gov

   The website for the Department of Homeland Security (DHS), which houses a number of predominant federal law enforcement agencies.

   Provide a general outline of the structure of the Department of Homeland Security. Then divide the class into groups, and have each group pick an agency housed within the DHS. Have each group prepare a handout for the class explaining which agency they were assigned, the function of that agency, and the career opportunities that agency provides for students with a criminal justice education. (OBJ 1 – 10)

3. *"Video Fusion Centers…Discussion and Debate"*
   "The Future of Fusion Centers: Potential Promise and Dangers". Retrieved from the Web Aug 21, 2012 at http://www.youtube.com/watch?v=FlHLXHg-bHk

   This video shows a government debating the future and functions of fusion centers in America.

Have students view the panel discussion, then discuss and debate the issues covered in the video. (OBJ 5 and 6)

4.   *"Current Events Article Summary with Peer Assessment"*

Use the Article Summary Template, which can be obtained on the instructor companion website, for this assignment. The template offers information on Internet research, outside resources, identification of credible sources, and detailed directions on completing an assessment of a news article. It also includes a peer evaluation tool.

Have each student comb the Internet for terrorism related news and select an article that relates to one or more of the chapter's core concepts. Be sure selections are an article of interest from a credible source (*more on credibility can be found in the article summary template above):* Fill out an article summary template. The *template asks for generic info about the article, a journalistic summary, as well as a personal opinion/reaction to the article.* Have each student summarize the article, present it orally to the class, and field Q & As from their fellow students. Have students complete peer assessments at the end of each presentation. Have students submit templates, original source article, and peer-reviews prior to the end of class. (OBJ 1 - 10)

Chapter 13—An Introduction to Homeland Security

TRUE/FALSE

1. In the 1950s the CIA tested drugs on Americans without their consent or knowledge

ANS: T   REF: p. 342   OBJ: 10

2. American policy guidelines for homeland security in the United States have been fully developed.

ANS: F   REF: p. 335   OBJ: 1 - 10

3. A major portion of homeland security involves civic responsibility.

ANS: T   REF: p. 336   OBJ: 1, 2, 5, 8, and 93

4. The essence of U.S. homeland security is to protect lives, property, and infrastructure - it is designed to secure the United States.

ANS: T   REF: p. 335   OBJ: 1 - 10

5. The New Jersey State Police have an extensive intelligence-gathering apparatus.

ANS: T   REF: p. 346   OBJ: 2 - 10

6. United States Attorneys are elected by the American public, with advice and consent of the United States Senate.

ANS: F   REF: p. 348   OBJ: 2 and 7

7. Less than half of the DHS agencies have police power.

ANS: F   REF: p. 349   OBJ: 2, 4, and 8

8. Researchers have suggested that the problem with intelligence-gathering is with the structure of the system, not with individual analysts.

ANS: F   REF: p. 349   OBJ: 3, 4, 5, 6, 7, 8, 9, and 10

9. According to Robert Poole, aviation security remains inadequate even after the 9/11 disasters.

ANS: T   REF: p. 335   OBJ: 2, 8, and 9

10. Most of the nation's infrastructure is privately owned and managed.

ANS: T   REF: p. 333   OBJ: 7 and 8

11. Spear-phishing has become one of most common methods of attacking private corporations.

ANS: T   REF: p. 333   OBJ: 4 and 9

12. Immigration and Customs Enforcement (ICE) is DHS's largest investigative arm.

ANS: T   REF: p. 336   OBJ: 2 - 10

13. The Transportation Security Administration is responsible for airport security.

ANS: T   REF: p. 336   OBJ: 2, 7, and 9

14. The Secret Service's only function is providing presidential security.

ANS: F   REF: p. 336   OBJ: 1 - 10

15. The Bureau of Alcohol, Tobacco, and Firearms (ATF) has played a leading role for years in counterterrorism.

ANS: T   REF: p. 338   OBJ: 1 - 10

MULTIPLE CHOICE

1. Civil defense evolved slowly from civilian functions during _____.
   a. World War I
   b. Korean War
   c. Vietnam War
   d. World War II

ANS: d   REF: p. 336   OBJ: 2, 8, and 9

2. Congress approved the creation of the Department of Homeland Security by uniting _____ agencies in 2002.
   a. 22
   b. 24
   c. 12
   d. 19

ANS: a   REF: p. 336   OBJ: 1 - 10

3. The DHS was created from the _____ in 2003 as a direct result of the 9/11 attacks.
    a. Federal Bureau of Investigation
    b. National Security Agency
    c. Office of Homeland Security
    d. The Bureau of Alcohol, Tobacco, and Firearms

ANS: c   REF: p. 336   OBJ: 1 - 10

4. Prior to 9/11, the U.S. Coast Guard was formerly under the _____, except in time of war.
    a. Department of Justice
    b. Department of Transportation
    c. Department of State
    d. Department of Labor

ANS: b   REF: p. 336   OBJ: 1, 8, and 9

5. The _____ provides protection to federal officials under threat from terrorism.
    a. Secret Service
    b. FBI
    c. U.S. Marshals Service
    d. NSA

ANS: c   REF: p. 338   OBJ: 1 and 2

6. The _____ counterintelligence program violated constitutional limitations on domestic intelligence-gathering and ultimately came under congressional criticism in the early 1970s.
    a. CIA
    b. FBI
    c. NIJ
    d. NSA

ANS: b   REF: p. 342   OBJ: 10

7. The New Jersey State Police Central Security Division is primarily concerned with maintaining civil peace, protecting dignitaries, and monitoring _____.
    a. Known hate groups
    b. Street gangs
    c. Organized crime
    d. Casinos

ANS: a   REF: p. 347   OBJ: 2 and 4

8. There are _____ U.S. Attorneys stationed throughout the U.S., Puerto Rico, the Virgin Island, Guam, and the Northern Mariana Islands.
    a. 90
    b. 93
    c. 98
    d. 85

ANS: b   REF: p. 348   OBJ: 1 - 10

9.   The Regional Information Sharing System (RISS) was created in what year?
       a. 2001
       b. 1996
       c. 1973
       d. 1960

ANS: c   REF: p. 344   OBJ: 2 – 7, and 10

10.   What is the lead agency in domestic terrorism?
       a. CIA
       b. DOD
       c. TSA
       d. FBI

ANS: d   REF: p. 338   OBJ: 1 - 10

11.   ATIX stands for _____.
       a. Anti-Terrorism Information Exchange
       b. American Terrorism Information Agency
       c. American Terrorist Informant Exchange Program
       d. American Terrorist Insurgency Axis

ANS: a   REF: p. 344   OBJ: 3, 5, 6, 7, and 10

12.   The California State Terrorism Threat Assessment Centers are staffed with local law
       enforcement, infrastructure protection personnel, and they work with local _____ field
       offices.
       a. FBI
       b. NSA
       c. CIA
       d. DOJ

ANS: a   REF: p. 348   OBJ: 1 - 10

13.   Which agency is NOT a part of the U.S. Office of the Director of National Intelligence
       (ODNI)?
       a. The FBI
       b. The CIA
       c. National Reconnaissance Office
       d. The National Security Agency (NSA)

ANS: a   REF: p. 339   OBJ: 2 - 10

14.   In time of war, the _____ plays the leading role.
       a. Department of State
       b. Department of Energy
       c. Department of Justice
       d. Department of Defense

ANS: d   REF: p. 338   OBJ: 2

15. The purpose of the _____ is to unite America's national security intelligence under one umbrella.
    a. Office of the Director of National Intelligence
    b. Office of National Security
    c. Central Intelligence Agency
    d. Department of National Defense

ANS: a   REF: p. 339   OBJ: 2 - 10

16. _____ is considered to be at the heart of local intelligence systems.
    a. Information hiding
    b. Information sharing
    c. Information coding
    d. Information retrieval

ANS: b   REF: p. 339   OBJ: 2 - 10

17. According to David Carter, intelligence works when information is based on _____ threats and shared among differing levels of government.
    a. Potential
    b. Confirmed
    c. Political
    d. Intangible

ANS: a   REF: p. 360   OBJ: 2 - 10

18. Created in 1973, _____ has six centers, each serving a selected group of states that share criminal information with investigators working on a variety of criminal activities, including terrorism.
    a. JTTF
    b. NCISP
    c. RISS
    d. TCI

ANS: c   REF: p. 344   OBJ: 2 - 10

19. According to the text, information from citizens defines the parameters of _____ problems.
    a. Foreign
    b. National
    c. Community
    d. Homeland security

ANS: c   REF: p. 352   OBJ: 1 - 10

20. The 9/11 Commission criticized the FBI for all of the following reasons, except _____.
    a. Not placing resources in intelligence-gathering
    b. The division established to analyze intelligence faltered
    c. The bureau did not have an effective intelligence-gathering system
    d. The bureau felt that shared no responsibility in dealing with terrorism

ANS: d   REF: p. 353   OBJ: 2 - 10

21. The number of U.S. top secret security clearances in 2010 was _____.
    a. 1,900
    b. 256,000
    c. 854,000
    d. 25,700

ANS: c   REF: p. 359   OBJ: 2 - 10

22. Regional Intelligence Centers were originally established to gather intelligence on what activity?
    a. Domestic terrorism
    b. International terrorism
    c. Espionage
    d. Drug trafficking

ANS: d   REF: p. 345   OBJ: 2 - 10

23. _____ has become one of most common methods of attacking private corporations.
    a. Spear-phishing
    b. Armed robbery
    c. Bombing
    d. Boycotting

ANS: a   REF: p. 333   OBJ: 8 and 9

24. Scholar Stephen Flynn's greatest criticism of homeland security is aimed at U.S. _____.
    a. Technology
    b. Borders
    c. Security analysts
    d. Military

ANS: b   REF: p. 335   OBJ: 1 - 10

25. Under whose administration did the government begin to limit the power of intelligence operations, unintentionally hampering their effectiveness?
    a. Jimmy Carter
    b. Bill Clinton
    c. George W. Bush
    d. Ronald Reagan

ANS: a   REF: p. 342   OBJ: 2 – 10

26. Which of the following is not one of David Carter's "R-cubed" to police intelligence? approach: reassess, refocus, and reallocate.

    a. Reassess
    b. Refocus
    c. Revise
    d. Reallocate

ANS: c   REF: p. 343   OBJ: 2 - 10

27.   _____ is/are responsible for breaking some of America's most formidable terrorist cells.
   a.   Foreign agencies
   b.   The general public
   c.   Government contractors
   d.   Police agencies

ANS: d   REF: p. 349   OBJ: 2 - 8

28.   What is HIDTAs?
   a.   The High Intensity Drug Trafficking Areas system
   b.   The Homeland Informants, Drug, and Terrorist Analysis Sector
   c.   The Highly Impact Department for Terrorism Assessment system
   d.   The Homeland Insurgency Deterrent Training Arrangement system

ANS: a   REF: p. 351   OBJ: 2

29.   Asymmetrical war is most often waged against _____ targets.
   a.   Systematic
   b.   Symbolic
   c.   Economic
   d.   Democratic

ANS: b   REF: p. 350   OBJ: 8

30.   _____ is specifically responsible for protecting nuclear materials, power grids, and gas lines.
   a.   the Department of Homeland Security (DHS)
   b.   the Department of Defense (DOD)
   c.   the Department of Energy (DOE)
   d.   the Department of the Interior (DOI)

ANS: c   REF: p. 335   OBJ: 2, 8, and 9

31.   Which of the following is NOT an example of a civil defense structure?
   a.   Missile silo
   b.   Private and public broadcasting
   c.   Evacuation routes
   d.   Fallout shelters

ANS: a   REF: p. 336   OBJ: 2

32.   What entity approved the creation of the DHS in 2002?
   a.   Congress
   b.   The President
   c.   Senate
   d.   The U.S. Supreme Court

ANS: a   REF: p. 336   OBJ: 2 - 10

33.	Who was the director of the FBI at the time of the 9/11 attacks?
	a.	Thomas Pickard
	b.	Robert S. Mueller
	c.	Louis J. Freeh
	d.	Floyd I. Clarke

ANS: b	REF: p. 338	OBJ: 9

34.	_____ are one of the most frequent weapons used in terrorism.
	a.	Biological agents
	b.	Bombs
	c.	Chemical agents
	d.	Nuclear weapons

ANS: b	REF: p. 338	OBJ: 8 - 9

35.	The Constitution forbids military forces from enforcing civil law except in times of
	_____.
	a.	Declared martial law
	b.	War
	c.	Attempted Presidential assassination
	d.	Natural catastrophes

ANS: a	REF: p. 338	OBJ: 2, 8, and 9

36.	COINTELPRO was the name given to what agency's counterintelligence program?
	a.	The FBI
	b.	The CIA
	c.	The NSA
	d.	The DOD

ANS: a	REF: p. 342	OBJ: 2 - 10

37.	JTTF agents may NOT use national security intelligence within _____.
	a.	Foreign operations
	b.	Terrorist identification
	c.	U.S. borders
	d.	Criminal prosecutions

ANS: d	REF: p. 348	OBJ: 3, 4, 8, and 9

38.	Despite confusion regarding counter-terrorist roles in Federal government, roles are
	divided into three distinct functions: preventing terrorism, responding to attacks, and
	_____?
	a.	Provision of funding for operations
	b.	International diplomacy efforts
	c.	Provision of technical support to local agencies
	d.	Civil defense measures

ANS: c	REF: p. 335	OBJ: 1 and 2

39. With the advent of radio-dispatched motorized patrol, _____ became the measure of police effectiveness.
    a. Interagency cooperation
    b. Arrest statistics
    c. Response time
    d. Successful prosecutions

ANS: c   REF: p. 349   OBJ: 2, 8, and 9

40. Indicators such as an increase in violent rhetoric, the appearance of extremist groups, and increases in certain types of crimes may demonstrate that _____ is on the horizon.
    a. A terrorist threat
    b. A natural disaster
    c. A Presidential election
    d. Martial law

ANS: a   REF: p. 351   OBJ: 1 - 10

Case 13.0

In the autumn of 2004, the Department of Defense (DOD) held a conference on special operations that combined the military's counterterrorism efforts with American law enforcement's. Three leading officials from the Presidential administration spoke about homeland security, outlining the national strategy. One of the speakers cited the three major elements of the administration's policy. Another official said that there were five major elements to President Bush's plans, and the last speaker, an advisor from the White House, said that there were four elements to the national strategy. A frustrated Army officer asked the last speaker if the United States had three, four, or five elements to its counterterrorist policy. The speaker answered that he did not know, but it was not important.

41. The scenario describes above demonstrates which of the following?
    a. A definitive hierarchy for U.S. homeland security
    b. A clear-cut description of the nation's counterterrorism strategy
    c. Why confusion surrounds the term *homeland security*
    d. The functions of DHS

ANS: c   REF: p. 334   OBJ: 1 – 10

42. Who was the President at the time of the special conference?
    a. George W. Bush
    b. Barrack Obama
    c. Bill Clinton
    d. George H. Bush

ANS: a   REF: p. 334   OBJ: 1 – 10

Case 13.1

One of most common methods of attacking private corporations begins with the attackers doing research on employees, generally through social network sites. The attackers devise a strategy to send e-mails to selected targets with lures to get them to open e-mails containing malicious software. The e-mails appear to be sent from close associates of the selected target.

When the e-mail is opened, a hacker can enter the system through the portal. According to Clayton's report, once the system has been compromised, the attackers seek to gain control of settings. Cyber experts said that control of gas flow and pressure could lead to disruption of services, systemic failures, and even explosions. The attack indicates that the infrastructure is vulnerable in the age of terrorism.

43. The attack method described above is known as _____?
    a. Identity theft
    b. Spear-phishing
    c. Earth First!
    d. Sovereign Citizen movement

ANS: b   REF: p. 333   OBJ: 2 and 8

44. Denial of Service attacks, such as the spear-phishing method outlined above, are classed as what form of terrorism?
    a. Narco-terrorism
    b. Racial terrorism
    c. Eco-terrorism
    d. Cyber-terrorism

ANS: d   REF: p. 333   OBJ: 4 and 8

45. Which of the following entities would be the LEAST desirable target for a Denial of Service attack?
    a. A local radio station
    b. U.S. Air Traffic Control
    c. The L.A. Freeway system
    d. The Nation's energy supply

ANS: a   REF: p. 350   OBJ: 8 and 9

46. Which of the following entities would be the MOST desirable target for a Denial of Service attack?
    a. A Disney cruise ship
    b. U.S. Air Traffic Control
    c. The Nation's Freeway system
    d. The Nation's water supply

ANS: a   REF: p. 350   OBJ: 8 and 9

47. Which of the following attacks would be classified as cyber-terrorism?
    a. Bombing of a University's computer lab
    b. Using a friend's Facebook account without authorization
    c. Release of animals from an animal testing lab
    d. Implanting a Trojan horse virus upon a company's network

ANS: b   REF: p. 333   OBJ: 4

Case 13.2

Homeland security also involves civil defense, that is, citizens engaged in homeland security. Civil defense did not develop overnight; rather, it emerged slowly from civilian functions during World War II. After 1960, civil defense structures were intended to help government protect citizens in areas, such as emergency communications, through private and public broadcasting, direct assistance during emergencies, evacuation routes, and fallout shelters. During the Cold War various organizations involved in civil defense gradually learned specific missions. The idea of "civil defense" will take on a new meaning in the coming years because the nature of conflict has changed. Homeland security is much more than the sum of agencies charged with protecting the United States. A major portion of security is a civic responsibility.

48. Which of the following is an example of civil defense?
    a. Defense contractors
    b. HAM radio operators
    c. Military operatives
    d. CIA agents

ANS: b   REF: p. 335   OBJ: 1 – 10

49. Which of the following groups would NOT be classed as civil defense?
    a. The Red Cross
    b. Community Emergency Response Teams (CERT)
    c. FEMA
    d. The Salvation Army

ANS: c   REF: p. 336   OBJ: 1 – 10

50. Fall out shelters were built during the cold war for fear of what type of attack?
    a. Chemical agent
    b. Nuclear
    c. Artillery
    d. Biological agent

ANS: b   REF: p. 335   OBJ: 1 – 10

COMPLETION

1. There are approximately _____ miles of interstate gas pipelines in the United States.

ANS: 200,000   REF: p. 333   OBJ: 8 and 9

2. The 9/11 Commission believed that America's multiple intelligence agencies did not see the attack coming because of the way the _____ was structured.

ANS: intelligence bureaucracy   REF: p. 335   OBJ: 2 - 10

3. The State Department had lost much of its ability to establish foreign policy because foreign policy planning had been shifting to the National Security Council (NSC) and the _____ since 1960.

ANS: DOD   REF: p. 355   OBJ: 2 - 10

4. The 9/11 Commission criticized the _____ of the government because there was no overall director of intelligence.

ANS: executive branch   REF: p. 355   OBJ: 2 - 10

5. The ODNI has also been able to attack the problem of _____ by placing analysts in critical thinking training during the first stages of their careers.

ANS: group think   REF: p. 358   OBJ: 2 - 10

6. _____ intelligence cannot legally be used for criminal prosecutions.

ANS: National security   REF: p. 341   OBJ: 2-10

7. Model systems for information gathering can be found in the New Jersey State Police, the California Anti-Terrorism Information Center, and the _____Police Department.

ANS: New York   REF: p. 348   OBJ: 2 – 7, and 10

8. Many counterterrorist experts believe that the southern border will become one of the main infiltration routes for _____ terrorists.

ANS: jihadist   REF: p. 335   OBJ: 2, 8, and 9

9. _____ refers to a system of agencies and networks that gather information about threats to the country.

ANS: National security intelligence REF: p. 339   OBJ: 1 - 10

10. The ODNI the CIA, the National Security Agency, the Defense Intelligence Agency, the_____, and the National Reconnaissance Office.

ANS: National Geospatial-Intelligence Agency   REF: 339   OBJ: 1 - 10

11. Some of the law enforcement agencies that report to the _____include the FBI's National Security Branch, the DOE's Office of Intelligence and Counterintelligence, and the DHS's Office of Intelligence and Analysis.

ANS: Director of National Intelligence   REF: p. 339   OBJ: 1 - 10

12. Human intelligence come from _____, informers, defectors, and other people.
ANS: spies   REF: p. 343   OBJ: 2 - 10

13. The Homeland Security Information Network (HSIN) is set up to connect all jurisdictions with ___ communication.

ANS: real-time   REF: p. 344   OBJ: 2 - 10

14. The Homeland Security Information Network (HSIN) is a computer-based counterterrorism communications system connecting all fifty states, five territories, Washington, D.C., and ___ major urban areas.

ANS: fifty   REF: p. 344   OBJ: 2 - 10

15. _____ intelligence is gathered to defend the nation. It is not used in criminal prosecutions, and it is not subject to legal scrutiny.

ANS: National security   REF: p. 341   OBJ: 3 - 7

16. Two types of private-sector organizations participate in homeland security: businesses providing _____ and businesses centered on security technology and service.

ANS: critical infrastructure   REF: p. 336   OBJ: 2, 3, 5, and 7

17. Homeland security also involves _____, that is, citizens engaged in homeland security.

ANS: civil defense   REF: p. 336   OBJ: 2, 7, 8, and 9

18. The Coast Guard and Secret Service may be found in the Department of Homeland Security, while the Federal Bureau of Investigation (FBI) and the Bureau of Alcohol, Tobacco, and Firearms (ATF) are located in the Department of _____.

ANS: defense   REF: 338   OBJ: 2

19. _____targets have limited military or security value to terrorists but represent the power of the state under attack.

ANS: symbolic   REF: 350   OBJ: 5

20. When raw information is analyzed to reveal patterns of suspicious activity, suspicious behavior, vulnerable targets, and probability of attack, it is called a(n) _____ product.

ANS: intelligence   REF: 346   OBJ: 6

ESSAY

1.   Why is there confusion in defining Homeland Security?

ANS:
- The reason for the initial confusion about policy is that America had no common definition of homeland security.
- Issues surrounding homeland security were confused because the country was dealing with a new concept, a new meaning of conflict, and a change in the procedures used to defend the United States.

- In the past, military forces protected the homeland, projecting power beyond U.S. borders, but the world changed with the end of the cold war in 1991.
- Another reason for confusion lies in the fact that the new Department of Homeland Security (DHS) was responsible for protecting the borders and the country's interior.
- Coupled with this state of affairs were bureaucratic efforts to redefine relations among agencies.
- The situation was further complicated when state and local governments became involved.
- Finally, a host of private businesses, nonprofit organizations, and health care systems were involved in security efforts. It was not easy to find a common definition for homeland security.
- Confusion remains. For example, there are debates about the constitutionality of some aspects of governmental functions and laws that followed the 9/11 attacks.
- There are tremendous differences of opinion about the use of the military in the war on terrorism, and this is highlighted in passionate debates about the effectiveness of the Iraq War.
- Foreign policy relationships and the use of intelligence also are debated within the homeland security discussion.
- Many federal, state, local, and tribal police agencies still search for their mission.

REF: p. 334   OBJ: 1 - 10

2. Explain how the federal government envisions the intelligence roles of the local government.

ANS:
- State, local, and tribal law enforcement agencies need to collect tactical intelligence for the prevention of terrorism and other crimes.
- They must also use intelligence for planning and the deployment of resources.
- Information sharing is at the heart of local intelligence systems.
- Chief Gary Vest says that agencies are sharing information at an unprecedented level, but they need to enhance the process by creating systems governed by policies.
- Chief Vest believes that agencies need to form associations with governing boards that have the power to enforce rules and regulations.
- This will regulate intelligence within the law, prevent leaks, and provide routine methods to share information.
- David Carter says the role of intelligence and information sharing among state, local, and tribal law enforcement agencies enhances counterterrorism efforts.
- Large federal systems operate on a global basis, and officers in local communities know their jurisdictions better than anyone.
- Community partnerships enhance the amount and quality of information they can accumulate.
- The federal government does not have the resources or the community contacts to develop these links.
- The National Criminal Intelligence Sharing Plan comes to the same conclusion.

- The ability of state, local, and tribal agencies to share information is at the heart of preventing terrorist strikes within the borders of the United States.
- When it comes to terrorism, state, local, and tribal agencies are crucial to homeland security.

REF: p. 339   OBJ: 2 - 10

3.   What did Nancy Tucker suggest as the failure of the 9/11 intelligence analysis? Discuss the response of Congress to these failures.

ANS:
- Nancy Tucker suggests that the failure of intelligence analysis is evidenced by two factors: the surprise attacks of September 11 and the prediction of the WMD program in Iraq.
- Congress created the Office of the Director of National Intelligence (ODNI) to address such flaws.
- ODNI was to be a vehicle for continuous reform, an organization to prevent bureaucratic goal displacement and organizational stagnation.
- This massive restructuring met all types of resistance.
- First, many people believed that the efficiency and methods of the intelligence community needed to be improved.
- Restructuring created another level of bureaucracy, but it did not address the need for accuracy and efficiency.
- Second, the new organization confused traditional lines of authority – more specifically the Director of the CIA was to be the one person who could synthesize information and present an apolitical, objective assessment of data to the executive branch of government.
- Tucker believes the reorganization of intelligence under the ODNI has signaled the beginning of improvement.
- The ODNI is able to balance the needs of information of all the intelligence agencies.
- In the past the CIA director performed this function, but was always forced to guard the interests of the CIA.
- The ODNI is able to avoid this bureaucratic pitfall producing a better balance in analyzed information.
- The ODNI has also been able to attack the problem of group think by placing analysts in critical thinking training during the first stages of their careers.

REF: p. 358   OBJ: 1 - 10

4.   List the reforms suggested by the 9/11 Commission.

ANS:
- Create a National Counterterrorism Center.
- Create a director of national intelligence to oversee intelligence gathering and all the agencies involved in national defense intelligence.
- Refocus the CIA. Reporting to the director of national intelligence, the CIA director should: build the analysis capability of the CIA; increase information gathered from

people; develop extensive language capabilities; recruit from diverse groups in order to have agents who can blend with a variety of cultures; establish routine communications with other agencies.

- Paramilitary operations should move to Special Operations in the Defense Department.
- Covert operations should move to the Defense Department, Northern Command should assume responsibility for military threats against the United States.
- Make the intelligence budget public.
- Demand that agencies share information.
- Streamline and strengthen congressional oversight of intelligence and homeland security.
- Accelerate the appointment of national security administrators during presidential transitions.
- Introduce new structures in the FBI: create career paths for agents and others assigned to intelligence and national security; create a culture of cross-fertilization between criminal justice and national defense; and restructure the budget to emphasize (1) intelligence, (2) counterterrorism and counterintelligence, (3) law enforcement, and (4) criminal justice services.
- The Department of Homeland Security should: assess threats, develop and test emergency plan, protect the critical infrastructure, and create a system for response to threats and attacks.

REF: p. 355   OBJ: LO7

5.   What is the Homeland Security Information Network? Discuss its purpose.

ANS:
- Carter notes that the Department of Homeland Security has also created an intelligence system.
- The Homeland Security Information Network (HSIN) is set up to connect all jurisdictions with real-time communication.
- It includes state homeland security officials, the National Guard, emergency operations centers, and local emergency service providers.
- HSIN provides encrypted communications on a secure network. Designed to combine the criminal information of RISS with critical infrastructure protection, HSIN is designed to unite all the different organizations involved in homeland security.
- Critics maintain that the system is underused and that it duplicates the functions of proven systems like RISS.
- The Homeland Security Information Network (HSIN) is a computer-based counterterrorism communications system connecting all 50 states, five territories, Washington, D.C., and 50 major urban areas.
- The HSIN allows all states and major urban areas to collect and disseminate information between federal, state, and local agencies involved in combating terrorism.
- It also helps provide situational awareness facilitates information sharing and collaboration with homeland security partners throughout the federal, state and local levels provides advanced analytic capabilities enables real time sharing of threat information.

- This communications capability delivers to states and major urban areas real-time interactive connectivity with the National Operations Center.
- This collaborative communications environment was developed by state and local authorities.

REF: p.344   OBJ: 1 - 10

6.   Explain the comparison of intelligence-gathering to academic research, as indicated in the text. Explain how this process is directly applicable to gathering intelligence.

ANS:
- Before beginning, a researcher needs basic knowledge of a field and an understanding of sub-disciplines.
- Much of this background information has no direct bearing on the actual question a researcher is trying to answer, but without background preparation, the researcher cannot address the question.
- Command of basic information allows the researcher to move toward applying results.
- Applied information, the specificity the researcher seeks, is divided into both in-depth knowledge about a specific topic and the latest information from the discipline.
- In the sciences and social sciences, this process leads a researcher from general concepts to applied ideas, from abstract principles to glimpses of reality.
- Although academic in nature, this process is directly applicable to gathering intelligence. Police intelligence systems can be modeled after academic research.
- Basic intelligence involves general information about a subject and its sub-disciplines.
- Applied intelligence involves gathering basic information about a target and real-time information about current activities.
- The practical application of this process comes through organizing structures aimed at collecting, analyzing, and forwarding information.
- Someone in every American law enforcement agency should be assigned to collect and forward terrorist intelligence.
- In small agencies this may mean assigning a person who represents several police and sheriff's departments, and in moderate-size agencies the function could be performed in the detective bureau or the planning unit.
- Large metropolitan and state police agencies need full-time intelligence units. At the state and regional levels, efforts must be made to assemble, categorize, and analyze information and place it within national and international contexts.

REF: p. 340   OBJ: 2 - 10

7.   Define national security intelligence and criminal intelligence, what is the difference between national security and law enforcement? According to Richard Best, what two channels of information should law enforcement plan and develop?

ANS:
- National security intelligence is gathered to defend the nation; it is not used in criminal prosecutions and is not subject to legal scrutiny.
- It is a system of agencies and networks that gather information about threats to the country – any threat or potential threat is examined under the auspices of national defense intelligence.

444

- Unlike criminal intelligence, people and agencies gathering defense information do not need to suspect any criminal activity.
- The FBI is empowered to gather defense intelligence.
- Criminal intelligence is gathered by law enforcement and prosecuting attorneys; it cannot be gathered, analyzed, or stored without reason to believe that a crime is about to take place or has taken place.
- Criminal intelligence is information gathered on the reasonable suspicion that a criminal activity is occurring or about to occur.
- It is collected by law enforcement agencies in the course of their preventive and investigative functions.
- It is shared on information networks such as the Regional Information Sharing System (RISS).
- Agencies must suspect some violation of criminal law before they can collect intelligence.
- Richard Best argues that national security differs from law enforcement.
- In police work, officers react to information provided voluntarily.
- Police actions are governed by the rules of evidence, and the ultimate purpose is to protect the rights of citizens, including those who have been arrested.
- National security intelligence, on the other hand, is used to anticipate threats.
- It uses aggressive methods to collect information, including, at times, operations in violation of the law.
- National security intelligence is ultimately designed to protect targets, not individuals' rights.
- Using Best's insight, law enforcement should plan and develop two channels for information.
- One channel should be aimed at law enforcement intelligence, that is, the types of information police agencies collect; this information is based on criminal activity and the protection of individual rights.
- It is governed by the rules of evidence; yet police agencies will inevitably come upon defense information, especially when monitoring community indicators.
- Much of this intelligence will not be used in criminal investigation.
- At this point, state and local police agencies should be prepared to pass such information along to defense sources.
- These two paths for information, one for criminal investigation and one for national security, can serve as the basis for dealing with intelligence collected by state and local police agencies.

REF: p. 341   OBJ: 2 – 10

8. Briefly explain the New Jersey Intelligence System and the California Intelligence System. Why are these agencies important when discussing the mission of intelligence gathering in a post-9/11 world?

ANS:
- The New Jersey State Police (NJSP) has an extensive intelligence-gathering apparatus made up of three main divisions; the Intelligence Bureau is the largest division, composed of six units.
- The Analytical Unit is responsible for reviewing data from organized-crime families and street gangs; it synthesizes information to produce a broad picture of the entire state, and it also conducts threat assessments for major public events.
- The Casino Intelligence Unit collects information on gambling affiliations of traditional and nontraditional crimes; it also serves as the government's liaison for regulatory agencies and conducts background investigations on contractors working in the casino industry.
- The Electronic Surveillance Unit conducts court-authorized monitoring and assists federal agencies in national security investigations.
- Critical information is shared through the Liaison Computerized Services Unit, including the sharing of information with agencies outside New Jersey; the Services Unit also codifies and organizes intelligence reports.
- The Street Gang Unit collects information and works with local gang task forces.
- The NJSP system is a model for gathering, organizing, analyzing, and sharing criminal information.
- The Central Security Division is responsible for New Jersey's counterterrorist mission; its primary purpose is the prevention of terrorist activities through intelligence operations; it is a proactive organization designed to prevent terrorism through interdiction.
- The Central Security Division is primarily concerned with maintaining civil peace, protecting dignitaries, and monitoring known hate groups.
- The Solid Waste Division, which gathers information about hazardous materials and keeps an eye on organized crime, and the Casino Bureau round out the organization of the NJSP Intelligence Service Section.
- The key to its organization and its preventive capabilities is the collection, analysis, and sharing of information.
- The California Anti-Terrorism Information Center (CATIC) was formed after September 11; this statewide intelligence system was designed to combat terrorism.
- The center linked federal, state, and local information services in one system and divided operational zones into five administrative areas.
- The design called for trained intelligence analysts to operate within civil rights guidelines and to use information in a secure communications system.
- CATIC combines machine intelligence, that is, the type of information that can be gathered by computers and other automated devices, with information coming from a variety of police agencies.
- The information was correlated and organized by analysts looking for trends; future projections were made by looking at past indicators.

446

- CATIC combined public information with data on criminal trends and possible terrorist activities.
- Processed intelligence produced threat assessments for each area and projected trends outside the jurisdiction.
- California created new systems under the tight control of regional law enforcement agencies and in partnership with four regional JTTFs.
- The State Terrorism Threat Assessment Center now coordinates the activities of regional threat-assessment centers; modeled after fusion center plans, the system works with only criminal intelligence.
- The regional centers are staffed with local law enforcement and infrastructure protection personnel, and they work with the local FBI field offices.

REF: p. 347-348   OBJ: 2 - 10

9.   What do symbols hold special importance for terrorism and counterterrorism?

ANS:
- Asymmetrical war is waged against symbolic targets, and homeland security is designed to secure symbols.
- Just because a target has symbolic significance does not mean it lacks physical reality.
- The bombing of the Murrah Federal Building in Oklahoma City in 1995, for example, had symbolic value, and the casualties were horrific.
- Attacks against symbols disrupt support structures and can have a high human toll. Defensive measures are put in place to protect both the physical safety of people and property as well as the symbolic meaning of a target
- Grenville Byford points out that symbolic attack may simply be designed to inflict massive casualties; that is, killing people has a symbolic value.
- Killing civilians serves a political purpose for terrorists – American citizens contribute economically to the well-being of the country, and because they participate in a democracy, they ultimately control military policy.
- Targeting them may have practical as well as symbolic value.
- Rather than engaging in political rhetoric about morality it is more productive to understand that Americans represent symbolic targets of military value.
- Symbolic terrorism is a dramatic attack to show vulnerability.
- Terrorists use symbolic attacks or attacks on symbols to achieve pragmatic or systematic results.
- Symbols can have literal and abstract meanings, such as a capitol that serves literally and abstractly as the seat of governmental power.
- The key to security is to offer protection without destroying abstract meanings.
- All societies create symbols, and American democracy is no different.
- In a time of asymmetrical war, American symbols demand protection; the key is to make symbolic targets as secure as possible while giving the illusion that very few security precautions have been taken.

REF: p. 350   OBJ: 2 - 10

10. Debate the reasons why Congress received special attention from the 9/11 Commission. Describe both sides of the argument and the key points used to defend one's stance in agreeing or disagreeing with this special attention.

ANS:
- The Commission said that Congress bore much of the responsibility for the state of affairs in government.
- It had failed to create an effective mechanism for protecting the country.
- It maintained a large bureaucracy with ineffective oversight and communication. Among the issues noted by the 9-11 Commission were:
- There were too many committees overseeing intelligence.
- Like the intelligence community, Congress was structured for a cold war enemy.
- Congressional priorities were in areas other than terrorism.
- Congress was slow to react to terrorism and favored local domestic issues over those of national security.
- The 9/11 Commission points out that it was easy to develop this critique with hindsight.
- As the jihadist network developed, only a few people, such as Dale Watson of the FBI and Richard Clarke of the White House staff, were focused on counterterrorism.
- American institutions and, more importantly, the American people were not overly concerned with jihadist terrorism.
- As the jihadist network grew, Americans looked the other way.
- Views will vary.

REF: p. 355   OBJ: 1 - 10

CHAPTER 14

Law Enforcement and Homeland Security

Learning Objectives

After reading this chapter, students should be able to:

1. Outline law enforcement's bureaucracy challenge.
2. Explain the ways homeland security represents Weberian bureaucracy.
3. Summarize bureaucratic issues within criminal and national security intelligence agencies.
4. Explain issues involved in border protection.
5. Discuss the ways the immigration debate impacts homeland security.
6. Define and describe infrastructure protection.
7. Describe the need for partnerships in homeland security.
8. Summarize the critical bureaucratic issues in law enforcement partnerships.
9. Outline Flynn's recommendations for effective homeland security.
10. Explain how the Joint Terrorism Task Force (JTTF) arrangement might become a model for law enforcement partnerships.

Chapter Key Terms

Bureaucracy, p. 365

1978 Civil Service Reform Act, p. 365

Government Management Reform Act of 1994, p. 365

Max Weber, p. 365

National Counterterrorism Center (NCTC), p. 367

Task orientation, p. 369

Threat analysis, p. 369

Goal displacement, p. 369

Mission creep, p. 369

Process orientation, p. 369

Pre-incident indicators, p. 369

Working group, p. 370

Actionable intelligence, p. 381

Bureaucracy: Governmental, private-sector, and non-profit organizations. It assumes that people organize in a hierarchy to create an organization that will solve problems.

1978 Civil Service Reform Act: A federal law designed to prevent political interference with the decisions and actions of governmental organizations.

Government Management Reform Act of 1994: A federal law designed to prevent political interference in the management of federal governmental organizations and to increase the efficiency of management.

Max Weber: (1864– 1920) One of the major figures of modern sociological methods, he studied the organization of human endeavours. Weber believed that social organizations could be organized for rational purposes designed to accomplish objectives.

National Counterterrorism Center (NCTC): An organization designed to filter information from the intelligence process, synthesize counterterrorist information, and share it with appropriate organizations.

task orientation: As used in this text, the ability to stay focused on the primary mission of an organization.

threat analysis: The process of examining a community to determine the areas that might be subject to attack and the criticality of those areas to the functions of the community.

Goal displacement: over emphasizing issues not associated with organizational goals

Mission creep: adding too many secondary tasks to a unit. Too many jobs divert a unit from its primary mission.

Goal displacement: favoring process over accomplishments. Process should be reasonable and efficient. Too much focus on the process, however, interferes with completion of job tasks.

pre-incident indicators: The criminal and social actions of individuals and groups before a terrorist attack.

working group: A term used in the federal government for a group of subject matter experts who gather to suggest solutions to common problems.

actionable intelligence: Information those law enforcement agencies, military units, or other security forces can use to prevent an attack or operation.

intelligence product: Any outcome or output of analyzed information that can be used by law enforcement agencies, military units, or security forces to take an immediate action.

Terrorism Screening Center (TSC): A multiagency operation in West Virginia that evaluates information gathered from a variety of governmental sources.

emergency-response plans: Preparations from any agency to deal with natural, accidental, or man-made disasters. They involve controlling the incident through an organized response-and-command system and assigning various organizations to supervise the restoration of social order.

Chapter Outline

I. **The Bureaucracy Problem**
    OBJ 1: Outline law enforcement's bureaucracy challenge
    OBJ 2: Explain the ways homeland security represents Weberian bureaucracy
    OBJ 3: Summarize bureaucratic issues within criminal and national security intelligence agencies

A. The federal government undertook massive reforms and reorganizations from 2002 to 2005, in the wake of 9/11.
B. Critics believe that the organizational problems involving federal, state, local, and tribal law enforcement cannot be handled until the nation's lawmakers restructure their own lawmaking *bureaucracy.*
C. Homeland security calls for new alliances among federal agencies, and cooperative relations among local, state, and federal levels of government.
D. The Weberian ideal
    1. *Max Weber* coined the term "bureaucracy" to describe professional, rational organizations.
    2. Every aspect of organizational structure was to be aimed at rationally producing a goal.
    3. Weber believed that impersonal, professional human groups (bureaucracies) converge to solve the problems of society.
    4. In Weber's ideal, labor is to be divided into specific functions or bureaus, and all the bureaus or functions of the organization are to assemble logically to produce the whole.
    5. Running an organization is a complicated affair, and the larger and more complex the organization becomes the more difficult it is to manage.
E. Bureaucracy and preventing terrorism.
    1. There are two views concerning expanded homeland security bureaucracy.
        a. Supporters of one position maintain that consolidating power is efficient.
        b. Proponents of a second position suggest that decentralizing power personalizes services and helps develop links to communities.
F. Intelligence and bureaucracy.
    1. The role of law enforcement and intelligence in homeland security is not exempted from the issues surrounding bureaucracy.

451

2. Both intelligence-gathering and law enforcement organizations operate within the American political system.
3. Internally, conflicts arise from personal rivalries, territorial fights, and power struggles.
4. In the United States, however, the lead agency for counterterrorism is the FBI; it has several charges in this realm:
   a. First, under Director Robert Mueller its charge is to prevent terrorism.
   b. Second, it is to coordinate intelligence-gathering and intelligence-sharing activities with the Border Patrol, Secret Service, and CIA.
   c. Third, it is to operate as a partner of state and local law enforcement.
   d. Fourth, because the FBI is in the Department of Justice, it is to coordinate its activities with Department of Homeland Security (DHS) and the Department of Defense (DOD).
5. This face of homeland security involves a new role for the CIA, which is to cooperate fully with the FBI on counterterrorism intelligence.
6. The DHS was created from the Office of Homeland Security in 2003, and is charged with counterterrorism; it is the largest organization involved in homeland security.
7. The Department of Defense has a limited, but critical, role in homeland security.
8. In theory, led by the FBI and the CIA, multiple agencies will work together to gain information, analyze it together, and share the results with every bureaucracy concerned with homeland security.
9. One of the top priorities of the federal government has focused on creating a system where information can flow among the various levels of government from and through America's police agencies.
G. State, local, and tribal law enforcement bureaucracies
   1. There are issues to overcome and partnerships with external agencies to be created.
   2. The first issue to overcome is to build a consensus among differing police agencies on the task to be accomplished.
      a. *Task orientation* will focus the actions of individual departments as they meet the homeland security needs within their communities.
      b. This is accomplished by *threat analysis,* information gathering, and information sharing.
   3. Officers need to become aware of the types of activities that take place before an attack; these are known as *pre-incident indicators.*
   4. Bureaucratic changes present challenges, but they also provide opportunities.
      a. Community Policing
      b. National Criminal Intelligence Sharing Plan (NCISP)

        i.   The concept of information gathering, analysis, and sharing began with the Global Advisory Committee to the U.S. attorney general, and moved to a working group of executives from all levels of law enforcement.

5. The many different organizations that compose state, local, and tribal law enforcement agencies face a daunting task in transforming bureaucracy, but ultimately it must be focused on preventing terrorism.

II.   **Border Protection**
      OBJ 4: Explain issues involved in border protection
      OBJ 5: Discuss the ways the immigration debate impacts homeland security

A. Besides the various law enforcement– and intelligence-related functions, the federal government has another major goal: to protect America's borders.

B. The main agencies responsible for border protection include Customs and Border Protection, Immigration and Customs Enforcement (ICE), and the Coast Guard.

C. American borders are vulnerable in several areas.
1. Long stretches of unprotected areas along the northern and southern borders are open to infiltration, and more than 300 seaports must be secured.

D. Policy disputes.
1. Critics say that DHS activities, broad as they may be, are not altogether effective.
2. Some DHS policies have not been popular with other countries.
3. Local governments have been asked to assist with border protection, but some of them have balked at the idea.
    a. Many local governments feel they need the trust and cooperation of foreigners living in their areas.
4. The 9/11 Commission Report addressed the issue of border security and suggested sweeping reforms.
5. The Commission recommended standardizing the bureaucratic response for monitoring the entry of foreign nationals.

E. The immigration debate.
1. One of the controversial issues surrounding border protection involves immigration.
2. Many elected officials argue that the United States cannot be secure unless its borders are secure.
3. Patrick Buchanan argues that by allowing the unregulated flow of immigrants from the southern border, the United States opens the door to terrorist infiltration.

4. Most of the people concerned with border security make the distinction between legal and illegal immigration, and their primary concern reflects a desire for the rule of law.
5. Kerry Diminyatz:
   a. The southern border is not secure, and DHS plans for securing the border have not been adequate.
   b. This is a security threat, not only in terms of terrorism, but also from a variety of other criminal activities.
   c. It is possible to secure the border, but it will take major reforms.
   d. The major issues involve economic, social, and political inequities and corruption on both sides of the border.
   e. Failure to protect the southern border presents four major national security threats:
      i. Terrorism and WMD
      ii. Drug Trafficking
      iii. Human Smuggling
      iv. Infectious Disease
   f. The most significant threat of unregulated immigration comes from terrorism and organized crime.
   g. The multiple bureaucracies responsible for border security are inefficient, and therefore fails to properly focus all efforts.
6. The federal government seeks to form partnerships with local communities so that state, local, and tribal law enforcement officers can act as an extension of agencies charged with border security.
7. Congress has considered a number of methods—national identification cards, laws regulating asylum for those from countries openly hostile to the U.S., and special laws or legal reviews for legal immigrants who pose a security threat.
8. Janice Kephart:
   a. There are holes in border security, and they come from lax enforcement of existing law.
   b. Border protection starts with rigorous law enforcement and background checks.
9. Sebastian Mallaby:
   a. The focus on illegal immigration is not important to homeland security; immigrants come to the United States because they want to live here.
   b. Security efforts should focus on two types of targets, those most likely to be hit, and those which will cause the greatest loss of life.
10. The debate about immigration reveals the problems inherent in law enforcement bureaucracy.
11. The immigration debate has grown more heated as the country continues to divide over ideological positions.
    a. The Arizona controversy.

III. **Infrastructure Protection**
OBJ 6: Define and describe infrastructure protection
OBJ 7: Describe the need for partnerships in homeland security

A. Another area concerning DHS is infrastructure protection –information, energy, communication, transportation, and economic systems are vulnerable to terrorist attack.

B. Private vs. government partnerships
   1. Jeanne Cummings points to two primary weaknesses concerning infrastructure:
      a. Even a year after September 11, the federal government had failed to release resources to state and local governments.
      b. The problem is even worse in the private security industry.
   2. Richard Clarke outlined many of the threats facing the nation's infrastructure:
      a. Most computer systems are vulnerable to viruses.
      b. The nation's power system, and technological organizations that support it, are vulnerable to disruptions.
      c. The internet and computer networks that support these systems are also vulnerable to attack.
   3. Following Clarke's recommendation, the Bush administration ordered the National Infrastructure Protection Center to move to the DHS.
      a. Extending Clarke's logic, it can also be argued that state and local law enforcement should not play the leading role in infrastructure protection.
   4. The key is to develop relationships so state, local, and tribal police agencies can support security functions.
   5. The problem is that private industry uses information for competition and profit.

C. The need for private partnerships
   1. All levels of law enforcement are faced with the problems of technical specialists and access to privately owned portions of the infrastructure.
   2. Protection of the infrastructure comes when specialists in crime fighting and protection establish critical links with the public and private organizations maintaining America's infrastructure.
   3. Linkages should be developed in two crucial areas:
      a. First, the police should be linked to the security forces already associated with infrastructure functions.
      b. Second, state and local law enforcement agencies must establish formal and informal networks with the organizations in their jurisdictions, and these networks should expand to a cooperative federal system.
   4. Michael Vatis points to another area: cyber-security.

a. Police agencies need to protect their own information infrastructures
b. Law enforcement agencies are not only unprepared to defend community infrastructures, but also unable to protect their own support systems.

IV. **Government Partnerships**
OBJ 7: Describe the need for partnerships in homeland security
OBJ 8: Summarize the critical bureaucratic issues in law enforcement Partnerships

A. One of the most important aspects of DHS's operations is communicating with local communities, law enforcement agencies, and private industries as they relate to intelligence gathering activities and infrastructure protection.
B. The federal mission:
1. As envisioned by federal bureaucracy, homeland security entails coordinating efforts from several local organizations, including private industry, public service, health care systems, and law enforcement.
2. Emergency response planning falls in two broad categories—prevention and reaction.
C. Expanding local roles
1. If engaged in homeland security, state and local police agencies will need to expand the role of traditional law enforcement.
2. Assuming that local law enforcement agencies will collect information only within the context of criminal investigations, bureaucratic problems remain.
3. Most law enforcement officers generally focus on crime elimination, not national defense.
4. Information about suspects, crimes, and criminal activity translates into power, successful individual performance with police agencies, and it helps solves crimes.
D. Thinking internationally
1. State and local officers are not rewarded for thinking in terms of international issues or national security.
2. To combat terrorism, security forces require groups of people with abstract reasoning skills, knowledge of international politics and history, and specialized expertise in particular regions.
3. Localized attitudes bring contempt from intelligence agencies.
a. Intelligence bureaucracies frequently question police competence.

V. **Bureaucratic Problems**
OBJ 8: Summarize the critical bureaucratic issues in law enforcement partnerships

456

A. Unlike the ideal rational organizations envisioned by Weber, public service organizations have foibles that emerge in the everyday social construction of reality.
B. Federal Rivalries
   1. Sometimes federal agencies act more like rivals than partners.
   2. The 9/11 Commission criticized agencies for not working together.
   3. Federal agencies mistrust one another at times, and their failure to cooperate in some circumstances influences local police relationships.
C. FBI versus locals.
   1. Many American police executives are not convinced that the FBI is in partnership with efforts to stop terrorism.
   2. Many state and local police executives do not trust the FBI, and the attitude extends down through the ranks of law enforcement agencies.
D. Local control and revenue sources.
   1. Some people feel cooperation between state and local law enforcement will result in the de facto concentration of police power.
   2. There is also frustration among local governments with the costs of their homeland security responsibilities.
E. Legal bureaucracy:
   1. Another factor inhibiting police cooperation is the legal bureaucracy of criminal justice.
   2. Each entity in the criminal justice system is independent, although it interacts with the other parts.
      a. There is no overall leader, and law enforcement, courts, and correctional agencies refuse to accept single management.

VI. **Bureaucratic Solutions**
OBJ 8: Summarize the critical bureaucratic issues in law enforcement partnerships
OBJ 9: Outline Flynn's recommendations for effective homeland security
OBJ 10: Explain how the JTTF arrangement might become a model for law enforcement partnerships

A. Bureaucracies contain inherent problems, but they too can work for solutions.
B. As law enforcement officers collect and forward information, analysts at local fusion centers turn the information into *actionable intelligence.*
C. This newly created actionable intelligence is returned to the fusion centers as an *intelligence product.*
D. When law enforcement agencies, and the other organizations focused on preventing terrorism, stay focused on the product, the process can produce results.
E. Border security: Critiques and reforms.
   1. Stephen Flynn:

     a. America has made two crucial mistakes.
       i. Homeland security has been separated from national security.
       ii. The infrastructure is vulnerable to attack.
     b. The reality is that the United States has not organized its resources for defense.
     c. Homeland security should be part of a national strategy to defend the United States.
     d. There is no central front, and America cannot always project its power to fight elsewhere – the U.S. has marshaled resources to fight overseas, while neglecting to protect the home front.
     e. The nation's critical infrastructure remains open to attack.
     f. The federal government has virtually ignored private industry, claiming that it is responsible for protecting its own infrastructure.
       i. Private industry is not doing this either..
     g. Jihadists are fully aware of vulnerabilities in the infrastructure, and they understand the economic effect of their actions.
     h. Development of an integrated system against terrorism would reduce the drug trade, contraband smuggling, and theft.
     i. There will never be enough security to prevent every attack, but the goal should be to follow the path of the aviation industry.
     j. In a system of civil defense, people have a civic responsibility to maintain the system.
  2. While not every attack can be prevented, most terrorism can be deterred through cooperative partnerships.
  3. It demands new skills for law enforcement officers, a culture of information sharing, and new bureaucratic relationships, but interdiction of terrorism is an attainable goal.
F. Preparing for successful law enforcement practices.
  1. Law enforcement bureaucracies and related agencies can develop procedures that solve problems.
G. New approaches to the law enforcement mission.
  1. The JTTF system might well serve as an example for the first step in law enforcement cooperation.
  2. The JTTF offers a sensible alternative by creating a system that separates criminal and national security intelligence.
  3. Another alternative for state and local agencies is to combine training in terrorism awareness, with specialized training for selected officers.
  4. On the surface JTTFs seem tailored to the needs of state and local law enforcement, but in some cases they meet opposition.
     a. Local governments have refused to allow their police forces to assist in counterterrorist activities.
     b. Some jurisdictions refuse to share criminal intelligence with federal law enforcement.

5. Police are in a perfect position to engage in intelligence-gathering activities and expand their role in national defense.
6. Partnerships with all types of formal and informal organizations, and cooperation among all levels of law enforcement in an environment that rewards information sharing, is the ultimate answer for preventing terrorism.
7. The final aspect of preventing terrorism involves applying crime prevention and detection skills.
   a. Many aspects of counterterrorism involve basic police work.

VII. **Responding to Disasters**
   OBJ 10: Explain how the JTTF arrangement might become a model for Law enforcement partnerships

A. No security system can completely stop terrorism, and law enforcement agencies will be called to respond when it happens.
B. The process for response and recovery involves planning.
C. Fire departments, regional disaster teams, the health community, and other agencies have *emergency-response plans*.
D. Law enforcement agencies have roles in these plans.
   1. Their primary responsibilities are to respond and restore order, assist emergency and rescue operations, and support health and human services.
   2. They also are charged with investigative and prosecutorial actions.
E. Multiple agencies, including police departments, respond to emergencies, and plan actions designed to stop terrorism.
F. Information gathering, analysis, and sharing findings among agencies are part of an intelligence process.
G. Law enforcement's primary role is to prevent terrorism and crime, and its secondary purpose is to react to an event to save lives.

Chapter Summary

- The problem of law enforcement bureaucracy, with respect to homeland security and the prevention of terrorism, is the sheer number of organizations in multiple layers of government. Bureaucracies can also become stagnate and more consumed with the processes of performing tasks than the actual goals of the organization.

- Max Weber's ideal bureaucracy rationally organizes people under goal-oriented leaders. Workers and managers are selected only according to their abilities. Most American governmental organizations—the military, and some private industry—base their structures on the Weberian ideal of bureaucracy.

- Many bureaucracies are involved in homeland security, and their most important functions center on law enforcement and activities related to intelligence. The federal bureaucracy is massive, which presents a problem for agency cooperation. Yet the bigger challenge is in coordinating the thousands of state, local, and tribal law enforcement agencies in the United States. DHS has assumed many roles in homeland security, but it has relatively little power in the intelligence community.

- Border protection involves ports of entry—seaports, border checkpoints, and ocean shores—and vast expanses of land on our northern and southern borders. Weaknesses in security develop because of the vast size of the borders and the multiple points of entry. Critics maintain that security checks in these areas are ineffective.

- Americans are divided on their approach to immigration policy. This division is exacerbated by the activities of interest groups among immigrant and anti-immigrant communities, and it is also compounded by the large pool of illegal immigrants living in the country. The debate about immigration is heated, interfering with attempts to create sound policies to protect the borders and points of entry.

- Infrastructure protection refers to security provided for the underpinnings of social life, such as roadways, computer networks, bridges, electrical grids, and pipelines. It is protected by government agencies, but most of the assets are owned by private corporations.

- It is not possible to secure the homeland with a single agency or small groups of agencies. Effectively, security can only come through partnerships among agencies. Barriers that separate bureaucracies need to be minimized. Partnerships also require cooperation between units of government and private corporations.

- If state, local, and tribal law enforcement agencies are to take part in homeland security, the mission needs to be reconceived. Making the needed changes seems to make sense, but several factors work against change.

- Flynn maintains that the focus on homeland security is misplaced. People and products coming into the country need to be checked and monitored. America needs to become resilient to recover from terrorist strikes.

- The JTTF system may serve as a starting point for cooperation among police agencies. In the final analysis, law enforcement agencies will need to create and sustain a variety of new partnerships in the public, private, and nonprofit sectors.

DISCUSSION QUESTIONS

1. Do you believe that it is efficient to have the FBI and CIA lead the counterterrorism effort at home and overseas? What challenges and/or opportunities do you foresee? Explain. (OBJ 1 – 10)

2. What do you believe the U.S. policy should be in terms of immigration and security? How would you implement this policy? Explain your rationale. (OBJ 1 – 10)

3. Do you believe that most terrorism can be deterred through cooperative partnerships? Why or why not? (OBJ 7 – 10)

4. Summarize Flynn's recommendations for effective homeland security. Do you agree with recommendations? What, if anything would you add or revise? Be specific in your answers. (OBJ 4, 5, 6, 7, and 9)

CLASS ACTIVITIES

1. Have the students break into two groups, assigning each group one side of the immigration issue. Give them time to research and prepare arguments for a mock debate. Have the class select a "judge" for the challenge, then have each group select one *panelist* from their respective group to be the debater. Recap, post debate, on the strengths and weaknesses of each of their arguments. (OBJ 4 and 5)

2. White addresses the bureaucratic inhibitors to homeland security. These inhibitors are apparent in every bureaucratic organization. Have the students brainstorm possible ways to overcome the obstacles of the current bureaucratic system. Afterwards, discuss why the inhibitors continue to exist. (OBJ 1, 2, 3, and 8)

3. Provide students with flipchart paper and have them list potential infrastructure (public or private) U.S. targets that they feel are most susceptible to terrorist attack. Poll the class offerings, and then reduce the list to their 'top 5'. Have them debate the reasoning for their selections. Time permitting; segue into possible solutions to mitigate terrorist attacks. (OBJ 6 and 9)

4. As a review, play jeopardy using key concepts and terms in the chapter. (OBJ 1 – 10)

5. Have each student comb through http://scholar.google.com/scholar?hl=en&q=immigration+debate+homeland+security&btnG=&as_sdt=1%2C5&as_sdtp= (or another website as approved by the instructor) for a current event and select an article that relates to one or more of the chapter's core concepts. Have students provide a journalistic summary and a

personal opinion/reaction to the article. Have students orally present the article to the class, field Q & As from their fellow students, and provide a copy of the original source article following the presentation. Optional: Have students complete peer assessments at the end of each presentation. (OBJ 1 - 10)

MEDIA TOOLS

1. ***"Wikis"***
    7 Things you should know about Wikis. Retrieved from the Web Jun 29, 2012 at http://net.educause.edu/ir/library/pdf/ELI7004.pdf

    This document offers easy to understand instruction on the history, development, and potential uses of Wikis.

    Have students develop (or make additions to a previously created one) a *Webliography* (resource list) using a Blog or Wiki that provides a short description, and link to a scholarly resource pertaining to course concepts. For example, have students add two to three resources each and ask them to add their assessment of at least one of their peers' contributions. If desired, allow time to discuss Blogs/Wikis. This activity can be reused throughout the course, by asking students to add/revise their contributions each week, bi-weekly, etc. (OBJ 1 – 10)

2. ***"Current Events Article Summary with Peer Assessment"***
    The Council on Foreign Relations. Defense/homeland Security Issues. Retrieved from the Web Aug 8, 2012 at http://www.cfr.org/issue/135/

    This website offers an exhaustive list of articles related to defense and homeland security issues, as well as information on other global issues. This resource can additionally serve as an example for media tool sample #1.

    Submit your template, attached original source article, and peer-reviews to your instructor prior to the end of class.

    Use the Article Summary Template, which can be obtained on the instructor companion website, for this assignment. The template offers information on Internet research, outside resources, identification of credible sources, and detailed directions on completing an assessment of a news article. It also includes a peer evaluation tool.

    Have each student comb the Internet for terrorism related news, and select an article that relates to one or more of the chapter's core concepts. Be sure selections are an article of interest from a credible source (*more on credibility can be found in the article summary template above*). Fill out an article summary template. *Your template asks for generic info about the article, a journalistic*

summary, as well as a personal opinion/reaction to the article. Have each student summarize the article, present it orally to the class, and field Q & As from their fellow students. Have students complete peer assessments at the end of each presentation. Have students submit templates, original source article, and peer-reviews prior to the end of class. (OBJ 1-9)

3. ***"Immigration Myths & Realities Quiz"***
   PBS. The New Americans: Immigration Policy – Past and Present. Retrieved Aug 16, 2012 at http://www.pbs.org/teachers/connect/resources/2012/preview/

   The website offers a variety of information on immigration issues in the U.S. The link directs students to a quiz, "Immigration Myths & Realities"

   Have students peruse the website gleaning information on the major issues in the immigration debate. Have students take the quiz, and then discuss their results. (OBJ 5)

Chapter 14—Law Enforcement and Homeland Security

TRUE/FALSE

1. The DHS maintains terrorist watch lists.

ANS: F   REF: p. 367   OBJ: 1, 3-10

2. Sexual assaults in federal prisons are a national problem.

ANS: T   REF: p. 363   OBJ: 1 and 3

3. Hundreds of immigrants are currently being held in federal detention facilities.

ANS: T   REF: p. 364   OBJ: 1 - 8

4. The creation of the Department of Homeland Security (DHS) involved one of the most massive reorganizations of government in American history.

ANS: T   REF: p. 364   OBJ: 1 - 10

5. The ideal projection of bureaucracy is a group of workers focused on solving a problem.

ANS: T   REF: p. 365   OBJ: 1 - 10

6. The DHS has spared no expense in securing every last U.S. seaport.

ANS: F   REF: p. 381   OBJ: 3 - 9

7. The DHS also uses technology, such as biometric measuring—identification systems based on body characteristics such as fingerprints, facial patterns, and\or DNA—to maintain records on aliens.

ANS: T   REF: p. 371   OBJ: 3 - 9

8. One of the controversial issues surrounding border protection involves immigration.

ANS: T   REF: p. 372   OBJ: 1 - 10

9. The federal government undertook massive reforms and reorganizations from 2002 to 2005, in the wake of 9/11.

ANS: T   REF: p. 364   OBJ: LO1

10. The southern border is very secure - DHS plans for continuing to secure the border have been more than adequate.

ANS: F   REF: p. 372   OBJ: 1 - 10

11. The most significant threat of unregulated immigration comes in the form of terrorism and organized crime.

ANS: T   REF: p. 372   OBJ: 1 - 10

12. Undocumented workers commit more crimes than U.S. citizens.

ANS: F   REF: p. 373   OBJ: 3 - 7

13. Information, energy, communication, transportation, and economic systems are unlikely terrorist targets.

ANS: F   REF: p. 374   OBJ: 3 - 7

14. America's power system and the technological organizations that support it are vulnerable to disruptions.

ANS: T   REF: p. 374   OBJ: 3 - 7

15. If electrical grids and computers stop functioning, transportation and communication systems can shut down.

ANS: T   REF: p. 374   OBJ: 3 - 7

MULTIPLE CHOICE

1. Who coined the term bureaucracy?
   a. Max Weber
   b. Karl Marx
   c. Steven Flynn
   d. David Carter

ANS: a   REF: p. 365   OBJ: 1 and 2

2. As American troops were preparing to enter Iraq in 2003, there was a tremendous dispute between what two entities about the validity of intelligence coming out of Iraq.
   a. The CIA and the military
   b. The FBI and the CIA
   c. The FBI and the military
   d. The NSA and the CIA

ANS: c   REF: p. 378   OBJ: 1 - 10

3. Former FBI executive Richard Marquise states which city is the best place to locate counterterrorist headquarters because it positioned the FBI for inevitable turf battles with the CIA and Department of State?
   a. New York City
   b. Washington
   c. Los Angeles
   d. Chicago

ANS: b   REF: p. 378   OBJ: 1 - 10

4. In the United States, what is the lead agency for counterterrorism?
   a. CIA
   b. Department of Homeland Security
   c. Department of Defense
   d. FBI

ANS: d   REF: p. 367   OBJ: 1 - 10

5. Which agency has the most limited role in homeland security?
   a. Department of Defense
   b. Department of Transportation
   c. Department of Justice
   d. Department of Energy

ANS: a   REF: p. 368   OBJ: 1 - 10

6. The FBI falls under the immediate umbrella of which department?
   a. Department of Defense (DOD)
   b. Department of Justice (DOJ)
   c. Department of homeland Security (DHS)
   d. Department of the Interior (DOI)

ANS: b   REF: p. 367   OBJ: 1 - 10

7. Under the intelligence reform law of 2004, all intelligence coordination must take place in the _____.
   a. National Counterterrorism Center (NCTC)
   b. New York Joint Terrorism Task Force (JTTF)
   c. Law Enforcement Information Network (LEIN)
   d. The National Crime Information Center (NCIC)

ANS: a   REF: p. 367   OBJ: 1 - 10

8. DHS uses technology, such as identification systems based on body characteristics like fingerprints or facial patterns, referred to as _____ to maintain records on aliens.
   a. Laser imprints
   b. Biometric measuring
   c. Computerized identification
   d. Digital monitoring

ANS: b   REF: p. 371   OBJ: 3 - 9

9. More than _____ U.S. seaports are at risk for a terrorist attack.
    a. 300
    b. 20
    c. 800
    d. 100

ANS: a   REF: p. 371   OBJ: 3 - 9

10. _____ refers to information that law enforcement agencies, military units, or other security forces can use to stop an attack or operation.
    a. Intelligence product
    b. Border security
    c. Actionable intelligence
    d. Covert intelligence

ANS: c   REF: p. 381   OBJ: 3 - 9

11. According to the CIA, the most likely route for smuggling WMD into the United States is by _____.
    a. Air
    b. Land-transport
    c. Underground tunnels
    d. Sea

ANS: d   REF: p. 381   OBJ: 3 - 9

12. The Department of Homeland Security was created from the Office of Homeland Security in _____.
    a. 2001
    b. 2003
    c. 1993
    d. 1988

ANS: b   REF: p. 368   OBJ: 1 - 10

13. The largest organization involved in homeland security is _____.
    a. The FBI
    b. The DHS
    c. The Department of Defense
    d. U.S. Customs

ANS: b   REF: p. 368   OBJ: 1 - 10

14. Emergency-response planning falls into two broad categories _____ and reaction.
    a. Orientation
    b. Purpose
    c. Prevention
    d. Action

ANS: c   REF: p. 376   OBJ: 3 - 9

15. Officers need to become aware of the types of activities that take place before an attack. Such activities are _____ indicators.
    a. Preemptive
    b. Offensive
    c. Pre-incident
    d. Intelligence

ANS: c   REF: p. 369   OBJ: 3 - 9

16. The Terrorism Screen Center is located in what city?
    a. South Carolina
    b. Washington, DC
    c. New York
    d. West Virginia

ANS: d   REF: p. 383   OBJ: 3 - 9

17. Border protection involves ports of entry including ALL of the following, except _____.
    a. Seaports
    b. Border checkpoints
    c. Airports
    d. Ocean shores

ANS: c   REF: p. 370   OBJ: 3- 9

18. The CIA was originally established at the end of _____.
    a. The Korean War
    b. The Viet Nam War
    c. World War II
    d. The Cold War

ANS: c   REF: p. 367   OBJ: 1 - 10

19. In the U.S., there are approximately _____ state, local, and tribal law enforcement officers.
    a. 500,000
    b. 800,000
    c. 600,000
    d. 900,000

ANS: b   REF: p. 368   OBJ: 1 - 10

20. Many state and local police executives have an above average mistrust of what government entity?
    a. DOD
    b. FBI
    c. ATF
    d. Military

ANS: b   REF: p. 379   OBJ: 1 - 10

21.   As law enforcement officers collect and forward information, analysts at local fusion
        centers turn the information into _____.
        a. Actionable intelligence
        b. Basic intelligence
        c. Practical intelligence
        d. Trusted intelligence

ANS: a   REF: p. 381   OBJ: 3 - 10

22.   Setting national criminal intelligence training standards is a suggestion of what body?
        a. American Police Chiefs Association
        b. International Police Chiefs Association
        c. Global Intelligence Working Group
        d. The Department of Homeland Security

ANS: c   REF: p. 370   OBJ: 1 - 10

23.   _____ refers to a federal law designed to prevent political interference in the management
        of federal governmental organizations and to increase the efficiency of management.
        a. 1978 Civil Service Reform Act
        b. U.S. Patriot Act
        c. Government Management Reform Act of 1994
        d. Border Security and Reform Act

ANS: c   REF: p. 365   OBJ: 1 - 10

24.   According to Max Weber, every aspect of an organization centers on _____.
        a. Rational efficiency
        b. Political influences
        c. Societal influences
        d. Economic influences

ANS: a   REF: p. 365   OBJ: 1 - 10

25.   According to the text, most terrorism can be deterred through _____.
        a. Military defense
        b. Cooperative partnerships
        c. Foreign assistance
        d. Civil defense

ANS: b   REF: p. 383   OBJ: 1 - 10

26.   The Civil Service Reform Act, a federal law designed to prevent political interference
        with the decisions and actions of governmental organizations, was enacted in what year?

        a. 1946
        b. 2003
        c. 1978
        d. 1967

ANS: c   REF: p. 365   OBJ: 1, 3, 7, 8, and 10

27. What is term applied to situations wherein too many jobs divert a unit from its primary mission?

    a. Mission fail
    b. Mission politician
    c. Mission creep
    d. Mission Multiplicity

ANS: c   REF: p. 369   OBJ: 1 - 10

28. Max Weber (1864–1920), one of the founding masters of _____?
    a. Economics
    b. Sociology
    c. Criminology
    d. Counterterrorism

ANS: b   REF: p. 365   OBJ: 2 and 3

29. Recent immigration law in what state spawned a heated national debate, lawsuits, demonstrations, and the deployment of National Guard troops on the border with Mexico?
    a. Arizona
    b. Texas
    c. California
    d. Washington

ANS: a   REF: p. 374   OBJ: 1 - 10

30. The Bush administration argued that counterterrorism is mainly a _____ problem.
    a. Military
    b. Foreign affairs
    c. Law enforcement
    d. FBI

ANS: d   REF: p. 367   OBJ: 1 - 10

31. The ___ and FBI compile the president's daily intelligence briefing.
    a. CIA
    b. NSA
    c. ATF
    d. DEA

ANS: a   REF: p. 367   OBJ: 1 - 10

32. _____ happens when managers begin focusing on issues other than the purpose of the organization.
    a. Goal displacement
    b. Mission creep
    c. Process orientation
    d. Task orientation

ANS: a   REF: p. 369   OBJ: 1 – 10

33. What agency has the leading role at the National Counterterrorism Center (NCTC)?
   a. NSA
   b. CIA
   c. DOD
   d. FBI

ANS: b   REF: p. 367   OBJ: 1 - 10

34. Currently, the main military role in counterterrorism is to _____.
   a. U.S. border protection
   b. Project American power overseas
   c. Counterterrorism
   d. Conduct wars

ANS: b   REF: p. 368   OBJ: 1 - 10

35. The National Crime Information Center (NCIC) maintains information on a (n) _____ basis.
   a. Nationwide
   b. Statewide
   c. International
   d. local level

ANS: a   REF: p. 369   OBJ: 3 - 10

36. The Intelligence Center (EPIC) is centered in what state?
   a. Texas
   b. California
   c. New York
   d. Virginia

ANS: a   REF: p. 369   OBJ: 1 - 10

37. Which entity bears responsibility for U.S. border protection ONLY when specially ordered by the President?
   a. Customs and Border Protection
   b. ICE
   c. The Coast Guard
   d. the military

ANS: d   REF: p. 368   OBJ: 1 - 10

38. An Arizona law centered on the issue of _____ spawned a heated national debate, lawsuits, demonstrations, and the deployment of National Guard troops on the border with Mexico.
   a. Narcotics
   b. Terrorism
   c. Immigration
   d. Gun control

ANS: c   REF: p. 374   OBJ: 1 - 10

39. The NIPC stands for the National _____ Protection Center.
   a. Infrastructure
   b. Information
   c. Informant
   d. Identity

ANS: a   REF: p. 374   OBJ: 2 - 9

40. Which of the following is NOT listed in the text as a "best practice" of security in the computer industry, as recommended by the Institute for Security Technology Studies at Dartmouth College?
   a. Biometric access requirements
   b. Update software
   c. Maintain firewalls
   d. Scan for viruses and use virus protection

ANS: a   REF: p. 376   OBJ: 3 - 9

Case 14.0

In the realm of terrorism and homeland security, the primary role of law enforcement is prevention. To fulfill their role, every agency involved in homeland security must deal with organization. The creation of the Department of Homeland Security (DHS) involved one of the most massive reorganizations of government in American history. It combined several agencies, ranging from the Secret Service to the Coast Guard. DHS is responsible for protecting almost every facet of American life, but it must coordinate its activities with other federal agencies. It has its own intelligence analysts and capabilities as do the other federal bureaucracies. DHS also coordinates activities with thousands of other organizations on state, local, and tribal levels as well as in the private sector. Every law enforcement agency—from part-time one-person police departments to the FBI—has some role in homeland security.

41. What catastrophe was the pre-eminent incident, which lead to the massive reorganization of government and the ultimate creation of the DHS?
   a. The bombing of the Oklahoma federal building
   b. The Katrina hurricane
   c. The 9/11 attacks
   d. The attack on the U.S.S *Cole*

ANS: c   REF: p. 364   OBJ: 1 – 10

42. Given the number of inter-related agencies responsible for homeland security noted above, what is the least likely challenge they likely face?
   a. Information sharing
   b. Unclear roles and responsibilities
   c. Inadequate skilled worker base
   d. Lack of funding

ANS: a   REF: p. 364   OBJ: 1 – 10

43.   In the massive restructuring of government described above, which agency replaced the Immigration and Naturalization Service?
        a.   Transportation Security Administration
        b.   U.S. Border Patrol
        c.   The U.S. Customs Service
        d.   Immigration and Customs Enforcement (ICE)

ANS: a   REF: p. 368   OBJ: 1 – 10

Case 14.1

The DOD has a limited but critical role in homeland security. Currently, the main military role in counterterrorism is to project American power overseas. DOD's military forces take the fight to terrorists in other lands, rather than letting terrorists become a problem within America's borders (Barnett, 2004, pp. 299–303). It also augments civilian defense and provides special operations capabilities. In some cases, military intelligence can also be used in counter-narcotics operations. Military forces can be used to protect the borders when ordered by the president.

44.   Which of the following is an example of how the military might augment civil defense?
        a.   Providing transport for emergency evacuation
        b.   Targeting terrorists with drone technology
        c.   Patrolling the Great Lakes for mines
        d.   The Christian Identity

ANS: c   REF: p. 368   OBJ: 1 – 10

45.   Which of the following scenarios would be LEAST likely to cause the President to direct the military to protect U.S. borders?
        a.   A nuclear attack off the coast of Florida
        b.   A shut down of New York's subway system
        c.   Mass assassination of the senior members of the Presidential administration
        d.   Terrorist hijacking of a major airliner

ANS: b   REF: p. 368   OBJ: 1 – 10

46.   Which of the following incidents would the military be MOST likely to engage?
        a.   The bombing of an American Embassy overseas
        b.   The bombing of a U.S. federal building
        c.   The takeover of an American high school by right-wing extremists
        d.   A lone-wolf sniper taking shots at Supreme court justices outside the High court.

ANS: a   REF: p. 368   OBJ: 1 – 10

47.   Which of the following incidents would the military be LEAST likely to engage?
        a.   A massive shutdown of the Nation's energy systems
        b.   The shooting of an American ambassador on a diplomatic tour
        c.   A hostile takeover of an American business overseas
        d.   Espionage on a U.S. based military encampment

ANS: c   REF: p. 368   OBJ: 1 – 10

Case 14.2

Task orientation keeps law enforcement focused on the problem of preventing terrorism. By focusing on the goal, law enforcement agencies avoid three common bureaucratic problems: goal displacement, mission creep, and process orientation. Goal displacement happens when managers begin focusing on issues other than the purpose of the organization. A good manager takes care of employee needs so that they can accomplish their tasks. Mission creep refers to adding to many secondary tasks to a group of workers assigned to an important task. Process orientation involves emphasizing the method of accomplishing a task over the completion of a job. All three problems divert a unit or organization from its goal. Unfortunately, these diversions are common at all levels of bureaucracy.

48. A manager emphasizing employee needs over a unit's purpose is an example of _____.
   a. Task orientation
   b. Process orientation
   c. Mission creep
   d. Goal displacement

ANS: d   REF: p. 369   OBJ: 1 - 10

49. A mission being approved with the understanding that it is to be aborted if it cannot be done legally is an example of _____.
   a. Task orientation
   b. Process orientation
   c. Mission creep
   d. Goal displacement

ANS: b   REF: p. 369   OBJ: 1 – 10

50. A U.S. Navy Seal team is dispatched to rescue a number of U.S diplomats being held hostage by terrorist and are asked to procure any documents they can from the location, take photos of the terrorists, and try to turn at least one of the terrorists as an informant. Such a scenario is an example of _____.
   a. Task orientation
   b. Process orientation
   c. Mission creep
   d. Goal displacement

ANS: c   REF: p. 369   OBJ: 1 – 10

COMPLETION

1. Max Weber's ideal _____ rationally organized people under goal-oriented leaders.

ANS: bureaucracy   REF: p. 365   OBJ: 2

2. _____ involves ports of entry, seaports, border check points, ocean shores, and vast expanses of land on the northern and southern borders.

ANS: Border protection   REF: p. 386   OBJ: 1 - 10

3. The ____Commission recommended standardizing the bureaucratic response for monitoring the entry of foreign nationals.

ANS: 9/11   REF: p. 372   OBJ: 1 - 10

4. The federal government seeks to form partnerships with _____ so that state, local, and tribal law enforcement officers can act as an extension of agencies charged with border security.

ANS: local communities   REF: p. 373   OBJ: 7

5. According to Richard Clarke, the FBI should not have been the lead agency for infrastructure protection; the role is more suited to _____.

ANS: technological specialists   REF: p. 374   OBJ: 4 - 10

6. _____issued a directive declaring law enforcement to be part of the nation's critical infrastructure.

ANS: President Clinton   REF: p. 375   OBJ: 6 - 10

7. Information that law enforcement agencies, military units, or other security forces can use to stop an attack or operation is known as _____.

ANS: actionable intelligence   REF: p. 381   OBJ: 3 - 10

8. Stephen Flynn believes that jihadists are fully aware of vulnerabilities in the Nation's _____.

ANS: infrastructure   REF: p. 382   OBJ: 3 - 10

9. The ___ is responsible for protecting almost every facet of American life, but it must coordinate its activities with other federal agencies.

ANS: Department of Homeland Security   REF: p. 364   OBJ: 1 - 10

10. _____refers to the criminal and social actions of individuals and groups before a terrorist attack.

ANS: Pre-incident indicators   REF: p. 369   OBJ: 4 - 9

11.   The _____ created the National Criminal Intelligence Sharing Plan.

ANS: Global Intelligence Working Group   REF: p. 370   OBJ: 1 - 10

12.   Many counterterrorist experts believe that the _____ border will become one of the main infiltration routes for jihadists.

ANS: southern   REF: p. 372   OBJ: 4 - 9

13.   _____ refers to a system of agencies and networks that gather information about threats to the country.

ANS: National security intelligence   REF: p. 376   OBJ: 1 - 10

14.   Law enforcement agencies need to have a _____ suspicion that criminal activity is taking place or has taken place before they can collect information.

ANS: reasonable   REF: p. 376   OBJ: 1 - 10

15.   The process of gathering _____ intelligence is not readily apparent in American policing.

ANS: defense   REF: p. 377   OBJ: 1 - 10

16.   Unlike analysts in defense intelligence, state and local police officers frequently exhibit no concern for in-depth _____information - the kind of information needed to understand intelligence.

ANS: background   REF: p. 377   OBJ: 4 - 10

17.   Intelligence analysts know that information is not usually _____ until it is categorized and placed within social and political contexts.

ANS: valuable   REF: p. 377   OBJ: 1, 2, 3, 4, 8, 9, and 10

18.   One of many strange uses of homeland security grants was $36,000 given to the State of Kentucky to keep terrorists from infiltrating _____.

ANS: bingo halls   REF: p. 379   OBJ: 1, 2, 4, 6, and 8

19.   Numerous criminal justice scholars make jest at the American_____ system, referring to it as the "wedding cake model."

ANS: Justice   REF: p. 379   OBJ: 1 - 10

20.   In the realm of terrorism and homeland security, the primary role of law enforcement is_____.

ANS: prevention   REF: p. 385   OBJ: 1 - 10

ESSAY

1. Compare and contrast the advocates and critics of public bureaucracies.

ANS:
- Bureaucracies work toward stagnation. Innovation, creativity, and individuality are discouraged.
- Career bureaucrats are rewarded with organizational power. Therefore, they look for activities that provide organizational power instead of solutions to problems.
- Public bureaucracies do not face competition.
- Within a bureaucracy, it is better to make a safe decision than the correct decision.
- Bureaucratic organizations protect themselves when threatened with outside problems.
- Bureaucrats postpone decisions under the guise of gathering information.
- Policies and procedures are more important than outcomes in bureaucracies.
- Centralized bureaucracy increases paperwork.
- As bureaucracies grow, simple problems result in complex solutions.
- View will vary.

REF: p. 386   OBJ: 1 - 10

2. Who was Max Weber? What is the Weberian ideal and how does it relate to modern bureaucracy?

ANS:
- Max Weber was one of the major figures of modern sociological methods; he studied the organization of human endeavors.
- The process is rational: there is a problem, people organize to solve it, they work together, and the problem is solved.
- Weber believed that impersonal, professional human groups (bureaucracies) converge to solve the problems of society.
- Weber argued that bureaucracy should be designed to accomplish specific purposes.
- In Weber's ideal, labor is to be divided into specific functional areas, or bureaus and all the bureaus of the organization are to assemble logically to produce the whole.
- The bureaus work together and produce a logical outcome. Management in the organization is rationally oriented and devoid of friendship, family, or political influences.
- Modern bureaucratic management ideally comes from leaders who excel at leadership.
- There is no place for inherited leadership or popular, elected managers in Weber's bureaucracy.
- Every aspect of the organization centers on rational efficiency

REF: p. 365   OBJ: 1 - 10

3. Discuss White's argument that the legal bureaucracy of criminal justice inhibits police cooperation. Do you agree or disagree with his statement that efforts to increase homeland defense efficiency will not change the relationships? Explain.

ANS:
- Many criminal justice scholars believe that the justice system is actually not a system at all but a multifaceted bureaucracy with intersecting—or not—layers.
- Drawing on earlier research, they refer to the justice system as the "wedding cake model."
- Rather than a smooth flow among police, courts, and corrections, they see a cake in which a large bottom layer represents misdemeanors, a smaller middle layer represents serious crimes, and the smallest tier at the top represents a few celebrated cases.
- Each layer has differing procedures for dealing with different types of crimes, and police departments, court systems, and correctional agencies work apart from one another in each layer.
- Each entity in the criminal justice system is independent, although it interacts with the other parts.
- There is no overall leader as law enforcement, courts, and correctional agencies refuse to accept single management.
- From a constitutional perspective, the courts are hardly designed to fit into a criminal justice system.
- Although police and correctional institutions represent the executive branch of government, the courts autonomously belong to the judicial branch.
- Views will vary.

REF: p. 379   OBJ: 1 - 10

4. Briefly summarize the current debate regarding immigration and homeland security. Explain your views on the immigration debate.

ANS:
- Some arguments claim that illegal immigration is not a problem, whereas the opposite side maintains that legal, let alone illegal, immigration is destroying civilization.
- Many elected officials argue that the United States cannot be secure unless its borders are secure.
- A few people want to eliminate immigration, but more want to stop only illegal immigration and install tighter controls on immigration from countries that may harbor hostility toward the United States.
- Other people believe the immigration debate is overemphasized.
- Most of the people concerned with border security make the distinction between legal and illegal immigration, and their primary concern reflects a desire for the rule of law.
- The southern border is not secure, and DHS plans for securing the border have not been adequate; this is a security threat, not only in terms of terrorism but from a variety of other criminal activities.
- The multiple numbers of bureaucracies responsible for border security are inefficient and the structure fails to focus all efforts.

- To correct the situation, U.S. military forces should be deployed along the border until civilian law enforcement can be consolidated and physical and technological barriers can be established to prevent illegal border crossings
- There is confusion about the relationship between local law enforcement and federal agencies.
- This is complicated by the number of federal agencies that have a role in border security and immigration.
- Finally, there are concerns with the efficiency of immigration laws; some people argue that they are not being enforced, some want tougher laws, and still others believe border security is not an issue in preventing terrorism.
- Views will vary.

REF: p. 373   OBJ: 1 - 10

5. Discuss why all levels of law enforcement should work with private agencies in order to protect infrastructure.

ANS:

- Protection of the infrastructure does not result with acquisition of technical expertise equivalent to that of industrial specialists; it comes when specialists in crime fighting and protection establish critical links with the public and private organizations maintaining America's infrastructure.
- Linkages should be developed in two crucial areas.
- First, the police should be linked to the security forces already associated with infrastructure functions.
- The American Society of Industrial Security has made great strides in this area, but more needs to be accomplished.
- Second, state and local law enforcement agencies must establish formal and informal networks with the organizations in their jurisdictions, and these networks should expand to a cooperative federal system.
- Michael Vatis points to another area: cyber-security. Police agencies need to protect their own information infrastructures.
- Following the trend of most American organizations, police agencies integrate electronic management and records systems in everyday routines.
- If these systems are disrupted, police agencies could lose their ability to function.
- Surveying major agencies throughout the country, Vatis argues that infrastructure defense begins at home.
- He worries that law enforcement agencies are not only unprepared to defend community infrastructures but unable to protect their own support systems.

REF: p. 375   OBJ: 1, , 4, 6, 7, 8, and 9

6. Why are abstract reasoning skills, and knowledge of international history, important in understanding and combating terrorism? What are your views?

ANS:

- Modern terrorism is an abstract, nebulous concept, which fluctuates according to historical and political circumstances.
- To combat terrorism, security forces require groups of people with abstract reasoning skills, knowledge of international politics and history, and specialized expertise in particular regions.
- If the police are to participate as full partners in this process, they must bring skilled specialists to the table.
- The philosophy behind policing, however, rejects this logic.
- American law enforcement relishes pragmatic information with immediate applicability on the beat.
- Localized attitudes bring contempt from intelligence agencies.
- Unlike analysts in defense intelligence, state and local police officers frequently exhibit no concern for in-depth background information, the kind of information needed to understand intelligence.
- As a result, intelligence bureaucracies frequently question police competence. Intelligence analysts know information is not usually valuable until it is categorized and placed within social and political contexts.
- If police agencies are unable to engage in this type of examination, intelligence organizations are hesitant to form partnerships with them.
- These factors present enormous problems as the DHS tries to create a network of information.

REF: p. 377   OBJ: 1, 3, 7, 8, and 9

7. Bureaucratic changes present challenges and opportunities, discuss the two recent national innovations White indicates as demonstrating this point. Explain working group and why you think it is important to bringing about bureaucratic changes.

ANS:
- The first innovation is community policing which began as an idea and spread with support from the federal government, research from university criminal justice departments, creation of community associations and partnerships and regional organizations, and participation of law enforcement executives who oriented themselves to the task of increasing police effectiveness.
- Homeland security presents the same opportunity, and community police networks are ideal for the functions it requires.
- The second recent innovation is the National Criminal Intelligence Sharing Plan (NCISP).
- The concept of information gathering, analysis, and sharing began with the Global Advisory Committee to the U.S. attorney general.
- It moved to a working group of executives from all levels of law enforcement.
- As the working group developed ideas for carrying the concept out, groups like the International Association of Chiefs of Police (IACP) reviewed and amended the recommendations.

- Like community policing, it was a national team effort of many different law enforcement agencies.
- When the NCISP was unveiled and endorsed by the IACP, a multitude of police agencies, law enforcement associations, intelligence organizations, and associated bureaucracies endorsed and adopted it.
- Working group is a term used in the federal government for a group of subject matter experts who gather to suggest solutions to common problems.
- Views will vary.

REF: p. 369   OBJ: 1 - 10

8. What is Stephen Flynn's argument regarding the national defense of the United States? Do you agree or disagree with Flynn? Explain your position.

ANS:
- Flynn says America has made two crucial mistakes.
- First, homeland security has been separated from national security.
- Second, the infrastructure is vulnerable to attack.
- Despite all the rhetoric and departmental rearrangements for homeland security, the reality is that the United States has not organized its resources for defense.
- Flynn argues that homeland security should be part of a national strategy to defend the United States.
- The United States has marshaled resources to fight overseas while neglecting to protect the home front.
- It is difficult to inspect all of the cargo containers arriving in seaports; therefore, the oceans represent an opportunity for terrorists.
- Flynn points out that very little has been done to protect the nation's 361 seaports.
- The nation's critical infrastructure remains open to attack, police and firefighter numbers have been cut even though they are crucial for security.
- Flynn also sees a problem in strategic thinking in DHS and other agencies; the federal government has virtually ignored private industry, claiming that it is responsible for protecting its own infrastructure.
- Flynn believes that jihadists are fully aware of vulnerabilities in the infrastructure.
- They will not simply let the United States bring the fight to them; they intend to strike, and the safest and most effective way to hit America is to strike the infrastructure.
- Views will vary.

REF: p. 381   OBJ: 1 - 10

9. Define emergency-response plans. Discuss law enforcement's role in emergency response plans.

ANS:
- Emergency-response plans refer to preparations from any agency to deal with natural, accidental, or human-made disasters.
- They involve controlling the incident through an organized response-and-command system and assigning various organizations to supervise the restoration of social order.
- Law enforcement agencies will be called to respond when an attack happens.

- The process for response and recovery involves planning – fire departments, regional disaster teams, the health community, and other agencies have emergency-response plans.
- Law enforcement agencies have roles under these plans – their primary responsibilities are to respond and restore order, assist emergency and rescue operations, and support health and human services.
- They also are charged with investigative and prosecutorial actions.
- With the exception of the last two functions, the procedures are similar when responding to natural disasters, civil disorders, or massive infrastructure failures.
- Response functions are critical and they save lives, but emergency-response planning differs from preventing terrorism.
- Multiple agencies, including police departments, respond to emergencies. Plans and actions designed to stop terrorism involve different skills.
- Gathering information, analyzing it, and sharing findings are part of an intelligence process.
- Law enforcement's primary role is to prevent terrorism and crime, and its secondary purpose is to react to it to save lives.

REF: p. 385   OBJ: 1 - 10

10. The National Criminal Intelligence Sharing Plan was created by the Global Intelligence Working Group. For what agency or agencies was the plan developed? List the points made by the group. Identify points you would add or delete, explain.

ANS:
- The group sought to create a system for state, local, and tribal law enforcement.
- Become a model intelligence sharing model for all agencies.
- Support and promote intelligence-led policing.
- Create a blueprint for enhancing or building an intelligence system.
- Develop model policies .
- Protect privacy and civil rights.
- Create technologies for sharing of information.
- Set national criminal intelligence training standards.
- Promote timely intelligence sharing.
- Allow for innovation and flexibility.
- Student responses will vary.

REF: p. 370   OBJ: 1 - 10

CHAPTER 15
Homeland Security and Constitutional Issues

Learning Objectives

After reading this chapter, students should be able to:

1. Explain the dangers of restricting freedom in the name of security.
2. Differentiate between civil liberties and human rights.
3. Describe the relationship between the idea of defense in depth and civil liberties.
4. Summarize the USA Patriot Act of 2001 and its renewal in 2011.
5. List the constitutional issues that affect homeland security.
6. Cite arguments to support and oppose increasing executive power to combat terrorism.
7. Describe court responses to attempts to counter terrorism with increased governmental executive-branch power.
8. Describe the role of law enforcement agencies in a social network opposed to terrorism.
9. Discuss the dangers of militarizing police work.
10. Summarize emerging criminal justice scholarship focusing on governmental power.

Chapter Key Terms

Military tribunals, p. 389

Civil liberties, p. 390

Bill of Rights, p. 390

Human rights, p. 390

Defense in depth, p. 391

USA Patriot Act, p. 393

Separation of powers, p.395

First Amendment, p. 395

Fourth Amendment, p. 395

Sixth Amendment, p. 395

Roving wire taps, p. 398

Enemy combatants, p. 399

Reasonableness, p. 399

Military tribunals: military courts trying combatants outside the civilian court system. Trials take place in front of a board of military officers operating under military law.

civil liberties: Individual rights granted to citizens under the U.S. Constitution.

Bill of Rights: The first ten amendments to the U.S. Constitution.

human rights: The basic entitlements and protections that should be given to every person.

defense in depth: Using social networks in national defense. It is based on Arthur Cebrowski's idea of operating at all levels of society.

USA Patriot Act: A law passed in October 2001 that expands law enforcement's power to investigate and deter terrorism. Opponents claim that it adversely affects civil liberties; proponents claim that it introduces reasonable measures to protect the country against terrorists. The act was amended and renewed in 2006, and the ability to collect and analyze domestic intelligence remained part of the law. Provisions for allowing roving wiretaps, the increased power to seize evidence, and increasing wiretaps were approved in 2011.

separation of powers: The distribution of power among the executive, legislative, and judicial branches of government. When powers are separated, there is a balance among the powers. No one branch can take control of the government.

First Amendment: guarantees the rights to speech, assembly, religion, press, and petitioning the government.

Fourth Amendment: particularly applicable to law enforcement and homeland security, it government search and seizure, including the elements of arrest.

Sixth Amendment: guarantees the right to an attorney and a speedy public trial by jury in the jurisdiction where an alleged crime occurred. The amendment also requires that a suspect be informed of any changes.

Fourteenth Amendment: A person cannot be deprived of freedom or property by the government unless the government follows all the procedures demanded for legal prosecution.

Roving wiretaps: a method of quickly intercepting disposal phone or internet traffic. A roving wiretap allows law enforcement officers in monitor new connections without returning to court for another search warrant.

enemy combatants: A legal term used to describe non-state paramilitary captives from Afghanistan. The term was later applied to all jihadist terrorists by the Bush administration. The Obama administration maintained detention centers after ordering the closing of Guantanamo shortly after President Obama took office in January 2009.

reasonableness: The actions an average person would take when confronted with certain circumstances. This is a Fourth Amendment doctrine.

militarization: Responding to social problems with military solutions. In law enforcement, militarization is usually characterized by martial law.

Field contacts: People encountered during normal patrol or investigative operations. Law enforcement officers frequently gather information from such people. The Nationwide SAR Initiative standardizes such information.

Chapter Outline

I.   **Security and Liberty**
     OBJ 1: Explain the dangers of restricting freedom in the name of security
     OBJ 2: Differentiate between civil liberties and human rights
     OBJ 3: Describe the relationship between the idea of defense in depth and civil liberties

   A. There are always trade-offs when considering security – this applies to social structures and to physical aspects of security.
       1. This is both an ancient and modern principle.
   B. The question of the suspension of liberty lies at the root of arguments concerning homeland security.
       1. Proponents at one end of the spectrum argue that the open nature of democratic societies make the social structure open to attack.
       2. On the other side of the spectrum, people argue that limiting civil liberties is far more dangerous than the more limited threats posed by terrorism.
   C. It is impossible to construct a counterterrorist system that ensures complete protection, allows for maximum civil liberty, and protects unrestricted freedom of movement. .
   D. Human rights and civil liberties:
       1. *Civil liberties* refer to the individual freedom people have under a system of law.
       2. Most people believe that all humans enjoy basic rights.
       3. *Human rights* focus on the legal right to exist in a society where people are free from arbitrary coercion.
       4. Human rights intersect terrorism and homeland security in two controversial areas:
           a. First, terrorist attacks on innocent civilians violate the human rights of people to exist apart from political violence.
           b. Second, governments must respect the human rights of their opponents.
       5. Proponents who favor strong security at any cost tend to overlook human rights abuses, and deemphasize civil liberties.
       6. Advocates who favor civil liberties tend to deemphasize security while emphasizing human rights.

E. Defense in depth:
1. Changes in how war is fought affect the structure of civil society.
2. Terrorism attacks *civil* society and *civilian* targets; to defend against terrorism, a nation or culture must use civil defense.
3. The idea of *defense in depth* implies that all levels of society must become involved in homeland security.
   a. This logic assumes that the community wants to fight for its existence, which implies that all members of the community are committed to preserving a similar goal.
   b. Defense in depth may require citizens to alter the way they live, and sacrifice the comforts of everyday life.

II. **Civil Liberties and Federal Power**
OBJ 1: Explain the dangers of restricting freedom in the name of security
OBJ 2: Differentiate between civil liberties and human rights
OBJ 4: Summarize the USA Patriot Act of 2001 and the renewal in 2006

A. After heated debate, the president and Congress reached a compromise in 2006, and the pattern was clear: the United States has increased restrictions on civil liberties after each major terrorist attack.
B. The USA Patriot Act of 2001
1. The *USA Patriot Act* has ten sections, or titles, outlining new powers for governmental operations
   a. Title I is designed to enhance domestic security, creating funding for counterterrorist activities, expanding technical support for the FBI, expanding electronic intelligence-gathering research, and defining presidential authority in response to terrorism.
   b. Some of the most controversial aspects of the Patriot Act appear in Title II, which aims to improve the government's ability to gather electronic evidence. It also allows intelligence and federal law enforcement agencies to share noncriminal information with each other.
   c. Title III empowers federal law enforcement to interact with banking regulators, and provides arrest power outside U.S. borders for U.S. agents investigating terrorist financing and money laundering.
   d. Title IV increases border patrols and monitoring of foreigners within the United States, and mandates detention of suspected terrorists.
   e. Title VII focuses on police information sharing, specifically targeting a nationwide police investigative network known as the Regional Information Sharing System (RISS)
2. Supporters of the Patriot Act believe it will increase federal law enforcement's ability to respond to terrorism, and will create an intelligence conduit among local, state, and federal police agencies.

486

3. Opponents of the law argue that it goes too far in threatening civil liberties while expanding police powers.
4. The most pressing concern centers on the increased power of the government to monitor the activities of its own citizens.

C. The debate about governmental power.
1. The most controversial facets of counterterrorism are symbolized by the USA Patriot Act. The most sensitive aspect of the law deals with intelligence gathering and sharing.
2. The American government was founded on the idea of civil liberties.
3. Increasing the ability of the government to collect information increases executive-branch power.
   a. When criminal justice and national security agencies gather information about organizations and people, they do so as an extension of the executive branch of government.
4. The U.S. Constitution separates the powers of the three branches of government: executive, legislative, and judicial, known as the *separation of powers*.
5. Powers not explicitly given to the federal government go to the states.
6. The *Bill of Rights* also comes into play by:
   a. 1st Amendment – protects freedom of speech and the right to assemble.
   b. 4th Amendment – prevents the government from performing illegal search and seizure.
   c. 5th Amendment – prevents self-incrimination.
   d. 6th Amendment – ensures that suspects have access to an attorney.
   e. *14th Amendment* – provides due process of law.
7. The Constitution guides the United States in war and peace, and it allows certain actions in times of emergency—actions that would be prohibited if there were no emergency.
8. Controversy arises when criminal systems and the defense establishment begin to blend their activities.
9. The law gives federal law enforcement agencies the right to monitor internet searches and to keep tabs on individual queries.
10. The government is allowed to conduct roving wiretaps without probable cause.

D. Debate and the 2006 law.
1. The 2001 Patriot Act was scheduled for renewal in 2005.
2. Although many Republicans wanted to pass the extension of the Patriot Act before the 2006 elections, senate leaders contacted President Bush and urged caution.
3. The reasons for reservations centered on concerns about how the Patriot Act had been used in prior years.
4. Critics were especially critical of "sneak and peek" provisions that allowed the government to search for information without informing the person who was being investigated.

5. In the spring of 2006, the White House and Congress reached a compromise on some of the controversial articles of the Patriot Act and new provisions were approved.
   a. When the government seeks information, the request can be challenged in court.
   b. When information is requested in a terrorist investigation, suspects and others involved, may talk about it.
   c. Suspects may also seek counsel from an attorney.
   d. The renewal also added provisions requiring retailers to maintain information on the sale of over-the-counter drugs that could be used to produce methamphetamines.
6. Laws that were renewed:
   a. The government has the right to intercept communications.
   b. Criminal intelligence can be given to agencies charged with national security, and the security community can openly communicate with the law enforcement community.
   c. The renewed law also extends the time suspects can be kept under surveillance, and allows the government to seize electronic or other evidence with a warrant.
   d. The law also requires internet and e-mail providers to hand over records.
   e. The renewed law allows federal law enforcement to collect national security intelligence if that is their "significant purpose."

III. **Terrorism and the Constitution**
      OBJ 1: Explain the dangers of restricting freedom in the name of security
      OBJ 2: Differentiate between civil liberties and human rights
      OBJ 3: List the constitutional issues that affect homeland security
      OBJ 6: Cite arguments to support and oppose increasing executive power to combat terrorism
      OBJ 7: Describe court responses to attempts to counter terrorism with increased governmental executive-branch power

A. One of the major stumbling blocks between civil rights advocates and the government, during the Bush administration, was the role of the president.
B. Constitutional concerns:
   1. David Cole and James Dempsey fear that federal law enforcement power is growing too strong in a wave of national hysteria.
      a. Their thesis is that antiterrorism legislation empowers law enforcement agencies to enforce political law.
      b. If terrorists are prosecuted under criminal law, the Constitution will be preserved.
   2. Cases to illustrate Cole and Dempsey's thesis:
      a. In the late 1960s and early 1970s, the FBI trampled the rights of suspects and citizens through COINTELPRO, its counterintelligence program.

488

    b. From 1981 to 1990, the FBI overreacted against U.S. citizens who expressed sympathy for revolutionaries in El Salvador.

    c. In the 1990s, Muslims and Palestinians were targeted by investigations, without reasonable suspicion to believe they were involved in a crime.

    d. During the 1990s, political investigations expanded against radical environmentalists and others.

3. The Cole-Dempsey argument is directly applicable to two critical arguments made during the Bush Administration.

    a. President Bush and Vice President Cheney maintained that the president had the power to designate certain terrorists as *enemy combatants,* and subject them to trial by special military courts.

    b. They also contended that the president had the authority to allow national security intelligence agencies to intercept telephone calls which originated in the United States, but were directed to suspected terrorists in foreign countries.

4. The issue of executive power forms the crux of the debate about civil rights and security.

C. Increased executive powers.

1. Lewis Katz:

    a. Argues that citizen protection under the 4th Amendment has been decreasing, and police power has been growing since 1971.

    b. The real test of the Fourth Amendment is *reasonableness.*

    c. Actions taken to prevent another September 11 do not violate the 4th Amendment if they are reasonable.

    d. There is no blanket policy of reasonableness, and care must be taken to balance security with civil liberties.

    e. Some governmental actions are unreasonable:

        i. Eavesdropping on attorney-client conversations, for example, violates the 6th Amendment, a suspect's right to counsel.

        ii. Military tribunals deny the presumption of innocence.

2. Sherry Colb:

    a. The scope of September 11 calls previous assumptions about profiling—or targeting specific groups of people on the basis of race, ethnicity, religion, or other social factors—into question.

    b. As police agencies assemble profiles of terrorists, one of the characteristics may be ethnicity.

    c. Any profiling system, including one having ethnicity as a factor, will yield many more investigative inquiries than apprehensions.

    d. If a terrorist profile develops, and it includes race as one of the characteristics, some opponents of racial profiling may find they endorse it for the sake of counterterrorism.

3. Ruth Wedgwood:

    a. The irony between Americans being detained militarily, and foreigners being held under civilian arrest.

           i. Al Qaeda attacked civilian targets, gaining an advantage in the U.S. criminal justice system.

           ii. Al Qaeda has learned it is best to recruit U.S. citizens for operations, because citizens are not subject to arbitrary arrest.

   b. Going to trial means exposing intelligence sources for the sake of a criminal conviction.

   c. The logic of the two situations:

           i. Terrorists are detained because no writ, no law, and no court order will stop them from attacking.

           ii. The purpose of detention is not to engage in excessive punishment, but to keep terrorists from returning to society.

D. V. Konotorovich:

   a. The stakes are so high that the United States must make all reasonable efforts to stop the next attack.

   b. Torture is out of the question in this country, but drugs are a viable alternative.

           ii. Drugs should not be used for prosecution, he says, but they are acceptable for gaining information.

   c. The threat is real, and legal arguments against obtaining information are illusory.

D. Limiting executive powers.

  1. Susan Herman:

   a. Urges a different approach to antiterrorism, believing the Patriot Act to be a law that throws the balance of powers out of kilter.

   b. Congress has relinquished its power to the president, and failed to provide any room for judicial review.

   c. She compares the USA Patriot Act with two previous sweeping pieces of legislation— the 1968 Crime Control and Safe Streets Act, and the 1978 Foreign Intelligence Surveillance Act (FISA).

   d. The constitutional concern partially focuses on judicial review.

           i. The courts have not been as vigilant in protecting individual rights during intelligence cases as they are in criminal trials.

   e. By increasing executive powers, the Constitution is threatened, and increased executive powers will be used to mask an attack on civil liberties.

  2. The American Civil Liberties Union (ACLU).

   a. Citing increased executive powers to detain immigrants, the ACLU charges the attorney general with trying to gut immigration courts.

   b. Attorney General Ashcroft sought to have the rules for detaining and deporting immigrants streamlined; wanting to make the process more efficient by decreasing the amount of judicial review involved in immigration and naturalization cases.

E. Executive powers and the courts.

  1. While the struggle between Congress and the president continued, and legal scholars argued positions about executive authority, the courts began to review some of the issues involved in counterterrorism.

2. One of the first issues involved the detention of enemy combatants in Guantanamo Bay, Cuba.

3. Both civilian and military courts, using similar language, handed down decisions blocking the government's authority to establish special military courts that violate the civil rights established in the American legal system.

4. There are several other cases where courts limited executive power.
   a. The Supreme Court ruled that the detainees in Guantanamo could contest the charges against them.
   b. The Supreme Court declared that the military tribunal system, established for enemy combatants, was illegal.

5. While the government won some of its early battles, the courts have been increasingly limiting executive power.
   a. One of the primary reasons is that the president acted without specific congressional authority.

6. Despite all of the political debate about increasing executive power, the courts seem to be demonstrating that any effort to fight terrorism will be done so within the rule of law.

IV. **Civil Liberties and Police Work**
   OBJ 1: Explain the dangers of restricting freedom in the name of security
   OBJ 2: Differentiate between civil liberties and human rights
   OBJ 5: List the constitutional issues that affect homeland security
   OBJ 6: Cite arguments to support and oppose increasing executive power to combat terrorism
   OBJ 8: Describe the role of law enforcement agencies in a social network opposed to terrorism
   OBJ 9: Discuss the dangers of militarizing police work

   A. The FBI conducted an internal audit to make sure that its actions were legal, and found that it might have violated its own rules or federal laws in national security investigations more than 1,000 times since 2002.
   B. Whether civil liberties are protected, or abused, most frequently depends on the way police officers handle their responsibilities.
   C. Controversies in law enforcement
      1. Effective counterterrorist policy is based on intelligence.
      2. The 9/11 Commission Report criticizes federal agencies for failing to recognize and share intelligence.
      3. The Patriot Act, before the commission's findings, was designed to facilitate intelligence gathering and to ensure intelligence sharing.
      4. The problem comes when the federal government requests assistance from state and local governments.
      5. Any attempt to use state and local law enforcement in intelligence-gathering operations will have constitutional implications.
      6. To gather counterterrorist intelligence, the police are forced to collect political information.

7. Any move to include the police in an intelligence gathering system alters the expectations local communities have about law enforcement.
8. Terrorism, both domestic and international, poses a variety of problems.
D. National security and crime
   1. Among the controversies surrounding the USA Patriot Act is the role of criminal justice, especially law enforcement.
   2. There are two general schools of thought about the role of the police in intelligence gathering:
      a. One position can be summarized as "eyes and ears" – state and local law enforcement officers should be used as extensions of, or the eyes and ears of, America's intelligence agencies.
      b. Another way of thinking can be called traditional crime response and prevention The fear is that police intelligence-gathering activities will interfere with the traditional police missions of fighting crime and providing a social service.
E. Intelligence, networks, and roles
   1. All levels of law enforcement form nodes in a network opposed to terrorism.
   2. While police agencies have a multitude of other functions, their primary roles in preventing terrorism involves information gathering and sharing, protecting citizens and property, and investigating criminal conspiracies.
      a. Under the Fourth Amendment, law enforcement personnel cannot collect intelligence without the standard of reasonable suspicion.
   3. Networks encourage the flow of information., When information is not shared it loses its value.
   4. Sharing information neither poses a threat to civil liberties nor reduces the effectiveness of partnerships.
   5. The civil liberties danger appears when agencies inside a network either act illegally or forget their role.
   6. Brian Jenkins, Frank Cilluffo, and Salam al Marayati:
      a. Rather than militarizing the problem, they presented terrorism, especially the jihadist movement, as a social idea.
      b. They equate terrorism to child abuse, illegal drug use, gangs, drunk driving, and family fights.
      c. Law enforcement agencies became involved in education, intervention, information gathering, and enforcement in each of these areas.
   7. Deeper community relationships will enhance law enforcement's role in national security by preventing crime, reducing fear, solving problems, and increasing the flow of information.
F. *Militarization* and police work.
   1. There are roles for law enforcement in homeland security, but there are questions about the necessity of developing these functions along military lines.

2. Some policymakers have responded by increasing the military posturing of the police.
3. The debate between these two approaches will become more intense as the police role in homeland defense is institutionalized over time.
4. Military forces are necessary for national defense, and they are organized along principles of rigid role structures, hierarchies, and discipline.
5. A military posture prescribes unquestioning obedience to orders, and aggressive action in the face of an enemy.
6. Two trends may be seen be seen in this area:
   a. The first comes from violent demonstrations.
      i. The Metro-Dade Police Department in Florida developed an effective technique for responding to urban riots called the Field Force technique.
      ii. A second source of militarization comes from police tactical units – tactical units use military weapons, small-unit tactics, and recognized military small-unit command structures.
7. Peter Kraska:
   a. Police in America have gradually assumed a more military posture since violent standoffs with domestic extremists, and terrorism, will lead to a further excuse to militarize.
   b. Police will picture their jurisdictions as war zones, and their mission as military victory.

Chapter Summary

- Increased intelligence activities, homeland security measures, and using governmental power in preventing terrorism must be balanced with the protection of liberty. Civil rights refers to protection from governmental power. The basic freedoms and protection that should be granted to all people are known as human rights.

- Changes in the nature of conflict bring about a need to operate deeply in the social structure. This concept can be called defense in depth. Because it encompasses civil society, it is not possible to talk about such a concept, with regard to homeland security, without discussing civil rights.

- The USA Patriot Act, first enacted in 2001, enhanced the gathering and sharing of intelligence. It increased executive authority. Several aspects of the Patriot Act were modified in 2006. Supporters of the Patriot Act believe that it gives the government tools necessary for combating terrorism. Critics maintain that the Patriot Act threatens civil liberties.

- The Patriot Act affects the doctrine of the separation of powers, *posse comitatus*, the Bill of Rights, and the Fourteenth Amendment.

- An increase in executive-branch powers makes criminal justice more effective, but it threatens civil liberties. There are arguments for both increasing and reducing the power of the executive branch of government in preventing terrorism. Recent court decisions have emphasized the importance of balanced power among the branches of government and maintenance of civil rights.

- Criminal justice agencies protect individual civil rights. The key for successful performance is to continue preventing terrorism by completing law enforcement functions and building community partnerships.

- Law enforcement remains a civilian entity. There is a danger when police work becomes militarized.

DISCUSSION QUESTIONS

1. In order to preserve the security of the United States, to what extreme are you willing to alter the way you live? Explain. (OBJ 1, 2, 3, 4, 5, and 6)

2. Do you believe that the Fourth Amendment has been violated in the wake of the "War on Terror?" Why or why not? (OBJ 1, 2, 3, 4, 5, and 6)

3. Explain your view on the role criminal justice plays in regard to homeland security. Do you a) feel criminal justice has a role in homeland security, b) do you believe criminal justice agencies want to assume this role, c) do you believe American society wants the police to assume a role, and d) how do you view the interplay between federal agencies and local law enforcement. Should local law enforcement agencies take a more active role? Be sure to explain each segment of the question. (OBJ 1 – 10)

4. White indicates that Title II of the USA Patriot Act contains "some of the most controversial aspects of the Patriot Act". Explain why he states this, provide examples. (OBJ 1, 2, 3, 4, 5, and 6)

5. Explain the relationship between the idea of defense in depth and civil liberties. (OBJ 1, 2, 3, 4, 5, and 6)

ASSIGNMENTS

1. Bring in excerpts from the U.S. Patriot Act. Have students discuss whether they believe the actions are a violation of our civil liberties or enhance our protection. (OBJ 1, 2, 3, 4, 5, and 6)

2. Separate the class into two teams. Have the students re-read the sections on executive powers. Have one side of the class debate from the viewpoint of

extending executive powers. Have the other side argue for the limitation of executive powers. After the debate, allow students time to discuss their own opinion regarding executive powers and the "War on Terrorism." (OBJ 6)

3. Break the students into four groups, and have them research the four cases David Cole and James Dempsey utilize to illustrate their fears regarding violation of Constitutional rights. Have the students combine their research into a Power Point presentation to share with the class. (OBJ 1, 2, 3, 4, 5, and 6)

4. Have each student comb through http://thephoenix.com/search/default.aspx?cx=017264708226751834838%3Apeu ly07layy&q=patriot%20act&sa=Search&cof=FORID%3A11#1156 (or another website as approved by the instructor) for a current even,t and select an article that relates to one or more of the chapter's core concepts. Have students provide a journalistic summary and a personal opinion/reaction to the article. Have students orally present the article to the class, field Q & As from their fellow students, and provide a copy of the original source article following the presentation. Optional: Have students complete peer assessments at the end of each presentation. (OBJ 1-10)

5. As a review, play jeopardy using key concepts and terms from the chapter. (OBJ 1-10)

MEDIA TOOLS

1. *"Wikis"*
    7 Things you should know about Wikis. Retrieved from the Web Jun 29, 2012 at http://net.educause.edu/ir/library/pdf/ELI7004.pdf

    This document offers easy to understand instruction on the history, development, and potential uses of Wikis.

    Have students develop (or make additions to a previously created one) a *Webliography* (resource list) using a Blog or Wiki that provides a short description and link to a scholarly resource pertaining to course concepts. For example, have students add two to three resources each and ask them to add their assessment of at least one of their peers' contributions. If desired, allow time to discuss Blogs/Wikis. This activity can be reused throughout the course, by asking students to add/revise their contributions each week, bi-weekly, etc. (OBJ 1 – 10)

2. *"Current Events Article Summary with Peer Assessment"*
    CNN. Domestic Terrorism. Retrieved from the Web on Aug 25, 2012 at http://articles.cnn.com/keyword/domestic-terrorism.

This website offers an exhaustive list of news articles related to terrorism and homeland security. This resource can additionally serve as an example for media tool sample #1.

Use the Article Summary Template, which can be obtained on the instructor companion website, for this assignment. The template offers information on Internet research, outside resources, identification of credible sources, and detailed directions on completing an assessment of a news article. It also includes a peer evaluation tool.

Have each student comb the CNN website above and select an article of interest. Fill out an article summary template. The *template asks for generic info about the article, a journalistic summary, as well as a personal opinion/reaction to the article.* Have each student summarize the article, present it orally to the class, and field Q & As from their fellow students. Have students complete peer assessments at the end of each presentation. Have students submit templates, original source article, and peer-reviews prior to the end of class. (OBJ 1- 10)

3. ***"Emergency Response Plans…Role Play Scenarios"***
FEMA. Emergency Response Plan. Retrieved from the Web Jun 29, 2012 at http://www.ready.gov/business/implementation/emergency

This site offers a substantial array of information on disaster preparedness and emergency response planning. It additionally provides links to a variety of supplemental related resources.

Have students review the elements of emergency response plans at the website above, then provide them with a scenario in which they must develop an emergency response plan. For example, a threat has been made to release a poisonous gas (similar to the Aum Shinrikyo attack in Tokyo) into the New York subway system during 5:00 pm rush hour. Break the students into groups, i.e. law enforcement, fire department/emergency responders, federal investigators, and the National Guard. Have each group present their plan to the class. Open the floor to critique and recommendations on the plans. (OBJ 1 – 10)

4. ***"Oyez Project…Legal briefs"***
"How to Brief a Case". Lloyd Sealy Library. John Jay College of Criminal Justice. Retrieved from the Web on Aug 1, 2012 at http://www.lib.jjay.cuny.edu/research/brief.html

The website offers simple to follow, detailed instructions on how to complete a legal brief.

Oyez. IIT Chicago-Kent College of Law. Retrieved from the Web on Aug 1, 2012 at http://www.oyez.com/cases/2012

The website offers ready access to all U.S. Supreme Court cases since 1850. In addition to digital versions, it offers downloadable audio files for each case.

Have students select a case from the OYEZ website above that has implications related to chapter concepts, i.e. wire tapping, illegal immigration, airport security screening, etc. Have students brief the case according the John Jay standards outlined above. (OB 1 – 10)

TEST BANK

Chapter 15—Homeland Security and Constitutional Issues

TRUE/FALSE

1.　　The USA Patriot Act of 2001, which made significant changes in the structure of federal law enforcement, was passed within weeks of the September attacks.

ANS: T　　　　　　　　　REF: p. 389　　　　　　　OBJ: 1 - 10

2.　　During the American Civil War, Abraham Lincoln suspended the right to habeas corpus.

ANS: T　　　　　　　　　REF: p. 390　　　　　　　OBJ: 1 - 2

3.　　Lewis Katz says the real test of the Fourth Amendment is reasonableness.

ANS: T　　　　　　　　　REF: p. 399　　　　　　　OBJ: 1 - 7

4.　　Following 9/11, many suspected terrorists were held at the detention facility in Guantánamo Bay, Cuba.

ANS: T　　　　　　　　　REF: p. 403　　　　　　　OBJ: 1 - 10

5.　　The 1968 Crime Control and Safe Streets Act and the 1978 Foreign Intelligence Surveillance Act (FISA) provides guidelines for domestic surveillance.

ANS: F　　　　　　　　　REF: p. 401　　　　　　　OBJ: 1, 2, 3, 6, and 7

6.　　In 2006, the Supreme Court declared that the military tribunal system established for enemy combatants was legal.

ANS: F　　　　　　　　　REF: p. 403　　　　　　　OBJ: 1 - 10

7.　　The IACP has traditionally favored the civil role of policing over a militaristic approach.

ANS: T　　　　　　　　　REF: p. 408　　　　　　　OBJ: 9

8.　　In the past few years, many of law enforcement tactical units (SWAT/TET) have abandoned the blue or brown tactical uniforms of police agencies for military camouflage, making it virtually impossible to distinguish them from military combat units.

ANS: T　　　　　　　　　REF: p. 408　　　　　　　OBJ: 9

9.   It is lawful to spy on American citizens engaged in political activity.

ANS: F   REF: p. 409   OBJ: 1 - 10

10.   Increased executive power has the potential to separate law enforcement from the public through militarization and surveillance.

ANS: T   REF: p. 410   OBJ: 1 - 10

11.   President Obama ordered the closing of Guantánamo detention facility within days after his inauguration.

ANS: T   REF: p. 412   OBJ: 1 - 10

12. Societies, even in times of emergency, are never willing to sacrifice personal liberty in the name of security.

ANS: F   REF: p. 390   OBJ: 1 – 10

13.   At the time of the birth of the U.S.A, property-holding white males governed, women were non-citizens, and slavery was acceptable.

ANS: T   REF: p. 391   OBJ: 1 - 2

14.   Many jihadists (who actually comprise a tiny minority of Islamic followers) believe that killing their enemies—Muslims who disagree with the jihadist philosophy and non-Muslims—is a sacramental act.

ANS: T   REF: p. 393   OBJ: 1, 4, and 6

15.   Title II of the U.S. Patriot Act gives the government legal authority to force Internet service providers to give information on their users to federal law enforcement agencies.

ANS: T   REF: p. 396   OBJ: 1 - 5

MULTIPLE CHOICE

1.   What year did the USA Patriot Act pass?
          a. 2001
          b. 2004
          c. 2005
          d. 2000

ANS: a   REF: p. 389   OBJ: 1 - 10

2.   Which of the following Titles of the USA Patriot Act is designed to enhance domestic security?
          a. Title I
          b. Title II
          c. Title III
          d. Title VII

ANS: a   REF: p. 393   OBJ: 1 - 10

3. Title II of the USA Patriot Act is designed to improve the government's ability to gather what type of evidence?
   a. Eye witness testimony
   b. Electronic
   c. Circumstantial
   d. Documentary

ANS: b   REF: p. 393   OBJ: 1 - 10

4. Which of the following Titles of the USA Patriot Act provides arrest power outside U.S. borders for U.S. agents investigating terrorist financing and money laundering?
   a. Title I
   b. Title II
   c. Title III
   d. Title VII

ANS: c   REF: p. 393   OBJ: 1 - 10

5. _____ of the USA Patriot Act focuses on police information sharing?
   a. Title I
   b. Title II
   c. Title III
   d. Title VII

ANS: d   REF: p. 393   OBJ: 1 - 10

6. Suspension of _____ lies at the root of most anti-Patriot Act arguments.
   a. Foreign diplomacy
   b. Civil liberties
   c. Free trade
   d. Government corruption

ANS: b   REF: p. 390   OBJ: 1 - 10

7. What Amendment seeks to prevent the government from illegal search and seizure?
   a. The First Amendment
   b. The Fourth Amendment
   c. The Fifth Amendment
   d. The Sixth Amendment

ANS: b   REF: p. 395   OBJ: 1 - 10

8. Strong advocates of civil liberties tend to emphasize human rights over _____ of the Nation.
   a. Terrorism
   b. The military
   c. The law
   d. Security

ANS: d   REF: p. 391   OBJ: 1 - 10

9. _____ ensures that suspects have access to counsel.
   a. The First Amendment
   b. The Fourth Amendment
   c. The Fifth Amendment
   d. The Sixth Amendment

ANS: d   REF: p. 395   OBJ: 1 - 10

10. ___ is the real test of the Fourth Amendment.
   a. Judicial review
   b. Reasonableness
   c. Security
   d. Protection

ANS: b   REF: p. 399   OBJ: LO6

11. The idea of _____ is that all levels of society must become involved in homeland security.
   a. Logic of conflict
   b. Defense in depth
   c. Protection of social order
   d. Arbitrary coercion

ANS: b   REF: p. 411   OBJ: LO3

12. _____ refer to the individual freedom people have under a system of law.
   a. Human rights
   b. Civil liberties
   c. Civil rights
   d. Civil society

ANS: b   REF: p. 390   OBJ: LO2

13. Some of the most controversial aspects of the Patriot Act appear in _____.
   a. Title III
   b. Title I
   c. Title IV
   d. Title II

ANS: d   REF: p. 393   OBJ: LO4

14. _____ focuses on the legal right to exist in a society where people are free from arbitrary coercion.
   a. Human rights
   b. Civil liberties
   c. Civil rights
   d. Democracies

ANS: a   REF: p. 390   OBJ: LO2

15. David Cole and James Dempsey fear that the power of the _____ is growing too strong in a wave of national hysteria.
    a. Military
    b. Federal law enforcement
    c. Local law enforcement
    d. Militias

ANS: b   REF: p. 398   OBJ: LO5

16. Between 1978 and 2001 FISA granted what percentage of warrant applications made by federal law enforcement officers?
    a. 10
    b. 50
    c. 75
    d. 100

ANS: d   REF: p. 402   OBJ: 1 - 10

17. In an internal audit, the FBI found that it may have violated its own rules or federal laws in national security investigations more than _____ times since 2002.
    a. 1,000
    b. 100
    c. 500
    d. 20

ANS: b   REF: p. 404   OBJ: 1 - 10

18. When criminal justice and national security agencies gather information about organizations and people, they do so as an extension of the _____ branch of government.
    a. Executive
    b. Legislative
    c. Judicial
    d. Congressional

ANS: a   REF: p. 395   OBJ: 1 - 10

19. The 2001 Patriot Act was last revised and renewed in _____.
    a. 2002
    b. 2004
    c. 2005
    d. 2006

ANS: d   REF: p. 397   OBJ: 4 and 7

20. According to _____, counter-terrorist legislation empowers law enforcement agencies to enforce political law.
    a. Lewis Katz and James Dempsey
    b. Sherry Colb and Lewis Katz
    c. David Cole and James Dempsey
    d. David Cole and Kerry Colb

ANS: c   REF: p. 398   OBJ: 1 - 10

21.　In the late 1960s and early 1970s, the FBI violated the rights of suspects and citizens through _____, its counterintelligence program.
　　a.　Crime Control and Safe Streets Act
　　b.　COINTELPRO
　　c.　FISA
　　d.　Counter Intelligence Enhancement Act

ANS: b　　　　　　　　　REF: p. 399　　　　　OBJ: 1 - 10

22.　Sherry Colb (2001) of Rutgers University School of Law argues that racial profiling (targeting specific groups of people on the basis of race, ethnicity, religion, or other violates the due process clause of the _____ Amendment.
　　a.　Fourteenth
　　b.　First
　　c.　Fourth
　　d.　Eighth

ANS: a　　　　　　　　　REF: p. 400　　　　　OBJ: 1 - 10

23.　The _____ gives the attorney general and the secretary of state the power to designate certain associations as terrorist groups.
　　a.　Patriot Act
　　b.　The Constitution
　　c.　The Crime Control and Safe Streets Act of 1978
　　d.　The Bill of Rights

ANS: a　　　　　　　　　REF: p. 402　　　　　OBJ: 1 - 10

24.　According to Herman, the USA Patriot Act places too little emphasis on _____.
　　a.　Foreign diplomacy
　　b.　Civil liberties
　　c.　The executive branch of government
　　d.　Terrorism

ANS: b　　　　　　　　　REF: p. 402　　　　　OBJ: 1 - 10

25.　Of the following, who sought to have the rules for detaining and deporting immigrants streamlined after 9/11?
　　a.　John Ashcroft
　　b.　George Bush
　　c.　Dick Cheney
　　d.　Alberto Gonzalez

ANS: a　　　　　　　　　REF: p. 396　　　　　OBJ: 1 - 10

26.　The United Nations adopted the Universal Declaration of ____ in 1948.
　　a.　Anti-terrorism
　　b.　Global Peace
　　c.　Anti-drugs
　　d.　Human Rights

ANS: d　　　　　　　　　REF: p. 390　　　　　OBJ: 1 - 10

27. The Universal Declaration of Human Rights was adopted by _____ in 1948.
    a. NATO
    b. The League of Nations
    c. The United Nations
    d. The United States

ANS: c   REF: p. 390   OBJ: 1, 2, 3, 5, and 7

28. Most terrorism analysts believe terrorism is best left to the _____ whenever possible.
    a. Citizens
    b. United Nations
    c. Police
    d. Military

ANS: c   REF: p. 409   OBJ: 6, 7, 8, 9, and 10

29. Criminologists, behavioral scientists, and civil libertarians have begun to question the new emphasis on _____ operations and the role of law enforcement in homeland security.
    a. Military
    b. CIA
    c. Intelligence
    d. FBI

ANS: c   REF: p. 409   OBJ: 1 - 10

30. The report by the _____ criticized federal agencies for failing to recognize and share intelligence.
    a. 9/11 Commission
    b. Senate Review Committee
    c. White House
    d. Judicial Review Committee

ANS: a   REF: p. 389   OBJ: 1 - 10

31. Though ultimately backing away from the effort, Attorney General Eric Holder tried to move a set of trials from military tribunals from Guantánamo Bay to what U.S. city?
    a. New York
    b. Washington, DC
    c. Richmond, Virginia
    d. Newark, New Jersey

ANS: a   REF: p. 389   OBJ: 1 - 10

32. Title II of the Patriot Act contains a passage that automatically ending the provisions of the Patriot Act unless it is renewed before a certain time limit. The passage is referred to as the _____
    a. Sunrise clause
    b. Moonlight clause
    c. Eclipse clause
    d. Sunset clause

ANS: d   REF: p. 393   OBJ: 1 – 10

33. The U.S. Constitution separates the powers of the three branches of government: executive, legislative, and judicial. This is known as _____.
   a. The church-state divide
   b. The separation of powers
   c. Federalism
   d. Bureaucracy

ANS: b   REF: p. 395   OBJ: 1 - 10

34. The criminal justice system is permitted to collect information only when it has _____ that people are involved in crimes.
   a. Clear and convincing evidence
   b. Reasonable suspicion
   c. Beyond a reasonable doubt to believe
   d. A Preponderance of evidence

ANS: b   REF: p. 405   OBJ: 1 - 10

35. In which title of the Patriot Act does the section which aims to improve the government's ability to gather electronic evidence appear?
   a. Title II
   b. Title I
   c. Title IV
   d. Title X

ANS: a   REF: p. 393   OBJ: 1 - 10

36. What section of the Patriot Act forbids discrimination against Arabs and Muslims?
   a. One
   b. Two
   c. Four
   d. Five

ANS: a   REF: p. 393   OBJ: 1 - 10

37. The USA Patriot Act has _____ sections, or titles, outlining new powers for governmental operations.
   a. Five
   b. Seven
   c. Twelve
   d. Ten

ANS: d   REF: p. 393   OBJ: 1 - 10

38. The United Nations adopted the Universal Declaration of Human Rights in what year?
   a. 2001
   b. 1918
   c. 1948
   d. 1967

ANS: c   REF: p. 392   OBJ: 1 - 10

39.   What Amendment provides that a person cannot be deprived of freedom or property by the government unless the government follows all the procedures demanded for legal prosecution?
      a. Fourteenth
      b. Fourth
      c. Eighth
      d. Eleventh

ANS: a   REF: p. 400   OBJ: 1 - 10

40.   Which innovative riot control technique was developed by Metro-Dade Police Department in 1980?
      a. Field-force
      b. Force- multiplier
      c. Tri-force
      d. Delta-force

ANS: a   REF: p. 408   OBJ: 8 and 9

Case 15.0

Some of the most controversial aspects of the Patriot Act appear in Title II, which aims to improve the government's ability to gather electronic evidence. In other words, it gives police officials expanded authority to monitor communications. It also allows intelligence and federal law enforcement agencies to share noncriminal information with each other. In addition, it forces private corporations to share records and data with federal law enforcement departments during investigations and allows the FBI to seize material when it believes national security is jeopardized.

Other sections of the law affect law enforcement and the criminal justice system in a variety of ways. Title III empowers federal law enforcement to interact with banking regulators and provides arrest power outside U.S. borders for U.S. agents investigating terrorist financing and money laundering. Title IV increases border patrols and monitoring of foreigners within the United States and mandates detention of suspected terrorists. Title VII focuses on police information sharing, specifically targeting a nationwide police investigative network known as the Regional Information Sharing System (RISS). Before the Patriot Act, RISS was used only in criminal investigations.

41.   Issues over roving wiretaps would be covered under what section the Patriot Act?
      a. Title I
      b. Title II
      c. Title III
      d. Title IV

ANS: b   REF: p. 411   OBJ: 1 – 10

42.   The CIA suspects a local grocery store owner to be a hawala dealer that is providing weapons to a local terrorist organization. What section the Patriot Act would give the CIA access authority to the store owner's records?
      a. Title I
      b. Title II
      c. Title III
      d. Title IV

ANS: c   REF: p. 394   OBJ: 1 – 10

43.   What section of the Patriot Act guides the operations of fusion centers?
       a. Title III
       b. Title IV
       c. Title VI
       d. Title VII

ANS: c   REF: p. 394   OBJ: 1 – 10

44.   What section of the Patriot Act guides the operation of terrorist detention centers?
       a. Title I
       b. Title II
       c. Title III
       d. Title IV

ANS: d   REF: p. 394   OBJ: 1 – 10

45.   FBI authorities seize the general ledger of a dry cleaning business that they suspect to be
       a front for a terrorist cell. Issues surrounding the FBI's actions would be governed by
       what section the Patriot Act?
       a. Title I
       b. Title II
       c. Title III
       d. Title IV

ANS: c   REF: p. 394   OBJ: 1 – 10

46.   Federal authorizes demand the attendee list of a meeting of a local charity suspected to
       have ties to Hamas. What section the Patriot Act would give the feds authority to make
       such demands?
       a. Title I
       b. Title II
       c. Title III
       d. Title IV

ANS: b   REF: p. 394   OBJ: 1 - 10

Case 15.1

In 1948, the United Nations adopted the Universal Declaration of Human Rights. The provisions
include the following ones:

1. All human beings are born free and equal in dignity and rights. They are endowed with
    reason and conscience and should act towards one another in a spirit of brotherhood.

2. Everyone is entitled to all the rights and freedoms in the Declaration; and no distinction
    shall be made on the basis of the racial, religious, political, jurisdictional or international
    status of the country or territory to which a person belongs.

3. Everyone has the right to life, liberty and security of person.

4. No one shall be held in slavery or servitude; slavery and the slave trade shall be prohibited in all their forms.

5. No one shall be subjected to torture or to cruel, inhuman or degrading treatment or punishment.

6. Everyone has the right to recognition everywhere as a person before the law.

7. All are equal before the law and are entitled without any discrimination to equal protection of the law.

8. Everyone has the right to a legal remedy if human rights are violated.

9. No one shall be subjected to arbitrary arrest, detention or exile.

10. Everyone is entitled in full equality to a fair and public trial.

11. Every defendant has the right to be presumed innocent until proved guilty according to law in a public trial.

12. No one shall be subjected to arbitrary interference with his privacy, family, home or correspondence. Everyone has the right to the protection of the law against such interference or attacks.

13. Everyone has the right to freedom of movement, and the right to leave any country, including his own, and to return to his country.

14. Everyone has the right to seek political asylum from persecution.

15. No one shall be arbitrarily deprived of his nationality nor denied the right to change his nationality.

16. Men and women of full age have the right to marry and to found a family. Marriage shall be entered into only with the free will and consent of the spouses.

17. Everyone has the right to own property and no one shall be arbitrarily deprived of his property.

18. Everyone has the right to freedom of thought, conscience and religion.

19. Everyone has the right to freedom of opinion and expression.

20. Everyone has the right to freedom of peaceful assembly and association.

21. Everyone has the right to take part in the government of his country, directly or through freely chosen representatives. The will of the people shall be the basis of the authority of government.

47. Mexican authorities expropriate the beach house of a foreign national for other than a public purpose. Which violation of the UN's Universal Declaration of Human Rights would such a circumstance best demonstrate?
   a. 12
   b. 17
   c. 20
   d. 8

ANS: b   REF: p. 392   OBJ: 1, 2, 6, and 10

508

48. The CIA *waterboards* a number of suspected terrorists in the hopes of gaining information about an impending nuclear attack on U.S. soil? Which violation of the UN's Universal Declaration of Human Rights would such a circumstance best demonstrate?
   a. 3
   b. 6
   c. 9
   d. 5

ANS: d   REF: p. 392   OBJ: 1 – 10

Case 15.2

The main body of the Constitution separates powers and prescribes duties for each branch of government. Powers not explicitly given to the federal government go to the states. The Bill of Rights also comes into play by protecting free speech and the right to assemble (First Amendment), preventing the government from performing illegal search and seizure (Fourth Amendment), and preventing self-incrimination (Fifth Amendment). The Sixth Amendment helps to protect these rights by ensuring that suspects have access to an attorney.

The Fourteenth Amendment, the most important amendment for law enforcement after the Bill of Rights, was added to the Constitution following the Civil War and ensures that suspects cannot lose their rights except by the due process of law. The interpretations of the Constitution and its amendments have protected American liberties for more than two centuries.NARREND

49. A group of suspected terrorists gather outside a mosque after performing their religious rituals. Local police demand they disband. Which amendment is potentially utilizable in the aforementioned scenario?
   a. First
   b. Second
   c. Third
   d. Fourth

ANS: a   REF: p. 395   OBJ: 1 – 10

50. A local resident befriends a known terrorist. Federal authorities show up at the local resident's home with a warrant and take several photographs he took of the two together. Which amendment is potentially at play in the aforementioned scenario?
   a. Second
   b. Third
   c. Fourth
   d. Fifth

ANS: c   REF: p. 395   OBJ: 1 – 10

COMPLETION

1. The Fourteenth Amendment ensures that suspects cannot lose their rights except by _____.

ANS: the due process of law   REF: p. 395   OBJ: 1 - 10

2. Critics argue that the provision in Title II forcing _____providers to give information on their users to federal law enforcement agencies is not acceptable.

ANS: Internet service   REF: p. 396   OBJ: 1 - 10

3. Based on Arthur Cebrowski's idea of operating at all levels of society, _____ refers to using social networks in a national defense.

ANS: defense in depth   REF: p. 411   OBJ: 6 and 8

4. _____ is a legal term used to describe non-state paramilitary captives from Afghanistan.

ANS: Enemy combatant   REF: p. 399   OBJ: 7, 9, and 10

5. The Nationwide SAR Initiative uses law enforcement information gathered through normal patrol or investigative operations. Such interactions are referred to as _____.

ANS: field contacts   REF: p. 410   OBJ: 2, 3, 4, and 8

6. Adam Liptak of the *New York Times* states, in reference to the Patriot Act that threats to civil liberties did not emanate from the law they came from _____.

ANS: attitudes   REF: p. 388   OBJ: 1 - 10

7. The sunset clause in Title II of the Patriot Act demands oversight by _____.

ANS: Congress   REF: p. 393   OBJ: 1 - 10

8. Civil liberty refers citizens as free from having their government infringe unreasonably on the freedoms guaranteed in the _____.

ANS: Constitution   REF: p. 395   OBJ: 1 - 10

9. Terrorists justify murders by stating that civilians are never _____ because they act within the governmental system.

ANS: innocent   REF: p. 391   OBJ: 6, 7, and 8

10. The UN has declared that persons have the right to a ____ remedy if human rights are violated.

ANS: legal   REF: p. 392   OBJ: 2, 3, and 5

11. Title I of the _____ creates funding for counterterrorist activities.

ANS: Patriot Act   REF: p. 393   OBJ: 1 - 10

12. Title III of the Patriot Act provides arrest power outside U.S. borders for U.S. agents investigating terrorist financing and _____.

ANS: money laundering   REF: p. 393   OBJ: 1 - 10

13. Before the Patriot Act, the Regional Information Sharing System (RISS) was used only in _____ investigations.

ANS: criminal   REF: p. 393   OBJ: 1 - 10

14. The _____ of powers acts as a check and balance to the amount of power wielded by each branch of government.

ANS: separation   REF: p. 395   OBJ: 1 - 10

15. The United Nations adopted the Universal Declaration of Human Rights in _____.

ANS: defense   REF: p. 390   OBJ: 1 - 10

16. The first ten amendments of the Constitution are collectively known as the _____.

ANS: Bill of Rights   REF: p. 390   OBJ: 1 - 5

17. The _____ is the law of the land in the United States.

ANS: Constitution   REF: p. 390   OBJ: 1 - 10

18. The basic freedoms and protection that should be granted to all people are collectively known as _____.

ANS: human rights   REF: p. 411   OBJ: 1 - 10

19. The Department of Justice program, Suspicious Activity Reporting (SAR), designed to systematically analyzes information gleaned from law enforcement _____.

ANS: field contacts   REF: p. 410   OBJ: 1 – 10

20. The IACP, America's largest association of state and local police executives, has traditionally favored the civil role of policing over a _____approach.

ANS: militaristic   REF: p. 408   OBJ: 9- 7

ESSAY

1. What is the difference between human rights and civil liberties? In what controversial ways do human rights intersect with Homeland Security and terrorism?

ANS:
- Civil liberties refer to the individual freedoms people have under a system of law.
- The first ten amendments, known as the Bill of Rights, further limit the power of government. Americans enjoy particular freedoms under the Constitution, and the government cannot take these freedoms away.

- Human rights focus on the legal right to exist in a society where people are free from arbitrary coercion.
- People have the right to be free, choose their religion, and have a fair trial; human rights refer to the basic entitlements and protections that should be given to every person.
- Decreasing civil liberties limits individual freedom and increases governmental power. It may increase protection from terrorism, but it increases citizen vulnerability to the abuse of governmental power.
- Human rights intersect terrorism and homeland security in two controversial areas.
- First, terrorist attacks on innocent civilians violate the human right of people to exist apart from political violence against innocent people.
- Second, governments must respect the human rights of their opponents. Ideally, they are not allowed to act outside the bounds of human decency and law when countering terrorists.
- Terrorists justify murders by stating that civilians are never innocent because they act within the governmental system.

REF: p. 390   OBJ: 1 - 10

2. Explain how "War against Terrorism" affects the structure of civil society. What are the issues associated with defense in depth as related to international terrorism?

ANS:
- Combating terrorism is not simply a matter of taking a battle to an enemy; it involves the preservation and protection of social order.
- Changes in how war is fought affect the structure of civil society.
- Jihadists believe they can use any method for disrupting their enemies' societies; the target of terrorism is social order.
- Terrorists fight against the way a group of people live.
- Terrorism attacks civil society and civilian targets.
- Defending against terrorism implies that military force must extend beyond the military – to defend against terrorism, a nation or culture must use civil defense.
- The idea of defense in depth is that all levels of society must become involved in homeland security.
- Defense in depth is designed to protect a community fighting for its way of life.
- In this instance, the community wants to fight for its existence, which implies that all members of the community are committed to a similar goal.
- At some point violence serves to justify violence.
- Defense in depth may require citizens to alter the way they live and sacrifice the comforts of everyday life.
- What about domestic terrorism? It seems to be inferred that all terrorism is international terrorism and domestic is not really addressed in these answers.

REF: p. 408   OBJ: 1 - 10

3. What is militarization? Explain the trends of militarization within law enforcement.

ANS:
- Militarization refers to responding to social problems with military solutions. In law enforcement militarization is usually characterized by martial law.
- Two trends may be seen in this area.

- The first comes from violent demonstrations.
- The Metro-Dade Police Department in Florida developed an effective method, called the field-force technique, for responding to urban riots.
- The technique calls for responding to a growing disorderly crowd, a crowd that can become a precursor to a riot, with a massive show of organized police force.
- Officers assemble in an area away from the violent gathering; isolate the area, providing a route for the crowd to disperse; and then overwhelm it with military riot tactics.
- A field-force exercise looks as though a small army has moved into an area using nonlethal violence.
- A second source of militarization comes from police tactical units.
- These special operations units are called out to deal with barricaded gunmen, hostage situations, and some forms of terrorism.
- Tactical units use military weapons, small-unit tactics, and recognized military small-unit command structures.
- In the past few years many of the units have abandoned the blue or brown tactical uniforms of police agencies for military camouflage, making it virtually impossible to distinguish them from military combat units.

REF: p. 408   OBJ: 1 - 10

4.   What is the USA Patriot Act? Explain why Title II has the most controversial aspects. What other sections of the law affect law enforcement and the criminal justice system?

ANS:
- A law passed in October 2001 that expands law enforcement's power to investigate and deter terrorism, the act was amended and renewed in 2006.
- Opponents claim that it adversely affects civil liberties; proponents claim that it introduces reasonable measures to protect the country against terrorists.
- Some of the most controversial aspects of the Patriot Act appear in Title II, which aims to improve the government's ability to gather electronic evidence.
- Police officials have expanded authority to monitor communications.
- It allows intelligence and federal law enforcement agencies to share noncriminal information with each other.
- It also forces private corporations to share records and data with federal law enforcement departments during investigations and allows the FBI to seize material when it believes national security is jeopardized.
- Title II also contains a sunset clause, automatically ending the provisions of the Patriot Act unless it is renewed before a certain time limit, and enacts congressional oversight of the act.
- Other sections of the law affect law enforcement and the criminal justice system in a variety of ways.
- Title III empowers federal law enforcement to interact with banking regulators and provides arrest power outside U.S. borders for U.S. agents investigating terrorist financing and money laundering.

- Title IV increases border patrols and monitoring of foreigners within the United States and mandates detention of suspected terrorists.
- Title VII focuses on police information sharing, specifically targeting a nationwide police investigative network known as the Regional Information Sharing System (RISS).

REF: p. 393   OBJ: 1 - 10

5.   Explain why there were reservations in regards to renewing the USA Patriot Act in 2005. What provisions were made in the 2006 version of the USA Patriot Act?

ANS:
- Although the House of Representatives voted to renew the law in December, in the Senate some believed the 2001 law passed too quickly.
- They argued that many of the provisions expanded governmental authority too far.
- The Bush administration contended that law enforcement agencies employed the provisions carefully, using them only to stop terrorist attacks.
- Congress accused the government of selectively releasing information and hiding unfavorable reports; they also said that agencies were classifying public documents in an effort to hide governmental activities.
- They were especially critical of "sneak and peek" provisions that allowed the government to search for information without informing the person who was being investigated.
- Concerns were raised about provisions for gathering secret information and the original Patriot Act stipulations about the denial of legal representation in terrorism investigations.
- Under the renewed act, when the government seeks information, the request can be challenged in court.
- When information is requested in a terrorist investigation, suspects and others involved may talk about it. Suspects may also seek counsel from an attorney.
- The renewal requires retailers to maintain information on sales of over-the-counter drugs that could be used to produce methamphetamines.
- The government has the right to intercept communications; criminal intelligence can be given to agencies charged with national security, and the security community can openly communicate with the law enforcement community.
- The renewed law also extends the time suspects can be kept under surveillance and allows the government to seize electronic or other evidence with a warrant.
- The law also requires Internet and e-mail providers to hand over records.
- Finally, the renewed law allows federal law enforcement agencies to collect national security intelligence if that is their "significant purpose."

REF: p. 397   OBJ: 1 - 10

6.   What is Cole and Dempsey's thesis regarding antiterrorism legislation? Discuss the evidence they use to support their thesis.

ANS:
- David Cole and James Dempsey sent out a warning after the 1996 counterterrorist law took effect in the wake of the 1995 Oklahoma City bombing and reiterated their warning after passage of the 2001 USA Patriot Act.

- Cole & Dempsey feared that law enforcement power is growing too strong in a wave of national hysteria.
- Their thesis is that counterterrorist legislation empowers law enforcement agencies to enforce political law.
- By contrast, terrorists must violate criminal laws to practice terrorism.
- Therefore, Cole and Dempsey argue, it is best to keep the police out of politics and focused on criminal violations.
- If terrorists are prosecuted under criminal law, the Constitution will be preserved.
- Cole and Dempsey point to four cases that illustrate their fears.
- In the late 1960s and early 1970s, the FBI trampled the rights of suspects and citizens through COINTELPRO, its counterintelligence program.
- Second, from 1981 to 1990, the FBI overreacted against U.S. citizens who expressed sympathy for revolutionaries in El Salvador.
- Third, in the 1990s Muslims and Palestinians were targeted by investigations despite there being no reasonable suspicions they were involved in a crime.
- Finally, during the 1990s, political investigations of radical environmentalists and others expanded.

REF: p. 398　　　　　OBJ: 1 - 10

7.　Compare and contrast the arguments of Lewis Katz and Sherry Colb in terms of reasonableness and increasing executive powers to combat terrorism. Do you agree with their arguments? Why or why not?

ANS:
- Katz says the real test of the Fourth Amendment is reasonableness.
- In normal times, police officers can be held to a higher standard of behavior than in times of emergency, and September 11 constituted an emergency.
- It was not unreasonable to interview Middle Eastern immigrants.
- A national identification system would not be unconstitutional, provided citizens were not ordered to produce identification without reasonable suspicion.
- Actions taken to prevent another September 11 do not violate the Fourth Amendment when they are reasonable.
- Katz does believe some governmental actions are unreasonable.
- Eavesdropping on attorney-client conversations violates the Sixth Amendment, a suspect's right to counsel; military tribunals deny the presumption of innocence.
- There is no blanket policy of reasonableness, and care must be taken to balance security with civil liberties.
- Sherry Colb applies a doctrine of reasonableness.
- Colb concedes that police in America are facing a new enemy.
- Racial profiling violates the due process clause of the Fourteenth Amendment; however, the scope of September 11 calls into question previous assumptions about profiling, or targeting specific groups of people on the basis of race, ethnicity, religion, or other social factors.
- Colb believes any profiling system, including one having ethnicity as a factor, will yield many more investigative inquiries than apprehensions

REF: p. 399　　　　　OBJ: 1 - 10

8. What is Susan Herman's argument regarding antiterrorism and the Patriot Act? Explain her legislation comparisons to the USA Patriot Act. Do you agree with Herman? Why or why not?

ANS:
- Susan Herman vehemently urges a different approach to counterterrorism, believing the Patriot Act to be a law that throws the balance of powers out of kilter.
- She asserts that Congress has relinquished its power to the president and failed to provide any room for judicial review.
- Proposals coming from the administration complement congressional actions by increasing the executive power to take actions without judicial review.
- Herman's argument is based in constitutional law. She compares the USA Patriot Act with two previous sweeping pieces of legislation: the 1968 Crime Control and Safe Streets Act and the 1978 Foreign Intelligence Surveillance Act (FISA).
- Title III of the safe-streets act mandates judicial review of police surveillance.
- Under Title III, criminal evidence cannot be gathered without prior approval from a federal court, and although a judge reviews a request for surveillance in secrecy, the police must prove that wiretaps or other means of electronic eavesdropping will lead to establishing probable cause for a crime.
- FISA surveillance differs from Title III warrants; under FISA, various forms of eavesdropping can be used to gather intelligence.
- A special judicial review is required before surveillance can be initiated, and any evidence gathered during the investigation cannot be used in a criminal prosecution.
- The constitutional concern partially focuses on judicial review; the courts have not been as vigilant in protecting individual rights during intelligence cases as they are in criminal trials.
- Herman compares FISA warrants to the type of surveillance proposed under the Patriot Act and concludes that the Patriot Act allows the government to watch its own citizens with similar rules.
- There is no guarantee that such surveillance will exclude evidence used in criminal prosecutions.

REF: p. 401   OBJ: 1 - 10

9. Explain how the courts have impacted the executive power to confront terrorism. Use examples from the text to illustrate your answer.

ANS:
- While the struggle between Congress and the president continued and legal scholars argued positions about executive authority, the courts began to review some of the issues involved in counterterrorism.
- One of the first issues involved the detention of enemy combatants in Guantánamo Bay, Cuba.
- The government contended it could try the defendants in special military tribunals, apart from normal criminal prosecutions and military law; judges were not swayed by this argument.

516

- Both civilian and military courts, using similar language, handed down decisions blocking the government's desire to establish special military courts that violate the civil rights.
- Defendants are entitled to contest the basis of their arrests; the government cannot hold a person without a hearing to ensure that an arrest is justified by probable cause – the Supreme Court ruled that the detainees in Guantánamo could contest the charges against them.
- The Supreme Court declared that the military tribunal system established for enemy combatants was illegal.
- A military court in Guantánamo dismissed cases against two defendants at Guantánamo Bay on the basis of the earlier Supreme Court decision.
- Although the Bush administration won some of its early battles to gain more power, the courts have been increasingly limiting executive power.
- One of the primary reasons is that the president acted without specific congressional authority; an analysis in the *Wall Street Journal* reported that the Bush administration did not seek such authorization after 9/11 because it feared Congress would not grant it.
- The courts seem to be demonstrating that any effort to fight terrorism will be done within the rule of law.

REF: p. 403   OBJ: 1 - 10

10.   Briefly describe the constitutional issues that illustrate points where homeland security and policies intersect with the Constitution.

ANS:
- The main body of the Constitution separates powers and prescribes duties for each branch of government.
- Powers not explicitly given to the federal government go to the states.
- The Bill of Rights also comes into play by protecting free speech and the right to assemble (First Amendment), preventing the government from performing illegal search and seizure (Fourth Amendment), and preventing self-incrimination (Fifth Amendment).
- The Sixth Amendment helps to protect these rights by ensuring that suspects have access to an attorney.
- The Fourteenth Amendment ensures that suspects cannot lose their rights except by the due process of law.
- The Constitution guides the United States in war and peace, and it allows certain actions in times of emergency—actions that would be prohibited if there were no emergency.
- This makes terrorism a constitutionally cloudy area obscuring the boundary separating war and peace, because many people disagree about the nature of terrorism.
- For example, America's enemies of September 11 used terrorists trained in military-style camps to attack civilian targets and military forces engaged in peacetime activities.

REF: p. 395   OBJ: 1 - 10

CHAPTER 16
Security, Terrorism and the Future

Learning Objectives

After reading this chapter, students should be able to:

1. Describe the purposes of the DHS quadrennial review.
2. Identify the factors that increase the future effectiveness of multi-agency anti-terrorism operations.
3. Explain the factors that complicate partnerships between units of government and private industry.
4. Describe the importance of foreign policy in homeland security operations.
5. Explain the necessity of creating a system that can absorb an attack.
6. Identify the value of liberal education as a means of countering future terrorism.
7. Outline probable future methods of terrorist attacks.
8. Summarize the developing law enforcement programs designed to prevent terrorism.
9. Describe probable future strategic directions in terrorism.

Chapter Key Terms

Homeland Security Act, p. 414

Quadrennial Homeland Security Review (QHSR), p. 415

9/11 Commission Implementation Act of 2007, p. 415

Janet Napolitano, p. 415

military-industrial complex, p. 416

force protection, p. 422

Mumbai, p. 423

Swarming attacks, p. 423

Raymond Kelly, p. 423

NYPD Intelligence, p. 423

Bureau of Justice Assistance (BJA) , p. 426

Smart Policing Initiative (SPI). p. 427

Communities Against Terrorism (CAT), p. 427

Targeting Violent Crime Initiative (TCVI), p. 427

Field contacts, p. 428

e-Guardian, p. 428

field training officers, p. 428

intelligence-led policing, p. 429

Homeland Security Act of 2002: A federal law created in 2002, and amended in the following years. It established the Department of Homeland Security, and reorganized the presidential cabinet. DHS's primary antiterrorism mission is to prevent attacks and respond to them when they occur.

Quadrennial Homeland Security Review: A requirement that the secretary of DHS conduct a review of the department's operations every four years. According to the first report, the Homeland Security Act of 2002, as amended, requires the secretary to "delineate and update, as appropriate, the national homeland security strategy," and to "outline and prioritize the full range of the critical homeland security mission areas of the Nation" (DHS, 2010).

9/11 Commission Implementation Act: A federal law requiring selected recommendations of the 9/11 Commission to be implemented. One of its provisions helped to create regional Fusion Centers.

Janet Napolitano: (1957–) the third Secretary of Homeland Security. President Obama appointed her while she was serving in her second term as governor in Arizona.

Military-industrial complex: A term coined by President Dwight D. Eisenhower (1890–1969) to describe the relationship between American military forces and private industry.

Force Protection: Refers to security operations by military forces engaged in securing bases, ports, other areas of operations, and personnel. Military personnel frequently operate with local law enforcement and other civil forces when engaged in force protection.

Mumbai: The LeT launched several attacks in Mumbai, India, in November 2008. Terrorists killed dozens of people and took several hostages. The attacks paralyzed the city for several days.

Swarming attacks: Launching attacks on multiple targets in the same time frame, or suddenly bringing several attackers to a single location and rapidly dispersing.

Raymond W. Kelly: (1941–) Became Commissioner of the New York City Police Department in 2002. A veteran New York City police officer, Kelley previously worked as the Commissioner from 1992-1994. A retired colonel from the United States Marine Corps Reserve, Kelly has served the NYPD for more than three decades.

NYPD Intelligence: After the 9/11 attacks, the New York City Police Department created a new intelligence operation to assess domestic and international threats to the city. Its first administrator was a former executive from the CIA. The NYPD sends officers overseas to gather information and assess terrorist threats.

Bureau of Justice Assistance: A division of the United States Department of Justice that assists state, local, and tribal law enforcement agencies.

Smart Policing Initiative (SPI): A federal program designed to focus law enforcement resources on a particular type of crime or community problem. Programs are evaluated by external research institutions, and modified based on the results of the evaluation.

Communities Against Terrorism (CAT): A law enforcement initiative that provides businesses with information about terrorist activities particular to that business or industry. Liaisons from local agencies contact businesses, provide information about the types of pre-incident activities employees might see in that type of business, and leave contact information.

Targeting Violent Crime Initiative (TVCI): A Department of Justice grant program administered through the Bureau of Justice Assistance. Its purpose is to fund multijurisdictional state, local, and tribal law enforcement teams that prevent selected violent crimes through intelligence-led policing.

Nationwide SAR Initiative (NSI): A federal program designed to develop common antiterrorism intelligence-reporting procedures among state, local, and tribal law enforcement agencies. SAR is an acronym for Suspicious Activity Report.

Field Contacts: Information recorded from contacts during patrol operations or investigations. Police officers come into contact with many people during the course of routine patrol or investigations. They frequently encounter suspicious people, but lack evidence to make an arrest. Field contacts refer to recorded information about such encounters.

e-Guardian: An FBI system to share information about possible terrorist threats.

Field training officers: Experienced senior patrol officers who ride with police academy graduates. They are responsible for on-the-job training. They mentor and evaluate new recruits.

Intelligence-Led Policing: A managerial model which focuses on the collection and analysis of information. After analysis, law enforcement resources are then deployed to prevent and disrupt crime, and to target specific crimes and offenders. ILP is an alternative to utilizing criminal intelligence to support investigations and other forms of reactive policing.

Najibullah Zazi: (1985–) A 1999 immigrant to the United States. Zazi was born in Afghanistan and raised in Pakistan. He was arrested in 2009 for planning suicide attacks in New York City, and pleaded guilty to charges of terrorism in 2010.

National Intelligence University: An in-service initiative standardizing training for the entire intelligence community.

Proteus USA: A project designed to identify future threats to national security by assembling panels of experts in various fields. It was developed by the U.S. Army War College and the National Intelligence University.

Enhanced interrogation: A process of questioning suspects by using physical duress. Supporters argue that such actions are necessary to gain information about future terrorism. Opponents argue that such actions constitute torture, thus, violating human rights.

Chapter Outline

I.   **Emerging Issues in Anti-Terrorist Security Policy**
    OBJ 1: Describe the purposes of the DHS quadrennial review
    OBJ 2: Identify the factors that increase the future effectiveness of multi-agency anti-terrorism operations
    OBJ 3: Explain factors that complicate partnerships between units of government and private industry

OBJ 4: Describe the importance of foreign policy in homeland security operations

OBJ 5: Explain the necessity of creating a system that can absorb an attack

OBJ 6: Identify the value of liberal education as a means of countering future terrorism

A. The *Homeland Security Act* of 2002 was touted as the biggest reformation of government since the Second World War.

B. The Department of Justice (DOJ), the Department of Defense (DOD), and the Department of Homeland Security (DHS) were given specific functions in national security, and their missions were to support overall direction of foreign policy and the Department of State (DOS).

C. Actual operations often become duplicative and inefficient.

D. Congress tried to create a method for ensuring cooperation, rather than confusion, on the national level when it passed the Homeland Security Act.

   1. Quadrennial Homeland Security Review (QHSR).

   2. 9/11 Commission Implementation Act of 2007.

      a. The DOD undergoes the same type of review every four years.

   3. The purpose of the four year review is to try to prevent the type of confusion and duplication that arises from overlapping roles.

E. DHS Secretary Janet Napolitano directed that her department focus on five areas:

   1. Counterterrorism and domestic security management.

   2. Securing U.S. borders.

   3. Enforcing immigration laws.

   4. Disaster prevention and management.

   5. Unifying the DHS mission with all other departments and national policy.

F. Multi-level communication and sharing.

   1. The most complex process in the DHS analysis is the implementation of a comprehensive strategy to ensure effective management of national policies.

   2. In addition to critical issues, practical aspects of operations and management become vital for policy success, implying three important areas for future security:

      a. All the federal agencies involved in terrorism prevention need to develop procedures to ensure that activities complement one another.

      b. Agencies need to develop methods for encouraging communication.

      c. It is necessary to share information.

   3. Agencies in Illinois developed a formal system of information-sharing that resulted in formal and informal communications.

G. The private industry problem.

   1. Effective preventative policies can be enhanced by private public partnerships.

2. This comes with two problems:
   a. Private businesses operate outside government, and they are not subjected to the same constitutional rules and regulations.
   b. Private businesses may use their relations with governments to win government contracts.
3. One of the emerging critical issues in anti-terrorism policy is the development of homeland security industries by private businesses.
4. Private businesses are replacing defense activities traditionally performed by the government.
5. Several units of government now simply outsource their work to private contractors, creating a "government-industrial complex". It is expanding into homeland security operations.
6. After 9/11, the nation's ten largest defense contractors immediately created homeland security departments in their companies, and they quickly became the largest contractors within DHS.
   a. Defense contractors possess skills most government agencies do not have.
7. Future security will be privatized by corporations unrestrained by constitutional limitations on government power.
8. Private companies often circumvent the constraints on government power:
   a. Private companies act within their own operational systems, and decide what they will and will not report.
   b. Private companies frequently act outside of the rules of warfare.
   c. The government has even intervened to protect civilian contractors who have broken local laws, giving them the same protection afforded to US military forces.
9. Private and public partnerships have resulted in some positive benefits.
   a. This approach involves sharing security information to benefit the entire community.
10. When cooperative relationships focus exclusively on community security, the risks posed by government-private industrial relationships are reduced.

H. Homeland security and foreign policy.
1. New military counterinsurgency policies suggest that approaches to terrorism require partnerships.
2. Future homeland security depends on the success of U.S. foreign policy.
3. Defense Secretary Robert Gates believes security begins by developing a concept he calls *partner capacity*.
   a. The prime goal of this policy is to help countries develop the means to defend themselves, and to create alliances to support them.
4. Partnerships require new cooperative intergovernmental relationships, assistance from allies, and pooling resources to solve security problems.
5. Three principles should guide this combined approach to foreign policy and anti-terrorism security:
   a. First, it must be agile and flexible.
   b. Second, Congress and the executive branch of government need to develop effective oversight mechanisms.

     c.   Third, it requires consistent long-term behavior in American foreign policy.

I. The Israeli-Palestinian conflict.

    1. Given the synergistic nature of the conflict between Israel and Palestine, attempts to secure the homeland must take the Middle East into account.

    2. Most jihadist movements come to embrace the Israeli-Palestinian conflict because it is a source of recruitment.

    3. The United States needs to refocus its peacemaking efforts in three areas:

        a.   First, it needs to avoid dumping all militants into a single camp.

        b.   Second, several countries have interests in Middle Eastern stability, and peacemaking policy should take their views into account.

        c.   Third, when other interests are taken into account, the U.S. should encourage Israel to make peace with the other regional actors.

    4. Daniel Byman says that Israel's future security, and by implication peace in the region, depends on the future of Hamas.

    5. Stephen Kinzer suggests a strategic partnership with Turkey to promote regional peace, democracy, and combat extremism.

    6. Law enforcement efforts to secure the homeland are part of a complex system of intergovernmental actions needed to prevent terrorism.

    7. Foreign policy and regional stability in areas like the Middle East are necessary to reduce future terrorist threats.

J. Absorbing an attack.

    1. The best anti-terrorism efforts will fail at points in the future.

    2. Democracies need to develop the ability to maintain social order without destroying the base of the democracy.

    3. Jakub Grygiel – the U.S. must not only work to prevent terrorist attacks, it must develop the capacity to absorb a major strike.

        a.   If a group launches a major attack when it has no visible geographical or political location, it is partially insulated from reprisal.

        b.   Non-state actors are not as vulnerable as recognized states, and the threat of retaliation does not diminish their willingness to engage in a massive attack.

        c.   The U.S. needs to develop the capacity to absorb a major attack on one of its cities or some critical aspect of the infrastructure.

        d.   The infrastructure needs to be decentralized; a central system can be disrupted when its control structure is destabilized and is vulnerable to attack.

        e.   An effective homeland security policy should be based on the ability to maintain social, political, and economic functions after a major attack.

        f.   Decentralization is necessary to maintain infrastructure in the event that a centralized center is destroyed.

K. Other critical issues.
1. The nation needs individuals who are broadly educated to deal with emerging complex security threats.
    a.. Higher education programs, especially at the undergraduate level, will better provide candidates for law enforcement, intelligence, and security force activities. They need to provide interdisciplinary, problem-solving based programs.
2. Another aspect of future policy should be aimed at settling the debate about the nature of the terrorism problem.
3. Richard Kohn argues that since the 1930s, the U.S. has become increasingly enamored by militarizing social problems. This presents some future problems.
    a. First, by militarizing the problem of terrorism, the United States follows a policy embraced by no other Western democracy.
    b. Second, civil liberties will be threatened, if in responding to a future terrorist attack, America moves beyond rhetoric to the reality of a militarized government.
    c. Third, the war metaphor does not work.
4. Terrorism is primarily a problem for law enforcement.
5. The military forces will increase use of non-lethal weapons in the future.
6. Jenkins states that the JTTFs represent the best counterterrorist tools in the legal system, but they have one significant drawback – they are based on criminal prosecution rather than gaining intelligence.
    a. The JTTFs should be expanded and driven by a focus on gathering criminal and national defense intelligence, as well as launching criminal investigations.

II. **Future Tactics**
   OBJ 4: Describe the importance of foreign policy in homeland security operations
   OBJ 5: Explain the necessity of creating a system that can absorb an attack
   OBJ 7: Outline probable future methods of terrorist attacks

A. The basic tactics of terrorism remain relatively constant, but terrorists continually develop innovative ways to use them.
B. Criminal and terror networks will intersect, even though they will probably not form a common front.
C. Cyber-terrorism has yet to reach its full potential, and the United States remains vulnerable to attack.
D. NYPD intelligence conducted a detailed analysis of the *Mumbai* and Lahore attacks and found similarities:
1. Both involved small unit assaults in densely population areas.
2. They were preceded by extensive preparation and surveillance
3. The actual attacks were coordinated by communicating through cell phones and small battery operated radios.

4. After the initial assaults, teams kept breaking down into smaller units.
5. Local police were outgunned at the time of the initial attacks.
6. The NYPD concluded that terrorist tactics from sophisticated groups will shift from emphasizing suicide bombings, to focusing on military-style assaults by small, heavily armed teams.

E. Terrorists do not need sophisticated weapons or WMD to create massive Chaos – small cadres of conventionally armed terrorists can wreak havoc in an urban environment through multiple random murders.

F. The FBI concluded that three future responses are warranted from the lessons learned from Mumbai and Lahore:
1. First, it is necessary to prepare for strikes from small groups operating without a central command.
2. Second, deep relationships with a local community will be imperative.
3. Third, since ideology and organizations transcend national boundaries, the FBI concluded that law enforcement agencies need to develop international partnerships and sources of information.

G. Another future mode of attack will involve employing multiple explosive devices. Bombs were present at the beginning of modern terrorism, and they will continue to be an important weapon in the terrorist arsenal.

H. Stephen Graham says that the military overview of conflict has moved from state-to-state confrontations, with a beginning and an end, to an ideology accepting perpetual warfare in a variety of civilian environments.

I. Blending criminal and terrorist networks.
1. Michael Stohl says conventional wisdom suggests that terrorist and criminal organizations are merging into common networks.
   a. The differences are often overlooked because both terrorists and criminals use similar tactics.
   b. The tactical objectives of terrorist and criminal networks differ, and law enforcement agencies need to understand the dissimilarities.
   c. There are other differences and similarities between terrorists and organized criminals:
      i. Terrorists seek media, criminals avoid media.
      ii. Both criminals and terrorists are frequently charged under the same criminal statutes.
      iii. Criminal groups employ terrorist tactics, and terrorists commit crimes.
      iv. Criminals and terrorists may form alliances, use the same underground networks, share operational motivations, and sometimes even combine operations.
   d. Networks should be understood as ever-changing structures that flow with social fluctuations.
   e. Law enforcement's eventual goal is not to categorize terrorists as criminals, but to create justice systems that can end violence and restore them to their communities.
2. One of the most important intersections between criminals and terrorists is in the field of finance.

3. Financial institutions will become more critical in the future because they are inevitably used by criminals and terrorists.
4. Future financial investigations will become more difficult as terrorists become more financially sophisticated.
5. Many terrorism analysts believe that the hidden nature of terror networks automatically give groups the ability to adapt to future changes.

J. Other tactical trends:
1. America's cyber systems are an infrastructure in need of protection.
   a. Nations seeking to attack the United States would achieve a strategic advantage, if they could disrupt communications, financial systems, data banks, and the information technology infrastructure.
   b. The .com, .org. and .edu environments are matters for the private sector, and they do not enjoy the same protection as the .gov systems.
2. Violent radicals are attempting to infiltrate military and law enforcement ranks, and this is primarily a domestic threat.
3. Explosives experts pointed to bomb data, demonstrating that "the philosophy of the bomb" will continue to remain a viable terrorist weapon.
4. Financial experts pointed to increasing uses of fraud to fund terrorist operations. Right-wing domestic experts note that many sovereign citizen fraud schemes are used for economic gain rather than for funding operations.
5. One of the greatest fears remains the use of chemical, biological, or radiological weapons.

III. **Law Enforcement and the Future**
OBJ 8: Summarize the developing law enforcement programs designed to prevent terrorism
OBJ 9: Describe probable future strategic directions in terrorism

A. There are several aspects of effective anti-terrorist activities that affect the future of American law enforcement.
1. They include initiatives such as the *Smart Policing Initiative* (SPI), *Communities Against Terrorism* (CAT), and the *Targeting Violent Crime Initiative* (TVCI).
B. Rivalries remain, such as the dysfunctional competition between the ATF and FBI over explosives investigations.
C. Agencies usually seek to control intelligence, or information about on-going suspicious activity, even when barriers to information sharing have been minimized.
D. The *Nationwide SAR Initiative* (NSI) is designed to overcome the danger of not sharing information about activities that might indicate a terrorist attack is in the making.
1. The idea is based on two key factors:
   a. First, *field contacts* are reported with standardized information gathered from a variety of law enforcement departments.
   b. Second, each agency retains control of the information.

E. Officials from the Department of Justice feared that the increased gathering and sharing of information would threaten to invade personal privacy.
   1. DOJ officials decided that no agency should participate in the SAR process unless it had a publically approved policy for collecting and sharing criminal intelligence that matched the standards set in the *National Criminal Intelligence Sharing Plan.*
F. The evaluation in 2010 demonstrated that SAR was effective, but it also revealed a few areas that needed to be addressed:
   1. First, criminal analysts needed to be trained.
   2. Second, patrol officers and investigators receive SAR training, but expansion of the system will require training supervisors.
   3. Finally, SAR works because it collects specific types of information about criminal activities associated with preparation for terrorist attacks.
G. The future challenge will be to utilize associations and concepts like SAR and fusion centers to ensure the flow of criminal intelligence.
H. *Total criminal intelligence.*
   1. Terrorism has presented new challenges for law enforcement, but diminishing resources and budget cuts result in fewer units for deployment.
   2. Law enforcement agencies are moving away from reactive patrol and investigative focused models of policing, to newer methods of deploying resources, based on known patterns of crime and criminal behavior.
   3. *Intelligence-led policing* (ILP) is a method of applying criminal intelligence and data analysis for the deployment of all law enforcement resources, targeting social problems, potential sources of crime, and offenders.
      a. ILP fits the model of terrorism prevention; under this concept, officers gather information and forward it for analysis.
      b. ILP is designed to disrupt criminal activities prior to a criminal act, identify community problems, and prevent crime.
   4. Terrorism is one aspect of criminal behavior, and TCI deals with all forms of criminal information.
   5. Another future trend in information gathering and analysis will be expanding community involvement.

IV. **Probable Strategic Directions**
   OBJ 9: Describe probable future strategic directions in terrorism

A. The *National Intelligence University* and the U.S. Army War College teamed together to create *Proteus USA,* an international think tank designed to consider future strategic problems.
B. Martin Cetron and Owen Davies suggest terrorism will grow in the future. – the three most important courses of future actions:
   1. Growing terrorist ranks.
   2. Probable access to WMD.
   3. Spinoff jihadist movements obtaining legitimate political power.

527

C. Democratic accountability.
1. As the United States continues to respond to terrorism, a number of concerns have surfaced and they remain to be addressed.
2. Future security policy should be developed within the body of existing theoretical literature.
3. Research also points to the growing loss of privacy and the inadequacy of current law.
   a. Governments will be able to build dossiers on individuals, and point to those most likely to engage in terrorism.
4. Future research should be conducted on the relationship between specific abuses of individual rights and a state's susceptibility to terrorism.
5. Terrorists should be handled in accordance with criminal law, and this position draws controversial practices like *enhanced interrogation* into question.
D. Domestic and international terrorism.
1. Ethnic and ideological confrontations will continue, and experts debate about the future of religious terrorism.
2. The course of international terrorism will be determined partially by the ability of the West to create alliances that bring regional stability and economic security.
3. Violent domestic extremism will continue to focus on ideology, and at least one leading expert, Bruce Hoffman, believes that domestic jihadists will base operations in the United States.
4. Domestically, right-wing violent extremism is growing in popularity.
5. The United States has created a blind spot; by focusing on operations overseas, and failing to account for the complexity of evolving jihadist organizations, jihadists have created bases of operations in the U.S.
6. Bruce Hoffman believes al Qaeda's campaign of religious terrorism will continue in the future.
   a. He recommends three steps to counter its effectiveness.
      i. First, America must seek to understand its enemy.
      ii. Second, the campaign to eliminate leaders and terrorists should continue, but it must be complemented with actions based on a more strategic effort.
      iii. The step that leads to victory will be countering al Qaeda's ability to recruit and radicalize jihadists.

Chapter Summary

- Several federal agencies have functions that could create needless duplication. The functions also complicate federal relations with state local and tribal police agencies. The DHS quadrennial review is supposed to assess the effectiveness of its own operations and the way it functions with other agencies.

528

- Three factors will help to ensure the effectiveness of anti-terrorism operations. Federal agencies need to ensure that their functions complement one another, and that they interface with state, local and tribal law enforcement. This implies that all agencies involved in anti-terrorism need to develop formal and informal communication networks. It also means that agencies must actually share information.

- Private-public partnerships are complicated because the Constitution limits the power of government, but the same rules do not apply to private industry. Companies may use information for economic advantages or gain actual control of national security.

- Anti-terrorism policy begins with united DOS and DOD efforts. The Israeli-Palestinian conflict illustrates this idea. State, local, and tribal law enforcement agencies lead homeland security efforts, and DHS and other federal departments and agencies coordinate the strategic role of law enforcement. Their efforts are dependent on the success of US foreign policy.

- The United States will continue to experience low level attacks, and it may experience a massive assault. When any terrorist attack occurs, the infrastructure must be designed to absorb the damage, and maintain social, psychological, and economic normality.

- Traditional liberal education programs, interdisciplinary approaches to problem solving, and developing critical thinking skills are necessary to understand the complexities of terrorism. Simplistic thinking leads to misguided solutions and militarizes social policy.

- Swarming attacks will become popular with large terrorist groups. Criminal and terror networks will join when they have common objectives, and cyber systems remain vulnerable to terrorist attacks. Domestically, right-wing extremism is growing.

- Law enforcement agencies are developing terrorism prevention measures. The SPI targets specific problems. The NSI is attempting to implement the SAR program. CAT gathers information specific to certain types of businesses. The TVCI identifies violent crime data that may impact terrorism prevention.

- Future terrorism will rely on technology. Radicalization is increasing along with the gap between rich and poor nations. The Internet will continue to be one of the most important vehicles in recruiting terrorists and planning operations. Government surveillance of private records are eliminating privacy. Right-wing domestic extremism is increasing, and homegrown jihadists have created virtual bases in the United States.

DISCUSSION QUESTIONS

1. Some researchers feel that terrorists and criminal organizations are merging into common networks, but some do not share this view. Which view do you believe to be the most appropriate? Explain why you hold this belief. (OBJ 7, 8, and 9)

2.   White reports that as the U.S. continues to respond to terrorism, a number of concerns have surfaced that remain to be addressed. Discuss these concerns. (OBJ 1 – 9)

3.   Discuss the positive and negative effects of the relationship between government and private industry. (OBJ 2 and 3)

4.   It is reported in the text that people charged with preventing terrorism should have critical thinking skills. Do you believe a liberal education will better provide these skills than a more focused education (i.e., a degree in Liberal Studies as opposed to a degree in Criminal Justice)? Why or why not? (OBJ 2, 6, 8, and 9)

ASSIGNMENTS

1.   Have students research varying policing styles, i.e. Intelligence-led Policing, Community Service Policing, Watchman Style, Legalistic, etc. Have the students prepare a PowerPoint presentation that describes and compares/contrast each. Have students imagine themselves in charge of a large law enforcement agency. Discuss and debate which style they would most likely employ. (OBJ 2, 8, and 9)

2.   Break the class into small groups. Provide each group with a flip chart and markers. Have them select a scribe and a presenter, then direct each group to identify factors involved in a counterterrorist public-private partnership and present to the class. (OBJ 2, 3, 5, 8, and 9)

3.   Have students research and report on any innovative law enforcement programs in their area designed to prevent terrorism. Students may present orally or in report form. (OBJ 8)

4.   As a review, play jeopardy using key concepts and terms from the chapter. (OBJ 1 – 9)

5.   Have each student comb through http://scholar.google.com/scholar?hl=en&q=americas+future+on+terrorism&btnG=&as_sdt =1%2C5&as_sdtp= (or another website as approved by the instructor) for a current event and select an article that relates to one or more of the chapter's core concepts. Have students provide a journalistic summary and a personal opinion/reaction to the article. Have students orally present the article to the class, field Q & As from their fellow students, and provide a copy of the original source article following the presentation. Optional: Have students complete peer assessments at the end of each presentation. (OBJ 1 - 9)

MEDIA TOOLS

1.   7 Things you should know about Wikis. Retrieved from the Web Jun 29, 2012 at http://net.educause.edu/ir/library/pdf/ELI7004.pdf

         This document offers easy to understand instruction on the history, development, and potential uses of Wikis.

Have students develop (or make additions to a previously created one) a *Webliography* (resource list) using a Blog or Wiki that provides a short description, and link to a scholarly resource pertaining to course concepts. For example, have students add two to three resources each and ask them to add their assessment of at least one of their peers' contributions. If desired, allow time to discuss Blogs/Wikis. This activity can be reused throughout the course, by asking students to add/revise their contributions each week, bi-weekly, etc. (OBJ 1 – 9)

2. ***"Current Events Article Summary with Peer Assessment"***

Global Issues. Social, Political, Economic and Environmental Issues That Affect Us All. Full List in War on Terror Section. Retrieved from the Web Jun 29, 2012 at http://www.globalissues.org/article/358/war-on-terror-articles. This document offers an exhaustive list of links to articles reposted from other sites that detail numerous terrorism related events that have occurred during America's "War on Terror". This resource can additionally serve as an example for media tool sample #1. (LO 2, 4, 5, and 9)

Use the Article Summary Template, which can be obtained on the instructor companion website, for this assignment. The template offers information on Internet research, outside resources, identification of credible sources, and detailed directions on completing an assessment of a news article. It also includes a peer evaluation tool.

Have each student comb the Internet for terrorism related news and select an article that relates to one or more of the chapter's core concepts. Be sure selections are an article of interest from a credible source (*more on credibility can be found in the article summary template above*). Fill out an article summary template. *Your template asks for generic info about the article, a journalistic summary, as well as a personal opinion/reaction to the article.* Have each student summarize the article, present it orally to the class, and field Q & As from their fellow students. Have students complete peer assessments at the end of each presentation. Have students submit templates, original source article, and peer-reviews prior to the end of class. (OBJ 1-9)

6. ***"America's Future Strategic Direction on Terrorism…Visual Aid"***
    "The FBI's Terrorism Screening Center. Retrieved from the Web Jun 29, 2012 at http://www.fbi.gov/about-us/nsb/tsc.

This site offers a substantial array of information on terrorism related topics, including postings of most Wanted Terrorists and Domestic Terror Fugitives. It additionally provides several links to related agencies in the War on Terror. In addition, the site also offers information on careers with the FBI, virtual tours, as well as a fun & games page.

Have students visit the photo gallery section and select three photos that they feel best represent America's future strategic direction on terrorism. Have students create a visual aid (flip chart, Bristol board, PowerPoint presentation, etc.) to display in class that includes each photo as well as commentary on why they chose the way they did. Be sure to give instruction on source citation for images. (OBJ 1 – 9)

531

7. ***"Intelligence studies….Analysis & Report"***
CIA. Studies in Intelligence. Retrieved from the Web on Aug 20, 2012 at https://www.cia.gov/library/center-for-the-study-of-intelligence/csi-publications/csi-studies/index.html

The website offers access to numerous studies in intelligence as general information on the Agency, policies, careers, publications, and related links.

Have students select and review one of the intelligence studies from the list above and provide a summary of the report to the class. (OBJ 2 – 9)

TEST BANK

Chapter 16—Security, Terrorism, and the Future

TRUE/FALSE

1.   Defense contractors possess the same skills as most government agencies.

ANS: F   REF: p. 417   OBJ: 2, 3, and 6

2.   Even the best anti-terrorism efforts will fail at points in the future.

ANS: T   REF: p. 420   OBJ: 1 - 9

3.   Criminal and terror networks often intersect.

ANS: T   REF: p. 423   OBJ: 2, 3, 5, 7, 8, and 9

4.   After witnessing enhanced interrogations of jihadists, a number of valuable agents left the FBI in disgust.

ANS: T   REF: p. 433   OBJ: 1 - 9

5.   Violence in Africa tends to be dominated by local political issues, making it an unlikely target for future al Qaeda footholds.

ANS: F   REF: p. 413   OBJ: 2, 4, 6, and 7

6.   A future trend is the continuing necessity to train law enforcement personnel in recognizing the indicators of terrorism and to develop effective interviewing techniques.

ANS: T   REF: p. 427   OBJ: 6 and 8

7.   . Despite the necessity to share information, law enforcement agencies are reluctant to do so.

ANS: T   REF: p. 427   OBJ: 1, 2, 3, and 8

8.   Military personnel frequently partner with local law enforcement and other civil forces when engaged in force protection.

ANS: T   REF: p. 422   OBJ: 2 and 3

9. The future of homeland security has no relationship with the success of U.S. foreign policy.

ANS: F   REF: p. 435   OBJ: 2, 3, and 4

10. DOJ officials decided that no agency would participate in the SAR process unless it had a publically approved policy for collecting and sharing criminal intelligence that matched the standards set by the FBI.

ANS: F   REF: p. 428   OBJ: 2

11. National defense and criminal intelligence operations are based partially on building background information to assess the probability of future pathways.

ANS: T   REF: p. 414   OBJ: 2, 3, 6 , and 7

12. The Senate has oversight of the Department of Justice (DOJ), the Department of Defense (DOD), and the Department of Homeland Security (DHS).

ANS: F   REF: p. 414   OBJ: 1

13. The most complex process in the DHS analysis is the implementation of a comprehensive strategy to ensure effective management of national policies.

ANS: T   REF: p. 415   OBJ: 1, 2, 3, 5, 6, 7, 8, and 9

14. Private-public partnerships reduce the effectiveness of preventive policies.

ANS: F   REF: p. 416   OBJ: 3

15. Private businesses are not subjected to the same constitutional rules and regulations as government entities.

ANS: T   REF: p. 416   OBJ: 3

MULTIPLE CHOICE

1. The Homeland Security Act of 2002 was touted as the biggest reformation of government since the _____.
   a. WWI
   b. WWII
   c. Viet Nam
   d. Gulf War

ANS: b   REF: p. 414   OBJ: 1 and 2

534

2.   _____ controls funding for the DHS.
    a. Congress
    b. Senate
    c. Law enforcement
    d. State government

ANS: a   REF: p. 414   OBJ: 1, 2, and 3

3.   _____established the Department of Homeland Security and reorganized the President's cabinet.
    a. 9/11 Commission Implementation Act of 2207
    b. Quadrennial Homeland Security Review
    c. Homeland Security Act
    d. USA Intelligence Act

ANS: c   REF: p. 414   OBJ: 1 and 2

4.   The November 2008 terrorist attacks in Mumbai, India were the responsibility of what terrorist organization?
    a. MeK
    b. The LeT
    c. Hamas
    d. Al Qaeda

ANS: b   REF: p. 423   OBJ: 4

5.   Military-industrial complex is a term coined by _____ to describe the relationship between American military forces and private industry.
    a. Lyndon Johnson
    b. George W. Bush
    c. Ronald Regan
    d. Dwight Eisenhower

ANS: d   REF: p. 417   OBJ: 2 and 3

6.   Private incursion in the public sphere has been expanded by the wars in _____ and Afghanistan.
    a. Iraq
    b. Iran
    c. Syria
    d. Saudi Arabia

ANS: a   REF: p. 417   OBJ: 3 and 4

7.   Logistical contractors have been given more freedom because the DOD has _____ in support and supply.
    a. Increased the number of regulators
    b. Reduced the number of regulators
    c. Increased funding
    d. Decreased funding

ANS: b   REF: p. 417   OBJ: 3, 4, 8, and 9

8. As used by Robert Gates, _____ refers to the ability of U.S. military forces to form alliances with security forces and civilian governments inside states threatened with destabilization.
   a. Cooperative relations
   b. Logistical contracts
   c. Allied support
   d. Partner capacity

ANS: d   REF: p. 418   OBJ: 2 and 3

9. Given the synergistic nature of the conflict between Israel and Palestine, U.S. attempts to secure the homeland must take _____ into account.
   a. Economics
   b. The European Union
   c. The Middle East
   d. Amnesty issues

ANS: c   REF: p. 419   OBJ: 1 - 9

10. Middle East peace talks can begin without _____, but they will not be successful if it remains on the sidelines.
   a. al Qaeda
   b. Hezbollah
   c. LTE
   d. Hamas

ANS: d   REF: p. 419   OBJ: 4 and 9

11. Stephen Kinzer believes _____ represents one of the region's greatest potential for establishing democracies.
   a. Iran
   b. Afghanistan
   c. Iraq
   d. Syria

ANS: a   REF: p. 419   OBJ: 4 and 9

12. According to the text, a majority of Iran's citizens dream of having what form of government?
   a. Dictatorship
   b. Democratic
   c. Theocracy
   d. Communist

ANS: b   REF: p. 419   OBJ: 4

13. Richard Kohn argues that the U.S. has become increasingly enamored by militarizing social problems since the _____.
   a. 1940s
   b. 1960s
   c. 1930s
   d. 1980s

ANS: c   REF: p. 422   OBJ: 2, 3, 6, and 8

14. Terrorism is primarily a problem for _____.
    a. Law enforcement
    b. The military
    c. INTERPOL
    d. Intelligence agencies

ANS: a   REF: p. 422   OBJ: 2, 3, 4, 6, 8, and 9

15. According to Brian Jenkins, what entity possesses the best counterterrorist tools in the legal system?
    a. JTTF
    b. CIA
    c. FBI
    d. NSA

ANS: a   REF: p. 422   OBJ: 2 and 8

16. Many terrorism analysts believe that the _____ of terror networks automatically give groups the ability to adapt to future changes.
    a. Political nature
    b. Tactical efficiency
    c. Hidden nature
    d. Infrastructure

ANS: c   REF: p. 426   OBJ: 5, 6, 7, 8, and 9

17. Former counterterrorism czar Richard Clarke and Robert Knake of the Council on Foreign Relations Nations state that Nations seeking to attack the United States would achieve a strategic advantage if they could disrupt a number of U.S. government systems. Which government system do the pair NOT mention?
    a. Transportation
    b. Communications
    c. Financial systems and data banks
    d. Information technology

ANS: a   REF: p. 426   OBJ: 1 - 9

18. Financial experts state that _____ is increasingly being utilized to fund domestic terrorist operations.
    a. Kidnapping
    b. Embezzlement
    c. Prostitution
    d. Fraud

ANS: d   REF: p. 427   OBJ: 7, 8, and 9

19. The primary purpose of the _____ is to fund multi-jurisdictional state, local, land tribal law enforcement teams that prevent selected violent crimes through intelligence-led policing.
    a. Communities Against Terrorism
    b. Homeland Security Act
    c. Targeting Violent Crime Initiative
    d. Quadrennial Homeland Security Review

ANS: c   REF: p. 428   OBJ: 2, 8, and 9

20. The e-Guardian system falls under the domain of the _____.
   a. FBI
   b. CIA
   c. JTTF
   d. NSA

ANS: a   REF: p. 428   OBJ: 2, 8, and 9

21. Police agencies that apply criminal intelligence and data analysis for the deployment of their law enforcement resources are using what policing style?
   a. Watchman
   b. Legalistic
   c. Community
   d. Intelligence-led

ANS: d   REF: p. 428   OBJ: 2, 8, and 9

22. The concept of intelligence-led policing (ILP) is a concept was developed in what country?
   a. The United Kingdom
   b. The United States
   c. Canada
   d. Israel

ANS: a   REF: p. 428   OBJ: 8 and 9

23. The goal of the Smart Policing Initiative (SPI) is to identify law enforcement tactics and strategies that are effective, efficient, and _____.

   a. Socially responsible
   b. Innovative
   c. Community-oriented
   d. Economical

ANS: d   REF: p. 429   OBJ: 2, 3, 6, 8, and 9

24. The National Intelligence University and the U.S. Army War College teamed together to create _____, an international think tank designed to consider future strategic problems.
   a. Intelligence Led Policing
   b. Proteus USA
   c. Probable Strategic Directions
   d. Nationwide SAR Initiative

ANS: b   REF: p. 431   OBJ: 2, 3, 6, 8, and 9

25. The _____ is designed to overcome both the danger of and the reluctance to share information about activities that might indicate a terrorist attack is in the making.
   a. 9/11 Commission
   b. Quadrennial Homeland Security Review
   c. Communities Against Terrorism
   d. Nationwide SAR Initiative

ANS: d   REF: p. 428   OBJ: 1, 2, 3, 5, 8, and 9

26. The process of questioning suspects by using physical duress is called _____.
    a. Enhanced interrogation
    b. Neuro-linguistic Programming
    c. Good Cop Bad Cop
    d. Enhanced interviewing

ANS: b   REF: p. 433   OBJ: 2 and 9

27. Leading terrorism expert, Bruce Hoffman, believes that domestic jihadists will base operations in _____.
    a. The United Kingdom
    b. Mexico
    c. Canada
    d. the United States

ANS: d   REF: p. 433   OBJ: 5 and 7

28. Israel has engaged in a series of targeted attacks upon terrorist _____for two decades with no visible reduction in terrorism.
    a. Training camps
    b. Leadership
    c. Communications
    d. Financing support

ANS: b   REF: p. 434   OBJ: 2, 4, 7, 8, and 9

29. The NYPD concluded that terrorist tactics from sophisticated groups like the LeT will shift from emphasizing suicide bombings to focusing on _____ assaults.
    a. Gang style
    b. Police style
    c. Military style
    d. Unit style

ANS: c   REF: p. 424   OBJ: 7

30. Where does the best source of information about potential terrorist violence come from?
    a. CIA agents
    b. Religious leaders
    c. Military intelligence
    d. Local citizens

ANS: d   REF: p. 424   OBJ: 2, 4, 8 and 9

31. Patrick Hardouin views one of the most important intersections between criminals and terrorists is in what field?
    a. Finance
    b. Narcotics
    c. Technology
    d. Operational strategy

ANS: a   REF: p. 426   OBJ: 7 and 8

32. American citizens who believe that the original citizens of the United States were free from all governmental control are known as referred to as _____ citizens.
   a. Sovereign
   b. Indigenous
   c. Native
   d. Nationalist

ANS: a   REF: p. 427   OBJ: 6, 7, and 8

33. One of the greatest fears remaining in the face of terrorism is the use of chemical, _____, or radiological weapons.
   a. Virtual (Denial of Service attacks)
   b. Biological
   c. Traditional
   d. Human (suicide bombers)

ANS: b   REF: p. 427   OBJ: 7

34. Experts have presented data to suggest that law enforcement officers will be increasingly targeted by _____.
   a. Hezzbollah
   b. Violent domestic extremists
   c. Al Qaeda
   d. Hamas

ANS: b   REF: p. 427   OBJ: 5, 7, 8, and 9

35. The most likely future trend of terrorists is the use of _____.
   a. Remote detonation devices
   b. Biological weapons
   c. Chemical weapons
   d. Nuclear weapons

ANS: a   REF: p. 427   OBJ: 7

36. As part of a Smart Policing Initiative focused on robbery and burglary, the Boston Police department has partnered with what academic institution?
   a. Harvard University
   b. Cambridge University
   c. Rutgers Universit
   d. Yale University

ANS: a   REF: p. 431   OBJ: 2, 3, 6, 7, 8, and 9

37. Barring nuclear war or some type of global plague, the world's population will reach 9.2 billion by what year?
   a. 2020
   b. 2080
   c. 2040
   d. 2050

ANS: d   REF: p. 432   OBJ: 4 and 5

38.   The law enforcement initiative Communities Against Terrorism (CAT) provides specific
        information about terrorist activities to what target audience?
        a. Academic scholars
        b. Federal authorities
        c. Media
        d. Business and Industry

ANS: d   REF: p. 428   OBJ: 2, 3, 5, and 7

39.   The secretary of DHS is mandated to conduct a review of the department's operations
        every ___ years.
        a. 10
        b. 2
        c. 4
        d. 7

ANS: c   REF: p. 415   OBJ: 1 and 2

40. The DOD undergoes a congressional review ever _____ years.
        a. 10
        b. 2
        c. 4
        d. 7

ANS: c   REF: p. 415   OBJ: 1 and 2

Case 16.0

The Homeland Security Act of 2002 was touted as the biggest reformation of government since
World War II, and it certainly changed the organization of the federal government. It also
increased potential confusion. In essence, the Department of Justice (DOJ), the Department of
Defense (DOD), and the Department of Homeland Security (DHS) were given specific functions
in national security, and their missions were to support the overall direction of foreign policy and
the Department of State (DOS). Each department also interfaces with the Office of the Director
of National Intelligence (ODNI) and the multiple agencies assigned to that organization. Since
Congress controls funding for all the departments and since it exercises oversight, it should be
expected to ensure that homeland security is guided by an efficient, comprehensive direction in
policy (see recommendations from the 9/11 Commission). A comprehensive federal direction in
homeland security, in turn, should help to clarify the antiterrorism role for state, local, and tribal
police agencies. In practice, actual operations often become duplicative and inefficient.
Therefore, some type of assessment is needed to increase future efficiency.

41.   The duplicity and inefficiency mentioned above can be primarily attributed to what
        concept?
        a. Lack of skilled workers
        b. Lack of resources
        c. Bureaucracy
        d. Terrorist infiltration

ANS: c   REF: p. 414   OBJ: 1 and 2

541

42.	The Homeland Security Act of 2002 came on the heels of what terrorist incident?
	a.	The 9/11 attacks
	b.	The bombing of the Alfred P. Murrah building
	c.	The Rajneeshee bio-terror attack
	d.	The U.S. embassy attacks in Kenya and Tanzania

ANS: a		REF: p. 414		OBJ: 2 – 5

Case 16.1

  The people who most frequently encounter terrorism are found in local law enforcement. This means that future antiterrorism activities must operate beyond the federal level and be effective among state, local, and tribal police agencies. Second, agencies need to develop methods for encouraging communication. Although procedures and personal rivalries frequently inhibit communication, organizational leaders need to develop formal and informal connections among agencies and encourage their personnel to use those networks. Third, it is necessary to share information. Policies will not work unless information flows through the system.

43.	Which of the following would most likely be the first responder to a terrorist incident?
	a.	A CIA agent
	b.	A police officer
	c.	A FBI agent
	d.	A military intelligence officer

ANS: b		REF: p. 415		OBJ: 2, 5, 6, 7, and 8

44.	Which initiative has been developed to enhance communication between law enforcement and the general public on methods of counter-terrorism?

	a.	Targeting Violent Crime Initiative (TVCI):
	b.	Nationwide SAR Initiative (NSI):
	c.	Communities Against Terrorism (CAT)
	d.	e-Guardian:

ANS: c		REF: p. 428		OBJ: 1 – 10

45.	Law enforcement agencies have historically held mistrust against what fellow agency that inhibits information sharing?
	a.	ICE
	b.	FBI
	c.	U.S. Border Patrol
	d.	ATF

ANS: b		REF: p. 427		OBJ: 1 and 8

46. Which entity exemplifies an information sharing network?
    a. e-Guardian
    b. Targeting Violent Crime Initiative (TVCI)
    c. Smart Policing Initiative (SPI)
    d. Proteus USA

ANS: a   REF: p. 428   OBJ: 1, 2, 8, and 9

Case 16.2

Tom Barry (2010) believes that one of the emerging critical issues in anti-terrorism policy is the development of homeland security industries by private businesses. He draws a parallel with national defense industries, saying that the term *military-industrial complex* is no longer applicable to the relationship between big defense contractors and the government. These businesses, he argues, have gone far beyond supplying weapons or goods; they provide command and control systems and perform military services. In other words, they are replacing defense activities traditionally performed by the government. Barry cites the increasing number of operations that corporations perform in the DOD and in the intelligence community.

47. Under whose Presidency did the term *military-industrial complex* first appear?
    a. Clinton
    b. Eisenhower
    c. Kennedy
    d. George W. Bush

ANS: b   REF: p. 417   OBJ: 1, 3, 8, and 9

48. Which of the following scenarios is NOT an example of the *military-industrial complex*?
    a. The military is ordered by the President to secure U.S. airspace
    b. The U.S. government hires a private company to escort U.S. diplomats
    c. The FBI, the CIA, and local law enforcement conduct a coordinated sting eration on a suspected terrorist cell.
    d. The CIA shares intel gained in Iraq with a local police agency that has been geted by Hamas for attack.

ANS: a   REF: p. 417   OBJ: 1, 2, 3, 4, 5, 6, 7, 8, 9, and 10

Case 16.3

Defense Secretary Robert Gates posits that one of the greatest threats in the coming decades is a city poisoned or reduced to rubble by a terrorist attack. The plan for this type of attack will most likely originate in a state that cannot secure its own territory. He believes that this is the main security problem of our times. The United States must approach this from a comprehensive perspective, combining defense policy with homeland security efforts and a renewed focus on foreign relations. Reestablishing failed states, Gates says, is beyond the capacity of the military.

49. The poisoning of a city, as mentioned by Gates, is what type of terrorist attack?
    a. Biological
    b. Radiological
    c. Symbolic
    d. Virtual

ANS: a   REF: p. 418   OBJ: 5, 7, and 9

50.   According to Gates' criteria, which nation would be the LEAST likely source for a terrorist attack, as described above?
        a. China
        b. Sudan
        c. Georgia
        d. Somalia

ANS: c   REF: p. 428   OBJ: 2, 4, 6, 7, 8, and 10

COMPLETION

1.   The _____ Review refers to a requirement that the Secretary of DHS conduct a review of the department's operations every four years.

ANS: Quadrennial Homeland Security   REF: p. 415   OBJ: 1

2.   One of the emerging critical issues in anti-terrorism policy is the development of homeland security industries by _____.

ANS: private businesses   REF: p. 416   OBJ: 3

3.   First responders to terrorist incidents are most often _____.

ANS: local law enforcement officials   REF: p. 415   OBJ: 2, 5, and 8

4.   Big defense contractors have gone far beyond supplying weapons or goods; they provide command and control systems and perform _____ services.

ANS: military   REF: p. 417   OBJ: 3

5.   Even though a WMD threat is real, it is balanced by the capacity for_____.

ANS: retaliation   REF: p. 420   OBJ: 7

6.   If a group launches a major attack when it has no visible _____or political location, it is partially insulated from a reprisal.

ANS: geographical   REF: p. 420   OBJ: 7

7.   Only after al Qaeda leadership could be pinpointed in the tribal regions of _____, did American efforts to kill or capture its leadership become more effective.

ANS: Pakistan   REF: p. 420   OBJ: 2 and 9

8.   _____ refers to launching attacks on multiple targets in the same time frame or suddenly bringing several attackers to a single location and rapidly dispersing.

ANS: Swarming attacks   REF: p. 423   OBJ: 4, 5, and 7

9.   The _____ University conducted an in-service initiative standardizing training for the entire intelligence community is referred to as the _____.

ANS: National Intelligence   REF: p. 431   OBJ: 2, 5, 6, 8, and 9

10. Law enforcement agencies are moving away from _____ patrol and investigative focused models of policing to newer methods of deploying resources based on known patterns of crime and criminal behavior.

ANS: reactive   REF: p. 429   OBJ: 2, 5, 6, 8, and 9

11. One of the most intriguing managerial concepts in modern law enforcement is the idea of _____.

ANS: intelligence-led policing (ILP)   REF: p. 429   OBJ: 2 and 8

12. TCI, in counterterrorism circles, stands for _____.

ANS: total criminal intelligence   REF: p. 429   OBJ: 2 and 8

13. Think tank members Cetron and Davies believe that jihadist veterans from ____ will return to their native lands and train future jihadists.

ANS: Iraq   REF: p. 431   OBJ: 4 and 7

14. Think tank members Cetron and Davies suggest that emerging technology will impact the effectiveness of security, but it will multiply the force of_____.

ANS: terrorist groups   REF: p. 431   OBJ: 5, 7, and 9

15. Experts suggest that the three most important courses of future action indicated by current behavior in the world of terrorism are: (1) growing terrorist ranks, (2) _____, and (3) spin-off jihadist movements obtaining legitimate political power.

ANS: probable access to WMD   REF: p. 431   OBJ: 5 and 7

16. Scholars Eller and Gerber suggest one of the things that bureaucrats do well is ____.

ANS: analyze policy   REF: p. 432   OBJ: 2

17. Researchers James Piazza and James Walsh (2010) discovered that restricting _____ does not lead to greater protection from terrorism.

ANS: freedom   REF: p. 433   OBJ: 5 and 9

545

18. Old racist elements are appearing within extremist groups, but many right-wing extremists have abandoned racial politics for _____.

ANS: antigovernment fanaticism REF: p. 433   OBJ: 7

19. According to the text, _____ is *the* new form of international conflict.

ANS: terrorism   REF: p. 436   OBJ: 4 and 5

20. Force Protection refers to security operations by military forces engaged in securing bases, ports, other areas of operations, and _____.

ANS: personnel   REF: p. 422   OBJ: 5

ESSAY

1. White reports that practical aspects of everyday operations and management become vital for policy, implying there are three important areas for future security. Discuss these areas, providing an example. Do you agree with White, do you believe that there are additional areas? Explain your position.

ANS:
- First, all the federal agencies involved in terrorism prevention need to develop procedures to ensure that activities complement one another.
- The people who most frequently encounter terrorism are found in local law enforcement, this means that future anti-terrorism activities must operate beyond the federal level and be effective among state, local, and tribal police agencies.
- Second, agencies need to develop methods for encouraging communication.
- Although procedures and personal rivalries frequently inhibit communication, organizational leaders need to develop formal and informal connections among agencies and encourage their personnel to use those networks.
- Finally, it is necessary to share information; policies will not work unless information flows through the system.
- These issues may seem overwhelming at first, but obstacles can be circumvented if multiple agencies establish and utilize a network of formal and informal relationships.
- For example, a study of five hundred law enforcement agencies in Illinois revealed that both police executives and local government officials believed that the probability of a terrorist attack was low.
- They also realized that if an attack were to happen, it would have massive consequences.
- Therefore, they expanded outreach to other law enforcement agencies and developed methods for sharing criminal intelligence.
- This information, in turn, can be passed on to various federal agencies and incorporated in national policy.
- Student view will vary.

REF: p. 415   OBJ: 1 - 9

2. Explain the three principles that Robert Gates argues should guide the combined approach to foreign policy and anti-terrorism security. Would you agree with Gates? Explain your view.

ANS:
- First, it must be agile and flexible.
- Threats from failed states do not match institutional planning goals or the congressional budget cycle.
- Gates says the United States needs to be able to respond immediately to emerging threats outside of bureaucratic norms.
- Second, Congress and the executive branch of government need to develop effective oversight mechanisms.
- Gates believes this would be enhanced by including the judiciary.
- This would have two effects, it would help to keep policy focused and it would limit opportunities to abuse power.
- Third, it requires consistent long-term behavior in American foreign policy.
- Gates concludes that convincing other countries and leaders to become partners with the United States depends on proving that the US will be reliable and consistent over a long period of time.
- Student view will vary.

REF: p. 418   OBJ: 1 - 9

3. Discuss why Daniel Byman states that Israel's future security depends on the future of a particular terrorist organization. What is this organization and why does Byman make this argument? Do you agree or disagree with his argument. Explain.

ANS:
- To date, Hamas' legitimacy has not been recognized and Israel has responded to its rule in Gaza with military force and a controversial blockade that has the support of Egypt; this according to Byman is ineffective.
- Middle East peace talks can begin without Hamas, but they will not be successful if it remains on the sidelines.
- The international community needs to engage Hamas where it is possible and exploit its weaknesses and vulnerabilities when it will not be engaged.
- Hamas's rhetoric is radical and uncompromising, but its political activities are more pragmatic.
- Military force has not undermined Hamas because it allowed the group to undermine its political rivals.
- Byman believes that if Hamas is given an opportunity to achieve some type of favorable outcome for Gaza, it might be willing to create a more stable relationship with Israel.
- Such an approach is risky as it might alienate moderates who feel that Israel is rewarding violence or allow Hamas to build its future military capacity.
- Refusing to deal with it will not enhance regional peace.
- Since future homeland security depends on a stable Middle East, Byman' approach seems to suggest that the United States should take a more pragmatic approach to Hamas and encourage its allies, including Israel, to follow the same path.
- Student view will vary.

REF: p. 419   OBJ: 1 - 9

4. Discuss Jakub Grygiel's proposed measure to deal with networked decentralized terrorist groups. What example does he use to bolster his point?

ANS:

- Homeland security strategies should involve defensive measures based on the assumption that a WMD attack will be successful.
- He suggests that the infrastructure needs to be decentralized as a central system can be disrupted when its control structure is destabilized and is vulnerable to attack.
- A segmented, dispersed infrastructure might be less efficient that a central system, but it is more likely to survive an attack on one of its control structures.
- Grygiel illustrates this by pointing to the electrical grid – if it is dependent on a few critical transfer stations, it is vulnerable.
- On the other hand, if its nodes are dispersed in regional networks, it is difficult to take the entire system off line by destroying a few critical targets.
- In addition, it is difficult for stateless groups to launch complicated simultaneous attacks against multiple targets.
- Grygiel says an effective homeland security policy should be based on the ability to maintain social, political, and economic functions after a major attack.
- Massed forces are of little value because they cannot protect all possible targets and they cannot be launched to destroy an identifiable political entity.
- He believes that creating regional counterterrorism centers in major cities like Los Angeles and New York City is a good beginning.
- Segments of the United States need to maintain their functions if one of its major cities suffers a devastating attack.

REF: p. 410   OBJ: 1 - 9

5. Explain the three future responses warranted from the lessons learned from Mumbai and Lahore, as indicated by the FBI. Would you agree or disagree with the FBI's conclusion? Explain.

ANS:

- First, it is necessary to prepare for strikes from small groups operating without a central command.
- Lahore demonstrated that a single unit can launch an effective attack, and an individual motivated by a radical ideology can do the same thing.
- Mumbai showed that larger groups can launch more complex operations.
- Security forces must prepare for both types of attacks.
- Second, deep relationships with a local community will be imperative.
- Local citizens are the best source of information about potential terrorist violence.
- They are in the best position to see activities that fall outside normal behavior.
- Third, since ideology and organizations transcend national boundaries, the FBI concluded that law enforcement agencies need to develop international partnerships and sources of information.
- Student views will vary.

REF: p. 424   OBJ: 1 - 9

6. Describe the similarities and differences between terrorists and organized criminals as indicated by Michael Stohl. Do you believe the similarities outweigh the differences indicating a growing collusion between the two groups?

ANS:
- Terrorists seek media coverage to enhance their aura, and they want their dramatic criminal activities publicized.
- Criminals avoid the media, seeking to operate under the public radar.
- Both criminals and terrorists are frequently charged under the same criminal statutes, but this is often because governments seek to discredit the political claims of terrorists.
- Criminal groups employ terrorist tactics, and terrorists commit crimes.
- Terrorists may associate with criminal groups to add to their reputation of ruthlessness.
- Criminals and terrorists may form alliances, use the same underground networks, share operational motivations and sometimes even combine operations.
  - Student view will vary.

REF: p. 425   OBJ: 1 - 9

7. Explain how the Nationwide SAR Initiative works. Who reviews the information? Do you believe this to be a viable system? Explain.

ANS:
- When an officer encounters activity that might be an indicator of potential terrorism, the officer gathers as much information as possible and forwards it in accordance with individual department procedures.
- The information is first reviewed by an intelligence analyst and then it goes to a supervisor.
- If the information appears valid, selected portions may be released on a secure computer server outside the agency's own system.
- Two more reviews take place before the information can be accessed.
- First, the local JTTF reviews the data to determine if it threatens any on-going secret investigation.
- This is followed by a review from e-Guardian.
- If both of these reviews are positive, the information can be reviewed by other agencies.
- Any investigator or analyst accessing the information is only able to look at material approved and released by the originating agency.

REF: p. 428   OBJ: 1 - 9

8. Define intelligence-led policing (ILP). What does ILP involve? What is your view of ILP?

ANS:
- A managerial model which focuses on the collection and analysis of information.
- Law enforcement resources are then deployed to prevent and disrupt crime and to target specific crimes and offenders.
- ILP is an alternative to utilizing criminal intelligence to support investigations and other forms of reactive policing.
- Deploying resources in anticipation of crime and social disorder.

549

- Utilizing deployed resources to gather new information.
- Organizing information for analysis.
- Analyzing information.
- Disseminating information to operational units.
- Re-evaluating information with incoming information.
- Planning and decision-making.
- Redeploying resources based on information and to gather new information
- Student view will vary.

REF: p. 428   OBJ: 1 - 9

9. What are the ten most important factors contributing to terrorism, as indicated by Cetron and Davies?

ANS:
- Western economic growth will spawn resentment and radicalization by populations who believe they are victimized by the West. Muslim countries present the greatest risk.
- Militant Islam will gain power and spread.
- Barring nuclear war or some type of global plague, the world's population will reach 9.2 billion in 2050. The United States will continue to prosper, while poverty will increase in poor nations, increasing resentment against the United States. America will remain an attractive terrorist target.
- Recent technological changes are just the beginning of a revolution that will grow exponentially in the coming decades.
- Americans will lose almost all privacy.
- The global economy will continue to grow and multinational corporations will expand. Economic crime and terrorism will continue to expand with the economy.
- Cities will continue to grow creating large pockets where religious radicalization will foster and terrorism will grow.
- Internet growth will slow, but it will remain the most important method for planning and administering terrorist operations. Almost all the world's population will have access to the Internet within twenty years. It will serve as a vehicle for recruiting terrorists and may be used for financial crimes to support operations.
- Communication technology will continue to expand and impact terrorism in a manner similar to Internet growth.
- The United States is losing its technical and scientific leadership to other countries. This has caused the growth of technicians and scientists in lands hostile to the United States. Some scientists will be able to supply terrorists with lethal technologies.

REF: p. 431   OBJ: 1 - 9

10. Name the Department of Homeland Security's five missions and their respective goals as indicated by the 2010 Quadrennial Homeland Security Review Report.

ANS:
- Mission 1: Preventing Terrorism and Enhancing Security
  Goal 1.1: Prevent Terrorist Attacks

- Goal 1.2: Prevent the Unauthorized Acquisition or Use of Chemical, Biological, Radiological, and Nuclear Materials and Capabilities
  Goal 1.3: Manage Risks to Critical Infrastructure, Key Leadership, and Events
- Mission 2: Securing and Managing Our Borders
  Goal 2.1: Effectively Control U.S. Air, Land, and Sea Borders
  Goal 2.2: Safeguard Lawful Trade and Travel
  Goal 2.3: Disrupt and Dismantle Transnational Criminal
- Mission 3: Enforcing and Administering Our Immigration Laws
  Goal 3.1: Strengthen and Effectively Administer the Immigration System
  Goal 3.2: Prevent Unlawful Immigration
- Mission 4: Safeguarding and Securing Cyberspace
  Goal 4.1: Create a Safe, Secure, and Resilient Cyber Environment
  Goal 4.2: Promote Cyber-security Knowledge and Innovation
- Mission 5: Ensuring Resilience to Disasters
  Goal 5.1: Mitigate Hazards
  Goal 5.2: Enhance Preparedness
  Goal 5.3: Ensure Effective Emergency Response
  Goal 5.4: Rapidly Recover

REF: p. 416   OBJ: 1 -9

Current Event Article Summary Assignment Description

Terrorism occurs every day! News reports often include articles about events that impact the field of criminal justice – terrorism, homeland security, crime, studies, research, careers, new technologies, etc. Your job is to find a recent, published article about any current event that relating to course topics, complete the article summary template, and orally present your article to the class – one presentation per class meeting.

Assignment Objectives
- Analyze the role current events plays in the criminal justice field
- Discuss and debate varying theoretical perspectives
- Examine societal response to criminal justice applications
- Critique credibility and synthesize information from a variety of sources

Deliverables
- Completion of template
- Submission of original source article
- Oral presentation

General Directions
1. Select an article of interest from a credible source. *For more on credibility, review the CARS checklist below*
2. Fill out an article summary template. *Your template asks for generic info about the article, a journalistic summary, as well as a personal opinion/reaction to the article.*
3. Present your article to the class. Be prepared to field questions from your classmates.
4. Complete a peer-review evaluation for each of your classmates' presentations.
5. Submit your template, attached original source article, and peer-reviews to your instructor prior to the end of class.

Additional Info
- There are several methods to access current event articles, here are just a few strong strategies:
- Talk to your local librarian and/or research your institution's virtual libraries
- Browse a newspaper or magazine. Cut out the article and include it with your template.
- Go to google.com and search for your topic by name or use keywords that relate directly to your topic. When you get the page of results, go to the top menu and click "News". Go to the Links page in the menu above. The first category of links is titled "News". Any one of those sites will be full of current events articles that you can either browse, or try searching on those sites using their search bar, which is usually in the right hand corner of the site. Be certain to evaluate your source for credibility. See more on how to evaluate Internet resources using CARS below. Examples of topics you might find in news articles (there are many, many more...include ~high profile crimes ~criminal investigations ~crime statistics ~new technologies ~program innovations

Summary of the CARS Checklist for Research Source Evaluation

Credibility	trustworthy source, author's credentials, evidence of quality control, known or respected authority, organizational support. Goal: an authoritative source, a source that supplies some good evidence that allows you to trust it.
Accuracy	up to date, factual, detailed, exact, comprehensive, audience and purpose reflect intentions of completeness and accuracy. Goal: a source that is correct today (not yesterday), a source that gives the whole truth.
Reasonableness	fair, balanced, objective, reasoned, no conflict of interest, absence of fallacies or slanted tone. Goal: a source that engages the subject thoughtfully and reasonably, concerned with the truth.
Support	listed sources, contact information, available corroboration, claims supported, documentation supplied. Goal: a source that provides convincing evidence for the claims made, a source you can triangulate (find at least two other sources that support it).

TEMPLATE
Current Event Article Summary

Title of Article

Article location
List the website, newspaper or magazine where your article was published. If unknown, use N/A (raises credibility concern –check CARS)

Article Date
List the date the article was published

Article Author(s)
If there is no author listed, just write "N/A".

Explain why you chose the article – what interested you?

Summary (Journalism Questions)

Who?
Who was involved/affected by the events reported in your article? This could be just a few people, or the residents of an entire region.

What?

What's the main idea or main point of the article?

When and where?
When/where did the incident occur?

Why?

Provide some background to the event. If the topic is something that we have already talked about in class, include what you've learned. If we haven't discussed
the topic, you may want to check a criminal justice reference in our libraries to deepen your knowledge of the subject.

In one – two paragraphs, take a stand and say what you really think about the event and its implications. You may say whatever you believe here, but make sure that you support your opinion with a good **supporting argument** with facts from the current event. You will be expected to field questions from your classmates. For this reason, I strongly encourage you to conduct additional research (read two – three more articles covering your topic). This will deepen your knowledge of the incident and increase your confidence and competence about answering questions relating to your article. It is not necessary to complete a template for your additional articles - these are simply for your own reference in assisting you with your presentation.

Peer Evaluation of Oral Presentation

Please complete a separate form for each presentation. Check only one box per area. Provide at least one comment on what you enjoyed most about your classmate's presentation and at least one specific, constructive comment on how (s)he might have improved his or her presentation. Please be respectful, fair, and honest in your assessments and commentary - you should expect the same from your classmates. The information will be shared with your classmates; however, the forms are anonymous.

Class Date:	Presenter		
	Very Good	**Satisfactory**	**Needs Improvement**
Gave an interesting introduction			
Presented clear explanation of topic			
Presented information in acceptable order			
Used complete sentences			
Offered a concluding summary			
Spoke clearly, correctly, distinctly, and confidently			
Maintained eye contact			
Posture not distracting			
Presentation was interesting			

Displayed enthusiasm for the topic			
Handled questions and comments from the class very well			

I was most impressed by:

I would have changed: